KU-215-909

THE HOUSE BOOK

The House Book

Edited by Beverley Hilton and Maria Kroll
Art director, Stafford Cliff
Associate editors, Ilse Grey, Lucy Oppé, Alexandra Towle

Contributors

Sheila Black – Buying a house
John Brookes – Outdoors
Caroline Conran – Batterie de Cuisine
Margaret Duckett – Bedrooms/One-room living/Attics
Kit Evans – Living-rooms (Floor levels)
Janet Fitch – Children's rooms
Stephen Garrett – Internal layout
Chester Jones – Living-rooms
Sally King – Bathrooms/Details/Finishes/ – Of course you can do it!
Maria Kroll – Things
Elizabeth Gundry – Going metric
Christopher Haines – Hi-Fi
Brenda Hall – Index
Claire Hunt/Russell Miller – Glossary
Joyce Lowrie – Elevations/Heating/Adding an extra room
José Manser – Work areas
Dawn Marsden – Windows
Russell Miller – Employing others
Barty Phillips – Floors/Walls
John Prizeman – Kitchens
Penny Radford – Halls, stairs and landings
Geraldine Ranson – Storage/Eating-rooms (Furniture)/Bedrooms
Martin Roberts – Bathrooms
Stella Samuel – Attics/Basements and cellars
Juliet Glynn-Smith – Colour
Peter Glynn-Smith – Lighting
John Vaughan – Eating-rooms
Cynthia Wickham – Indoor plants, Window boxes, Roof gardens

Designed by Conran Associates
28 Neal Street, London WC2H 9PH
and produced by Mitchell Beazley Publishers Limited,
14-15 Manette Street, London W1V 5LB

© Mitchell Beazley Publishers Limited 1974
First Published 1974
Eleventh Printing 1986
All rights reserved
ISBN 0 85533 649 8

Type set by Foremost Typesetting Limited, London
Colour reproduction by Fotomecanica Iberico, Madrid
Printed in Spain by
Printer Industria Grafica S.A.
Sant Vicenc dels Horts Barcelona 1978
Deposito Legal B-48.200-1977

THE HOUSE BOOK

Terence Conran

Mitchell Beazley Publishers Limited
London

Contents 1/2

Contents 3/4

Once the people employed in furnishing stores could be relied on for comprehensive advice. Nowadays, there is too much information for anyone to have at his fingertips – but the House Book is here to bridge the gap.

Having a warm home that looks good and works well and that you, your family and friends enjoy must be one of the most worthwhile things in life; and to help you achieve it is the object of this book.

Most people will have an inheritance of furniture and furnishings, and an arrangement of rooms that is short of ideal. This book will help you get the best out of what you've got, and will open up possibilities in areas where you'd given up hope. If you are just beginning to set up house, be prepared to start with the absolute minimum of possessions.

Two good chairs, a table, a bed, pillows, sheets and duvet, a heavy frying-pan and saucepan, and an excellent kitchen knife, one wooden spoon, two plates, two knives and forks and a couple of mugs and a teapot are almost enough to start your home. Certainly, this sparseness will allow you to consider how you want your home to be planned, and encourages you to think out carefully what you really need and want, before you rush out to the shops.

But what is it going to look like when it all comes together? Will it give you the sort of place you have in your mind's eye? To help you do this, you'll need to be able to make a workable plan, to understand the minimum and maximum sizes that your furniture can be, know what styles will or won't work together. You'll interest yourself in colours and textures, in fixtures and fittings, and you'll have to be clear in what order to do things.

Once the basic planning is done, then is the time to consider the wall finishes, flooring, the major pieces of furniture, the main light sources, and after that your attention should turn to the pictures, rugs, blinds or curtains, objects, lamps, and even waste-paper baskets. The purpose of this book is to help you come to all these decisions. But what no book can do is to ensure that your home reflects your own personality. That's your job.

Terence Conran.

Style/1

Do you know how you want to furnish your home? If you do, don't read on. But if, although you know what you like, you are not sure how to set about getting it, and if you find the avalanche of suggestions in books and magazines as muddling as it is inspiring, then you may think it useful, as I do, to analyse the various current "looks" in terms of their main components.

Obviously, different rooms in your house can be different in style: the sort of atmosphere that you like in your kitchen may not be what you want in your living-room. So, don't be afraid to diversify: the one most important thing about your house is that it should be yours, and not a kit picked up lock, stock and barrel from a book, magazine or designer.

Remember, if you can afford to employ a designer he will only be as good as his brief. Make your requirements clear, and be clear too about what you want to spend. Sort out your own mind first: (people who treat their consultants like a mixture of pet poodle and father confessor must be prepared to pay for the privilege).

If you do employ a designer you'll probably arrive, together, at a style that's partly his, partly yours and wholly to your liking. However, there is usually neither need nor opportunity to call in outside help, and you will have the task of clarifying your ideas by yourself.

Your own taste will dictate the general style. The first step then is to examine the specific things that go into making it up. You will find that it is not the individual pieces of furniture that add up to a look, but the way in which things come together, the background (in terms of both colour and material), and the sort of accessories with which they are combined.

The six main styles from which most current interiors seem to be derived, I have called farmhouse, town-house, country-house, Mediterranean, international and eclectic simply to define them. Each can be transplanted – but I am certainly not proposing straitjackets from which escape is impossible. Different styles from different periods can live happily together, blending into a look that reflects your own individual personality, and this is what really matters.

The hub of the farmhouse is its kitchen, and the hub of that kitchen is the table: old, huge and scrubbed, a reminder of endless gargantuan meals that have been prepared and eaten there. Here, all abiding warmth and comfort comes from an Aga recessed into the beautiful old chimney breast – such a welcome for a farmer returning from his fields – or a fugitive from the city rat-race.

Style
2/3 Farmhouse

A manifestation of the wave of nostalgia which is sweeping through every developed part of the world. The feeling for natural materials, textures and simple, comfortable furniture does not, however, mean a return to nature by latter-day Rousseaus; it means having one's cake and eating it too. Brick, slate, wood and tiles are used in conjunction with new, man-made materials all over the house; kitchens with traditional central tables are no less friendly if they also contain washers and freezers.

Rush-matting and cane-seating are part of the farmhouse style. Natural wood, especially pine, belongs to it, but never fake pine plastic laminate. Part of it, too, is the sort of furniture that was once found in the servants' attics or below the stairs in their kitchens and pantries – much more part, in fact, than that in the masters' rooms. And "farmhouse" does not on any account mean over-wrought iron, mock-rustic accessories or horse brasses; it does mean an atmosphere of casual comfort and sturdy solidity.

(*Above*) *The essential farmhouse elements are all present here: slate and brick floor, wooden beams, rough-rendered walls, all natural-looking materials which seem to connect the interior with the garden.*

1 *Real farmhouse windows are often rather small and can't always readily be flung open. This does not matter when the best part of the day is spent outside in any case, but "farmhouse" in town needs windows that can open wide. Here, the outside comes into the room, making a perfect, simple country bedroom.*

2 *The fireplace must always be large – capable of burning apple logs at least. Seating should never be arranged in a formal manner – the thought of "farmhouse" living-room furniture conjures up old sofas and floppy armchairs. But cushions and mattresses, giving the same sort of relaxed comfort, can successfully be included.*

3 *Textures more than anything else foster the style. Massive timber staircases and beamed ceilings are examples par excellence and would not be at home anywhere but in the country; but stone floors, whitewash and natural woods can be used anywhere.*

(Below) Farmhouse style used in the conscious manner : exposed bricks, beams, large open fire, simple, ladder-back chairs with rush seats carry on the tradition. Architectural features, such as the missing walls on either side of the chimney breast and the large window, however, are of today, as is the blind, edged with the same small print that covers the table.

1

2

1 *This kitchen could be equally at home in a cottage or a modern town block of flats – for all that the table is not scrubbed but varnished wood.*

2 *The unpretentiousness of this kitchen corner is the point to note. Things have happened sensibly and naturally, and no excesses of modern technology have been allowed to confuse the issue.*

3 *The visible relish that the owners of this kitchen take in the objects with which they surround themselves makes for comfortable chaos, but with all its clutter this kitchen is strangely efficient.*

3

Style
4/5 Town house

A smart style much influenced by famous decorators such as François Catroux, William Baldwin, David Hicks and Jon Bannenberg, relying on a soothing mixture of unaggressive, comfortable, modern furniture and one or two antique pieces. The best features of the room are picked out and emphasized – perhaps a good fireplace or cornice. Colour is usually subdued but quite rich. Luxury is the keynote.

There is not much pattern on the walls. Materials like natural hessian or ordinary brown wrapping paper are quite often used to good effect. Curtains are also likely to be of a plainish fabric but might be bordered with bright-coloured webbing. Judicious combinations of rough and smooth textures are important factors in the town-house style.

The floor is usually carpeted, quite often in a small neat pattern, but there

1 *Typically town-house are these dark walls with mouldings left in place, the chrome-framed graphics and the shiny white painted fireplace, well-used to house a hi-fi speaker. The silver and black bird sculptures are very deliberately positioned.*

might be an old, richly-patterned rug on a plain carpet.

Lighting is always very carefully considered. Twelve-volt high-intensity spots will highlight pictures and objects, while the background is often lit by large, drum-shaded lamps.

The living-room is often dominated by one or two large, traditional, feather-filled sofas, perhaps covered with a natural linen piped in a contrasting

2 *Sybaritic voluptuousness is the essence of this metropolitan bedroom. This style is often reinforced by a collection of carefully-arranged objects – in this case ostrich eggs and amber beads.*

3 *Rough fabric walls and a tousled rug, contrasted with the smoothness of marble, characterize this rich, small, comfortable corner. Another point to note is the contrast between the simple, cotton-covered cushions and the elegantly upholstered sofa.*

colour. Modern chrome-and-slab coffee tables, or perfectly plain, white, lacquered square-legged tables fit in well. But the room usually relies on at least one good and rather rococo chair or cupboard to relieve the austerity.

Collections of carefully-arranged objects are vital to this sort of interior: antique stone or ceramic heads, beautiful shells, obelisks. Flowers often provide brilliant patches of colour. At times there will be neither stems nor foliage showing, just their heads, massed tightly together; or perhaps a single lily in a simple stylish vase.

4 *Saarinen-sculptured fibre-glass chairs are an important ingredient for town-house dining-rooms, as is the very traditional floor-length tablecloth. Its tiny print matches the roman blind at the french window. Also note how the cheap, herringbone-patterned coconut matting forms part of this expensive-looking room.*

The very synthesis of the town-house – executed by that past master of the style,
David Hicks, in his own dining-room. It is the combination of the colours that gives this
quite simple room its air of luxury, to which painted panels add hard-edged prettiness.

Style
6/7 Country house

Unlike farmhouse, which draws inspiration from peasants' dwellings seen through the rose-coloured spectacles of urbanites bent on recapturing the simple life, the country-house style looks to the rich-man-in-his-manor rather than to the poor-man-at-his-gate.

"Country-house" suggests house-parties; space, or the illusion of it; cucumber sandwiches after tennis; drawing-room rather than family-room, with furniture handed down through several generations in turn.

Victorian and Edwardian accessories, such as fire-screens or cushions embroidered by gentle girls during long winter evenings years ago, or water-colours by long-forgotten maiden aunts all play a part. Ancestors, gilt-framed, foster the look, as do all portraits, no matter of or by whom.

It is a soft-centred style, with a touch of faded gentility – bright, solid splashes of colour are counter-productive. Charm is the thing that most immediately registers, and airiness, though when the garden comes into the house, it is by way of flowers straight from the herbaceous border and, probably, floral print fabrics.

Country-house has no use for hunting-print table-mats, or those scarlet cardinals who seem, mercifully, to have quaffed their last. Gentle colours, un-aggressive objects and a sense of the past are the crucial elements of this style.

---

1 *The romantic, creamy cotton canopy and drapes make this room fresh and airy. This atmosphere is helped along by walls of pine and simple, subtly painted rush-seated furniture. It is the sort of bedroom a Ruritanian princess might dream in.*

---

2 *Peacefulness is of the essence: pretty, stripped pine chest, and dressing table together with its jug of iris, as well as coarse net curtains, provide it here.*

---

3 *This is the country-house treatment interestingly applied to a modern house. The crucial elements are the antique oak chairs, the candlesticks, the chandelier, and the Andy Warhol Marilyn Monroe prints. On the face of it they may make an incongruous collection, but they combine successfully to make a grand, modern country dining-room.*

1

2

3

1 *Chinese Chippendale, a polished floor, wickerwork, drum-shaded lamp, and, most importantly, a superb, gentle colour-scheme, make this soothing bedroom an excellent example of the country-house style.*

2 *A really comfortable sitting-room. Curvy furniture and fireplace work surprisingly well with patterned rugs and upholstery. Rush matting underneath it all keeps the room firmly in the conntry.*

3 *Stripped pine chests and beams, white-painted wicker chairs, a collection of pretty shells and butterflies and sunshine through white calico curtains add up to a charming, comfortable bedroom in which to have breakfast.*

Style
8/9 Mediterranean

In terms of interior design, this style does not echo the playgrounds of millionaires, but the relaxed, occasionally spartan, habitations of the indigenous population. The keynote is simplicity, lack of fuss and an absence of accessories. Efficient central heating helps "Mediterranean" in non-balmy climates, but colours are predominantly cool – white and more white, blue and green. Tiles form a part of this style, as do arches and rough-plastered walls.

Kitchens respond particularly well to "Mediterranean" treatment. A "farmhouse" kitchen with less wood, more tiles and much more white becomes "Mediterranean" by another name.

Crisp fabrics, especially cottons, in simple checks, stripes, or tiny Provençal prints, all foster the look. So does peasant embroidery – especially when it comes in borders of traditional design.

While wrought-iron work and, in the case of the southern shores of the Mediterranean, filigree masonry, are in evidence *in situ*, these things are best ignored during transplant operations, since their beauty depends on a long tradition of local craftsmanship. Also unconducive to the pleasant sort of atmosphere I have in mind is an undue reliance on things like Chianti-flask lamps and bullfighting posters brought back from holidays.

The quality of light, such an essential ingredient, can, on the other hand, be recreated without too much difficulty. Translucent or venetian blinds can make even northern light filter into the room or admit it in shafts, and in the evening the intense beams of silvered spotlights help enormously to create the illusion.

It is also possible for anyone with access to a yard or an area to enjoy a bit of Mediterranean indoor/outdoor life. There is no need to invest in a special patio suite; a stout table and chairs will do. The trick is to place them close up to the house, so that not only meals, but chores – preparing the vegetables, darning – can take place out of doors with a minimum of fuss, whenever it's sunny. (Sadly, no way has yet been found to produce Mediterranean summer weather in northern latitudes.)

The very essence of Mediterranean life – one can almost smell the suntan-oil and see the bronzed bodies. The light filters through white calico, the glazed floor tiles gleam, the white-painted, rough-rendered walls and ceiling are kept looking alive through the play of reflections. But where would the room be without the marvellous blue-and-white striped cushions? They really are the crucial elements that make this room feel so Mediterranean.

1 *Important here are the colourful seating units, which give a summer look regardless of the season.*

2 *The subtle colour of the shutters, and the window set into an ice-cream plaster wall would make this a "Mediterranean" window even if there was no view over a calm blue sea.*

3 *A beautiful, simple, four-poster with calico drapes. The peasant embroidery, repeated on the table-cloth, show the affinity between crafts the world over.*

4 *Mediterranean indoor/outdoor living can be recaptured with a covered patio like John Stefanides's plants in tubs and a number of oil-lamps for glow-worm lighting.*

5 *Blue need not be the colour of the sunlit sea. It might be slate or indigo, colours that go particularly well with the tones of terracotta.*

6 *Vast expanses of white and cream, used with mellowed, natural wood and embroidered textiles in strong colours make this room feel Mediterranean for all that it is part of Geoffrey Bennison's Brighton flat.*

7 *The quintessential rough plaster wall, here partly covered by a wall-hanging under intricately-worked metal framed mirrors, would be effective in any part of the world.*

8 *Arches and half-arches, features of Mediterranean architecture, work best in rooms deliberately left stark and unaccessorized.*

9 *Serenity comes from being surrounded only by the essentials of life, as in this small kitchen/eating area of ecclesiastical simplicity.*

1

2

3

4

5

6

7

8

9

Style
10/11 International

This style takes a great deal of skill and money – but it makes for rooms of great tranquillity, allowing a depth of concentration only rarely encountered outside monasteries.

The very best (which, sadly, means the most expensive) furniture from international designers will dominate the room. There may well be a beautifully-detailed storage unit of Mondrian-like simplicity to act as a foil to the voluptuous leather-covered sofas or the sinuous, elegant chromium chairs.

Colour, though practically non-existent, may be found in large, cool, abstract paintings.

There is often a natural-coloured close-fitting carpet, but occasionally there might be a long-haired rug on fine maple boards. Blinds or curtains are usually creamy white.

The shape of the light fittings is usually considered before the quality of light – that is to say, the highly-stylish lamps work well individually, but seldom produce a restful all-over scheme.

Background lighting will probably come from fittings recessed into the ceiling. Objects as contemporary as the furniture may be carefully displayed. Flowers are not much in evidence, but large plants do occur, chosen more usually for their sculptural qualities than as reminders of the great outdoors.

1 *Le Corbusier and Mies van der Rohe furniture is set off by chesterfields and an antique rug. The way it all seems to float on a pale wooden floor gives the sensation of international opulence.*

2 *The simplicity and purity of this room gives it a heavenly calm, where every object is thrown into sharp relief.*

3 *The international kitchen to end all international kitchens. Judiciously borrowed from hard-working restaurant kitchens are the extractor hoods, the tough tiles and travertine floors and surfaces. The light is particularly well considered: one can imagine Escoffier creating some of his sophisticated dishes here.*

4 *Extremely elegant, small dining area with all the components of the jet-set style. Beautiful chrome and black plastic work well with the greens of the fern which in turn echo the Richard Smith picture. The Art deco bowl gives an important accent.*

5 (*opposite*) *The raw-silk covered sofa, the herringbone rough-wool carpet, and the woven cane of the Mies van der Rohe chairs are the important factors in this restful room which is dominated by a powerful Frank Stella painting.*

1

2

3

4

Dictionary definition: "borrowing freely from various sources; not exclusive in opinion or taste...".

This style is highly personal, and the mark of people who are supremely confident of their own taste. They may be, and usually are, associated in some way with the arts, and it is they who are the creative innovators, discovering, as it were, the styles that in a short space of time are imitated, simplified and absorbed into styles that will be generally accepted.

That is not to say that every novelty is bound to take root. But it is a fact that all unfamiliar sights – whether in art or in decoration, whether truly new or revived – seem eccentric before one has got on to their wavelength.

The chief eclectic style poised on the brink of "mainstream" at the moment is not quite op, or pure pop, pure deco, pure Bauhaus, or *art nouveau*, but a blend of all of these. It will, in time, acquire a name of its own. Already, the junkshops of the world cannot yield enough 20s and 30s miscellanea to satisfy the demand: new Bauhaus furniture and art deco textiles, carpets and rugs are again being manufactured, and so are the accessories to go with them.

One thing is certain: while yesterday's eclectic choices get synthesized into the currency of the day after tomorrow, the creative innovators, antennae quivering, will pick up new ideas out of the air, realize them in their own houses, and so continue the process.

1 *The objects in David Hockney's living-room all relate to each other having been lit on by his trained and selective eye. Although they stem from many schools, they are placed in a way that is part of none and add up to a very positive style of their own.*

2 *In this scheme the objects are what might loosely be termed "contemporary", but the gentle lilac-and-apricot colour scheme adds a note that is anything but: it is reminiscent of a chiffon-clad production of an elegant 20s drawing-room comedy.*

3 *Lamp and dove are witnesses to Art deco, zebra skin and coffee table are from a different world, and the 30s blackamoor, himself the heir of an eighteenth-century ancestor, strikes yet a different note; but the whole is as homogeneous an arrangement as it is possible to find.*

4 *This desk area exemplifies perfectly how things from various sources and periods, judiciously assembled and given room to breathe, add up to a style that is perfectly of itself, benefiting from every area from which it has "borrowed".*

Style
14 Eclectic

1 *Rietveldt chairs and panelled tallboy: their makers would not have visualized them in conjunction, but they work beautifully together.*

2 *Sculptured table and antelope-legged chairs underline the special qualities of the sensitive display of traditional kitchen utensils that form a decorative wall behind the sink.*

3 *Floor cushions, used in this disciplined way and combined with tables reminiscent of the 30s, are a far cry from the "ethnic Oriental" that undoubtedly inspired them.*

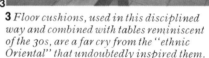

4 *Wall decorations, too, can be highly personal – and although one can't quite see "mainstream" mittens, there is a growing tendency to mount collected objects of strange provenance side by side on vertical surfaces.*

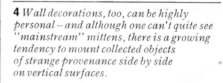

5 *Splendid Charles Rennie Mackintosh chair by a bird's-eye maple fireplace assumes, by juxtaposition, the character of a David Hockney linear still-life.*

6 *Pure pop with a vengeance: smiling lip sofa, seen here through an Odeon arch of twinkling lights.*

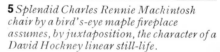

7 *Highly stylized interpretation of deco in a colour scheme that gives it a special edge.*

8 *Printed bedspreads make these cusions to flop back on – there's a debt to those rooms full of Eastern mystery and promise. In this case, however, they've been used so cheerfully that the effect is one of Provençal prints and the atmosphere is of the Midi rather than the Middle East.*

9 *The feeling of Stars and Stripes, but the idea is so ingeniously used that it's stylish and, thank goodness, owes nothing to the overused notion of nationalism in interior design.*

Elevations/1

Appearance, like a pretty face, isn't everything. It's what goes on behind it that matters. When buying a house, you have to take into account so many equally important considerations, that by the time you have found what you need, it is possible that the outside appearance is not absolutely what you had imagined. However, just as a plain face can be improved by clever make-up, so a house can be improved, either cosmetically with colourful paints and plants, or by giving it a structural face-lift.

We get disturbed by the wanton demolition of handsome old buildings, forgetting that we ourselves contribute to the erosion of the environment by the unthinking way we replace a decayed old timber casement by an incongruous modern form when it is possible to retain the character and balance of the façade by fitting an off-the-peg version of the original frame.

First of all, think about the setting of the house. Unless you live screened in by trees or a high wall, take a good look at your neighbours. Do you live in a hybrid collection of individual houses? Then you can simply treat your house on its own merits. If you live in a group that has some common character, then it will be to everyone's advantage if you respect this neighbourly relationship.

If you live in a terrace you might suggest to your neighbours that you get together to decorate the outsides of your houses. It will certainly reduce costs all round and add considerably more distinction to the houses individually and collectively. The same suggestion holds good if your house is semi-detached. One way to do this is to have the same colour scheme for the main architectural features of both units – stucco work, porches, window frames, shutters and metalwork etc., and simply paint the front doors different colours.

If your house owes no special loyalty to its neighbours, walk all around it and try to sum up its good and bad features. Your object should be to give order, to simplify and to clarify. This means being true to the house's essential character, or the character it's trying to assume.

---

1 *A fussy Victorian exterior given an air of distinction with a coat of paint.*

---

2 *A dingy Edwardian terrace house simplified and given a startling face-lift.*

---

3 *Brilliant red Virginia creeper covers dull, bricked-in windows.*

---

4 *A Victorian bow window with white curtains stands out boldly from the dark walls.*

1

2

3

4

Weatherboarding

(Essex and Home Counties). The tiled roof is brown-red, and the small windows are set within the structural framing on which the horizontal boarding is fixed. In the country paint walls white, pale cream, pale grey etc.; in town, dark brown, dark grey, dark blue or sludgy green. Contrast with white timber trim and black metalwork. Where orderly, paint drain and rain-water pipes black as well, otherwise merge with wall colour.

Timber framing

(Hampshire). Here infilled with herringbone brick-work. When possible leave the frame exposed, treat timber with colourless preservative or preservative plus an appropriate staining, if the colour is patchy. New windows or any other opening should be matched to the existing ones and formed within the framework, extend-ing to entire width or height of panel opening. Take care also when repointing brickwork – don't let the builder make it look too crisp and new.

Cotswold stone

Usually coursed rubble, ideally with a stone slate roof. Good reconstituted versions of both blocks and slates are available for repair and new work. The steeply pitched roof provides attic room with windows in gables or gablets, as well as pitched dormers. Windows are casement type, metal or wood framed. Where window units are in groups of threes they are usually separated by stone mullions, with double units timber framed. Add windows to match existing unit size and pro-portion, including leaded lights where they exist. Moulding details can be copied in reconstituted stone.

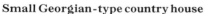

Small Georgian-type country house

This basic form has been copied up to the present day. If in brick, later examples often need greater emphasis on doors and windows. A parapet cornice, mouldings, louvred shutters or a porch or canopy over the door may help. Stone mouldings should be left unpainted, plaster ones finished in white or cream. Woodwork should be white except where the walls themselves are white, when black or grey could be used for the outer or entire frame. If genuinely Georgian, maintain small window panes, otherwise match to existing ones. The ground floor is sometimes covered in rusticated rendering to simulate stone blocks. This should be painted to match other rendering in a matt finish.

Regency stucco

On the whole both mouldings and wall surfaces on this type of house should be painted the same colour. In the country, choose whites and pastels but not blue-greens or blues as these may not fit in with the surroundings. In towns, dark browns, blues and greens and greys can look handsome but need the sparkle of large areas of white. If woodwork is not sufficient to provide this, the ground floor or mouldings around windows and doors could be painted. Windows will be sash type; copy these where more light is needed. Window frames, door frames and doors and any other woodwork should be painted white, unless the house has white walls when black or grey outer framing is an alternative.

Victorian gothic

These may be brick, stone or plaster. They invariably have steeply pitched slate roofs, often with carved bargeboarding trimming the gables. Doors usually have pointed arches, and so may windows. Do all you can to lighten the mood. If stucco, paint a pale, light-reflective colour; all wood work should be white. Copy the existing sash windows and french doors where you want more light. If there is any ornate cast iron, clean thoroughly, rustproof it and paint it black or white. If you want to use the roof space, skylights would be acceptable at the back of the house, pitched dormers in the fronts or windows in the gable walls.

Small artisan terrace house

These can be of brick, stone or plaster. To look pretty they must look modest and unfussy. Unless there is an original or absolutely "in period" porch, strip it off. The front door should have six panels or two vertical ones, or be tongued-and-grooved vertical boarding. This can be painted black, white, or a colour to contrast with the walls. All other woodwork should be white and the reveals of the windows and door openings can be white to give extra emphasis and sparkle. The window on the ground floor may be a large sash or casement. Those on the upper floor should be modest and smaller versions of the same type. Dormers or skylights are best added at the rear if the roof pitch allows space for an attic room.

Georgian cottage

Usually red brick with symmetrically placed windows and centrally placed front door. This can be boarded or panelled but rarely has a porch. Some openings have elliptical arches over them which should be preserved, and windows are multiples of the same unit grouped in twos or threes. Never add beyond this width; where more light is needed, insert new window in side wall or drop an existing one at the back of the house to form a french door. Match proportions and pane sizes carefully. Traditionally all woodwork should be white, except for doors which could be black or some other solid colour. Where brickwork has been painted white, window frames – but not sashes – could be painted black.

Georgian terrace house

The brick upper floors are usually topped by a cornice which conceals a shallow sloping roof; ground floor and basement are often stucco. This should be painted white, pale stone or pale grey, always lighter in tone than the brickwork above, with cornices, window sills and any other mouldings matching. Window frames are generally better white, with the reveals of the window painted white also where they are not already framed with a moulding. Front doors can provide a colour contrast. Windows should be sash type with small panes (these get larger the later the date). Any replacements should match the existing ones if in period, or those of the terrace generally. Basement windows alone can be altered without destroying the consistency of the façade, although skylights could be inserted in the roof behind the parapet. But whatever you do, keep it in proportion and if it is in a terrace maintain the general appearance of the whole.

Edwardian terrace house

These are usually built of brick with stone trim around windows and doors, and frequently have bay windows. The bay may have a mock gable above eaves level which is better trimmed off. Leave the stone trim unpainted, replacing damaged sections with reconstituted blocks. Where there are plaster mouldings or the stone is already painted, use a matt, slightly textured paint in a soft pale stone colour. Woodwork should be painted white, front door a colour to tone with the brick, or white. Paint metalwork black.

Surburban semi

Many detached and semi-detached houses built between the wars pretend to be cottages with their half-timbered gables, weatherboarding, tile-hung bay and areas of stucco. Do all you can to emphasize this cottage character, and accent the horizontal. Strip what you can and paint the rest white or cream to simplify the appearance as much as possible. If the tilehanging of the bay clashes with the roof tiles try to replace them with matching ones. All woodwork including the front porch will look prettiest white, the front door could be white too or black or a muted green or blue. Although often poorly designed, it is worth remembering that the inspiration behind these houses was well-intentioned (the architect Voysey for instance) and an effort should be made to create a rural mood.

50s, 60s, 70s detached house

Owing allegiance to no period or region, these houses are often built of unsympathetic as well as too many materials. Frequently the windows are overlarge and of unpleasant proportions. This can be offset by painting window frames white and hanging white venetian blinds inside or fitting white louvred panels over the narrower panels outside. Redress the boxy look by linking ground floor windows with areas of squared timber trellising and plant with evergreen creeper. A pergola running across the entire face of the house will do the same, especially if you can link its framing with a side garage.

Elevations

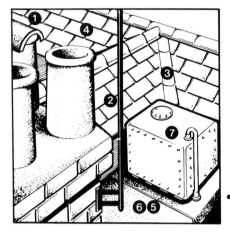
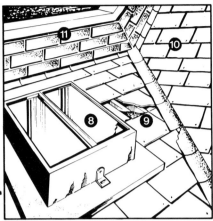

1 Are any of the chimneys leaning – does the brick or stonework need repointing? If the chimneys are pointed with cement at their junction with the roof, does this pointing appear to be intact? If less than perfect, replace with metal flashing. If the fireplaces are blocked up, replace the pots with half round ridge tiles to permit ventilation whilst preventing rain falling down the chimney.

2 Are there television aerials and to what are they attached? Heavy ones attached to chimneys can weaken them seriously.

3 Are there valley gutters between sections of the roof? If they are flat, they can be protected against being clogged by snow and leaves by a raised slatted board over them.

4 Does the ridge line sag, or any other sections of the roof? In old houses a slight sag need cause no worry; in a newer house it is more serious, but in any case check the roof structure inside.

5 Check asphalt roofs for cracks as these will need specialist attention. Surface crazing is nothing to worry about for the time being, but can lead to leaks in the future.

6 With bituminous felt roofs, check joints for good adhesion – specialist skill will be needed for splits and serious blistering.

7 Is there a cold water tank on the roof? Is it effectively insulated or will it need replacement and possible removal into the house? Is it accessible for valve washer replacement?

8 Are there any skylights or dormers? Because they are hard to reach, they sometimes do not get repaired and painted with the rest of the house and are a common source of damp penetration.

9 Check whether any tiles or slates are missing. Look at the ridge as well as the body of the roof.

10 Do all the tiles or slates on the different slopes of the roof match?

11 Check whether all the coping stones on parapets and gable walls are there and whether the pointing looks secure. Do they have damp-proof courses? If the parapet is damp or stained, have one inserted.

12 Are there overhead electricity and telephone cables? If so, are they unattractively conspicuous and are the junctions ugly?

13 Check that every section of the roof drains to a gutter. One piece of roof may drain on to another piece of roof but water should ultimately reach a gutter and not splash upon the ground around the house. This applies to all roofs except thatched ones.

14 Is the house covered with creeper? Creeping plants grown on wires and trellises will do no damage nor will the lighter deciduous climbers such as Virginia creeper. Ivy is a different matter as its rootlets penetrate the joints and can dislocate bricks and blocks.

15 If there is any half-timbering, is it an intrinsic part of the structure or simply surface decoration?

16 If the house has gables trimmed with a barge board, does this appear to be in good repair? This would need careful copying if replacement was necessary.

17 If the house is plastered, are there cracks and bulges? Small cracks are not serious; large cracks may indicate movement of structure; bulges and areas broken away suggest serious dampness behind plaster. Old patching need not worry you; recent patching should be investigated.

18 Are the finishes consistent on all exterior walls? If not, do they blend or is decoration required to pull the appearance together?

19 Are there shutters on the house? If they are attractive enough to leave, are they in good condition? Are hinges or other fixings rusty, or in good repair?

20 The odd broken window does not matter but several over a long period could have let damp into the house as well as vandals.

21 Are there any ground floor bay windows? They often have inadequate foundations so that they sag forward pulling their roofs away from the house to let damp penetrate.

22 Check whether gutters and rain waterheads are clogged with leaves. These can cause overflows in storms which will result in damp penetration through walls or roof. Downpipes should have mesh guards over the gutters to prevent leaves washing down.

23 Porches and extensions, as well as having inadequate foundations, may be poorly connected. Check whether they are pulling away from the main structure or allowing rain to penetrate through defective joints or pointing.

24 Check whether cornices and mouldings around doors and windows are plaster or painted stone. If plaster, is the plaster in good condition or will these details need remaking? You might find glass-fibre alternatives.

25 Where mouldings are made of painted or natural stone and are either broken or flaking and crumbling away, replacement in reconstituted stone is the answer for natural stone, and not too expensive. If painted, they can be rerun in cement.

26 Are the household waste pipes on the outside, and festooned across the house in an untidy fashion? If at all possible rerun them in a duct inside the house to improve appearance and avoid frozen pipes.

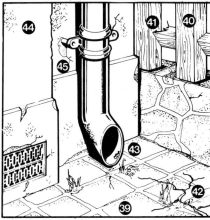

27 Check whether the walls of the house are true vertically and horizontally with plumbline and spirit level. In old houses, a little discrepancy will not matter. In a newer house the cause of this will need checking.

28 Check if you can the thickness of external walls. You can do this by assuming that the window frame is roughly 4 in./102 mm; stone walls are usually 18 in./457 mm; 4½ in./114 mm brickwork will need lining or an external waterproof layer; 9 in./229 mm brickwork will probably need weather protection and insulation; 11 in./279 mm – 12 in./305 mm will indicate a cavity wall, 13½ in./343 mm – 14 in./356 mm solid brickwork.

29 Test the balustrades, railings and framework of any balconies or verandahs to see whether they are secure or would need dismantling or replacing. Check condition of their flooring and that rain-water drainage is provided for.

30 Does the woodwork look as though it has been recently painted? Look closely to see whether it is smooth and the paint has gone on a well-prepared base. Where paintwork looks poor, poke it with a penknife to see whether wood is soft and has actually rotted.

31 Is there efflorescence on the brickwork? This will need persistent dry brushing to remove it.

32 If the house is of unpainted stonework or brickwork, will it need repointing? Scrape at the joints with a penknife to see whether it is very crumbly.

33 If the house has a timber floor it should be ventilated underneath. Check whether there are air bricks or similar ventilators at ground level in every outer wall, and that these are clear of debris: they could have been covered over to prevent draughts from floorboards. You may have to poke around to find them.

34 Is there a damp-proof course? Houses built since the 1914-18 war are likely to have one though it may be broken or concealed behind banks of earth, rockeries etc. Look for one about 6 in./152 mm above ground level – generally shown by a thicker horizontal joint in the wall.

35 Are there paving stones or areas of concrete tight up against the walls of the house? Check by the sills of external doors whether there is a step down in level from the floor level inside and that the paving is not masking the damp-proof course or air bricks provided for under-floor ventilation.

36 Check for dropped and cracked lintels and sills, and drooping lines in brick and stone courses or stepped cracking – these may indicate a failure of foundations. In an old house the settlement may well be over; in a newer one these could be serious symptoms. But if the foundations are on clay the movement will be seasonal as the clay shrinks and expands in which case the foundations should be reinforced.

37 Trace which side of the house the manholes are and try to relate the waste pipes and drains of the house to them. Are the manholes rusty and difficult to lever? Is the interior of the manhole in good repair? Are the pipes clear of obstruction?

38 Are oil storage tanks and coal bunkers disagreeably obvious? Could they be screened or moved to a less disturbing position?

39 Will the existing garden paths, paved areas and terraces need repair or relaying?

40 Check who is responsible for the party walls on both sides.

41 Are the garden walls or fences in good condition? Are they high enough to give sufficient privacy from the neighbours?

42 Are there large trees close to the house? Check if their roots have affected the foundations of walls closest to them.

43 Check that any solid paving – this includes paving slabs with mortar joints – is laid to drain either away from the house or to a trapped gulley.

44 If the wall surfaces have been painted, is the paint in good condition or is it flaking or mouldy demanding considerable preparation before repainting can take place?

45 Are gutters and downpipes firmly attached to the walls? Plastic gutters will mean a recent replacement and these should be in good order. Do metal ones look rusty and are there damp patches on the walls behind and around them? Because it is difficult to paint the backs of pipes, they often rust and crack, leaking into the wall. If they are broken, replace them. It is better for downpipes to discharge over an open gulley than for them to run directly underground. They are less likely to be clogged by leaves.

46 What sort of front fence or wall is there? If it is in poor condition, is it worth repairing or so inappropriate that it would have to be removed or altered?

47 Note the front steps: apart from general condition are they rather steep or made of slippery tiles which could be dangerous in icy or wet weather? Is there a handrail to grab?

48 Is there a basement or cellar? Is this ventilated by windows or grilles? Has it an area access and are the steps and railings to this sound? Is there a drain to prevent flooding?

49 Check where external drains are. Are the gratings there and intact and is the concrete around them cracked and in need of repair?

50 Is there an area of tilehanging on the walls? Are any of the tiles missing? Do they blend with those used on the roof or clash enough to need replacement, and are the junctions with the body of the house adequately protected with flashings?

Elevations
6/7 Emphasizing good features/removing bad ones

If the attractive old tiles or slates on your roof are broken and letting in the rain, do not be tempted to have them brushed over with one of the patent water-proofing materials now around, as it will ruin their appearance. If you cannot face up to having the roof stripped, and the slates or tiles relaid, have them lined from behind by the new systems available which many Local Authorities now employ.

Tilehanging

Some late Victorian and Edwardian houses have handsome red tilehanging on the upper floors, but because of the hot red shade of brick used on the ground floor the tiles are never seen to full effect. They will be seen to far better advantage and the proportion of the house frequently improved, if you paint the brickwork white, ochre, pale cream or a cool pink.

Stucco

If you live in a town and the walls of your house are plastered, a smooth-textured paint will accumulate soot and dirt more slowly than a coarse-textured one, and darker colours will be more serviceable. White paint on mouldings and features such as shutters and window boxes will offset any heaviness and demand far less upkeep than if the whole wall were a pale colour.

Porches

Where you have a deeply recessed porch, infilling the opening with glazed doors will provide a draughtproof lobby but can destroy the emphasis the porch provides, It is better to find room for double doors in the hall, and then to paint the door and door frame white and the recess itself white to make it appear more inviting.

Blank walls

Exploit large areas of blank wall by growing a wisteria or creeper against them. Only ivy is dangerous to the structure. Some creepers such as Honeysuckle halliana and the rose Mermaid are evergreen and will thrive happily, flowering all summer through. As a support, plastic-coated wire netting comes in a variety of gauges and colours or you can use framed panels of trellis.

Brickwork

Many houses in the Midlands are built of a hard red smooth-faced brick which never weathers. Make the most of it by painting with a matt-textured paint to soften its appearance. The colour you choose will depend on the setting and situation. If you are surrounded by dark trees, paint your house a pale but warm colour – sugar pink or a delicate apricot can look very good. Dark ochres and brown-reds will look handsome against the lighter tones of silver birches.

Bargeboarding

If you have a Victorian house or cottage with carved bargeboarding trimming the gables, paint them white if the walls are of a natural material or painted a colour – or black if the walls are white, so that the shape of the profile is set off to best advantage.

Formal façades

When houses have a formal orderly façade with a central front door, do all you can to emphasize the symmetry. Where the front path is set at one side move it to a central position. The front door can be further emphasized by a hood carefully matched to the period of the building. Although windows of varying sizes can be acceptable on the ground floor – they are often masked to some extent by shrubs and trees – the windows on the upper floors should all be the same size and type. The only permissible exceptions are the ones directly over the door itself.

Simplification is always a good policy but do not trim back a building so that it becomes characterless. If you have an 18th century house with a handsome but shaky cantilevered bay on the first floor, this is probably just the feature that gives the house its character, so it is worth investing money in getting it into perfect order. In the same way, if you are lucky enough to have an old conservatory, treasure it and have it restored, even at some cost.

Doors and door furniture

In-period panelled front doors should be restored, if possible, or replaced with modern equivalents. Tarnished brass door fittings can be cleaned in an acid bath, and rusted iron work can be given a new lease of life by treatment with caustic paint stripper.

Clumsy dormers

Old dormer windows are usually charming; modern versions are nearly always too wide and too solid. Inserted into the roofs of old houses and cottages they can overwhelm the entire façade. Ideally, where headroom will allow, they could be replaced with a double glazed roof light or the roof developed to form a mansard. Otherwise make them merge with the roof finish as much as possible, hanging the sides and all solid parts with the same tiles or slates as are used on the main roof and painting all woodwork a colour to match this finish. Alternatively, strip out all solid parts including the sides and glaze to achieve as light an effect as possible, with no curtains or blinds visible; paint all woodwork including window frames dark grey. Then focus attention on the colour and features of the wall below.

Planting quick-growing trees can sometimes help, but tree roots must be kept well away from the house to prevent damage to foundations by the roots.

Castellated brick/concrete garden walls

First slice off the castellations and as many courses as necessary to give the height you want. Then using a good reconstituted stone, cap the wall with coping units wide enough to overhang it 1 in./25 mm on both sides. Paint – or cement render and paint – the wall to blend as unobtrusively as possible with the walls of the house. Alternatively, drop to about 12 in./305 mm or less from the pavement and use the coping as a base for metal railings.

Unnecessary pediments

Although houses built before the 1914-18 war are generally of a sufficiently consistent style to look best left as they stand, trimming can help. Pediments and other ornaments above the line of the eaves are better and safer down, unless they are essential elements of the design.

Prefabricated boiler flues

Heating contractors unthinkingly install these asbestos cement and concrete block flues against any wall that suits them. Where such a flue is disfiguring one of the main walls of your house you have three choices open to you: you can switch to a boiler with a balanced flue (gas and oil) – this will require only a 9 in. × 9 in./ 229 mm × 229 mm hole in the wall and a small unobtrusive terminal; keep the boiler but build the flue internally; or move the boiler so that it links up with an existing internal flue. Whichever alternative you choose should make for more efficient boiler operation, but you must have a reliable professional installation to make sure there is no fire hazard, and if using an existing chimney, make sure this is lined to prevent spread of damp from flue gases.

Clumsy bay windows

The late-Victorians and Edwardians were particularly fond of adding enormous bay windows to houses of an earlier period. To restore the former elegance of your façade you may have to replace them with a window in style and scale with those on the upper floors. If major surgery is unacceptable, trim off the grosser features such as heavy roof or clumsy window frames. The windows will almost certainly be sash, and an attractive solution is to fill the wide gap with a triple sash.

Unwanted chimney stacks

Where fires and flues are no longer used, consider removing unwanted stacks and roofing over the gap. Unless the chimney forms an integral part of the composition this can tidy up the appearance considerably as well as reduce maintenance. If the flue is still providing room ventilation, cap the stacks with rain-resistant ventilators.

Tangles of drain pipes

If you are replumbing, try to lose any outside drain pipes in ducts inside, or at least convert them to the simpler single stack system which is now allowed. Rainwater pipes look neatest set at the corners or tucked into angles.

Television aerials

The older kinds of television aerials are monstrosities and should come down. Check whether an aerial in your roof space would be adequate. However, if you have foil-backed bituminous felt under your roof tiles or wire-secured thatch, this will screen out the signal. Where the aerial has to be outside replace it with one of the new types which are much smaller and far less hazardous to your building in high winds.

Mock half-timbering

Unless the house is a serious effort at reproduction Tudor design or the genuine article strip off the fake timber beams. Where this seems too formidable an operation, choose an acrylic-based finish and paint the timber in with the wall colour.

Additions by previous occupiers

Anything that is out of character with the house or is pretentious is best removed. This also applies to minor items such as modern wrought iron gates and coach lamps.

Mock stone blocks

In an effort to achieve rustic charm, builders often cut back and emphasize the joints between these blocks producing a clumsy effect. Where blocks are a pleasant colour, get your builder to point the joints with mortar which will match the blocks when dry, letting it extrude and smoothing it over the edges to give a softer effect and blur the pattern. Where blocks are a dull grey, point as above and paint.

Architect's plan superimposed on this façade shows that no detail should be left out.

Elevations
8/9 Walls

If you have pleasant coloured brickwork, stonework or any other permanent finish, there is almost everything to be said for simply putting it into good order and leaving it at that. The two main reasons for decorating the external walls of a house are either to rescue its appearance or to provide protection against the weather. This was done in the past with lime wash and paint, soft plaster as well as weatherboarding, slate and tilehanging and coating with tar – all methods still relevant today. But before you consider any external treatment you should treat your walls against rising damp, otherwise your protective finish will simply trap the damp inside so that its only means of escape is into the house. Where you have an existing attractive wall surface you can deal with penetrating damp by providing ground floor walls with a waterproof lining on their inner face or treating them with a colourless silicone finish on their outer face which, while protecting the fabric from driving rain, allows any residual moisture in the walls to escape. Remember too that repointing brickwork when necessary can often remove the main cause of damp penetration, depending on the relative porosity of bricks and mortar.

Brickwork

Bricks can be brushed down with water to clean them. If you are troubled with efflorescence continue doing this regularly until it disappears. Applying a coat or two of colourless silicone will then keep brickwork clean and stop rain penetration while still allowing the wall to breathe. Some of these silicone seals help to hold friable mortar together and may make repointing unnecessary.

Where repointing cannot be avoided, insist that the new mortar matches the old in strength and especially in colour. With new building, to get the richest effect mortar should be a little darker in tone than the brickwork. Avoid paler or very dark jointing which looks harsh and makes the bricks stand out unnaturally. The character of the joint is important too; with handmade and sandfaced bricks a flush joint looks best but with hard machine-made bricks a "struck" joint will give the wall a more interesting texture.

Where a number of bricks have disintegrated badly and the house is distinguished architecturally or the brickwork particularly handsome, try to replace the worn bricks with matching secondhand ones. Otherwise replace with bricks of matching texture, repoint and paint; or, if the brickwork is thin and in an exposed position, a coat of soft render (1 part cement, 1 part lime to 6 parts sand)

will cope with patching and repointing in one operation as well as making the wall weatherproof.

Stonework

How stone behaves depends on its type. Whereas granite is almost indestructible, an acid-polluted atmosphere can build up a surface skin on limestone and calcareous sandstone which will eventually blister and flake off, causing serious erosion. In such cases it is always worth bringing in a specialist firm rather than the local builder, so that both repairs and any new work is carefully matched in.

Stonework can be steam cleaned to improve its appearance and bring out its colour. Depending on its chemical character it may then be possible to apply colourless silicone to prevent further decay and accumulation of dirt.

Where mouldings and sills need replacing, it is often possible to find a firm which can produce an exact match of the originals in form, colour and texture at a reasonable cost. A number of good-looking reconstructed stone blocks are available in a great variety of colours and textures, and so long as both the coursing and pointing are carefully matched to the original stonework these can be used for extensions. They should weather and marry in with the old work fairly quickly, if brushed with manure water.

Concrete blocks

If these are simply painted, the scale of the block may seem rather clumsy and the texture rather mean. The pattern of the blocks can be softened considerably if a coarse-textured finish is used, or it can be totally disguised if the blocks are given a coat of soft render.

For new work some blocks such as Lignacite come in a good self colour which needs no painting. It is worth noting that the new metric ranges relate much more closely to traditional stone sizes and are more sympathetic in their proportions than the old imperial size blocks.

Plaster

Old lime plaster is soft and flexible and sufficiently porous to absorb a degree of water which in turn prevents more penetrating. More recent plaster is much harder because of its high cement content. This hardness makes it inflexible so that with the inevitable movements of the structure due to changes of temperature and moisture content, cracking occurs letting rainwater penetrate. This moisture gets trapped behind the plaster, causing the wall to deteriorate.

By far the best cure for cracked and crazed stucco is to chisel it off and replace it with a lime stucco to which very little

cement has been added. Cutting open the cracks in stucco and pointing them with strong cement mortar, though often done, is not a cure because the trouble will simply recur.

Unless the house is a formal one or you are matching up with existing fine plaster, roughcast finishes with a generous proportion of lime, applied by throwing rather than by trowel, are most effective and longest lasting.

An enemy of plaster is streaking from projections and this can be avoided by protective flashings and mouldings. Sills, for instance, can be sloped on the central face only (known as stooling) so that water is thrown off instead of creeping down the sides.

Pebbledash

Pebbledash consists of small pebbles or crushed stones thrown on to a fresh coat of mortar and left exposed. It can look dull and depressing if dirty or where the surrounding woodwork has been painted a dreary colour. However, brushing down gently with plenty of clean water will remove dust deposits, and painting all the woodwork white and the metalwork black can often transform it into a pleasantly textured warm neutral. Pebbledash can be painted – one manufacturer recommends that you mix their finishes with silver sand so that only a few coats will be needed to reach the deeper crevices.

Flints

Flint walling is found where flints are readily available, in chalk and limestone areas or on the coast. They are either split so that their bright faces show or left undressed to give a knobbly texture.

If repair work needs to be done or a new wall added, compare examples of the craftsman's flint work with good traditional work before taking him on. The mortar should be carefully mixed to match the existing texture and colour, and the appearance is considerably improved if mortar joints are well raked back with a pointed stick.

Half-timbering

This is found all over Britain but more particularly in areas where little natural stone is available. The framing is sometimes infilled with brick, sometimes with wattle and daub. Because wood tends to shrink, this form of construction becomes draughty and leaky in time so sometimes the entire face is found plastered over.

Silver grey oak in good condition should be left unstained but where the colour is patchy you could apply a black preservative wood stain to give a uniform colour.

Where half-timbering is in a very poor state, weatherboarding or tilehanging will provide an insulating and waterproof skin.

Weatherboarding

Weatherboarding can either be painted or, if it is elm or cedar, left to grey down to pretty silvery tones. Never use preservative on cedar weatherboarding or on shingles; it is totally unnecessary and simply maintains the unattractive hot ginger colour. Weatherboarding can be used to provide a waterproof skin on most types of structure and is set on vertical battens at roughly 2 ft/610 mm centres. It should be laid on bituminous felt and if you add a quilt of 2 in./25 mm fibreglass at the same time you will add considerably to the insulation of the building. A plastic version (which comes in white but can be painted) is now available, and has the advantage of requiring no maintenance.

Tilehanging

Tilehanging is another useful traditional way of providing an existing building with a waterproof skin or creating a sympathetic link for a new extension. Tiles chosen for wall hanging should relate in colour and texture to those used on the roof, although a different pattern may be used. There is a great variety of pretty traditional shapes such as diamonds and shields. Tiles can be hung on brick, stone, block or timber framing by means of horizontal battens with bituminous felt and glass quilt insulation behind.

Slatehanging

This is used in the southwest of England, particularly Cornwall, as protection against driving rain. Sometimes a slurry of plaster is used to fill up the joints. It can provide an excellent waterproof skin. Slates are hung on horizontal battens in the same way as tiles.

Painted surfaces

Where surfaces are already painted, you should check what kind of paint has been used. If your decorator is uncertain, the technical department of the firm whose finish you plan to use will take samples of your present wall finish and recommend how you should strip down and treat the surface before repainting.

In the past it was common to paint outside walls with a glossy, oilbased paint, as old plaster was soft and flexible and there was less danger of cracking to tear the paint film. The problem with using oil-based paints on walls is that they are not permeable – this means that any moisture trapped in the wall is unable to escape through it. Most of the new exterior finishes are either semi-permeable or permeable and you should take particular care to choose a permeable one if you suffer from rising damp.

Do not skimp on external wall finishes. It is better to pay quite a lot more for the job than need to have it redone in two or three years. Labour costs will continue to increase and for any buildings taller than two storeys painters will demand scaffolding to gain access and this too adds quite a bit to the basic price, so while you are about it get the job done as well as possible. This means the most thorough cleaning down of the surface to remove dirt, moss, lichen, flaking and powdering paint. The surface may need a stabilizing coat and treatment with fungicide, unless you choose a finish that includes its own. In many cases, you can use the little man around the corner for internal work but it is wiser to go to a reputable firm for external decoration. State in writing the make and type of finish you want used, that you want the manufacturers' instructions carried out to the letter and that your acceptance of a price is on the basis of the work being done with the materials you specify applied in the way you specify.

Types of finish available

A wide range of exterior finishes is now available, many of which can be applied to a great variety of surfaces.

First of all come the permanent treatments which once applied to the outside of the house should last for most of its natural life. These are products made from crushed natural stone (which provides the colour) set in a colourless matrix, and in all cases are specialist applied. Both black and white as well as a good selection of attractive subtle colours are available.

The spirit-based textured types which are sprayed on by either the manufacturers' own team or a specialist firm are the next most longlasting. These are totally permeable and usually come with a ten or fifteen year guarantee, and experience shows they will last considerably longer than that without needing retreatment.

Then come the brush-applied semi-permeable emulsions – textured finishes with a life of some seven to ten years. Slightly less longlasting are the good exterior quality emulsion paints or cement-based paints, all of which should give you a dependable life of up to five years if properly applied.

A nondescript façade becomes a work of art by brilliant use of colour. White curtains emphasize the treatment of the white painted window unit.

Elevations
10/11 Before and after

1/2 *A miraculous transformation has been achieved with this gloomy Victorian house. A very dark coat of paint over walls, drainpipes and projecting brick features gives an even, flat effect because shadows are eliminated. By contrast the detail is painted a sparkling white. A new, wider front door adds dignity to the entrance porch. Blinds and curtains have been considered as an integral part of the colour scheme and are kept drawn at a becoming level.*

3/4 *Structural alteration may not be necessary to upgrade a house generally and greatly increase its value. It can be done by a judicious application of paint in the right colours – when in doubt stick to black and white.*

5/6 *The only structural difference between this house and its neighbour is a large dormer window making use of the top floor. The main transformation has been effected by painting all woodwork yellow and everything else slate colour to match the roof.*

7/8 *The main trouble with this house was extreme damp, so the face-lift has been designed to counteract this. The broken slates were replaced with red tiles, the front door was moved to garden level so that rickety and rotten steps could be removed. The basement was tidied up and tarred to look like a neat, solid plinth to the white painted weather-boarded upper floors. This weather-boarding provides a weather-proof skin and extra insulation when laid on battens and bituminous felt.*

9/10 *A good neighbourly relationship could result in a much more dignified and formal appearance to your semi-detached house.*

1

2

3

4

5

6

7

8

9

10

1

2

3

4

5

6

7

8

1 The charm and dignity of this early 19th-century terrace has not been affected by the fact that each house has been painted a different colour. The pale colours chosen have the same tone values.

2 As a contrast, bold, brash contrasting colours can look equally well providing the houses have some common denominator – here the fact that all architectural features are kept a uniform white.

3 In order not to spoil the formal front elevation of this house, the extra windows that were needed have been built into the end wall. Though placed in a rather haphazard fashion, they have acquired architectural merit by being strongly emphasized with extra thick white frames. These contrast excitingly with the unusual dark navy blue of the walls.

4 Georgian sash windows with small panes are usually painted white for maximum definition and light. If you wish to paint the walls white as well, you could outline the windows in black.

5 This rather underlit and nondescript house has been given considerable distinction and a larger window area by means of new traditional triple-sash windows of the correct proportions. A new and imposing panelled front door has also been added.

6 A wall, built to protect this house from noise and traffic, has been lowered to show off a sufficient proportion of the ground floor windows.

7/8 Bold, strong colours look well when architectural features, such as sills, quoins, arches, door and window reveals are picked out in white.

33

Elevations
12/13 Roofs/windows

The shape of the roof does more to establish the character of a house than any other single feature. Climate dictates form. Heavy rain and snow produced the large sheltering roofs of Scottish crofts and Swiss chalets; a minimal rainfall and hot airless nights, the flat roofs of the Middle East. Although any roof form can be made watertight these days, both character and value can be lost unless new work is consistent with the old.

Pitched roofs are found on larger houses built before the end of the sixteenth century and on all regional cottages. With the Renaissance, in more sophisticated houses, the roof disappeared behind a parapet. The Victorian Gothic Revival brought back the steeply pitched medieval roof and the Modern Movement of the 1930s introduced the flat roof.

The size of the roofing unit governs the pitch: the smaller the unit the steeper the pitch. Slate can be laid as low as 22 degrees whereas a small clay-tiled or thatched roof should never have a pitch of less than 45 degrees.

Roof tiles can be painted, to blend in with neighbours, as in a terrace, or if you find their colour unbearably brash. Brushing with manure water helps organisms to grow and will darken the tone. Avoid mixing old and new tiles or slates on the same plane of the roof; patch with matching secondhand ones. Where these are not available, strip one side and use for patching, reroofing the stripped side with new ones.

Clay tiles

A builder who specializes in conversions should know where matching ones can be found, and a wide range of concrete tiles in colours, shapes and sizes which marry in well with the old traditional clay ones are available.

Pantiles

Secondhand red pantiles are usually easy to find – the East Anglian shiny black ones are however hard to come by. So choose as smooth and dark a tile as possible of the same pattern and paint to match the existing ones.

Slates

New and secondhand slates are still available. Individual slate replacements are fixed with lead or zinc clips. As a cheaper alternative, black asbestos cement slates are made to the same sizes as traditional ones and look enough like them to be used for renovation work by the National Trust. Do not be inveigled into having black clay tiles as an alternative – they have a thicker edge than true slate and give the roof a different texture.

Typical northern European roofscape. In countries where the stork is a regular visitor, special frames are placed on unused chimneys to encourage nesting.

Stone slates

Real Stonesfield slates are made from laminated Cotswold stone, and laid graded, small ones at the top, large ones at the bottom. Virtually the only way to get hold of secondhand ones is to buy the building they are on. However, very good reconstituted stone copies are available which will become virtually indistinguishable after a year or two of natural weathering.

Ridge tiles

Frequently, Victorian and Edwardian houses have pretty ridge tiles; where one is missing or the terminals at the end are broken, it is possible to buy modern reproductions of traditional patterns in red, black or buff.

Thatch

Even if a thatch roof is in poor condition it is worth restoring. If replaced by any other roofing materials (except shingle or asbestos cement slates, which are extremely light) the rafters and other roofing timbers will need strengthening. A thatched roof certainly adds capital value to a property, but may attract higher rates and insurance premiums. Norfolk reed lasts between fifty and sixty years, combed wheat reed twenty-five to forty years, and long straw ten to twenty years. Whichever one you use can be treated with a retardant to discourage fires. (Plastic thatch is also available!). A fine wire mesh will hold thatch in place and prevent birds from taking advantage of a ready-made nest.

Corrugated roofs

You may find outhouses with corrugated asbestos or iron roofs. Corrugated asbestos comes in a range of good profiles and weathers well, and you can paint it. Where corrugated iron is rusty and in bad condition, strip it off and either replace it with corrugated asbestos or, if the pitch is adequate, the same finish as the main roof of the house.

Sheet metal

Aluminium, zinc, copper and lead are often used in large flat sheets to cover roofs. The metals oxidize on exposure to the atmosphere and this patina acts as a protective coating. Walking on sheet metal roofs is the most common cause of damage, but this can also be caused by defects in the decking. The repair of sheet metal roofs should always be left to an experienced plumber.

Glazed roofs

If you are incorporating areas of glazed roof in outhouses or in sunrooms, it is better to invest in glass rather than plastic which yellows, gets brittle and loses its transparency. Glass is more expensive initially, and it will require stouter framing, but barring accidents it should last for ever. The framing for a transparent roof can be either stained or painted timber or made up from commercial aluminium sections.

Asphalt roofs

As a finish for flat roofs asphalt has the great advantage that it forms a continuous skin over the entire roof surface. Surface crazing does not matter but cracks are more serious. These can be caused by movement in the supporting structure, or could be the result of a coat of paint applied to the asphalt some time in the past. Although cracks can be temporarily repaired by filling with bitumen paint, a specialist contractor needs to be brought in for permanent repair jobs.

Bituminous felt

This can be laid almost flat; a fall of about 2 in. in 10 ft/51 mm in 3 m will allow rain to drain safely away. Blistering is a common defect and results from the sun heating the roof and causing any moisture trapped beneath to vaporize and expand. For this reason, felt roofs should always be covered by white spar chippings to reflect heat and the sub-layers ventilated by various patent methods. Splits can be caused by movement in the supporting structure and temporary or minor repairs can be carried out with bituminous paint – major ones should be left to the roofing contractor.

There is a dangerous assumption around that the first step in modernizing your house is to rip out the windows and replace them with modern wood and metal designs. This can in fact be the quickest way to devalue your property. If you want to retain your house's character you should replace or add with designs consistent with the basic style.

Timber and steel framed windows and french doors in traditional casement and sash shapes are available ready-made, either plain-glazed or with small Georgian panes. Or you can match up with panels of lead lights, diamond or rectangular-shaped, to fit your frames.

Where sash windows need replacing, and unless they have small panes when you have no alternative but to use a timber version, aluminium sashes make a good alternative. These come both single and double glazed and have slim sections which match more closely the sections of traditional ones than do today's heavier timber ones.

Remember, when you are adding windows or enlarging them, that it is not only the size and type but the balance of window to wall that determines the house's character. It is on the whole better to have too little window than too much, though in some modern houses large areas of glass can be an essential element of the façade.

Too big windows

Unnecessarily large windows in many recently built houses can give rooms too much light and overwhelm the façade. A panel of louvred shuttering fitted over one or more of the sections of the window and painted in with the wall colour, or to match the window frame, will offset that void empty look. White venetian blinds with horizontal slats are almost as effective. Sheer curtains are not sufficiently architectural to do the job. Pergola framing, covered with creeper, spanning the whole width of the window – or better still the whole ground floor – will distract the eye by its strong horizontal emphasis.

Too small windows

Where the problem is not so much a matter of insufficient light inside but a mean-looking façade, painting the reveals and sills of the windows white, as well as all the doors and window frames, will give them more emphasis, and also help to reflect more light into the house.

Where additional light is needed, add another window of the same size and type at the side or back of the house. It is far less disruptive to drop the window sill than to make a window wider, which demands the insertion of a new lintel; at the side and the back of a house sills can often

Bricked-in windows give a blank, faceless look. This is one way of coping with them. Brightly painted blinds would give a similar effect.

be dropped and french doors inserted in the opening. These of course should be matched in material and pane size to the windows of the house. If at the front, where there is no alternative but to widen a window, a two-unit casement can be extended to accommodate three, so long as the centre remains the same. With stone or brick buildings, unless the stone or brick is used to provide mullions, four sections are not traditional, but in a timber-framed house, provided that they fit into an existing opening in the framework, there is no argument against using them.

A sash window can be widened by replacing it with a triple sash, in which case the side sashes should not be more than half the width of the central one. With a formal façade, try to maintain the window pattern, lining up the centres of windows on the different floors.

Too wide or too narrow windows

Where windows are tall and narrow and look rather mean, louvred shutters will make them appear wider. Each shutter should be half the window size: otherwise, they will look disconcertingly bogus. With any but a white-walled house, both window frames and shutters should be painted white for maximum effect. With a white-walled house, colour should be used on the shutters and the window frames.

Where window sills seem high and the windows themselves too wide for their height an alternative to replacing them with a taller window, is to paint the frames and the sill white and set white-painted window boxes the width of the sill on brackets beneath it. If the character of the house will allow, some decoration over the lintel can add to its apparent height.

Mis-matched windows

Where windows are all shapes and sizes you can marry them up to some extent by a unifying treatment such as painting all the outer frames white and the casement and sashes black. Glass appears as dark grey or black, and the black-painted glazing bars will accordingly disappear.

The alternative is to hang sheer white curtains or venetian blinds at every window and paint the inner frames white. Replace as and when you can with appropriate window forms but do your homework first – check with houses of the same period in the area.

French and glazed doors

These are an easy way not only of introducing more light but of improving the circulation in a house. Introduced on the ground floor, or on a first floor opening on to a verandah, they need not unbalance the appearance of a house so long as the framing and glazing is consistent with that of the rest of the windows. Where you are using aluminium sashes, horizontally sliding aluminium-framed glazed doors marry in well if they are on the ground floor, at the side or the back, or in a partially masked basement in the front of a house.

Dormer windows and skylights

These enable you to put your roof space to useful purpose. With dormers, match either the frames of existing dormers or the existing windows on the same wall. To let in maximum light, fit a top-hung or centre-pivoted single casement, or a panel of louvred glazing. Glazing the cheeks of the dormer will let in even more light. Where headroom is no problem, skylights are useful and far cheaper to fit. Use a double-glazed type: one comes draughtstripped with a roller blind fitted between the two sheets of glass. These skylights, unlike many of the old kind, do not leak and for further insurance come with their own prefabricated flashing.

Painting your windows

Unless the walls of the house are themselves white, painting both inner and outer frames of windows and french doors white is difficult to beat, although grey on the outer frame can look well with some grey random rubble stone walls. White provides sparkle and definition even on the greyest days and gives full value to the glazing pattern. Where walls are white, so long as there are not too many windows, painting the outer frames black or grey and the inner ones white can look crisp and trim and underline the window pattern attractively. Otherwise *never* use two colours.

Windows should always be painted in good quality gloss paint specifically recommended for outside use. The traditional treatment is one priming coat, two undercoats and one top coat of gloss, but you will get better weathering if you replace one of the undercoats with an extra top coat.

The front door needs to be sufficiently emphasized so that when you look at a house the way in is immediately apparent. This is not to say that the main entrance should always be at the front, but if it is at the side of the house, the path from the front gate, some kind of porch, canopy or an entrance courtyard should indicate that this is the main way into the house.

Front doors

You may feel that you cannot afford to change out-of-character windows, but if the front door is wrong this is worth changing. The job need not cost you a fortune. A front door of the right period or style immediately starts to pull the façade together.

If you have a Georgian, Regency or classical (as opposed to Gothic) Victorian house in need of a new door, search through manufacturers' leaflets and you will find several well-proportioned six-panelled doors which could be appropriate.

If you have a modern house, your choice will depend on whether you want a solid or glazed front door. Plain flush doors look pretty dull if they are merely painted; if you want a door of this type choose one with an interesting looking timber veneer but not a hot colour if your bricks are red.

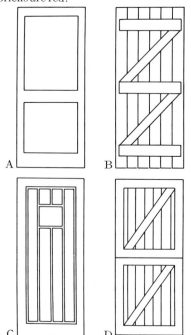

Four types of classic panelled front door.

A *Modern type.* B *Ledged and braced door.* C *Framed and ledged door with glazed panel.* D *Framed, ledged and braced stable door.*

Solid front doors certainly make more impact and if there is no room in the hall for a window or a glazed side panel it might be possible to take the door frame up to ceiling height and fit a panel of glass above the door. If you paint your door number on the glass in white it can be seen both by day and by night if you leave your hall light on. If you are going to glaze the front door of a modern house, a door with a central locking bar and a glazed panel above and below usually look best.

Side and service doors

Ledged and braced doors are useful for outhouses, but for house doors, framed, ledged and braced types are more weatherproof. Where some light is wanted, the framed type will take a diamond pane in the upper half and this is a traditional treatment for cottage front and service doors. A further variation is the stable type (both halves hinged separately) with or without a small glazed panel in the upper half. Painted louvre doors for both old and new houses not only provide an attractive texture but can be useful for outside stores as they allow ventilation.

Garage doors

These are so large in area that with small houses it is important to stop them overwhelming the façade. One way of reducing this effect is to paint the door itself to match the wall colour – a warm soft grey with Cotswold stone, for instance, or a bluer grey with Cornish granite. Where you have bright red or brown/red brick, sealed timber often looks the most unobtrusive: where garage doors are hidden from the road use a dark neutral-grey, beige, black or something appropriate to your general scheme.

Hinged timber garage doors, with vertical boarding for cottages, come either with or without glazed upper panels and could match up with side and front doors of the same type. Up-and-over garage doors in either timber or metal with horizontal ribbing are also suitable for cottages. A panelled garage door (7 ft/2.13 m or 14 ft/4.27 m wide), which would marry in well with a six-panel Georgian door, comes in maintenance-free white glass fibre, and can be electrically operated.

Sliding folding doors are the other alternative for wide garage openings. These can be metal but are usually in timber, either panelled or vertically boarded.

Canopies and porches

Quite often some moulding or a canopy is all that is necessary to emphasize an insignificant front door. For more formal older houses there are hoods, columns, pilasters and classical porches in white glass fibre which are based on authentic period originals, as well as classical surrounds for panelled front doors. But there is something rather tawdry about a glass fibre reproduction of a wood, plaster or stone original.

For cottages, look at local examples. A simple sloping roof set at right angles to the house, or a double pitched porch carried at its sides on timber brackets and roofed over to match the main roof, are attractive traditional forms found all over the country. In Victorian and Edwardian houses you sometimes find two little bay windows and a separate hood over the front door. In such cases the façade is often improved by stripping off the three separate roofs and running a single sloping roof across all three features, matching its finish to that of the main roof. This again is a traditional form. A characterless modern house can often be improved by running a flat canopy across the front, linking front door, side passage and garage.

A porch can be used not only to give emphasis to a front door but to provide practical amenities. Glazed in, it provides a useful draught lobby. In Scotland and Cornwall the entrance to the porch is often set at right angles to the front door to prevent through draughts – an idea worth copying in any exposed situation. On any side of the house, if it has a sunny aspect, and it is architecturally appropriate, the porch could be totally glazed to double as a small greenhouse or conservatory. In the country it is useful to have porches large enough for locker seats to store gum boots and so on. Deliveries can be left there safely out of the rain – you could if you wanted incorporate a lockable delivery cupboard. If you are rewiring the house you might put your meters in the porch so that they can be read while you are out.

In a semi-detached house or one at the end of a terrace, the main entrance can sometimes be moved from the front to the side, the old front door being remade as a window – but this would of course involve a major re-plan inside to put the hall space to better use.

Painting

All outside woodwork should either be painted with a full gloss paint or be treated with some kind of preservative which soaks into the fibre (except for cedar which needs no preservative). There are now excellent stain preservatives which are cheaper and longer term alternatives to paint if a colour is wanted for new work.

Where porches, pilasters, canopies, etc., are made of plaster they should be painted the same colour as the walls (if the walls are painted) or to match any other mouldings. Timber porches should be painted the same colour as the outer window frames, i.e., in a white-walled house where the outer frames are black and the inner ones white, the porch woodwork should be black, the front door white. However, in a white-walled house where the entire window frame is painted black, both porch and front door should be black. Where you have timber balconies, the same principle applies. With pergola framing it depends on what looks least fussy, either white paint or preservative, a brown or black stain, or natural weathered wood; all make an attractive foil for climbing plants. If you are concerned with ease of maintenance, it is worth remembering that preservative tends to need renewing less often than paint.

1/2 *The advantage of a top hung pivoting door is that it can be much wider than a side hung door and there is no door frame.*

3 *Victorian door and porch painted white. An extra-large house number has been painted on to the lantern and it can thus be read by night as well as by day.*

4 *Subtle colours highlight the renovated entrance of a New York brownstone building.*

5 *The top two panels of these doors have been glazed. Stripping a door down to its natural wood can be an effective treatment.*

6 *This blue door has a frame of white tiles. The French enamelled number plate echoes the general colour scheme.*

7 *Well-placed door furniture and the oval glazed panel give this its special character.*

8 *Neat shutters frame this door. They can be closed in the owner's absence to protect the entrance from weather and intruders.*

9 *Honeysuckle is a most suitable plant to grow round a front door. It is more or less evergreen and smells marvellous.*

10 *Trees in tubs, roses, ivy, fuchsia and a few boulders of marble to make you feel you are really going somewhere.*

11 *Bushes of white marguerites soften the soaring lines of this imposing entrance.*

12 *Ferns, pots of geraniums and clematis, and on the threshold of this formal front door, stands an example of topiary.*

1   2   3   4

5   6   7   8

9   10   11   12

Elevations
16/17 Door furniture

Even though good door furniture tends to be expensive do not be mean about it: once on it will last virtually for ever, and give distinction to the house. It must be in character both with your house and the front door itself.

Brass, bronze and iron are the traditional materials. Brass adds great richness and sparkle to any old and formal front door, and it can now be lacquered to avoid daily cleaning.

Solid bronze looks very handsome and has the added virtue that it needs absolutely no attention. Although both brass and bronze fittings of authentic period design are fairly easily available, iron ones are harder to come by. The "period" patterns often have a bogus rustic finish and where you can find second-hand ones these are normally a better alternative.

For newer houses, bronze is still a good choice and is available in strong, simple, modern forms. The other alternatives are matt chromed steel and aluminium. Whatever metal you choose, match it through in letterbox, knocker, door handle, keyplate and bell push. It is important to remember that door furniture must be fitted in the correct position on the door.

Letterboxes

If you are cutting a hole through a door to fit a letterbox, you must not weaken the framework.

It should be at a height that won't make the postman slip a disc when he bends down or pull a muscle if he has to reach too high. Recommended heights for letterboxes are between 2 ft 6 in./762 mm minimum and 4 ft 9 in./1.45 m maximum.

A letterbox can be sited almost anywhere on a flush door, as the load is evenly distributed. Panelled doors are constructed of lengths of wood forming a framework that supports the panels. As they are usually symmetrical, a letterbox will look best placed somewhere on the vertical axis rather than to one side. This means either in the middle of the central bar, or in the vertical bar between the panels.

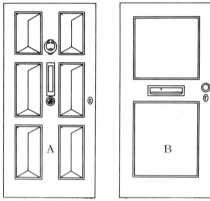

A *Vertical letterbox in a six-panelled door.*
B *Horizontal letterbox on the central bar.*

This brings us to the size of letterbox you will need. Is your household likely to get a lot of large envelopes or magazines – or the fatter Sunday papers? Get a letterbox that is large enough, but remember that if it is too big wily thieves with supple wrists · might be able to reach through and unlock your door. You could of course foil them with a letter basket hooked on to the back of the door. These are useful as long as the door does not open directly against a wall.

Knockers and bells

Bells come in two types: electrically operated from a battery, or off the mains via a transformer unit; or mechanically operated, i.e. wound up like a clock. Electric bells should be sited on the frame of the door on a line with the cylinder lock or the door handle. Those that incorporate a light are particularly useful in this position where there is no outside light, as they indicate the key hole. The mechanical kind can be fitted on the door itself. But even the best bell fails and some sort of knocker, whether it is an independent one or incorporated in the letterbox, is worth having.

Where you have a six-panel Georgian-type door, an independent knocker looks well set in the framing at the junction of the top four panels. Where you have a door with a central bar only, it is better to incorporate the knocker with the letterbox. When you are thinking about knocker positions remember that you might want to fit a spyhole.

Handles

If you have a knocker this gives something to pull to shut the door firmly behind you; without one it is useful to have a handle. It may be useful to combine this with a mortice latch and deadlock. Often in the country people are happy to leave the door unlocked and use the latch only during the day, using the lock at night. In such a case a neat alternative is the type of knob handle which incorporates a lock in the spindle.

Except for cylinder locks, door handles and mortice latches and locks should be set on the axis of the middle bar of the door where there is one. Where a handle is not combined with a mortice latch and lock, the knob can be set in the centre of the door. In this position a larger and more substantial knob is required.

Burglar precautions

Burglars are less likely to bother you if you use a combined cylinder and deadlock, as by double turning the key you ensure that only a key will open the door from either inside or out. However, it is always wise to call in expert advice.

Spyholes are comforting if you are often alone in the house, and are effective at night too as long as you have an outside light. A good chain is worth fitting – cheap ones are useless and easily forced. The best firms also give whole house advice on protection against burglars as well as supplying a wide range of door, window, skylight and garage door locks. They will install too, and their work and fittings meet the most stringent requirements of insurance companies.

Names and numbers

As in every other field of design, simplicity is all. Resist mock rustic and whimsy nameplates which seldom do anything for a house, and are illegible into the bargain. Simple, unpretentious names and number plates are the best choice. Bronze, brass or iron numerals can be easily screwed on and the blue and white French enamelled plates look crisp and pretty. Site names or numbers at a reasonable height, preferably near the gate so they can be seen from the road.

Outside lights

Unless you have a street lamp just outside your gate, a light by the front door is welcoming to guests and discouraging to burglars, quite apart from its practical value of leading anyone safely to the front door on a dark night. Outside lights are not extravagant to run – a 25 watt bulb shines remarkably brightly in the dark.

Blue and white French enamelled plates.

Old brass letterbox / door handle.

A vertical letterbox set into the central bar.

A smart modern "carriage lamp"

G.P.O poster 1965.

When deciding on door furniture – knockers, numbers, letterboxes – stick as far as possible to one style, making sure that it suits your style of door.

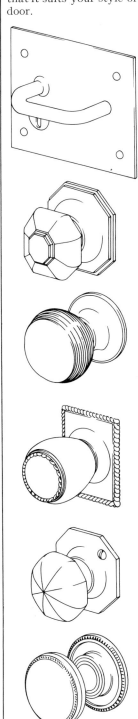

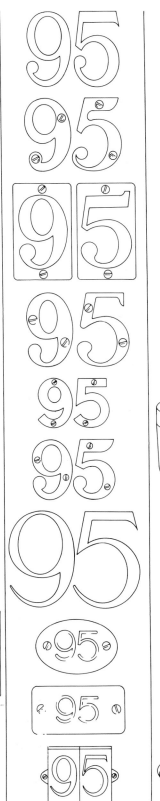

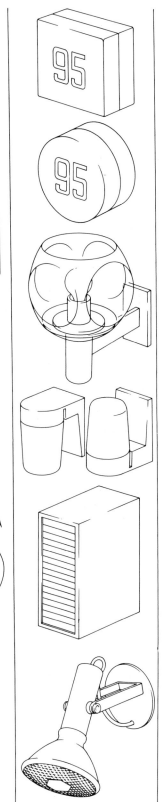

Elevations
18/19 Front of house services

Drainpipes, dustbins and fuel stores tend to get pushed aside by most people while they concentrate on the more attractive aspects of exterior decorations such as colour schemes and planting, but this is a mistake. If you take services into account right from the start a great deal can be done to minimize their clutter, either by incorporating them into the structure itself or exploiting them to positive purpose in the treatment of the areas around the house.

Cables and aerials

Cables can usually be laid underground even for existing installations. This will cost more than an overhead connection but the absence of wire can mean much to the appearance of the house, so consider this seriously before laying the turf and paving. Television aerials, even if they have to be outside, can often be unobtrusively placed, but make sure that yours is adequately supported.

Downpipes and gutters

If you have to replace downpipes and guttering, remember that the plastic types are maintenance free. They are available with the standard round sections or with square or ogee sections which are often more suited to older houses. Generally available in grey, they can also come in black or white. If you need to paint them to merge into the wall colour, this is easily done, and as there is no problem of rusting the paint will last longer than on metal. On a particularly handsome old house, clearly you should replace defective downpipes and gutters with new ones to match the old ones as closely as possible, in material and form.

Drainpipes also come in plastic; try to bring them inside the house or at least rationalize them. Pipes from kitchen sinks often trail unnecessarily across the outside wall when they could easily be tucked away at the back of the cupboard below the sink, to appear immediately over the drain as a tiny outlet spout. External drainpipes, whatever their material, should be painted to merge with the wall colour, irrespective of the colour of the rainwater pipes.

Drains

Where you are adding drains and require new manholes, be sure to position them so that they relate to the paving pattern surrounding them. It is not necessary to have a cast-iron top: you can get a tray top which can be infilled to match the paving treatment.

Where you have no main drainage, septic tank covers will need masking if they are in a prominent position in the garden. Brown plastic-covered wire netting, laid over them and staked alongside, allows evergreen creepers to run rampant over them. Choose the sort that will not mind being turned back if you have to get at the tank.

Where manholes are visible, one or two tubs or large earthenware pots filled with shrubs and flowers will disguise them, as long as they are not too heavy to move.

Dustbins

Unless you are a trainee weight lifter, dustbins need to be housed as near as possible to the point from where the dustman collects. Sometimes they can be recessed through the wall into the kitchen, accessible from the inside by means of a hinged, lockable section of work-top. You will probably need more than one bin, and as the amount of waste products we shed each week increases, we will soon be in the position where we will also have to house compactors. These will press paper and rags, or metal, or plastics, into neat parcels ready for recycling.

Fuel stores

Metal oil storage tanks are most unobtrusive when painted a dark brown/green and surrounded by shrubs and trees or trellis screening covered with evergreen creeper. This allows enough air circulation to discourage rusting. Where a new tank is needed, avoid maintenance completely with a glass fibre tank.

If you can, avoid having coal bunkers outside; find space for them in a garage or outhouse, or knock an access door through the wall of the house and make a store that is also accessible from inside.

If you have to house coal bunkers and dustbins outside, try to incorporate them in one neat waist-high unit built of materials that blend in with the house sympathetically, with matching boarded doors and a neat sloping lid. Utilities of this kind – and this includes oil tanks as well – should be treated positively. Screened with trellis or fencing as high as neighbouring walls, they can not only provide interesting vertical elements dripping with flowers throughout the summer, but also help define the different areas of the garden, masking a sandpit or the compost heap, or sheltering the terrace from cold east winds.

Garages

Often a pleasant-looking house is flanked by an ugly garage. It may have a silly little gabled roof or fussily panelled door. If its condition is shaky, consider dismantling it and building something more substantial and better related to the house.

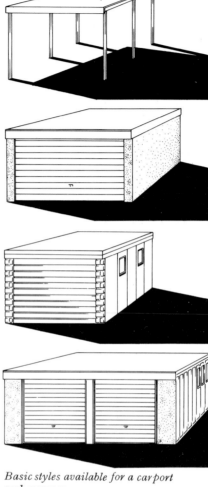

Basic styles available for a carport and garages.

Garage built on to a garden wall.

Sculptural Spanish carport.

If the structure is fairly sturdy, it may be possible to adapt it. Where the front of the garage lines up with the house, you could link the two by means of a new flat roof, providing yourself at the same time with a covered way to a side or back door. If the garage projects forward and is on the same side as the front door, you might run the flat roof across the front of the house to provide a porch, and a strong horizontal linking line. But in either case be careful not to obscure any light to the windows.

Where the structure can take it, and you need the space, the most successful way of integrating a garage with the house is to build a room over, and to run the main roof across.

New garages

Anyone who has ever tried to buy a garage will know that it is a fairly depressing business. They come in timber, concrete or asbestos, and one seeks in vain for a sympathetic material that will blend in with the existing house.

The vast majority of house owners have a single-car garage built on to their house, or at least a garage sited alongside it – but for some the problem of what to do with a second car arises. Does one build another garage, enlarge the existing one, or make do with a carport?

Although more expensive, consideration should be given to building a new structure altogether, if only in concrete block. These blocks are now cast to a much higher standard of finish than they were formerly, and come in a variety of colours. They are therefore quite acceptable as a material, and can also be colour washed. The roof of the structure can either be flat or pitched.

Doors can open outwards, be up-and-over, wrap around, or, when you have a double garage, slide to left or right for access to the appropriate half. The latter method looks far better, since the area of door is broken up.

Carports

We are told that it is far healthier for a car to stand under a carport, with a free circulation of air around it, than be penned up in a garage. Standard size carports are available with a roof of clear rigid vinyl sheeting, although these only cover the area of one car. It is now possible to buy opaque and matt vinyl sheeting in a number of different profiles.

A carport, by its structure, can link together house and garage, neighbouring houses, or just visually expand the house itself. Properly surfaced and planted, a functional car area can become a positive addition to the house's elevation, rather than an unconsidered excrescence.

1

2

3

4

5

6

7

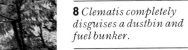

8

9

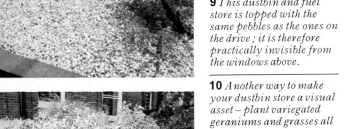

10

1 *A parking bay defined by a brick plant box which has been built up to the original level of the tree it surrounds.*

2 *Parking bays and garages for a terrace of houses have been broken up by beds of plants and small trees.*

3 *Parking bay and steps have been designed as one unit broken up with railings and plants.*

4 *Grass between the York paving stones of the drive has been taken right up to the building. A plant pergola forms the carport.*

5/6 *A grass bank, set-in shallow concrete steps and ramps separate this modern house and garage from the road.*

7 *Pebbles, low decorative trees and paving stones designed to break up this front garden and carport. Specially designed stone buffers keep the car off the flower beds.*

8 *Clematis completely disguises a dustbin and fuel bunker.*

9 *This dustbin and fuel store is topped with the same pebbles as the ones on the drive; it is therefore practically invisible from the windows above.*

10 *Another way to make your dustbin store a visual asset – plant variegated geraniums and grasses all over the top.*

41

Elevations
20 Under cover

Polygonum or mile-a-minute is perhaps the cheapest total solution if you really do not like the look of your house. Unlike ivy it drapes itself around the structure and has no sucker roots to pull the mortar away from the bricks.

Internal layout/1

How many homes ever come up to all our expectations? What happened to those dreams of grand and spacious living? But wait a minute: let your imagination go, and think how the existing space in your house or flat could be re-thought to work better, look better.

Can you use the rooms differently?

Most of us are slaves to tradition, taking it for granted that living-rooms are downstairs, bedrooms upstairs. But something as simple as rearranging the way you live in a house can make all the difference.

If there's a better view from the upstairs window, why not live up there and enjoy it, and sleep downstairs?

Using the existing space better

There are arguments for keeping within the existing structure if you can – you won't be adding to your external maintenance expenses, services will be easily available, heating should cost only a little more, and you won't be eating into your garden.

You can often increase the apparent size of your home simply by replanning and simplifying your furniture layout; making new doors where there were none before; blocking up others; opening two rooms into one, dividing others into two, and rationalizing the way you store things; inserting a gallery into a high-ceilinged room, or exploiting a dark, dead centre area, using artificial ventilation.

Adding on

If all else fails, you may be able to increase the actual floor space of your home by going up (see Attics), out (see Extensions), or down (see Basements).

The creative use of space can make a vast difference to the appearance and enjoyment of a home which no amount of tinkering about with cushion covers and saucy gadgets can ever equal. This creative use of space is the prime service of architects and designers, but developing, enhancing and fulfilling it is the prerogative of the householder.

Before you get out your hatchet, consider the following points:
- ☐ Can your house or flat be improved by just changing the function of the existing rooms?
- ☐ Is what you plan to do legal?
- ☐ Will your projected improvements prove practical in terms of services, circulation, storage, cost?
- ☐ Will the inside and outside benefit aesthetically?

The carpet links the separate areas and its pattern is repeated in the louvred doors.

Internal layout
2/3 Basic thinking

In theory it should be possible to raise the roof, excavate a new basement, change all the walls to glass, or convert the house into one big space with all facilities available.

In practice there are problems in producing even simple solutions: however, the recognition of a problem is halfway towards solving it. What are these problems? Perhaps cost, maybe permissions, how will you get along while the work is being done, and will the changes that might suit you add to the value of the house?

As in all other aspects of life it is essential at the outset to establish your family's particular priorities, and then to list them in order as a measure to be applied to possible solutions.

The choice

There are few hard and fast rules and these will be obvious to you. The location of the house will have a bearing on the matter – for what might suit in a town house could be very different for a country house – and also the pattern of your family life; most people will have to balance conflicting demands from the priority list and provide some general, family areas with adequate "private" spaces as well.

Perfection is for the gods – so, ensure that the improvements you make will achieve some real successes, albeit at the expense of some unfulfilled wishes. A pocket knife with five blades, a corkscrew, screwdriver and various other gadgets probably does nothing very well. You should aim at doing one or two things marvellously well.

Free-range living or monkish cells

Glossy illustrations tend to stress the attractions of open-plan living: one room opening generously on to another; spiral staircases rising from living areas to give access to landings and internal balconies suggesting joyous community between parents and pretty children; bachelor flats where magnificent views can be enjoyed while lying in the bath a suite of rooms away.

The advantages of opening up a house, room to room, floor to floor, inside to outside, can be very considerable. Some account of them comes later. But there can also be disadvantages such as lack of privacy and conflicting activities; and incorrectly grouped furniture may "float" without unifying walls. Before you become fired with the possibilities of tearing down walls and ripping great spatial chasms through your floors consider all aspects of your requirements.

When thinking of an open-plan house, it is important to consider what furniture you intend to use. However expansive the view through the house that you wish to create, you are sure to find that certain areas are "zoned" for particular uses. These zones are best defined either with furniture (which does not obstruct the view) or with decorations, or by the forming of windows or ceilings which define their position.

Cellular living

The advantages of having a house or flat where all of, or at any rate a major part of, the rooms are self-contained and shutable (or even lockable) can be summarized:

Members of a family will not always want to be exposed to the view and the noise of others. There can be problems in an open-plan house in providing the facilities for both play and work, adult and child, cooking smells and sweet-scented living areas.

The need for isolated activity – silent or noisy, active or contemplative – is too important to ignore and must be provided in a balanced home.

Much of the information in this chapter deals with ways in which houses can be opened up. But there are some cases where it may be appropriate to erect some walls.

Suggestions

So you have the urge to make changes, but you are not quite sure what you would like to do. How can you explore and get your ideas straightened out?

Make a model

It is often helpful and not difficult to make a small model of one room or more. By reducing the problem to the size that you can have in your hand, and being able to look up, through, down, into the spaces, you will see the problems as a whole as an aid to a coherent solution.

Imagine the difference

You are thinking of forming a new window and do not know how it will look: cut a piece of paper of the right size and stick it on the wall; stand back and see. If you are thinking of knocking a big hole through a wall between two rooms, rearrange all the furniture that would be displaced if you did this and pin a piece of string round the outline of the proposed new opening.

How to read a plan

A plan is a diagrammatic view seen from above showing the correct geometric form of a building layout. In order to show door and window openings it is generally taken as a horizontal "cut" at about 4 ft/1 m above floor level.

This means that walls are shown solid (because they carry on up above the hypothetical cut) and features below are shown in outline. In plans of buildings, symbols are used to signify door swings, sanitary fittings, electrical sockets, and so on. Other information can be: arrows to show the rise of staircases; compass points to show the position of the sun; arrangement of furniture.

Electrical symbols

Main control ⊡ *Tubular*
Main switch ◻▸ *heater* ⟊
Switchboard, *Fixed radiator or*
distribution board *heating panel* ⊠
or fuse board ◻ *Convector*
Meter ◼ *heater* ▤
Ceiling outlet lighting *Electric unit*
filament lamp ○ *heater* ▥
Wall outlet lighting *Immersion*
filament lamp ▸○ *heater* ⟊
One-way switch ✓ *Thermostat* ⟊
Two-way switch ↗ *Bell* ⌓
Socket outlet ▷ *Buzzer* ⌓
Switch socket outlet ▷ *Telephone point* △

A plan enables us to see the relationships between the adjacent spaces (rooms, corridors, etc.) and to make decisions concerning their disposition.

So that the effect of these decisions on other areas can be seen at a glance, we draw plans at a fraction of the actual size of the building: they are "to scale". This also makes the plans easier to handle. In this way an area actually 8 ft/2.4 m × 10 ft/3 m may be represented by an area of 8 in./203 mm × 10 in./254 mm, or a detail which needs to be seen more clearly, and may contain more information at a larger scale, perhaps 2 ft/610 mm to 4 in./102 mm.

How to draw a plan to scale

Plans are invaluable aids, not only in making layout decisions but also as subsequent instruments of instruction to builders, furniture movers, or even the bank manager who may be lending money for the work. The first step is to assemble the information that you will be showing on the drawing – make a survey.

Using firm, clear lines, make freehand drawings of the shapes of your rooms and how they relate one to the other. Then measure the lengths of walls, widths of doors, thickness of partitions, positions of fittings and mark them clearly on the sketch.

Next the scale to which you will be drawing must be decided, and as a guide take a scale of 1:48 for general areas and 1:24 for places like kitchens, laundries and bathrooms that have to accommodate a lot of fixed items. This is where inches count, and you can see them at this scale.

For your scale you will need a ruler marked in the units that represent feet (or metres), that is to say quarter inches or half inches (or centimetres), whichever you choose. An excellent method if you are working in inches is to use graph paper with the inch squares divided into eighths, and then take two, i.e. a quarter inch, for a foot; four divisions will represent two feet, and so on.

Lay a sheet of tracing paper over the graph paper and pin or tape it down on a hard, flat, smooth surface. Using a sharpened, fairly hard pencil (H or 2H) draw a line that will be one of your walls. From your survey notes measure its length and draw a line at right angles for the next wall; a set square is useful. Scale it off and continue to form the perimeter of the room. Mark on the doors, windows and other features, then draw in the thickness of the walls to the next room, measure from the connecting door to the corner and repeat the process. With accurate notes and reasonable luck you will end up with a floor plan. If it lacks precision don't worry overmuch . . . at least you will have a fairly accurate diagram of your domain.

You may also find it a good idea to draw the shapes of your furniture to scale on a piece of coloured paper and cut these out.

These shapes can then be moved around on the plan you have drawn to experiment with furnishing arrangements. It's lighter work than humping the actual furniture around from room to room. Do remember to write on each paper shape what it represents, or you might finish with an unidentifiable pile of square confetti.

How your scale plan will look

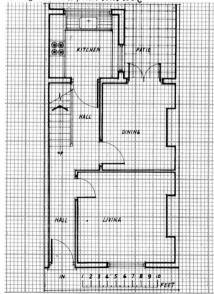

Visualizing a plan

If you are presented with someone else's plan of your home remember what we said about making one yourself. A plan is a diagram in two dimensions of a three-dimensional space. Think of the walls enclosing rooms, the stairs going up into upper levels, openings in solid walls for entries, views, light (and sound!).

Consider how floor finishes carry from one room to the next; how the colours and textures should create positive and continuous experiences, instead of either isolating one area from another or, worse, creating visual traffic accidents.

Making a model

This is fun with a serious purpose. A good working model is a design tool, not a doll's house.

Your plan will become a recognizable series of spaces and, if you are contemplating opening one area into another by removing all or part of a wall, it is much less trouble to cut a hole in a model than in a brick wall – particularly if you then change your mind.

You will need a sheet or so of fairly stiff cardboard, big, sharp scissors or a model knife, glue and sticky tape. The walls will be cut out and fixed together, so first of all measure the room heights and take the lengths from your survey plan.

Draw all the walls on the cardboard with windows, doors and other important fixtures marked on. Cut them out and, to help with assembly, note on the back of each one which wall it is. Mark and cut out the whole plan of each floor on one piece with positions of walls marked on. Position the cut-out walls and fix them with quick-setting glue or sticky tape.

Leave peep holes at the equivalent of eye level or omit whole walls to give an interior view. Lay a piece of paper over the top as a ceiling to give a complete effect.

Furniture can be cut out of block balsa wood or polystyrene – so much easier to move about than the real thing.

1 Measure up the heights

2 Draw & cut out the walls

3 Draw the plan

Stick walls onto plan with glue or tape

Balsa wood furniture

peepholes at eye level

paper on top as a ceiling

Beneath the smooth surface of your walls, floors and ceilings there lurks a network of pipes and cables, conduits and wires. These carry the lifeblood of your house and you should take into account their location and type during the planning stages of work to be done.

Heating

This is dealt with fully elsewhere in this book, and you will be able to identify the system that you have or intend to have. If your new layout involves making holes in walls, ensure that pipes, radiators, cables and so on can be moved, and that the new heating requirements can be satisfied. If they cannot find out whether the system has enough capacity to be extended.

Electricity

The main supply arrives from outside at a switch and fuseboard, from where it is distributed by wires to the various outlets. These wires are run in the floor and ceiling spaces, and where they are actually embedded in plaster they will be protected by conduit pipes. In this way there will be a conduit from a light switch up to the ceiling for a pendant light fitting or wall bracket, and another from a socket outlet down to the floor and back under the floor to the fuseboard.

If your installation is fairly old it may be wise to have the wiring replaced, as old, worn cables are a fire hazard. Even if you only need some more fittings and lights, or a cable re-routed, always be sure to employ a qualified electrician – this is no job for amateurs.

Other wires that you find are either telephone cables, television aerials or leads to hi-fi. Plot the new positions of your equipment and these wires can be neatly tucked away.

Water

Most houses have a storage tank in the roof. The water comes in the main pipe under pressure and is pushed up to the tank. Pipes then run down the building and the water runs by gravity to the taps, cylinders and boilers.

Hot water can either be supplied from one cylinder with pipes to the taps, or you can have individual heaters – gas or electric – close to the bath, sink, basin or bidet. If you are going to have extra, new fittings – basins in bedrooms, sinks in utility rooms – do make sure that water can be run to them and drained away.

Gas

The supply pipe arrives at the meter and is distributed in steel pipes to the fittings. They are generally run under floors; being too large to be buried in the wall plaster, vertical pipes are usually hidden in ducts and cupboards. Connections are pipes of flexible plastic with self-sealing clip-on ends. If you find an old gas-lamp pipe buried in the middle of a wall, get a plumber to remove it – it may still be connected. Should you install a new gas fire into an old fireplace, the flue will have to be specially lined to prevent flue gas vapour soaking into the brickwork.

New gas-fired boilers are very small and efficient: on an outside wall they don't need a flue, just an outlet.

Drainage

Local authorities' regulations are very strict about this, and natural laws even stricter. Water will not flow uphill except under pressure, so drainpipes have to slope downwards until they reach a position that will permit a vertical pipe where gravity will take over.

Drainpipes are bigger than supply-pipes, which are under pressure, and they can gurgle and make other alarming noises so that, even if you can hide them, you may still hear them.

It's when the drains go into the ground that the cost really will bring you out in a nervous rash, so be warned before you draw in something as simple as a new basin in the bedroom.

The law says that pipes must be inside the building, so look for places to hide them: in cupboards, under worktops, behind bathpanels, in the depths of hollow floors. Bends, traps and junctions can get blocked up and should be accessible for rodding out.

Ventilation

Fresh air in and stale air out is usually achieved by opening a window. If the room is internal it must be artificially ventilated. This is usually done by running a duct from the outside with a fan to force the stale air out, while fresh air is drawn from the rest of the house. In the case of a wc the fan must be connected to the light switch so that both come on at the same time.

Fan units are available that connect to ducts made of plastic drainpipes: they are neat, efficient and easy on the eye and pocket. Run the pipe/duct between floor joists or in the roof space.

One of the main drawbacks to open planning is the smell and steam from cooking. There are hoods made to fit over ovens, and hobs that filter out these undesirable by-products. If you prefer, you can take them to the outside air by means of a hood, duct and fan, but don't have the outlet placed near to opening windows – this would mean the defeat of the entire exercise!

Visual treatments

The scope for dramatically changing the form of a house is limited for most people, so it's sensible to start with the simpler aspects of interior design where you have more control – and which can have considerable effect on the sense of spaciousness. So before you take a sledge-hammer to a warren of tiny rooms or plan to cut up huge, barn-like areas, see whether some simple visual treatments or a serious re-think about furniture will help.

Furniture

If the aim is to make a home, or room, look as big as possible, then most of us have far too much furniture. Spare a moment, just to look around you. Did you actually buy it all? Or did it just arrive, bit by bit, gradually to accumulate and silt up the house? We tend to be highly emotional about furniture, which means that we cannot actually bring ourselves to throw anything away. But a house, like a garden, needs regular pruning. And if you want to get as much space as possible – both physically and visually – reducing the amount of furniture can help enormously.

Combining and unifying furniture help as well: a pair of two-seater sofas rather than four chairs; one complete storage wall rather than umpteen tables for record players, cabinets for drinks, free-standing bookshelves, a separate desk; down-lighters and spotlights rather than table lights and their tables. Of course, it can't all be done at once, but bear it in mind as a goal.

When the rag-and-bone man has made off with your surplus furniture you will be left with what you wanted – space. Don't be overwhelmed by all that air, use it wisely. Within the volume you will want to enjoy different activities, so break it up into these – but gently. Don't arrange the remaining furniture like wallflowers around the perimeter, group it in a way that will define the areas: lounging, eating, sleeping, etc.

Storage

There is no single feature in a house which will do so much to help to create a sense of spaciousness as good storage. Nothing detracts from spaciousness so much as a clutter of things (which may be very nice for other reasons) and there

This bathroom shows the number of services that may have to be thought of in replanning an interior. On the surface it looks smooth, clean and simple: below the surface run pipes, wires and drains – all of which influenced the design and had to be thought of at the beginning. See diagram opposite.

is usually no better way of concealing things than putting them into a cupboard. Do not underestimate the advantages of built-in cupboards. Ideally any house or flat would, at the design stage, have a generous complement of cupboards integrated into the plan. Apart from anything else cupboards make very good walls between bedrooms, where they provide excellent sound insulation. One of the things that an ingenious architect should do when faced with designing a new house or altering an old one is to start thinking where storage units can be worked in as discreetly and inconspicuously as possible, so that they become working walls that define space, rather than massive pieces of furniture that occupy spaces.

Decorations

The decorations that you apply to the walls and ceilings, and the choice of furnishings, can dramatically affect the sense of space of individual rooms as well as the house as a whole. They can also actually alter the appearance, the struc-ture and physical form of the house. So it is necessary to decide whether you want a room – and even the whole house – to look as large or as restricted as possible, and whether you want one room to relate to other rooms or not. Here are a few basic rules:

(a) The fewer changes there are in colour, texture and pattern, the bigger the place will look.
(b) The lighter the colour schemes, the larger the rooms will look.
(c) Strong colours come towards you, pale colours recede. If a ceiling is too high, or the end wall of a passage too far away, a bright colour will reduce the apparent distance.
(d) A picture rail or continuous band of colour will appear to draw the room in.
(e) If a room has awkward features, these can be partly lost by running a strong treatment (colour or pattern) straight over them.
(f) A big pattern makes a room look smaller; a small pattern makes a room look bigger. A pattern on a lighter ground gives an impression of "space beyond"; a pattern on a darker ground of enclosure.
(g) A pattern with a strong "direction" leads the eye. For example, a striped paper hung with the stripes running up the wall will make the room look higher.

Have you thought of blurring the shape of a room with pattern and colour? Take a bold colour up a section of wall and run it over part of the ceiling. Run a pattern up a wall, across a ceiling and down again the other side. Take a carpet with a bold directional pattern part way up a wall, and the room takes on a new dimension.

Mirrors

The judicious use of mirrors can do miracles to open up dark corners. You can use a mirror to make a dull, boxy room more interesting, or to widen a mean hall. It doesn't involve using acres of the expensive material, however – the secret is to use as little or as much as you like, so long as you run it right into a corner, or floor to ceiling. And that means all the way to the ceiling and all the way to the floor if you want an illusion of floor and ceiling continuing round a corner, or right into a corner if you want a wall to appear to run on into a further area.

You will have to be careful with vacuum cleaners and floor mops, which can be shattering in vigorous hands.

Two disadvantages of mirror glass are that it is heavy and that in bathrooms it steams up. You can buy feather-light "mirror" made of plastic film on polystyrene sheets that was designed to counter these faults of mirror glass in aeroplanes, where weight is crucial. Advantages are: one, minimal support is needed; two, being warm, it doesn't steam up.

Light and shade

The quality and quantity of light is the rock on which many interiors founder. You should be aware of where it comes from, how strong it is and how adaptable your light sources can be.

Light from windows can be controlled by curtains, blinds or shutters; these will affect both quantity and feeling of light. Colour reflected from surfaces or filtered through fabrics will give subtle tone changes to the rest of the room.

Making full-height, glazed panels in internal partitions not only adds light to inner halls and corridors, but also combines the spaces visually while keeping noise, smell and heat where they are wanted.

If man can ever be said to have got the better of Nature it must be in the field of artificial light: the variety of fittings available is immense. Colour, strength, direction, control – take your pick. It should be possible to define with reasonable precision what light you need where: bright directional light for clear vision or soft, misty, indirect light for dreamy, relaxing situations.

A room with bright overall light is there for all to see; there is no mystery, and if that's what you want and need, then have it. But what about the soothing effect of pools of light only where really needed, with warm mysterious shadows around? Then pick out special features, such as pictures, bowls of flowers and so on, with dramatic spotlights. But be practical; you don't want to break your neck stumbling down a subtly-lit staircase, or be forced to wear sunglasses to read a book in the living-room.

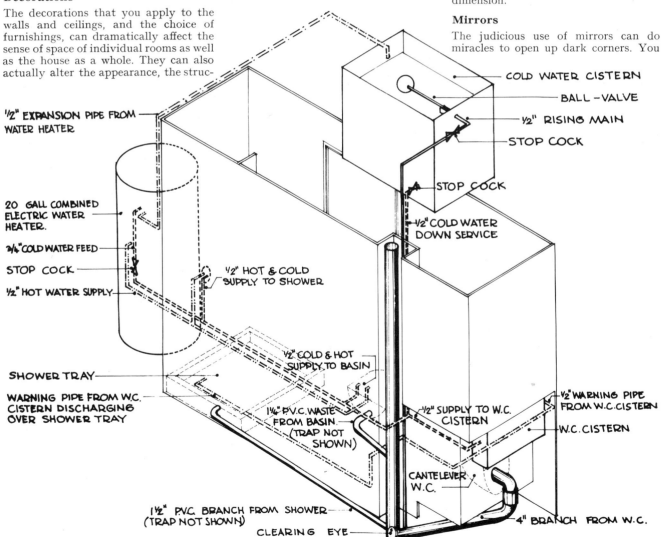

½" EXPANSION PIPE FROM WATER HEATER

20 GALL COMBINED ELECTRIC WATER HEATER.

¾" COLD WATER FEED

STOP COCK

½" HOT WATER SUPPLY

½" HOT & COLD SUPPLY TO SHOWER

SHOWER TRAY

WARNING PIPE FROM W.C. CISTERN DISCHARGING OVER SHOWER TRAY

½" COLD & HOT SUPPLY TO BASIN

1¼" P.V.C. WASTE FROM BASIN. (TRAP NOT SHOWN)

1½" P.V.C. BRANCH FROM SHOWER (TRAP NOT SHOWN)

CLEARING EYE

4" SOIL & VENT PIPE IN P.V.C.

½" RISING MAIN

COLD WATER CISTERN

BALL – VALVE

½" RISING MAIN

STOP COCK

STOP COCK

½" COLD WATER DOWN SERVICE

½" WARNING PIPE FROM W.C. CISTERN

½" SUPPLY TO W.C. CISTERN

W.C. CISTERN

CANTELEVER W.C.

4" BRANCH FROM W.C.

Internal layout
6/7 Minor operations/simple structural improvements

There are a lot of relatively minor structural ways in which the layout of a room can be improved or the apparent size increased.

Fireplaces

Block over a fireplace or remove a chimneybreast and the room looks simpler and consequently bigger. It also means you can rearrange the furniture radically.

Alternatively, strip away the fire surround, fire-back and grate, box around the inside of the fireplace and put shelves across for books, TV or drinks.

Rehanging doors

The direction in which a door opens should ease the flow of traffic between rooms. If your new layout changes this flow, or if it is already awkward, then consider altering the door swings. These can be in either direction from each side.

Doing the job is quite a tricky task, so if you are not a DIY expert, call in a joiner.

Space-saving doors

There are often situations where space

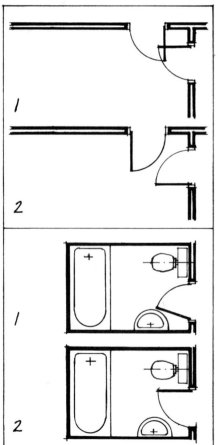

is so limited that rehanging the door is not the answer. If this is the case we can consider doors that occupy minimal space when they are open.

One method is to split the door in two with one half opening from each side; alternatively it can hinge in the centre and fold to one side. A run of folding doors hung from a sliding track could be the answer for wide openings to wardrobes, kitchen recesses or between rooms.

If space is really cramped there are patent doors that concertina into almost nothing, but the choice of appearance is mostly limited to the plastic sheet with which many of them are covered.

Should you have a clear space to one side you can hang a door on track and slide it away; and if you are building a new wall it can even slide into it.

If all else fails, consider curtains, which might be made of anything from fabrics to bead or bamboo.

Removing doors

Do you actually need a door?

It may well be that it can be taken away to leave the opening. Either repair the frame in places where hinges and locks are removed or take out the frame as well. In this case the opening will have to be repaired and, while you are at it, think about the possibility of rounding off the top to form an arch.

Conversely, do you actually need the opening at all? Some old houses have doors in all directions; so the door may be in an inconvenient place, and you may need to move it to another part of the room. Your friendly builder will take away the lot and fill the opening flush with the wall surface.

Windows

Windows, like doors, can be a matter of either minor or major surgery (depending on whether a steel beam or concrete lintel is necessary).

The effect of windows on the appearance of space in a room, and the way their positions affect the layout of that room, is considerable.

This has led in recent years to a fashion for huge picture windows which merge living areas with the landscape outside – fine if it's a beautiful day but not so cheerful if it's pelting with rain. But though large windows do increase the apparent amount of space within a room, they also bring problems of security, heating costs, and possible lack of privacy.

While you are on the subject of windows consider also the possibilities of raising the sill level of a window so that you can place furniture, or a sink, more satisfactorily underneath it.

See whether there is an opportunity of making some small windows – for example, to the side of a fireplace. They may give only a glimpsed view and little light, but they can greatly increase the interest within the room itself.

A tall, narrow slot of a window can be most exciting, especially if you allow it to run the entire height of the room, so that the light runs right across the ceiling and floor.

Internal windows

You can sometimes relieve claustrophobia and let light into a dark, internal part of the house by making an internal window, say from a hall into a dining-room. This still leaves wall space to range furniture against.

Rounding off angles

Ask a child to draw a room and he will draw a box with square corners. We all tend to imagine that a room will have square corners because almost every room we know has them.

The reason is a matter of cost. It is cheaper to make a square corner. Houses are built of square elements like bricks; builders are accustomed to working with them, and of course in terms of furniture they have many advantages.

In relation to spaciousness, however, round corners are often better than square ones. The more the delineation of the room is blurred, the bigger it will look. Lose the line between wall and wall,

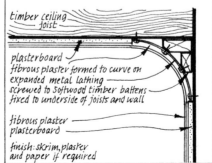

timber ceiling joist

plasterboard
fibrous plaster formed to curve on expanded metal lathing screwed to softwood timber battens fixed to underside of joists and wall

fibrous plaster plasterboard

finish: skrim, plaster and paper if required

wall and ceiling, and the eye drifts and the apparent size of the room increases.

Consider whether there are not places in the home where you might not round off the corners – not with an ineffectual tennis-ball radius, but a radius more comparable to a bicycle wheel.

Not a cheap exercise! It would probably be easiest to form the arc in expanded metal lathing which would then be plastered to merge into the existing plaster on the walls, and this will tend, being a fiddly and complicated little job, to be rather expensive. But it's worth looking into and the resulting benefits would be far greater than you might expect.

Ceilings

We think of ceilings as flat, level things. Why? Because they nearly always are so (being cheaper to build), but they do not need to be in your house. Providing you maintain the minimum heights that are required under the bylaws, have you ever thought what the effect would be, on the sense of space and the quality of light, of sloping the ceiling, or having it all rising towards the centre, or in an undulating wave-pattern from side to side? The way that you would do this would depend on the surface finish that you want. If you want smooth plaster finish, it would be constructed with plaster board (if level), or plaster on expanded metal if curved or shaped. If you are thinking that you might surface the new ceiling in boarding, the builder would put up a timber framework to accept the boards suspended from the ceiling. And if you were concerned about noise in the room, you could use an acoustic tile which would also be suspended from the ceiling.

Have you thought of lowering part of the ceiling only? This also can have a dramatic effect on the apparent size of a room and can help to define a particular area. You might lower the ceiling over a dining recess, or over a work area, and use the space for storage.

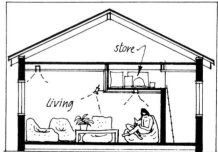

Storage space can be created by partial dropping of the ceiling.

Dropped ceiling with recessed lights provides demarkation for dining area, and space for a sunken bath above.

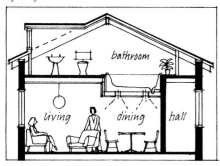

1 *The wall that used to hold up the roof has been removed, so that an alternative support had to be provided. A new beam has been run from the centre of the recess arch to make a visual connection between old and new. The strong lines of the new boarded ceiling run in the opposite direction giving a feeling of strength whilst complementing the shape of the roof. The soft yellow of the beam removes any possible feeling of heaviness.*

2 *Without the undulating ceiling this room would be too sparse. As it is, texture and proportions give a subtle balance to the open space below. Fittings are carefully considered and built as part of the spatial composition. Decoration is provided by the variation of movable plants and sculptures.*

3 *Three separate areas have been created in a calm yet contrasting way. To one side the large, semi-circular arch makes a dramatic opening in the wall. At the end of the room the low ceiling defines an eating area. One method vertical, the other horizontal. Polished floorboards tie the entire room together and the wood colours are continued in the fabrics and decorations. Gentle pools of light illuminate objects of particular interest.*

1

2

3

Internal layout
8/9 Major surgery

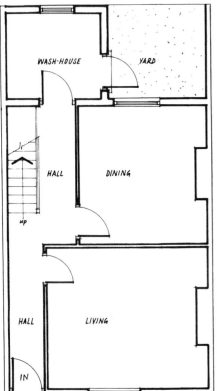

Opening up a traditional terrace house.

If limited knocking-about isn't the answer, you may need to consider making bigger decisions, to knock down or put up walls, go up into the roof space, excavate the basement or change the floor levels.

Knocking down walls

Before imposing your will on the house, give the place some sympathetic consideration. The layout of most pre-1918 houses was usually more formal and rigid than that of newer homes. These days, most people want some informal areas, some more formal areas. With an older house, you may often do better to leave intact the more formal living-room and dining-room arrangement and add on, say, a family room to the kitchen area.

Which rooms to combine

Here are a few of the rooms that can often be combined in older houses:
(a) Dark, narrow hall plus living-room or dining-room.
(b) Kitchen plus dining-room.
(c) Lavatory and bathroom (preferably if there is another separate lavatory elsewhere). You may well be able to fit a clothes-washing machine into the space gained.
(d) Living-room and "morning-room".
(e) Scullery plus kitchen.

After 1945 the pattern of cheaper housing changed from a scullery/back parlour plus front parlour to a minute kitchen, separate dining-room and living-room. You may well think it's worth combining the living/dining-room or kitchen/dining-room so that the dining space can be of use all day.

Which walls are "load-bearing"?

Alteration work to buildings is often dangerous and more complicated than would appear, so if this is what you have in mind leave it to a competent builder.

Nevertheless you will want to know what are the possibilities, so that you can instruct him.

The problem with knocking down walls is that they might be supporting something, and the first step is to find out if this is so.

How to find out

To find out if a wall is supporting the one above, measure from a point common to both of them – a staircase or outside wall for example. If one is directly below the other it is almost certainly bearing the weight. Floors are usually made up of boards nailed at right angles on to wooden joists. This makes the task of finding out which wall is holding up the joists an easy one. See which way the floorboards run: the joists must go in the other direction, and the wall on to which

they run is bearing the load of that floor.

If neither of these situations occurs it will be fairly safe to assume that the wall can be removed.

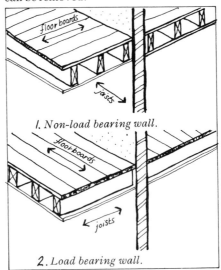

1. Non-load bearing wall.

2. Load bearing wall.

Concrete lintels and RSJs

If the wall cannot be removed because it is carrying a load, an opening can usually be made by inserting a steel beam or concrete lintel. There are concrete beams stocked by builders' merchants in various sizes, generally 4 in./102 mm wide and 6 in./152 mm – 9 in./229 mm deep by any length required. Concrete lintels have generally replaced steel beams in domestic work, since they are easily available and fire resistant, which may be required by law. It is difficult, and not generally practicable, to try to install a lintel so that it is flush with the ceiling – a downward projection usually has to be accepted. There are various ways in which you can treat the beam. In older houses the cornice can be maintained if the work is done carefully. If not, you can either box around the beam and treat it as part of the ceiling to combine the two rooms, or you can treat it decoratively to form a visual break. Should your proposal call for this sort of structural work the local authorities will come into the picture, so it is advisable to employ a professional engineer or architect to work out the information they will need.

What sort of opening?

If you have determined that the wall is not load-bearing, you can take it all away. On the other hand, if it does carry a load and you have to put in a beam, you will almost certainly have a down stand from the ceiling, and possibly a section of the old wall at each end of the opening will have to be left for the beam to sit on.

With just the beam and supporting "nibs", the basic opening will be square, but it doesn't have to stop there. A square opening is abrupt and positive and this may not be what you want. Other shapes can be formed with framing and plaster: arches, both round and pointed, or gentle flat ones. Just curving the corners can soften the impact.

The finishing materials used will also vary the degree of transition. Continuing the wall surface treatment and colour or pattern eases the flow, but if you want to make a visual break, the opening can be lined with panelling or treated with contrasting textures and colours.

Matching up mouldings

If you knock down a wall in an older house, you will need to match up any picture-rail and skirting mouldings – most timber merchants will copy the section exactly off a sample.

Cornices can also be matched, but this is a costly, specialist operation. If you have beautiful cornices, consider making a large arch rather than opening up the two rooms completely.

Marrying plaster

Without replastering the whole wall, it can sometimes prove difficult to marry up the old plaster and the new, because the level of the surfaces may vary. If you want a paint finish, wallpaper first with a heavy covering material to conceal any unsatisfactory joins.

---

1 *The wall running the length of the hallway in this house has been removed and a simple arch was knocked through from the living room to the dining room, thus opening up three rooms into one. The arch remains unobtrusive as it is not highlighted by any change of colour and, while defining areas, does not break up the unity.*

2 *To place modern furniture into a traditional interior calls for the firm approach demonstrated in the handling of the arch between these two rooms. The wide opening has really made these rooms into one. The moulding round the arch balances the ceiling mouldings and makes the opening a positive feature in tune with the classical proportions of the room.*

3 *The depth of this arch was dictated by the dimensions of a reinforced steel joist which supports the load of a wall on the floor above. The vertical supports are of the same width making a rectangular opening which underlines the proportions of the room and the formality of the setting. Lighting gives an almost theatrical effect to the area contained by the proscenium arch.*

1

2

3

Internal layout
10/11 Take out a wall

1 *The combination of accentuated forms and decoration gives this opened out interior a 1920s look. The opening in the staircase wall runs from an angular top into a curved sill. The door into the hall has been taken out, and the wall between the two main rooms has been cut away to form a rectangular opening.*

2 *Only just enough of the wall between kitchen and dining area has been removed. The ceiling of the kitchen has been lowered to create a more intimate scale in the smaller space.*

3 *The problem of cutting away only half of a wall has been solved here with advantage by balancing the size and shape of the opening with a shelving unit.*

1 *The dining area here is defined by a curved wall finished off with a triangular column which encloses a circular table. A passageway has been created to the side of the dining area, and a painted reinforced steel joist runs across the centre of the room to support the load of the floor above.*

2 *An elegant solution to opening up a loadbearing wall which must have a framework of steel beams and columns. The steel structure has not been plastered over and hidden, but left bare and painted to show off the grace of the classical capitals.*

3 *In order to balance the flowing shape of the chimney, a formal screen has been built. The end columns which frame the screen echo the vertical square flue, leaving space above the screen that permits the ceiling to run through uninterrupted, uniting the entire room. The area between the chimney and the screen is infilled to form a hatch.*

Internal layout
12/13 Grafts and transplants

Firstly you could consider whether it would be practical to form an extra room in the roof. Whether this makes sense largely depends on the height of the existing ridge of the roof above the ceiling joists. In order to be able to make a reasonable room, this dimension cannot be much below 8 ft/2.5 m, if you are going to end up with adequate (and legal) headroom below.

There are a number of firms that specialize in forming rooms in roofs and are familiar with the special problems that this kind of work involves. You would be wise to consult one of them at an early stage to establish whether it is sensible to proceed in your particular case. (See *Attics*.)

Windows: It is usually found that the major part of the room – the fully useful part, where there is adequate headroom and not a sloping ceiling angling down to the eaves – is best formed by having new dormer windows, in which the glass is vertical and a new section of horizontal roof is formed above, projecting from a point a little below the ridge line of the roof. Planning permission needs to be obtained before embarking on this job.

Stairs: The biggest problem that you will find in forming a room in the roof is likely to be how you are going to get up there. There is not the slightest doubt that a good fixed staircase is by far the best solution. The usefulness of the new room will greatly depend on the ease with which you can get up there. While it may appear fun, and seem amusing in other people's houses, to gain access to the roof by going up vertical ladders or pulling down collapsible ladders from trapdoors, it can prove very boring and restrictive in one's own home. And the snag is that an adequate staircase is a space-consuming thing; but, if you can manage one, you will find it the ideal answer.

Another possibility is not to form a room in a roof, but to open up some of the roof space to the room, or rooms, below. It is worth bearing in mind that it is often easier to remove upper storey walls than ground floor ones. It may be possible to remove the existing ceiling joists (though this should be checked with an architect or builder).

If it is feasible, you will be able to achieve a very considerable increase in the spaciousness of the room below: the underside of the rafters can be covered to continue the wall up, or treated as a separate surface. But even if some (or all) of the joists have to remain, you will find that by removing the plaster to the ceiling (and being willing to lose storage space you previously had in the roof) you will be able to give a new dimension to the room.

Changing levels

It is all too easy to think that the only things that can be changed in a house are the walls and the ceilings – but why not the floors? It may be possible to have them raised or lowered, depending on their structure or the heights of the rooms below.

Supposing that you have sufficient height in a room, why not lower part of the ceiling by dropping the level of the floor in the room above?

Or supposing that you have sufficient height in the room itself, why not consider having part of the floor raised?

Even in quite small rooms, such as a bathroom, quite dramatic changes can be made to the appearance of the room by changing the floor. In a bathroom, lowering the bath can have the effect of dramatically increasing the apparent size of the room. A bath takes up an awful lot of space – lower it and you will find that the apparent floor area, which now includes the bath, has greatly increased, and a sunken bath can make the smallest, pokiest bathroom look luxurious.

Floors will usually be composed of timber joists at approximately 16 in./406 mm to 18 in./457 mm centres, on to which will have been laid floorboards, with the ceiling being usually of plaster.

Holes of fairly large dimensions, e.g. to take a dropped-in section or to insert a staircase, can generally be cut in timber floors, but expert advice is essential.

Dividing rooms

Sometimes the space occupied by a big room can be employed better if divided into two: one big bedroom divided to provide a smaller bedroom with connecting bathroom, or a large sitting room with a small study/den self-contained within it.

There are two main ways of dividing up a room: (a) to create two rooms, each of which needs daylight, and (b) to create

two or more rooms, some of which will be internal, with electric light and artificial ventilation. If it is merely a question of rooms to satisfy both you and the law, separation, e.g. between bedrooms and dressing-rooms, or living and study areas, need not be complete. Wardrobes or bookcases, about 7 ft/2 m high or less, leave enough space at the top for light and air, and valuable wall space is left clear for things like Vanitory units or desks.

Platforms and balconies

Do you have a high room? It could be possible to introduce an extra floor level, such as a balcony for a sleeping or working area, slightly withdrawn from the main room.

One way would be by using metal scaffold tubing, boarding it over and having a ladder up to it. This is a relatively cheap method, but be sure that it complies with the local bylaws. Alternatively, you could have a balcony in timber joists and boarding, with a staircase up to it; a permanent method, but costing more, and you might well find that the staircase takes up a lot of space.

Even if the height is not enough for a balcony, you can still alter part of the level with a platform. It can be any manner of shape, running around the room (if it is large enough), across one section of the room, or in the centre. Storage cupboards can be fitted underneath, and a rail or run of shelving along the edge. The platform doesn't have to be very high and is an excellent way of dividing activities within one open-plan space, such as dining, sitting and cooking.

Getting into both rooms conveniently

Privacy of access is a problem to be overcome if you want to avoid early risers in one bedroom waking sluggards in the next, on the way to the bathroom. Try to plan a common entrance lobby or approach corridor, remembering to provide light and fresh air.

Internal rooms

Legally, only "non-habitable" rooms can be internal, like bathrooms, laundry-rooms, stores, etc. Make sure that you can run the necessary ventilation ducting and that you obtain local authority approval.

Making two rooms with daylight

Will there be enough light in both new rooms, to satisfy both you and the law? All habitable rooms in Britain must have a required amount of light (see *What's Legal?*, at the end of this section).

Always try, if humanly possible, to avoid dividing a window, bay or otherwise. It will look like what it is: a poor compromise.

Be prepared if necessary to cut another window (or, if on the top floor, install a rooflight), but consider the position of it in relation to the exterior of the house. You may need permission for this too. (*See Elevations.*)

Proportion

The main problem with divided rooms is that the proportion is usually wrong in both the new rooms, which are often too high. You may well have to form suspended ceilings to cope with this – either flat, or "barrel-vaulted", which can look pretty in a small bathroom and is a relatively simple affair with a few battens and some hardboard.

Remember too that, if the room has an attractive cornice, it will prove costly to carry it across the new dividing wall.

What sort of wall?

The form that the dividing wall might take will be dictated by the uses to which the two new rooms will be put. For two bedrooms, or study divided from sitting-room, it would be wiser to consider a relatively solid wall constructed in insulation blocks. Remembering the problems encountered in removing a wall, if you build a new one, make sure that the weight can be carried from below. If it can't, a beam will have to be inserted below to take the weight. If the noise transmission through the wall is unimportant, it would be cheaper to build the new wall in timber-framing surfaced in plasterboard or pine-boarding, or to use patent preformed panels.

Doors and screens

If you think that you may sometimes want two rooms and sometimes one, explore the possibilities of the sliding doors, folding doors and panels which can be fixed and unfixed.

Experience shows, however, that few people make much use of the flexibility which they have often gone to great pains to provide. So think first. Sliding doors, which it was fondly imagined would be pushed back and forth as the mood took one, often remain firmly shut (or open) year in, year out. Still, it can be a good solution between, say, a dining-room and living-room, where once or twice a year you want to join up the two rooms for really large parties.

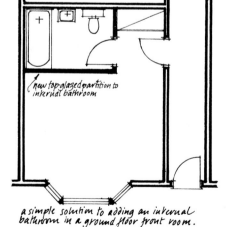

new top-glazed partition to internal bathroom

a simple solution to adding an internal bathroom in a ground floor front room.

(Opposite) This two-storied room benefits from various levels of light source: a dormer window in the vaulted ceiling, a window on the galleried staircase as well as a low level window. Vertical and horizontal features are so balanced that you lose neither the sensation of intimacy nor the feeling of space.

Internal layout
14/15 Going up/cutting up

1 *In this spacious interior the bold sculptural form of the balcony balances on the wall screening off the kitchen from the rest of the living area. The delicate lines of the spiral staircase make a direct contrast.*

2 *Building a balcony into a classically proportioned, high-ceilinged room demands a bold approach. Here standard industrial units form an elegant framework. Light colouring softens the mechanical quality of the construction and is echoed in the verticals of the radiator and pedestals.*

3 *The top floor and attic have been combined to form one huge space. The staircase from below comes up between the two central shelf units. A ladder gives access to the balcony, which provides more space for the display of books, pictures and artefacts. The minimal handrail permits a total view from below adding to the spacious quality of the room.*

4 *Simplicity of construction emphasizes the flow of space from this room on to the balcony. Furniture and wall decorations seen from above achieve qualities of pattern not normally appreciated at one level.*

1

2

3

4

1 *From the photographs on this page we can see how the designer has doubled the height of this living area and created a separate sitting or sleeping area which benefits from the overall spaciousness.*

2 *Underneath the upper level in an intimate dining area. It is partially screened by the supporting wall which divides the activities without destroying the spacious quality of the whole. Access to the balcony is by way of simple, unobtrusive, open stairs.*

3 *A large horizontal slatted blind floods light into the entire space. At the same time it forms a visual barrier, enclosing the upper level.*

4 *The flow of space above and below the balcony is amply illustrated from this point of view. By simplifying the form and detail of all new work the designer has concentrated attention on the spaces created.*

Internal layout
16 Is it legal?

We seem to live in a country with a legal system that has tied itself round its own neck a few times. Explaining simply what can and cannot be done is, therefore, more complex than might be supposed.

Broadly, when talking about altering a house, the things the law will prevent you from doing are those that are dangerous; anything that could be injurious to health, or anything which is detrimental to the general enjoyment of the area by others.

Load-bearing walls

Thus, you must not remove a wall in a house which might endanger the stability of the house. In general, this means that you must not remove a wall that is load-bearing, i.e., one on which either the roof or the floors above depend for their support, unless you provide alternative support.

Ventilation and light

There are also a number of regulations concerned with health, which affect what you might consider doing in relation to the design of bathrooms, windows, the height of rooms, and so on. Generally these are concerned with ensuring that a room is provided with adequate ventilation and sunlight, and that the danger of ill-health from faulty drains is reduced to a minimum.

The kind of alterations that you might consider, but for which you would need to establish that you could get the necessary permission, includes:

(a) Changing the way that a room containing a wc is linked with other rooms.

(b) Lowering ceilings (below 8 ft/2.5 m on ground floors and 7 ft 6 in./2.3 m on upper floors) or making a mezzanine balcony.
(c) Reducing the area of window serving a room (in general a room must have glass equivalent to 1/10th of its floor area, and half of that must be able to open).
(d) Making a room smaller than about 80 sq ft/7.4 sq m (if you do, you cannot legally use such a room as a bedroom).
(e) Internal rooms must be non-habitable – such as bathrooms, landing, etc. Ventilation in a wc must be connected to the light-switch.

Fire Precautions

The prime aim is to prevent a fire starting, so regulations control electrical wiring, positions of fuel-burning appliances and so on. If a fire does start it must be contained; other regulations cover the combustibility of surface-covering, such as boarding and wallpapers. And, of course, the structure of the building has to be fireproof to certain specified standards. Smoke from fires is a big danger, and people must be able to escape from the burning building by way of strong, smoke-free stairs and passages.

Planning Regulations

Here, broadly, the intention is that you do not do things, by way of altering the appearance or form of your house, in a manner which could be detrimental to the enjoyment of the area by others.

Ways in which the Planning Regulations might restrict the alterations that you have in mind include adding another floor, if the result is regarded as unsightly, and building close up to a boundary.

If you add to the number of rooms, even by dividing a big one, you may be making way for an increase in the potential number of occupants. This is regulated by a specified "density", or the permitted number of people per acre/hectare. Density is calculated by complicated sums worked out by planning experts.

It is a mistake to imagine that all local authority officers are soulless officials whose purpose in life is to restrict rather than to help. If you have any doubts about whether you would be allowed to do what you have in mind, you should go and ask, and you are likely to get most helpful advice. Do a little homework first. Make some simple drawings of what you want to do. Take any architect's drawings that may exist. Take some photographs which, even if they don't show exactly what you want, indicate the sort of house that it is.

To sum up

Before calling in the builder, surveyor or architect, take a look through the sections covering Flooring, Walls, Windows, Lighting, Colour, Heating and Storage. Then read the chapter on Co-ordination, which is about getting all the overlapping, and often conflicting, layers of decisions into some sort of order. Then come back and see how the suggestions in this chapter are affected.

If you can find an architect or interior designer to discuss your problems, and you decide to hand the whole thing over to a professional, you will at least have a very good idea of what is involved, and can provide that rare and lovely thing – a perfect brief.

Floors/1

Before you start thinking about textures and colours you must consider the practical problems. Flooring can be one of the biggest expenses, so mistakes could be costly. Certain types of flooring may not be suitable for the construction of the house. If you have solid concrete floors you can put down almost any flooring provided a damp-proof course is incorporated, but you cannot for instance put quarry tiles on the average domestic timber suspended floor without taking expert advice on floor loadings.

In deciding what floorings are suitable for your home, you will have to take into account the kind of wear the floors will get. Where there's likely to be a lot of mess, the situation calls for a tough washable floor finish, not a carpet. Kitchen floors should always be easy to clean and resistant to water and grease. Living-rooms, halls and stairs get a lot of wear, but bedrooms hardly ever do. Those doubling as a playroom or teenage room do, however, need a tougher floor, because they'll have to take an extra-hard beating.

There are other things you have to consider: comfort, warmth, quietness; whether it should be professionally laid, how much it will cost, and, of course, what it will look like. The cost of laying will vary, but it is worth remembering that a well-laid flooring will last longer and is likely to give less trouble than a cheap badly laid one. If you decide to lay the floor yourself, follow the manufacturers' instructions throughout.

Warmth

Very hard floors can be cold and tiring to stand on for long periods of time. If your family likes to walk about barefoot, this might be a good reason for carpeting the whole house or, alternatively, installing underfloor heating.

Safety

Avoid slippery finishes, for these can be dangerous, particularly for older people. Loose rugs on polished floors are a hazard, so never polish under rugs and make sure you have non-slip underlays where possible.

Noise

Ceramic tiles and stone can be very noisy. Cork and rubber both have good sound absorbence, and cushion-backed vinyl is much quieter than the flat vinyl sheet or vinyl asbestos floorings. Noise and reverberations can also be transmitted through the structure, either through walls or from one floor to the next, and are more difficult to deal with.

It is very much worthwhile to insulate a floor before laying a new finish both to

reduce the transmission of noise and to help keep in warmth. This can be cheap and quite easy to do.

Choice

If the existing floorboards are sound, and you haven't much money, you can sand and seal them. (Sanders can be hired, or you can employ a contractor.) Use a clear seal to bring out the colour and grain of the wood; or for a bleached, cool look a white seal; or colour-stain the boards. Large expanses of bare floor can be softened with rugs.

Vinyl is the fastest growing development in flooring materials, and takes on many guises. Some of the better tiles and sheet floorings are now designed by well-known designers, but, particularly at the cheaper end, many patterns imitate other materials. Many patterns have embossed or textured surfaces; better qualities are usually cushion-backed.

There are so many qualities of carpet and different fibre mixtures that it can be difficult to make a choice. Even all-wool carpets differ greatly in wear and general quality. It is not always necessary

to buy the most expensive; light traffic areas don't require the same hard-wearing carpets as the hall or living-room. The choice of colours and patterns is very wide, but shop around before you decide.

Planning

Having decided on the type of floor you need, you are left with the task of choosing makes, colours, textures and patterns. This is where you have to sit down and work out your own preferences, so refer back to the Colour and Pattern chapter. Go round showrooms and shops, snoop through your friends' homes, ask questions, test and feel. Sometimes finding out what you don't want can be helpful, too. Take with you any samples of fabrics you know you will want to use and look at the colours together, but remember that colours seen in small squares look different in large areas, and that they change under different lights.

If you have a small house or flat you might be wise to concentrate on making small areas look larger by carrying the same flooring right through.

A larger house has rather different problems. Here you have to decide whether you want each door to open on to a separate world of its own with its own identity or whether you want the whole house to work within a uniform framework. Individual members of a family should not have to be imprisoned by one person's taste, and the main house could fall into a fairly precise and specific scheme, with a variety of different schemes in the individual bedrooms. Rooms seen through open doors, passageways leading to staircases or rooms, and the problem of how two different floor finishes can meet successfully in a doorway are other points to bear in mind.

Briefly, these are some of the points that you'll need to check out:
- [ ] Is the floor solid or suspended?
- [ ] At ground level, is there a damp-proof course?
- [ ] What kind of wear will the floor get?
- [ ] Will it be easy to maintain?
- [ ] Can you lay it yourself or should you call in a professional?
- [ ] Will your choice of colour or pattern fit into the general scheme?
- [ ] Are you aiming at an all-over co-ordinated scheme, or decorating each room separately?
- [ ] Have you taken into account thresholds – the changes from one material or colour to another?

The lozenge-shaped quarry tiles add character to a white-painted room. The carpet softens the line, adding warmth and comfort. Its design is based on the medieval labyrinth on the floor of Chartres Cathedral.

Non-porous floors (slate, ceramic and quarry tiles): There is no point in putting a seal on a non-porous floor; it is already waterproof and impervious to most household liquids. Anyway, sealers would soon peel or chip off. Non-porous floors are usually the most durable, but they are non-resilient, and china or glass is more likely to break when dropped.

Semi-porous floors (marble, terrazzo, rubber, most linoleums, vinyl, vinyl asbestos, thermoplastic): Waterproof and resistant (not impervious) to oils and grease, they tend to react badly to spirit solvents such as petrol, paraffin and white spirits, and most of them should not be sealed as this can irreparably damage the finish.

Porous floors (unsealed wood, cork, concrete, chipboard, some older linoleums): These are not waterproof or greaseproof and are likely to stain. Sealed, this kind of floor becomes a non-porous surface. The softer and more porous the floor, the more sealer is needed.

Sealers, cleaners, polishes, stains: To be on the safe side, ask the manufacturers which products to use on their floorings (they will sometimes even send representatives to advise you). Or ask the product manufacturers if theirs is suitable for a specific floor. As a rough guide, we indicate suitable types of sealers or polishes in each case.

Sealers: Domestic ones are usually oleo-resinous, containing oil and slower to dry, or polyurethane in one-can or two-can form. The two-pack version has a separate hardener to mix with the seal just before application, and gives a tougher finish. Urea formaldehyde, which contains an acid hardener (and will not do for concrete), is sometimes used instead. Some varnishes and lacquers are suitable for floors, but not as tough.

Most sealers have a gloss finish, but some are semi-gloss or matt and preserve the original look of a finish. Generally, any seal will change the colour slightly; oleo-resinous ones, particularly, tend to darken in time.

The main difference between oleo-resinous and polyurethane seals is that the former partly soaks into the grain or surface, while the latter forms a hard skin on top. It dries to a harder finish but on a new wood floor which is subject to shrinking, the polyurethane skin may crack while an oleo-resinous seal would move with the wood.

Polishes: These come either spirit-based (liquid or solid wax) or in emulsion (suspended in water). It is important to know which to use. Plastic, asphalt or rubber floors do not like petrol, paraffin or white spirit, and anything containing these chemicals should be avoided. Over-application of spirit wax polishes leads to a slippery build-up of dirt.

Some emulsions are self-polishing; others are really water-based seals, stronger and longer-lasting, which can considerably improve the look of worn marble or stone.

There are also a number of *cleaners/polishes* which can be effective, but tend to build up if used too often – so that you end up with a yellow layer of polish and dirt. If this has happened, ask the makers of the polish for advice on how to clean it off. On no account try to tackle it with wire wool – you may ruin the surface.

Stained wood

Floor stains are available in wood tones, and also in colours like blue, red and green. There are various chemical dyes and water-based or spirit-based stains. The latter contain oil, and if the floor is also going to be sealed, be very careful that the sealer is compatible with the stain, otherwise you might land up with a sticky mess. On the whole, it is safest to use a water-based stain, which can be sealed without chemical reaction. It also has the advantage that you can thin it for a lighter stain, or mix it to make your own colours. However, water-based stains will raise the grain of the wood and the floor must be sanded smooth before and after sealing. If you don't seal water-based stains, they will eventually wash off.

Painted wood

Although any gloss paint can be used on the floor, paints made specifically for floors will dry harder and wear better. They usually contain polyurethane, acrylic or epoxy resin and come in a fairly wide range of colours. (The kind used for yachts is particularly hard-wearing.) There are also special paints for concrete floors, made for industrial use, but most ordinary floor paints can be used on concrete in a domestic situation. It is absolutely essential that all grease, oil, dirt or old polish is thoroughly removed before the floor is painted, as these may affect the adhesion and drying of the paint.

Softwood boarding

Description: Spruce, fir, pine. This is the most common timber surface. In newer houses the boards may be tongued and grooved; in older ones they will usually be butt-jointed.

Advantages: If your existing timber floor is in good condition it can be sanded and sealed. The rich natural colours show up the grain and look attractive as a background for rugs and loose carpets or, alternatively, boards can be coloured with pigmented translucent wood sealer; with a water-based stain then sealed; or painted.

Disadvantages: Butt-jointed boards may have shrunk or twisted and the resulting gaps will collect dust and dirt. They may also be draughty.

Care: Seal with oleo-resinous or polyurethane sealer. Sweep, mop and polish with emulsion polish. Unsealed boards can be wax polished. Make sure that ground floors are well ventilated under the floorboards. Clean out vent bricks regularly.

Hardwood

Description: The hardwood strips or blocks are laid in herring-bone, basket or brick patterns. Traditional parquet floors are made of short strips laid individually or glued in panels pre-mounted on ply. Wood mosaic squares are made up of fingers of wood in a basket pattern and backed with felt or hessian or faced with paper which is peeled off after laying. Long narrow hardwood strips can also be glued to concrete and sometimes come sealed.

Advantages: Resilient, good looking, warm, and hard-wearing. Improves with age. Can be sanded and resealed.

Disadvantages: Dry heat may cause shrinking, dampness swelling – and parquet can be expensive.

Laying: Wood block and mosaic should be laid on screeded concrete, ply or chipboard. Parquet and wood strip need a level timber, ply or hardboard sub-floor. Seal with polyurethane or oleo-resinous sealer.

Care: Sweep, mop, and emulsion-polish occasionally if sealed. If not, polish regularly.

Plywood

Description: As well as being a good sub-floor, $\frac{1}{8}$ in./3 mm thick plywood can be used as surface covering. (In new houses $\frac{3}{4}$ in./18 mm or 1 in./25 mm thick squares or rectangles of tongued-and-grooved ply are now used directly on timber joists instead of boarding.) In various timber finishes, unsealed or pre-sealed. Can be stained.

Advantages: Comparatively inexpensive, attractive. Dearer than softwood but quicker to lay in larger sheets.

Disadvantages: It is not very impact-resistant (i.e. dents) but better than softwood. If the seal wears off, the ply will stain and deteriorate.

Laying: Fix to level board floor with panel pins at 6 in./152 mm to 9 in./229 mm intervals with paper underlay. Or bed in bitumastic on a screeded concrete sub-floor.

Care: Seal with oleo-resinous or polyurethane sealer. Sweep and mop. Occasionally emulsion-polish. If staining before sealing, check that stain and seal are compatible.

Chipboard

Description: Made from varying sizes of wood-chips mixed with urea formaldehyde resins bonded under pressure. Like ply, it can be used as a surface covering or it is available tongued and grooved for use directly on timber joisted floors. In squares of varying thicknesses, unsealed or sealed. Clear seal gives it a palish honey-coloured cork look.

Advantages: Inexpensive, attractive. Reduces sound transmission.

Disadvantages: Non-sealed chipboard is very porous and stains or discolours considerably, so seal must not be allowed to wear off (i.e., re-seal before this happens).

Laying: As for ply.
Care: As for ply.

Hardboard

Description: Can be used as an inexpensive surface covering in the same way as ply or chipboard. It is cut to order and sealed *in situ.* There are light and dark hardboards to be found or you can easily stain them. Oil-tempered hardboards can't be sealed but can be waxed to give a pleasant finish.

Advantages: Very inexpensive, useful short-term floor which could later have carpet or other material laid over it. It is also good for making a level base over old warped floorboards.

Disadvantages: It is not very hard-wearing. May stretch a little so don't butt edges too close together. Will rot if water gets underneath and stain if the seal is allowed to wear off.

Laying: Can be laid on slightly uneven floorboards with paper underlay. Nail at 6 in./152 mm to 9 in./229 mm centres round and across the board to avoid drumming.

Care: As for ply.

Ceramic floor tiles

Description: Made of clay, pressed into tiles and fired at a high temperature. The tiles can be hand- or machine-made and some have a non-slip finish. Vitrified tiles are frost-proof. There is a wide choice of colours, glazed and unglazed surface patterns, finishes and textures. Sizes and thicknesses vary and tiles can be square, rectangular, hexagonal, Provençal, etc.

Advantages: Tough, waterproof and impervious to almost all household liquids. Suitable for underfloor heating and the vitrified tiles can be used outdoors.

Disadvantages: Can be cold, noisy and rather tiring to the feet.

Laying: On concrete sub-floor with cement and sand screed, but as long as the floor is flat you can also lay them on other smooth sub-floors, using latex screed.

Care: Sweep and wash but do not polish, as they can become dangerously slippery.

Quarry tiles

Description: Made from a high silica alumina clay to an almost glass-like hardness. Usually square or rectangular, in various sizes; buff, yellow, various reds or browns and dark blue or black. Tiles in blended colours look more mellow. Check whether the tiles are genuine quarries.

Advantages: Impervious to water, grease and all household liquids. Tough British quarry tiles are made to high standards and are very tough and easy to clean. Suitable for underfloor heating. It is sometimes possible to buy cheaper "seconds".

Disadvantages: Cold, hard and fairly noisy.

Laying: Lay on a screeded concrete sub-floor. Seal immediately with a mixture of 1 part linseed oil to 4 parts turps. Then cover with brown paper and leave for a couple of days. Don't let anyone walk on an untreated floor.

Care: Sweep and wash. Very worn quarries can be given a coat of water-based sealer, after cleaning off all grease or dirt.

Mosaic

Description: Can be made of glass silica but are at most 1 in./25 mm square. Glazed or unglazed, semi- or fully vitrified. Usually sold mounted on paper to make them easier to lay. Also clay or marble mosaic. Various sizes and a wide colour range. The floor above is a mosaic design by Picasso.

Advantages: As for ceramic tiles. Suitable for underfloor heating.

Disadvantages: Cold, hard, and rather noisy.

Laying: Lay on a screeded sub-floor. Coved skirtings make cleaning much easier.

Care: Sweep and wash, but do not polish.

Brick

Description: Usually buff, purple, blue and a variety of browns.

Advantages: Most types of hard brick make good floor surfaces and some pre-war houses without damp-proof courses have this kind of floor. As bricks can be used both inside and out, they look well in rooms that open into the garden or courtyard. Suitable for underfloor heating.

Disadvantages: Hard, fairly noisy.

Laying: On concrete, inside, or in sand or weak cement on level ground outside. May be sealed.

Care: Sweep and wash. May be polished.

Granwood block

Description: Tiles made from cement, wood and linseed oil with a keyed underside, twelve colours. Non-porous.

Advantages: Combines resilience and warmth of wood with hard-wearing qualities of concrete.

Disadvantages: Expensive in small areas.

Laying: Should be laid by Granwood expert.

Care: Sweep and wash. Polish occasionally.

Terrazzo

Description: Marble chippings set in cement, plain or coloured, then ground smooth. In tiles or large slabs or laid *in situ*; chippings vary in size to make colourful patterns. Not often used domestically because laying and finishing small areas is expensive.

Advantages: It is fairly hard-wearing and maintenance free. Used for visual effect. Suitable for underfloor heating. Good in bathrooms.

Disadvantages: Fairly hard, noisy, sometimes slippery.

Laying: As for mosaics and ceramic tiles. The joints between the chippings can be sealed with silicone.

Care: Sweep and wash but do not polish. Do not use acid cleaners, which can affect the marble.

Marble

Description: Hard-wearing natural material in many beautiful colours. Can be bought now ¼ in./7 mm thick and laid on block-board or chipboard if this is firm and flat.

Advantages: Lasts a very long time.

Disadvantages: It is cold and hard underfoot. Rather expensive.

Laying: In a cement bed on concrete sub-floor.

Care: Can be swept and washed or scrubbed. Don't use acid cleaners. Polish worn marble with a water-based sealer.

Concrete tiles

Description: Made of cement and aggregate on ordinary concrete backing. Natural or grey and reds. Usually square.

Advantages: Suitable for underfloor heating and for patios, showers.

Disadvantages: Very hard and cold.

Laying: Lay on concrete sub-floor. Can be sealed – a sodium silicate or chemical sealer which combines with the surface is recommended – or an occasional coat of water-based emulsion polish.

Care: Sweep and wash.

Stone

Description: Sandstone, yorkstone, granite and limestone slabs; also cast slabs made of chippings mixed with cement.

Advantages: Extremely hard-wearing.

Disadvantages: Hard, cold and noisy.

Laying: Lay in a cement bed on a concrete sub-floor. It is sometimes possible to seal stone with a varnish or a water-based sealer though this will change its colour; get expert advice because stone varies in porosity.

Care: Sweep and wash.

Granolithic

Description: Superior and less porous kind of concrete made from cement, granite chippings and granite dust.

Advantages: It is very hard-wearing. More often used in factories than in the home, but when sealed is easy to maintain. Use in workrooms, garages, etc.

Disadvantages: Very hard and not generally suitable for living areas.

Laying: On a concrete floor by an expert. Seal as for concrete.

Care: Sweep and wash.

Slate

Description: A dense, non-porous stone which varies in colour from dark blue (Welsh) to the heather colours and grey-green (Westmorland). It looks best in square or rectangular (here separated by wood surround) rather than random pieces; sawn or polished finishes, or available with a non-slip riven surface.

Advantages: Beautiful, easy to care for and exceptionally hard-wearing.

Disadvantages: Very expensive, fairly noisy, cold, hard, can be slippery when wet (except non-slip variety).

Laying: In a cement bed on concrete.

Care: Use linseed and turps mix as for quarry tiles. Sweep and wash or scrub. Emulsion polish or water-based sealer can be used occasionally, but sawn or polished slate becomes slippery.

Cork tiles

Description: Made from cork granules and natural or synthetic binders, compressed and baked. Beige to dark brown.

Advantages: Good insulation qualities, warm, resilient and quiet. Hardwearing. Sealed floors easy to maintain. Unsealed, good for bathrooms.

Disadvantages: With relatively light wear, no grease or heavy splashing, looks attractive left natural. However, manufacturers recommend seal or polish. (Matt seal looks better than gloss.) Tiles chip or crumble at edges, fade in strong sunlight.

Laying: Lay with adhesive on even sub-floor.

Care: Seal with oleoresinous or polyurethane sealer; wash, and occasionally emulsion-polish, or don't seal, but maintain with spirit-based wax. Old cork can be sanded and resealed by an expert.

Vinyl cork tiles

Cork tiles are also available with a laminated top layer of vinyl. This makes them tougher, non-porous. They can be kept clean by damp mopping.

Linoleum

Description: Made of ground cork, wood, flour, linseed oil and resins, pressed on to a jute or hessian backing. There are different grades and thicknesses. Generally harder-wearing and less porous than some years ago, but beware of cheap versions which are really a printed felt base. Usually treated with a surface dressing. In sheet or tile form, in a good range of plain colours, also marbled or patterned.

Advantages: It is hardwearing. Thicker qualities have a high resilience and are warm underfoot.

Disadvantages: It is inclined to rise, peel, rot if water gets beneath. Sensitive to alkalis.

Laying: Lay tiles with adhesive on any dry, even sub-floor with a damp-proof course. Floorboards need a layer of hardboard or a latex screed. If sheet linoleum is laid loose you can use felt paper underlay but the linoleum may stretch and need to be trimmed.

Care: Should not be sealed but can be polished with an emulsion polish.

Rubber

Description: Often a combination of natural and synthetic rubber. Traditionally in sheets or tiles in plain colours, mottled, or with inlaid patterns. Industrial forms – ribbed, studded, etc. – are now coming into homes.

Advantages: Hardwearing, resilient, quiet, waterproof.

Disadvantages: Natural rubber is difficult to lay. It reacts badly to grease, fruit juices and spirits. Rubber heels make black marks. Synthetic rubber now often replaces natural rubber.

Laying: Lay on screeded concrete or ply or hardwood sub-floor. Synthetic rubber can be laid loose on cement screed.

Care: Rubber is sensitive to spirit solvents – only use emulsion polish. Wash with warm water and mild detergents.

Rubber cork

Description: A mixture of rubber and cork granules. Limited range of colours: plain, mottled, dark. Has the same advantages and disadvantages as rubber and is laid and maintained like it.

Thermoplastic tiles

Description: Early tiles were made from asphalt, mineral fillers and pigments. Modern tiles contain synthetic resins and a vinyl binder which makes them more resistant to oils and grease.

Advantages: Cheap and tough. Abrasion-resistant. Easy to clean.

Disadvantages: They are not very heat-resistant. Fairly cold.

Laying: Lay on a smooth sub-floor with a damp-proof course.

Care: Sweep, wash, use emulsion polish, not spirit wax. Do not overwet your floor when washing, as water may seep under the tiles.

Vinyl asbestos tiles

Description: Made from asbestos fibres, minerals, pigments and up to 30% plasticized PVC. Flecked or marbled patterns.

Advantages: More resistant to oils, grease, etc. than thermoplastic tiles.

Disadvantages: Rubber heels tend to leave black marks (remove with fine steel wool and soap). Low radiators sometimes soften tiles underneath.

Laying and Care: As for thermoplastic.

Vinyl sheeting

Description: The better qualities usually have a cushioned backing. The term vinyl is used rather loosely; often a top layer of vinyl is backed with another material, but this also provides a durable surface. Vinyl flooring is as expensive as a medium-grade carpet. Wide range of colours, patterns, textures and prices.

Advantages: Waterproof, resistant to oil, fat and grease and most domestic chemicals. A textured finish shows up marks less and is slip-resistant. Cushioned vinyl is quiet, resilient and warm underfoot. Can be used over underfloor heating up to 80° F (27°C).

Disadvantages: Unbacked vinyl over concrete can be hard and cold.

Laying: See vinyl tiles. Some sheeting can be cut with sharp scissors. Unbacked vinyl sheeting may shrink if laid loose, but most vinyls with cushioned backing are dimensionally stable. Some sheeting can be left loose, or fixed with double-sided tape. Avoid ugly joins.

Care: As vinyl tiles.

Vinyl tiles

Description: They come in many different colours, textures, patterns and grades. Decorative tile designs are an acceptable and resilient alternative to ceramic tiles.

Advantages: As for vinyl sheeting. You can make up your own patterns from different-coloured or different-sized tiles of the same thickness and quality.

Disadvantages: Needs very accurate laying both for pattern continuity and to avoid gaps; and also to prevent corners lifting.

Laying: Stick tiles to smooth, even sub-floor. Follow manufacturers' instructions as there are different types of vinyl and the chemicals in some products may damage them.

Care: Manufacturers also make different recommendations about cleaning, so check. Most of the textured and some flat vinyls only need washing, but rinse well or a film of dirty suds dries on the surface. Most flat vinyls respond to an occasional emulsion polish but avoid a build-up of polish.

Floors
6/7 Soft floors/carpets and rugs

The fibres used in the making of carpets can be either natural (animal or vegetable) or man-made (regenerated fibres or synthetics). Different fibres have different advantages and disadvantages. They may be very hard-wearing but attract dirt through static electricity. Research is reducing this problem and many synthetic carpets are specially treated to make them anti-static. If you walk across an all-nylon carpet in dry weather or in a centrally-heated room, the charge accumulated by the nylon may be released through a metal door handle. To avoid nasty shocks, change the handles to china or the carpet to wool. By mixing two or more fibres you may increase the carpet's durability.

The following is a brief description of the main carpet fibres, but new ones are constantly being developed.

Natural fibres

Wool: Used particularly in woven carpets, either on its own or in mixtures; the most popular being 80% wool, 20% nylon, which adds extra strength from the nylon to all the advantages of wool. Quality and price vary, but wool carpets are warm, soft, resilient, fire-resistant, and do not attract dirt.

Animal hair: Goat, cow, horse or pig hair is used in hair cords and carpet tiles, sometimes blended with viscose, rayon or wool. Very hard-wearing, does not attract dirt; fire-resistant.

Jute: Brown hard fibre from plant stem. Used in the backing of carpets, but in tufted ones polypropylene is now often used. Occasionally blended with viscose rayon in cord-type carpets.

Sisal: Plant fibre used for cord carpets and carpet tiles. Less expensive than hair or wool but harsher.

Coir: Comes from the coconut, is similar to sisal. Often used for mats and runners (coconut matting) or in better-quality carpet widths (coir matting).

Cotton: Used for rugs, in the foundation of some woven carpets, and occasionally also in cheaper pile carpets. Although hard-wearing, it soils easily and the pile tends to compress. Twisted pile cotton makes a good washable bathroom or nursery rug or carpet.

Silk, linen and asbestos: These can be added to carpet mixtures. Silk is sometimes found in Chinese carpets or rugs.

Metal: Very fine metal fibres are sometimes used in blends to cut out static charges which tend to build up in synthetic carpets.

Man-made fibres

Acrylic: (Acrilan, Courtelle, Dralon, Orlon) Nearest to wool in many ways and used particularly in woven and tufted carpets, either 100% or blended. Wears well; warm and resilient; soils easily but easy to clean; not fire-resistant.

Nylon: (Bri-Nylon, Enkalon, Du Pont 501, etc.) Used in woven and tufted carpets, needleloom felts and bonded carpets, either 100% or blended with wool or viscose rayon. Nylon is very tough and blends well with other fibres to give increased durability. It attracts dirt but is easily cleaned; is liable to static electricity in 100% nylon carpets (though non-static ones are being developed). Melts when in contact with direct flame; a cigarette will leave a burn mark if dropped on it.

Viscose rayon: (Evlan) A regenerated fibre which is inexpensive and not very hard-wearing, and is used mostly as bulk in blends. Also used as a main fibre in cheaper carpets, sometimes strengthened by nylon. It is not dirt-resistant.

Polyester: (Terylene, Dacron) This is often blended with nylon. Waterproof, easy to clean, soft, hard-wearing.

Polypropylene: (Merkalon, Fibrite, etc.) Widely used in backings for tufted carpets and for needleloom felt, or in small quantity in pile blends. An all-polypropylene cord carpet is now available. It is hard-wearing, resistant to stains, and is easily cleaned.

Pile

There are three main types of pile:

Cut pile: Where all the ends are cut on the surface of the carpet, as found in Axminsters, Wiltons and tufted carpets, and in some bonded carpets. Cut pile can be long and shaggy, short and smooth, or stubbly where a hard twist yarn is used. It can also be cut long and short to give a sculptured effect.

Looped pile: Is uncut and available in Wiltons, all cords and some tufteds. Textures, depending on length and type of yarn, can again be shaggy or smooth.

Cut and looped pile: Is available in Wiltons and tufted, and is used effectively (if not always aesthetically) in sculptured or carved patterns.

Quality

How well a carpet wears depends on the type of fibre used, the density and height of the pile and whether it has been well-laid on a level surface, either with a good

underlay or a foam backing. The density of the foam backing can affect the wearing qualities of the carpet. Generally, prices vary with the quality: the better the carpet, the more it will cost.

The British Carpet Centre has a standard labelling scheme for Axminster and Wilton carpets and rugs, worked out in collaboration with British carpet manufacturers, which is a classification guide plus guarantee covering weave, construction and materials. There are five classifications from light domestic to heavy contract use and approved carpets carry a guarantee/classification label.

Underlay

To get the best and longest wear out of your carpet, and also a softer tread, you need a good underlay. Also, if the floor is slightly uneven a thick underlay will take up minor differences. Some carpets come with their own foam backing and do not need an underlay. For narrow-width carpeting a felt-type underlay is still the best, since rubber-type ones tend to push the seams upwards so that they get worn. However, there are now felt and rubber combinations where the lower rubber layer allows the seams to embed themselves. Other materials include PVC or latex foam, foam rubber, wool blended with other fibres, 100% acrylic fibre, felt and jute. There are special stair-pads. Never use newspapers or old carpet.

Widths

Narrow-width carpet is usually 27 in./686 mm or 36 in./914 mm and can be used as runners in the hall and on the stairs, or seamed together for wall-to-wall coverage. Broadloom carpeting comes in various widths from 6 ft/1.8 m to 15 ft/4.6 m or even 18 ft/6 m. All kinds of carpet are woven in broadloom, but you may not get the same designs in the narrow and broad widths. Broadloom carpet can be bought in squares or rectangles and laid loose.

Measuring and laying

We are not recommending that you lay your own fitted carpets. Unless you have ideal conditions – rectangular rooms, smooth, even floors, no stairs, no odd corners – you are liable to run into snags, both in the measuring and the laying. Most carpet stores have their own floor-laying specialists who measure the floors, work out the amount of carpet needed and the cost of carpet, underlay and installation. Check estimates carefully, however, as some firms over-provide for the amount required. Complicated patterns need more than plain colours, due to pattern matching. Carpets can be

laid on dry screeded concrete provided there is a sound damp-proof course, or over a latex/cement screed which is the cheapest way to smooth out an old wood floor or stair treads. Timber floors may need to be covered with ply or hardboard unless they are very smooth and close fitting. *Don't* have a carpet laid on a damp or uneven floor.

Edgings

Use self-adhesive linen carpet binding tape to bind raw carpet edges, and also for sisal, rush and other matting.

Tackless installation

Fitted carpets can be effectively laid with carpet grippers which eliminate the use of tacks and are easy to take up if you move. These grippers are strips with angled pins fixed to the floor and which grip the carpet from underneath.

Stairs

The carpeting on stair treads gets heavy wear, and the risers none at all. Carpet grippers nailed in the angle of tread and riser hold stair carpets in place invisibly from underneath, and make it easier to move the carpet from time to time to spread the wear.

Thresholds

Where two different carpets meet in a doorway, or where one type of floor meets another, use aluminium threshold strips screwed into the floor to trap the edge of the carpet.

Cleaning

New carpets tend to fluff. For the first few weeks they should be cleaned only lightly with a hand brush, after which they can be suction-cleaned once or twice a week. If a few single tufts stand out, don't pull them, but cut with scissors to the level of the pile. If you shampoo your own carpets, use recommended strengths and follow the instructions exactly. Most shampoos produce only a foam which is rubbed into the carpet with a special applicator and left to dry to a powder, then suction-cleaned. Never overwet a carpet, as this may cause shrinkage, or, if jute-backed, or on a hair underlay, the colour may stain through. Spills need speedy attention, and an emergency carpet stain-removal kit is useful to have on hand. First quickly blot up the spilled liquid with tissues, then use the recommended method of stain removal.

Axminster

Woven carpet with a cut pile. The different-coloured tufts are inserted into the weave from above so that they make up the pile but do not run in the back. For this reason it is possible to use any number of colours and the majority of Axminsters are patterned. Quality depends on the type of fibre and the amount used per square inch. Fibres can be anything from 100% wool, acrylic, nylon and rayon to blends of any two or more; one of the best blends for durability and general wear is 80% wool, 20% nylon. Available in broadloom and narrow widths or as rugs. All price ranges, depending on the quantity of fibre used. Patterns and textures are very varied. Pile can be long or short, smooth or shaggy, pebbly or carved.

Wilton

Woven carpet with cut, looped, or cut and looped pile. Here the carpet-yarn is woven in continuous strands and only a limited number of colours can be used on the loom – usually no more than five, but occasionally up to eight colours. The pile yarn is woven so that colours not showing on the surface lie in the back (like Fair Isle knitting). Patterned Wiltons are consequently only available in better-quality grades. Patterned Axminsters can be very cheap, but even so a patterned Axminster and a patterned Wilton of the same high quality and fibre will cost the same. However, the majority of Wiltons are plain, many with a smooth velvety surface and in hundreds of colours. The textured Wiltons include sculptured, carved or embossed surfaces. Fibres as for Axminsters. Available in broadloom and several narrow widths.

Tufted (Above)

Made by needling the tufts into a backing then securing by a latex coating. The pile is looped, cut or a mixture of both. Textures include sculpturing. Fibres as for Axminsters. Available in broadloom and narrow widths. A stabilized foam-latex backing is often added to prevent stretching; acts as an underlay.

Cord (Below)

Normally made in a similar way to plain Wilton carpets but the pile is left uncut, giving the carpet a corduroy look. Hair cords are made of animal hair and are very hard-wearing, but cords are more often in man-made fibres. Broadloom and narrow widths.

Indian (not shown)

Off-white comes both in broadloom or rug form, hand-made in wool, with the pile looped and knitted into the backing. Good qualities wear well.

Needleloom (Above)

These have no pile and are made by needle punching and entangling a mixture of fibres through a backing fabric and impregnating it with an acrylic resin. Fibres used include nylon, jute, and polypropylene, and layers of different fibres used together combine economy with durability. ICI have also developed a process whereby nylon and Terylene are welded under heat without the need for resin adhesive, which makes it much softer than an ordinary needleloom.

Bonded pile (Below)

There are various ways of bonding a sheet of yarns or fibres to an adhesive backing to produce pile carpets. These include short cut piles and loops or cords, and also electro-static flocking. New processes are perpetually being developed.

Carpet tiles (Above)

These used to be made of animal hair pile, especially pig bristle, in a wide range of colours; now tiles are available in woven, tufted, cord and bonded carpets in a variety of fibres. They can be laid to look like one carpet or different colours used together to form chequer-board or other patterns. They can be laid loose and moved or exchanged if one area gets worn or stained. However, if the worn area is very worn, new tiles will stand out and make the others look even worse – particularly if they are all one colour: the answer is to switch them around regularly.

Rush matting (Below)

Natural rush is woven into squares and continuous lengths. It is sold either by the square or made up. Inexpensive and useful laid loose over stone or screed floors. Dust and dirt are trapped underneath so that you only have to lift and sweep it away. Should be gently watered in very dry conditions.

Carpet felt (Above)

Thick carpet felt will provide a warm, colourful floor covering for a bedroom or other room which gets light wear. Spills are difficult to remove. Spot clean with household cleaning solvent.

Sisal carpeting (Centre)

Cheap and hard-wearing – harsher than rush matting. Also comes latex-backed for ease of laying.

Coconut, Coir (Below)

Coconut matting is still used for doormats, hall runners, etc. Coir matting is a better version and can be bought in carpet widths. Usually natural in colouring. Sometimes comes backed with vinyl. When dirty, loose matting can be scrubbed with soapless detergent.

Floors
8/9 Rugs

True oriental rugs are hand-made with patterns which are hundreds of years old. They come mainly from Iran (Persia), China, Turkey, Morocco, Afghanistan, India and the Caucasus. They are extremely hard-wearing, and many people buy them not only for their beauty but also as an investment.

The craft of rug-making was practised by the nomadic tribes of these countries, as well as in the Imperial "factories" where the carpets and wall-hangings of the Emperors were made. The nomadic tribal rugs are woven, whereas those traditionally made in the towns are knotted carpets with a dense pile. Chinese rugs are of a very fine wool with an embossed traditional design.

It is possible to buy good rugs at reasonable prices, but go to a reputable dealer or take expert advice. Loose rugs or carpets should have a non-slip underlay, to ease the wear and to stop them from slipping.

Persian rug from the old walled town of Qum in Central Persia, where the basic designs have not varied for hundreds of years. This classical design is one of the traditional patterns.

These carpets are among some of the very finest now made in Persia, having an extremely high density of knots to the square inch. The carpets are made of silk and wool knotted by hand on to a firmly woven base.

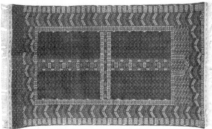

Hutchli Bokhara finely-knotted carpet of wool and goat's hair made in the Bokhara region of Russia. The Hutchli (cross) pattern is one used throughout the Orient. The background colour is traditionally red, signifying happiness.

The Afghanistan Kelim is a tapestry-woven rug traditionally used for wall-hangings or bed covers, but they are quite sturdy enough to use as floor coverings. This Kelim, or prayer rug, is coarsely woven from a fairly harsh, thick wool.

The Kurdish Kelim is more brightly coloured than the Afghan version, the wool used is softer and glossier, and the designs are embroidered.

Berber rug from the Sahara. A woven rug in which the design for the most part adheres to stripes. The wool lacks the high gloss of the Persian rugs.

Iraqi rug, similar in design and texture to the Kurdish Kelim.

Figga rug, from Iraq, another example of geometrically-patterned Kelim rugs made mainly in muted colours.

Ethiopian rug – a coarse, woven rug. The triangles in the design are an Abyssinian symbol of happiness.

Beni Menel. A flat-woven rug made in the Lower Atlas mountain area of Morocco by Bedouin nomads. These rugs were originally designed as wall hangings and floor coverings for the nomads' tents and made useful camel blankets when the tribe was on the move. The outstanding features are the highly-stylized geometric patterns in sharp, contrasting colours.

Dhurry. The ubiquitous, hand-made Indian cotton woven rug in bright stripes. Used for wall hangings, bed and sofa covers as well as floor rugs.

Rya shaggy pile Finnish carpet (now machine-made). This example is hand-made, designed by Peter Collingwood.

Peruvian woven rug of traditional South American design – a smiling yellow sun and orange sun rays.

Mexican serape. A coarsely woven rug with fringed ends. Traditionally, this kind of fabric was made for wearing, in the form of ponchos.

(Opposite) An extravaganza of oriental patterns and colours combine to give this room a rich, warm unity.

Floors
10/11 Practical choices

Check which floor coverings can be laid on your existing floors. There are basically two types of floor construction: suspended and solid.

Many floors are constructed of softwood (usually deal) boards laid across timber joists. In older houses, the ground floor is often constructed like this, with the joists resting on short brick walls and the space between ventilated by air bricks. Any draughts from ill-fitting boards can probably be overcome with an appropriate floor covering. Other pre-war houses may have brick or stone ground floors without a damp-course and without protection against rising damp.

In more modern houses or conversions, instead of a suspended timber structure there is often a solid slab of concrete incorporating a damp-proof membrane. Although relatively unusual in individual houses, it is quite common in blocks of flats for upper floors to be constructed of reinforced concrete.

Suspended floors

Floorboards can be tongued-and-grooved or butt-jointed. In older houses they are usually butt-jointed, which may have caused warping and shrinkage. If vinyl or lino were laid on top it would very soon crack or wear unevenly. An underlay of hardboard or ply can prevent this. Tongued-and-grooved floors are likely to be flatter. In new houses flooring-grade plywood or chipboard is sometimes substituted for deal boards, which means that vinyl, linoleum or carpet with suitable underlay can be laid directly on to it.

N.B. Hard floors like stone, marble or quarry tiles should not be laid on a suspended floor without taking expert advice on floor loadings, as these materials are heavy, have no give and may crack if the floor below them moves.

Solid floors

Unless there is an old brick or stone floor, solid floors are likely to be of concrete. A good smooth surface suitable for most coverings is a cement and sand screed. Some hard floorings are set into a cement mortar bed, and decorative wood floors can be set on an asphalt base or "secretly nailed" to floor strips. Almost any flooring can be laid on a solid floor provided that there is a proper, sound damp-proof course.

General condition

If you bought a house with fitted carpets, check the floors underneath for any woodworm, rot, etc., which might have been missed in the initial survey. (It is also worth checking this if you are exchanging your old carpet for a new one.) If in doubt call in a specialist firm for advice.

It is worth getting several estimates for removing dry rot or pests as quotations can vary enormously.

Is the ground floor properly ventilated? Sometimes a previous owner may have built up the level of the ground outside, and inadvertently blocked up the vents, which could cause condensation under carpets or vinyl tiles and lead to rotting of both floorboards and carpet.

Damp

If you have no damp-proof course because your house was built before the First World War be careful what you put on the floor, or get expert help. Do not cover a perfectly good quarry, brick or stone floor with unbacked vinyl or linoleum. The quarry, brick and stone are porous enough to allow the damp to evaporate, but vinyl or linoleum will prevent this process so that after a while the sheet will start rotting and lifting.

Something loose like rush matting is best as it can be taken up and dried.

Heating

Different forms of heating will react differently on various materials. Always check with the installation people, or the manufacturers of your flooring, or both, that the material you have chosen is suitable. Underfloor heating, for instance, is not at its best with a wood block floor and should not be used with fitted carpet.

Skirtings

Wooden skirtings are available in several widths and styles. Some are grooved to carry electric wiring, etc. behind. A competent carpenter is needed to fit them, as few walls and floors are at right angles. Many floors are matched by coved skirtings – for example, quarry tiles, ceramic tiles and vinyl asbestos, which look neat and make cleaning easier. Vinyl skirting in black or white can be purchased by the yard, and is easily fitted because it has a flanged edge to compensate for slight inequalities in the wall. Marks can be rubbed off easily, and the surface does not need re-painting. Good, too, for floors with rising damp as they don't rot, unlike timber, but they don't look very nice.

Consider areas separately

Ask yourself what each room or area is for and the sort of wear it gets. If a room has more than one function, like a dining-room/kitchen, then you must consider all of these. Check that your flooring can be laid on the existing floor (see above); if you already have underfloor heating this affects your choice. (See also sections on individual rooms.)

1

2

3

Dining-room

1 *Provençal ceramic tiles are a real decorative asset to any dining-room and easy to clean. However, ceramics or quarry can magnify the noise of conversation and scraping chairs. A tile-patterned foam-backed vinyl would be quieter, if its unaesthetic qualities don't offend you – and more suitable if you feed the baby there or the children play trains on the floor. Other alternatives are linoleum, cork, wood block, sanded and sealed boards, or a good quality carpet – one not too difficult to wash should you spill soup.*

Living-room

2 *A long-pile carpet looks and feels comfortable – essential if your guests sit on or near the floor. Most living-room floors also need to be tough and resistant to dirt and stains. This could mean good-quality carpets, timber (with luxurious rugs), cork, or a warm-coloured, cushion-backed vinyl. If noise is no problem and your house is well heated, ceramic tiles or marble look handsome. Remember to take into account sparks from an open fire. If you have children, a dog, and french doors to the garden, think again before buying a pale carpet which shows up every mark.*

Kitchen

3 *Here a brick floor is matched by the peninsular work unit, dividing kitchen from dining area. Kitchen floors must be tough, easily cleaned, non-slip, waterproof, stain- and grease-resistant. Brick, quarry, non-slip ceramic, stone and riven slate all comply with these requirements. Cold hard floors can be warmed with underfloor heating. More resilient are linoleum, synthetic rubber, cushion-backed vinyl, sealed cork or vinyl cork.*

Bedroom

1 *Fitted carpet is a good choice where you need comfort and warmth to walk in bare feet. Less durable qualities of carpet are usually adequate as the room is unlikely to get the same wear as living or circulation areas. Floorboards may also be in better condition than elsewhere and could be sanded and sealed (or painted) and rugs added. Cork is a good alternative to carpet and makes a nice background for a shaggy bedside rug.*

Nursery or playroom

2 *Sealed chipboard, used in this playroom for both floor and furniture, decoratively incorporates Nine Men's Morris and a chequer-board. Small children spend much of their time playing on the floor and need something warm, smooth, easily cleaned, preferably quiet, and resilient – it hurts to fall on a hard floor. It should also be resistant to water, paint or ink stains, and glue. Suitable materials include linoleum, foam-backed vinyl, sealed or vinyl-backed cork, or sealed wood. Some flat-surfaced carpet tiles can be washed, dried and replaced.*

Circulation

3 *White vinyl tiles with a black inlaid pattern complement the elegant black and white scheme of a hall cum dining area reflection in the full-height mirror. Halls and stairs get a lot of wear and may get wet or muddy, particularly in the country. You have to weigh noise against wear and choose between a tough quality carpet, coir matting and quarry tiles, stone, brick, vinyl or well-sealed timber. Often a good combination is a hard floor in the hall with carpet on stairs and upper landing.*

Bathroom

4 *Natural cork, here also taken up the side of the bath, is warm to bare feet and non-slip – important if there are very young or old people. Rubber, vinyl and vinyl-surfaced cork are all suitable. The floor should be waterproof in case of accidental flooding and be thoroughly stuck down, otherwise water will penetrate to the boards underneath, which may eventually rot. Coved edges overcome this. Carpets – man-made fibres if you want to be sure of no rotting – do not use jute.*

Workroom

5 *Fitted coir matting in a herringbone pattern is a tough but comfortable flooring for this study workroom. In sewing-rooms it is easier to clean up bits of cotton and material from linoleum or polished wood than carpet. Avoid rough surfaces which snag. Laundries are similar to kitchens but can be less resilient, so concrete, ceramic, or quarry are suitable. Carpentry work-shops can take most hard floors, but concrete could be cold and tiring to stand on unless you put duck boarding on top. Metal workshops need an oil-resistant floor finish.*

Hall

6 *Another black and white floor, this time in a traditional design, in the hall of Zimmie Sasson's London flat. The tiles are self-adhesive and have been cut at the corners to take small black key tiles. The floor of the dining alcove leading off the hall is carpeted in sisal cord which is carried through to the living-room. Often, in small flats, it is best to treat the floor as a single area with the same, or related, flooring throughout.*

Floors
12/13 Practical choices/planning visually

Even in a smallish house or flat the amount of floor area to cover comes as a shock. The ideal floor usually turns out to be more expensive than your budget allowed for. However, since your floor is expected to last for years and will get the hardest wear of any surface in the house, it is worth making sacrifices elsewhere and adding to your floor budget rather than making do with second-best.

Buy the best quality of carpet or flooring you can afford, bearing in mind the amount of wear each area is likely to receive. You may find you can renovate an existing floor surface in a spare room and add some inexpensive rugs.

It helps to take a scale drawing of the floors before you decide on something, and work out comparative costs.

Could you use your existing floor?

Before deciding to lay something else over them, it is worth taking a good look at your existing floors. If these are timber boards and in reasonable condition without large gaps or bits missing, you could sand and seal or polish them. Even if some areas, such as in front of a doorway, are soft or worn, they can be cut back in a stepped pattern and replaced with similar boards from another room where you intend to close-carpet. Before doing this, check that they are the same width and similar in colour: new boards could stick out like a sore thumb (though it is possible to stain them to colour-match). Fireplace hearths (cement or tiles) can usually be removed and replaced by boards in the same way. Sanders can be hired or you can employ a contractor to do the work for you. For do-it-yourself, select a sander with a dust bag attachment (like a suction cleaner bag) which will reduce the mess of sanding. Each room should be sealed by taping round the tops and bottoms of doors to avoid the dust spreading. If you are doing the job yourself remove *all* tacks (often left from old lino) and punch nails below the surface of the boards.

When the floor is clean and smooth, you can choose a clear seal for a natural look, or a light to medium combined wood dye/sealer if the wood looks insipid. Most sealers are suitable for timber, but check with the retailer or manufacturer if you are not sure. If you polish the boards instead, use a spirit-wax polish as the water in an emulsion polish affects untreated timber. Alternatively, the boards could be painted with floor or yacht paint. If you want a light-coloured surround to a loose carpet, this is a good way of doing it.

Replacing tiles is more difficult, even if you can find ones that match. If the floor is in a generally good condition and only one or two tiles are cracked, you might be able to exchange them with whole ones from a part of the floor which will be having a cupboard or other furniture on it (providing you can prise them up in one piece). But check the reason for the crack first – it may be that the floor is uneven or there is a loose tile.

If many of the tiles are breaking up or otherwise in poor condition, it is better to rip them up and start again, even to the extent of putting down a new sub-floor.

Will you do the work yourself?

Make sure before you start that you are quite sure you know exactly what to do. Mistakes could be costly. Work out the correct area with the help of the scale drawings and your retailer. Don't forget that rooms with right-angle corners are much easier to cope with than ones which slope or have lots of odd corners.

Make sure all the boards are secure. Loose boards can creak or squeak. However, don't rush round banging nails into old floorboards indiscriminately. Find out, first, where the wiring or the water pipes are: you don't want to end up dead, and a burst pipe makes an astonishing amount of water. To remind you, make chalk marks along the line of the wires or pipes. Sometimes electricians or telephone engineers cut boards between the joists when rewiring or laying cables; make sure these are properly resecured.

Follow the manufacturers' instructions faithfully for laying, cutting, joining and so on. Vinyl tiles with self-adhesive backs are far and away pleasanter and easier to lay than the kind with separate adhesive. Floors like wood block or mosaic must be laid professionally.

N.B. Remember to check that doors clear the laid floor. If not, trim them *before* putting down the new floors. It is possible to get lift-off hinges for doors.

Planning visually

First choose a flooring for its practical qualities, *then* choose the colours, textures and patterns to fit within the overall decoration scheme.

Starting from scratch

When you are planning a completely new home – or a room – without having any existing furniture or other items to consider, you may start by choosing the floor covering and then relating walls, paintwork, curtains, furniture and accessories to it. The floor is one of the biggest and probably most expensive items – and therefore the most difficult to change if you make a mistake. It is unwise, for instance, to cover a large living-room floor with multi-coloured floral carpet unless you are sure that is what your family wants to live with for a number of years. If, on the other hand, you plan the floor as a pleasant background, it is possible to change the colour scheme and mood of a room without too much disruption and expense.

If you have no definite ideas, start by thinking of natural or earthy colours on the floors. Peaty browns, moss, oatmeal or terracotta are all colours you won't tire of easily.

Cleaning problems

If you have a house prone to dog hairs, solid-fuel dust, town filth, endless pairs of dirty boots, you will bless yourself for choosing a smooth floor which you can easily clean. Most floors which used to be polished can now be sealed with a clear seal and need only be damp-mopped.

The cleaning advantage of having fitted carpets is that you can go through the whole house with a vacuum cleaner and not keep stopping to sweep in the corners. But some carpets, like the cheaper Indian ones, have a tendency to moult. The latest carpet sweepers deal equally well with pile carpets and flat surfaces, and have a lever mechanism for raising or lowering the brushes.

Matching up to what you've got

Having a starting point such as an existing piece of furniture is often easier than having *carte blanche*. Supposing you already have a sofa and chairs in striped blue, brown and cream, you might match the carpet to the brown or cream and echo the blue in the curtain or accessories. As plain carpets come in a wide range of colours it is often easier to match them up than, say, a chair which comes in only three or four colourways. If the kitchen already has built-in units, say of orange and white laminate, you could choose a floor tile that combines these colours.

Another kind of limitation is if you have one favourite object which you want to make a focal point. Here you have to think of the weight of colours you choose, otherwise they will take your eye away from the object to the floor.

Plain or patterned

In small areas, plain colours appear less busy than patterns. Plain floors also allow a greater freedom in choosing the rest of the furnishings. First of all you should examine your reasons for choosing a pattern. Many people choose patterned carpets not so much because they like them better, but because they think the dirt is camouflaged. But for that reason you are less likely to bother to keep them at their best and a dirty patterned carpet looks just as dirty as any other.

If you decide on a patterned floor, look for one that doesn't hit you in the eye the moment you walk into the room, but relates to everything else.

Textured unpatterned carpets, for instance, are patterns of a sort. So are wood mosaic blocks, or sanded and sealed timber boards. A hard-twist Wilton will not show foot-marks or dirt in the same way as a smooth one of the same colour. A shaggy pile goes well with smooth leather upholstery.

Surrounds

There are several alternatives to what you can do with the borders round loose carpet squares or rugs, or in a hall and stairs with strip carpeting. If it is a timber floor, it can be stained or painted to either match or contrast with the carpet – for instance, white to match the wall and skirtings. Or it can be left natural, such as a sanded and sealed or polished floor. A pale border can help to expand a small room. Remember that a shiny dark surround will show up every speck of day-to-day dust as well as creating a "void" feeling around the rug – with the rug or carpet like an island in a dark bottomless sea.

1 *Cross-grain wood blocks and quarry tiles are used in the kitchen and dining areas of this open-plan Swedish studio house to define the different areas.*

2 *A threshold is left bare to show stained floorboards beneath. It visually separates the landing carpet from the bedroom carpet and adds to the medley of colours.*

3 *Off-white Indian rugs are used in the living area and the eating area, forming a border round the white-painted floorboards.*

4 *Thick Wilton carpet tailored to fit the curved steps which lead from one level to another in this open-plan room.*

5 *A lighter-coloured strip set into the main carpet leads through to the living-room.*

6 *White ceramic tiles visually separate kitchen and passageway from the carpeted seating area.*

7 *A patterned floor, a practical choice for the eating area, has a mosaic effect. It is made up of a combination of two-colour square tiles which form patterns when laid together.*

8 *The green Wilton carpet square under the dining table defines the eating area in an open-plan room, and contrasts with the white ceramic tiles and white walls.*

1 2 3

4 5 6

7 8

Floors
14/15 Vistas

Before you put any of your ideas on flooring into practice, consider your house or flat as a whole. Whether you are revamping the decorations from top to bottom, or deliberating over a new rug for the bedroom, remember that no room is a watertight compartment, that doors are more often than not left open, and a vista of rooms opening off the hall is the first thing to greet you every time you walk through your front door.

Unity of design

You can achieve great unity of design without sacrificing interest or excitement; on the contrary, you will find the whole will be greater than the sum of the various parts. You can carry out your colour scheme on every floor surface of the house, from expensive, luxurious floor coverings to cheap, hard-working ones, as all floorings, even tough ones, come in a great variety of colours.

On the following pages we show plans for two houses with schemes suggested by architect/designers James and Valerie Bath. Our first example is a fairly typical three-bedroomed, three-storied modern house for a family of four. The key colour in this house is olive green, a colour which is easy to live with and easy to accent.

White looks wonderful with it, and these colours, picked by our designers, show just how interesting a range of contrasting and complementary colours can be devised.

1 *Curled pile carpet will wear well in areas of heavy traffic, such as the stairs.*

2 *Ceramic tiles with a non-slip finish.*

Ground floor

In a hall, take the long view. First impression for visitors, so it's got to look good: and be tough enough to take a family pounding. Spend money for long-term saving on non-slip ceramic tiles with a handsome, ageless design (won't show dirty footmarks nearly as quickly as would a plain floor).

That dining-room door is going to be more often open than closed. The view through is important. Keep hall, kitchen, dining-room floors the same.

Stairs are in a hard-wearing curled pile carpet in a good olive green all the way up to include the first landing, and pick up the green on the tiles.

First floor

Through-views here are from bedroom to sitting-room. If the floor is polished boards in the sitting-room, you won't want to cover them except, perhaps, with a long-pile white Greek rug, so "project" the olive green from the landing on to walls or curtains.

Master bedroom might well have the same carpet as stairs and landing. This is a good "space-making" trick. You'll probably get a discount for buying so much carpet in one colour or design.

Bathroom needs a PVC floor with kids around. A small tile design is the answer, following the green theme.

1 *Stair and landing carpet runs into master bedroom.*

2 *PVC flooring for the bathroom – waterproof and easy to clean.*

Second floor

Children's floor. Here's where the noise comes from and whatever is on the floor is going to have to be strong, shrug off marks and give some noise insulation. Sisal is the answer, preferably with a woven design.

Stop the stair carpet on the last riser; start the sisal on the landing and run it on into both children's rooms. Give them a change in the wall colours.

Shower-room floor of self-adhesive PVC tiles echoes the new, blue tones, still conforms the whole scheme with some olive green in the design.

3 *Tough sisal carpeting with woven design.*

4 *Self-adhesive PVC tiles are easy to lay, and could also be used on the walls.*

Floors
16/17 Vistas

Ginger is the key colour in this two-storied conversion. On the open-plan ground floor "pools" of pattern and texture have been used to define areas but the vista is kept "long" by relating colour.

Stairs, which mount from long-pile carpeted "well", are clad in a similar colour, different curled pile carpet.

Kitchen/dining-room and border around the sitting area carpet, in geometric design PVC tiles in orange and white, tone with the long-pile carpet.

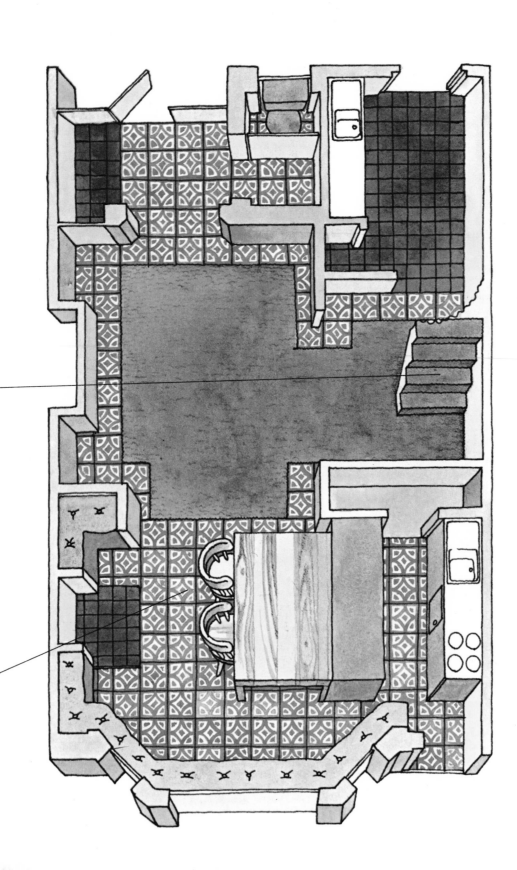

Hard-wearing curled pile carpet to withstand wear and tear on the stairs and landing.

Luxurious long-pile wool carpet in the key colour for the sitting area.

PVC tiles . Bold orange and white design for kitchen and conservatory.

Tough and scrubbable sisal carpet in related colours for the children's room.

Interchangeable carpet tiles, plain and patterned for the master bedroom.

Cork tiles. The natural colour of these cork tiles relate the bathroom to the hall.

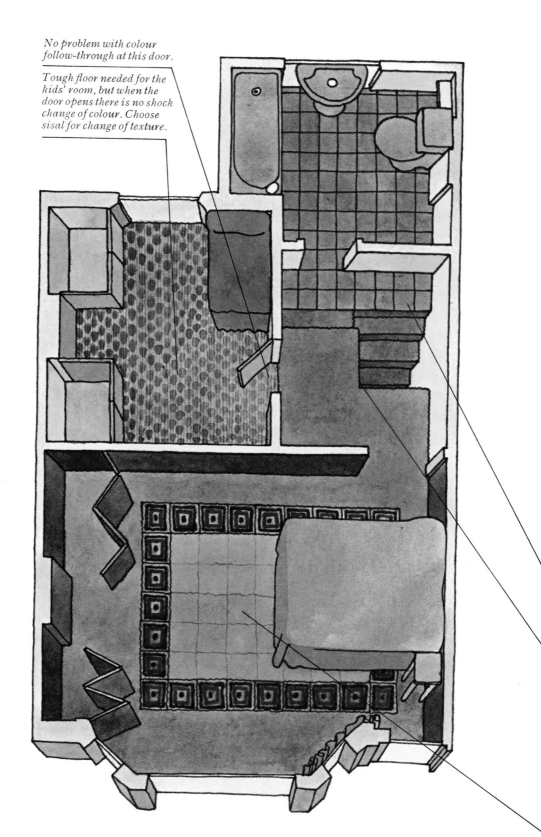

No problem with colour follow-through at this door.

Tough floor needed for the kids' room, but when the door opens there is no shock change of colour. Choose sisal for change of texture.

Colours that go. A terrific range of blues, mauves, pinks and browns all go well with ginger so that you can ring the changes with interesting colour accents without spoiling the unity of the whole.

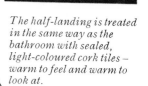

The half-landing is treated in the same way as the bathroom with sealed, light-coloured cork tiles — warm to feel and warm to look at.

Follow-through. Stairs go up, so colour must mount too and resolve itself all over the landing.

Master bedroom. Lush carpet tiles in a very interesting design outline a central square of plain carpet tiles in hot orange. The border is made of the stair and landing carpet. Carpet tiles are a good idea because you only need to take up one or two if someone spills the milk, or red wine.

Floors
18/19 Pattern on floors

1 *A simple rug is all that is needed to add colour and pattern to the sanded and sealed wood floor and elegant lines of chromed steel and leather furniture.*

2 *A geometric pattern on the fitted carpet adds emphasis to the symmetrical arrangement of Breuer chairs and other furniture.*

3 *Oriental rugs and cushions provide the only applied patterns in this room, though the framed drawings and watercolours and venetian blinds create patterns of their own.*

4 *A bold circle of green dominates the centre of this room in Karen Radkai's flat. The flowing line of the painted metal rocking chair is in marked contrast to the rectangular lines of the sofas and low table at the other end.*

5 *Patchwork floor-covering is perhaps a little delicate for daily wear, but the idea could be adapted using carpet tiles of various designs.*

6 *Well-defined areas in a multi-level room. The carpet in the conversation pit is repeated under the dining table surrounded by a tiled floor. Steps are edged in plain carpet – a good safety point. Note the repetition of the table shape on the sofa cushions.*

(Opposite) Three different floorings in an all-white scheme. A shaggy long-pile carpet lies loosely on the short-pile fitted Wilton which in turn leads through to a vinyl floor in the adjoining room. The dividing doors have been glazed with mirror.

Floors
20/21 Using tiles/creating patterns

Patterned floors have been a popular form of decoration for centuries, going back to the staggeringly intricate mosaic floors and pavements of the Greeks and Romans. Clay tiled floors were used in Europe in the 12th and 13th centuries, sometimes laid in intricate patterns but using only a few colours such as red-brown and yellow.

Many traditional patterns, particularly the simpler geometric ones, are still very popular today, not only in tile form, but also on carpets and sheet flooring.

All sorts of geometric patterns can be made by arranging tiles of one or more colours or designs in a variety of ways. Shapes and sizes vary, too, from squares and rectangles to hexagons and octagons. On a floor made up of tiles in a single colour you can emphasize the shape of the tiles by using grouting of a lighter or darker colour. Wood parquet is also laid in various different traditional patterns.

A careful choice of pattern can sometimes help to hide or reduce a visual defect, particularly where the proportions of a room are unsatisfactory. For instance, wide horizontal stripes across the floor of a long thin room visually shorten the distance. Or where there is more than one activity – as in a kitchen/dining-room – each area can be, as it were, outlined and defined at floor level.

1 *Alternating stripes of vinyl tiles have been laid to form a right angle and take the eye round the corner of an L-shaped kitchen with a breakfast bar in the middle. The colour-scheme is carried through to the fittings, work-tops and blinds.*

2 *Here wide stripes of light and dark ceramic tiles break up a long and fairly narrow floor area.*

3 *A tessellated pattern of brown and white Provençal tiles provide a softer line to a bedroom floor than would a diamond pattern of squares. This shape of tile is an old Moorish one much used in Spain and France.*

4 *Black triangular corners to light square tiles together form a traditional pattern of octagons and squares.*

5 *The patchwork effect of these hexagonal tiles in two colours is repeated in the multi-coloured patchwork tablecloth.*

6 *Eight-sided quarries with small square infill tiles make an attractive pattern heightened by the use of a lighter colour for the grouting. The leather upholstery provides a textural contrast within a consistent earthy colour scheme.*

1

2

3

4

5

6

A simple alternative would be to use one colour for the room in general with a block of a second colour in the sitting and dining areas.

As well as making designs from differently coloured tiles of the same size, some manufacturers make matching tiles – vinyl or sometimes ceramic – in different sizes so that you can lay a rectangular border, say, round a plain floor, or alternatively, hexagonal tiles with square key ones.

Vinyl sheeting or tiles are often easy to cut. Here are some suggestions for patterns you could achieve yourself with the aid of a metal straight edge, T square and sharp knife. Measure the floor area first and work out the design on graph paper. This is important, not only to get the pattern right, but also to calculate the number of tiles you will need.

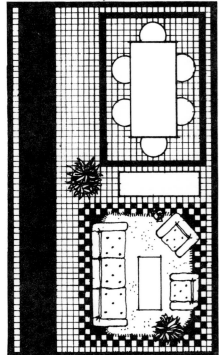

Cutting lines and angles must be absolutely accurate so that the tiles butt up neatly without any gaps. If your floor is not rectangular, think carefully before embarking on a geometrical design. A room which has to cater for more than one function can be visually defined by changing the pattern of the floor. In the plan of the living/dining-room (above), the sitting area has a chequer-board floor in two colours. The lighter colour is used on its own between the different areas of activity and the darker one is laid to form a border both round the dining table and round the edge of the room. Dark tiles also form a gangway.

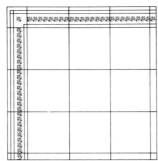

Plain tiles with a patterned border of rectangular tiles.

Diagonally laid squares, plain and patterned, with a border of small tiles.

Two designs of geometric border tiles laid round harlequin patterned tiles.

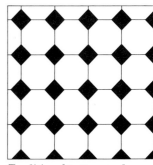

Traditional pattern made with standard tiles trimmed to take key squares.

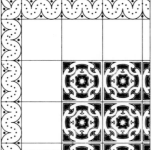

Pattern tiles with a plain border edged with half pattern tiles.

To align these tiles correctly, place quarter tiles at corners.

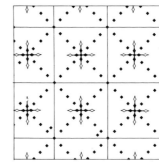

Tiles with a diagonal design form a larger, all-over pattern.

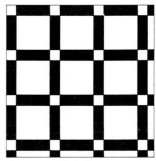

Even rows of plain squares separated by strips of another colour.

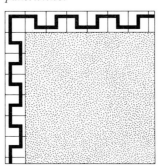

One-colour textured vinyl sheeting has a border of small squares.

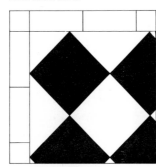

Standard black and white squares laid diagonally with a border of rectangles.

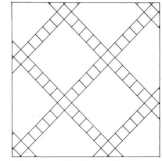

Squares laid diagonally with a surround of small tiles of the same colour.

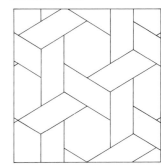

Hexagonals and strips laid to look like an interwoven basket-weave pattern.

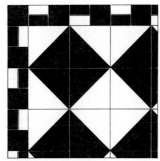

Squares form diagonals and have a border of whole and half tiles.

Border of rectangles make a new shape where tiles meet the edging.

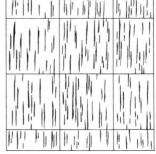

Marbled tiles should all face the same way so the pattern is continuous.

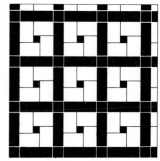

Rectangles with a central infill laid to form squares and edged with strips.

Floors
22 Details that count

1 *A threshold strip between rooms – where a fitted carpet meets a harder surface (or another carpet in a different colour) – is not only a neat solution, but also protects the edge of the materials in a heavy traffic area.*

2 *Stepped-back honey-coloured bricks matching those on the floor have been used to build a raised hearth.*

3 *Quarry tiles laid diagonally in the half-level dining-room change direction across the steps leading down to the lower level.*

4 *White ceramic floor tiles have been taken up to form a plinth which doubles as a shelf.*

5 *Fitted carpets can unify a change of level. Here a Wilton broadloom has been cut and fitted down vertical surfaces as well as the steps.*

6 *27 in./686 mm carpeting, again used for more than one level, is defined by dark, narrow-painted skirtings.*

7 *Patterned carpet inset in a tiled floor has a brown carpet border stitched to it. The same brown carpet is used as a stair nosing.*

8 *A neat steel edging divides the vinyl floor in the kitchen area from the short-pile carpet elsewhere.*

9 *Dark grouting emphasizes the scale of the light coloured pre-cast concrete slabs.*

10 *Quarry tiles have been carried over the threshold of a sliding glazed door to link the patio with the wood board floor inside the house.*

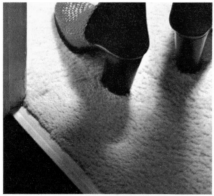

1

2

3

4

5

6

7

8

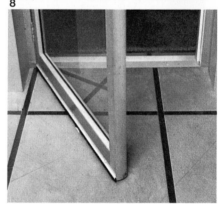

9

10

Walls/1

Wallpaper and paint are still the quickest way to revamp an existing scheme, or make a dull room exciting.

The way you deal with walls will make the difference between being interesting or fussy, bleak or calm, exciting or overpowering.

First you must get the practical choices right. Check what is available and what is structurally practical, and whether you can do it yourself or will need an expert.

Then pause and think about the visual decisions. Get the feel of the proportions. If you're moving into a new place, or have lived so long with a room that you've stopped seeing it, it sometimes pays to paint everything white or cream to obliterate all past decisions and take in the room's shape and potential. After a while you will know whether walls need warming, a ceiling needs lowering visually, or architectural features need emphasizing or removing.

Practical choices

The choice is enormous, but your decisions will be restricted by the character and condition of the house – and money. If walls are rough, but not bad enough to replaster, choose something other than paint; wood-chip paper, hessian or Lincrusta, for instance.

If the house suffers from condensation, and you have already put in extra ventilation and stepped up the background heat, surface the walls with a warm insulating finish. Thick wallpaper, backed fabrics or wood-panelling all help to counteract heat loss.

Paint is relatively cheap, but avoid distemper, which has to be completely removed before you can paper or repaint.

Wallpapers can be thick or thin, plain, patterned, embossed or textured. Many are washable. Fabrics, tiles, wood panelling, cork, felt, foil are all suitable wall coverings in the right circumstances.

Occasionally it is sensible to do things quickly and cheaply, because the result needs to last for only a year or so – for instance, in short-term accommodation. If rooms for small children have an inexpensive finish, you won't be upset if they scribble on the walls. Children care much more about colour than quality.

Colour and texture

These are equally important. A colour changes dramatically according to its texture and depending on whether it absorbs or reflects light. Don't be afraid of deep colours; it's much easier to get a good effect with one strong colour than with just a bit here and there. Pale walls and ceilings, particularly white, help to lighten a badly lit room. A plain wall is often the best background for good-looking furniture or accessories.

Textures show up more if light falls on them at an angle to throw them into relief than if they are flattened by diffused light.

Visual choices

Think of the house as a whole and follow your ideas through. Your walls, curtains and carpet can act as a sympathetic background to your possessions and way of life, or they can take on a dominant role in creating the mood and style.

Here are some questions to ask:

- [ ] Are the walls damp-proof and sound?
- [ ] Which walls are structural and which partitions?
- [ ] What are they made of?
- [ ] Can present finishes be used as a basis for future decoration?
- [ ] Could your home do with more warmth or sound insulation?
- [ ] Do you have a family with grubby fingers?
- [ ] Do you prefer plain colours or patterns on your walls?
- [ ] Could proportions or messy areas be improved visually?

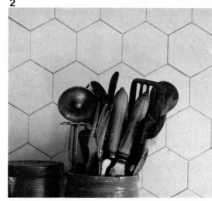

1 *Wood provides a warm insulating surface and reduces condensation. Tongue-and-groove panelling can be horizontal, vertical or diagonal. Seal to preserve appearance.*

2 *Plain paint in a positive colour is an admirable background for good furniture, objets d'art or a vase of flowers. Paint is one of the quickest and cheapest ways of changing a colour scheme.*

3 *Patterned wallpapers can help pull together a bitty room. Waterproof ones are particularly useful for kitchens and bathrooms.*

4 *Ceramic wall tiles are durable, easily cleaned and heat-proof – particularly useful behind the cooker or sink.*

5 *Textured wallpaper, like Anaglypta, helps disguise rough wall surfaces. A well-placed light will throw texture into relief.*

6 *Hessian comes in plain colours, stripes and patterns. Backed hessian is not much harder to hang than wallpaper.*

7 *Cork is warm, handsome and a good noise insulator. Tiles are glued to the wall – some are self-adhesive. Hang paper-backed cork like wallpaper.*

8 *Exposed brick can be painted without plastering, provided both bricks and pointing are in good condition.*

Recent developments have improved the looks, quality and performance of most paint. The addition of synthetics such as polyurethane, vinyl or acrylics has made it tougher, more washable, quicker drying, smoother and easier to apply.

Preparation for painting

The quality and type of paint are important, but equally important is their application and the quality of the surfaces you put them on. If you are doing it yourself, follow instructions carefully. If you are employing a professional painter make sure his written estimate gives details of making good, preparing the surfaces, any primers or undercoats and number of top coats. In this way you have a comeback if he has skimped anything. It is not fair to say vaguely you want it done as cheaply as possible and complain later because the results aren't first class.

Colour

Manufacturers' names for colour differ widely, and one firm's "Guardsman" is another firm's "Pillarbox"; so when buying paint always take with you a sample of the colour you want. In Britain most manufacturers carry the British Standard range, which is numbered so that it is possible to match different firms' paints accurately.

Drying

The time needed for paint to dry depends not only on the type of paint, but also on the surface to which it is applied and on atmospheric conditions. Any grease or dirt left on the surface can slow down drying. If the room is cold and damp, thinners in both oil and emulsion evaporate less quickly and the paint dries more slowly.

Safety

Paints for interior use now contain either no lead or only tiny amounts of it. However, some paints for exterior use may still contain quantities of lead which could make them toxic. Check that the paint you buy for the nursery is lead free; the label should give this information.

Oil-based paints

Made of natural or synthetic resins, colour pigment, oils and white spirit solvent. Synthetic resins include alkyds (for flexibility) and polyurethane (for toughness). Oil-based paints generally take longer to dry between coats than emulsions, though some dry faster than others. Improvements in the making of white paint mean there is less tendency for them to go yellow. Use white spirit for thinning and cleaning.

Gloss: On the whole the toughest and most durable finish. Used on doors, window frames, skirtings, radiators, and woodwork and metal generally, also on walls and ceilings if you want them shiny. Semi-gloss (a term not used much now) – about half-way between gloss and eggshell.

Eggshell: Also called satin, silk, sheen. Anything from almost matt to almost semi-gloss comes under this heading. Ask to see samples before buying to make sure it is what you had in mind. Use anywhere a tough, washable, non-gloss surface is required. Suitable for both wood and metal.

Matt: Absolutely matt oil-based paint is not used much these days and is often available in white only, but some eggshells are almost matt.

Non-drip: Thixotropic (jelly-like) paint is used straight from the tin without stirring and does not drip or run. It is applied thickly, and often one coat is sufficient on a previously painted surface. Some types can be used as their own undercoats. Polyurethane non-drip gloss gives a hard, durable finish. Beware of the so-called "non-drip" paint which, though thicker than ordinary paint, is not thixotropic: read the small print.

Advantages: Oil-based paints are washable and durable, especially when made with synthetic resins. With possible exceptions, the glossier the paint the more hardwearing it is. Very wide range of colours. With proper primers and undercoat they protect wood and metal. No special undercoat needed for some thixotropic paint. Oil-based paints stop moisture penetrating to the plaster.

Disadvantages: Gloss tends to emphasize surface imperfections and irregularities. It also shows up condensation in steamy conditions. Oil-based paints generally take longer to dry between coats than emulsions and they have a stronger smell and need good ventilation.

Application: On clean, dry surfaces. Use a matching or slightly lighter undercoat and one or two top coats. In kitchens or where the previous colour was much darker, you may need a third coat. New surfaces need a primer.

Emulsion paints

Synthetic resins and colour pigment suspended in water: when the water evaporates a resinous film is left on the surface. Some emulsions are made with acrylics, others with vinyl. Some are also used as undercoats or primers. Thin and clean up with water.

Eggshell: Most emulsions have a satin or silk-type finish, but this varies from paint to paint. Used on ceilings and walls. Tougher, improved ones can be used in heavy-wear areas such as kitchens and bathrooms.

Matt: As eggshell, but usually not washable, only spongable. Fingermarks tend to show and are difficult to clean off.

Non-drip: A softer consistency than the oil-based kind – usually called "structured" in the trade (rather than thixotropic). They contain vinyl instead of polyurethane and do not come in gloss. Should not be stirred or thinned.

Fungicidal and anti-condensation: Some emulsions have properties which reduce condensation, others prevent fungus or mould.

Advantages: Easier to use than oil-based, particularly over large areas. Needs no special undercoat, easier to clean up afterwards. Dries quickly with little or no smell. Alkali resistant, so suitable for new plaster walls containing lime. If for some reason a new wall has to be painted before the plaster has completely dried out, emulsion is less likely to flake or blister than oil paint because it is porous. Acrylic emulsions are more waterproof. Vinyls give a smooth finish.

Disadvantages: Not as washable or as tough as oil-based paints, but new developments are improving them all the time. Because they are water-based they should not be applied direct to metal surfaces. They tend to raise the grain on new wood and are not ideal as a finish on wood, though some acrylic emulsions can be used as a primer.

Application: On clean, dry surfaces. Two coats are usually sufficient on plaster or other new surfaces. If very absorbent, an additional first coat of thinned-down emulsion should be applied first. On painted surfaces of a similar colour in good nick, one coat may do.

Distemper

Although it is cheap, distemper is to be avoided except in outhouses. It cannot be cleaned or washed and comes off if you try. However, many ceilings and walls have been painted with it in the past, so check; if the finish starts crumbling and coming off on a wet rag then it's distemper, and should be removed completely by washing and scraping.

Primers

These can be oil-based or emulsion and are used to seal porous surfaces and bind loose, chalky or powdery ones (but not distemper). There are many different types, and you should get expert advice on the correct one to use. Briefly they can be divided as follows.

Plaster, etc.: Alkali resistant primer is for use on dry new plaster, brickwork, concrete and all surfaces likely to contain alkaline salts. An oil-primer sealer binds powdery surfaces and friable brickwork, and seals porous surfaces. Oil-based paints are more likely to need a primer than emulsions; previously painted or paper-lined surfaces generally don't need primers. A thinned-down coat of emulsion paint can also act as a primer sealer on porous surfaces. Where there are bad water stains, they tend to bleed through paint. An aluminium primer will prevent this.

Wood: Non-resinous hardwoods or softwoods can be painted with a leadless wood primer or an acrylic primer undercoat. Resinous or old creosoted wood can be primed with an aluminium sealer and wood primer. Woodwork treated with a fire retardant should be primed with an alkali-resistant primer.

Metal: Metal primer chromate can be used on iron, steel or aluminium. Lead and copper do not need a primer and can be painted with gloss after etching with wet or dry abrasive paper, using white spirit as lubricant.

Application: Primers are best applied with a brush and worked well in rather than just brushed on. Wood and metal should be painted as soon as possible after the primer is dry.

Undercoats

Used under gloss or eggshell oil-based paint, undercoats provide a non-porous surface to ensure that the top coat retains its colour and original shine. Allow the undercoat to dry, then rub down and dust off between coats.

Synthetic varnish

Fast drying, clear gloss or satin varnish made of polyurethane or polyester is on the whole better than traditional varnishes, although atmospheric conditions can affect the drying of *all* varnishes, especially the Z-pack variety. Use it to seal wood panelling, ply, etc. Ordinary wallpaper can be waterproofed, but only if the pattern is colourfast.

Wood stains

To colour wood and yet retain the grain – on wood panelling or screens – you can apply a coloured wood stain. If you use a polyurethane stain which has a tough waterproof finish, you eliminate the need for varnish.

Aluminium paint

This is used as a finish on metal and is particularly recommended for heated surfaces (up to 260°C (500°F)). It can also be used on wood as a finish.

One strong colour used boldly to pick out architectural details can change a room's whole character. Here beams are painted red.

Walls
4/5 Wallpapers/other coverings

Decorative wallpapers have been in general use for over 350 years; the earliest included flock and painted papers from China. Today the choice is enormous, and covers a very wide range of patterns and textures in paper and other materials.

A patterned wallpaper can brighten up a dull, featureless room or add interest where there are few other decorations. Where you have a slightly uneven, rough or cracked wall a thick wallpaper can hide the defects – it needn't be patterned – a plain textured one will do just as well.

Most papers come in standard rolls of 21 in./533 mm × 11 yd/10 m – allow 5% in length either way. Some, especially hand-printed ones, may need trimming. The manufacturers specify, and often also market, the correct paste to use, and this can vary with different types of paper – for instance vinyls should be hung with a fungicidal adhesive.

Wallpapers are available in such a variety of qualities and prices that you will almost certainly find one you like and can afford. If you are doing it yourself you may consider that the money saved on workmen's time justifies the purchase of a self-adhesive paper which only needs to be wetted and then stuck on. These give you about 20 minutes to put right your mistakes in matching before the adhesive refuses to let go.

Machine printed

The cheaper papers are printed with rollers on to a white ground. The more expensive ones are coated with a ground of colour before the design is printed on. Cheaper, thinner papers are harder to hang – they may stretch when wet and shrink or distort in drying. They are not suitable for rough treatment, but are all right for bedrooms. Thicker papers help to hide minor defects and blemishes. A special sealer protects non-washable papers, but rub a wet finger on the pattern first to see if the ink smudges.

Hand printed

Hand-printing is done with blocks, screens or stencils and is sharper than machine printing. It is also more expensive. Some small firms specialize in modern hand-printed designs, but traditional patterns, like those by William Morris, are still produced – some from the original wood-blocks.

Washable

A transparent plastic coating (matt or glossy) makes this paper water-repellent so that it is suitable for bathrooms and kitchens. It can be washed, though it is not as tough as vinyl. Wash with soapy water, not detergents or abrasives. Once up, it is difficult to remove, because the coating prevents water soaking through. However, there is a version with a vinyl coating which can be peeled off the wall.

Embossed

A metal roller is used to press the design into the paper to give it a raised surface. Look for simple geometric or plain textures rather than imitation leather and wood grain effects. Embossed paper should be hung on a previously lined wall with a thick, not watery, paste to prevent stretching (some papers are of double thickness to counteract this). Do not flatten the relief by pressing too hard.

Ingrain paper

This has small wood chips and sawdust added to the paper pulp during manufacture. It is greyish and is called donkey paper in the trade. There is a white version. Usually it should be painted; it is useful for covering uneven surfaces.

Marble paper

Marble patterns are available in printed papers, but there are firms that still do hand marbling to order. Although expensive, this is worth having because the marbling is not a regular repeat as in the printed version and you can sometimes get very large sheets.

Lining paper

Although you don't always need this thin underpaper, it helps to give a first-class finish. Lining papers are available in various weights, and although you only need the lighter papers on normal walls, the heavier the paper the better it will hide cracks, unevenness and other flaws. It should be hung horizontally and carefully butt-jointed. Pitch-coated lining paper can be used on dampish walls – paste it on the pitch-coated side.

Ceiling paper

Sometimes paper is the only way to cover a ghastly ceiling. Cracks which have been filled in may open again slightly, or the surface may be rough or stained. Where lining paper is too thin to hide the defects, plain embossed paper is often used instead – some have a bubbly texture, almost unnoticeable.

Flock

One of the oldest types of wallpaper. It is made of wool, silk or nylon fibres on a paper backing and has a velvety pile. Usually inappropriate in modern houses.

Vinyl wallcoverings

These are tough and waterproof and can be gently scrubbed if they get grubby. They are made from PVC with a paper or cloth backing with a printed or textured surface and come in many designs and colours, but always with a characteristic sheen. Because they are water- and steam-proof they are ideal for bathrooms, kitchens, playrooms; but because they are impervious they need a special fungicidal adhesive so that no mould can form underneath.

Anaglypta

This is made from cotton fibre with an embossed design and looks like plaster. It is strong and will successfully cover cracked walls and ceilings. It is sold in rolls or panels and should be painted.

You can also get Anaglypta decorations, and though most of these are like the icing on a wedding cake, they can be useful for patching a bit of moulding.

Foil

A comparatively new wallcovering, this looks like baking foil but is in fact silver-sprayed polyester on a paper backing. It comes in $3\frac{1}{2}$ yd/1 m or 11 yds/10 m rolls, 25 in./635 mm wide.

Hessian

Available backed or unbacked in lots of colours; also in stripes and patterns. It also looks good painted. This is often done in Scandinavia.

Unbacked hessian can be quite difficult to hang if you are inexperienced, and it sometimes shrinks. Hessian backed with foam, paper or latex (or self-adhesive) is more expensive but easier to deal with, stable and very tough. Some colours tend to fade in strong sunlight. If you are a compulsive rearranger of pictures, hessian is a practical wallcovering because it won't show nail holes (or you can cover softboard panels in hessian fabric and use them as pinboards). Some backed hessians are flame-resistant.

Fabric by the yard

This is usually fixed to a framework of narrow battens at ceiling and skirting heights. Any kind of fabric which doesn't stretch or distort too much, even ginghams or ticking, can produce successful results. The only way to clean it, however, is to take it down and wash or dry clean it. You also have to remember to fix battens to the walls where pictures are to be hung, before the fabric is put up.

Backed silk

Finely woven silk cloth is glued to a background paper for a luxurious environment (with bank balance to match). Cheaper vinyl "silks" look similar.

Moires

Paper embossed to look like watered silk. Some cheaper papers are moisture printed.

Felt

There is a paper-backed felt in good colours which can be hung like wallpaper. Felt tends to pick up dust, but can be vacuum cleaned. It cannot of course be washed, but there is a special cleaner for wall-hung felt.

Linen, wool, jute

There are a number of backed wallcovering fabrics similar to hessian. These include open- and slub-woven linens, jute/linen mixtures, and vertical wool, natural jute or linen yarns laminated to kraft backing paper. Some of the natural beige and brown colours are particularly attractive. They can be vacuum cleaned and some can be sponged. (Woven glass fibre fabrics are unbacked.)

Japanese grasscloth

Dried grasses are sewn closely together and glued to a paper backing. They can be expensive and are not easily cleaned.

Lincrusta

This is a putty-like material made from linseed oil and fillers bonded to a flat backing paper. It can look like wood panelling, tiles or hessian, and comes coloured or ready for painting. Like Anaglypta, it covers up defects.

Cork

Available glued to a backing paper to hang like wallpaper, or unbacked in tiles or panels to glue to the wall, or in self-adhesive tiles. Cork looks best in natural colours – from very pale to dark brown. It is made of compressed granules, small squares, strips or random chips. Those with a thick layer of transparent PVC or polyurethane are more suitable for heavy wear.

Polystyrene

Reduces noise, heat loss and absorbs a certain amount of condensation.

Tiles usually measure 12 in./305 mm square, but they are also available in 9 in./228 mm and 2 ft/610 mm squares. They can be painted (with emulsion or fire-proof paint, never oil-based), but they dent easily, which makes them less suitable for walls. Flexible sheeting, such as Kotina, can be hung like lining paper and wallpapered or painted. Some polystyrene is flame-proof, but it emits dense smoke and poisonous fumes; it should never be put near fire exits. N.B. You should cover the whole back of each tile with non-combustible adhesive, not the five dabs often suggested.

Stainless steel tiles

Expensive but not ruinous if used only as a splashback behind a stainless steel sink.

Ceramic tiles

Wall tiles are available plain, textured or patterned, glazed or unglazed, machine- or hand-made. They are usually $4\frac{1}{4}$ in./ 105 mm or 6 in./152 mm square, and some have spader lugs so you can line them up accurately. (There are also other tiles in various sizes and shapes.) If applied to dry, smooth walls, tiles are long-lasting, hardwearing, easy to clean.

Plastic laminate

Formica and other laminates are rigid sheets made from resin-impregnated layers of paper, bonded together under pressure. They are stuck down, but as they need a perfectly flat surface (rare in walls) it may be better to fix them to a framework of battens, or better still, to buy them pre-bonded to hardboard or chipboard and then to fix to battens.

Vinyl tiles (see also vinyl wallpaper)

In bathrooms, vinyl flooring tiles are often used on the bath panel as well as the floor to give continuity. For a unified look they can be used on the walls as well, but do not use vinyl tiles behind cookers, as they are not completely heatproof.

Mirror

Large panels of mirror can create an illusion of space. Cheaper than real mirror (though not cheap) is plastic mirror, or coloured acrylic.

Tongue-and-groove boarding

Interlocking boards, usually of pine or cedar. They are fixed to battens on the wall or ceiling – horizontally, vertically or diagonally – and are usually V-jointed (i.e. with a chamfered edge), which exaggerates the joints and helps to hide bad registration.

Panelling

Whereas this used to be solid oak it is now more likely to be natural or veneered ply. It can be fixed to battens or used to make partition walls or sliding doors. Tongue-and-groove ply panels are also available.

The most common facings are birch or beech. Veneered ply comes in wood finish or in melamine and other plastic surfaces, some with imitation wood grain.

Softboard

Covered in felt, hessian or linen, soft-board can be used as whole wall surfaces or as pin-up boards. It comes in sheets 8 ft/2.4 m × 4 ft/1.2 m. The fabric is tacked to each board and these are then nailed through to the wall.

If a room is high and light a big panel of mirror and all-over creamy walls will create a marvellously luminous background.

1 *Walls and ceiling treated as one with an old-fashioned floral paper to complement the old-fashioned wardrobe and bedstead.*

2 *An attic room with sloping ceiling and dormer windows unified with a patterned paper on all surfaces and a matching blind. White-painted frames make the green look greener.*

3 *Staircase walls and landings often have awkward shapes and angles, which again benefit from an all-over treatment.*

4 *Richly patterned paper, and a collection of dolls' furniture behind glass, get away from the clinical bathroom image. But white tiles round the bath are practical and so is the towel rack.*

5 *Hand-printed marble paper in David and Sue Gentleman's bathroom covers walls and cupboard doors.*

6 *An original idea by Shirtsleeves Studio for brightening up a dull hall – a patchwork of many different patterns and dark plain colours cut out of wrapping papers.*

7 *Softboard panels covered in felt can turn a wall into a pinboard.*

8 *Some wallpapers have a matching or co-ordinating fabric. Here home-sewn bedspreads match the wall and covered headboards.*

9 *Alternatively, curtain fabric can cover the wall too. This is usually done by nailing battens to the wall and fixing the fabric to these.*

10 *Here fabric (in the form of Indian bedspreads) is used on walls, sofa and as a tablecloth : for relief, the window has a plain blind.*

1 *White tiles with a simple flower motif look pleasantly crisp above the kitchen work-top. Note the single line of plain white tiles bordering the work surface.*

2 *A wall of mirror tiles at right angles to the window gives the illusion of double the window length – and twice the view.*

3 *Tongue-and-groove boarding is not only handsome but is also a good insulation material. Here it has been used vertically on walls and kitchen units, and painted.*

4 *Lapped boarding is similar in effect to tongue-and-groove but joint recesses are deeper. It is normally used horizontally and can help to make a high room less lofty.*

5 *Boarding can also be stained and used diagonally for a decorative effect as across this fireplace wall.*

6 *Another example of diagonal boarding, this time clear-sealed to give it a warm honey colour.*

7 *Three floor-to-ceiling mirror panels reflect the adjacent stainless steel trestle desk and stool in a cool all-white room.*

1

2

3

4

6

5

7

Walls
8/9 Practical decisions

Before you rush out and buy an expensive wallpaper, or order gallons of paint, you must check the condition of the walls.

Damp and condensation

Even if the house has been surveyed, or you are having structural alterations made, it is worth checking each individual wall to make sure it is dry – to save yourself possible trouble later on. If there are stains on the ceiling, check whether the cause has been dealt with. If there is a condensation problem, you will have to consider some form of insulation on the walls. In cases of slight damp it is possible to paint with an anti-condensation paint or to fix boarding to battens treated with a preservative.

Noise

You can help to reduce noise through walls or ceilings by insulating them in the same way as for condensation or to avoid heat loss The denser the material, the less sound will get through – though vibration-type noises are more difficult to deal with. Remember that next door's noise is more easily muffled if *they* insulate *their* wall; in other words, you are stopping noise getting out of a room, not coming in.

Money

Get your priorities right. If you are short of cash, you can spend your money on good quality paint, do the job yourself and add texture with curtaining, cushions, and accessories. Even if you get the builder to plaster and make good first, and then do your own painting or wallpapering, you will save quite a bit. If you can save in one area, spend the extra on areas where you will appreciate it most. A hessian wall in the living-room for warmth and a feeling of well-being; an area of ceramic tiling behind the cooker which is practical and looks luxurious.

Types of wall

Here is a run-down of the kind of walls you are likely to encounter:

Brick: If unpainted, check that mortar is in good condition, otherwise you will have to point it. Brick walls in new houses are sometimes left unpainted for decoration and these can be covered with a clear sealer to stop them from crumbling or becoming a dust trap. If the wall was previously plastered and has been exposed (e.g. because of dampness) it will probably not be in good enough condition to be left and could be painted white, but make sure the dampness has been cleared up first. Or you could fix plasterboard, tongue-and-groove wood panelling or other rigid sheet to battens.

Old plaster: Good plaster is a suitable surface for most wallcoverings or paint. Bad plaster needs checking. If damp, it will probably need stripping and renewing, after the damp has been treated. Or it may only need replastering in patches. If uneven, or cracked, use wallpaper or other covering or line with lining or ingrain paper and paint.

New plaster: Must be allowed to dry out thoroughly before decorating. If for any reason you have to paint it before it is absolutely dry, emulsion paint is the least likely to blister and allows the wall to breathe. Don't try to paper until bone dry. Plaster with lime in it should be treated with an alkaline primer. Plasterboard should be sealed before papering.

Matchboarding or wood panelling: If in good condition it is probably worth stripping or sanding and then staining or sealing with a clear sealer. Or wash thoroughly to remove dirt and grease, sand or rub down and paint. Previous varnish may have to be removed.

Temporary or permanent?

The answer to this doesn't necessarily depend on money. You may be decorating for the first time, in which case a temporary scheme will allow you to change parts of it later on if you get tired of it. You may be the kind of person who tries out new ideas all the time, in which case you won't want to go to vast expense to get a perfect finish. And of course if you are in short-term rented accommodation you will want to make the place as habitable as possible without wasting money or effort.

Previously painted walls: Emulsion paint can be washed thoroughly with water and detergent to remove marks, then painted with emulsion or oil paint, or wallpapered. Oil paint should also be sanded with an abrasive paper to remove shine and provide a key for the new paint. If the paint is crazed, after too many coats of different paints, you may have to strip it down before repainting. (For small patches, try sanding it with wet-and-dry paper.) You can wallpaper over gloss paint as long as it has been properly keyed. Line the walls first.

Previously papered walls: Paper in good condition can be painted over, but check first in case the colours are not fast and bleed through. If this happens you may be able to use a sealing primer before painting, otherwise the paper will have to be stripped off. Emulsion paint may cause bubbling, but this will probably go when the paint is dry. It is always wise to try a small area first – also to make sure the paper won't peel off. If you are repapering, strip off all the old paper and wash the wall thoroughly to remove all the size.

Ceilings

These can be treated in the same way as walls. Old wallpaper should be stripped off, distemper removed, emulsion paint washed. Bad stains should be treated with an aluminium primer before lining, and then painted. Cracks, even if filled in and made good, may open up again, so it may be better to paper the ceiling first.

Woodwork

New wood should be sanded and primed, painted with undercoat and top coats. Previously painted wood can be washed and then sanded, but particularly on skirtings and windows new paint on old tends to chip more easily, and it may be better to burn or strip the old paint off. Too many coats of paint on windows may make them stick.

Suitable finishes

Some areas of the house have problems which need special consideration.

Kitchen: Liable to condensation. Walls tend to get greasy and dust sticks to grease. A washable surface is therefore almost a necessity. An oil-based eggshell paint is one answer, or one of the tougher plastic emulsions. Vinyl or washable wallpapers are suitable, or sealed tongue-and-groove boarding. Ceramic or stainless steel tiles are practical behind the sink and cooker.

Bathroom: Tends to steam up. Water gets splashed about. The same surfaces as for the kitchen are suitable here. Also cork, vinyl tiles, plastic laminates in the shower, plastic mirror tiles, and tongue-and-groove panelling.

Passages: Narrow passages get dirty quickly – a washable surface is useful. Pale colours and metallic surfaces reflect light, and mirrors create a spatial illusion.

Playroom: A wall which can get dirty without a fuss. Vinyl, washable paper, oil-based paint all do the job. Or use any emulsion which can be changed at the slap of a brush – to a different colour. A wall of insulating cork, or softboard covered in felt or hessian, makes a pin-up area, and is a good sound absorber. You could also paint the lower half of one wall with blackboard paint.

---

1 *A wall of exposed brickwork painted white provides a strong textural contrast to smooth furniture surfaces.*

---

2 *Sometimes the bricks look better unpainted, as this pale-coloured fireplace wall.*

---

3 *Random stone wall encloses an area.*

---

4 *Rough plaster can be indented with a diamond pattern.*

1 *Chipboard on walls matched by adjustable shelves can be sealed to protect it against dirt, and is a good insulator.*

2 *Hollow blocks in pre-cast concrete, more often used outdoors as a garden screen, make an original room divider.*

3 *Primitive structural materials, like old rubble and brickwork left exposed, are an effective foil to the polished craftsmanship of traditional furniture.*

4 *Kitchen gadgets are always to hand if hung neatly behind the kitchen work-top on pegboard, here painted red and white to match the units.*

5 *Horizontal boarding on walls and ceiling with the joints picked out in black makes a virtue of the narrow passageway. Note Christmas pudding light.*

6 *A wall of bookshelves can house a complete library and looks better than shelves or bookcases dispersed around the room. If you site it along a thin party-wall, it also affords insulation against noise.*

Walls
10/11 Visual choices

Having decided on such practical matters as types of wallcoverings and general colour schemes, you can start to think about the purely visual aspect of each room. A boring shape can be livened up with bright colours and warm interesting textures. Proportions can be changed visually (see overleaf) and faults disguised where necessary. Nothing helps a small room more than a well-placed mirror to make it seem larger and brighter and full of interest.

However, before you plunge into a riot of colour and pattern, consider what is to go into each room – if you have beautiful antique furniture or modern classics, or if you have a large collection of decorative treasures, it may be unwise to marry them to wall surfaces which compete for attention. In such cases it is much better to use the walls as a plain backcloth and let your possessions dominate the room.

1 *White paint over rough plaster here results in a solid sculptured look, accentuated by the high, deep-set window and the chunky shelves.*

2 *Pictures, arranged against a darker background in this traditionally furnished bedroom, are themselves framed by the formally patterned frieze and skirting.*

3 *A painted horse-chestnut tree, always in leaf and with its own permanent fauna, partners live pot plants so effectively that the room seems filled with leaves.*

4 *Warmly painted door and panelling across the end of a corridor-like cottage lean-to contrasts sharply with the lighter-coloured wall. The frame of the doorway on the left is picked out in the same colour.*

5 *A full-length panel of mirrored glass at right-angles to the window creates the illusion of extra space and a second identically shuttered window.*

6 *A stylized landscape of flowered meadow, house, trees and sky adds fantasy to the children's bathtime.*

7 *Here the room is divided horizontally into a blue-and green landscape. Trees are silhouetted on the "horizon", the door is painted over in the same way as the walls.*

8 *Mirror tiles, arranged geometrically at various angles, reflect different areas of the room as a glittering patchwork of patterns.*

9 *Traditional American wall-stencil design behind a fourposter at the American Museum in Britain.*

1

2

3

4

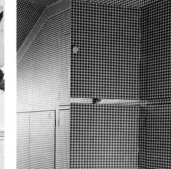

5

6

7

8

9

Another way to draw attention to the wall is to use a material not usually associated with wallcoverings – such as dress fabric or carpeting. Sometimes this also has practical advantages: for instance if it is a good sound absorber or reduces condensation.

Trompe l'oeil murals are a traditional form of wall decoration and have in the past been brought to such a fine art that the eye is deceived even after the mind has registered that it is an illusion – for instance where a colonnaded passageway is continued in paint on the end wall, perfect in perspective and every detail!

You can also carry the eye from one point to another by the use of colour or pattern, as when you pick out the skirting and ceiling moulding in the same colour and continue them up the staircase.

1 *A glimpse of the seaside – holiday postcard style – through a painted "hole" on an otherwise plain wall.*

2 *Dried leaves, pages of flower paintings cut from a book and other objects decorate a white-painted wall.*

3 *Gingham wallpaper, used to cover walls, ceiling and cupboard doors in a hall, has a neat border of smaller checks where wall and ceiling meet.*

4 *Another mural, this time a pastel-coloured tree, keeps company with a china dog and miniature air balloon light fitting.*

5 *Silver foil can sparkle up a dull little lavatory or cloakroom, though it isn't all that easy to put up. You need a stronger foil than ordinary kitchen foil, which tends to crumple and tear.*

6 *Vertical striped wallpaper has been taken up the walls and over the ceiling in a large living area. The stripes are repeated in the vertical louvred sliding door screen.*

7 *Large oriental carpet emphasizes the height of a room in designer Geoffrey Bennison's Brighton flat, and adds grandeur to the Eastern-style decoration.*

8 *Cord carpeting, more usual on the floor, covers the wall and shelves – a possible solution for a small study needing warmth and quiet.*

9 *Tiles with a geometric design are enclosed on each wall of this bathroom by a border of plain brown tiles. Note the "cut off" corner of the bath and the wall-mounted taps.*

Walls
12/13 Visual problems

Very few of us live in perfect houses. But with a little cunning you can achieve the atmosphere and effect that you are after: odd corners, sloping ceilings or awkward storage can all be improved visually (see below).

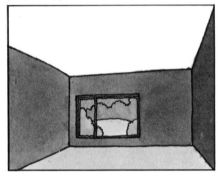

This ceiling is low, and the walls are short. A lighter colour on the ceiling and floor makes the room appear higher. This is because darker tones seem to draw inwards and lighter tones to "fall" away.

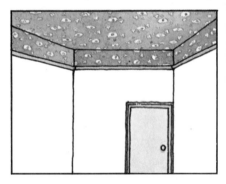

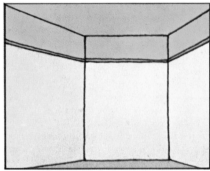

If the ceiling is too high, make it a tone or two darker, and it will seem lower. Don't make it too dark though, because at night, with low-placed lighting, the ceiling will vanish upwards. Paint or paper the ceiling down to picture-rail height – if you are using a paper choose a bold non-directional pattern, and be sure to echo the colour scheme in the rest of the room.

 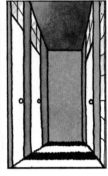

Long, narrow corridors can be opened with a striking focal point at the far end. Alternatively, choose dark colours for walls, floor and ceiling and highlight doors and window with mirror glass on the opposite wall.

An irregular, bitty area, such as a hall and staircase with several landings and passageways leading off it, can look confused if you change the decorations at each level. Work out carefully how the different surfaces could be co-ordinated. Often the surest way is to use a basic scheme of only one or two colours, and tones of those colours, for all the walls, floors, ceiling and paintwork.

An uninspiring box-shaped room can be quite a problem. Try painting it all white, then adding colour in bands, working up from the skirtings and building stripes of contrasting or blending colours.

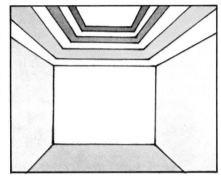

The ceiling of this box-shaped room has been lifted and the shape of the room seems to alter thanks to a huge coffer of decreasing squares. To paint this yourself you will need a steady hand, plenty of masking tape and some scaffolding.

1 *Frequent changes in direction or levels, together with odd architectural features such as beams and arches, can be treated as one to make them less prominent. Here an arch which breaks the otherwise pleasing line of the staircase has been papered to merge with the walls. The eye registers the pattern before taking in the shape of the wall it covers. An all-over non-directional design is best as a geometric one would tend to emphasize the changes in direction.*

2 *Fireplace surround and ornate Victorian overmantel have been painted brown to match the walls, ceiling and wooden shutters. Any danger of gloom is dispelled by the white sofas, and by carefully placed lighting from spots on a ceiling-mounted track, the internally lit cabinet and the blazing fire.*

3 *Where dark walls meet a light ceiling, horizontal bands of a pale colour below the cornice can make the ceiling seem lower than it really is.*

4 *Colour and pattern have been used to impose symmetry on a tall, narrow stairwell with off-centre landing doors and a high, irregular sloping ceiling. Height is less apparent after a coat of a dark colour, and the addition of the broad flame-pattern frieze at the top of the wall accents the basic rectangular shape of the area. White-painted doors and dado rail bring the colour to life.*

1

2

3

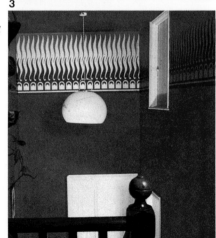

4

Narrow bands of tape turn large, plain painted walls into interesting "panels".

Walls
14/15 Ceilings

So often the ceiling is a large, blank surface, forgotten and unused. Here are some suggestions for ways of making a ceiling contribute to the decorative effect of the room. Sometimes it can help the proportions if you expose the beams or install a lower, false ceiling. How you light the room can also make a deal of difference.

1 *Exposed beams and timbers in an old farm house, infilled with plaster.*

2 *This room has been heightened by removing the ceiling, leaving the beams exposed and panelling in between with plasterboard.*

3 *The timber of both the joists and the floorboards above has been left uncovered. A thin coat of white stain takes the hot yellowness out of the pine.*

4 *Sealed pine matchboarding lines the exposed butterfly roof supported by a yellow painted RSJ.*

5 *Painted matchboarding used to line both ceiling and walls.*

6 *Acoustic tiles made of pre-finished slotted insulation board form a geometric pattern on the ceiling.*

7 *Papering the ceiling to match the walls makes any room look cosier.*

8 *The ceiling echoes the carpet, but in muted colours as though it were a pale reflection.*

9 *Tongue-and-groove boarding along the length of a kitchen ceiling is sealed to protect the wood.*

(Opposite) White paint with a very high gloss in this dramatic Italian room is achieved by repeated rubbing down between coats, on a very smooth surface.

Walls

Wallcoverings

To calculate the number of rolls of paper or other covering, measure the height of the room, then work out how many lengths can be cut from one roll. A standard roll measures 11 yd × 21 in./10 m × 533 mm. It usually comes trimmed, with the exception of some hand-printed papers. Allow for pattern-matching, cutting, and ignore windows and doors.

When buying, check each roll for colour variation; they may vary slightly from batch to batch, so it is better to buy all you need in one go.

To help you, here is an estimate of how much wallpaper you need for different sizes of room. Measure the height from the skirting and ignore doors and windows when going round the perimeter.

Paper Height of Walls	Perimeter					
	32 ft 10 m	40 ft 12 m	48 ft 15 m	56 ft 17 m	60 ft 18 m	74 ft 22 m
7–7½ ft 2.1–2.2 m	4	5	6	7	8	9
8–8½ ft 2.4–2.5 m	5	6	7	8	9	10
9–9½ ft 2.7–2.8 m	5	6	7	9	10	11
10–10½ ft 3–3.1 m	5	7	8	10	11	12
11–11½ ft 3.3–3.4 m	6	8	9	10	12	13
Ceiling	2	2	3	4	5	7

Numbers refer to how many rolls you need.

Paint

The spreading capacity of different types of paint can vary considerably – if in doubt consult the retailer. First multiply the height by the length of each wall and length by the width of the ceiling. Add these together to get the total area of the surface to be painted. Don't forget to allow for each coat of paint separately. Where a surface is porous you will have to allow for more paint.

Here is a rough guide to the spreading capacity of different sorts of paint in commercially available quantities.

Paint	Primer		Gloss		Emulsion	
	sq yds	sq m	sq yds	sq m	sq yds	sq m
½ litre	7	6	9	7½	10	9
1 pint	8	7	10	8½	12	10
1 litre	14	12	18	15	21	18
1 quart	16	14	20	17	24	20
5 litres	72	60	90	75	108	90
1 gallon	64	54	80	67	96	80

1

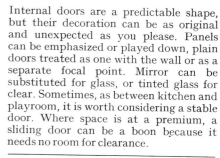

Internal doors are a predictable shape, but their decoration can be as original and unexpected as you please. Panels can be emphasized or played down, plain doors treated as one with the wall or as a separate focal point. Mirror can be substituted for glass, or tinted glass for clear. Sometimes, as between kitchen and playroom, it is worth considering a stable door. Where space is at a premium, a sliding door can be a boon because it needs no room for clearance.

1 (*Opposite*) *Wallhung patchwork – not a mistake in the calculations but walls as environmental works of art.*

2 *If you have original pine doors in good condition, it is worth stripping off the old paint to expose the honey-coloured wood. This is very hard work and takes quite a long time – and is perhaps a case for calling in specialist help.*

3 *A garland of fruit and flowers, painted and varnished, decorates this door.*

4 *The door of the patchwork room shown opposite has fabric over panels framed by a narrow border which helps to "contain" it.*

5 *This clear pink door shows how to use colour imaginatively. The glass panes of the double doors between rooms are covered in mirror foil to create an illusion of greater space.*

6 *In an institution type corridor, paint doors in clear colours, then add giant numbers which will look like an abstract, graphic design.*

7 *A sunny, translucent effect is created by painting a mural on to a glass panel.*

8 *A door painted in strong glowing colours – repeated in cornice, frieze and skirtings – can add warmth and gaiety to a child's room.*

9 *Doors are painted to match walls with lighter mouldings. A narrow band of white round the frame makes for clean yet subtle definition of the space.*

10 *The door, frame and wall above are painted the same colour to give the impression of greater size. (Both sides of the door are painted red to maintain the effect when the door opens.)*

Walls
18 Screens

Screens come in many shapes and materials and can be either free-standing or permanently fixed, opaque or partly see-throughable. They are useful in a number of ways – as an informal alternative to a door, as a room divider in open areas, to protect your privacy from the street without taking away precious daylight, or to turn a corner into a cosy niche. Covered in felt they can become an office pin-board; fretworked and painted, they might become a decorative element in the room.

1 *A movable hinged screen gives some privacy between the various activities in a large area, though it is not a sound barrier.*

2 *A fixed wooden lattice screen divides dining from living area. Note the cantilevered shelf and intertwining snake light fitting.*

3 *Concertina door screen between two areas takes up little space when opened back.*

4 *Three-quarter height semi-circular white screens divide the office and dining area. It's made on the principle of a model aeroplane wing – i.e., a 3- or 5-ply frame with a ply skin stretched over it, then the whole thing sprayed with melamine.*

5 *White-painted fretwork-tree screen in an arched doorway of Jane Kasmin's house in London.*

6 *Mirror screen with piano hinges hides the stereo equipment from the rest of the room.*

7 *Printed cotton fabric is used to cover a screen protecting the sitting area from the door and circulation areas.*

1

2

3

4

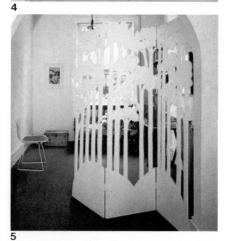

5

6

7

Windows/1

With window treatments, as with many things in life, the simplest ideas are usually the best. You can have curtains, of course, but have you thought of roller or roman blinds, shutters, louvres or screens? If you like big, bold designs, you'll find they work much better used flat, as in blinds, so the pattern isn't distorted. To give a room a modern, uncluttered look, shutters or screens may be the answer.

Since window treatments contribute to the exterior as well as the interior of the house, you should consider them from the road too, not only during the day but also at night. When choosing curtains you must also decide which headings and rails are right for your windows, taking into account length and weight of fabric and anything that may have to be sited under the window sill.

To let in the maximum of light and air during the day you should avoid anything that covers the windows unnecessarily. And where privacy is not a problem you could leave a handsome window uncurtained. Net curtaining, though efficient, can look dreary, but there are several attractive alternatives.

Lack of money needn't be too great a hindrance as there are helpful aids – efficient heading tapes, roller blind kits, off-the-peg louvre panels, and so on. Warmth is an important factor. A heavy curtain will not solve a heat-loss problem, although it may cope with minor draughts. You may need to draught-strip, renew the frames or even double-glaze.

Before you start plunging into major expense, ask yourself:

- ☐ Does every window really need a curtain – what about blinds, shutters or even nothing at all?
- ☐ Do you need to shut out every scrap of light in bedrooms?
- ☐ Will you need some form of sheer for daytime privacy or to block out a dreary view?
- ☐ Have you considered all the up-to-date types of headings, rails, tracks? Especially as alternatives to pelmets?
- ☐ Will the various window treatments add up well when seen from outside both during the day and at night.

1 *One way to prevent passers-by from peering in without resorting to net curtains – hang up a large paper daisy.*

2 *You could cheer up the outside of your house by painting a design on the roller blind material before it is hollandized.*

3 *Big, bold Marimekko fabrics look great at night with the light glowing through.*

4 *Attractive night-time windows do a lot to make a house look more welcoming.*

1

2

3

4

Windows
2/3 Curtains/how to hang them

There is always the exception that proves the rule, but if you follow these guidelines you won't go far wrong. There are only two lengths to which curtains should be hung: to the floor, or to the sill. Any other arrangement is unlikely to look good.

The top of the heading can be at ceiling height, above or at the top of the frame or flush with the reveal of the window. Should you use café curtains, the top pole or track would usually come about half-way down a window. The choice you make will depend on whether you want to emphasize the height or the width of the window. Let floor-to-ceiling curtains drop to within half an inch of the floor; curtains which drop to the window sill should be about $\frac{1}{4}$ in./5 mm above, so that they don't pick up dust.

What fabrics?

Next, consider your room and your choice of fabrics. On the practical side you have to decide (a) how much the budget will allow, (b) whether the fabric is suitable for the treatment, (c) whether you want lined or unlined curtains, (d) whether you need insulation against cold or noise, either by lining the curtain or using a heavy fabric, or both, (e) whether you need to keep out light at night or only screen the room from the street, (f) fire hazards.

On the visual side you need to think about (a) colour, texture and pattern, (b) whether floor or sill length, (c) what kind of headings, (d) fullness of the folds. This last affects your budget, and generally speaking it is better to choose a generous amount of a cheaper fabric than to skimp on a more expensive one.

Should you decide on short curtains, avoid particularly heavy fabrics, or very large patterns; keep them for full-length curtains. You can get away with a large pattern if you match it very carefully to the rest of your scheme: for instance, if the wallpaper is a large all-over pattern, and you want the curtains to match. Adding a neutral border in a colour picked out from the pattern, or a plain blind under the curtain, can help to soften an over-large effect.

Pattern repeats

Always take into account the fabric repeat, which means the length of each pattern before it starts all over again. Since both curtains should have the same pattern each side, this can mean ordering an extra pattern length per curtain.

Plain or patterned?

For most people it is easier to try to tone things in, that is, match things up. So if in doubt, play safe and start with one colour. Remember, if you feel the tones you want

are getting a bit dull, you can always brighten up a room with cushions in more positive colours: but you cannot so easily take away a brilliant and costly curtain once it is up.

You could cover your walls in beige hessian and have richly patterned curtains in beiges, browns and creams. If you have already decided on a patterned fabric, you could pick out one or more of the colours to use in the rest of the room. Don't go overboard for very expensive, multi-colour contrasts unless you are quite convinced you are right, or have the help of a decorator. Pattern on pattern – using different patterns for curtains, walls and upholstery – can produce beautiful effects if properly used, but it can also look more dreadful than less adventurous schemes ever would.

Use fabrics generously: a cheap gingham can look just as good as an expensive silk, as long as you use enough of it. Skimped curtains without enough fullness look mean even if the fabric has cost a fortune. You don't have to break the bank, especially when you make your own curtains, but do be a perfectionist.

If you buy cheap fabric and want to give it quality, line and interline it. It will last for years, and the lining gives it the generous bulky look that expensive curtains have. Be sure, however, lightly to iron the finished curtain into the folds you want it to assume when it is drawn open.

Some colours fade more than others, so check with the salesman or the manufacturer whether a fabric is liable to fade. This is not always easy, but perseverance should be your watchword: it will pay off in the end.

1 *Floor-length curtains with pinch-pleated headings that draw well back to frame the French windows and the lovely view beyond.*

2 *Unlined sill-length curtains which filter the daylight into the room can create a pleasant soft atmosphere.*

3 *Crocheted café curtains give a pleasant period look to the window of this restaurant.*

4 *Sheer café curtains that let in the light, but block out the view of the houses opposite.*

5 *Boldly patterned curtains with a matching wallpaper look very dramatic.*

6 *These bright bedroom curtains are bordered with a contrasting colour that matches other elements in the room.*

7 *Effective and cheap curtaining, using Indian bedspreads. A very large one can be cut in half and turned "sides to middle" so that the border meets in the middle.*

1

2

3

4

5

6

7

Curtain headings

Decide on the sort of heading you want to use. A heading is the term used to describe the sort of pleat, or gather, at the top of curtains, Different headings need different kinds of heading tape.

Types of tapes

There are many heading tapes available, but they vary only slightly from manufacturer to manufacturer, so keep to the product of a well-known firm.

There are two basic types of heading tapes: with one, for pencil pleats and gathered headings, you pull a draw-string after you have sewn your tape to the curtain, then thread through hooks at various intervals, and hook these to your curtain track. With the other type – for pinch pleats – there is usually no draw-string. You set in long hooks through the back of the tape which folds the fabric into pleats, which may be single, double or treble. You then fix these hooks on to the track.

Professional curtain makers still make curtains all by hand and do not use tapes, but tapes give a neat look to any curtain and are so easy to use that making your own curtains is quite simple these days. Some tape manufacturers have printed leaflets, and in the DIY chapter we give you instructions on how to make curtains using the simpler headings.

Types of hooks

Standard curtain hooks (A) now come in plastic as well as metal, which eliminates rusting. There are also hooks which slide directly into the track (B).

Where tracks are sold with their own special hooks, buy extra hooks just to be on the safe side.

For some headings special hooks can make the job that much simpler: for instance, hooks for deep pinch pleats (C) are inserted into pockets on the tape.

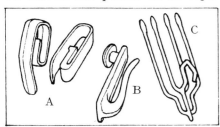

Measuring up for fabric

It is a good idea to make a note of your window measurements on a diagram. If possible use a steel rod or wooden rule to measure with, since they are more accurate than tapes. Fix your curtain track in position before you take curtain measurements. (If you are going to have your curtains custom made, don't take the measurements yourself. Get a professional to come along and do it. Then if there are mistakes you are not to blame.) Always take into account your headings and choose the tapes when you buy the track. In this way your retailer will be able to help you decide the correct measurements for both these before you finally buy the fabric.

Some fabrics are not pre-shrunk, so check on this. It could be disastrous if either the main fabric or the lining shrank after the curtains had been made. If in doubt, try washing a small square of fabric before you cut the lengths – if it shrinks, wash all the fabric. Or leave long hems (tacked) until after the first wash.

Width

Curtain width depends on the type of heading and fabric. The following is a guide to the minimum number of widths you should allow for; but allow also for overlaps, plus approximately 1½ in./38 mm for each side hem and 1¼ in./32 mm for each join.

The chart below is to help you work out the width for different track lengths.

Gathered	1½ times track length
Gathered (nets and sheers)	2 times track length
Pencil pleats	2 times track length
Pencil pleats (nets and sheers)	3 times track length
Pinch pleats	2 times track length
Pinch pleats (nets and sheers)	2½–3 times track length

Length

Measure the length from curtain runner to sill or floor (a b or a c – see diagram). Add 6 in./152 mm to 10 in./254 mm overall for hems and heading (6 in./152 mm for lightweights and sheers, 10 in./254 mm for heavy fabrics). On patterns that need to be matched (which should run on the same level on all curtains) allow one pattern repeat per curtain length.

Calculating

The number of yards you need is calculated by the drop of the finished curtain times the number of widths. Thus for a 4 ft/1.2 m track and 8 ft/2.4 m drop you would need two widths of a 4 ft/1.2 m fabric (giving you a generous allowance for turnings and overlap) times 8 ft/2.4 m plus about 8 in./200 mm hem and heading allowance. So you need approximately 6 yds/5.5 m of fabric. But don't forget to add to this if you have a pattern repeat. Always check your yardage with your retailer to make sure you've got it right.

When making curtains the one thing to remember is that hanging fabric is likely to stretch at the beginning. So tack the hem when hanging the curtains for the first time, and allow one or two days or longer, depending on the fabric, before finally sewing the hems.

Pinch pleats

If you are not used to making curtains, and want to play safe, stick to pinch pleats. Deep pinch pleats look best when used on a relatively heavy fabric hung from ceiling to floor, though a short curtain made of finer fabric can also look good, and there is a narrower tape for this.

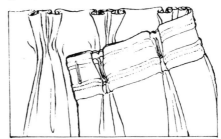

Pencil pleats

For pencil pleat headings use a Regis tape which looks well on most types of curtains. This type of heading looks especially nice when used on lightweight net (there are special lightweight tapes to use with net) teamed with a heavier pinch-pleated curtain.

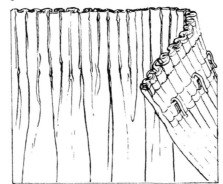

Gathered headings

There is a standard tape, 1 in./25 mm, which plain-gathers the heading. It can be a bit sparse and tends to look skimped except on very short, lightweight curtains. But this is a matter of taste. This is one time when a valance or pelmet can look appropriate.

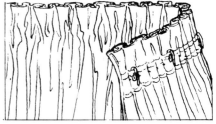

Looped headings

There is no short-cut to making these headings: it's a case of DIY or having them made professionally. These headings are particularly useful if there is a radiator behind the curtain because they let the warm air into the room. They are also often used on café curtains.

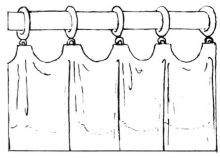

Lining tape

Lining tape has two decks for hooks: one to take the hooks for the curtain, the other to take the hooks for the lining. Sew the tape to the curtains, hang them up; then sew 1 in./25 mm tape to your lining fabric, pull the draw-string, insert hooks, and hook on to the main curtain tape. In this way the lining is removable for washing – which is sensible as linings always pick up dirt first, being nearest the window. Although they don't hang quite as well as a lined and interlined curtain, this is a good compromise for a medium-priced, practical, lined curtain.

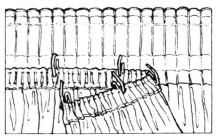

Windows
4/5 Rods, rails and poles/radiators

There are two basic ways of hanging your curtains, either with an "invisible" track so that you see neat headings and nothing else, or with a pole which is there to be seen.

Measuring

If possible, curtain tracks should be at least 18 in./460 mm wider than the window frame (i.e. 9 in. or 229 mm either side), so that the curtain can be drawn back clear of the window to let in the light. Very thick curtains across a wide window may need as much as 2 ft/610 mm either side.

Tracks

There are simple, plain and efficient tracks on the market, which will take even the heaviest curtains so long as they are fixed securely to the ceiling or window. Many tracks are now made in plastic instead of metal; they don't corrode and, though lightweight, can usually take heavy curtains. Ask the retailer whether the track you choose will take the curtain fabric you have in mind. (Helpful hint: spray regularly with silicone furniture polish to ensure smooth running.)

A bay window was once rather a problem, requiring a custom-made track that curved and hugged the shape of the bay. Now you can buy tracks which you bend to the required shape or lengths which are already shaped in sections for you to fix together. These come with an extension bracket which projects them 3 in. to 5 in./76 mm to 127 mm from the wall on to which they are fixed.

Double tracks

These are useful for straight runs or bays when you want to use two sets of curtains. Another type of double track enables you to use a pelmet on the front strut with curtains underneath. This can be quite attractive in a bedroom bay with pencil pleat or pinch pleat heading on a crisp cotton gingham or madras. A useful point is that the curtains can tuck round at each end, so not a chink of light shows through.

Ceiling-mounted track

A ceiling-mounted track looks neat if your window goes right up to the top of the wall or if you have a wide window sill half-way down and want the curtain to hang well out into the room: it can also be useful when the fabric is very heavy, since there is more strength in a ceiling mount than a wall mount.

Tension rod

A tension rod, for lightweight curtaining, is sprung inside at each end so that when it is fitted into a recessed window the pressure will hold the rod firmly in position. It's useful for people who move

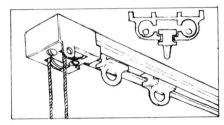

Ceiling - mounted track.

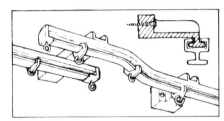

Wall- fixed track.

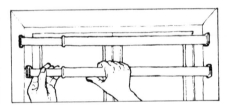

Tension rod.

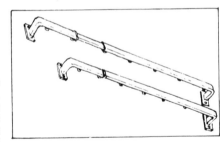

Extendable track.

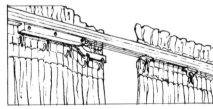

Central overlap on single track.

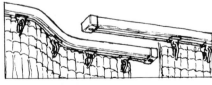

Track curved to make an overlap.

about a lot and don't want to buy new curtains and tracks each time they move.

Extendable track

Where a track has to fit exactly, there is one with an extendable piece which can be adjusted to fit a window which does not fall into any standard size category. These are useful when moving house, as they can easily be adapted to different widths of window.

Ultra-slim tracks

For reasonably lightweight curtains there are very slim tracks sold as pelmet tracks, which can be wall or ceiling mounted. They are easy to bend and absolutely inconspicuous once they have been put in position – almost invisible.

Lastly, there is a track which is only $\frac{3}{8}$ in./10 mm deep and is ideal for use in a bathroom or kitchen when you need every scrap of available light; it fits to the underside of the window frame.

Cords and overlaps

Cording sets are available with lots of tracks and poles; they cost a bit more but are well worth it. They protect curtains from constant handling, and as you pull them open from one position the drapes always fall well, which is not always so when operated by hand. Most tracks, including corded ones, are available with centre overlaps if required.

Hinged track

Hinged tracks are wall-fixed and the track swings outwards so that the curtain opens away from the window.

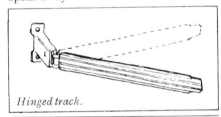

Hinged track.

1 *It's quite possible these days to buy neat, slim tracks strong enough to support heavy, interlined curtains – and if a ceiling is interesting, it's particularly important to avoid heavy or fussy window headings.*

2 *If curtains are bunched into bay window corners, light gets blocked out and the fabric doesn't look its best. Run the track round the bay and on the flanking walls so that the curtains can be drawn well clear.*

3 *It would be a shame to spoil the arched tops of windows like these – much better to fix the track on the wall or ceiling above. Or incorporate a pencil-slim track in the window-frame moulding.*

1

2

3

Poles

Many people still buy traditional brass poles with pole ends and brass rings. You can buy them in wood, too; you can even get wooden poles mitred at each corner to go round a bay.

If you need only a short, slender pole you can buy dowels very cheaply from most hardware stores. Finish off by buying two wooden door knobs to screw into each end of the pole; then you can paint or stain or polish it. You can also get a brass pole with a cording set fixed inside the pole, for heavy curtains.

Helpful hint: wax polish is the old-fashioned cure for sticky brass poles. But it is better to have your poles polyurethane treated (this stops them tarnishing), and occasionally to use a silicone wax polish on them to stop the varnish from scraping off.

Radiators

Sited under a window, these can be a problem. There will be no heat from them at all at night if you have heavy curtains from floor to ceiling. Overcome this by having a brass or wooden rod and curtain rings so that the warm air can flow up and into the room.

If you have a radiator that projects right into the room, the most obvious thing to do is to alter the projection of the curtain track. There are tracks available with extra-long brackets, and also some that can be clipped to the original track. Alternatively any handyman should be able to construct a simple device such as a batten supported on brackets, so the track can be fixed to the front of it.

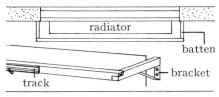

1 *Sheer sill-length curtains have a cool airy look when hung on slim wooden rods with matching knobs and rings.*

2 *Stained dowelling makes a cheap and simple pole to hold up mock curtains.*

3 *A wall-to-wall pole can be lifted off its brackets when the curtains need cleaning.*

4 *Looped headings on curtains in front of a radiator will let the hot air into the room.*

5 *The pulley arrangement on these wooden rings means the curtains can be drawn easily, without dragging the material itself.*

6 *Wooden poles look best when teamed with matching rings and supports.*

Fabric blinds are easy to make and easy on the purse because you need so much less material than you do for a curtain.

Roller blinds

Roller blind kits are readily available and are simple enough for anyone to make a success of. They blend well with any scheme; for example, you can use a material that tones exactly with the wallpaper or paint colour of your windows and walls or one that stands on its own, almost like a picture.

Because of their neatness, they are exceptionally useful for giving a crisp, modern look to Victorian bays. You can also team them with curtains – for instance under sheers when darkness is needed at night. Many are washable or can be sponged; waterproof blinds are useful in bathrooms. If you buy a ready-made plain roller blind it is very simple to trim it either with coarse lace along the bottom, or by sewing on strips of ribbon, braid or border tape. Or you can use the curtain fabric as a border to link your blind to the room scheme. When choosing your own fabric for a blind you must make sure it is suitable for the job, otherwise it may sag or roll unevenly. A tightly woven, flat cotton is usually most reliable.

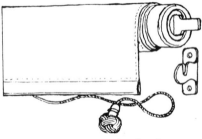

Roller blind spring mechanism is contained in the end-piece with a flat pin.

Roman blinds

Roman blinds are similar to roller blinds, but pull with cord into accordion pleats, which, when fully up, make a neat pleated pelmet. And when let down have a good-looking, sophisticated effect with their gentle pleats.

You can now make roman blinds at home, and though they are not quite as simple as rollers, the effort is well worth while. They, too, are cheaper than curtains because they take up less fabric, and can be made up in any kind of fabric, including sheers and dress materials. They can be wall or ceiling mounted and look equally well dropped to the sill. If they are to be used over a large expanse of window it is best to group several of 48 in./1.2 m wide

each – or the same widths as the glass panels, rather than one wide one which is difficult to handle.

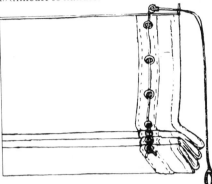

Cords go through eyelets in the tape at the back of the blind.

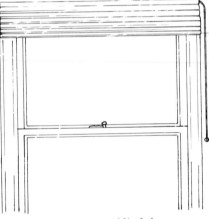

When pulled up, roman blinds have a pelmet effect.

1 *Slick new look for a pleasant old window – a pair of blinds rather than just a single one. Note how the window frame is subtly pointed up with a fine black outline.*

2 *Roller blinds lend themselves to dramatic treatment if you're handy with fabric paints. (These were painted by Olivia Brett.)*

3 *You can have virtually any closely woven cotton hollandized, and turned into a roller blind – good for big designs which lose so much if they are bunched up into curtains.*

4 *This ingenious blind pulls upwards to make the bedroom private while letting in light at the top. The cord runs from the centre top of the blind to the top of the window frame, on to a ceiling pulley and is then wound round a cleat near the bedside light.*

5/6/7 *Roman blinds can be made in both thicker and flimsier fabrics than rollers and in virtually any width.*

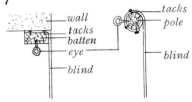

wall
tacks
batten
eye
blind

tacks
pole

blind

Two ways of fixing roman blinds.

Pinoleums, slatted wood and quills

Pinoleum blinds have moved out of the conservatory and into the house to provide a reasonably cheap solution for large expanses of glass where curtains are not needed. They are also useful because they can be fixed to sloping ceilings, as can roller blinds. They are made of very fine strips of wood, woven together with cotton, usually in natural pine or stained green. A white plastic quill version is also available. They do the same job as romans, rollers and sheers, and allow a soft light to filter through.

Similar to pinoleum are the coarser, wooden slat blinds; these are sometimes used as screens.

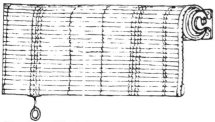

Pinoleum blinds have the same spring mechanism as roller blinds.

Balastores

Balastore blinds are old fashioned, charming and inexpensive. They are made of especially strong treated paper fibre, accordion pleated, and usually cream. They have small holes punched out all over, so that they restrict glare but allow plenty of warm light to filter through. The top wooden lath screws to the ceiling or wall. A point to remember when measuring is that the fixing lath is 2 in./51 mm wider than the actual blind, so allow enough room. They come in widths from 18 in./460 mm to 104 in./2.7 m and drops of up to 6 ft 6 in./2 m.

Pleatex

Pleatex blinds are made from tough super-calendered, wet-strength craft paper, permanently pleated in 1 in./25 mm pleats. They come in orange, green, parchment and blue, are cheaper than roller blinds, and have a five-year guarantee. Sizes are from 2 ft wide by 2 ft 6 in./610 mm by 760 mm drop to 10 ft wide by 8 ft 6 in./3 m by 2.5 m drop.

Venetians

Venetian blinds are made in plastic, metal or wood. They are available in a large variety of sizes, from about 10 in./254 mm wide, with any length of drop. They can be wall or window mounted.

The slats come in various widths, usually from 1⅜ in./35 mm up to 2 in./51 mm, and the very slim ones look neat and architectural. Unfortunately, the slats in some venetians make a noisy clatter when the window is open, or if there's a through draught.

They control the light coming into a room, which prevents your furniture and cushions from fading; the light they do allow in has a cheerful brightness without dazzle. At the same time, they are good heat controllers, insulating the room in winter, reducing heat in summer. At night time, the closed blinds keep out light very effectively. They can also be used on sloping windows, or even fitted into the deep frame of a pivot window. For appearance's sake, you should give venetians a regular dusting, or go over them with the appropriate attachment on your vacuum cleaner.

Vertical louvre blinds

These blinds are made of vertical strips of canvas, wood slats, silk or man-made sheers, which are attached at top and bottom. They pivot open and shut and are either fixed or can be pulled back. They are usually floor to ceiling and are more often seen in offices than private homes, though they can be very effective across a window wall.

Wooden blinds

Wooden blinds give a warm and agreeable light. The snag is that they cost a lot – but are worth it if they're just what your scheme needs, as they last for ever. They're made to order in pine or western red cedar, then stained or coloured to the customer's own requirements.

1 *Pinoleum blinds look particularly good made up to fit the sections of a window frame.*

2 *They are also a relatively cheap way of coping with large expanses of glass.*

3 *Pleatex blinds look like a cross between a venetian blind and a roller blind – and cost much less than either.*

4 *Vertical louvre blinds made in broad bands of creamy fabric manage to combine a strong, architectural line with a gentle way of transmitting light.*

5 *Venetian blinds can look quite lovely on sunny days, especially if the quills are slim and white – and used as simply and elegantly as in this long slot of a window.*

6 *Venetian blinds offer another solution to the problem of sloping attic windows.*

7 *Wooden venetian blinds give a warmer glow than the usual metal or plastic, but they cost considerably more.*

Windows
8/9 Shutters and screens

There is something extremely comforting about old-fashioned internal shutters folded neatly across windows or a door. They look secure and attractive, and one hopes that they also repel burglars. An old shutter looks particularly well during the day when folded back on either side of a splayed recess, and there is no need for an extra window treatment except for daytime privacy. Old-fashioned French shutters on the outside are practical and look good. They keep out the light when you want them to, but otherwise do not restrict the window at all.

You can also buy doors in sections which fold forward and back in the same way as louvres. These can be kept plain, stained or painted to match any decorative scheme.

Louvres

The louvre has to a large extent replaced the old shutter. It is made in a variety of natural woods like pine and mahogany, or in wood which can be painted or stained. There are a multiplicity of shapes, sizes, widths and depths of louvres; some are half-louvre, half-plain; some are even one-sided, which means they are plain on the reverse side and don't let in the light, draughts or dust. Louvres can look good used full-height across one end of a room which has French windows. They can also be useful where you have oddly-shaped adjacent windows which are too much of a problem to deal with separately. Besides being used for windows, they can be used in front of storage units, as cupboard or wardrobe doors, or as partitions and screens.

Screens

Screens can be made to slide clear of the windows or they can be fitted into the window recess if you want to veil an uninspiring or downright ugly view. Hardboard panels with cut-out designs look very good as fixed screens, and you will find that old-fashioned garden lattices, which let in a great deal of light through the large holes, will effectively fragment the view outside. If you leave enough room between the screen and the window for a row of pot plants, so much the better. If privacy is what you are after you can fix half screens, taken up the window, say 2 ft/610 mm.

There is now a track which allows you to ceiling-mount all kinds of screens, like pinoleum, widths of thick fabric, blinds, or anything else that is suitable, so that they can be pulled to one side when an unrestricted view is needed. They can be hung in front of windows, round a bay, over storage, or used to divide a dining area from a living area – in fact they are the ideal means for visual partitioning.

1

2

3

4

5

6

7

1/2 Surprise! Plain day-time shutters open out at night to reveal a mural.

3 Piano-hinged panels which fold flat on top of each other to save wall space either side.

4 Shutters can be shaped to fit unusual windows – even turned into wing mirrors for a bathroom "porthole".

5 Louvres needn't always be horizontal, as these Swedish windows show.

6 Bi-fold shutters don't need to be folded back against the reveals since they are supported by top and bottom tracks.

7 Painted louvres are perfect for French windows.

8 Small, hinged panels let in light and air.

9 The panels in the shutters are sympathetic in shape to the central table and carpet.

10 Fixed timber grille designed by Clendinning brightens up this dark basement window.

11 Detail of a painting – Mr. & Mrs. Clark and Percy – by David Hockney, proving just how cool painted shutters can look.

12 Neat treatment for a kitchen window with cupboard below: louvred shutters for both.

13 Punched, white painted hardboard panelling makes a cheap, DIY way of screening a dreary view.

14 Break up large expanses of picture window with wall-to-wall louvre panels.

15 These smoky acrylic screens reduce glare in the daytime.

16 A half screen of translucent material is a smart solution for street-side privacy.

9

10

12

13

14
15

16

Windows
10/11 Handling sheers

The term "sheer" covers a variety of translucent fabrics – ranging from nylon, cotton or terylene net to heavy woollen or Dralon tweed.

How to hang them

Hang sheers in the same way as you would all other curtains. If you are using them with heavier curtains, use a double track. Heavy cotton lace as a main curtain looks handsome hung from a dark brown wooden pole. And translucent tweeds hung wall-to-wall, floor-to-ceiling are extremely effective against large expanses of glass – the more open the weave the more handsome they look.

Sheers don't have to be curtains: you can use fabric as fixed panels if you make a 1 in./25 mm hem each end, thread curtain wires through and fix to hooks at either side. Or sew tape (as for a pencil pleat heading) to the top and bottom, then fix as above.

Texture and pattern

The texture or weave of the fabric will show quite clearly against daylight. So when buying a sheer, always look at it against the light. The colour and pattern also take on a different dimension. A lacy, textured fabric or a softly patterned cheese cloth gives a room a refreshingly airy, light look if you use them as curtains and install a light-obscuring blind to pull down at night. Don't choose green net unless you fancy an underwater look.

Alternatives

Sheer fabrics can also be used for roller or roman blinds, or stretched across a frame as permanent window panels or screens. Venetians, shutters, Panelaire, pinoleum, Pleatex or Balastore blinds all do a similar job. Or you can fit frosted or stained glass, or buy special glass paint and stencil an all-over design, which will not be washed off when you clean the windows.

---

1 *This screen is designed by Nicholas Hill. It is of muslin, stretched over a wooden frame.*

---

2 *Frosted bathroom window is right up to date with a design etched into the glass.*

---

3 *Fixed panel of French caning lets the daylight in and smudges the view opposite.*

---

4 *While a creamy blind lets in plenty of light, the tree cut-out makes a movable, decorative screen.*

---

5 *Translucent Marimekko printed cotton makes a pretty alternative to net.*

---

6 *Victorian-style coarse white cotton curtains can be bleached snow-white.*

1

2

3

4

1 *It is possible to make roller blinds from some plain or patterned sheers. However, if the sheers seem liable to sag or stretch, it is usually more satisfactory to stretch and tack the fabric over a light wooden frame and leave it up as a permanent screen (of course you can untack the fabric and wash it when necessary). Many white-on-white sheers, whether they are woven or printed look much more effective seen flat, instead of bunched up as curtains. (There are several other practical ways of using white, as shown in this pretty room: washable tile floor, PVC-covered sofa, mop-down plastic tables and light, airy wicker chairs. The whole character of the room can be changed just by altering the colour of the lampshades and cushion.)*

2 *More useful light comes into a room through the upper part of windows, so this cunning scheme makes double good sense. Pinoleum is fixed as panels at the bottom half of the bay window for privacy, while roller blinds pull down from the top to meet half-way.*

3 *Gauzy light-filtering long curtains look much more effective if they have well-made pleated headings rather than skimpy gathers.*

4 *This window was a real challenge, since it looked out into a gloomy, internal light-well full of dustbins and dead leaves. Designer Raymond Elston made the room permanently, happily sunny by building an inner false window with an opaque blind and lighting it from the other side. The diffused light gives good all-round illumination for working, while the panels of glass have a pleasantly Japanese look about them.*

Windows

Individual and unusual treatment can disguise a dreary outlook or provide a focal point in a room. Here are a few examples, giving various degrees of privacy where it is needed, and a high degree of interest, achieved by simple means.

1 *Mirror glass can be fitted to plain glass in lower sashes and make a small bathroom or bedroom seem larger, and it's useful for shaving, or making up, as the light still comes in at the top.*

2 *If you are lucky enough to find, or inherit, a stained-glass masterpiece, it can look marvellous set into a new or existing frame.*

3 *Where the proportions of wall to window do not seem quite right, and you want another window to look at, why not hang a tapestry or a painting of a window. This is a woven tapestry by Edith Carruthers.*

4 *Windows facing a depressing blank wall can be covered from the outside by climbing plants: light filtering through the leaves looks sensational, although it must be admitted that the greenery will block out some of the light.*

(Opposite) If you fit shelves across a dull window and grow plants which enjoy the sunlight, it becomes a sort of one-sided greenhouse. The shelves, of course, must lift out easily for window cleaning, but the extra bother is amply repaid by the pleasant looks of thriving growing things.

Windows
14/15 Types and treatment

Bay Windows

Plan the treatment thinking of the whole bay as a single unit.

Curtains: Floor-length curtains on a track following the line of the windows to draw back to walls at the side of the windows during the day. (Avoid bunching curtains at the edge of each pane.)

Floor-length curtains on a track straight across the bay, cutting it off at night, drawing back to side walls by day. Track can be mounted in ceiling.

Nets/sheers: Can either be in addition to or instead of floor-length curtains. Use slim track following line of windows.

Sill-length curtains to reveal either window seat and/or radiators beneath window bay. Use track following line of windows. Use double track if nets/sheers are to be mounted as well.

Blinds: Plan to have one blind per window, checking that the fittings will not overlap or snag in the angles of the bay. Choose from: roller blinds; roman blinds; venetian blinds; Pleatex blinds; vertical louvres.

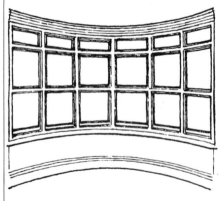

Bow windows

Again plan the treatment, thinking of the whole bow as one unit.
Curtains: As for bay windows.
Blinds: Vertical louvres, curved track.

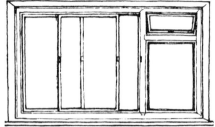

Horizontal windows

Typical of modern houses. Often the curtains/blinds have to correct proportions of window/room.

Curtains: If windows are deep set with wide sills, sill-length curtains inside the window frame are possible.

Full-length curtains on decorative poles or on invisible tracks above the window are better for shallow windows, or those whose proportions need correcting. The track can be placed way above the window or even in the ceiling and extended either side as necessary.

Nets/sheers: Mount inside the window frame or parallel (on double tracks) with full-length curtains.

Blinds: Roller blinds, roman blinds, Pleatex, venetian and vertical louvre blinds can all be used. Fit over window area. If width of window is more than 48 in. have two or more blinds of equal width side by side. Large areas of venetian blinds look warmer if wooden slats are chosen rather than metal ones.

Sliding panels or louvred pine shutters can be arranged to stack up against, or beside, the inside wall of the window.

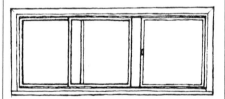

High clerestory type

If these are not overlooked and light coming in is no problem, these are best left uncurtained.

To keep light out: Venetian blinds (with wooden slats) with cords and cleats for ground-level control, or roller blinds with extra-long pull-cords.

Casement Windows

In groups of one, two, three or four, usually outward opening.

Curtains: If windows are deep set, curtains can be mounted inside the window frame on invisible track.

Sill-length or floor-length curtains can be mounted outside frame on visible track or on a decorative pole. Preferably without pelmet.

Nets/sheers: Mount inside frame on invisible track or expanding wire.

Blinds: Any blinds can be mounted inside the window frame close to the window. The smaller the window the simpler the blind should be.

Inward-opening casements:

Mount nets/sheers on expanding wire on to the windows themselves, or choose French-type wooden shutters that are fixed on or into the outside wall.

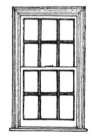

Georgian sash windows

Make the most of the proportions of these windows. No need for frilly tricks.

Shutters: Occasionally Georgian windows still have their original shutters. If so, no other covering is necessary; they just need stripping, or painting like the rest of the woodwork.

Curtains: Floor-length, mounted outside and above the frame on invisible tracks or decorative poles.

Sill-length curtains can be considered for windows with frames deep enough for window seats and/or radiators.

Nets/sheers: Mount inside the frame on invisible track or expanding wire.

Blinds: Roller blinds are best, others may detract from the line of the window.

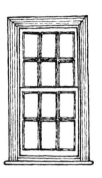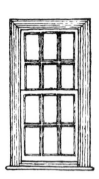

Pairs of windows

Plan to treat as a single unit, especially if they are a well-proportioned pair.

Curtains: On one track across the top of both windows, either on an invisible or a decorative pole track. Curtains should draw back symmetrically at either side or in centre as well. Floor-length curtains look best.

Nets/sheers: If windows have good surrounds, fit these inside the frames, otherwise run as curtains above them.

Blinds: Use matching pairs of roller blinds, roman blinds, Pleatex, venetian blinds or vertical louvres.

Fabric screens: Fabric panels mounted on sliding screens are an expensive solution, not worth doing unless the pattern on the screens is sensational.

Uneven pairs of windows

Treat as one unit – see above.

Curtains: Use an invisible track or a decorative pole and have full-length curtains which cover the whole wall when drawn, and pull back well to each side when they are opened.

Nets/sheers: Double up with full-length curtains.

Blinds: Choose roller blinds or roman blinds and match to wallpaper and curtains, to make the separate windows into one pleasant unit.

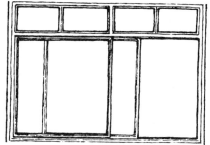

Picture windows

A modern type of window which reaches to the floor and opens to provide access to a garden, patio or balcony.

Curtains: Full-length to cover whole wall or section of wall in which windows feature. Mount on a decorative pole or invisible track, and extend so curtains draw back to leave opening clear.

Curtains provide useful insulation if they are lined and interlined; this is necessary unless windows are going to be double-glazed.

Nets/sheers: Can be doubled up with the curtains, but are not recommended for picture windows which open.

Blinds: Roman blinds or roller blinds mounted inside the window frame, usually in sets of two or more.

Shutters: Full-length fold-back or slide-back pine louvre panels.

French windows

If inward-opening single door, fit door-sized curtains on a hinged rod which will swing the curtains clear of the door, or fix curtains on to the door itself by mounting on expanding wire.

If a complex of doors and windows leads into a garden, treat them as if they were one single unit.

Curtains: Mount above the frame on an extended pole or track so that they draw back against the wall.

Blinds: Sets of roller, or roman, or pinoleum blinds mounted above doors and windows.

Shutters: If the complex is neatly designed and deep set, shutters can fold back into the sides of the frame.

Arched windows

These windows are best left alone. If curtains and blinds are necessary they should be planned to show the arch top as much as possible.

Curtains: Mount sill- or floor-length curtains on invisible track or a decorative pole well above top of window, long enough for the curtains to be drawn well clear of the window.

Nets/sheers: Not suitable.

Blinds: Roller blinds fixed to the sill can be pulled upwards by a cord and pulley to cover the window.

Shutters: Custom-made half-arch wood shutters can fold against the wall by day, close over window at night.

Moroccan grille: For a window with a poor outlook, fix a shaped screen of decoratively perforated hardboard in front of the window, and a light behind.

Semicircular window

If not overlooked, leave. If overlooked put in pearly or sandblasted glass, or decorate with semi-permanent artwork.

Round windows

If not overlooked, leave. If overlooked treat as above, or put in fabric panel or Moroccan grille.

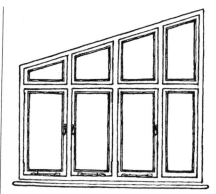

Windows with sloping top

Usually caused by a sloping ceiling.

Curtains: Hang from top horizontal line on invisible track or decorative pole (café curtains). Keep track length within width of frame. Leave top bare.

Nets/sheers: Could cover whole window if fixed along top on expanding wire. Not advisable if windows are constantly opened and shut.

Blinds: Roller blinds, roman blinds, venetian blinds can all be mounted at the horizontal level, leaving top part bare.

Vertical louvres could be mounted and fixed to cover whole window.

Shutters: Custom-built panels (wood) in two parts: one to hinge over rectangular part of window, the second attached to top slope and pulled up during day to rest against ceiling.

Pivot windows

Total privacy is impossible unless the pivoting window is to be opened only on warm, sunny days, in which case treat as sash or casement windows.

Horizontal pivots: Curtains can be fixed to the pivoting window on rods or expanding wire, so that when the window opens, the curtains do, too. Café curtains can be mounted on a decorative pole across the pivot level.

Blinds: A Pleatex blind can be fixed to the pivoting window, top and bottom.

Vertical pivots

Fix curtains or Pleatex blind to window frame as above.

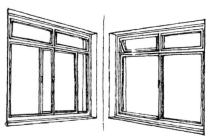

Corner windows

Where the windows meet at the corner with minimum space in between.

Curtains: Mount above on invisible track, to draw back to the outside edges of windows. Floor-length or sill-length (if there is a window seat and/or radiator beneath) with nets/sheers on a separate, inside track if required.

Blinds: Vertical louvres only: other types of blinds will snag each other where they meet at the corner.

Dormer windows

Treat as casement windows if the sides are not glazed. Fit tracks or blind fittings inside frame. Nets/sheers can be mounted on double track with curtains.

For glass sides: leave bare if not overlooked. If curtains are essential, run track right along top of window, doubling up with nets/sheers if desired.

Skylight

Privacy is seldom necessary, but often light has to be prevented from entering.

Curtains: Fix on to window itself on expanding wire, or mount on decorative poles fixed on to ceiling beside window.

Blinds: Pleatex blinds, roller blinds or venetian blinds can be mounted on special fixings.

Windows
16 Leave it alone

Some windows look best without curtains or blinds, for example, picture windows with a panoramic view or windows which overlook a beautiful garden, which can be floodlit at night.

1 *An eye for an eye : brilliant Italian view framed by a window shaped like an eye. Just imagine how a curtain would spoil the whole effect.*

2 *This deep-set little window with its pretty arch, green-stained wood, and etched glass would be quite spoiled by curtains.*

3 *Tiny windows should be treated like miniature pictures in a frame.*

4 *If the window frame itself is beautiful . . . if the top of it is curved . . . if glass is delicately tinted . . . if there's a beautiful vine outside . . . try to leave it alone.*

5 *Windows that give a tantalizing sliver of a view are often the most exciting. And notice how beautifully light floods straight across the floor from this full-length window. The only possible treatment here would be a roller blind.*

6 *Instead of always shutting out the outside world at night why not give the neighbours a treat by burning candles in the window. Their bright reflection in the glass makes it hard to see in anyway.*

7 *Sometimes an old window has charming panes of etched or richly coloured glass. Once again, consider leaving it bare and simple.*

8 *This window is made from a single pane of glass set into the wall. What makes it so effective is the crisp white reveal against the bright ochre wall.*

1

2

3

4

5

6

7

8

Lighting/1

The way colours, forms and textures appear to the eye depends upon light, either natural or artificial. Used imaginatively, in the ways that lighting can be deployed, it can make the most contribution to the look of your home. Bad lighting can make a beautifully furnished home dull and grey, but good lighting can add excitement, drama and warmth to even an ordinary interior.

At the same time that light illuminates, it creates shadows, and the stronger and narrower the beam, the more shadow is created. For instance, a tree in bright sunshine will cast a strong shadow, but on a cloudy day, when light is dispersed over the sky, there is no shadow. In the same way, a spotlight throws a piece of sculpture into relief, while a row of fluorescent lights flattens the form.

This chapter is primarily about how to use electric light, but the effect of daylight is equally important, and you need to plan a room to work for both.

Methods of lighting

The visual shape, size and atmosphere of any space is directly dependent on the quality of light introduced into it. There are various methods of lighting a space, ranging from a single lamp bulb hanging from a flex in the middle of the ceiling (the film cliché of poverty) to an array of table, standard and picture lights dotted around a room, or a sophisticated combination of devices, such as spotlights, downlighters, wallwashers and moving-effects lights. If a room is too high, too large or too small, lighting can do a lot to help correct the shape – for example, lights washing the walls will make a room seem larger, while low lamps that let no light out at the top will make it seem lower. The problem is to decide what is most suitable for you.

Different functions demand different lighting solutions. Spotlights, floods, downlighters, low-voltage spots and dimmers are among the comparatively recent developments which are now available for the home, and the main types of fittings are described and illustrated here.

Planning

It is essential to work out a furnishing plan before deciding on positions and types of light fittings. Allow for greater flexibility in the living-room than you would in the kitchen, say, where the light is directly related to specific jobs.

Make sure that switches are where you need them; within easy reach of the front door; by the bedside light; at the top and bottom of your stairs. (Two-way switches are essential in halls and

Pools of subdued light from low-level lamps give this high-ceilinged room a friendly look. A ceiling spot turns the table into a focal point, another washes the wall .

staircases. Nothing is more frustrating than having to feel one's way along a dark passage to turn on the light.)

Remember also to take into consideration outside areas such as the front porch, back door or garage.

Any electrical work, such as putting in extra sockets, must be done by a qualified electrician. Don't despair if you can't afford to install a whole new lighting scheme or if it's not allowed, as in some rented accommodation. Flexible lighting can be achieved with the help of standard lamps, each carrying a number

of adjustable spotlights, or by using a light track on the ceiling which co-incides with an existing central outlet.

A word about terminology. What the Trade calls a lamp, most ordinary mortals call a bulb. In this chapter the part that lights up is called a bulb and a fitting is called a lamp.

How to decide

Many rooms are multi-purpose and the use to which they are put by family or friends should be analysed before making any decisions.

This may mean several different kinds of light distribution. For instance, in just one room you may need a light over the dining table, another on a desk, a separate reading light and a more general light.

Since eyes deteriorate with age, the average 60-year-old person needs about twice as much light as a 30-year-old for the same job. Dark walls/floors provide less reflection and require more light if the same degree of general illumination is required as for light-coloured walls.

You also need to balance light and shadow so that shapes aren't flattened. An evenly lit room with little shadow can very quickly become depressing. On the other hand, one or two areas of strong light and shadow can give interest to a room at night.

The type and angle of a light source can affect texture and colour. Light shining directly at a heavily textured wall effectively removes the texture; so will badly positioned fluorescent tubes. But if you mount a downlighter on the ceiling, above and close to the wall, the downward beam will accentuate the texture. Colour, too, can be enhanced or degraded, depending on the choice of bulb.

When choosing a lamp, ask yourself whether it harmonizes with the general decoration scheme; whether it is reasonably efficient in terms of bulb life; and whether it is easy to maintain and clean as well as being able to withstand the hazards of normal domestic activities.

How do you decide which type of light to use when working out the scheme for each area of your house? The selection depends on the answers to several important questions which you first need to ask about each space which you have designated to your various activities.

- [ ] To what use will the various areas in your home be put?
- [ ] What type of light is needed – direct, indirect, static, adjustable, strong or background light?
- [ ] Will the amount of light on all horizontal and vertical surfaces be sufficient for your purposes?
- [ ] Will sufficient shadows be created to avoid flatness and enhance colour and texture?
- [ ] Are there enough existing sockets, outlets and switches? Are they in the right place?
- [ ] If you are re-wiring from scratch, have you worked out the best position not only for sockets and switches, but also for wall and ceiling outlets?
- [ ] What kind of lamp-shade or fitting will suit the style of your room?

Lighting

Before any decisions are made about individual fittings, each room has to be planned according to its functions and layout. At this stage, it is useful to have an overall picture of what is available.

The many different shapes and sizes of fittings in the shops can be confusing, although the ways in which they distribute light are really very few. Once they are grouped under simple headings, as here, it becomes much easier for you to decide what fittings are suitable for which purpose.

The many technical terms used by the lighting industry have been known to confuse even designers and architects, let alone the layman; so again we use the simpler classifications.

General light

By general light we mean light that shines unhindered in all directions from the source. This can mean a bare tungsten or fluorescent bulb, or one with a diffuser shade – a translucent covering over the bulb which distributes the light without glare.

Under this heading come paper and glass globes, table and standard lamps with glass or other translucent shades, and ceiling or wall-mounted opaline lights. A paraffin lamp also gives a general light, although anyone who has ever tried to do a job of work by one may be surprised to hear this.

Many rooms are lit solely by general light, frequently from one central pendent fitting, but this often results in monotony, with dull forms, little shadow and no highlights, and produces an inefficient light to work by.

Directional light

Any light beam that is trapped by a solid baffle or reflector shield, so that the light is forced to travel in one direction, is a directional light. This heading includes any light which shines straight at a person or object, and it may be a pendant, a table or standard lamp with an opaque shade, a jointed lamp, or an adjustable or fixed spotlight of any kind.

Reflected light

Where a light is bounced or reflected off a wall or ceiling instead of shining at a person or object, it is no longer a direct light. But it does come from a directional source. To get a clear understanding of this, think of an adjustable spotlight shining down on the book you are reading – this is direct light. Now think of it turned towards the wall so that you are reading by the light bounced back at you from the wall – this has now become reflected light. However, the light-source is still the spotlight, and so

the beam is directional, as would be the sheet of light from a fluorescent tube behind a pelmet.

Two-directional

This is a way of describing a fitting which has direct light shining out at both ends, such as a standard lamp with a drum shade. The light shining out at the top will probably be directed on to the ceiling or walls, and bounced back.

Some light fittings combine directional and general light. For instance, a pendent light with a semi-translucent shade throws a strong light downwards but also allows a certain amount of light out through the shade.

Spotlights

A spot is a particular type of directional light, projecting a controlled, intensified beam on to a object. It can be used for dramatic display effects as well as in situations where a strong, direct light is essential for some specific job or work. There are three main types of spotlight. The simplest sort has a reflector fitting which takes an ordinary domestic filament bulb. More sophisticated ones hold specially-designed spot bulbs and many of these are internally silvered with built-in reflectors for extra intensity. The third kind is fitted with low-voltage transformers for narrow beams on small objects. They can be fixed or adjustable, and can be used singly, in groups clipped on a ceiling track, or in twos and threes on a standard or table lamp.

Uplighters and downlighters

Downlighters are forms of spotlights that provide narrow beams spreading down to the floor, the width of the beam varying according to the fitting. They can be fully recessed in the ceiling, semi-recessed so that some of the fitting protrudes, or mounted on the surface, and are often designed with some form of anti-glare device.

Multigrooves, spillrings and pinhole spots are all forms of downlighters. They are called wallwashers when angled to "wash" or bathe a wall in light.

There are also uplighters and other specialized spotlights, such as "eyeball" or framing spots, for lighting defined areas – paintings for instance, which can be lit only over the actual image.

Decoration and effects

Some fittings are designed to be decorative rather than useful. For instance, coloured lights can be projected on to a wall via a spotlight and colourwheel unit, or by strobe lights flashed at irregular intervals. Or the fitting itself can become a piece of light sculpture.

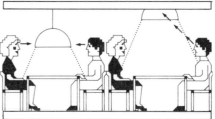

Directional pendant has opaque shade to shine downwards in a pool of light. Practical for dining as long as light is kept out of diners' eyes. A deep shade and adjustable rise-and-fall fitting will ensure this.

A directional standard makes a good reading lamp and can be moved where needed. It can shine over the reader's shoulder on to the page, or be turned towards the wall for a more comfortable light.

Directional table or desk lamps should light the work in hand without dazzling the user. The light should shine down, as here, and is often best when adjustable. A clamp is practical where space is limited.

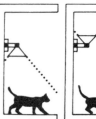

An adjustable directional wall light can be positioned to light a picture, or a table below, to bounce light off the ceiling or wall. If you only need it to do one constant job, a non-jointed spotlight will do.

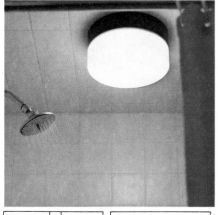

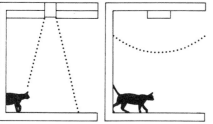

A ceiling-mounted light with a translucent shade gives an overall general light, best teamed with other types to avoid flatness. Some ceiling fittings are semi- or fully-recessed, which restricts downward light.

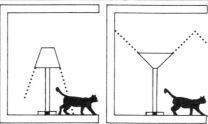

Standard floor lamps are useful in changing situations. They give general or directional light depending on shade – up, down or up and down. Semi-translucent shades let a little light through sideways.

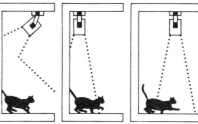

Ceiling-mounted spotlights – here fitted to a traditional ceiling rose – must be carefully positioned to avoid a searing glare in some-one's eyes. Adjustable spots can be directed on to pictures, a wall, or downwards.

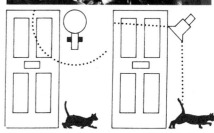

Porch lights welcome you home and help keep burglars away. They can be combined with the house number and be operated on a time-switch or photo-lens control. Choose one specifically designed for exterior use.

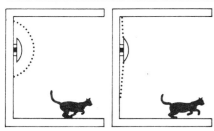

Bare bulbs round the mirror give a clear shadowless light for making up. For a softer light the bulb can be hidden behind an opaque reflector; the light is concentrated on to the wall.

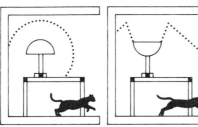

A general table lamp rarely lights a whole room but provides rather local areas of light. A restricting shade concentrates the light downward on to a bowl of flowers or other objects, or up to reflect off the ceiling.

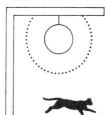

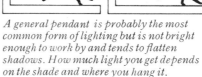

A general pendant is probably the most common form of lighting but is not bright enough to work by and tends to flatten shadows. How much light you get depends on the shade and where you hang it.

An open fire is also a form of light source, particularly comforting as daylight fades on cold winter evenings. Even if the fire gives off little heat the red glow can make you feel warmer.

Lighting
4/5 Fittings/types of bulbs

Dimmers (1–5)

Most dimmers are combined with the normal on/off switch and are easy to install. By turning the knob you can control the level of light from full brightness to a soft glow. Should a larger number of lights need to be controlled from one switch, there are units with higher loadings.

If you want to avoid re-wiring, or if you live in rented accommodation, choose a dimmer plug. This is rather like an adaptor. It plugs into 13 amp sockets and controls one or two fittings. Alternatively there is a bayonet-type adaptor which fixes into the bulb socket. However, both this and the dimmer plug use as much electricity when dimmed, whereas the switch/dimmer uses only the relative amount of wattage.

Anti-burglar lighting (6)

A determined burglar won't be put off by a landing light burning twenty-four hours a day while you are on holiday. Better to install a time-switch which turns lights on and off at certain times, or a more elaborate one to turn on lights at different times in different rooms.

Door switch (7)

Saves fumbling for a switch inside dark cupboards. A button set in the door frame turns the light on and off as the door is opened, or closed. Cars use the same device.

Photo-cell control (8)

Light-sensitive units can replace the switch of a porch or hall light, turning the light on at dusk, off in the morning. Usually fixed on a north-facing outside wall or where headlights cannot interfere with the control. Useful indoors, as an anti-burglar device.

Lamp clamp (9)

Many lamps, particularly spotlights or jointed lamps, are available with fitments for clamping them to a desk or shelf.

Detachable ceiling rose (10)

A two-part device that is useful if a lamp fitting needs to be cleaned occasionally. The lower part slides out; the upper, which is connected to the mains, remains fixed to the ceiling.

Light spreader (11)

Used to carry lamps to various parts of a room from a single centre outlet. The flexes (up to five) can be fixed to the ceiling immediately above the points where light is needed.

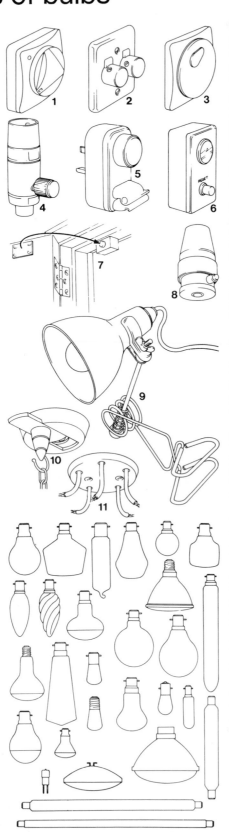

Rise and fall fitting

Pendent lamps can be raised or lowered with this fitting, which is particularly useful over dining tables. Finger-tip control is provided by a counterweight.

Incandescent bulbs

Most bulbs used in the home are tungsten wire inside the glass bulb: the hotter the wire, the brighter the light. A low voltage transformer can be used to produce the same amount of light from a lower wattage of bulb. Lower heat makes a higher level of brightness possible.

G.L.S.: General Lighting Service bulbs (15-200 watts) come clear, pearl or silica-coated. Clear bulbs are best where the fitting has an efficient reflector; the silica-coated bulb provides greater diffusion of light. Average life, 1000 hours.

I.S.L.: Internally Silvered Lamps (40-150 watts) have a built-in reflector, giving an accurately controlled beam, and are used for spotlighting and general floodlighting. Average life, 800 hours.

Standard Par 38 (Coolbeam): A pressed armoured glass reflector (100, 150, 300 watts), specially designed to reduce heat output in the beam. The heat is transferred to the holder and therefore these bulbs should be used only in specified fittings. Also suitable for outdoor use. Average life, 1500 hours.

Crown silvered: Also known as top silvered, or bowl silvered (100 watts). When used with a specially designed parabolic reflector these bulbs provide an accurately controlled and adjustable beam with little spill or glare. Average life, 1000 hours.

Tubular filament: Gives a warmer light than a fluorescent fitting, but is less efficient and shorter lived. Various sizes.

Fluorescent bulbs

(From 40 to 125 watts.) Fluorescent light functions by arcing between two cathodes at each end of a tube, the quality and colour of light depending on phosphor content. Tubes can be straight or circular. Very efficient light, providing about three times as much light as a tungsten bulb of the same wattage and an average life of 5000 hours. However, because there is no single light source as in a filament bulb, the overall flood of light reduces form and shadow. This can be an asset in a kitchen or workshop, where shadow is a nuisance. It also tends to distort colour, and it is therefore essential that the correct colour tube is chosen for each particular task. They can be masked either by a baffle or by a panel of milky Perspex to avoid glare.

Colour 27 de luxe warm white: This is the nearest to tungsten and can be used in conjunction with it. It can be used, if diffused, in bathrooms and kitchens.

De luxe natural: Provides reasonably good colour quality with some warmth. The colour of meat in supermarkets is improved with this lamp! It can be used in kitchens, but might be too cold for bathrooms.

Colour 34 natural: This simulates daylight, and is useful in areas where there is not enough natural daylight and artificial lights are required at all times.

Note: Fluorescent tubes with the misleading names like "warm white", "white" and "daylight" are also available but they emphasize greens and yellows while killing pinks, and that means complexions. To be avoided.

How bright a bulb?

Unless a fitting specifically requires lower wattage, try to use bright bulbs. For example: table lights – 100-150 watts. Floor standards – 150 watt or 2 × 60 watts. Spots – wattage depends on the reflector, so check.

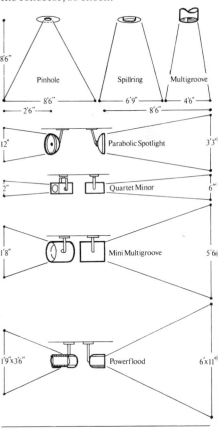

(*Opposite*) *The exception which proves the rule – a beautiful bare bulb. But these handblown bulbs designed by Castiglione glow like candles and are pleasantly irregular. Decorative rather than effective, they need other light in a supporting role.*

Lighting

How much and what kind of light you need depends on what you want it to do. For specific jobs, like writing or carpentry, you need a bright light, free from glare. Listening to music or watching television is more comfortable with a softer, background light. Below are suggestions on how to handle some typical lighting situations.

Reading

The light should be a reasonable distance behind the reader, otherwise the page becomes too bright. It should shine down over his shoulder. If there is no other light in the room, you may get "discomfort-glare", as a result of the harsh contrast between light and darkness. Some background light from another source will balance the two.

Writing

A right-handed person should have light shining down over his left shoulder. Alternatively, an adjustable desk- or wall-mounted light should throw light on to the work in hand. But make sure that the bare bulb cannot be seen by the user; too much contrast between the light and the shade will again cause discomfort-glare.

Reading in bed

The most considerate kinds of lights for reading in bed are wall-mounted, individual swivel spots, one on either side. Alternatively, you may prefer a table lamp – tall enough to throw light on to the page. Switches should be by the bed.

Sewing

Most modern sewing machines have their own light. You may find this enough with other light nearby. Otherwise, use a jointed lamp with a wide beam, clipped to the table or wall-mounted with a swivel arm.

Making up

Don't put a light above the mirror as it will make shadows under the eyes, nose and chin. It is better to put fairly strong lights on either side of the mirror, positioned so that they shine on you, not on it.

Shaving

Lighting that's suitable for making-up will do for shaving as well. You can get lighting and shaver sockets combined in one unit.

When you dress, the light must illuminate you, not the mirror. A ceiling-mounted light should come between the mirror and where you normally stand, nearer you than the mirror.

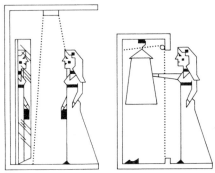

Cupboards and closets

Fix tungsten strip lights behind a batten just inside the top of a clothes cupboard, so that light shines on to the clothes. Then install a door switch which will operate automatically as you open and close it.

Dining

A pendent light with an opaque shade over it, fitted to a rise and fall mechanism, must throw light on to the table, not into the eyes of the eaters, without obscuring the view across the table. A rectangular table may need two pendants, or two downlighters. If you have candles, make sure that they are above or below eye level. You need a reasonably well lit area for serving, so that you can tell the difference between a sauté potato and a pickled walnut.

Washing up

A light in the middle of the ceiling would throw your shadow over the washing-up. Fix a downlighter or ceiling-mounted light with spot diffuser above the sink, or lengthen the flex from the centre rose and run it over a ceiling hook, to drop down over the basin.

Worktop below storage

A tungsten or fluorescent colour strip light, fixed behind a batten on the underside of high level storage, makes a good work light.

Television

Never view with all the lights off, as this is a severe strain on the eyes. However, a light near the viewers reflects on the screen. If the set is on a shelf, a tungsten strip-light concealed behind the set, or on a different level, is adequate.

With a free-standing set, choose a standard lamp with light directed to the floor or wall. Best of all are ceiling downlighters which illuminate the floor without interfering with the screen.

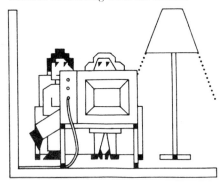

Pictures

Traditionally, a picture is lit from above, and you can buy specific fittings to do this. You can also use parabolic spots fixed to the wall or ceiling, or a specially designed framing spot which can be adjusted to the exact size of the picture. Glass-covered pictures or prints often have a mirror effect, especially if dark paper or inks have been used. Non-reflective picture glass is available, though it has a slightly dulling effect.

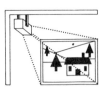 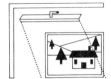

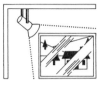

Halls and stairs

Lighting should make a clear distinction between tread and riser. Therefore, you need a strong light above the stairs, and a lesser one below, for balance. Never let light shine directly into anyone's eyes. A low-cost light near steps or landings can be left on all night if there are children or old people.

Alcoves (aerial view)

How you light the inside of an alcove depends on the effect you are after, on what you mean to display and the type of shelving.

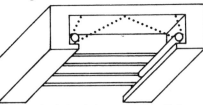

Wooden built-in shelves can all be lit by a vertical fluorescent strip on either side of the front hidden by battens which can be papered or painted to match the wall.

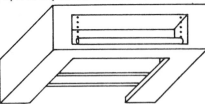

Where there are glass shelves, a single horizontal strip light can be concealed behind a baffle-board at the top of the alcove.

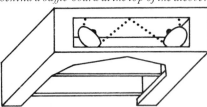

If the back of the shelves does not go to full depth, spots on either side at the top can be adjusted to light the wall behind.

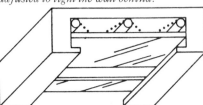

Vertical strip lights fixed to the back wall concealed by translucent glass or Perspex give a good glare-free background light, perhaps for a collection of glass objects.

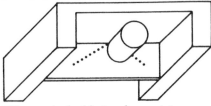

Where a single object such as a statue or a flower arrangement is to be lit, this can be done with a central top-mounted downlighter.

1 *Adjustable standard gives good direct light for reading, plus an extra bounced light for fill-in softness.*

2 *Dining by candlelight for atmosphere – low enough not to dazzle the diners – and candles, too, in the summertime fireplace.*

3 *Corridors need light on the floor to show changes of level or surface – and on walls at least as far up as the door handles and light switches.*

4 *Downlighters for working by need to be positioned at least 12 in./305 mm in front of you so that you don't get in your own light.*

5 *Strip lighting concealed by a batten, underneath the shelves, spreads light on to a working surface. Another above the shelves reflects light on to the ceiling.*

6 *As sunshine makes the relief of a facade come alive, so lighting can make the nooks and crannies of storage and display more exciting, as in this room by Max Clendinning.*

7 *Bedside lighting should be high enough to read by when well tucked up. An electrified oil lamp can add to the old-fashioned air of brass bedstead and Victorian oval mirror.*

8 *Pictures grouped on one wall are illuminated by a wash of recessed tungsten strip lighting.*

9 *A washer spotlight pointed at the sloping white ceiling makes all sorts of cool, sculptured planes appear in the room. Candles by the fireplaces give a contrasting gleam of warmth.*

Lighting
8/9 Creating mood and atmosphere

Ceiling recessed spotlights and a bold table lamp give an awareness of texture.

Bright pools of light alternating with shadow can give a warm welcome on a dark night.

Table and wall lights wash the walls, while a few areas only are put into sharp focus by spotlights.

Maximum candle-power from these low, fat candles bathes diners in a romantic light.

(Opposite) Angled spotlights have the advantage of being flexible, so that you can move them to illumine different objects and textures.

Lighting
10/11 Planning each room

Once you have decided how your rooms will be furnished, use your room plans to work out the lighting. Bear in mind how the natural daylight source relates to the lighting scheme. Make a list of the various goings on that have to be catered for, homework, sewing, cooking, and so on, then decide what fittings you need. To be efficient, they must be fitted with the right type of bulbs of the correct wattage. If you are re-wiring, adding socket outlets, re-positioning or changing switches, make all your decisions before the electrician starts work. Then give him the clearest possible instructions. And make sure he does the work before the room is decorated!

The room plans with suggested lighting schemes shown here may not match your requirements exactly, but the principles remain the same.

Living room

Since this is where most of your life will be spent, it is where your lighting needs to be most adaptable. At any given moment there may be several people all doing different things.

To start with, you probably have an outlet in the middle of the ceiling, and a socket or two in the skirting. To get away from a central light, you might loop a long flex from the centre to a ceiling hook at one end of the room and suspend a pendent light over a coffee table. (Be sure you don't overload the sockets if you are adding TV, heaters, or other gadgets. From each socket, you can draw 3120 watts, and a one-bar fire will use 1000 watts, colour TV uses 350 – black and white 150 – an electric iron 1250 watts.)

Dimmer switches enable you to ring the changes: think of the living room as a kind of theatre.

1 *Downlighters take over from decoratively screened windows as daylight fades.*

2 *Wall-mounted fitting adds light relief to a room designed by Quasar Khanh.*

3 *Table lamp with two-directional drum shade lights both shelves and tabletop.*

4 *Individually lit areas combine to provide a dramatic scheme.*

5 *Ceiling-mounted adjustable spots show up the wall-texture ; the low lamp produces a pool of gentler light.*

6 *Chrome tub-shaped uplighters under dried cow parsley make interesting patterns. Downlighters and standard lamps give directional light where needed.*

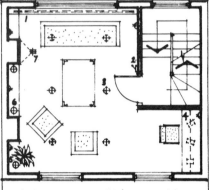

1. full length discreet pelmet lighting – over curtain.
2. switch panel – dim for 3 downlights, pelmet and lykespan.
3. 6 downlight fittings with dimming facility.
4. lighting track over with 3 spot-lamps.
5. uplight fitting behind plants.
6. double socket for occasional lamps. 7. picture spot over.

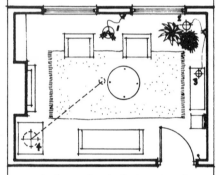

1. 2 spot adjustable floor-standing lamp. – for reading.
2. uplight fitting behind plants. – for dramatic effect.
3. small spot-lamp or standard shaded lamp on sideboard.
4. low-level pendent lamp (eg: Japanese paper shade) – flex extended across ceiling from centre rose.

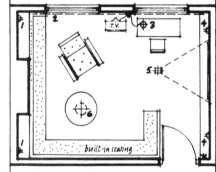

1. double sockets to take spot-lamp fittings or alcove standard lamps :– bookshelves and storage in alcoves.
2. full length discreet pelmet lighting – over curtain.
3. adjustable desk lamp.
4. double sockets to take HI-FI etc – storage-shelves unit.
5. ceiling mounted picture-framing spot-light.
6. Rise and fall low pendent fitting over table.

1

2

5

3

4

6

Main bedroom

Bedroom lighting should be flexible – warm and relaxing, yet bright enough to let you see the creases in the clothes you are putting on. You need a good general light to dress by; if there's a long mirror, position the light to shine on you, not the mirror. A dressing table light needs to be strong enough to make up by, and bedside lights should be set high enough to illuminate the page of your bed-time book but not shine on your sleeping partner. Lights inside your cupboard are a worthwhile luxury, but a ceiling spot, angled to shine into the cupboard, is an adequate substitute.

You can change atmosphere and mood completely with dimmer switches, or low wattage coloured lamps.

Single bedroom

This needs more or less the same kind of lighting as the main bedroom. If the room is also used for working or studying you will need a good direct light, preferably adjustable on or over the desk or table. An Anglepoise could double as bedside and desk light.

Child's room

Make sure that the light fittings are out of reach. If you have socket outlets they should be child-proof. Use safety plugs; children are naturally inquisitive and given to poking things into sockets.

Small children spend a lot of time playing on the floor, so it should be well lit. A dimmer control could be a useful alternative to a night light.

Older children are going to read in bed, so provide adequate bedside lights.

---

1 *Pivoting lamps, fixed high for bedtime reading, can swivel round to illuminate other parts of the room.*

2 *The darker the decorations, the more dramatic are shafts of light from spots set into the ceiling.*

3 *Anglepoise lamps successfully come out of the study and into the bedroom.*

4 *Two spotlights, fixed to point downwards, give an excellent light to make up by.*

5 *Interior wardrobe lighting, from a source that is well-concealed.*

6 *Well spaced wall-mounted lights around the mirror look pleasant.*

7 *Pliable lamp with silvered reflector bulb needs no shade.*

8 *For children's bedtime reading, a lamp mounted on the wall.*

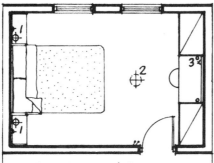

1. individually switched bed-side table spots.
2. pendent or ceiling mounted diffuser.
3. tungsten strip dressing table lighting.

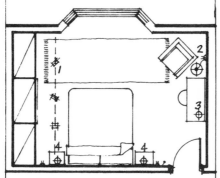

1. Lighting track and 3 spot lights over.
2. adjustable floor-standing lamp.
3. adjustable desk lamp.
4. wall mounted reading lights.

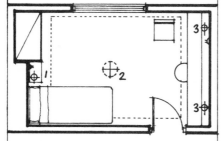

1. adjustable bedside reading lamp.
2. centrally mounted diffuser fitting.
3. adjustable desk lamps over worktop.

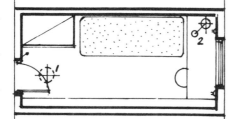

1. general diffuser fitting ceiling mounted.
2. adjustable desk lamp.

Lighting
12/13 Planning each room

Since lighting, more than any other element, contributes to the atmosphere of a room, it needs to be especially carefully planned for eating rooms.

For family meals and dinner parties, concentrate the main light on to the table, having only a very low background light for the rest of the room. No background light at all is too great a contrast and a strain on the eyes.

A rise-and-fall pendant over the table does this job well, though you must choose a deep shade for it.

Where the room will be used in a more general way, you may need a higher level of lighting. This can be provided by a series of lights round the room, adjustable spotlights on a single track or downlighters above the dining table. Dimmer switches enable you to change to more intimate lighting or even to dim them down to background level and put candles on the table.

Your background light can come from wall-washers, downlighters over a sideboard, strip lights behind a shelf or pelmet, spotlights aimed at pictures, or an illuminated alcove or glass cabinet.

Hall

As often as not, the hall has one ceiling outlet and that probably in the wrong place. Although it is feasible to light the hall with one general pendent light, if this is dreary (or even unsafe) it is simple to take a second flex from the same outlet, loop it across the ceiling, and hang a second light from a ceiling hook.

A more sophisticated way to light the hall is with a series of downlighters and wall-washers. The wiring for these will have to be chased into the wall, unless you have them mounted on a light track.

As well as good general light in the hall you will probably need subsidiary lighting by the telephone, coats, any mirrors you have, and under the stairs.

Hanging cupboards could have interior lights, or a tungsten strip on the ceiling above.

1 *Pendent light over a circular dining table in all-purpose family room where a non-glare direct light will be needed.*

2 *A ceiling spot angled at the wall bounces light back to the eating area of an open-plan flat designed by Santa Raymond.*

3 *A semi-recessed ceiling spot in designer John Stefanides's room highlights picture and sideboard.*

4 *The focal point here is a beautiful mahogany chest set into a built-out recess and lit from above by two concealed strip lights.*

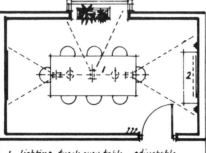

1. Lighting track over table — adjustable spot-lights to illuminate table, plants, walls and pictures: dimmer controls by door
2. shaded fluorescent picture lamp.

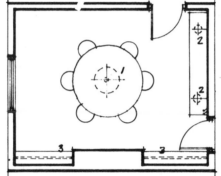

1. Rise and fall pendent fitting over table
2. 'wall-washer' spot lights over sideboard
3. concealed tungsten strip lighting in alcoves

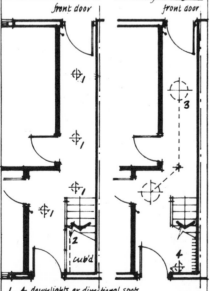

new wiring — front door
existing wiring — front door

1. 4 downlights or directional spots
2. concealed tungsten strip switched on by door opng.
3. Jap. paper shades from common rose point
4. wall fitting for cloak room area.

1

2

3

4

If a room is going to perform several different functions your lighting needs exceptionally careful planning.

Bed-sitting-room

A bed-sitting-room is equal to three or four rooms rolled into one, so you will need a very adaptable lighting plan.

In a room with cooking facilities you will need a good light over the cooker and sink-unit. If you have high level cupboards over a work surface, you could fit tungsten strip lights underneath them behind a pelmet board. You are also going to need a pleasant light to eat by, a bedside light, and a reading light in the sitting area, as well as a general one. A rise-and-fall pendent on a ceiling-mounted track could be the answer, as it would be mobile, variable in intensity, and more versatile than anything else.

Bathroom

A small bathroom may need only one general light, such as a ceiling-mounted glass or plastic diffuser. If you intend to make up in the bathroom, you will need a light on either side of the mirror; for shaving only, a light above it will do.

Special safety regulations apply to all fittings and switches in bathrooms, and you must check these before making any changes to your existing fittings. If you are short of space, you might consider some of the bathroom equipment that does more than one job, like a medicine cabinet with its own mirror and a built-in light, or a fluorescent tube fitting with a built-in shaving socket.

1 *A bed-sitting-room has an adjustable lamp clamped on to a high shelf which will serve as a general light and can be lowered to provide glare free lighting to eat or work by, or angled to shine on the seating area.*

2 *Bathroom mirror with glare-free lighting; you don't see the bulb itself because it is hidden behind a baffle board, and you don't see its reflection because of the narrower baffle which is placed between bulb and mirror.*

3 *An Edwardian-style bathroom has period light fittings of opaque glass. A modern downlighter and a concealed fluorescent tube discreetly drive away the shadows.*

4 *Bulbs set into a mirror surround give a "Star" dressing-room touch. The bulbs should be small, of a low wattage, and give off a white light.*

5 *Simple fluorescent strip displayed – with no attempt at concealment – above a bright, modern mirror.*

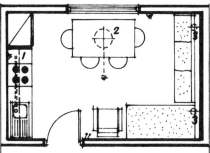

1. tungsten strip under wall cupboards over sink
2. Rise and fall Pendent fitting connected to centre rose fitting.
3. bed-head height adjustable spot lights.

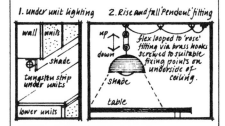

1. under unit lighting   2. Rise and fall Pendent fitting

wall units
shade
tungsten strip under units
lower units

up
down
flex looped to 'rose' fitting via brass hooks screwed to suitable fixing points on underside of ceiling.
shade
table

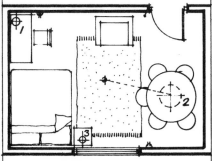

1. Adjustable desk lamp.
2. Rise and fall Pendent fitting or Jap. paper shade.
3. bedside reading lamp.

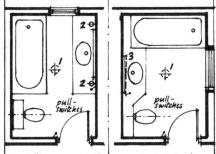

pull-switches
pull-switches

1. Ceiling mounted diffuser or simple shade fitting.
2. Tungsten strips or 'theatre' dressing room bulbs on either side of mirror.
3. diffused light/shaving point unit over mirror.

1

2

3

4

5

Lighting
14/15 Planning each room

As a rule, it is best to provide good general light, with stronger light for specific work areas, in all the rooms in which you are planning to do any sort of precision work.

Kitchens

Storage cupboards should, if possible, have lights inside them, just like the refrigerator and the oven.

Ceiling-mounted diffusers are a good source of general light; you may need more than one, depending on the size of your kitchen. However, ceiling light on its own can lack warmth and friendliness, and is sometimes hard to position so that no shadows fall on the surfaces where you are preparing food, cooking, or washing up. Strip lights fitted under the front of high-level cupboards and concealed from view make good worktop lights. If you use fluorescent tubes, make sure they are colour 27 de luxe warm white, as this is the colour of light that makes food look most appetizing and this is an important consideration, as any cook will know.

1 *An alternative to a central diffused light is this "halo" of low wattage bulbs, which provides plenty of light and is enhanced by its own reflection in the ultra-glossy ceiling.*

2 *Work-surface is lit by fluorescent strips concealed under the storage cupboards, which accentuate the change from light horizontal to dark vertical surfaces.*

3 *Pendent lights dropped low enough to shine on the work-surface and the sink. A fluorescent strip concealed in the alcove lights up the cooker.*

4 *The warm light in this pine kitchen comes from a downlighter over the work-surface and a pendent light in the eating area.*

5 *This stainless steel extractor hood above a stainless steel cooker/sink unit was designed by Gio Ponti. A light set into the hood provides a good light above the working-surfaces to light up the surface while coping with the steam and smells.*

6 *Two fluorescent strips above the sink wash the walls in this small kitchen while ceiling-recessed downlighters (not shown) provide a stronger light to work by.*

(Opposite)
A bright, cheerful kitchen with diffused lighting from above the false, slatted ceiling. The work areas are well lit by fluorescent tubes concealed under the storage units, and the central pendant hangs low enough not to glare in the eyes of of anyone working or eating.

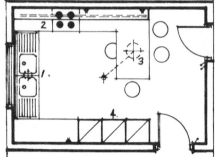

1. diffuser fitting over sink.
2. tungsten strip lighting under wall units.
3. adjustable pendant or downlighter.
4. wall oven and refrigerator with interior lights.

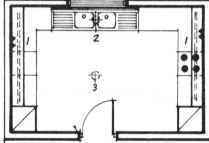

1. tungsten strip lighting under wall units.
2. diffuser fitting over sink.
3. central rose - diffuser or similar fitting.

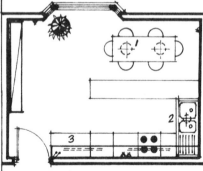

1. pendent fittings over table.
2. diffuser over sink.
3. tungsten strip lighting under wall units.

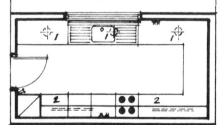

1. 3 diffusers over worktop and sink.
2. tungsten strip lighting under wall units.

1

2

3

4

5

6

Lighting
16 Something different

There is yet another way of using light – purely decoratively.

You can create a kaleidoscope of moving colour on wall or ceiling with a spotlight shining through a rotating wheel of coloured lenses. Perhaps you'd prefer a non-moving light sculpture in one corner of the room. There could be fat coils of light which weave in and out of open shelving or wriggle along the floor, or those outer space feeler-like waving wires with twinkling lights. Here are some more ideas:

1 *A garland of bulbs, hung at intervals along a continuous flex (needing only one socket outlet).*

2 *Flexible, tubular lighting-sculpture, with internally silvered bulbs.*

3 *Coloured spiralled flex-housing makes simple fixture into decorative feature.*

4 *Sun-King motif around opaline plastic fitting.*

5 *Internally-lit table pedestal with neon flower-sculpture.*

6 *Table with translucent acrylic top illuminated from within; flower lamp with stamen-shaped bulb.*

7 *Arc of white neon tube tops sculpture.*

8 *Tall arum lily makes clever use of elongated bulb.*

9 *Low voltage uplighters and "kinematic" display unit create flame patterns against the wall.*

10 *Earthenware drain-pipe; bulb bounces light off the ceiling. Lighting fixture can be set into concrete or braced against the inner walls.*

1

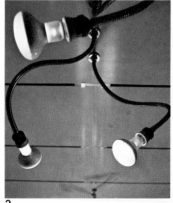

2

3

4

5

6

7

8

9

10

Colour/1

What is colour? To the scientist it is reflected light which, viewed through a prism, breaks into the visible spectrum.

To most of us, however, colour is a highly evocative and individual thing. What we associate with it as much as its appearance affects our reaction to it: even people who claim to hate, say, pale green, live happily with it when it is called "Avocado". Cream paint, for a time, was thought exceedingly boring, but lovingly applied by the gallon to acres of walls and called bamboo – a case of "a rose by any other name" such as "crushed raspberry" smelling a good deal more sweet.

Colour is potentially the most exciting and rewarding, as well as the most inexpensive, ingredient that goes into the making of a home. Used with flair, it can transform any interior. Conversely, insensitively handled, it can destroy even the most beautifully proportioned room.

Planners of colour schemes, however, must not be carried away by emotion alone. They must consider colours (and non-colours) in terms of materials: paint, stains, textiles, skins, leathers, marble and metal, before deciding on, say, a purple bathroom, a pink bedroom or a green kitchen.

Before you even start collecting paint samples of snips of colour, try to clear your mind of prejudice.

If you think you hate yellow, remember sunflowers, primroses, mimosa, honeysuckle, golden syrup, bananas, saffron.

Don't think Cream, Beige, or White – think bamboo, Mermaid roses, Iceberg roses, meringues chantilly, young walnuts, tobacco, French breakfast coffee.

The same goes for all the other colours. Make up your own associations, and allow your reactions to surprise you.

(Above) An object lesson in the use of colour that is simple, subtle and surprising.

Colour
2/3 The spectrum

Colour schemes fall, roughly, into groups: monochrome, related or contrasting.

Theoretically, a monochrome scheme features one basic colour in a variety of shades and textures. In practice, pin-prick accents of contrast tend to emphasize its monochrome nature.

Related schemes are made up of a combination of colours lying close together in the spectrum of the rainbow. Contrasts happen when the colours, or their weights, are widely different.

However, in decoration schemes, there are many subtleties to consider. They are hard to visualize beforehand, and difficult to put right once they have gone wrong, so it is as well to have some idea of how colours affect each other, and how the variation of a single detail can change the feel of the whole design.

The rules applied here to small sets can be applied to large areas; the principle remains, whether you're dealing with a small table or a grand piano.

The blacks, greys and whites.

(i) Dark on dark and silver – perhaps for a room that comes into its own at night. The print is translatable into curtains or cushions. The braid between wall and carpet gives a subtle but definite division.

(ii & iii) The same grey wall, with a paler carpet. Shiny white and chrome further dramatize the partnership. Where wall and carpet meet, bold stripes emphasize the colour-change in (ii).The skirting in (iii) is plain : the shaggy carpet provides tonal changes. Tiny red touches keep the set lively.

(iv) White on white : shaggy carpet as above – but the wall is not smooth. There are touches of pink and yellow. This can translate into textured whites, and bits of soft, related colours.

Browns, beiges and cream.

(i) The same principles as in the first of the greys apply, but the range of textures used is larger. This makes for richness, and can adapt to any monochrome scheme.

(ii) Compare this set with that on the left : the balance is altered, calling for an enlivening bit of colour at ground level : perhaps rugs or floor cushions.

(iii) The same warm brown wall looks cooler against stripped, waxed wood. Small coloured pattern might be interpreted in fabric. The hat suggests that darker pieces look well in this combination.

(iv) Beiges and whites are easy to live with. The paler the all-over scheme, the more responsive it becomes to colour accents.

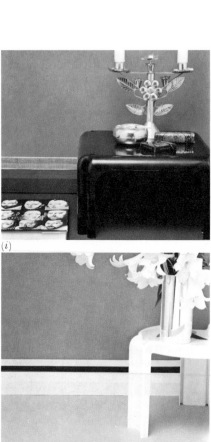

(i)

(ii)

(iii)

(i)

(ii)

(iii)

(iv)

(i)

(ii)

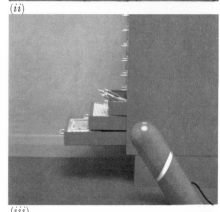

(iii)

(iv)

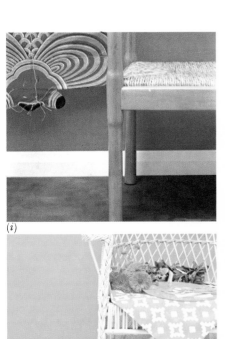

(i)

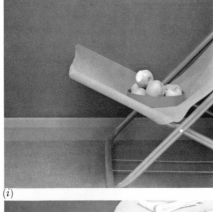

(i)

(i)

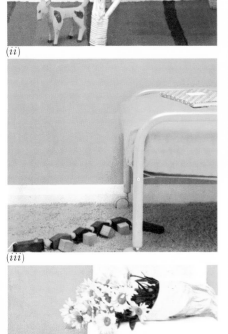

(ii)

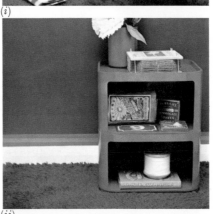

(ii)

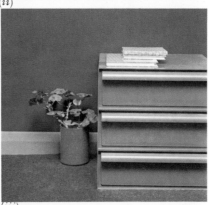

(ii)

(iii)

(iii)

(iii)

(iv)

(iv)

(iv)

The reds and the pinks.

(*i, ii, iii & iv*) all show various colours commonly thought not to "go" together. Although (*ii & iii*) share both wall and carpet colour, the respective weights change with the different skirting board treatments. (*iii*) is sparked up with chrome, and (*iv*) shows how cool pinks and whites look when there's a little creamy yellow to point them up.

Red, orange, yellow to green.

(*i*) Orangey reds can partner sharp pinks, other reds and russets. The glossy skirting prevents any Windsor Soup feeling where red meets brown. Further coolness is provided by natural wood and the rush seat, which could translate into straw or cane.

(*ii*) Yellow, contrary to rumour, is flattering. Here, the striped red carpet gives it warmth · the print brings out the sunshine quality. So does orange and chrome, as in the marigolds, the toy and the plate.

(*iii*) Yellow-on-yellow-on-yellow needs more courage than other schemes except perhaps one in greens alone. To intensify warm yellows, use sappy greens or olives.

(*iv*) For a look that is summery even in midwinter, think of a bunch of daisies. Use the clear yellow and the green, separating the two colours by the white for crispness.

Greens and blues.

(*i & ii*) Schemes made up in different shades of a single colour need the greatest variety of texture, so that light and shade come fully into play. Very striking colour arrangements are best kept to rooms not too frequently used, because one hardly wants to be overwhelmed by the effect from morning to night.

(*ii & iii*) When whites and yellows enter the green scene and the blues make their appearance, the atmosphere lightens and becomes less dramatic.

(*iv*) The green wall has been retained, but it looks paler because of the dark blue carpet, the chair and the shiny brown coffee pot.

The blues and their friends.

(*i, ii, iii & iv*) Unlike yellows and greens, the blues are mistakenly thought to be easy and commonplace. There is, however, nothing "safe" about any of these blue schemes; they are frankly dramatic, whether they are deep blue and white, or whether they contain areas of green, of purple and red, or, as in the bottom set, a deep blue carpet is teamed up with deep brown walls. The very nature of the blues seems to change according to the way in which they are used, and this applies to all the other colours in the spectrum.

Colour
4/5 Texture/pattern

Texture plays an extremely important part in the planning of any room. Consider, for example, the multiplicity of wall, floor and ceiling finishes on the market today and contrast the textural qualities of rough hessian with smooth plaster, a thick pile carpet with sealed cork tiles or an Anaglypta ceiling paper with tongued-and-grooved boarding, and you will see the variety of different surface effects you can achieve in a single colourway. Study this simple board presentation of some of the textured surface materials available to the interior designer of today – all composed in a related colour scheme of brown, beige and white.

Take soft floor coverings. Nowadays, carpets are available in a vast range of different qualities and designs ranging from herringbone textured ship's matting to softly looped Berber designs and loose long-haired rugs. Ceiling and wall cladding materials are equally varied and here we show the different textural effects of travertine marble matched with pitted insulating cork, rough brick and chunky insulating tiles – which in turn contrast sharply with the tough surface textures of wool wall cloth, natural hessian and sisal braids.

Lastly, from the host of different furnishing materials now in the shops, we have chosen to group quilted chintz with embroidered cotton; traditional English lace, a loosely woven Irish tweed upholstery cloth and a fine example of Indian crewel work. All add up to a striking display of texture on one board and show that there need be no lack of variety in a pale monochrome room scheme.

1 Irish tweed	**9** Wool wall-cloth	**17** Textured insulating board
2 Quilted chintz	**10 & 11** Hessian	**18** Cork
3 Long looped-pile	**12** Two-tone looped carpet	**19** English lace
4 Short curled-pipe	**13** Unglazed tiling	**20** Coarseweave linen
5 & 6 Quilted PVC	**14** Sisal matting	**21** Wool embroidered fabric
7 Flockati rug	**15** Wool braid	**22** Cut pile
8 Long pile rug	**16** Marble	

Pattern is as important as texture when it comes to planning a total room scheme. Examine the effect of a multi-striped fabric with a highly patterned Moroccan rug; look at the traditional William Morris wallpaper with a Liberty country cotton, and contrast a bold Marimekko furnishing textile with the intricate patterns on a Mexican blanket. You will realize the potential of pattern in a room, but remember, the success or failure of your scheme depends as much on the balance and proportions of the patterns used as on the actual patterns themselves.

Now look at this sample board presentation and consider each individual pattern in terms of its colour, scale and design as well as general relationship to the whole.

You will see, in skilful juxtaposition, a primitive Indian hand-printed silk with a bold, striped carpet design, a fragment of mirror embroidery from Kashmir, and a coarsely woven Moroccan braid. A fresh daisy-patterned fabric from France harmonizes superbly with a group of mini-prints from India, a square of traditional cotton gingham and a bold Art deco rainbow design – and elsewhere bold flower prints contrast well with striking geometric textiles in a well-balanced essay of pattern and colour.

Pattern, however, does not rest purely on textiles and carpets. Furniture and accessories make patterns of their own. Books on shelves, an arrangement of pictures, cane bentwood, collections of china and glass, multi-drawer storage units – all must be taken into consideration. Before you rush out and invest in yards of patterned curtain fabric or select a dizzy wallpaper design, make up a pattern board like this and study the effect they make together.

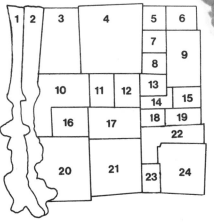

1 & 2 Mexican braid
3 Indian silk
4 Kashmir embroidery
5 Printed linen union
6 Geometric fabric
7 Wrapping paper
8 Woven upholstery cloth
9 Indian mini-print
10 Tufted carpet
11 & 12 French patterned fabric
13 Art deco fabric
14 & 15 Indian mini-print
16 Marimekko
17 Liberty cotton
18 Gingham
19 Geometric fabric
20 Liberty cotton print
21 Cotton fabric
22 & 23 Printed wallpaper
24 Cotton print

Colour
6/7 How to decorate one room

Working out a colour scheme for a whole house or flat is a daunting task, particularly if you are doing it for the first time. So, although you should think of the whole before planning any individual areas, try tackling one room first to give yourself confidence. In principle, the technique of interpreting a colour scheme can then be applied to any interior part of the house, from a guest bedroom to a children's bathroom. By using the methods and equipment of professional designers and translating them into simple domestic design terms, you can build up a visual plan of possible solutions.

Plans-boards

In the case of boards prepared by interior designers, these would constitute alternatives for their clients to choose from. In the case of home-made boards, it will be more a question of discarding schemes that fail to please, and the aim should be to come up with a single one that is liked by one and all of the inhabitants.

How to make up your own

Having examined the room in terms of its functions, and decided what sort of wear it is likely to get (and by whom), assemble the following items: white cards in sheets measuring approx. 18in. × 12 in./450 mm × 305 mm; scissors, pins, a plan of the room and, perhaps, a photograph of the existing interior, catalogues with pictures of the selected furniture; samples of curtain and upholstery fabrics.

Fix each of your proposed floor coverings to one of your cards. (If you are thinking of sanded boards, wood-grain paper can be a help, although it will not look exactly as your floor will.) Then, having grouped your other swatches and samples into congenial "families", see what seems to go with what. Consider the stuff for the important areas first – walls, curtains and sofa coverings will set the tone by virtue of their acreage.

Settle on your basic scheme: it is important to get it absolutely right; if a different shade of, say, beige is needed, get yet another paint chart before you start pinning the accessorizing colours to your board.

The examples

Scheme 1, like Scheme 2, is an alternative for the same basic interior: a garden-room for a couple with one child.

The first scheme differs largely in atmosphere from the second, but the basic facilities are the same: there is plenty of storage space, provided by the extension of the plinths on two sides of the room, which at the same time creates the sitting area, in each case topped with a mass of cushions.

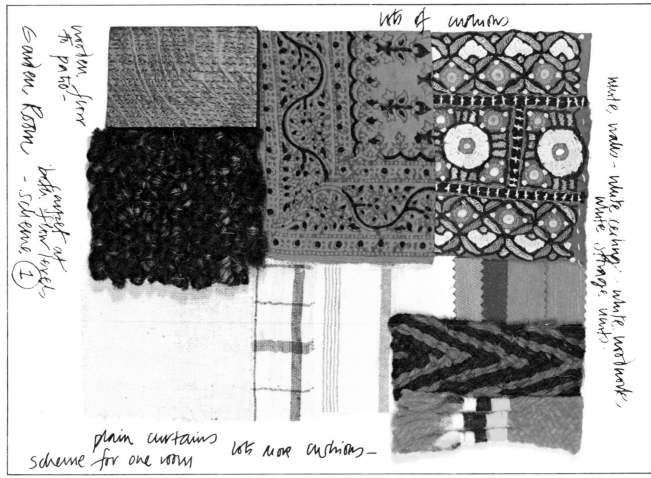

Scheme 1

Floor and plinth are covered with a thick loop-pile carpet in rich tobacco brown, which is dark enough to disguise the odd coffee spill as well as bicycle track marks over the floor and, at the same time, contrasts well with the superb collection of seating cushions. Indian mirror-work, handwoven cheese cloth, tough Irish linen and silky cotton twill in boiled-sweet colours are carefully arranged together to create a vivid splash of pattern and texture – splendidly offset by natural coloured curtains and white glossy paintwork.

Scheme 2

Although the basic design approach is the same, a totally different atmosphere is achieved by a different colour plan. The success or failure of a design is often determined by the quality and choice of floor covering, and since this can be one of the most expensive items on the budget, it is essential to select a suitable flooring first. In this case, a honey-coloured hardwood flooring was chosen. It is tough, easy to maintain and practical enough to be extended out into the patio, so adding a further spatial dimension to the room. At the same time, a chrome yellow Flokati rug contrasts well with the hard surface of the floor and also sets the pace for a decoration scheme of sharp primary colours interpreted in Marimekko patterned fabrics on the cushions.

Short-cuts

Designers, of course, always have a great mass of samples and swatches in their offices, while most of us have to go out to get them piece by piece. To save one's feet, it is not a bad idea to arrive at the basic accessorizing scheme via bits of coloured paper, foil and ribbon. It is then easier to match these colours in the actual materials or at least get very close to them.

Testing

When you have assembled a board that perfectly pleases you, with all the materials pinned on to it, be sure to look at it both in daylight and artificial light. If you are planning fluorescent lighting, carry your board to a place where it is already installed so that you can judge the effect – some colours do not work too well in some lights.

Colour
8/9 Scheme for the whole house

Once you have got the hang of doing the colour plan for one room, you should be able to organize a colour scheme for a whole house. Even if you cannot afford to carry out the entire project at one time, it is important to assess each room as part of a total-look colour plan so that you will eventually achieve a well-co-ordinated series of interiors.

Colour-planning the whole house

How do you start off? First of all, consider the project as a simple extension of a one-room scheme. Assemble the same materials and equipment – this time creating a larger sample board that will act as a master colour plan for the house. Next, analyse each room in terms of function and select a series of colour themes that also relate well to one another. Examine the meeting points of different wall and floor finishes and make sure that they work well together in terms of colour, texture and pattern.

Continuity

Consider the view from one room to another and select colours that co-ordinate successfully without introducing too many different surface finishes at key meeting points, such as an entrance hall or first-floor landing.

Lower ground floor.

Garden Room

tile to landing area.

Laundry + stairs up to ground floor

floor

wall.

blinds.

Kitchen and Dining area

Complete house scheme

Ground floor.

floor.

Sitting Room

sofa + curtains.

cushions.

walls.

bedspread and curtains.

cork walls.

First floor

Master bedroom and ~

Bathroom.

wall covering

walls.

bedspread.

Hall and landing area.

Nanny's bedroom.

bedspread + cushions.

walls + ceiling

pin up board

walls + ceiling

Daughter's bedroom.

2nd Bathroom

To illustrate these basic rules, here is a master colour plan showing the floor, wall and surface treatment of the interiors of a small three-storey town house, including the garden room scheme already discussed.

Colour emphasis

In the average house, the design emphasis should be on easy-to-live-with colour schemes, incorporating a practical overall surface treatment and simple choice of materials. In this scheme, for example, the main colour plan centres on shades of brown and cream; linking areas such as the landing and stairs are clad with camel-coloured wool cloth, and a bitter chocolate carpet unites the main circulation areas with the bedroom floor.

Accents

Meanwhile, the first-floor sitting room scheme features a lively exchange of patterned fabric cushion covers, which contrast well with the soft-textured upholstery materials, wool wall covering and carpet design. In the master bedroom the same basic colour theme is beautifully interpreted in a hand-embroidered crewel-work bedspread, textured natural linen curtains and chocolate-coloured carpet, whereas the nanny's room, child's bedroom and second bathroom provide great scope for a series of sharp primary-coloured design schemes and a bold interplay of patterns.

Lastly, and from the practical point of view, hard-working areas, such as the laundry room and kitchen, both feature tough tiled surfaces and colour schemes that are essentially simple and easy to live with.

Colour

It is important to remember that colour schemes in much-used areas of the house, such as the family room, kitchen and family bathroom, should be relaxed and all the material should be practical and simple to maintain. This does not mean that these areas need to be dull or colourless; the test of a successful scheme is that the room should look perpetually fresh, cheerful and inviting.

Schemes for hard-working areas

1 Kitchen: *The traditional concept of a pretty country kitchen, complete with sealed timber units and a tough quarry-tiled floor, is brought up to date here with a sharp red PVC roller blind, smooth laminate working surfaces and practical recessed ceiling lighting.*

2 Family room: *A buttercup yellow ceiling, white emulsion walls and a practical polished cork floor, create a relaxed country-style family room in this Victorian town house.*

3 Hall: *Yellow emulsion paint covers the walls; the floor is sealed oak. Brown sisal staircarpet carries the yellow-brown scheme further, and white gloss painted woodwork brings it all alive.*

4 Children's room: *A patriotic red, white and blue colour scheme, interpreted in fresh gloss paint, is teamed with a sealed timber floor and spongeable holland blinds to create a lively, practical children's bedroom/play area.*

1

2

3

4

Little-used areas of the house, however – spare rooms, the dining-room and guest bathroom – offer far more scope for lively, even eccentric colour planning. It is here that brilliant combinations come into their own, and here that one can go in for the pale, pale decorations that would not stand a chance in the family areas.

Schemes for little-used areas

1 Living-room: *This adults' sitting room is essentially an escape area from the rough and tumble of family life. It has creamy hessian-covered walls, thick white carpet, ivory-coloured upholstery and white woodwork.*

2 Bedroom: *English mustard coloured walls, teamed with a brilliant embroidered bedspread and matching wall hanging, create a happy balance of colour and pattern in this bedroom interior.*

3 Dining-room: *Mint green felt walls decorated with giant appliqué cotton panels, bright blue blinds, a white ceiling and smooth white vinyl floor, all add up to a lively interior for dining in.*

4 Master bathroom: *A stylish use of cork wall cladding, teamed with cigar-coloured towels and accessories, creates a superb atmosphere of luxury, combined with quiet practicality, in this bathroom.*

Colour
12/13 Ideas/solutions

Colour can contribute an exciting surprise factor: monochromatic schemes can be just as exciting and successful as multi-coloured ones – but in both cases, the approach must be wholehearted and bold.

1 *Take a brown cord carpet and contrast it with a sharp white bedcover trimmed with a maroon and pink border.*

2 *Colour a sparkling white table with poppy red mats and place it alongside a barrage of chrome yellow cushions.*

3 *Revitalize a Victorian whatnot with sharp lime green paint and blend it with peppermint green gingham walls.*

4 *Take a white room – add a Victorian mahogany bench and scatter cushions in fruit colours over it.*

5 *Surround a seascape picture window with rock pink striped walls and contrast it with a bold checked working surface.*

6 *Take a primary school lesson in colour and translate it into a series of alphabet cushions in red, yellow and navy blue, fire-engine red accessories and a bull's-eye table.*

7 *Practise elementary geometry in a plain white interior. Here a striking black and white blind, bedcover and cushions are brilliantly foiled by a gleaming silver lamp.*

1

2

3

4

5

6

7

1

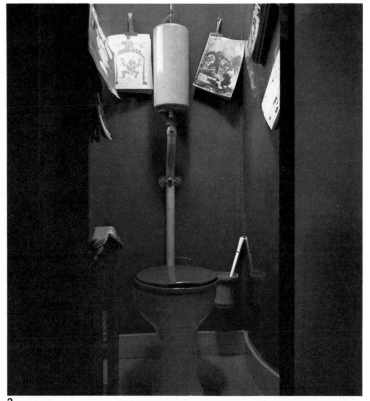

2

1 *Newsprint is the key ingredient in this total-look monochromatic interior. It not only provides fascinating reading with reports from all over the world but is one of the cheapest, most effective and most readily available wall coverings on the market today. Here, the black-and-white theme is accentuated with a black lavatory seat, black-and-white towels and matching accessories.*

2 *A small lavatory offers great scope for eccentric colour planning. Here, a red floor is teamed with blue and green walls, a red and yellow cistern, scarlet radiator and purple seat to create a wild scheme accentuated by the colours of the horror comics bull-dog clipped to the wall.*

3 *This living area is essentially for purists, with its stark white walls and floor, bare windows and country-style furniture in honey-coloured wood.*

4 *In contrast, cushions, soft drinks, marzipan sweets, striped Moroccan blankets and accessories all add up to a kaleidoscope of colour in this plain white interior.*

3

4

Colour
14 Pepping up last year's scheme

The advantage of a neutral colour scheme is that it is flexible and easy to revive. Pep up last year's white-painted interior with gaily-coloured accessories, introduce a collection of bright lithographs, a fresh plant or a striped blanket, and you will see how it revitalizes a tired scheme. Look at the transformation of this one-room living area : the white painted shell and tough ship's matting remain the same, but the room looks new through the addition of a pepper green canvas sling chair, a potted palm and some fresh flowers, Indian rug, new pictures and things on shelves, and cushions in a fresh spring colour theme.

Heating/1

For readers who do not wish to be blinded by science when talking to heating consultants, here is a dictionary of the jargon with which you may be faced.

Air-changes

Necessary for both your health and comfort. One-and-a-half changes an hour in living-rooms and two an hour in kitchens/bathrooms are recommended.

Back boiler

A boiler incorporated at the back of the living-room heater – solid fuel, gas or oil-fired – to provide domestic hot water and/or central heating.

Background heating

A system which keeps the temperature around 55°F/13°C, using individual heaters to bring each room up to a more comfortable temperature when in use.

Balanced flues

An alternative to the traditional flue, available with many gas boilers and heaters and some pressure-jet, oil-fired boilers. The flue unit enters through any outside wall and terminates in a cowl or grille.

Both incoming air for combustion, and out-going fumes, are ducted through the unit so that the combustion chamber is sealed off from the room itself, and the effect of variations in wind pressure and direction are balanced.

Bottled gas – Butane and Propane

Cooking, water heating, heating and lighting can all be run on bottled gas with appliances like those used with town and natural gas.

British Thermal Units

One British Thermal Unit (Btu) is the amount of heat required to raise one pound (450 grammes) of water 1°F. One hundred thousand Btu's equal 1 Therm.

Ceiling heating

Heating elements, enclosed in plastic sheet, fixed to the ceiling joists. The sheet is backed by a layer of insulation, and covered with plasterboard. The elements can be controlled by individual thermostats in each room.

Centigrade and Fahrenheit

At present, the heating industry still seems to be using the Fahrenheit scale but the metric Centigrade measure will undoubtedly take over.

Central heating

From a central boiler or heating unit, by hot-water radiators or ducted warm air; do not confuse with background heating.

Circulating pumps

These pumps force heated water through the radiators and pipes in micro-bore and small-bore heating systems. The pumps are also used to boost circulation of primary and secondary circuits in domestic hot-water systems.

Condensation

Moisture, carried by warm air, that forms droplets on cold surfaces.

Conduction

Method of heat transfer in liquids or solids.

In solids, heat is transferred from one object to another when a warm object touches a colder one. The warm object could be your body, the cold one a floor or wall.

Consultant heating engineer

A professionally qualified person, who is employed directly by you and is not a member of the firm who does your heating installation. He can design your heating scheme, help you select contractors, supervise the work done by the heating contractor, and check the bill.

Convection

Heated air expands and rises, creating air currents which can warm a room. This is natural convection and is provided by electric, gas and oil convector heaters, by standard as well as convector radiators, and any warm surface. Some convector heaters and most warm-air systems are fan-assisted to accelerate this warming-up process.

Direct cylinder

A simple tank, storing domestic hot water.

Domestic hot water

As used for washing, cooking, and so on.

Ducted warm air

A form of central heating.

Feed and expansion tank

Small tank off the main water supply which keeps radiators in a central-heating system topped up.

Finned tubes

Pipes with radial fins along their length to extend their heating surface. Skirting radiators have them; but they can be used independently as well, recessed in the floor or walls, and masked by grilles.

Floor heating

This heating system is used most generally with off-peak electricity. Elements are laid in the concrete floor slab so that the floor itself acts as a low-temperature radiant panel. Check that the floor finish you want is suitable for under-floor heating.

Flue lining

A modern boiler, using an existing flue, should be fitted with an asbestos or steel inner flue, or lined by a specialist firm with an insulating cement.

Full heating

When all the rooms of the house are as warm as you want, all the time.

Heating contractor

A person or firm who installs the heating system. He may be a qualified heating engineer: but remember, he is not an independent consultant heating engineer.

Humidifier

A device for adding moisture to dry air, by means of evaporation from the humidifier itself. Types vary from simple radiator-mounted ones to electric humidifiers with a fan or heating element to accelerate evaporation.

Immersion heater

An electric element inserted into the hot-water cylinder that uses either on- or off-peak current.

Indirect cylinders

These protect against scale or corrosion in a heating system, and should always be used where water is hard or where there is a combined heating and domestic hot-water system. They work by means of a "closed circuit" of hot-water pipes running through the cylinder.

Kilowatt

A kilowatt is 1000 watts and indicates the heat output given by the appliance. 1 kWh = 3412 Btu.

Main cold-water tank

Filled direct from the mains, it provides replacement water for the hot-water cylinder and, frequently, cold water to baths and basins, but not the kitchen sink, which is invariably fed direct from the mains.

Micro-bore systems

Small-bore piping that uses soft copper or ductile steel tubes of approximately 6, 8 and 10 mm diameter. They can be easier to install and less obtrusive than larger pipes. Lower water content often provides quicker heat-up period. These systems have a low water content and a high water temperature, so that panel radiators are too hot to touch. Finned tubes, skirting and convector radiators, and forced fan convectors, are more generally used with these systems.

Natural gas

This has twice the calorific value of town gas, different flame characteristics, and is non-toxic.

Off-peak electricity

Current available at a cheap rate during some night hours. Floor heating, warm-air and radiator systems, storage radiators, and domestic hot water can take advantage of it.

Package deals

Supply a standard installation at a set price. They are cheaper than an individually designed system, but make sure they are adequate for their purpose.

Radiation

Directly heats objects and not the air through which it passes.

Low-temperature radiant heat is provided by heated floors, ceilings and radiators. Coal, gas, electric and oil radiant fires provide high-temperature heat.

Radiators

Boiler-run radiators have water pumped through them; electrically-run ones contain heating elements still oil.

Small-bore systems

These have superseded the old gravity systems, as the use of a small pump to circulate the water through the pipes and radiators allows much smaller piping (about ½ in./12 mm) to be used.

Storage radiators

Are made of fire-bricks which heat up with off-peak electricity.

Smokeless zones

Areas where only appliances which are capable of combusting the major part of their fuel may be used. Oil and gas meet these requirements, but only smokeless fuel may be used in solid-fuel appliances.

U-value

The measure of the rate at which heat will flow through any material. The lower the U-value, the higher the insulation value of the material.

Warm-air heating

Central heating by means of a warm air heater circulating hot air to individual rooms through ducts and grilles.

White meter

This replaces the old type of on-peak and off-peak meters by one meter, which records all consumption during a set period on one on-peak dial, and all consumption for the rest of the 24 hours on a separate off-peak dial.

Heating

You must consider heating and insulation from the very moment that you take over a new house, or decide to update your existing one.

While heating installations are becoming much more unobtrusive, you will still get the best results if you plan them in relation to all the other changes you are making.

This applies equally to insulation, and in many cases the decorative finishes can themselves provide the insulation you need.

Central heating is too expensive, and too disruptive an exercise, to entrust to anyone but specialists. Too many incompetent firms have jumped on to the heating-installation band-wagon, so it is advisable to go to the National Heating Consultancy, who will recommend a consultant heating engineer in your area; or use the invaluable advisory service offered by the National Heating Centre (see Yellow Pages).

By getting help of this kind you can be sure that you will arrive at the most appropriate installation for your house and its occupants, that the work will be done to a guaranteed standard, and that you will be insured against subsequent failure of materials, equipment and workmanship.

If you have your house or flat on a short lease, or if you are only renting it, you can build up a heating system with independent units that you will be able to take with you when you move on. Suitable systems might comprise electric storage radiators, on-peak heaters or individual gas and electric fires.

Whatever heating system and appliances you decide on, make absolutely sure that they are completely safe. Not only must your system and appliances comply with safety regulations and be properly installed, but they should also be checked to make sure that small children or elderly people cannot be hurt by them. It is not enough to say that you would never leave a child alone in a room with an open fire – you must make doubly sure and get a proper fireguard.

The priorities

Whether the house has full central heating, partial central heating, or no heating at all, before deciding what changes you want to make in your home, check whether you have your priorities right.

Avoid heat loss

Effective insulation should be your first aim because, however warm the air, if large areas such as walls, ceilings, windows and floors are cold, you yourself will feel uncomfortable. This is easily explained by the simple fact that warm objects (including you) lose heat by radiation to cooler things near them. This is precisely what happens to your body whenever you enter a room which contains any cold surfaces.

Most bodies maintain a temperature of around 98.6°F/37°C; but most people can feel perfectly comfortable in considerably lower air temperatures, providing that the surrounding structures are well insulated, and reflect back the radiant heat given out by the body and any heater in the room.

Controlling the temperature

The average human body is comfortable between about 67–72°F/20–22°C – i.e. within a range of about 6°F/3°C. By maintaining the constant level of heat in your rooms within a degree or so of the temperature required, by means of today's sophisticated controls, you will not only be much more comfortable, but also reduce your running cost.

Temperature requirements vary with different households, but a good basis to work on is 70°F/21°C for living-rooms and bathrooms, and 65–68°F/18–20°C for the rest of the house during daytime hours, with an 8°F/5°C or 10°F/6°C setback during the night.

The important thing to remember about temperature levels is that these must be capable of being maintained when the outside temperature drops to below freezing.

Keeping a good heat gradient

Human beings are happiest when their feet are warmer than, or at least as warm as, their heads; but, as every child knows, heat rises, so insulate your floors and choose heating systems which either heat the floor, or have their heat output close to the ground and spread around the room (such as skirting heaters, radiators, low-level grilles). Curiously, ceiling heating, as long as the ceiling is not lower than 7 ft 6 in./2.2 m does not make for hot heads and cold feet as you might think, because most of the heat is reflected back off floors and walls.

Heat volume

The surface area of radiators has to relate to the volume of the room they are heating. For this reason, the relative outputs of different kinds of radiators should be carefully considered whenever wall space is at a premium, or if the visual effect is of special importance.

Spread your heat

One large, single radiator will provide very much less warmth and comfort than skirting radiators of the same total capacity which have been spread around the room. Draught-stripping and double-glazing will go a long way towards making every part of the room comfortable to use.

Ventilation

You need to provide for enough air movement and fresh air without losing too much of the warmth you have created. Controlled ventilation is the answer.

Humidity

Dry air can irritate the skin, eyes, nose and throat; can damage antiques and paintings, and cause shrinkage in wood panelling and furniture. Low-temperature heat sources cause less dryness than high temperature ones, which argues again for spreading your heat. With a warm-air system, try to build in a humidifier.

Clean air

Apart from easier maintenance of decoration, less frequent cleaning and redecorating, clean air is also an important consideration for bronchitics and asthmatics. Air cleaners can be incorporated in ducted warm-air systems and there are portable models too.

Effective draught-stripping, double-glazing and controlled ventilation will do a lot to reduce incoming dirt.

Quietness

Make it clear to your installer that this really matters to you, and is a condition of your paying the bill. Before having a boiler, a circulating pump or any fan-assisted system installed, check its noise-level. See that the clips that fix pipes to the floors/walls are padded with sponge-rubber, and find out whether the heating controls will affect things like your hi-fi or television, since they can cause interference.

Convected and radiated heat

For maximum comfort, look for a form of heating that combines both types, such as water or electric radiators, heated floors or ceilings. A radiant heater (electric, gas, oil or coal fire) should be available in the home to offset severe chilling in very cold weather; this is particularly important in rooms where old people or children are living. Well-insulated surfaces will help too, since they reflect back low-temperature heat.

Convenience

This covers many things: trouble-free maintenance, freedom from servicing, a quick warm-up, speedy response to controls, no smells or noise, no flue, safety, reliability, and availability of a good service contract, and most important of all, comfortable warmth throughout the winter.

Condensation and ventilation

Because of the prevailing humidity of our atmosphere, condensation can be a problem for many households in the British Isles. Condensation is the result of moisture, always present in the air as water vapour, forming into droplets when it touches a cold surface, such as window glass or the cold walls of your bathroom or kitchen. This is much more than just a nuisance, for if it is not dealt with immediately it can cause serious damage, such as rotting window-frames and floor-covering, if they are on a concrete base, causing paint to blister and peel, mould to develop, and wallpaper to discolour and finally come away from the wall surface altogether. If plaster has been soaking up condensation over a long period of time, it will explode and crumble, and if this happens will need to be hacked off and renewed completely or be the cause of dry or damp rot.

Curing condensation calls for a three-fold attack. First, good ventilation, to get steam out of the house as quickly as possible, must be installed. Second, good insulation of structural surfaces, to prevent the moisture in the air condensing on them, must be assured. Finally, sufficient background heating, to warm the air to a point where it will help to keep the structural surfaces from getting too cold, and to absorb any residual dampness, should be incorporated into your heating system.

Bathrooms, kitchens

Your first step is to improve your ventilation where you can. In bathrooms, kitchens and laundry rooms try to avoid creating unnecessary steam. When you run a bath, turn on the cold tap a bit before, or at the same time as, you turn on the hot – not afterwards. Set the thermostat on your water cylinder to 140°F/60°C. This is a safe temperature when there are children about, and does reduce the amount of steam created.

In your kitchen, if you do the sort of cooking that keeps saucepans boiling away on the stove for hour after hour, adapt yourself to different methods – try out new ones that require low simmering. If your family insists on plum duff, buy yourself a pressure cooker. If you are the kind of person who sometimes turns on a kettle and forgets about it, leaving it to steam away unnoticed, buy the type that switches itself off automatically once it has boiled. Let a dishwasher take over as much washing up as possible, and use a fully automatic washing machine; this way you'll reduce the amount of steam getting into the atmosphere. If you have blocked up a chimney in a bathroom or kitchen, put a louvred vent into the wall connecting the stack with the room as this will draw air out of the room.

Extractors

One way to get the steam out of the bathroom, kitchen and similar rooms quickly, is to use an extractor fan. If you want your fan to do its job properly, it will need to be powerful; you will probably find that getting one that's too small for the job will turn out to be an expense rather than an economy. The sizes of fans are rated according to the volume of the room in which the extractor is to be placed.

It is well worth remembering that a fan inserted through the wall is quieter when it is in operation than one set in a pane of glass, as the wall absorbs the vibrations. Don't site it too far away from the cooker, the bath, etc, since ideally it should be directly over the source of steam. The familiar "hit or miss" ventilators set in window-panes will ensure some air movement.

Strips, louvres, extractors

A very neat alternative is aluminium strips which are slotted over the top edge of the glass before it is fitted into the window-frame. These can provide either permanent or controllable draught-free ventilation.

Louvred windows also give you easily adjustable ventilation. There has been some criticism that this type of window is draughty, but there is at least one firm which makes a version that is designed to stand up to British weather conditions. Flues will provide ventilation where fireplaces are not used, if a "hit and miss" ventilator is fitted into them as high as possible.

Clearly one of the very real advantages offered by double-glazing is its ability to prevent condensation because the warm air in the room never comes into contact with the cold face of the outer skin of glass.

Surface finishes

There is also every argument for getting your main structure as dry as possible which will make it warmer and then adding as much insulation as you can. Even then, some surface finishes will offset condensation better than others. To prevent trickles and rivulets avoid glossy paints, paper and tiles and try instead to find matt or semi-matt alternatives which will temporarily mop up any condensing moisture until it is absorbed back into the room. A useful alternative to ceramic tiles is to use cork tiles or sheeting

usually used for floors or tongued-and-grooved boarding for the walls of kitchens and bathrooms, particularly when they are in extensions with thin brick walls.

Anti-condensation paints

Some paints deteriorate much more quickly in steamy atmospheres than others and you should check this when you buy paint. One firm makes a special anti-condensation paint which has the appearance of a good emulsion paint and comes in a good range of colours.

If you are seriously troubled by condensation don't make the mistake of using a flueless paraffin heater in your effort to provide background warmth. One gallon of paraffin produces one gallon of water vapour in burning and this will aggravate the problem rather than help to cure it.

The heating system which best prevents condensation is the kind that prevents the house from ever getting absolutely cold. If you are installing central heating it is better to use a day/night set-back thermostat which will turn the temperature down, but not off, when warmth is not required, rather than a programmer which will turn off the heating completely for certain periods, and let the structure of the house get cold.

Where there is no whole-house central-heating system, it is worth fitting some form of low background heat. In kitchens a small night storage heater, or a 300 or 500 watt electric skirting heater, left on continuously won't cost you much to run, and will prevent walls streaming and towels staying cold and clammy. In bedrooms a 500–1000 watt heater run continuously should be enough to offset condensation unless the room is very large. This can always be topped up with a fan or radiant heater when more heat is needed.

Insulation

For every £100 that you spend on heating your home, £75 of it could be wasted. Effective insulation will reduce your running costs if you have an efficient heating system, and probably enable an otherwise inadequate system to provide full heating Where there is no heating at all, it will allow you to put in a smaller system initially. With the world's supply of fuel dwindling fast, insulation can be your contribution towards conserving what we have left. Remember, the lower the U-value, the better the insulation.

Roofs

Roughly a quarter of the heat that escapes from your house does so through the roof; this is even more applicable if you live in a bungalow. Attend to insulat-

ing the roof before you tackle any other part of the house, as this is the easiest part of the building to insulate yourself, and the cheapest.

If you are replacing or renewing the roof-covering, the problem of providing insulation is lessened, as it is easier to lay insulation quilt or board above the rafters than below or between them.

If you can get into the roof space, and can see the underside of the tiles, tack or staple heavy polythene sheet to the underside of the rafters to keep out draughts, snow and rain. If the roof needs retiling, lay aluminium-backed felt and 2 in./51 mm mineral quilt before the tiles are relaid.

Lofts

If you should want to use your loft for storage, it would be a good idea to pack your insulation between the joists, and then board them over to spread the load of storage while protecting and improving the insulation.

If you don't intend to use the loft for anything, simply lay the insulation across the joists.

When installing central heating, aim for a U-value of .10 or less. *Which* Magazine (August 1972) carried out tests which showed that:—

2 in./51 mm mineral or glass wool gives .10;

3 in./76 mm vermiculite gives .10;

2 in./51 mm non-flammable polystyrene gives .09;

3 in./76 mm mineral or glass wool gives .08.

Once it is insulated, your roof space will be colder than before – since the heat will now be trapped below it – so don't forget to insulate over, not under, your cold-water tank as well as its connecting pipes.

Lagging

It is essential to lag all pipes in the roof space and under the floorboards of a suspended ground floor. In both cases any heat that is lost will be lost to the house completely. Whether you lag any other pipes will depend on whether the heat loss will be inconvenient; for example, when they run through a cupboard which you need to keep cool because vegetables or other perishables are stored there. Otherwise, any loss of heat from piping will simply contribute to the general warmth of your home.

Ceilings

If you can't get up into the roof space, or you have a flat roof, insulate the ceiling of the top floor. You could use an insulating material that provides an attractive permanent finish in itself, such as cork

board, birch-faced ply, chipboard or flaxboard or tongue-and-groove boarding, to name only a few alternatives.

Walls

The greatest proportion of heat lost goes through the walls of a house. Older houses have solid walls; if stone, they will be thick, and – once dry – provide good insulation in themselves. Brick walls can be 4½ in./114 mm, 9 in./229 mm or (in very old strongly built cottages) 13 in./343 mm thick.

Protection brickwork

Even if there is a damp-proof course, 4½ in./114 mm brickwork needs both positive insulation and protection from penetrating damp. Damp-proofing could be provided by brushing with a colourless silicone waterproofer or, if the place needs a face-lift, hanging with tiles, slates or weather-boarding – whatever is appropriate locally.

Internal panels

Otherwise, the internal face of the wall could be damp-proofed and panelled with insulating material. Such treatment could equally well be used for 9 in./229 mm brickwork in a poor state.

Finishes

With 13½ in./343 mm brickwork, once it is dry, try to use wall finishes that provide some insulation in themselves, as this will offset condensation as well as trap heat. Consider for instance vinyl, t&g or cork floor-tiles for bathroom and kitchen walls, as an alternative to ceramic ones. Line wallpaper with a thin polystyrene sheet.

Cavity walls

Most of the houses built since 1920 have cavity walls, two skins of brick or blockwork with a 2 in./51 mm gap between them. This gap prevents damp penetrating and improves insulation. In new work, if insulating blocks are used for the inner skin, the U-value can be reduced from about .26 to .20, providing the air in the cavity is still, which it rarely is. However, it is becoming popular, following the example of Scandinavian countries, to trap the air and add further insulation by filling the cavity. This can reduce the U-value to as low as .10 – but beware of fly-by-night installers and choose a firm that has an Agreement Certificate. Rentokil's mineral-wool filling appears least likely to give trouble, and ICI's method seems the most reliable method of using formaldehyde. Poorly installed, this form of insulation can result in damp penetration across the cavity.

Heating
4/5 Insulation

Windows can be doubly responsible for a considerable loss of heat – they let in draughts, and heat is lost through the glass itself. Draught-stripping is an inexpensive remedy, and one which, being quite simple, you could probably do for yourself. Double-glazing, while giving you a smaller return on your investment than other forms of insulation, can prevent condensation and cold draughts.

In addition, if you choose a double-glazing system which provides you with a sufficient gap between the two skins of glass, it may very well provide sound insulation. A gap of 2 in./51 mm will take off the sharp top notes of traffic; 4 in./102 mm will almost muffle it; 8 in./203 mm will cut out noise from low-flying aircraft.

Check first to see whether or not there are any old shutters still in place that could be put to use as insulating agents. They can be found not only at the sides of windows, but occasionally also in the panel below the sill of sash ones.

Double-glazing

1. Factory-sealed units. These are roughly $\frac{5}{8}$ in./16 mm thick, and are formed from two sheets of glass which have been sealed at the edges to sandwich either dry air or a vacuum between them. The sandwich is fitted directly into the window-frame, just like a single sheet of glass. This form of double-glazing provides an inexpensive kind of heat insulation, although you will not get too much sound insulation this way.

2. Coupled sashes. In this case, two glazed frames are joined together to move as one unit. The gap between them is enough to provide some sound insulation. Suitable for conversions and new building, and a roof-light version is available.

3. Secondary frames. This third method of double-glazing means fitting an additional frame into the window recess. The new frame is either hinged or slides independently of the existing frame, so that it will provide ventilation and make cleaning easier. This is by far the best way to obtain sound insulation as well. Although it is usually installed only by specialist firms, DIY versions are also made.

4. Attached frames. This is far and away the easiest method of double-glazing to do yourself. A plastic, metal or wooden strip is used to attach a second sheet of glass directly into the frame of the existing window.

Draught-stripping (windows)

This is essential, not only to keep out draughts, dust and dirt, but to give full value to double-glazing. Window-frames must fit reasonably well to begin with.

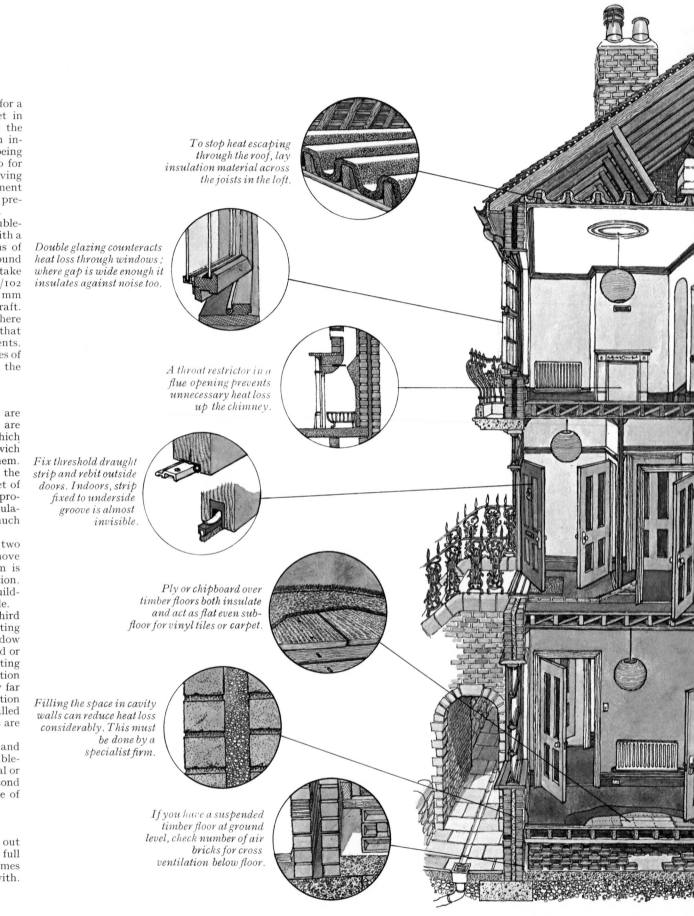

To stop heat escaping through the roof, lay insulation material across the joists in the loft.

Double glazing counteracts heat loss through windows; where gap is wide enough it insulates against noise too.

A throat restrictor in a flue opening prevents unnecessary heat loss up the chimney.

Fix threshold draught strip and rebit outside doors. Indoors, strip fixed to underside groove is almost invisible.

Ply or chipboard over timber floors both insulate and act as flat even sub-floor for vinyl tiles or carpet.

Filling the space in cavity walls can reduce heat loss considerably. This must be done by a specialist firm.

If you have a suspended timber floor at ground level, check number of air bricks for cross ventilation below floor.

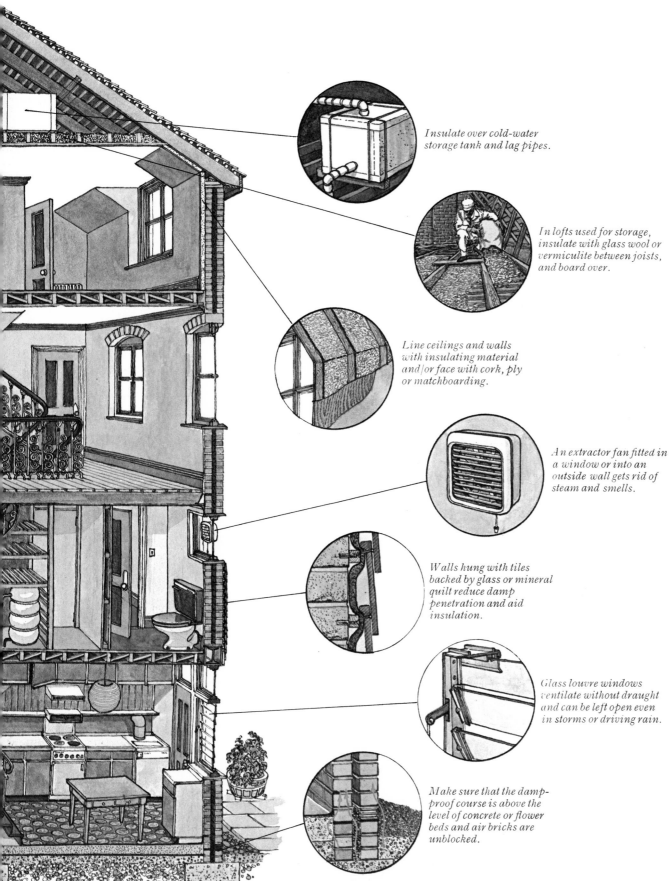

Insulate over cold-water storage tank and lag pipes.

In lofts used for storage, insulate with glass wool or vermiculite between joists, and board over.

Line ceilings and walls with insulating material and/or face with cork, ply or matchboarding.

An extractor fan fitted in a window or into an outside wall gets rid of steam and smells.

Walls hung with tiles backed by glass or mineral quilt reduce damp penetration and aid insulation.

Glass louvre windows ventilate without draught and can be left open even in storms or driving rain.

Make sure that the damp-proof course is above the level of concrete or flower beds and air bricks are unblocked.

Where there is a small and regular gap along the window-edge, the best draught-stripping is the bronze-spring kind which is tacked on to the frame, but where windows are shut most of the time, or when they are set into metal frames, self-adhesive rubber or plastic-foam stripping is easiest to fix, especially when you are going to do it yourself.

Draught-stripping (doors)

Door frames can be draught-stripped in the same way as windows, and threshold strips can be fixed to the bottom edge of the door itself, or to the floor.

Draughts: lobbies and porches

Cold air gets in and warm air gets out through outside doors. If your hall is large enough, add an inner frame and door to provide a draught lobby. An existing open porch could be glazed in or you could build one on.

Flues and fires

Warm air gets lost up the chimney. Fit a throat restrictor and tray to provide an under-hearth draught which draws air for combustion from the outside, instead of warm air from the room itself. Where fireplaces are not used, block them up and seal off the chimney-pot, or insert a "hit and miss" ventilator into the flue at ceiling height for controlled ventilation.

Floors

One-sixth of the heat lost goes through floors. Damp floors lose more heat than dry ones, as well as encouraging condensation. When floors are damp, have them up and re-lay them, incorporating a damp-proof membrane and a layer of 1 in./25 mm non-flammable polystyrene or glass quilt, which is put down before the top screed is laid. Alternatively, mix vermiculite into the screed itself to improve its insulation.

The next step is to use an insulating floor-covering, such as foam or felt-backed linoleum, vinyl sheeting, thick foam underlay or foam-backed carpet, wood blocks or cork.

If you don't want to disturb handsome old brick or stone floors, a transparent polyurethane finish will seal off rising damp, and give a pleasant sheen to the floor too.

Should you have suspended wood floors on the ground level, check that there are enough air-bricks to provide cross draughts and keep them unblocked. Otherwise you will get dry rot in the joists, and even in the floorboards themselves. Once you have taken this precaution, wall-to-wall finishes will prevent draughts from penetrating upwards.

Type of installation	Hot Water Boiler with Radiators	Back or Hearth Boiler and Radiators	Warm Air – Perimeter ducted
Solid fuel	Gravity-fed or manual. *Fuel Storage :* The larger the better. *Flue :* Conventional – insulated lining. *Installation Costs :* Average. *Attention :* Automatic feed – none. Hopper fed – 24–36 hours. Other types from 6 hours. *Control :* Semi-automatic or manual. *Domestic Hot Water :* Can be provided.	Open fire or closed stoves. *Fuel Storage :* The large the better. *Flue :* Conventional – with insulated lining. *Installation Cost :* Low to average. *Attention :* Hopper fed, 24–36 hours. Other types variable. *Control :* Semi-automatic with fan-assisted type and manual. *Domestic Hot Water :* Can be provided.	Boiler-run. *Fuel Storage :* The larger the better. *Flue :* Conventional – insulated lining. *Installation Cost :* Average to high. *Attention :* Automatic feed ⎱ as boilers *Control :* Automatic ⎰ *Attention :* Automatic feed. *Control :* Automatic. *Domestic Hot Water :* Can be provided.
Oil	Pressure Jet – large to medium output, very efficient, many now made for internal use but some need separate boiler room. Wallflame and Dynoflame – large to medium output, very efficient, quieter. Vaporizing, fan-assisted – less efficient but quieter. Vaporizing, natural draught – as fan-assisted but silent. *Fuel Storage :* Large. *Flue :* Conventional with insulated lining – some have balanced flues. *Installation Cost :* Medium to high. *Attention :* Little to none. *Control :* Semi-automatic, others automatic. *Domestic Hot Water :* Can be provided.	Appliance incorporates a radiant panel to heat living-room. *Fuel Storage :* The larger the better. *Flue :* Conventional type with insulated lining. *Installation Cost :* Low to average. *Attention :* Little or none. *Control :* Automatic or semi-automatic. *Domestic Hot Water :* Can be provided.	Can be boiler-run or direct-fired. Some types can be developed into full air-conditioning units. *Fuel Storage :* As large as possible. *Flue :* Conventional with insulated lining. *Installation Cost :* Medium to high. *Attention :* None. *Control :* Fully-automatic; gives quick response. *Domestic Hot Water :* May be provided as well.
Gas	Largest output are floor-standing; others can be floor-standing or wall-hung. *Fuel Storage :* None. *Flue :* Conventional or balanced flues. *Installation Cost :* Average to low. *Running Cost :* Average. *Attention :* None. *Control :* Fully-automatic. *Domestic Hot Water :* Can be provided.	Appliances available with radiant fire in the living-room. *Fuel Storage :* None. *Flue :* Conventional type with insulated lining. *Installation Cost :* Low to average. *Attention :* None. *Control :* Automatic. *Domestic Hot Water :* Can be provided.	Can be boiler-run or direct-heated. Some types can be developed into full air-conditioning units. *Flue :* Conventional with insulated lining. *Installation Cost :* Medium to high. *Attention :* None. *Control :* Fully automatic; quick response. *Domestic Hot Water :* May be provided.
Electric/on peak	Electrode boilers are available which can be used to run radiator systems. *Installation Cost :* Average. *Attention :* None. *Control :* Fully-automatic. *Domestic Hot Water :* Not usually from the same boiler.	No system available.	*Tronicair system :* Can be used with standard warm-air ducting installation full air-conditioning with automatic control. *Elvaco system :* $1\frac{1}{2}$ in./38 mm diameter pipes; provides easily installed, inexpensive system giving room-by-room control with ventilation in summer, but not full air-conditioning. *Either* can provide domestic hot water.
Electric/off peak	Electrode as on-peak. Could have on-peak boost used with White Meter. Centralec units (not strictly boilers) can run radiators. *Installation Cost :* (Centralec) : As gas. *Attention :* None. *Control :* Fully-automatic. *Domestic Hot Water :* Not provided from Centralec unit.	No system available.	No system available.
Will it suit us?	Suitable for medium to large houses where full central heating is needed. Installation in existing house not too disruptive with small-bore or micro-bore systems. Fully-automatic whole house or room-by-room control possible with most systems but humidification or summer cooling not provided.	Suitable for country cottages used full time, bungalows, small houses, terrace and semi-detached houses with up to three to four bedrooms. Gas type useful in upper floor flats.	Due to size of ducts required, use mostly confined to new houses or those being radically converted except for Elvaco system which uses $1\frac{1}{2}$ in./38 mm pipes and can be installed in an existing house or flat. Particularly valuable in town as most systems can include air-cleaning, heating, cooling and humidification.

Warm Air – Stub duct	Under Surface Heating	Unit Heaters – Convectors	Unit Heaters, Radiant
Closed stove/back-boiler versions are available. *Fuel Storage :* The larger the better. *Flue :* Own insulated flue. *Installation Cost :* Average. *Attention :* Variable. *Control :* Semi-automatic or manual. *Domestic Hot Water :* Can be provided.	Boilers can be used in conjunction with hot-water pipes embedded in floor slab. *Fuel Storage :* The larger the better. *Flue :* Conventional – insulated lining. *Installation Cost :* Average. *Attention :* See hot-water boilers. *Control :* As hot-water boilers. *Domestic Hot Water :* Can be provided. Systems for ceilings are possible.	*Closed stoves* provide convected heat. *Fuel Storage :* The larger the better. *Flue :* Conventional – insulated lining. *Installation Cost :* Low. *Attention :* Hopper fed – 24–36 hours. Otherwise 6 hours upwards. *Control :* Manual.	*Closed stoves* also provide low temperature radiant heat. *Open fires* provide both high temperature radiant heat and some convected heat. Otherwise as Unit Heaters – convectors.
Brick central units are available; can have radiant panel. *Fuel Storage :* As large as possible. *Flue :* Conventional with insulated lining. *Installation Cost :* Low to medium. *Attention :* None. *Control :* Automatic or semi-automatic. *Domestic Hot Water :* May be provided as well.	A hot-water boiler can feed hot-water pipes set in concrete floor to give fairly responsive system. Ceilings, as above.	As well as the familiar portable oil stove, larger continental versions are available requiring flue and which can be linked to an oil storage tank. These will give background heat to whole floor of small house if set in central position. Semi-automatic control.	*Oil convector stoves* give some low temperature radiant heat. *Radiant heaters* requiring no flue. Manual control.
Run from centrally-placed direct heating units. *Flue :* Conventional type. *Installation Cost :* Low to medium. *Attention :* None. *Control :* Fully-automatic. *Domestic Hot Water :* May be provided as well, but usually not.	Ceilings, as above.	Fan-assisted and most natural convection types have to be linked with a flue. Most appliances have balanced type. Fan-assisted type can have fully-automatic control. High-output versions of these can background heat whole floor.	All radiant gas fires require a flue. Manual, semi-automatic and fully-automatic control available.
The *Tronicair system* can be used with stub ducts in a central position in a house or flat. Its great advantage is that it is a very small unit. *Installation Cost :* Low. *Attention :* None. *Control :* Fully-automatic; quick response. *Domestic Hot Water :* None.	Cables embedded in floor slab (not usual). *Installation Cost :* Low. *Attention :* None. *Control :* Fully-automatic; somewhat slow response. *Installation Cost :* Low. *Attention :* None. *Control :* Fully-automatic; quick response.	A great range of panel, skirting convectors and fan-assisted heaters are available, many of which can be thermostatically controlled.	Both floor-standing and wall-hung radiant fires are available. They give more comfortable heat if they incorporate a convector as well. Semi-automatic. Skirting radiators, free-standing oil-filled radiators and slim wall-fixed panels give off low-temperature radiant heat and are available with semi-automatic and automatic control.
Electricaire unit *Installation Cost :* Low. *Attention :* None. *Control :* Fully-automatic. *Domestic Hot Water :* Not provided.	Electric cables embedded in floor slab. *Installation Cost :* Low. *Running Cost :* Low to medium. *Attention :* None. *Control :* Fully-automatic with external sensor. *Domestic Hot Water :* Not provided.	Storage radiators are now available with a natural convector afternoon and evening boost period, and fan-assisted capable of fully-automatic control.	Night storage heaters of the simple storage and afternoon boost kind provide low-temperature radiant heat. Any portable or unit electric heater can benefit from cheaper off-peak rates if used with a White Meter. Best used with some convected heat as well.
Suitable for small cottages both full-time and holiday use, square-shaped bungalows, small houses or flats where unit can be set in central position.	Floor heating can be installed in new houses or where a floor slab is being put down in an old one – particularly bungalows, ground floors of old cottages and basements to keep the structure warm and dry. Ceiling heating is suitable in new houses or where old ceilings are being renewed (7 ft 6 in./2.2 m or more high).	Convector unit heaters are valuable – even if you have a full heating system – to warm up individual rooms quickly on cold summer days. Fan-assisted types give quicker warm up, but check noise. For longer term comfort, convector/radiant heater is preferable.	Low-temperature units are very useful where there is no central heating – especially in babies' and old people's bedrooms to ensure constant background heat. Could provide full heating in small house or flat.

Heating
8/9 Improving an existing system/hot water

Your new house may already have a full heating system, or partial heating giving background warmth only. Try to find out from the previous owner the name of the firm who did the installation, whether there are any guarantees, or a maintenance and servicing contract in operation. Check, too, arrangements for fuel delivery, annual fuel costs, what temperatures the different rooms were kept at and for what proportion of the year the heating was kept going.

Next, check the insulation. This can reduce running costs or may enable an inadequate system to provide full heating. Have the system checked by a heating engineer, to see whether any improvements or alterations can be made, such as fitting more sophisticated controls, a different burner, etc.

Insulation and controls should always be thought of together as allies in improving comfort and reducing costs. Controls won't enable a system to produce more heat but will allow it to distribute the heat it does produce more advantageously and economically.

Retaining the existing boiler

More radiators can be added to the system, depending on its capacity, or you could change existing radiators to a larger size, to a convector type with a greater output, or to fan-assisted convectors. An accelerating pump in the primary circuit of the domestic hot-water system may enable you to make better use of the existing boiler capacity. Or you might take domestic hot water away from the boiler completely to make all its output available for the radiators. The cost of this should be checked against replacing the existing boiler by one with larger output.

Changing the existing boiler

Modern boilers take up much less space so you should be able to replace your elderly boiler with one of larger capacity, without disturbing the kitchen lay-out.

You can make the present installations trouble-free by getting rid of an attention-demanding old boiler and fitting an automatic or semi-automatic gas solid fuel or oil-fired one that can be fully controlled. Such a boiler could use the existing flue. Alternatively, you could save space in the kitchen by moving the boiler out altogether, or choosing a gas or oil-fired boiler, with a balanced flue, which could be wall-hung or tucked in a cupboard (providing it is against an outside wall).

If the house is not large and you want an open or radiant fire in the main living-room, you could switch to a high-output back boiler system. A solid-fuel back boiler system with an inadequate capacity can easily be replaced by one of the new high-output solid-fuel back boilers, or with one using gas or oil; pipework and radiators can stay or be added if necessary. Gas boilers are extremely flexible as the radiant panel, domestic hot water and central heating can all be operated independently (this also applies to many oil-fired units).

The Centralec system runs water-filled radiators by electricity, and can be used to replace a traditional boiler. The system is run off the White Meter cheap night rate (a).

Warm air

Perimeter ducted systems: These probably don't need improving, but for further comfort add humidification (b), air cleaning and cooling. Beneficial especially in cities where windows have to be kept closed against dirt and noise. Humidifiers can be bought separately and sometimes disguised as flower troughs (c). *Stub duct systems* are most commonly gas

fired or electric. They seldom provide full central heating, though proper insulation will improve their effectiveness. You can top up with radiant heater units.
Gas systems: Add some radiant gas fires where flues are available.
Electric systems: Add night storage radiators, as the house will be already wired for off-peak electricity; or add day rate radiant heaters, radiators or skirting heaters.

Night storage

Floor heating: Top up with electric radiant heaters, or fan-assisted night storage ones with flexible control room temperature.
Night storage radiators: Where you find just a few of these, it may be worth extending the system by adding more and linking them together with an external thermostatic control. They then store up more electricity on very cold nights and so relate to the house temperature on the following day. Or you could add fan-assisted ones to the existing radiators. (Diagram d shows a cut-away elevation with embedded elements, air input, output and controls.)

Day rate electricity systems

With radiators or skirting heaters, you can increase the warmth by adding further radiators, with a good room stat for temperature control.

Ceiling heating

Except perhaps in small rooms, ceiling heating is not likely to be adequate. Top up with oil-filled radiators or skirting heaters.

Controls

Effective controls will enable you to get the most comfort out of any heating system, and soon pay for themselves by keeping down running costs. A sensitive room thermostat can control room temperatures within $2°F/1°C$, much more accurately than the human body. Since even $1°F$ of unwanted heat over the year will increase the fuel bill by roughly 5%, you could save up to 30% by fitting an efficient control system.
Boiler stat: All central-heating boilers now have one of these to control the water temperature, and by manual adjustment it can be used to control the temperature of the house as well. However, it is a pretty rough and ready method and demands constant intelligent attention. It also wastes fuel.
Room stat (e): This is more reliable. Fitted in a room which maintains a fairly constant temperature, e.g. a living-room, when the required temperature is reached the control shuts off the pump which circulates the hot water through all the radiators (or warm-air system) and turns it on again when the temperature drops. Separate areas of the house can be controlled by installing more than one room stat. This is known as a zone-control.

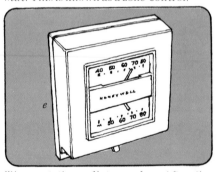

Thermostatic radiator valves (f): Can replace on/off control knobs to give more precise temperature control

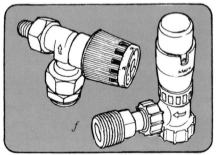

Time controls (g): Can be used with most heating systems: the most simple can be set to turn on the heating for two separate periods each day. Others have day-omission devices, and can be switched off for up to six days at a time while you are away, switching on automatically to warm the house for your return. They can also control hot water.
External sensors (h): These are fitted to an outside north wall and forewarn the heating system of outside temperature changes before the inside of the house has begun to react.

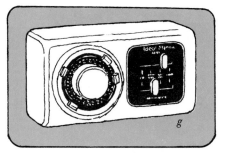

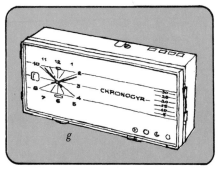

g

h

Programmers (i): These allow for a wider range of combinations; heating on, water on, both on, and so on. But as different makes vary, shop around.

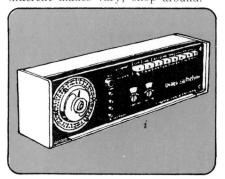

i

Frost stats (j): Frost stats override the time-switch clock and turn the boiler on to protect the heating system from freezing on cold winter nights.

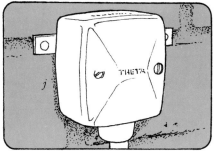

j

Day/night set-back thermostats: These work with a time clock to give two pre-set temperatures – normal daytime and lower at night for background warmth. Heating engineers prefer this to the complete shutdown of the system at night, and by avoiding dramatic temperature changes, you get considerably greater comfort for the same running costs, plus an in-built precaution against freezing.

Hot water "pumped primary" controls (k): A pump fitted in the primary circuit between boiler and hot-water cylinder.

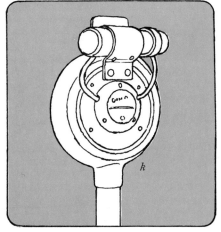

k

The hot water in this primary circuit heats the water you actually use. The pump operates only when the water in the tank has dropped below the necessary temperature. This can save on fuel bills, and means that a smaller boiler can be installed. The forced circulation is particularly useful where there is the problem of lack of gravity.

Hot water

With some heating systems water heating has to be undertaken separately. Water heaters need no longer be an eyesore. Many tuck away in cupboards. Wall-hung ones look much nicer than they used to.

Boiler systems: As with room heating, the hot-water system could be improved by insulation. Lag the lengths of pipe running from the boiler to the hot-water cylinder, and lag the cylinder thoroughly

as well, either by boxing it in or with two overlapping insulating jackets. Even if it is in the airing cupboard, the pipes alone will provide sufficient heat for airing clothes.

It is important to have a thermostatic control on the hot-water cylinder itself to ensure that the cylinder stays hot, prevent wasted fuel and avoid the danger of scalding; in addition, it stops fur and scale developing in hard water districts. Aim at a water temperature of somewhere around 140°F/60°C.

With a boiler system, you can improve the hot-water supply by incorporating a pump in the primary circuit. Or in large houses a pump in the secondary circuit will keep hot water immediately on tap.

Where a central-heating system provides hot water, check whether it is economic to keep it running for hot water only in summer. Sometimes it is less wasteful to turn it off and rely on an electric immersion heater.

A solid-fuel back boiler should also have an immersion heater so that you are not bound to keep the fire going in order to have hot water. But with the gas and oil-fired versions, domestic hot water works independently.

Storage or instantaneous heaters: Storage systems are generally cheaper to run, but in a household where heavy demands are made on hot water at limited periods of the day, an instantaneous heater may well be more convenient. As a rule you will benefit from more advantageous tariffs if you can use the same fuel for water and space heating.

Storage heaters are available to run off gas and day and/or night rate electricity. Gas instantaneous water heaters come with single or multi-point outlets which serve the bathroom as well as the kitchen. Remember that where a water heater has a traditional flue, permanent ventilation of the room to the outside is essential to prevent serious accidents.

Electric instantaneous heaters are as yet available with outputs sufficient only for sinks, basins and showers; it would take too long to fill a bath from one.

Types of hot-water heaters:
l Combined cold and hot water tanks with electric immersion heater.
m Electric slim-line cistern.
n Electric oversink water storage heater.
o Floor model.
p Gas multi-point, sometimes with swivel spout.
q Gas circulator connected to storage cylinder.
r Electric undersink heater.
s Combined cooker/water heater, solid fuel, gas or oil-fired.

Heating
10/11 Appearance

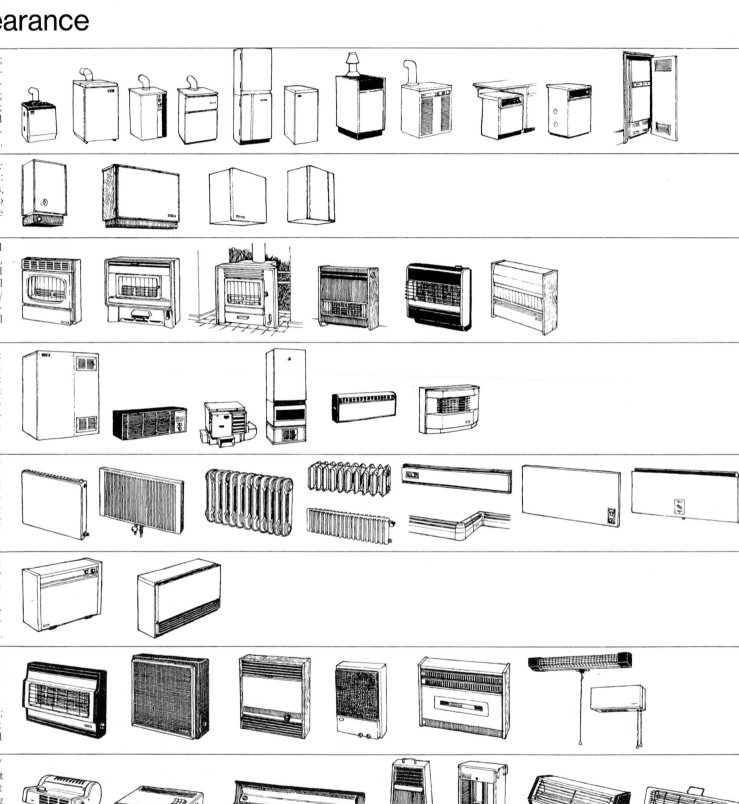

Floor boilers: Solid fuel; solid fuel gravity feed; oil-fired pressure jet; Dyno-flame with drying cabinet; compact gas; larger gas; combined gas boiler and calorifier; gas below work-top; free-standing gas.

Wall-mounted boilers: gas fired balanced flues: space saver, in three sizes, square with dimensions to co-ordinate with storage cupboards; fan-assisted.

Hearth boilers: Solid fuel for hot water, solid fuel, up to eight radiators; solid fuel free-standing, partial central heating; radiant/convected gas fired; radiant gas fired, full central heating; oil-fired hearth.

Warm-air heating: Unit for ducts and hot water; fan convector run off hot water; unit for stub duct or full heating; Electric-aire off-peak; room diffuser run from central unit; oil-fired back boiler.

Radiators: Flat convector; ribbed convector; steel column; stubby steel column; low-height convector; electric skirting panel; hot-water skirting radiator; electric closed panel, thermostat control.

Storage heaters: Off-peak electric storage radiator with booster control, three sizes, grey and white white electric storage radiator also with booster control, four models.

Non-portable heaters: Built-in radiant gas fire; gas convector heater and fan-assisted gas heater; similar, not fan-assisted; two-burner paraffin heater; wall-mounted electric fire; electric fan heater and light unit.

Portable heaters: 1 or 2 kW electric fan heaters for hot or cool air, thermostat control; 1 kW free-standing low-line electric convector; paraffin heater; "greenhouse" paraffin.

However intent you are on installing the most efficient central-heating system of all time, don't rip out every fireplace without some hard thought – not so much for practical reasons, but so that sometimes you can enjoy the magic of a real live fire. On dank and gloomy winter afternoons, there is nothing nicer than toasted marshmallows or buttered crumpets in front of an open fire.

If you are choosing a new fireplace, converting an old one, or just re-thinking a nasty, mean, little war-time grate, think big. Everything that goes with fires wants to be as generous as space will permit – a large rush basket for logs, decent-sized fire-irons, a coal hod or brass bucket that doesn't need to be refilled after every topping up.

Fireplaces don't have to look bleak and empty when not alight; in the summer fill them with interestingly shaped logs, great big fir cones or the kind of soft-foliaged plants that don't need too much light.

If your house is an old one and you are going to furnish the room in a fairly formal way, then a fireplace will provide a fulcrum about which the room can be balanced. Think twice before replacing it with a modern type. Unless you are replacing your panelled doors and sash windows at the same time, it is better to keep a consistency in the main architectural features of a room.

However, if the original one has been succeeded by a castellated brick or porridge tile job, what should you replace it with? Here scale is the important thing, and it's best to avoid the mock Adam pine ones, the phoney Tudor repro, and go for something much more robust. It is worth buying a few hours of an architect's time to have him design something in period or at least in scale. You may be able to pick up a marble or wood surround of the right period that has been taken out of another house. Or the Solid Fuel Advisory Service will give you the names of firms which make good-looking and efficient reproduction grate and hood sets.

Some of the best-looking modern fireplaces are those that are inserted in the wall above floor level. They are available with reflective surrounds and are simply slotted into the brickwork with the plaster taken right up to them. This is a useful treatment if you are disregarding the period character of a house, or in rooms with no marked architectural style.

Fine free-standing chimney breast with circular fireplace opening and stainless steel surround in an all-brick extension designed by Max Clendinning. The wide brick hearth has a clear seal finish.

Heating
12/13 Fireplaces

One of the very simplest things to do is remove the fireplace completely, and either fit a free-standing fire in the recess, or simply burn logs. Whether the latter is possible depends on whether you live in a smokeless zone or not, and this will affect the type of grate you can install.

Mantelpieces can usually be pulled away from the wall. Behind is the recess containing the grate itself usually fixed roughly in position by bricks which can be pulled out with little trouble. Trim the recess opening with a wood or metal frame and plaster up to this, or strip the plaster off the whole chimney breast for a rough effect.

The draught which provides air for combustion is an important aspect of fireplace design. If you can bring in air from outside, you will avoid the fire drawing air across the room from under doors and cracks around the windows.

Pipes to provide underfloor draughts can be inserted between the joists of a suspended ground floor. Or, if the fireplace is on an outside wall, they can be introduced from behind and beneath the hearth.

1 *A stag's head crowns the hood of this stone fireplace which has a raised hearth. A raised hearth looks attractive, but does not warm cold feet.*

2 *A wooden Victorian mantelpiece has been painted dark brown to match the room.*

3 *This kitchen stove with exposed stainless steel pipe has been placed on a raised tile platform which can be cushioned for comfortable seating.*

4 *Backing fireplaces have been converted into one. Created by removing the dividing wall between two rooms, it is now open to both sides of a large room.*

5 *Exposed brick surrounding this fireplace adds to the cosy atmosphere of log fire and bentwood rocker.*

6 *In this all-white room, black edging round the mantelpiece, door frame, skirting, etc., accents the interesting shapes they form. The fire is an electric radiant one.*

7 *A cottage fireplace, open to the room on three sides and with a roasting spit over it. The floor and steps are tile.*

8 *An old-fashioned stove rests on a slate shelf in this Scandinavian house. The pipe goes out through the white brick wall behind.*

9 *Small, portable coke-burning stove is framed by the old iron fireplace behind it. The wall is of tile.*

Raised fires and hearths also allow for a sunken ash-pit, which means that the grate needs clearing only once a week. Where the fire is against an outside wall, you can build an access panel through the wall so the ashes can be lifted directly out, not carried through the house.

If you have a large fireplace opening, and you're going to burn logs, you will need a relatively large flue opening for smoke to escape up the chimney. But where you have central heating this means that a lot of warm air from this escapes too although you do get ventilation. When there is no fire you should fit a metal panel into the flue-opening partially to block the upward flow of air. With a coal-burning fire, a much smaller flue-opening is required and the one in your existing grate may well be unnecessarily large, so you may be losing more heat up the chimney than necessary. The size of flue should vary with the type of fuel – large flue for logs, medium for coal, coke, etc, small for slow burners such as anthracite. You can narrow the opening with a throat restrictor, either fixed or with a damper to shut it when the fire is not lit.

Modern fires and closed stoves need a much gentler flow of air through them than the old-fashioned type. Asbestos flues can be threaded into the existing flue and sealed off for closed stoves only, or the existing flue can be lined with an insulating cement.

1 *A corner has been specially constructed in this room to make a fireplace.*

2 *An elegant modern fireplace and hearth of marble and stainless steel.*

3 *Here candles give an interesting lighting effect and flowers give colour.*

4 *The white-painted brick fireplace wall frames a raised hearth with a grate.*

5 *This square, concrete fireplace has been built out from the wall.*

6 *In summer, this modern fireplace with metal surround holds decorative, pretty-shaped logs.*

7 *In their country cottage, the Conrans removed the wall between two rooms, leaving a central fireplace supported by wooden beams.*

8 *This raised fireplace has the hearth in front built out so that it doubles as seating and work area.*

9 *If you haven't a fireplace, you could have a tapestry instead.*

157

Heating
14 Integration

The least visible heating is often the most successful and the least conspicuous are floor and ceiling heating. Next come warm-air and skirting systems. All have the advantage of allowing you to place furniture where you like.

Some column or panel radiators are much better looking than others and some pipe connections are neater and project less than others. Many radiators, particularly bulky night storage ones, can be incorporated in recesses or built-in shelving. Flat-faced panel ones can be painted or papered to match the walls.

1 *Panels of French caning hide a finned radiator under the window seat.*

2 *Warm-air grilles under the bathroom window stop cold down-draughts and reduce condensation.*

3 *A white-painted metal screen can conceal a radiator or warm-air unit.*

4 *Panel radiator built into a recess under the window offsets down-draughts.*

5 *Fat column radiator, in a dark colour, becomes just another decorative object.*

6 *Radiator under kitchen worktop island circulates heat from the room centre.*

7 *Warm-air grille in the quarry-tile floor.*

8 *A really well-designed radiator used as a bath panel.*

9 *To cheer up a radiator which looks bleak and cannot be concealed, paint each section differently.*

1

2

3

4

5

6

7

8

9

Co-ordination/1

When redoing a whole home, or just a single room, so many decisions depend and impinge on so many others, and so many different kinds of workmen, services and goods may be involved, that the problems can become hopelessly tangled. To eliminate confusion, double work and irritation, keep track of who and what have to be chased and when.

Systematic planning is needed. Before you alter your home, you must first of all know precisely what there is to be altered. To assemble this information, begin by making a survey of the various aspects of the building.

Space

Measure the dimensions of the rooms, marking windows and doors (don't forget to draw in "haloes" for their swing, if any).

Services

On a copy of this plan (known in the trade as a "space survey"), mark the position of the existing services.

Electric: meters, switches, sockets, light fittings
Gas: meters, pipes, outlets, fittings
Water: rising mains, stopcocks, tanks, pipes, outlets, cylinders
Ventilation: fans, ducts, outlets, grilles
Heating: boilers, radiators, fires, heaters, fireplaces
Plumbing: waste pipes, gutters
Drainage: gullies, manholes

Condition

Referring to the drawing, make a list of all the defects that you have discovered under three headings:

Structural: cracks in walls and ceilings, broken roof coverings, damaged exterior walls, broken or worn floors.
Services: antiquated electrical circuits, redundant gas pipes and outlets, leaking tanks and cylinders, suspect water pipes.
Natural attacks: wet and dry rot, damp patches, woodworm (call in an expert for diagnosis and free estimate for cure if in doubt, as they will all require specialist treatment anyway).

Layout

Measure all the pieces of furniture that you own or plan to acquire, draw them in plan or on coloured bits of card, cut them out so that you can move them about on your space survey, to arrive at your definitive layout (bearing in mind all traffic routes, relationships between zones and focal points).

Your normal planned activities will indicate where your lighting points should be, and the variously planned areas will suggest desirable finishes for floors and walls.

Draw in the positions of all the lighting points, and chart your requirements for floor and wall finishes.

Requirements

Collect brochures of all that you are going to need in the way of kitchen units, sinks, baths and other sanitary fittings; assemble all possible information on what is on the market.

Co-ordinate the colours of your fittings, having planned your general colour-scheme; decision-chains between floors/windows/walls are so interlocked that you can't consider one without the other.

Checklist

Draw up an enormous list for each room, which should show every single item that you require.

Draw up six blank columns beside the first, heading them as on the prototype (right). Fill in the relevant details. Also attach a large envelope for colour samples and brochures. Into this will also go your receipts, and on the outside of the envelope you'll keep a note of what money you've spent.

Although the installation of equipment and the finishes of walls and floors will come last in your scheme of things, almost everything on these lists will have to be ordered as early as possible to ensure delivery at the right time in the building sequence – and even if you do not immediately place a firm order, it is worth checking at once on the delivery dates. Do not place undue reliance on these, for three months can easily stretch to five, but at least you'll have a vague idea. Confirm everything in writing, keeping copies of your letters in the big envelope, and wherever possible find out the name of the person dealing with your order – the personal touch marginally helps to reduce delays.

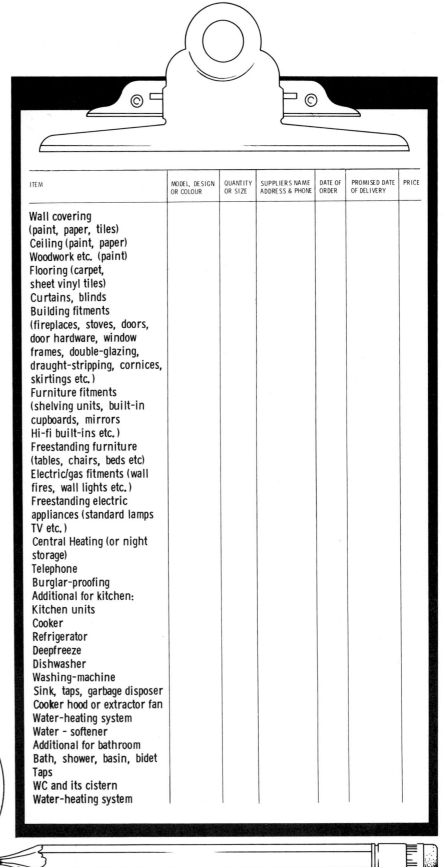

ITEM	MODEL, DESIGN OR COLOUR	QUANTITY OR SIZE	SUPPLIERS NAME ADDRESS & PHONE	DATE OF ORDER	PROMISED DATE OF DELIVERY	PRICE
Wall covering (paint, paper, tiles)						
Ceiling (paint, paper)						
Woodwork etc. (paint)						
Flooring (carpet, sheet vinyl tiles)						
Curtains, blinds						
Building fitments (fireplaces, stoves, doors, door hardware, window frames, double-glazing, draught-stripping, cornices, skirtings etc.)						
Furniture fitments (shelving units, built-in cupboards, mirrors Hi-fi built-ins etc.)						
Freestanding furniture (tables, chairs, beds etc)						
Electric/gas fitments (wall fires, wall lights etc.)						
Freestanding electric appliances (standard lamps TV etc.)						
Central Heating (or night storage)						
Telephone						
Burglar-proofing						
Additional for kitchen:						
Kitchen units						
Cooker						
Refrigerator						
Deepfreeze						
Dishwasher						
Washing-machine						
Sink, taps, garbage disposer						
Cooker hood or extractor fan						
Water-heating system						
Water - softener						
Additional for bathroom						
Bath, shower, basin, bidet						
Taps						
WC and its cistern						
Water-heating system						

Co-ordination
2/3 One jump ahead of the problems

Whatever you are going to do, for economy and speed you must ensure that it is done in logical order. A badly-leaking roof or a broken ground floor window may well have to take priority. A small, inaccessible window can wait until the rest of the house has reached the glazing stage.

Priorities

It is frequently necessary to give notice to the local authorities or other statutory bodies before you start. From then on, apart from your own particular priorities, the building sequence is fairly obvious. But there are frequent cases of bad co-ordination – if the walls are papered before the electric cables are run, the result often is that a channel for the circuit has to be cut out of the wall, which then has to be patched over – extra dirt and extra expense.

If your job is a large one, your builder will probably sub-contract all the electrical, plumbing and carpentry work, and so become responsible for the smooth flow of the job. But you may feel brave, or impecunious, and decide to do your own sub-contracting.

Service list

You'll need another list for services to be estimated for, commissioned and carried out.

Column 1 will contain some or all of the services listed overleaf together with names of the people you're dealing with, their addresses and telephone numbers. Column 2 is for the dates on which estimates are due, Column 3 for the amounts quoted and Column 4 for estimated dates of completion.

Estimates do take time, and may turn out unsatisfactorily, so that you may want more than one for purposes of comparison. Get moving on this as early as possible too.

Your services list and your requirements list will be interdependent at many points. Once you have decided on your plumber, for instance, and a date has been fixed, you'll have to get the arrival of your bath, basins, lavatories, taps and plugs timed to coincide with the planned date of his appearance. This should also coincide with the departure of the structural crews.

More important still, you must get the various craftsmen booked in the right order. Most craftsmen are in such demand that you need to pin them down months ahead, and then keep on checking and confirming all through the sequence.

Note also that if you have put in for an improvements grant, work should not start until the premises have been inspected and the plans okayed.

Telephone. Wallphone or variety of models available (consult Telephone Manager Sales). Consider press button type or warbler with or without volume control. Bell can be remote from the instrument.

Polystyrene or other insulation .

Extractor fan. Cut hole and chases for wiring and position fan control and reversing switch. Choose model with automatic shutter.

Clear finish to matchboarding to be wax-polished or varnished to prevent staining.

Wall Boiler. Cut hole through external wall first to allow for balanced flue terminal. Also cut chases for all pipes (i.e. gas and water) which are to be buried. To provide central heating & domestic hot water it is possible to install this balanced-flue wall boiler on an outside wall and supply all heating requirements. Pipes for gas and water should be chased or ducted in.

Sink. Drinking water supply from mains supply: note all other cold water should be from "down service", i.e. the storage tank.

Under work-top electrics. Provide fused socket outlets for any appliances which are required under work-top with switches located in convenient position above work-top height, e.g. dishwasher, waste-disposal unit, washing machine, fridge.

Stopcocks. Place stopcocks in supply pipes under the sink to both cold and hot taps. This enables the sink or taps to be disconnected without disabling remainder of house.

Service duct. Allow space at rear of cupboards for all service pipes, esp. $1\frac{1}{2}$ in./38 mm diameter waste pipe.

Dry rot. Spray underfloor voids with proprietary liquid before fixing carpets or other floor finish.

Floor. Check dpc, wall-plate, floor joists and floorboarding. Also ensure an adequate cross-ventilation of underfloor voids, cleaning out blocked air-bricks or providing new ones.

Heating pipes. Complete all underfloor pipes and other services before fixing down floorboards.

Wood treatment. Expose timber where rot or fungicidal attack is suspected. Treatment by specialist firm recommended. (Examination and guarantee included.)

Ceiling. Badly cracked ceiling: pin through new plasterboard into existing ceiling (use galvanized clout nails). Finish with skim coat of plaster or scrim to joints only, and line with paper.

Door. Form door opening much as for window, and fix $2\frac{1}{2}$ ft $\times 6\frac{1}{2}$ ft/0.76 m $\times$ 1.98 m or other door, complete with lining, architrave, ironmongery, etc.

Lighting. Allow for lighting electricity supply and fixing mountings. This could possibly be associated with curtain pelmet for effect.

Window. Insert new lintel after first propping up, or in some way supporting loads over. Cut out brickwork to form jambs and sill, then fix window frame and glass. Remember to build in vertical and horizontal dpcs. and to seal gaps with suitable mastic gum.

Wall lining. Consider first lining wall with pre-compressed polystyrene before applying wallpaper, as this will inhibit condensation and increase the warm feel of the room.

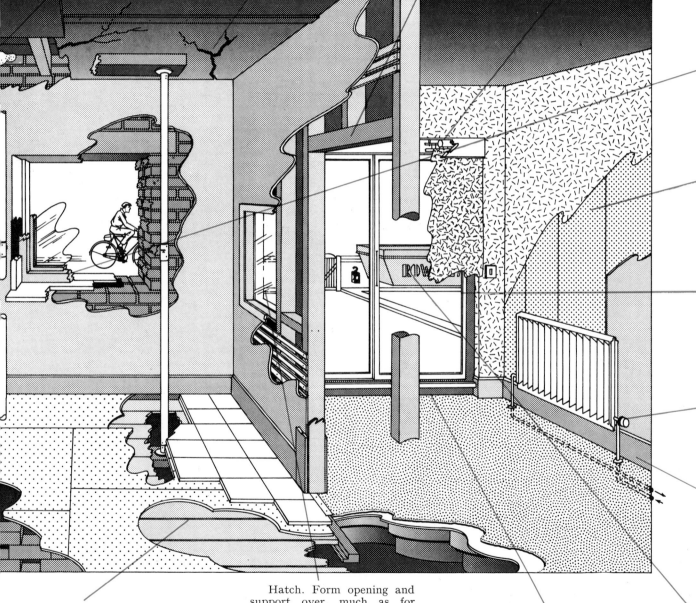

Patio door. Select left or right hand opening panel, and single or double glazing. There is a great variety of standard opening sizes.

Thermostat. Cut-out for electricity service to thermostat and boiler control unit; these should be placed away from boiler and the thermostat should not be in direct sunlight.

Skirting. Use stick-on plastic skirting where walls have been damp-proofed. If timber skirting is used treat back against rot.

Floorboarding. Carefully fix down loose boarding, and if fixing hardboard or ply sheeting over to receive tiles, ensure that correct screw nails of right length are used. (Too long nails will endanger pipes, wires, etc., underneath.)

Hatch. Form opening and support over, much as for window. Line opening with 6 in. $\times$ 1 in./150 mm $\times$ 25 mm board and fix grooved track to receive sliding panels, possibly in $\frac{1}{4}$ in./6 mm ply, or frosted glass. Fit architrave (moulded or chamfered) round both sides of lining.

Threshold. Decide on finished floor levels and detail threshold to accommodate junction of dissimilar floor finishes.

Skip. Arrange first with local authority to obtain permission for skip to be placed in the road. They give you a certificate number on the 'phone which enables you to place an order with a Road Haulage Contractor. They will provide you with red lamps to illuminate the skip at night, but you are responsible for lighting them.

Co-ordination
4 The work plan

The work plan is the order in which things actually get done. Your thinking and decision-making started from the outside in, but the work will be done from the inside out. Find out at which point on this list the jobs become relevant to your particular needs and work from that point onwards. Work through in this order even if you are only revamping a kitchen because the sequence will not change however large or small the job.

If you are your own contractor, then you will obviously be responsible for hiring each workman in the correct sequence. If your builder acts as the contractor, then this will be his responsibility, but you may require some services (removal firms, upholsterers etc.) that you'll have to contact directly.

In many cases the relevant workman should be able to produce his own materials and you will not be responsible for ordering or checking on deliveries.

Symbols

The symbols in column three indicate your involvement at each stage.

★ You must specify and order the model or design of a particular item.

! Beware – unless you specify, the workman may automatically supply you with standard fittings, when you may want a particular product which will have to be ordered.

O Delay installation until Stage 7.

Work sequence	Workman	★ ! O
Stage 1. Clear the decks		
(a) Get rid of things to be thrown out		
(b) Remove and store furniture, carpets etc.	Storage firm	
Stage 2. Knocking down		
(a) Arrange for a rubbish skip if needed	Builder/Waste clearance contractor	
(b) Prop up floors that are supported by walls that will be removed	Builder	
(c) Knock down any structure as required and remove rubble	Builder	
(d) Take out redundant pipes, wires, metres, sockets and tidy up	Builder/electrician/plumber	
Stage 3. Special treatments		
(a) Put in damp proof course and deal with other damp problems, such as rising damp	Builder/damp-course contractor	
(b) Remove worm-eaten or rotten timber and treat for dry rot. This can be a major operation, so make sure your survey is comprehensive	Dry rot contractor	
(c) Sweep out chimneys and flues	Chimney sweep	
Stage 4. Basic construction		
(a) Dig new foundations and drains	Builder	
(b) Lay foundations and drainpipes to ground level		
(c) Build up new walls to ground level		
(d) Form new ground floor		
(e) Fill in trenches back to ground level		
(f) Carry on with walls		
(g) Put in, or replace or mend beams, window frames, door frames, floorboards	Builder/carpenter	!
(h) Build upper floor or roof structure as necessary and put the roof finish on	Builder	
Stage 5. Services		
(*Repairing or installing.*) *These are the pipes, conduits and wires that are hidden behind the finishes wherever possible*		
(a) New meters	Relevant board	
(b) Electrical runs to all lighting points, heating points, cooker points, air extractors and fans, waste-disposal units, fridges, deep freezers, dish-washers, washing machines, spin dryers, tumble dryers, general socket outlets	Electrician	O
(c) Hot and cold water supply to storage tanks; water softeners; boilers and hot water cylinders; washing machinery; sinks; basins; WCs; bidets; baths; showers	Plumber	
(d) Gas to cookers; fires; boilers	Gas fitter	★
(e) Heating pipes to radiators and water cylinders	Central heating firm/plumber	★ ★

Work sequence	Workman	★ ! O
(*Stage 5 continued*)		
(f) Drains from all sanitary fittings; gutters and yard gullies to drains below ground	Plumber/builder	!
(g) Telephone cables for Post Office telephones; intercoms; entryphones	Post Office Engineer	★ O
(h) Cables for TV aerials	TV engineer	★
hi-fi speakers	Electrician	★ O
burglar alarms	Electrician/specialist	★ O
Stage 6. First finishes		
(*Either new or to be renovated.*) *Permanent finishes covering the rough surfaces to hide the services*		
(a) Plaster walls and ceilings: wall tiling	Builder/plasterer	!
(b) Floor tiling, laying sheet vinyl etc.	Flooring contractor	★
(c) Boarding and panelling walls and ceilings	Builder/carpenter	★
(d) Glazing or double glazing to existing windows	Glazier/double glazing specialist	★
(e) Doors, skirtings, architraves, window sills	Carpenter	!
(f) Sanding floors, applying sealer	Flooring contractor	!
Stage 7. Fitting out		
Permanent "Furniture" is fixed in position and, where relevant, connected to the services installed at stage 5		
(a) Kitchen and bathroom units installed	Carpenter/specialist	★
(b) Sanitary fittings fixed in place: baths; showers; basins; sinks; WCs; bidets; washing machines, dish washers; waste-disposal and extractor units	Plumber	★
(c) Cookers, electric or gas	Fitter	★
(d) Fuel supplies connected: oil; gas; solid fuel; bottled gas	Fuel supplier	★
(e) Built-in wardrobes, cupboards, shelves	Carpenter	★
(f) Draught-proofing	Builder/carpenter	!
Stage 8. Decoration		
(a) Backgrounds to final finishes: lining papers; paint undercoats; battens for stretched fabrics	Decorator Carpenter/specialist	★
(b) Final finishes: paint on ceilings, woodwork, walls; paper or fabric on walls and ceilings; mirror cladding	Decorator	★
(c) Last fittings: switch cover plates; door handles, window catches, locks	Electrician Carpenter	! !
(d) Curtain tracks	Carpenter/specialist	★
Stage 9. Furnishing		
(a) Put down underlays; carpets	Floor contractor/carpet firm	★
(b) Hang curtains and blinds		★
(c) Hang light pendents	Soft furnisher	★
(d) Bring furniture out of store and position. Hang pictures and mirrors	Electrician	

Storage/1

Those households which always seem to run smoothly with everything in its place and a place for everything, have one common feature: well-planned storage throughout the house. Remember, one always tends to underestimate one's needs; twice as much as one thinks is usually about right. (And remember, too, that dead storage can be invaluable provided that it holds domestic expendables bought in bulk. Things tucked away and not used for years are best got rid of.)

The only way to provide enough storage space in a small house is to get it against walls. "Working walls" for storage are discreet and self-effacing when closed, but everything is to hand when you open the doors. And the secret of making a room *look* spacious rather than crammed with cupboards is to keep the outside finish simple and avoid unnecessary knobs, moulding and contrasting materials.

Good storage is usually expensive, so expect to spend at least as much as you would on carpets or floor covering in most rooms and, of course, many times more in the kitchen.

Insist that storage meets your needs. This means keeping an open mind. If a system works well in one room, there is no reason why it shouldn't be suitable in another. Could the kitchen units be continued into the dining area? Why not use one and the same system in the living-room, the bedrooms, and on the landing? Why must shirts and jerseys go into wooden drawers rather than into wire baskets? Or on open shelves? If no manufacturer offers what you want or if it looks as though it would be too expensive, settle for manufactured cupboard fronts only and think of having the inside made up to your own specification.

Before making your choice of storage system, check out these points:

☐ Are you likely to move house in the foreseeable future? (This will help your decision regarding fixed v movable storage.)

☐ How many different kinds of storage system will you ideally need?

☐ In how many rooms will you need storage? Which of your possessions seem habitually to billow over?

☐ Have you considered how wall-storage would affect the proportions of your room?

☐ How much you can afford to spend.

☐ Do you like to see all your possessions on display, or would you prefer to have them all neatly out of sight?

This system is made up of cubes, fitted with drawers or open shelves, which are stacked one above the other.

Storage
2/3 What are you storing?

Before starting on a project, most interior designers send their clients a questionnaire, asking all members of a household exactly what they intend to store in their home.

Most of us do not employ professional designers, but this is no reason why we should adopt a haphazard approach to our storage problems. So get out pencils and paper, and ask each person in the family who is old enough to write to list his or her possessions.

Bedroom storage

Start in the bedroom. Although there are statistics on the average volume of clothes owned by any one person at any one time, none of us is as average as all that when it comes to the actual countdown. However, no matter how many suits, ties or pairs of pants a man may own, or how many maxi-mini-micro garments fill a girl's wardrobe on a given date, the basic unit measurements are pretty static. To work out how much space is ideally needed, add up the basic units, and do not forget that hemlengths change all the time while wardrobes' innards will not do so unless you keep the shelving adjustable.

Children's storage

Children change their sizes so fast that there is no way of giving a precise guide for their storage needs. Whenever possible, provide as much space as for an adult.

Bathroom

Razors and medicines should be stored in a special cabinet or drawer. If there are children under ten in the house, have a childproof catch or lock. Allow extra space for a supply of lavatory paper, soap and toothpaste.

Linen storage

Sheets and towels are all right in the airing cupboard, provided that they do not stay there too long. But if your airing cupboard doubles as a drying cupboard, the damp conditions will in time rot the fibres, and anything not in regular use must be stored elsewhere. When you calculate the quantity of linen that you need (ideally four sheets, four pillowcases, two towels, two duvet cases for each bed) don't forget that half of this is likely to be in use and will not require storing. But you should provide summer storage space for things like eiderdowns and blankets.

Kitchen/dining-room

What you store where will depend on your way of life, but most people find it convenient to keep china and cutlery in general use in the kitchen, close to the dishwasher or sink. To give exact figures for the space taken up by a dinner-service is impossible because of the variety in sizes of the plates alone (the difference in diameter between meat-plates and, say, pudding plates is approximately 6 in./152 mm), not to speak of the possible differences in serving dishes.

But it is worth noting that it is the width of the shelving that is crucial; it is much neater to store small items on narrow ledges just wide enough to take them, than to have them sitting at the front of full-depth shelves.

Cups, say the manufacturers, should never be stacked (unless designed for the purpose), nor hung by their handles. They should be placed on their sides, nestling in groups of four; this will prevent much accidental chipping.

Pots and pans should of course be near the cooker, and again it is impossible to say just how much room they will take up. There are storage units especially designed to take the average requirement for a family of four – the magic number as far as statisticians are concerned.

They also tell us that such a family requires at least 10 cu ft/.3 cu m of space for dry food storage, i.e. the staples. The amount of fresh foods you can store will be governed by the capacity of your refrigerator and/or larder.

Cleaning materials

Whether these go in a separate cupboard in the kitchen or under the stairs, allow space for at least a vacuum cleaner, broom, mop, dustpan and brush and a bucket. Poisonous cleaning products must be kept out of children's reach. There is, of course, no reason why all cleaning things should live in one and the same place (a small extra vacuum cleaner upstairs is worth its weight in trouble saved and takes up little space).

Living-room

Permanent storage in the communal living area should be for shared possessions only. Parents of small children might make some provision for storing toys in the living-room – in a drawer or perhaps a window-seat, where the available space dictates what can be stored.

Seldom-used things

Suitcases, bowls for bulbs that bloom in the spring, camping and sports gear that is seasonally needed, can go into "dead" storage – tops of cupboards, or attics, or even drawers in spare rooms. For anything else, it tends to be a case of out of sight, out of mind, and these spaces are not really useful.

How much space do you need for your possessions?*
Each square equals 4 inches square.

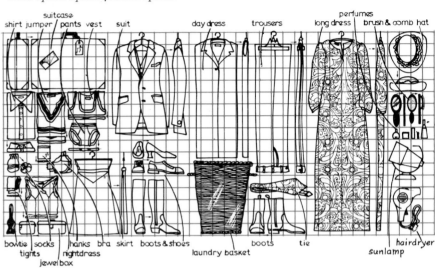

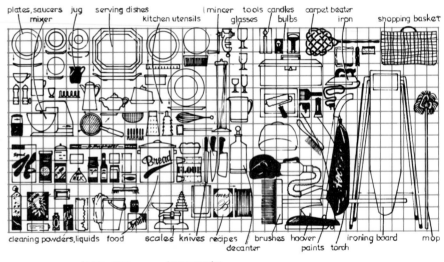

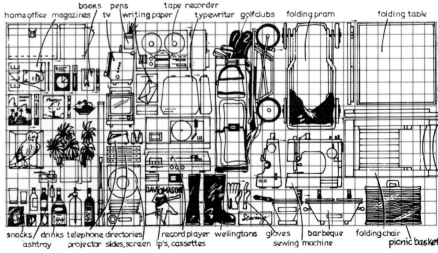

Organize the storage space at your disposal so that you make the best use of it.

1 Wardrobe fitted with clear plastic drawers – one for each shirt – makes selection easy and keeps clothes dust free and uncrushed.

2 Open shelves inside a cupboard can take the place of drawers. Here larger garments are folded and placed direct on the shelf while small things are collected together into wire trays to keep them tidy.

3 Flat baskets in an open slot under a work-surface not only keep small articles tidy but help to make them quickly accessible.

4 The inside of a really well planned wardrobe. Note how well the space is used. There are no large unused areas above or below the hanging clothes.

Storage
4/5 What is there to choose from?

The choice is likely to lie between free-standing, built-in or modular storage. Freestanding cupboards, bookcases and wardrobes tend to be the heirs of traditional, craftsman-made furniture – acquired usually for their looks rather than their capacity. Built-in storage on the other hand, together with shelving, is the basis of the "working-wall". Its function is to conceal or display your possessions, and it should merge with the walls, becoming an architectural feature.

Modular systems

Modular storage fittings usually comprise units of standard height and depth and two or three different widths, designed as to fill almost any given space within a few inches the remaining space filled in with a scribed panel. These storage units tend to come in several finishes: natural wood, white or coloured.

The carcass, the doors and panels are often veneered chipboard, because it stands up to central heating better than solid timber, which may warp and crack.

The most popular veneers are teak, sapele, rosewood and mahogany, but too much of these rich woods up the walls of a small room could be overpowering. Solid beech, oak, ash and pine lend themselves to large flat areas better than these richer woods.

Check on the finish of any furniture before you buy. Laminate is the toughest followed by lacquer and veneer and then paint. Painted furniture chips and usually does not take so kindly to washing. Coloured finishes can be exciting, if restrictive, and there are coloured stains which cannot chip.

Metal storage units are usually intended for contract use, but can provide tough, inexpensive domestic storage. Be sure to inspect the inside. The finish often differs from the outside even if the colour is the same.

Look at the handles, hinges and catches. Handles are often simple to replace, but hinges and catches must be strong or it will not be long before the doors do not shut properly.

If you are buying more than one unit, get the manufacturers' catalogues to see full ranges with all the details.

Corners

Not all storage ranges are designed to turn a corner. Some cupboards can be butted up to form a neat right angle leaving a dead area in the corner which it is difficult to reach from outside. Some manufacturers overcome this difficulty by cutting across the corner. This wastes some of the space, but makes the whole area more accessible. In kitchen units the problem is sometimes solved by a fitting of circular baskets which swing out.

Comparing prices is difficult because each manufacturer's goods are a different size and each unit is priced separately. Ask your retailer to give you an estimate or price several different ranges to fill the alloted area yourself.

Free-standing living-room units

These are made either in one piece with the base fixed to the shelves above or as stacking units. A compromise between the two systems offers a choice of base and top units, and maximum versatility for arranging a variety of heights.

Built-in living-room units

These range from simple storage walls, which can be used as see-through room-dividers, to units which make up the core of a room. Some of these (notably the German ones) are so thoughtfully designed that they go far beyond solving simple storage problems. It is worth studying these systems, even if there is no immediate prospect of acquiring one, because they do suggest many new possibilities of streamlining one's ideas. When ordering this sort of storage, it is essential to do one's sums correctly, to give the proper space to each item.

Continuity

In small houses or flats storage figures large, and it is worth considering using the same units throughout the house to give a feeling of continuity.

Few units are designed for overall use, but some kitchen units can be used in other rooms. The clinical ones with shiny laminate finish and metal trim can look stunning in a dining room, while some of the pine or matt white units can be used throughout, especially if they include open shelves and full-length cupboards.

Inside fittings can be bought separately from carcasses and include plastic drawers, wire storage baskets and shelves of related sizes which can be used throughout the house.

1 *A roomy wall system for bedroom storage unit with link dressing table, wardrobes and linking top cupboards.*

2 *The same system composed of top units superimposed on a base made of drawers and a cupboard.*

3 *Interlübke fitted wall units include over 700 variations, which can be tailored to fit the walls of any room in the house. The desk folds up into the wall and the filing cabinet slides away into the space beneath.*

3

1

2

1 *Palaset cubes. Each cube is complete in itself so the units shown here could be arranged in many different ways. The cubes can be free-standing, wall mounted or used with a bridging top to form a table.*

2 *Wall storage made up of four units, each complete in itself. The advantage of these units is that they are easy to rearrange and can be used back to back as a room divider.*

3 *Habitat shelving – simple, strong and inexpensive. It can be used against a wall or, as here, free-standing to form a room divider.*

4 *A built-in wall system. The construction is divided into cubes which are fixed, but the shelves within the cubes are adjustable.*

3

4

Storage
6/7 Covering up

When you place your order for ready-made storage furniture you often have a choice of doors – not just of their styles but also of how they will open. And if you are having the units built to your own specification, this latter point is something you will need to consider carefully.

What sort of door you choose, and how you want it to open, will depend on how much space there is in front of it, and on how much clearance the door will have over the contents of the cupboard.

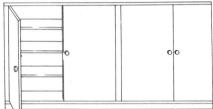

Hinged doors undoubtedly have the advantage of giving the maximum access to the inside of the cupboard. But they require a semicircle of the radius of the door left clear in front of them to allow for opening, which often annoyingly limits the arrangements of the furniture.

Saloon doors can be a satisfactory compromise. They obviously require less room to open (about half as much) but slightly limit the opening into the cupboard. A further disadvantage is that since you need two doors in the space of one, your costs will obviously increase in proportion.

Sliding doors slot into two top and bottom parallel channels sometimes with roller-bearing backs, if they are heavy. They overlap slightly where they meet and so, again, access is limited. This means that the width of the items to be stored is somewhat limited, unless you don't mind manoeuvring them a bit when you take them out. The advantage of these doors is that since they open on each other, no extra floor space needs to be left in front of them.

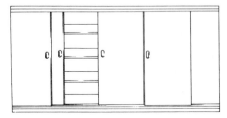

Hinged concertina doors require special top and bottom fixing gear linked to metal channels so that they can slide smoothly. This type of door is particularly suitable for a long run of cupboards where unobstructed access is essential to all but the very end sections. The disadvantage of these doors is that since they are hung from the centre of each panel, when they are open they project equally into and out of the cupboard. It is essential therefore that the cupboard is several inches deeper than usual, because any shelves within it must fall short of the total depth. A similar door made of battens covered in simulated leather, is sometimes used but since it is not particularly attractive it is mainly for business and hospital buildings. It looks better painted white or, for that matter, in any other colour, and could at a pinch be used in a domestic situation.

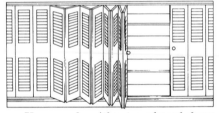

You can do without cupboard doors altogether if you use roller blinds which again need no floor clearance. They do not obstruct access on either side, only at the very top, where rarely used items could be stored.

In the case of bedrooms, where clothes are hung on a wall-to-wall rail or on one running the length of a recess, simple unlined floor-length curtains (perhaps matching those by the windows) would do. Large Indian bedspreads, side-to-middle, would also make good, cheap curtains of this sort, which should clear the floor by $\frac{1}{4}$ in./7 mm.

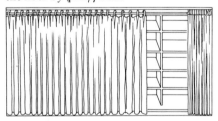

1 *Louvred doors are inexpensive and widely available in a good range of sizes. Here they are used in pairs. The pine doors have been lacquered and fitted with brass knobs.*

2 *Large sliding doors conceal a dressing area with open shelves, a dressing table with a mirror and light. The door closes, hiding away all the paraphernalia of clothes and dressing, leaving the bedroom immaculate.*

1

2

1

2

3

4

5

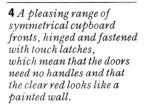

6

7

8

9

1 *Wall completely covered from floor to ceiling in simple white cupboards. The top cupboards make "semi-dead" storage for possessions not in everyday use – suitcases, perhaps, or out-of-season clothes. The doors are hinged.*

2 *Cupboard discreetly built into a wall and concealed by a flush door papered to match the surrounding walls.*

3 *Sliding doors on a range of well-fitted cupboards. The carefully fitted interiors ensure that no valuable space is wasted.*

4 *A pleasing range of symmetrical cupboard fronts, hinged and fastened with touch latches, which mean that the doors need no handles and that the clear red looks like a painted wall.*

5 *Plain white doors, arranged in pairs with brass handles and decorated with panels of chair caning trimmed in split bamboo.*

6 *A wall covered in shelves which are protected from dust by red roller blinds which also help to conceal occasional untidiness.*

7 *Sliding kitchen doors clad in mosaic mirror tiles provide a surface which is washable and helps, by reflection, to light the room.*

8 *A pine-clad bathroom with a wall of pine doors concealing floor-to-ceiling storage.*

9 *Another false wall made from felt-covered panels. Large panels such as these must be thick enough to be stable and besides making a handsome background for pictures, would make good pinboards.*

Because shelves are the simplest, cheapest and most versatile form of storage, they are too often treated without the respect that their usefulness deserves. So before you place your order for timber, spare a little time to think about shelving. You will be amazed what a difference a little extra planning can make.

First decide what you want to store on the shelves, and which wall you are going to fix them to.

Check that the wall is made of solid bricks or breeze blocks, as flimsy partition walls usually cannot stand the weight of shelving plus content. Next find out if any electric cables or gas pipes are concealed in the plaster, as it is obviously essential not to drill holes for the fixings in these areas. If you are in doubt get expert advice.

Positioning shelves

Make a scale drawing of the whole wall. Draw in the door and windows and any furniture that stands against the wall. In coloured pencil add the light switch or electric points and then in dotted lines the position of concealed gas pipes or electric cables.

Make an assessment of the possessions to be stored on the shelves. Which is the best way to place them for your convenience and to obtain the best visual effect? Will the contents of the shelves remain the same or will it change and be added to later?

Measuring up

Sort your books into piles as they will be arranged on the shelf and measure them. Very large books can be laid flat on top of each other.

As each LP record sleeve measures $12\frac{1}{2}$ in./318 mm square, you will be able to stand about 80 on every linear foot of shelf. Eighty records in their sleeves weigh about 45 lb, so make sure that the shelves can take the weight.

If you plan to intersperse records or books with china or glass, again measure up. Will the shelves need a lip to prevent the china from slipping off or a narrow beading to make plates stand up? Do the shelves need or merit special lighting?

Brackets

If you are reasonably sure that the contents of your shelves will remain the same, there is no point in fitting uprights and *adjustable* brackets. Either use brackets screwed into the plaster at either end of the shelf in an alcove, or from side to side below it on a flat wall. On unplastered brickwork, glass shelves can be set into the wall, between bricks.

If the shelves are long, you will need inconspicuous supports.

Adjustable metal shelving, originally intended for office use, makes attractive, inexpensive and strong home storage.

Tebrax uprights and adjustable brackets. Position of the brackets is governed by slots in the uprights.

Click upright and adjustable brackets, which slide up and down, can be locked at any chosen position.

Partitions, other than load-bearing ones formed by the supports, are not necessary unless the shelves are to form a display case. If this is so, make sure that the size and shape of each "box" relates to the object it will hold.

Wall-mounted uprights with brackets provide strong and adjustable shelving. The brackets either fix into one of a series of slots in the upright or lock into positions anywhere on a track.

Brackets usually hold the shelves at a right angle to the wall although some, designed initially for shop displays, incline the shelves downwards; these might be useful for holding magazines.

How close together you should place the uprights on the wall will depend on the width of the shelf and the weight of its contents. The heavier the load the more uprights, and brackets, you need.

Sizes

Shelves come in a number of standard widths similar to the size of the brackets, and DIY shops will cut them to the length you require. You can choose from natural timber or plywood, blockboard and chipboard, which are also available with wood veneers or white melamine finishes. If you choose one of these, buy the self-adhesive finishing strip to complete the cut ends. These strips are also available for the most popular plastic laminates which are ideal for kitchen shelves.

A thick shelf with added hooks will store half the clutter in the kitchen. Square hooks on the side for cups and jugs are best in case the handles are wide, but fit round hooks underneath for the can opener, cheese grater, saucepans, egg whisk and slice. Light plastic drawers with their own runners can be fixed to the underside of the shelf for storing clean tea towels, greaseproof paper and very small kitchen utensils (see diagram C). Add air-tight storage jars for dry goods and, for very little money, you have fitted up a very serviceable kitchen.

A similar shelf about 12 in./305 mm wide is very useful in a study. Scissors and keys along with unpaid bills are less easily mislaid if they are automatically put on a special hook. Paper clips, glue and staples can be stored in the drawers.

Plan your own cupboards

Shelves inside cupboards are very important. Make sure that you are not wasting space. Unless you need them that way, avoid deep shelves and shelves that are too far apart. You should never need to move one row of things to reach another.

Shelves for china should be fairly close together. It is more convenient to have two piles each of six plates than one

Shelves recessed into the wall. Note the small lips built into the plaster on each side, to support the shelf.

of twelve. However, make sure that the shelves are not so close together that you cannot see what you are doing, as this can cause breakages.

In an old cupboard with deep shelves spaced far apart, fix another narrow shelf between two of the old ones and then use only the front of the wide shelf, transferring the china from the back to the mezzanine. Glasses can be stored on narrow shelves.

Although you may prefer to store underclothes and sweaters in drawers where they are better protected from dust, they can be stored on shelves inside a bedroom wardrobe.

Simple but effective storage for a child is an arrangement of uprights with adjustable brackets on the inside back wall of the wardrobe area. Add two wide shelves, one with a hanging rail screwed to its underside. For a little child, hang clothes out of reach or keep them folded on the top shelf. Use the bottom part for toys, but as soon as the child is big enough to take care of his own clothes, move the hanging rail down to within his reach. As he grows up adjust his storage to his needs. A curtain on a ceiling-mounted track will take the place of doors.

Both adjustable and fixed brackets come in large enough sizes to support a wide shelf which can be used as a work-surface. This can be a dressing table or desk in a bedroom, a play surface in a child's room or a breakfast counter or cooking area in a kitchen.

(Opposite) Simple and inexpensive shelving provides attractive storage for books, records, record-player, bric-a-brac.

Storage
10/11 Relating to architecture

Furniture that is set against the walls tends visually to become part of the fabric of the house and unless positioned with care can upset the balance of the room.

Anyone who has planned a kitchen will know how difficult it is to fit in the electrical appliances, provide enough storage, and have everything in the most convenient position. But don't lavish all your ingenuity on the kitchen. The rest of the house needs just as much care and thought.

In old houses with tall ceilings, cupboards should be added with extreme care. If the architectural proportions of the rooms are very fine, it may be preferable to stick to a free-standing wardrobe rather than risk building in cupboards which will wreck the symmetry of the layout. However it is often possible to build in storage that blends with the room, but it is essential to allow the room itself to dictate where and how you fit it.

Sit in the room. Ignore any furniture or curtains and note the architectural details. Make a plan showing the position of the door and windows and then an elevation of each wall. Look out for the moulding and skirting and the details of the fireplace. Search for strong horizontal lines (like the mantelpiece) which you should consider when you position work-tops and shelves.

Next look at the furniture. Is the storage you are planning complementary to its style and function? Carefully located, storage can add visual interest to a room and improve its proportions.

Bedrooms

The bedrooms of modern houses are rarely larger than 12 ft/3.7 m × 10 ft/3 m, allowing enough space for one or two beds and little other furniture. Here the best answer is to devote one entire wall to built-in cupboards. If you are short of room, dispense with a chest of drawers and order shelves and drawers for the inside of the cupboard.

Divide the hanging space into long and short areas, the former for dresses and coats and the latter for suits and skirts. Use the free space under hanging clothes for extra drawers or hang one row of clothes above another.

Spare-rooms

For very small bedrooms, either build in all the furniture like a ship's cabin or try to site the hanging space on the landing outside. In many modern European flats, the corridor in the bedroom area is lined on one or both sides with floor-to-ceiling cupboards, leaving more space in the adjacent bedrooms.

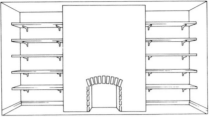
Open shelves fitted into the recesses either side of the chimney-breast.

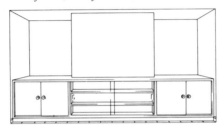
Low level cupboards that incorporate narrow shelves for glasses.

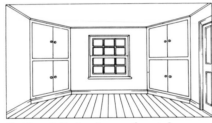
Cupboards that make use of wasted corner space, and continue the skirting.

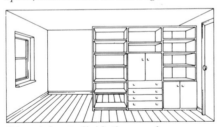
Open shelves to divide the room for different uses.

Moulding continued along the front of full-height units.

1/2 The recess each side of a chimney-breast is one of the natural places for fitting shelves, which can successfully return around the corner. The position and size of the windows often help to suggest where shelving might be placed. It can go either into existing recesses, or, as here, the uprights themselves may create the effect of recessed windows.

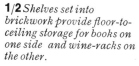

1/2 *Shelves set into brickwork provide floor-to-ceiling storage for books on one side and wine-racks on the other.*

3/4 *Storage recess is fitted with pigeon-holes and shelving above cupboard with louvred doors. These are held in place by magnetic touch-points and are entirely removable for easy access to the radio, record-player and tape recorder which they conceal.*

5/6 *Storage relating to the room in which it is situated. Doors, cupboards and drawer-fronts all match to make a good-looking panelled wall at one end of the room.*

7 *Shelves built across a cupboard door will mask it; the inside of the door frame provides storage. In this drinks cupboard, built into a recess in the wall, a drop-down flap makes serving easier. When the door is closed, the entire cupboard is invisible.*

8 *An ingenious treatment of floor levels provides storage beneath steps as well as seating.*

9 *Books here placed at ceiling height on a run of shelving make a continuous frieze around the room – uninterrupted by doors or windows.*

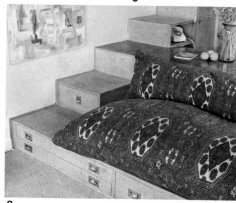

173

Storage
12 Show what you've got!

Kitchen dressers are natural display areas (as well as providing useful cupboard and drawer space). If the china on the shelves is in regular use, it will not have a chance to gather dust.

Kitchen utensils often need to be air-dried before they are put away, so why not do two jobs at once and store them on hooks on the wall? The arrangement here has the quality of a mural in 3-D.

If you are living in a furnished flat, you may find the hanging space provided inadequate. These metal rails on castors are the answer. Strong and inexpensive, they dismantle when you move house. Valuable clothes less frequently used can be protected from dust with plastic covers.

A plastic wall tidy with a place for everything that usually clutters up a desk drawer saves time and tempers.

Halls/stairs/landings/1

Halls, staircases and landings can be difficult areas to handle well. First and foremost they are, by their very nature, traffic routes, designed to get you from one part of the house to another as simply and easily as possible. That means no chance of stumbling over obstacles like pieces of furniture, of slipping on highly polished floors, skidding on loose rugs or mats, or tripping on badly lit stairs.

But while halls and landings are important as traffic areas they can become uninteresting and wasted spaces unless they are planned in a positive way to work well with the rest of the house.

They may be roped in for all sorts of jobs that need not interfere with the through traffic; they may combine the function of telephone booth, art gallery, laundry, library, storage area or home office – separately or together – but they need to be carefully planned, and their main function must be kept in mind.

The hall is the first place your guests (and you) will see on entering your house, so it should be as friendly and welcoming as you can make it. It will colour everyone's reaction to the rest of your establishment, and since it is usually the one place where visitors will spend comparatively short stretches of time, the decoration can afford to be on the dramatic side. However, you yourself are likely to be in and out of the place a lot and the excitement will, in time, fail to register; when it does, think again.

Above all, don't forget the practicalities. But keep an open mind about the extra uses to which you might put your circulation areas. In rethinking them, and especially if you suspect that a bit of surgery is indicated to make them adequate, be clear about your personal needs and priorities. Be sure that you have exploited all the possibilities of the existing layout before embarking on any major operation. Check out the points below – they may help you to analyse the problem and, together with these suggestions, point the way to a cure.

☐ Would you like to take the load off some overworked room?
☐ Would you like your hall occasionally to double as an extra room?
☐ Can it provide additional storage space?
☐ Could you put the wall space on the staircase to some better use?
☐ Could you improve circulation?

1 *Shallow 3-D objects take the place of pictures in this town-house hall. Furniture is slim so as not to impede the circulation.*

2 *In wider halls, there can be more furniture, and more objects, which in this case reinforce the country-house feeling.*

1

2

Halls/stairs/landings
2/3 The hall as a hall/as an extra room

You may be one of those lucky people with plenty of space, who can afford to use the hall purely to give a warm welcome. Or you may have only a narrow passage with doors leading off it. Either way you will have to plan it carefully. Start by making a list of all the things you will want in the hall.

The necessities

There should, obviously, be a place to park coats. Umbrellas must have somewhere to drip. A looking glass in reasonable light, either natural or artificial, with a clothes brush in the vicinity, is helpful. So is provision for a stiff brush and scraper for getting mud off boots and clothes.

Make arrangements to have somewhere on which to drop the parcels you've dragged home; if there is no room, quite a narrow shelf might do, and provide a place for leaving letters and messages for absent members of the household. If your hall is too narrow even for this, you might put up a pinboard, latticed with tape, where correspondence could be tucked.

Circulation

Plot – as for all other rooms – how the necessities can be fitted in, making sure that you leave all the traffic routes clear. You will be surprised how neatly a little chest of drawers can sit in a recess, but remember when you consider your traffic system that it will not just be a matter of unencumbered pedestrians.

You may have, or acquire, a bicycle or pram that might have to live indoors, or you might be carrying trays from the kitchen to the living-room, so you don't want to block the way.

Telephone

If there is only one telephone in the house or flat, the hall is probably the best place for it so that conversations won't interfere with what is going on in the rest of the household. If there is room, provide a comfortable chair and a telephone table with space to store directories vertically. If the hall is tiny, have a wall-mounted telephone, a shelf for directories and a slim stool or even a flap-down chair.

1 *Little chests of drawers can sometimes be fitted into surprisingly small recesses.*

2 *Two-way telephone – use it from hall or from the adjoining living-room, depending on the amount of privacy that you require.*

3 *The end of a passage becomes a cloakroom, where coats can hang well out of the way.*

4 *Cupboard-lined wall in the hall can solve storage problems in other rooms.*

Nothing looks worse in a hall than a line or hooks with hats and coats hanging limply on them and an array of Wellington boots underneath. (Coats should always be on hangers anyway.) Try to make use of irregularities in your hall to accommodate such things. An alcove bridge with sliding doors can become shallow storage for coats by wall-mounting shelves above for hats, and perhaps a shoe rack underneath. Or you could build hanging space across the end of a passage or along the length of a wide corridor. If you are left with a fairly narrow space, sliding or concertina doors or even just a curtain across will ensure that when someone is rummaging in the cupboard, other people are not prevented from getting past the open door.

Walls

Even in a small hall there is usually quite a lot of wall space which it would be a pity to waste. Quite often, the top of the stairwell is the only place of sufficient height to take a really large painting or tapestry. Collections of narrow objects, like plaster seals, corn dollies, patchwork or African masks, lend themselves to being displayed in the hall, and look particularly nice if they are specially lit.

Wall space could be used to take books for which there is no room elsewhere – but make arrangements for some steps or a sturdy stool, otherwise you will have difficulties in reaching those on the top shelves. Landings and the wall space below the stairs can be used for this purpose, too. If the banisters are unprepossessing, make "steps" of bookshelves which rise with the staircase and double as a handrail.

Pram park

Small modern homes are just not designed for baby carriages. One answer is a carrycot with a folding chassis which can be stored in a cupboard or under the stairs. If you have to manoeuvre a large pram in the hall, at least be sure to choose a tough durable wall finish, because it is quite certain to get bumped and dirtied.

5 *Boxed-in radiator becomes hall table, and wall space above it a picture gallery.*

6 *Telephone table neatly incorporates umbrella stand and other storage facilities.*

7 *Shallow bookshelves, floor to ceiling and extended above the door, for library/hall.*

8 *Small folding prams can often be parked in the space under the stairs. When there are prams about, make sure of a tough wall finish because of the inevitable scuffs.*

Hall/kitchen

If you are really pushed for space, and can ensure ventilation by, say, installing an extractor fan, you might even fit a two ring cooker and fridge into this area, and use the room once designated as a kitchen for another purpose.

Hall/dining-room

A fairly large hall can be a convenient place for meals. For a permanent arrangement, treat this area as you would a dining-room, making sure it is out of the way of the main traffic routes. Even where there isn't a lot of space, you may still come up with a workable solution: cushioned cantilevered benches take up much less room than chairs. For occasional use, you might decide to make a wall-hung grouping of folding chairs and tables (reminiscent of those relief sculptures), or have stacking chairs that store away and a drop-leaf table.

However, if your dining table has to stand in the centre of your hall or landing, make it a narrow one, with no corners to bump into. You won't want to be clobbered with extra side tables, and there should be no awkward thresholds to impede the trolley.

Improving circulation

The problems of moving easily from place to place in a house are often left unsolved by the designers, and you may only discover them after living there for a bit. Doors may be badly positioned, or hung inwards instead of outwards (which can be easily remedied) or perhaps there are too many doors altogether. For example, if rooms are connected, one of the doors to the hall may be redundant. You could block it up; put a mirror or shelves on it; or use the gap as a coat-hanging place.

Moving walls

You may be able to steal space from the hall for one of the surrounding rooms, or vice versa, by partially removing walls. By breaking through you may also be able to borrow or lend light. Remember, though, that the minute you start playing with the structure, you must

1

2

3

4

1 Under-the-stairs kitchen includes all that is needed for preparing light meals: two-ring cooker, refrigerator, sink.

2 Hall/dining-room: in a narrow space, use a table that is as narrow as possible, and chairs that fold up between meals.

3 Under-the-stairs home-office: strategically placed mirror prevents claustrophobia.

4 End-of-hall laundry makes for more room in the kitchen.

consult an architect or builder about the safety of your proposals, building regulations and possible planning permission.

Landings

Upper landings can often be improved. If they are dark and cramped, a small room might be opened into the area, at the same time giving light from its window.

Under the stairs

Under-the-stairs is often just so much wasted space in which junk accumulates. But it could be transformed into a really useful spot. It is, of course, not a bad place for storing cleaning materials or hanging outdoor clothes, but if there is enough clearance, it could become a small cloakroom with a hand-basin and hanging rail. With adequate lighting, you could also hang a long mirror, preferably on the inside of the door for a good head-to-hem view when it is open. With proper plumbing and ventilation facilities, you might also install a lavatory (with an extra slim cistern).

Hall/study

Or you might fit in your study, though that would depend on how much other activity there is likely to be and how much quiet is needed. But if it is just a case of doing the household accounts and writing letters, then a properly lit desk, a chair and perhaps some shelves are all that is needed. If you don't want to tuck your desk under the stairs but still mean to put it into the hall, it is best to keep it as far away as possible from all doors and from the foot of the stairs. A folding screen would be useful for a little extra privacy and draught-proofing.

Hall/laundry

If there is no room to squeeze washing machine and tumble dryer in the kitchen, perhaps one or both could be fitted in along a passage, on a landing, or at the back of the hall, if the water supply can be provided. By building them in – complete with a work-top, storage cupboard, and if there is room, a fold-away ironing board – this area could become an inconspicuous, but efficient laundry.

5

6

7

8

5 By breaking through the wall between hall and living-room, both gain space and light.

6 Partial removal of the hall wall appears to throw the ground floor into one; the "balustrade" becomes a means of area demarcation.

7 Desk-and-sitting area on the landing extends upstairs living space.

8 Under-the-stairs spare low-level bedroom.

The rule about doormats is "the bigger the better". They not only look silly when they are little and mean, but they are awkward to use. Recess the mat into the floor wherever possible. This is easier when the floor is tiled, but it is rewarding even on an existing board floor, because it is safer and looks tidier. It also means that when you are cleaning, you can vacuum right over the mat. If it isn't recessed, you will need a raised threshold for the door to clear the mat. Sisal doormat carpeting comes in a range of colours in tile form or by the yard, and can look splendid if used wall-to-wall.

Letterboxes

Choose a large one; it's maddening having to answer the postman's knock for everything larger than a middle-sized envelope. Those cages which are supposed to save you a lot of bending down aren't such a good idea if you are often away from home – they quickly clog up, and corners of mail sticking out of the slot outside are a positive invitation to burglars.

Hall-floors

The floors in circulation areas are going to get very hard wear, so whatever you choose should be durable and easy to keep clean. Whatever you are thinking of – treated wood, quarry tiles, sealed cork, vinyl or good, old-fashioned linoleum – first read *Floors*.

If you live in the country and mud is a problem, think in terms of a washable hard floor. In a town flat, you may need a thick pile carpet to deaden the overhead noise downstairs. (Rugs are impractical and dangerous unless they are heavy and on a non-slip underlay.)

Any carpet contractor will tell you (and not just for the sake of his sales figures) that for this area you need the very best quality carpeting. If you are budget-watching, good quality haircords, all-synthetic needlelooms or non-woven carpets may be the answer. Also useful are carpet tiles which can be swopped from heavy to less heavy traffic routes, as can strips of rush matting – be sure, though, to buy a few spare ones from the start, for possible replacing later.

1 Recessed matting covers entire floor of draught lobby – the larger the doormat, the less mud gets into the house.

2 Whatever the size of the well, doormats can be made, or cut, to fit into it exactly so that there's no danger of tripping up.

3 Rush matting looks friendly and welcoming, and easily sheds dust. Tiles and/or strips are easy to replace.

1

2

3

Stairs

If you are close-carpeting the hall and landing, close-carpet the stairs too, both for continuity and for cleaning. Even if the hall has a hard covering, you may want carpet on the stairs to counteract noise; you then have to choose between close-carpeting and using strips. If you choose traditional strip carpeting (27 in./686 mm) you must decide what to do with the borders. You could sand and seal the wood, or paint them to match either the carpet or the wall. Professional carpet layers usually recommend close-carpeting on half landings, but if you prefer a hard floor, the carpet will need a nosing on the top stair, or a beading strip between carpet and hard floor; this could be taken round as a neat finish where there are balustrades. Buy an extra bit of carpet so that it can be occasionally shifted.

Methods of fixing

Ordinary rods are rarely used nowadays, except for brass rods, decorative but expensive. The usual method of fixing strip carpet on wooden stairs is to use tacks, or fittings such as Gripperods. These are L-shaped little metal sections with spikes to hold the carpet in place, fixed between treads and risers. Tacking is cheaper; it shows the creases less after the carpet has been moved.

Open treads

Many open-tread stairs are made of hardwood; these can be sealed and polished with non-slip polish. For something softer, have each step made with a recess into which pieces of non-woven carpet or grooved rubber can be stuck. Or use the wrap-round method.

Carpet laying

A badly laid carpet can cause accidents and will not wear well. Unless you are experienced, employ a professional.

4 Multi-coloured stairs have none of that look usually associated with naked flights.

5 Wooden open-tread cottage stairs, designed by David Hicks, are flanked by square steel railings, floor to ceiling.

6 Texture and colour contrast: shiny white woodwork, carpet edged with thin strips of more carpeting in a different colour.

7 Winders can present problems. But quite thick carpet, cut to shape and fitted in wrap-around fashion, works well.

8 Carpet off-cuts left over because of non-standard width of tread, are here utilized to cover the sides of the stairs.

4

5

6

7

8

Many halls are welcoming enough by night, but dreary and ill-lit by day. In such a case it might be possible to let in more light by putting glass panels into a solid front or back door (but check that it is strong enough to stand slamming) or, more structurally, by building in a roof-light or an extra window.

Windows

Because circulation areas are essentially "busy", it is best to keep window treatments simple. This could mean blinds, vertical louvres, roller or roman blinds, or no curtains at all, especially as privacy is hardly ever a serious consideration in this context.

If a window gives really very little useful light, you might find it more satisfactory to panel it in, to hang a mirror or picture over it, or to fill it in with plants on shelves.

Lighting

Where there is little or no daylight, the hall will have to be lit by electricity by day as well as by night. Existing daylight can be boosted by artificial light in the dark corners – for instance, a small passage might be lit by tubular tungsten lights concealed by shelving or a pelmet, or an uplighter placed behind a large potted plant in the hall. Since this is a traffic area, it is no place for free-standing lights which may be in constant danger of being knocked over.

Ordinary wall brackets are not really suitable either, as they tend to light the walls rather than the traffic lanes. For an all-over light, pendent fittings with diffuser shades, such as paper globes, are adequate, but a low-wattage lamp may give a light that is dreary as well as unsafe. Really, any bulb under 100 watts used on its own tends to look depressing and institutional, and will make little saving on electricity.

If you are keeping the background light low, light up individual areas with adjustable spots, wall or ceiling mounted, or clamped on to furniture.

1 *Circular roof-light dome traps all available daylight so that porch and hall become nurturing ground for plants.*

2 *Little stair window has been left severely alone, so that nothing interferes with the pleasant curve of the half-landing.*

3 *Half-landing bay is another case of non-window treatment; all the decorative effect is concentrated in the plants.*

4 *Dramatic lighting effects created by lights emphasize the qualities of this beautiful staircase.*

For an architectural approach, you could have fixed direction downlighters recessed in (or mounted on) the ceiling, but watch out that heads are not obscured by strong shadows.

Recessed eyeball spots could highlight your pictures or plants; or a light track (there are some very inexpensive ones about) might have a series of lights directed at all the essential features.

Stair safety

Stairs should be lit to make for a clear distinction between tread and riser. A strong light from above lights the treads leaving the risers in shadow, and any lighting from below should preserve this balance. On a half-landing, for instance, there could be a light-fitting with a downwards directed beam, which might allow some light to bounce off the walls. Avoid glare at all cost, and never let lights shine directly into people's eyes.

Where there are elderly or very young people consider installing a time-switch, so that the staircase is automatically lit at dusk, and there will be no groping about and no chance of accidents.

Walls

Bear in mind the constant rubbing and scraping they will get. Small children in particular hold on to walls for support and leave grubby marks. If you want a wallpaper, choose a washable or a spongeable one. In family houses, use gloss or eggshell paint rather than emulsion paint in a hall.

Heating

The hall must act as a sort of airlock of warmth. It is most important to have adequate heating, or the house will be depressing to come into, and the temperature of all the other rooms will be affected. Check that the front and back doors fit well and don't let in draughts. If there is no draught-lobby, and you can't fit draught-excluders, consider a heavy internal curtain across the front door. Fix it on the sort of rod which lifts the curtain off the floor as the door is opened.

Whatever you decide, remember that heat rises, and that a warm hall makes the whole house feel more comfortable.

5 *Here, uplighters and downlighters have been skilfully placed.*

6 *Staircase art gallery: pictures lit by beam directed from opposite wall.*

7 *Shiny paint reflects light, as does mirror placed near the door.*

8 *Two-tone treatment, defined with shiny metal strip at dado height.*

6/7 Stairs

Unless you are gutting the house, it is difficult to change the position or type of the stairs. But if you do put in a new staircase, be sure to comply with local building regulations. These lay down the maximum number of risers in a flight, the steepest permissible angle of the nosings, maximum riser and minimum tread sizes, headroom over stairs and the height and widths between handrails.

Some stairs are extravagant with space, particularly if they curve, but you must weigh visual against practical advantages. Some are too beautiful to sacrifice (perversely, usually those which take up the most room). In any case, you might gain space in one way, only to lose it in another.

A spiral staircase may seem more compact than a straight flight, but you still need an area of about 6 ft/2 m square to allow for wide enough treads, and you lose under-stair space, while still needing a clear access area. Installing a spiral staircase can be a problem: where you land on the first floor depends on the ceiling-height; if there is more than one flight, you may land in yet a different direction on the next floor. (In pre-fabricated spiral stairs, each tread section rests on the previous one and can be adjusted.)

Where a staircase with a half-landing has to be removed, think of replacing it with one with winders or balanced treads – this shortens the runs.

If you are converting a basement into a self-contained unit with its own front door, consider removing the bottom flight. That will create more space in the basement, as well as on the ground floor, where you would put a floor over the gap.

Types of stairs

These diagrams show the types of stairs used in domestic housing. The choice will be determined by the position and direction of access at the top of the stair related to that at the bottom, and access at half-landing.

It is usual to have the space of the hall directly in line with the foot of the stair, and the landing with the head, taking the change of direction upon the stair.

Winders are tapered treads radiating from a common point (often the newel post). They are too narrow to stand upon at the inside edge (and a danger to very young and old people).

Balanced treads provide a more comfortable turning angle; the inside edge tapers, but is at least 3 in./76 mm wide and can be used without danger.

Spiral stairs are most commonly used where the available space is square in plan (for other types, the space must be two to four times as long as it is wide).

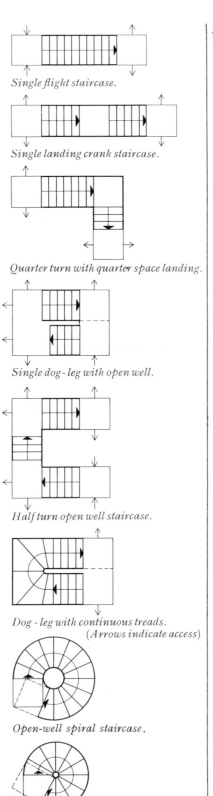

Single flight staircase.

Single landing crank staircase.

Quarter turn with quarter space landing.

Single dog-leg with open well.

Half turn open well staircase.

Dog-leg with continuous treads.
(Arrows indicate access)

Open-well spiral staircase.

Spiral with newel post.

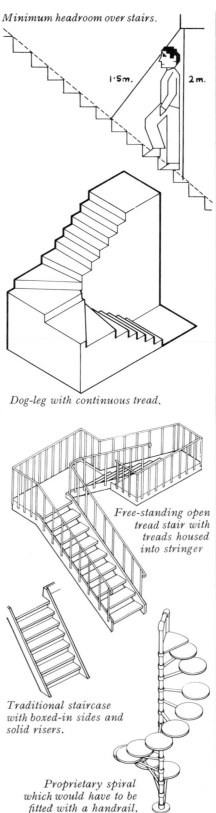

Minimum headroom over stairs.

1·5m.   2 m.

Dog-leg with continuous tread.

Free-standing open tread stair with treads housed into stringer

Traditional staircase with boxed-in sides and solid risers.

Proprietary spiral which would have to be fitted with a handrail.

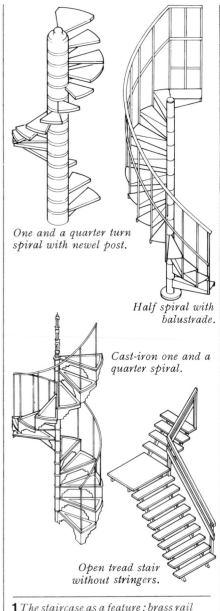

One and a quarter turn spiral with newel post.

Half spiral with balustrade.

Cast-iron one and a quarter spiral.

Open tread stair without stringers.

1 *The staircase as a feature: brass rail and banisters and, for added lightness, open under stairs.*

2 *Space-saving staircase with open treads.*

3 *White banisters, panelling: a staircase designed in the grand manner.*

4 *These steep and narrow stairs are divided into two, like stepping stones.*

5 *Decorative iron spiral staircase, with infilled risers for greater safety.*

6 *Pine staircase with open treads is easy to clean, needs no carpeting.*

1

3

5

2

4

6

The hall, stairs and landing of your house are its crossroads. You pass through from one part of the house to another and there are likely to be several, or many, doors leading off these central areas. This is important to remember because in a well decorated house you should always be able to leave doors open and find that the colour scheme of one room complements the other ones.

Colour

The colour should also be related to the shape of the hall and landing. If these are narrow, you might fight shy of strong, bright colours, which seem to crowd in on you as you pass, and choose recessive, neutral tones to make the area seem larger. Or you might deliberately refuse to play safe and plump for a really sizzling scheme to dazzle the eye.

The effect of colour depends on light, so if the light is poor and grey, quite common in halls, remember that the colours will be seen, as it were, through a grey filter (unless, that is, you use artificial lighting during the day too). Even white, commonly thought to brighten up dark areas, does not always look all that cheerful if the light is poor, and neither do very pale pastel colours.

Patterns

The pattern that you use should be considered in conjunction with those in the adjoining rooms. Either blend them, or, if your preference is for Art deco or flowery fabrics, wallpapers and carpets in the living room, you might keep the hall disciplined with a strict, linear treatment, for contrast.

Geometric designs always seem to impose their own symmetry on their surroundings, which makes them particularly useful for hallways which are ugly or irregular in shape.

Tiles or a carpet with a geometric pattern can do wonders for spaces which are all ins and outs and odd corners. But remember, when you choose tiles or patterned carpets, to lay them so that they lead your eye in the desired direction – say to the stairs or to the living-room door. Don't let the shape of the room dictate the run of the pattern, or you might finish up gazing at a corner leading to nowhere.

In a narrow hall, an open wallpaper design on a pale or white ground will create an optical illusion of space by making you feel that you are looking through the pattern. If you can afford it, cover one whole wall in mirror; it will make the space seem infinitely larger. (Plastic mirror, or mirror foil, is infinitely cheaper and creates largely the same effect as the real thing.)

1

2

3

4

5

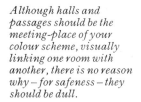

6

7

8

9

10

Although halls and passages should be the meeting-place of your colour scheme, visually linking one room with another, there is no reason why – for safeness – they should be dull.

1 *Zigzag stripes painted up the walls and over the ceiling transform this staircase into an exciting tunnel.*

2 *Small landing at top of stairs being fully used with a partition dividing the small area into two. The central area is wallpapered with little pink flowers, matching the lampshade.*

3 *Door graphics as staircase decoration.*

4 *Have the colour of your convictions. Bold red of the walls is continued, and the staircase and the strong line of the banisters echoed in the band on the wall.*

5 *The louvred door echoes the circular balustrade in this quietly comfortable top-landing dining-room.*

6 *The lowered ceiling and the shelf, which replaces the conventional hall table, make this corridor seem wider than it is.*

7 *The side of this curved staircase is painted in sympathy with the treads, and matches the skirting on the other side.*

8 *The colour-treatment links a narrow hall with the outside of the house.*

9 *Design by John Stefanides in primary colours; fresh, clean, light and airy.*

10 *Tones of colour banded in white cheer up "under-the-stairs". Dog food bag adds a touch of pop art.*

1 *Moulding around door and wall panelling is picked out to make a decorative feature.*

2 *Visual co-ordination: the predominating colour of the living-room reappears in the hall wallpaper.*

3 *Louvred "supraportas" above slim louvred doors solve the problem of organizing a tall hall.*

4 *"Framed" walls and strong diagonal design for a geometric feeling.*

5 *Taking the place of "marble halls" statuary, a shop-display figure from the thirties has found a new lease of life.*

6 *Staircase in Corfu, painted jet black all over with extra tough paint.*

7 *Spanish stair treatment: plaster banisters and handrail in one, gently rounded, are in sympathy with the curved stairwell. Tile treads, wide nosings.*

7

Halls/stairs/landings
12 Doing away with the hall

Living-room hall : extra heavy curtains pull right across front door and window, wall to wall, to exclude possible draughts.

Hall-wall gone, and the living-room has extra light and air.

The hall and stair area are opened up for maximum light and space, the living-space is screened from the stairs by ceiling-height banisters, and the serving-counter in the foreground helps to organize the space for circulation.

Out of the garden and straight into the heart of the house, where the spiral staircase, tucked into a corner, contributes to the air of spaciousness.

Living-rooms/1

No other room in the house needs to work quite so hard. The living-room has to be both private place for being peaceful in, and public platform where you can sparkle when you are, as it were, at home to the world. It must be a place where you can relax, and it must, moreover, enable you to recharge your energies. You will want the room to reflect your tastes and your personality (or at least the facets that you choose to put on display).

Whether you are entertaining, doing the accounts, writing, reading, sewing, having a meal, watching the box, the physical arrangements should help to make your life run smoothly. You will

want the right sort of light in the right place, at the right time.

The softness (or otherwise) of the seating should be appropriate to your prospective concentration or relaxation. The TV should be properly positioned in relation to light sources, and people. It is not a good idea to place it with its back to the light (too much glare), and, at the same time, the machine should not cast a baleful blind eye over the proceedings when it is not switched on.

Your living-room has to function pleasantly and unobtrusively, whether you are settling down to a quiet game of backgammon with an adult or a brisk

round of carpet bowls with the young, and it has to go on functioning even as your demands on it change and continue changing as time goes on.

If there are young children about, they will want a good deal of floor-space, but should not be able to get at dangerous or breakable objects. As they grow older, they will need additional seating because, although they will spend increasing amounts of time on their own, you will presumably still be glad of their company in your living-room.

Seating arrangements, in any case, need to be flexible, so that varying numbers of people can be accommodated

without making small groups seem lost, or large ones squashed up together, and if you can arrange the seats to make more than one conversation possible at the same time, so much the better; groups of six are the most satisfactory.

In the course of time there will inevitably be new acquisitions, like pictures, rugs, objects or pieces of furniture. These will impose their own demands on the existing order, and lead to alterations.

(*Above*) *Comfort, controlled casualness, flexibility and prettiness; the Conrans' living-room scores high on all the important points without being over-designed.*

Living-rooms
2/3 Design for living

Your own and your family's interests and activities are likely to undergo changes, and your living-room will be expected to be all things to all men, women and children. Its success, however, will depend not so much on the excellence with which it copes as on the atmosphere that you create in it.

Designers say the living-room invariably poses the most complex of their problems. It is a room which should reflect the interests and aspirations of all its users, and be the social and recreational centre of the house; but most people find it remarkably difficult to pin-point their requirements, and rarely come up with a comprehensive brief.

The sitting area will naturally be the first consideration, but most living-rooms are nowadays expected to house activities to which series of smaller rooms used once to be dedicated, and secondary uses must also be thought out carefully so that the various inhabitants can go about their business without disturbing each other.

Eating

If main meals are to be served, it is best to organize a dining area. The chairs may at times provide extra seating, and the dining table could double up as an additional work-surface. The kitchen itself may form part of the room, to be divided off – perhaps by sliding screens – on appropriate occasions, and on others to enlarge it for family togetherness. This is especially useful where there are small children, because they can play under their mother's eye without getting under her feet.

Studying

Study areas may form part of the layout. Place desk, files and reference shelves as far away as possible from the core of the room, where others may be pursuing their own distracting activities. Since not much desk-work will get done while the television/record-player/tape-recorder is in operation, it may be a good idea to put all such equipment in this part of the room, and to use it at the times when things are quiet, peaceful and conducive to concentration.

Sleeping

Sleeping facilities may have to be considered – not the odd kip but the real sheet-and-blanket thing, invisible during the day, comfortable at night. A sofa can often satisfactorily convert into an additional bed for an unexpected guest, but if the living-room is fairly regularly used to accommodate sleepers, both layout and storage arrangements should take this into account.

Preparing the brief

Family requirements vary just as much as families themselves: to find out exactly what's needed, a professional designer would begin by asking questions: age, sex, interests and habits of each family member. What sort of entertainments? How many visitors at a time? He would assess available space, possessions – whether to be displayed or stowed away – and take due note of the climate. For fine-weather areas, where the garden or terrace becomes an extension of the room in the summer, he would plan floor finishes and furnishings reflecting these agreeable conditions, but before he would get down to details he would spend a great deal of time on preliminary studies. So, examine and analyse your own way of life.

Practical checklist

Start with an open mind. Instead of just listing your prospective activities and the furniture and equipment you have or think you will need, work from the checklist below. Relate the "activities" to "furniture" and "equipment"; add any of your possible activities, and extra pieces of free-standing furniture you own, and go on from there.

Activities
Sitting, talking, party-giving, disco sessions, watching TV, snoozing, studying, writing, projecting slides or films. Listening to music, making music, card playing, board games, playing with children. Sewing, embroidery, crafts, painting. Eating. Sleeping.

Furniture
Sofas, chairs (occasional, dining, folding, desk), chaise-longue.

Tables (low, occasional, folding, dining), desk, music stand.

Equipment etc.
Books, magazines, records and record-player, tapes, projector, musical instruments, writing things, eating accessories, drinks (possibly fridge and sink), sewing things, objects, collections, blankets. Wastepaper basket, telephone, directories, ash-trays, vases.

1 *The island unit in the middle of this living-room, upholstered in the same cord carpet that covers the floor, surrounds a huge, cushioned lounging area.*

2 *A two-storey living area seen from the upper landing, which forms a useful gallery. The eating area, placed beneath the gallery, benefits from the lower ceiling.*

(Opposite) Cool, creamy comfort in this monochrome scheme, where every item has been picked for shape and texture.

2

Living-rooms
4/5 Zoning and traffic

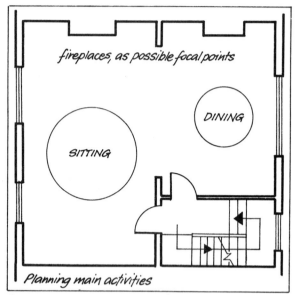

fireplaces, as possible focal points

DINING

SITTING

Planning main activities

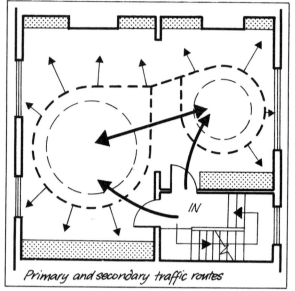

IN

Primary and secondary traffic routes

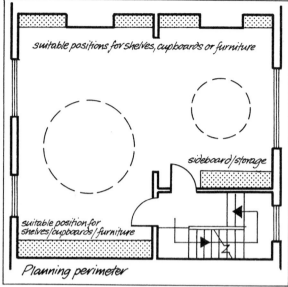

suitable positions for shelves, cupboards or furniture

sideboard/storage

suitable position for shelves/cupboards/furniture

Planning perimeter

Draw out a scale plan of the living-room. Rough in the main traffic routes (see above) and define the various areas. Repeat this exercise until you have tried all reasonable permutations, by which time the best solution will probably have emerged.

Now draw in the secondary traffic routes – from door to television set, door to seating area, door to serving place – and to all the points that people are likely to approach. Note how much movement there is likely to be within the different zones, and whether the various zones work next to each other. If you have to walk through the seating area to get to the drinks, or the telephone finds itself next to the television, try again, even if you have to jettison pleasing parts of your plan; they won't please you for long if they do not work.

Main sitting area

First think about the position of the principal sitting area. This is the core of the living-room, where people should be able to relax and to talk to each other. This area should be seen to dominate the room, and access to it should be direct from the entrance. No through-traffic should interrupt it. Bear in mind at this stage what form of seating you will use: sofas, easy chairs or cushions, because what you choose will obviously affect the space which you will need. If seating is too far spaced out, people have to shout or feel awkward; if it's bunched up too close, their feet get entangled. And don't, for heaven's sake, range all the furniture round the four walls like a dentist's waiting room. (By the way, the most comfortable way for talkers to sit seems to be at right angles to each other.)

If the room is to be shared at various times by adults and children, do try for the sake of both age groups to arrange for grown-up conversation in one part and for the children's activities in another – perhaps around the dining table if it's to be an all-purpose family room, or maybe in a window seat. Try to keep the floor as clear as possible – older children practically live at floor level, and younger ones need lots of play space.

Study area

For what further purposes are you going to use your sitting-room? If you need a study or quiet area, place it in such a way as to enable you to cut out distractions, and to hide any possible muddle of papers or bits and pieces. You might plan the various activities at opposite ends of the room or use a screen, or the layout might be suggested by the architectural plan. A sewing or study area, for instance, needs good natural and artificial light, preferably from the left of a right-handed person. Bookshelves and reference storage need to be close at hand, and this area is often the sensible position for the telephone.

Dining

If there is a dining area in the living-room – for occasional or general use – consider whether it can absorb any of the other intermittent activities, and bear in mind that you might want to use it as a useful extension of the principal sitting area when lots of friends are invited.

The choice of chairs and table for a living/dining situation needs special thought. You don't want a large, useless lump of furniture using up space between meals. Go either for a table which looks elegant and sculptured in its own right (with chairs that either melt into the rest of the room-scheme or can fold away), or make a point of bringing it into the general scheme of things (as they do in many European countries, where they use it all the time).

Work out how meals can best be served from the kitchen. Will food be trollied in or passed through a hatch? Is the table in the right relationship to hatch or door? What about dinner-parties? Will you need a serving table or a sideboard? In each case, both design and positioning will have to be carefully thought out.

Improving the basic structure

Once you have established the living-room's basic organization, it's worth considering whether this could be improved by changing or removing such elements as doors, fireplaces and non-loadbearing partitions. A door in the corner of a room, close to flanking walls, can often be moved over so that built-in units or free-standing furniture can be placed against the liberated wall without inhibiting access. Bear this in mind during the zoning operation – a moved door sometimes makes all the difference to the organization and spaciousness of the living-room.

Fire-places

Fire-places are usually very difficult to reposition, as this entails extensive structural alterations to the building. But they can often be blocked up and stripped of their overmantels – an operation usually undertaken where more wall – or floor – space is needed, or where the design of

the room provides some other focal point. Moreover, alternative forms of heating have, alas, made fire-places obsolete in many cases.

Opening up the living-room

If there is need for more wall and floor space, the non-structural partition between two adjoining rooms can sometimes be removed; so may the wall dividing living-room from hall and staircase, which will increase the floor area, and give more freedom in planning, although landing or hall will become shared circulation space.

A partition wall between living-room and kitchen might be replaced by sliding or folding doors, so that the whole area can become one large space. Perforated or glazed screens are often effective for creating the illusion of space and light.

Finally, your floor plan: the best one will probably be the one which is the simplest, provides most floor-space, arranges for traffic-flow where the routes do not cross sitting areas, and where there is generous provision for seating.

1 *The living-room is screened off from the dining-room by a partition which stops short of the facing wall.*

2 *A really flexible low-level setting by Max Clendinning uses a floor cushion sitting area, which can contract or expand according to need.*

3 *The furniture has been set at angles to the walls, adding a whole new dimension*

4 *Shiny white tiled surround defines a passage-way from the sitting-room to the dining-room.*

1

2

3

4

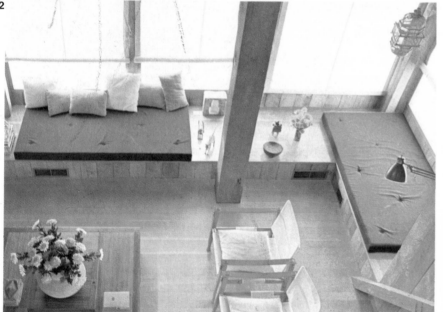

1 *Seating for six formed by a built-up base plastered to match the walls. The seat and back-rest are upholstered with simple foam cushions.*

2 *Window seats on a wide platform, which introduces a new level into this pine-clad room. The platform runs from wall to wall along two sides of the room and, apart from providing plenty of table space and casual seating, houses the heating ducts. A narrow sill above the platform supports the cushions.*

3 *Three-seater sofas are pushed against the walls and piled high with bright cushions to become the focal point in this monochrome colour scheme.*

4 *Something very different for the agile and the young in heart. A huge, foam-filled sausage which turns this room into something like an adventure playground.*

(Opposite) A pair of matching, low-backed sofas set at right angles with a central table; the seating area is self-contained, and the dining table is screened off.

Living-rooms
8/9 Detail planning

When you start planning the room, all pieces of furniture have to be related to each other and to the space for the most usable and/or most interesting scheme.

Fittings

First, examine the positions of existing fittings. Will the radiators exude your heat where it is needed?

Light switches should be by the doors, and when a door is moved or "handed" (rehung to open the other way) they must follow. Ceiling spots, pendent lights and downlighters may, repositioned, contribute more to your scheme, and any ceiling light that does not fulfil a definite purpose should go. Arrange for plenty of power-points, so that there will be no trailing flexes.

Furniture

Measure all your furniture and draw it in plan to the same scale as the room plan, then cut it out and move it around on the plan. Then, if you mean to acquire new pieces, it will be easier to determine their optimum size. Avoid cramming the room – people must be able to move around easily; conversely, avoid dotting things about or they will look unrelated. Check that side-tables are within easy reach of the seating, and that there is adequate space in front of bookshelves and storage units. Work out the positions of essential equipment – TV, hi-fi, drinks table or cupboard – and how all these facilities relate to their users.

Focal points and lighting

At this stage, focal points and lighting need to be roughly planned. Will the fire-place be the focal point? What will replace it if it is blocked up? Will you put up pictures or prints? Consider how they will be lit; and remember that large pictures emphasize the areas where they are hanging.

Your lighting layout will be determined by the uses of the living-room; indeed, it can help you to achieve greater definition of the important areas.

Summing-up

When all the requirements are catered for and the layout settled, the scheme is ready for a final critical survey. Look at every decision objectively and test its viability. Is the best use being made of the space? Can the circulation be improved by moving a particular door after all, or should a fine view be further exploited? All through this process, apply your personal preferences. What suits your way of life best? Will you feel at home with your arrangement? If you are not completely satisfied, start the whole zoning and planning process over again.

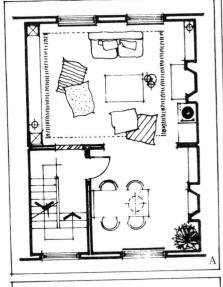

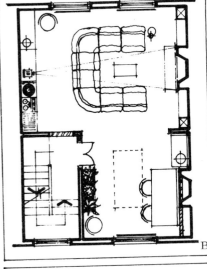

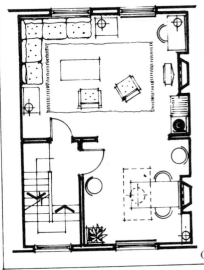

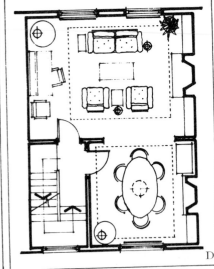

Two basic areas of activity are marked on the plan. Note the easy access to both these areas from the doors, and from one another. The recesses beside the two chimney-breasts are likely to be useful for shelving, storage or furniture. The fire-place in the living-room should be considered as an important focal point. The recess opposite the door to the dining area is ideal for a sideboard or serving table as it is also adjacent to the likely table position. It could also be handy for serving drinks as it is fairly close to the seating. The long wall in the sitting-room could become a focal point – perhaps with a display unit or a large painting.

Plan A is a traditional interpretation of these two rooms. The fire-places retain their chimney-pieces. The furniture is arranged symmetrically about their axes, giving them added importance. The desk or bureau bookcase is on the same axis and positioned to balance the room. The occasional chairs on either side contribute to the composition, again arranged symmetrically around the axis W-X of the centre panel of the window wall. This is a formal layout which allows little flexibility. Low tables or perhaps lacquer boxes could be conveniently placed by the sofas and chairs. Standing or table lamps are placed on, or close to, most tables. Small objects, patterned upholstery, curtains and/or rugs would contribute to an overall impression of cosiness. The dining area is approached in similar fashion (with the table placed on the axis Y-Z of the window), but might well be screened off from the sitting-room.

Plan B is approached much more freely. The banquette seating in the corner immediately establishes a strong asymmetry. This allows other elements to be placed with greater ease. The desk, which is positioned to the left of the chimney-breast and by the window, does not have to balance the units on the other side. The fire-place is best blocked up as its implied axis would conflict with the rest of the composition. The focal point under these circumstances would be the large rectangular table in the centre of the seating group. The dining area is designed to be an adaptable area for general use when not required for meals.

Plan C is an attempt to unify the two spaces even further. The arch between the rooms is removed completely, and the one entrance is widened for greater emphasis. The storage of all books and objects is confined to the recesses on either side of the fire-place. Activities other than the seating are located in a unit running the full length of the wall opposite. This would contain desk, audio-visual equipment and drinks cupboard.

The sitting area, which comprises one huge U-shaped seating unit, is the focal point of the whole area.

The dining area is an adaptable space, used generally as a study area and as an extension to the living-room. The fire-place and the far recess are both blocked up, so any conflicting second axis is disbanded.

Plan D is an informal centralized plan, a scheme which relies very little on expensive modern or antique furniture.

The door to the living-room is blocked up so that a more economic traffic flow can be achieved and so that shelves 15 in./381 mm high × 20 in./508 mm deep can be built around the periphery. These will take all the books, objects and equipment. Standing lamps can be freely moved to light what is interesting or amusing. The furniture layout consists of one large, low table, perhaps a chopped-down Victorian one, with seating arranged around it.

The door to the dining/study area is "handed" for easier access to the seating group. The dining table, with a paper lantern over it, can be informally pushed against the wall, the folding chairs stored or hung in the far recess. A tree in a tub, or potted plants, can contribute significantly to the room's mood.

(Opposite) A black and white living-room making the most of its garden setting. The shelving unit divides the areas without blocking the view. Tough studded rubber flooring looks attractive and makes sense in a room that has access to the garden.

Living-rooms
10/11 Focal points

In order to relax, people need to have their gaze directed to something pleasant. The lack of any focal point tends to make people feel ill at ease, particularly in surroundings that are not familiar to them. The sitting area, especially, needs some point of visual reference; it is uncomfortable to be forced to stare unceasingly at the person opposite one.

Traditionally, the fire-place is the chief focus in the living-room. Firelight in itself induces a feeling of well-being, and when seating is grouped around it, the whole area becomes an expression of hospitality at its warmest.

However, since the general use of central heating has sadly made so many fire-places obsolete, alternatives have to be considered. A low table set with an arrangement of short-stemmed flowers, books or other objects may become the focal point in the sitting area – or the seating itself may have enough visual impact because of its design, mass or colour scheme.

Television and hi-fi, provided that they play a large enough part in your life, can be used as focal points. In this case the housing of equipment needs very careful consideration (see Hi-fi). It may mean designing a special stand for such things, or building them into a wall, so that they become an architectural feature, or you might consider making them part of a storage/display unit.

Question the relevance of all traditional focal points. like pictures, or side-tables used for the display of objects. You may think up amusing and imaginative alternatives, and produce a room which is the visible reflection of the inhabitants' interests and a real expression of their personalities.

Focal points related to architecture

Focal points can also emphasize a room's structure and add to its intrinsic quality. They may vary in scale and in importance, and are generally arrived at quite unconsciously.

In classical Georgian rooms, the symmetrical arrangement of traditional furniture complements the architectural features and emphasizes the features of the room. An asymmetrically placed picture, on the other hand, may underline the freer plan of a living-room in a modern house, where surprise views and vistas can be one of the real treats.

When the positioning of furniture and objects complements the shape of the room, the arrangement is usually successful, provided that the various elements are kept in scale to each other. The test is whether your things look as though they belong where you have placed them: pictures above fire-places, furniture be-tween windows or set into recesses, are examples of this sort of traditional integration. Occasionally, a piece of furniture is sufficiently dominant and interesting to be used independently, without obvious reference to any architectural elements. This can be very successful, provided that the other things are placed in relationship to it. Long walls without architectural relief are often well tackled in this way. For instance, one huge canvas or a group of assorted small pictures can be used to create a splendid effect on a long expanse of wall, and make the room look larger into the bargain.

Change and variety

Secondary focal points, arrangements of smaller objects, flowers and other accessories to go on shelves and table-tops, warrant the same kind of careful attention. The interplay of all these items, their grouping, form and colour, will give the living-room much of its character. However, there is the risk that if they remain static for too long, they become so familiar as to be invisible to you. To be a continuous source of pleasure, they should every now and then be rearranged.

Emphasis through colour

Contrasts in colour, pattern and finish play an important part in building up and heightening a focal point. A piece of furniture may be painted or lacquered in a primary colour to make it stand out; the strong geometric pattern of a Kelim rug may be used to offset a predominance of plainer fabrics. A tray of green ferns can give living, coloured, patterned emphasis to a low table in a neutrally coloured room.

Lighting

Lighting can make furniture, pictures, sculptures and groups of objects look more important. Use it to underline your layout and the areas of different activities. At night, the mood of the principal area can be made to dominate all others by the flick of a switch, and dimmers especially come into their own as do all the various kinds of spots.

1 *Beautiful rugs above a low shelf dominate this room, and the neutral hessian wall-covering shows them off to best advantage. Heavy wall-hangings are best mounted on to battens so that they hang straight.*

2 *A magnificent display of avocado plants and other greenery placed at floor level on a piece of slatted timber. The plants will get plenty of sun here, but will need to be turned frequently so that they do not grow lop-sidedly towards the light.*

1

2

(*Opposite*)
1 *If the television is going to be the focal point in your room, try and find one that is good to look at when it's turned off.*

2 *Green borders round the windows, green apple print; colours are brought together simply and dramatically on the two-toned fire-place wall.*

3 *Large, bamboo-framed mirror over a traditional fire-place is surrounded by prints, photographs and objects to create a point of interest.*

4 *A mirror over a mantelpiece is a conventional focal point. Instead of a mantelpiece, however, a wide side table is used for display purposes.*

5 *The cool, sculptural feel of this classically proportioned room is enhanced by the arrangement of pictures in the arched alcove.*

6 *The original brick fire-place wall, old-fashioned log-burning stove and slate hearth offset this modern conversion of a high-ceilinged, galleried room.*

7 *The focal point in this room is the fire-place wall with a cluster of framed drawings and an array of treasures on the mantel-piece. The plant and flower arrangement can be changed about to keep the wall alive with interest.*

8 *Updated Victorian whatnot is a small round table with a round motif completely covered in round earthenware bowls and small lacquer boxes.*

1

2

3

4

5

6

7

8

Living-rooms
12/13 Furniture

There are two categories of living-room furniture: the elements that form the room's basic organization – sofas, easy chairs, dining/work tables, and storage units, all fairly permanent because their size and weight means that they don't get moved around much; and the smaller things – sidetables, sofa-tables and the drinks tables, occasional chairs and standard lamps – that help to make pieces in the first category more effective. It is these smaller things which will give each zone in the room its immediate and changeable character, since they can and should be moved about to suit any number of people on any occasion at a moment's notice.

Flexibility

The essence of a multi-purpose living-room is that it should be able to accommodate any number of activities, and each piece of furniture should make a positive contribution to this. Not only should it fulfil its specific function, but it should adapt easily to a variety of others. Keep the scheme as flexible as possible. A desk chair can occasionally form part of the general seating; a table might be used for dining, study, board games or sewing. The more potential uses you assign to any one piece of furniture the better; to over-furnish is death to flexibility, quite apart from the claustrophobia it induces.

Seating arrangements

As we have said earlier, seating arrangements, which should be conducive to conversation and relaxation and further the feeling of pleasant togetherness, are the nucleus of a good living-room. This means chairs and sofas to suit different tastes and purposes: a sofa on which one can stretch out; a chair offering head and neck support with perhaps a foot-rest; a chair that is comfortable for needlework or reading. Think out all possible ways of sitting and relaxing before making a final choice – and bear in mind that the old three-piece-suite routine is the least flexible of the lot.

Sofas and chairs

Two-seater sofas are useful because they take up much less space than do two easy chairs. They also give mass and weight to the composition of your furniture, which might otherwise look disjointed. Bear in mind that while three-seater sofas will look nice in a large room with generous proportions that need to be complemented with a large furnishing element, neither great comfort nor any real conversation is achievable by three people in a row – two talkers are all that they will happily accommodate,

although they will, of course, take three TV watchers or listeners to music.

Seating groups

L-shaped seating, wall-fixed or free-standing, makes the most economical use of space because quite a large group of people can sit in comfort, leaving the rest of the floor free for circulation (see planning diagram).

It is not necessary for all your upholstery to match, but if you are trying to achieve visual continuity, you might cover all seats in related fabrics. The effect will be pleasant, particularly if your chairs are of various ages, shapes and sizes (and you would further unify the scheme by relating the curtain fabric to it as well).

Expanding the group

A seating group of more than three or four permanent pieces, including sofa or wall-seating, tends to look rather overwhelming. Whenever there is an unusually large number of people present, occasional chairs can come and join the party from another part of the room. An upholstered desk chair is especially useful here, or perhaps chairs that fold away when they are not in use. If dining and occasional chairs can be co-ordinated it makes for maximum flexibility in your seating scheme, always provided that they are light enough to be carried about without too much fuss or upheaval.

High or low – broad or narrow?

There are no hard and fast rules relating the dimensions of easy chairs and sofas to comfort: people's tastes vary as much as their shapes. The only way is a personal test, so before acquiring anything new, take as many members of your family as you can muster to play musical chairs in a furniture department. Dimensions, however, are very important in terms of style. Low seating of an exaggeratedly soft appearance may look fine in most modern rooms but not necessarily in all traditional ones. These sometimes seem to ask for higher, more upright sofas with arms, or for a mixed bag of seating, arranged so as not to destroy the spatial proportions. Chaise-longues, giant cushions, sagbags and environmental seating (areas where the entire floor is upholstered), are all possibilities that can be used to very good effect in the right place.

Full-size tables

The height of full-size dining-room tables – about $28\frac{1}{2}$ in./724 mm – will generally be governed by the height of chairs. But how large your living/dining/playing/multiple everything table will be,

and whether it will have drawers for knives and forks or for papers, games or what have you, you will have to decide in the light of the layout you have planned for the room in general.

The table's uses will be determined less by its dimensions than by its design and position in the room. If the table surface is both pleasant and tough, its use will be practically unlimited, provided it gets natural light in the day-time and efficient lighting at night.

Smaller tables

Generally speaking, these come in two sorts of height. Side-tables, meant to be used for serving or carving, will relate to standing rather than seated people. In the case of low tables which relate to sitters, consider not only the space you have got alongside sofas or chairs but also what is to be placed on them: ash-trays, flowers, lamps which must provide light for reading, and the odd plate of food. A shelf under the top is enormously useful for all sorts of things that would otherwise clutter up the surface.

The height of adjacent seats should always be considered. Table-tops next to armless seating should be level with the bottom of the seat-cushion. Next to, say, a sofa with arms, the table-top should come $\frac{1}{2}$ in./13 mm to 2 in./51 mm below the arms for comfort.

A central table is inevitably a focal point of some importance. It should be pleasant to look at when not in use, and when it is, people should be able to see their opposite numbers across whatever objects may be placed on it. It should be high enough for informal eating without anyone having to bend double (its plan dimensions will depend on the available space). There should be enough room to allow people to circulate even when the seats around it are occupied.

Materials and finishes vary enormously: you can choose between metal, glass, Perspex, wood veneers, paint, plastics or marble, depending on the effect you are after, and the use to which you mean to put the surface of the table.

Shelving and storage

Decide which of your possessions you want to conceal. Remember that the paraphernalia of living can grow quite amazingly in quite a short time. In principle, the greater the possibility of storage, the greater is the living-room's adaptability. An increasing number of splendid storage units are coming on to the market, as are systems consisting of brackets, ladders or frames to which shelves and cupboard units can be fixed. In the larger units, desks, drinks cupboards with refrigerators, television,

hi-fi equipment plus speakers, can all be built in. If you plan such an elaborate scheme, check that you have an adequate number of power and lighting points, and a point for the telephone, and remember that TV, hi-fi and refrigerators all need adequate ventilation to function properly; if in doubt, call in specialist advice.

1 *Display storage blends with the room. The central, wide shelf is just the right height for the television and record player. The low table is big enough for casual family meals. The light, airy feeling of this room is emphasized by the plants and the simple cane chairs.*

2 *All the furniture in this room is related not only in colour but also in shape. The low, simple, sturdy lines are enhanced by the geometric arrangement of the pieces. Two tables have been pushed together to make one large one to sit in the area between the sofas and the moulded partition wall.*

3 *In an essentially Victorian room, the period feeling is reinforced by the patterned curtain fabric, the delicately turned chair, and the pedestal table.*

4 *A dramatically lit pine desk, which fits perfectly into this setting, can double as a sideboard when the living-room is used for eating or drinking.*

5 *If you do not want a low central table to dominate the room choose one topped with glass. Here, a chrome and glass table enables visitors to admire the beautiful Persian carpet, and the low-level light won't prevent them from admiring each other.*

6 *An antique-shop atmosphere is created by an assortment of period pieces. The collection of framed pictures and prints complement the moulding of the wall panels.*

7 *Habitat's Palaset units are a bright and attractive idea for building up an individual storage system to suit the proportions and style of any room. The table is constructed of four units, one of them with the open side facing upwards, making a built-in plant holder.*

8 *Flexible conversation well is composed of modular seating units upholstered in related colours, easily rearrangeable to suit the occasion. Another flexible and dramatic element is the lighting – ceiling spots are mounted on an overhead track so that light can be angled to bathe the whole seating area or to highlight just one unit.*

1

2

3

4

5

6

7

8

Living-rooms
14/15 Furniture styles

Before acquiring furniture, don't lose sight of the look at which you are aiming. What is your objective? This is a decision only you can make. Some of the basic ingredients for a number of

1 *The furniture here has been chosen to complement the classic proportions of this room. The heavy, dark leather sofa is counterbalanced by the lightness (actual or apparent) of the table and occasional chairs.*

2 *Minute attention has been given to every detail of shape, texture and contrast from the positioning of the furniture to the angle of the reading lamp. The small coffee table means that plenty of floor space is left free.*

3 *Bench-type sofa running along the wall is the main, solid feature in this individually-styled room with its air of well-organized clutter and splashes of bright colour. Bentwood dining chairs double as occasional seating.*

4 *In this open-plan living-room, dominated by a huge, sculptural fire-place, the seating platform is incorporated in the sweep of the rounded, rough-plastered walls. Only cushions, round table and floor rug have been added.*

1

2

3

4

1

2

3

4

1 *For dedicated loungers – a cross between a seating platform and a huge bed, supported by units which house record-player, books and the telephone. When more floor space is needed, the four large mattresses can be taken up, leaving the raised, carpeted back-supports for casual seating.*

2 *A simple and cheap way to create a modern, relaxed seating area is to build up a low-level seating platform in the corner of a room and to scatter floor cushions over it. As people will spend quite a lot of time near to the floor it is a good idea to keep the decorative interest, as well as the lighting, at the same level.*

3 *Far Eastern influences are at work here. A batik fabric panel balances the dark curtaining material, and the texture of the rush matting is taken up by the hessian walls. The simple shape of the high-sided wicker sofa is a perfect foil for the richness of the colours.*

4 *A circle within a circle within a square. The circular seating unit is more flexible than it appears, as it is divided into two free-standing sections on castors.*

We are *not* talking to, or about, the dedicated hi-fi addict who would sacrifice all to technical performance, nor his opposite number who completely subordinates performance to appearance.

Fortunately you can have excellent hi-fi which looks good. What you get in sound quality depends on how much you can afford to spend. But even on a reasonably low budget you will be able to get better sound and, arguably, better appearance than is available from the traditional radiogram or record player.

Basics - choosing the equipment

The information which follows is not technical, but shows how hi-fi can be fitted into decorative schemes and even enhance them. However, some decisions, unrelated to design, must first be made.

Most of these are concerned with cost versus quality. Decide what you want to spend and then aim at the best quality for that price. A good retailer (and there are some) will understand this. Also be clear about what sort of music you want to hear and where, and analyse your listening habits (for instance, if you like "background" music, tape/cassette will be more convenient than disc). You can get a lot of help in these areas from hi-fi magazines, good retailers and books.

However, you will *not* get much help from any of these on design and so you must make some basic decisions before you go out shopping.

(a) Will you display or hide your hi-fi? It will affect the sort of units you get.

If you want to *display* the amplifier, tuner or tape recorder, make sure that you like its casing. Equipment such as the Quad 33/303 is difficult if you don't like the look of the power amplifier, which is separate from the control unit and is usually stored away.

If you want to *hide* your hi-fi make sure that turntables, amplifiers, tuners, tape recorders can be built into an enclosed area, and are sold with the fittings to make this possible. Loudspeakers are dealt with below, but it is obvious that small bookshelf speakers are less obtrusive (and more flexible) than large free-standing ones.

(b) How much room have you for your equipment? Again, this relates particularly to speakers, but as far as size goes it also applies to all the other units. A tuner/amplifier (the Americans call it a receiver) is more compact than two separate units. And there is an enormous difference in size between the largest and smallest units, which is not necessarily related to quality.

Specially-designed unit includes TV, and complements existing furniture.

(c) What sort of design do you like? More important, what sort of style will you like in, say, two years' time? Equipment should last for several years. Today's "new fashion" can look awfully dated in three years' time. The best rule (if you don't trust your own predictions) is to use the manufacturers' skill. Some change their range every five years or so, and some stick with their designs for far longer, making only small modifications. It is these manufacturers who produce what is almost a classic look.

Fitting your hi-fi into the home

Once again you will have to make some decisions. Most of these relate to the importance of hi-fi in your life; a large part of the discussion will revolve around loudspeakers. Here are some tips:
(a) Decide where you want to listen to music and where to control it. You may want to listen in one room and put the control units in another (this is feasible if you have only tape which runs for a long time). But normally the speakers should be opposite to where you sit, and the control units close to you.
(b) The speakers should usually be about 6 ft/2 m to 10 ft/3 m apart for stereo, but you might consider omnidirectional speakers, where placing is less critical.
(c) The usually disproved rule, the bigger the better, applies with some exceptions, to speakers. But small bookshelf speakers can produce excellent results.
(d) The most critical item is the turntable. This must be (a) level, and (b) as far as possible unaffected by movement in the room. In old houses, where floorboards are liable to move, this may need specialist insulation.
(e) If you are considering hi-fi while building or converting, think about building it in. Advantage: it's hidden. Disadvantage: difficulties if you want to change it – and don't forget access for service is needed.
(f) Don't necessarily think about hiding hi-fi equipment. If listening to music plays an important part in your life and you like the technical look of the best equipment, then show it off. You can display it elegantly, whether you disguise its technical nature, or even feature it by showing the wires and all.
(g) Perhaps the simplest solution, though, is to steer a path between reticence and ostentation and let the equipment simply become part of the room; neither more nor less obvious than other furnishings.

Housing hi-fi

Shelf mounting: Either DIY shelving or standard shelving/storage units accommodate most of the control equipment; the speakers, if they are small, can go at the ends of the shelf. Your collection of records and tapes can go alongside.
  Cabinet mounting: Controls can be mounted in the side or top of existing, or new, cabinets; records go below.
  Table mounting: Small units can be mounted on coffee tables or on special furniture made for this purpose.
  Cube mounting: Cubes make an excellent display system which is particularly flexible since new cubes can be added as you go along. In the Palaset system, amplifier, tuner and control panel can sit in ordinary drawers, which are pulled out for servicing.
  Custom-built cabinets: Specially made cabinets can be obtained. Design standards are not very high, but one or two companies do produce interesting models.

Living with hi-fi

Finally, a few pointers on how to make the most of it:
(a) If you want to listen to music in more than one room, you can put up extension speakers using the same amplifier and record deck. Most retailers will help you with a switching system if there isn't one on your amplifier.
(b) Dust is the enemy of good record reproduction. You might like the casual look of exposed record sleeves, but it is better to keep them in a closed cupboard.
(c) If your record deck is in a family area with children around, fit a cheaper stylus for them to use – the stylus is the most easily damaged piece of equipment.
(d) Hi-fi works best in a room with a balance between hard and soft surfaces. If you change your furnishings, say, from rugs and blinds to carpet and curtains, it may make the sound very dull. But you may be able to compensate by adjusting the amplifier controls.
(e) Don't feel that you must keep your hi-fi up to date, even at the price of altering your original concept of fitting it into your room. If you are happy with the sound, stick with it and make a change only when you are convinced it is for the better. The obvious example is Quadrophonics using four speakers. No one knows at present how important this will be, but our advice is, resist it – it may go away – and if it does it will save you a lot of space and money.

1 *A custom-built shelving system which holds equipment, speakers, TV and books. A flap hides equipment not in use.*

2 *How to use hi-fi housings: one unit for equipment, and speakers used as shelves.*

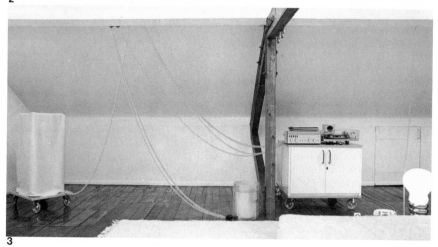

3 *Hi-fi as an essential in bare-minimum living scheme. The speakers are hooded to soften their shape.*

Living-rooms
18/19 Hi-fi display/camouflage

1 *A neat shelving system which can be adjusted if equipment is changed.*

2 *Equipment hung from a centre column. Possible problems with rigidity of record deck support; speakers must be moved apart to achieve stereo effect.*

3 *Ringo Starr and Robin Cruikshank suggest a stylish answer to storage.*

4 *The cheapest you can get : a home-built cabinet for a Planar expanded polystyrene speaker, surprisingly good sound.*

5 *A room-centre unit with equipment, records and built-in plug sockets.*

6 *Equipment blends in with books, flowers, ornaments.*

7 *A colourful unit using Palaset cubes. Amplifier, tuner and controls neatly slot into drawers.*

8 *The centre unit holds the record deck and amplifiers, set into drainage pipes and chip-holders. They work perfectly.*

1

2

3

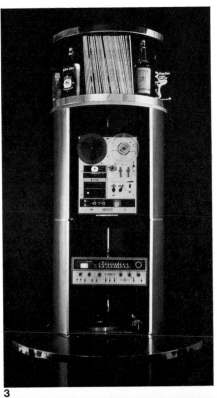

6

4

5

7

8

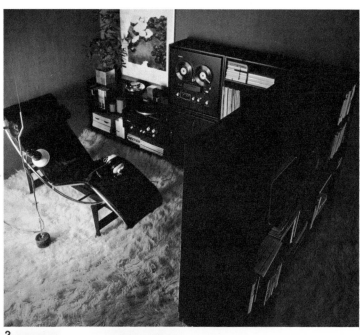

1 *An island unit built to match the equipment that does not pretend to be 19th century.*

2 *A room designed around the hi-fi and the listening chair.*

3 *A casual, relaxed approach with no attempt to regiment the equipment.*

4 *Simple mounting on built-in cabinet for record storage.*

5 *Hinged flaps on this cabinet capable of completely hiding hi-fi equipment, records and TV.*

6/7 *A low-level storage answer which can be completely hidden even when in use – one of the advantages of cassette over disc.*

8 *Speakers can be beautiful as well as of excellent sound quality.*

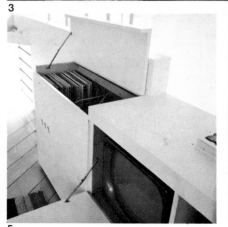

1 2 3 4 5 6 7 8

205

Living-rooms
20/21 Floors/levels

All sorts of different effects can be achieved by different floor treatments. Carpets will soften the look of the room and muffle sound; the more carpet and the deeper the pile, the softer the sound and the cosier the feeling. Wall-to-wall carpet helps to unify the space – this is worth remembering when a room is small or awkward in shape. And if there is a great deal of bitty furniture, it helps to have the upholstery in the same colour as the carpet. For floor finishes, your design ideas can be emphasized with appropriate flooring. Wall-to-wall rush matting, for instance, will give a day-in-the-country feeling, as will ceramic tiles. Finishes such as rubber, cork or thermo-plastic tiling, normally picked for tough-ness and laid in other parts of the house, now come in such good colours that they can hold their own on looks alone. This makes them a perfect choice where the living-room is also a through-way.

Rugs isolate the sites they occupy and can add significance to a piece of furniture or accentuate areas of activity.

3-D Floors: changes of level

A more dramatic way of creating a special place within the room is to introduce a change in the floor level. Modulations of the floor-plane can be simple or complex, occasional or progressive, subtle or striking; but all can contribute special qualities to a living-room not readily achievable by other means.

If you are starting from scratch, your architect will be considering levels as part of a total spatial concept. But if you are contemplating alterations to an existing floor, be clear about the prospective advantages before embarking on what might be a costly operation.

The easiest change of level, a simple platform dais at one end of the room, is a way of gaining a continuous seat without obvious "furniture" connotations. Or it can create a special place within the living-room for a particular activity – dining, working, meditating – as an alternative to physically dividing it off with walls or screens. Or it might simply provide a focus within a dull space that lacks something like a fireplace or a bay window. Depending on the use or combination of uses, the size of the raised area might extend from a couple of feet to half the length of the room.

1 *The mirrored ceiling above this multi-level platform gives an illusion of height.*

2 *Steps lead to a change of level.*

3 *A cushioned seating well within the platform shown above.*

1

2

3

Seating wells

A more fundamental change of level, at least in structural terms, results from sinking part of the floor to create a well. The depth of this could vary from a single step down, deep enough for cushions around the edge to provide rudimentary seating, to the full-size "conversation pit" which contains all the seating within the well. This sort of feature demands a room of reasonable size if the well is to be adequately large and the space around it is not to be reduced to a strip unusable for anything but circulation.

Is it structurally feasible?

The size problem can sometimes be resolved by considering a group of rooms together. As well as amending the existing walls and doorways to enable you to move about easily from space to space, the floor levels of each room can in some cases be varied to produce a quite complex range of spatial effects.

None of these major alterations can be undertaken without considering the structural complications that are involved. Generally speaking, positive additions to the existing floor-plane, in the form of platforms or wholesale raising of the total floor, are unlikely to be ruled out simply in terms of weight, since the overall load of a timber-jointed boarded platform placed on top of the existing floor structure should not exceed 5 or 6 lb per sq ft/25 to 30 kg per sq m. This is not excessive because the weight is distributed over the whole existing floor, and not concentrated in a small area. A limiting factor in a floor-raising project will probably be height. If you start with a room not more than about 8 ft/2.5 m high – a common modern room height – not only will building bye-laws limit the floor area over which you can reduce that height, but you will have to consider if you can bear a reduction in ceiling height above the platform. People vary in their reaction to low ceilings, and what is cosy to one will seem unbearably oppressive to another.

As far as the structure of floor wells is concerned, each case has to be considered individually. In a ground floor without cellar or basement, any sort of well should be physically possible; though it may be complicated if the existing floor is of timber (depending on the structure), and expensive if it is concrete. Possible alterations to drain runs and damp-proofing must also be taken into account.

Foam cushions create further changes of level on this carpeted platform.

Living-rooms
22/23 Floor levels

On upper floors, the first factor to be considered will be the effect of a well on the ceiling height of the room below it. Some serious thought will also have to be given to the possible need for extra structural supports for the floor of the well in this lower room. In such cases it is probable that the existing floor structure of the building will have to be altered, perhaps fundamentally, and it is obvious that professional advice must be sought; also, bye-law permission will probably be required.

Construction methods

The new floor level, whether well or platform, can be made with traditional tongue-and-groove softwood boarding, about 1 in./25 mm thick, ¾ in./18 mm plywood or chipboard sheets or panels. It is likely to contrast visibly with the old floor around it, and this contrast can be emphasized by the finish chosen. Old and new levels may be united by choosing one material to cover everything in a continuous surface. Carpet is ideal for use in this way, but most other floorings are normally suitable if careful attention is paid to exposed edges and corners.

Safety

The safety aspect of these changes of level should never be ignored. While it is often a special requirement that alterations in level should occur almost imperceptibly, this can mean that they are easily overlooked by strangers who are not used to them and may trip over them. So it is important to consider whether any proposed change of level could produce a potentially dangerous situation in an important route through the house. In such a case, it would be advisable to arrange for some subtle change in the covering materials, and/or to arrange for the lighting to illuminate the tread portion, while leaving the riser part in the shadow. Of course all sorts of handrails or parapets can be employed to overcome this problem, but these are rather powerful elements which can act against the primary appeal of the change of floor level – the ability to re-define an existing space in a positive but unobtrusive way.

1 *Steps down to the living-room, and down again to a rectangular seating well.*

2 *Sturdy hardboard boxes covered in carpet are another way of changing floor levels.*

1

2

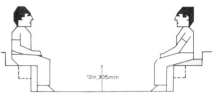

Simple conversation well.

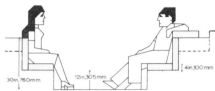

Conversation well with backrest.

Split-level living-room incorporating built-in table on upper platform, seating on lower deck.

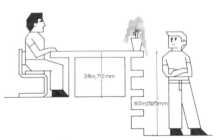

Top bookshelf continues on to upper level, becoming table.

In some parts of the country, bye-laws specify that risers must not be more than 8⅝ in./220 mm if they form part of a stair system. In others, they can be as high as you consider safe, probably not more than 9½ in./250 mm.

Armi Ratia's house in Finland has a raised sitting area and fire-place with storage for logs.

Living-rooms
24/25 Walls/ceilings/windows/lighting

Wall treatments, in traditional room-design, owe a debt to the columns of classical architecture. The skirting derives from the plinth, the dado and dado rail from the base, and above there is the architrave, the frieze and, finally, the cornice at the junction with the ceiling. The different parts are often emphasized by changes of colour and tone, so that the wall's proportion becomes a delight in itself, and not just the background for whatever else is going on in the room.

In modern interiors, when they are not used for display storage, walls are generally seen as sheer slabs of colour or texture. See *Walls* for finishes, and bear in mind that in a much-used room, plain or tone-on-tone colours are easier to live with than a very contrast-y scheme.

Walls which you want to make look less solid might be mirrored, or, if you're starting from scratch, they might be constructed as perforated, glazed or sliding folding screens.

Ceilings

For a feeling of day-time spaciousness, paint the living-room ceiling a few shades lighter than the walls or use a high gloss paint, so that it reflects what's going on.

If the room is meant particularly to come into its own at night, dark ceilings with judicious lighting arrangements can create a marvellously intimate atmosphere (see *Lighting*). If there is to be a lot of entertaining and/or music while people upstairs are meant to be asleep, acoustic ceilings will help to contain the noise within the four walls of the living-room.

Windows

All windows act as focal points and if there is a roofscape, gardenscape or any other sort of view you are happy to look out on, think hard how much privacy you actually need before embarking on a curtaining scheme. If you decide on patterned curtains, consider them carefully in relation to the other things in the room. Make a point of dealing with glare, especially if you are using window seats, and in deciding where to position the TV.

Lighting

Consider the living-room lighting scheme as soon as the furniture layout is settled. It's mainly a question of common sense: bright lights for working and reading; pleasant lighting, suitably muted, for conversation and relaxation; flattering light for parties.

For all the ways to achieve dramatic lighting effects, see *Lighting*.

Silvered wall panels reflect light and warmth and gently distort the image of the room, adding a new dimension.

1

2

1 *Simple, effective and flexible lighting shines on a wall of storage which acts as a room divider.*

2 *Daytime brightness has been achieved by painting walls and ceiling white. Roller blinds leave the windows uncluttered during the day to let in the maximum of light. The feeling of airiness is further emphasized by the lines of the furniture.*

3 *A room which springs to life at night. Dark, subtle colour for the walls, and a pool of light illuminating a picture.*

4 *A light, bright room with a warm, cosy corner. Cork tiles have been taken up to picture-rail height. The tiles have been spaced out at the far end to accommodate the wall-fixed brackets supporting the book shelves.*

3

4

Living-rooms
26 Room for change

Living-rooms work well only if they are given a chance to evolve. Each new acquisition will suggest changes – some small, some large – in the surroundings. The Conrans' living-room has had a long career, which emphasizes this point.

1/2 The bentwood chair (above) used to live happily with the long-haired tousled carpet. But then the carpet was replaced by a patterned rug – a Kelim with which it would not have looked well. So the chair moved to another part of the room, and in its place stands a low, white table to complement the rug.

3/4 Changes in the furniture arrangement transform a room. Above, the Conran living-room as it looked in its last incarnation. (Its present one, with the yellow sofa re-covered in white, is shown on the first page of this section.) Below left`, it becomes the scene of a fireside shot for the Habitat catalogue, and the emphasis is on comfort instead of the spatial quality.

5 Drinks table now – circular pedestal, white top with coloured rim and black base. The old drinks table (above), low and white, has become a coffee table by the sofa.

6/7 An armoire, newly acquired, and placed against the end wall, focuses new interest and adds richness to an area which had been the background to a handsome linear metal bench. The new arrangement complements the armoires' proportions.

Don't let your living-room become a permanent unchanged environment. Keep arrangements mobile, allowing them to evolve along with your own life, your changing ideas, and the changes of taste that are occurring all around you all the time.

Eating-rooms/1

The social patterns of eating used to be pretty clear-cut. The well-off ate in formal splendour in a well-appointed dining-room, their children well out of the way in the nursery. The rest ate less formally around the kitchen table. Today, with less room and even fewer helpers, people have to plan to eat as pleasurably as possible according to a vastly different set of circumstances. We like to have it both ways – a bit of elegance and formality when it is called for, and a cosy place for an easy-going family meal. In either case the eating place must be close to the kitchen.

The chairs must be comfortable for any type of eating, and the table surface durable for the inevitable fall-out from the family meal. When the occasion is a more formal one, the room should at least *feel* isolated from the practical world of cooking and washing-up and become a relaxed place where good food and conversation can be enjoyed by guests and hosts alike. The stronger the impression that the food has been cooked by invisible experts in the kitchen, the more successful the party.

It helps if dishes can be brought in with the least possible panic. If, because of the immovable walls of your house or flat, the dining-room is up a tricky step, it is worth while arranging a wooden ramp so that there are no trip-ups. Doors should be easy to open and close, and a metal kick-plate on the kitchen side helps when hands are full.

With space at a premium, the dining-room is usually the first to be squeezed out. Whether you have a kitchen/dining-room (probably best where there are young children, as spills matter less on vinyl than on carpet) or a living-room/dining-room depends as much on the size of the room as on the degree of formality you are after. The list below should help to clarify this point for you:

☐ Are you happy eating in the kitchen?
☐ Do you enjoy having people in for meals?
☐ When you entertain, do you like to be seen attending to dishes, or do you prefer having the paraphernalia of cooking out of sight?
☐ Do you and your family and friends enjoy long leisurely meals with a lot of conversation?
☐ If you entertain business associates do you take them to restaurants, or do you feed them at home?
☐ Does the family assemble for meals, or do members fend for themselves?

Main ingredients for a meal (besides good food): togetherness and a happy atmosphere. Here they are concentrated around a giant table covered in a bold print.

Eating-rooms
2/3 Furnishing/decoration

The choice of the style of furniture and decoration is very personal and will be influenced to some extent by the sort of house you live in. But the problem of decorating a dining-room is rather a special one, different from other rooms in the house. Because the room is used largely for entertaining, with the focus on the table itself, colours and lighting can be a bit more dramatic, the style a bit more of a surprise, since it is not a room used for hours and hours on end. As in the theatre, lighting is important. A beautifully set dining table can be ruined by clumsy lighting. Harsh lights blazing directly down can turn a dining table into an operating theatre and make everyone look at least ten years older. Too many bright spots of light around the walls can distract from it.

If, when you sit at the table, you can see any part of a naked light bulb, something is wrong. Candlelight, the traditional romantic illumination, is marvellous, providing that the candle flames are above eye-level and not hypnotic points of light bang on the sightline. And candles too low throw shadows upwards and make even young faces look tired.

Dining styles

As in decorating every other room, what's best is what's most comfortable. With flair and self-confidence you can mix styles, and this is sometimes inevitable where expensive items cannot be replaced all at once. A heavy oak table can look great with modern scarlet chairs (though you may get tired of the combination in time). Or curved Regency chairs can look perfectly all right set around a modern white melamine table. It is all a question of having a good eye for line and proportion, and it is fairly safe to say that well-proportioned furniture of any style will mix so long as the pieces are of sympathetic sizes and are given breathing space. There is, however, one thing that can be said with complete confidence. When choosing a style for furniture, pick one in which you feel completely at home. Rooms that work best are the ones that suit the people who live in them.

With the table the focal point of the room, the rest of it should not be too distracting. Pictures should be lit discreetly by strip-lighting – not dazzlingly illuminated. Whatever the style of furnishing, make sure that there is a table, with durable top, on which to put dishes brought from the kitchen. The single-handed hostess can also use this table to avoid trips to the kitchen, by putting on it things to come later in the meal. This makes things more restful for everyone.

All the decorative details should be chosen to enhance the mood of the meal, not to overwhelm it. Central flower arrangements should be below eye-level – or small sprays or sprigs, in egg cups, can be put beside each place.

The more formal the furniture the more formal the details should be. Starched white damask goes with mahogany and rosewood, though you might choose place mats (but choose these with care). In either case, however, see that this type of table is well protected from hot plates. Put felt or a blanket under a damask cloth and make sure mats are heatproof.

For less formal dining, table cloths may be coloured, and pink or apricot or terracotta are very becoming and give a look of warmth in winter. For summer dining, though, a pale blue cloth, perhaps with green napkins and glasses, can look enticingly cool. Make sure that napkins are large enough. Linen ones, at least 27 in./690 mm square, are a "must" for dinner, but coloured paper napkins, so long as they are thick and absorbent, can be used for luncheon.

Always have a coaster for the wine; however careful you are, drips and rings are inevitable. Glasses and cutlery need not match the style of the furniture. Some people, who like everything else modern, love Georgian silver, while those who like early oak may go for steel and chunky glasses. And however comfortable your chairs, always keep a few small cushions handy (as the best restaurants do), as there is often someone with a bad back or some other ache or pain. And have a supply of thick paper napkins so that, in case of a spill, there is no panic rush for a mop-up cloth.

1 *Rush-matting and chairs, both traditional though from widely different backgrounds, live well together in this friendly setting.*

2 *White floor, assorted chairs, walls and shutters, lacy curtains, adjustable Edwardian lamp and broderie anglaise tablecloth show how inviting a monochrome dining-room can look.*

3 *Deep-pile rugs won't do for messy eaters, but give a feeling of cosiness and luxury.*

4 *Unplastered walls, ladderback chairs and print tablecloth make for a rural scene.*

5 *Coffee-and-cream scene: the long-haired carpet sets off clean-cut Bauhaus chairs.*

6 *Architect Norman Foster's virtually noiseless rubber floor is good-looking and easily cleaned if there is fall-out from the table or bits of garden come inside.*

1

4

2

3

5

6

Attitudes to furniture are increasingly informal. Instead of buying a full suite, combining furniture to your own taste and to fit the needs of your home often works out to be more visually stimulating, as well as being more useful and more comfortable.

Choosing tables and chairs

These should fit your home and members of your family. Human beings are bulky. Ask an adult member of your family to sit in a dining chair with his feet on the floor in front of him. Get her to sit well back in the chair so that it supports her back and then measure. You will be surprised how much space she takes up (diagram A). Houses and furniture are

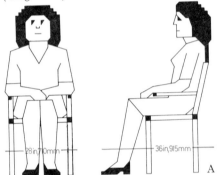

made for human beings, and it helps to know a few facts and figures. Look at a standard dining chair standing beside a dining table (diagram B).

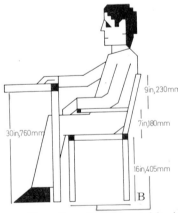

You will notice that the table is 30 in./760 mm and the chair seat 16 in./405 mm from the floor, so the space allowed for your knees is 14 in./355 mm. If you decide to buy a higher or lower table make sure that you will still have this precious 12 in.–14 in./305–360 mm of leg room or you may not be sitting comfortably.

Our diagram also shows where most people need support for their backs. Comfort is a very personal thing and the

same chair does not necessarily suit everyone. The only way to choose a chair is to sit in it – and for long enough – so that if it is going to dig into your back, you begin to notice it.

Dining chairs with arms cost more than their armless counterparts and take up more room. However, many people find them more comfortable. The position of the arms is very important. You must either be able to rest your hand and forearm comfortably on the arm of the chair and move your elbows above it when you eat *or* have space to manoeuvre comfortably inside the frame.

Chairs – in and out of use

What do you intend to do with the chairs when they are not in use? Will you push them under the table, stack them in a corner or fold them up?

Consider how the chair backs will look in relation to the table top. Will the line and design of the chair look good with the table? If the chairs have arms will they go under the table?

Stacking chairs no longer look like refugees from the church hall and can be great space savers in small homes; they are particularly useful with a table which will open out to twice its size.

Folding chairs should be chosen with care. Although they are space saving, they frequently look untidy in the folded position, though there are exceptions, like the Italian acrylic *Plia* chair, which has its own simple rack.

Dining chairs plus

Living/dining-rooms are here to stay, but if they are to look good and the room is to remain uncluttered they need careful planning. In this solution your choice of dining chairs is crucial. Are they intended for the sole purpose of eating or do you wish them to double as extra seating?

Plia chairs hang flat on their own hook.

Dual-purpose chairs must be high enough to use at your dining table and easy to move. Choose chairs which can be easily carried (like those made of cane or willow) or chairs with large free-rolling

castors. There is a new generation of neat armchairs which are high enough for dining but so comfortable that you will be pleased to stick to the same chair for the evening.

With a chair that is to be used for eating be sure to check that the seat is not tilted so that you are *forced* to sit back in it. These chairs are fine for reading the evening paper but impossible to eat in.

Many people, especially elderly people, find a higher, firm wooden or cane-seated chair more comfortable than a low, softly upholstered chair, but remember your female guests, and if short skirts are in fashion provide squab cushions to go over the cane.

Dining at low level

Another approach to eating in the living-room is to dine off a lower table sitting on your easy chair or sofa. This requires a very careful choice of furniture, but can mean that all your furniture, including your table, is dual-purpose. The sketches show what happens to the human body when it sits in a lower chair. As you see, it takes up more floor space (diagrams B, C and D).

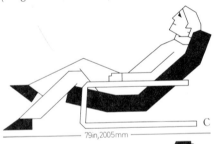

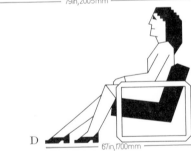

You will need a wider table or you must plan for people not to sit opposite each other if there is insufficient leg room. Chairs or sofas should be without arms or, if you plan to use a large conventional sofa, choose a table with a centre support.

Eating comfortably in limited space

Banquettes are upholstered benches in restaurants, usually with a wall-fixed padded back panel. The principle can be adapted for homes too.

Bench seats are simpler – a fixed wooden or chipboard bench, preferably

with a loose cushion running the length of the seat and a cushion panel fixed to the wall behind. In a small dining recess this fully built-in furniture may be the answer.

Diagram E shows such an arrangement to fit into quite a small area if the bench seat is a little higher than the standard chair so that eaters make small laps. (The height of the table should be adjusted accordingly.)

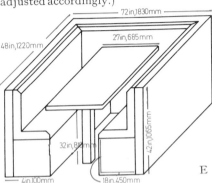

Free-standing benches seat more people than do chairs. They are best used with tables with a central support. As a bench cannot be moved once two or more people are sitting on it, it must be positioned in advance. The diners must either be able to climb over it from the back or duck their knees under the corner of the table and slide along. Corner-placed table legs are therefore impractical. Central pillars or crossover "refectory" legs are best.

If you already have a table which is unsuitable for use with benches, wooden stools are an alternative, at least for the young.

Choosing a dining table

There are two factors which will determine the size of the dining table you choose: the space you have allotted for eating and the number of people you wish to seat at the table.

Sizing up the table

Let's start with the people. Set the table for one to include a side plate, meat plate, glass and cutlery and measure the space it occupies (diagram F).

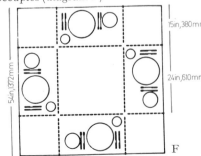

As you will see, you need about 2 ft/610 mm width and 1 ft 3 in./380 mm depth. However for optimum comfort allow 2 ft 2 in./660 mm per person if you are using ordinary dining chairs and 2 ft 4 in./710 mm for armchairs. If you are sitting on both sides of the table, the table should be at least 2 ft 6 in./760 mm wide. To seat one person at each end of a rectangular table allow an extra 1 ft 7 in./480 mm each (diagram G).

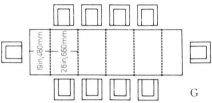

G

But what about round tables? How can you calculate accurately how large a table you will need to seat your family and friends? If you are a mathematician, multiply the number of people by the size of the place setting and divide by $\frac{22}{7}$ or 3.14 (π) which gives you the diameter of the table. For example, a table for six people sitting in armchairs –

$$= \frac{6 \times 2\,\text{ft}\,4\,\text{in.}}{22/7} = 14\,\text{ft} \times \frac{7}{22} = \frac{4\,\text{ft}\,5\,\text{in.}}{(\text{approx})}$$

So a table about 4 ft 6 in./1.3 m in diameter will seat six people comfortably.

What about a square table? This time go back to your place setting and arrange it for using the minimum amount of space so that nothing overlaps. You will find that you need a table 4 ft 6 in./1.3 m square for six people.

You have just proved an important fact; that in a given floor space you can seat more people comfortably at a round table than at a square one (diagram H).

How big a table can you reasonably fit into the space available? Remember that in addition to the width, or diameter, of your table you must add at least 1 ft 4 in./406 mm for each chair. Also a further 1 ft 6 in./460 mm (a) for the chair to be pushed back when the diner stands up to leave the table, and (b) to provide a passage round the back of the chairs for serving. If two people serve you will need at least a 3 ft 2 in./965 mm passage (see drawing next column).

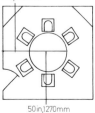
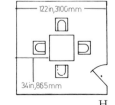

H

It is often best not to place the table in the centre of the room but to one side. This allow a wider passage along the wall.

This sort of calculation is particularly important if you plan to buy an expanding table with extra wings or leaves.

Calculate the minimum passage-way to allow with the table fully extended, so that when it is closed up for everyday use you have plenty of extra space without the table looking too small for the room.

There are two ways of extending a table – either (a) the top slides apart on a fixed underframe, or (b) the underframe and top slide open together.

Choose a table which provides storage for the extra leaves inside the table top. Rectangular tables can be made with an extra leaf at each end slotted above drawers which push into the main body of the table and store the leaves when they are not in use.

Where to put the table

Dining tables are rarely best placed in the centre of the living space. Try experimenting with the table up against a wall. When you have guests pull it out (I).

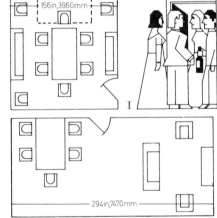

I

Finally drop-leaf tables. These are ideal for families where everyone is out all day and the evening meal is eaten on coffee tables in front of the television. For Sunday lunch the table that has stood folded flat against a wall all week can be opened out to seat a party.

American-type supper parties call for small, low folding tables for everybody sitting around in the living-room; the hostess puts a tray of food on each low table in front of each guest.

Eating comfortably at the counter

Counter tops, or breakfast bars, are a standby in kitchens which are too small for a table. The height is usually determined by the kitchen units or equipment – often 36 in./915 mm high. To be of any use the counter must be at least 8 in./203

mm deep, but a deeper top is more convenient. Your stool should be 10–12 in./254–305 mm lower for leg room. Make sure it has a footrest, or provide one under the counter 8 in./203 mm from the ground (diagram J).

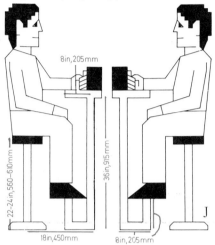

J

Serving

Conventional sideboards have fallen into disrepute. Often expensive and cumbersome, the storage space they offer is inconveniently low and not geared to the size of the china and glasses usually kept in the room.

How much space you can allow for serving depends on what you can spare. If space is tight, a stout trolley which can also be used for clearing the table may be the answer.

Many people prefer to carve and serve food from a work-surface higher than the standard table, say 36 in./915 mm from the ground. Sideboards usually provide this high surface, but an alternative is to fit a shelf 14–18 in./355–460 mm deep, painted to match the walls or coated in melamine or plastic laminate, and run it wall to wall (diagram K).

Whatever you choose to serve from, if it is not heat-resistant it must be protected by a heavy wood (scrubbable) or cork mat.

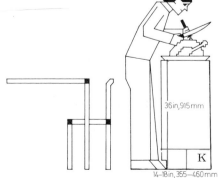

K

Storage

Some families prefer to store all their glass and china in the kitchen, putting it straight back into the cupboards after washing up. But in many households extra storage in the dining-room is welcome. Unless solely for display, china, glass and cutlery are best kept covered. Floor-to-ceiling cupboards, with either hinged or sliding doors, can be built on either side of a fireplace or across a whole wall, if necessary (diagram L).

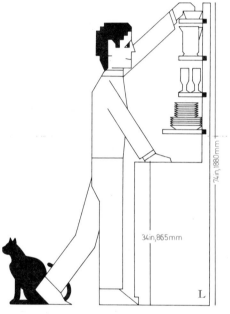

L

The narrow space in front of the chimney is ideal for glasses. Fit plenty of shelves fairly close together. It is far more practical to have three piles of six plates each than one of 18. Standing, the average person can comfortably reach up to 6 ft 2 in./1.9 m and down to 34 in./865 mm from the ground. Use the centre of the cupboard for the things you use most: china, glasses and serving dishes.

Store cutlery in a partitioned basket which can be carried to the table in one piece. This is more convenient than keeping it in a specially fitted drawer.

For a narrow cupboard in a small room make the door in two halves (called concertina hinged doors) so that it folds in on itself or opens from the centre like a saloon door.

Finally, a two-way storage wall which opens both into the kitchen and into the eating area is probably the most efficient. The beauty of this kind of storage is that it need be only about 14 in./355 mm in depth so that it does not protrude far into either room.

Eating-rooms
6/7 In the kitchen

The traditional country kitchen, the walls hung with gleaming pans and a huge scrubbed table groaning with food, is a fantasy to which most of us are susceptible, judging by the TV commercials. Unfortunately, for most of us it has to remain a fantasy. All that space is just not available, and we have to create our dreams in miniature. But there are ways of both economizing on space and making the kitchen/living/eating-room warmly attractive, and if we are cunning the results are well worth while. The kitchen/dining arrangement is the best solution for the family with children. It makes for sociability and the food can be served quickly with the minimum of fuss, and as the floor is likely to be washable, young eaters will be able to learn tidiness without spoiling any carpets.

Central tables

If you like the idea of a central kitchen table, remember that you do need generous space around it – at least 4 ft/ 1.2 m from the edge of the working-top to the back of the nearest chair, so that there is enough room for people to pass around the table in comfort.

Ideally, the table should be well out of the way of the cooking area, and screened, if possible, from the chaos. Eating jammed against the stove may be cosy for the family, but it will drastically limit your guest list.

If you try to squash the table and chairs into a narrow space, either your family will be jammed up against the person who is preparing the meal or the table will have to be reduced in width. A better solution, where space does not permit a central table, is to use a narrower table and to have the seating on one side only. This is perhaps not quite so conducive to general conversation, but a practical solution in a small kitchen.

Wall seating

A table at the side of the kitchen, with wall seating behind it, has obvious advantages: food can be served directly on to the table, the table can be narrower than one intended for all-round use (2 ft 3 in./690 mm is adequate) and the seating can be fixed to the wall, which results in great savings of space.

But most wall seating has to be tailor-made, i.e. exactly fitted to the space available. Constructing a wall seating unit is fairly simple, however, though it is important to get the overall dimensions right. The height of the seat will depend on the height of the table, i.e. the top of the seat should always be so far below the underside of the table as to accommodate every possible size of

1

2

thigh. Cushions, which should be of plastic or material that can be easily removed for cleaning must allow for this, too. Seat cushions ought to be 3 in.–4 in./ 76–102 mm deep. The back cushions should be equally thick to be comfortable. They can be fixed to the wall – in which case they should be of spongeable plastic or tied to a rail. The height of the back cushions is important. Sit the tallest member of the family down and measure his back height from the seat to the middle of his shoulder blades. The back cushion should end either well below or well above this part of the anatomy. Anything else is uncomfortable. (See previous pages for measurements.)

Corner tables

A corner, or a bay window (if your kitchen is endowed with one), is an ideal place for a small table. Space can often be made for one by building all the kitchen units out into the room, leaving enough room for table and benches.

Folding tables

A table that is made to fold upwards on to a wall or storage unit is a useful idea where space is really short. It can be covered with a laminated plastic and double as the cook's additional working-top, for homework, or any other activity, no matter how messy.

Bar counter

The counter of the type found in snack bars is a solution for the quick and easy meal – particularly for breakfast and for children's snacks. A snack bar top can act either as part of the working space or as a counter at right-angles to the wall. And the seating at this kind of counter must, of course, be higher – e.g. stools, if possible with adjustable seat heights. If they are backless, they can be pushed under the bar, and right out of the way, between meals.

---

1 *Out-of-doors eating is such a joy that it seems a pity not to cater for it, at least on clement days. French windows in the kitchen are rare, but achievable and delightful. They could lead out to a covered patio, like in John Stefanides' Greek island indoor/ outdoor eating-kitchen.*

2 *It is worth knocking down a wall to make one spacious kitchen/dining-room. Here, heavy curtains keep out the winter, when meals are taken in the kitchen-end.*

(Opposite) In the Conrans' basement kitchen, a long narrow table seats eight and (a very important point) this still allows room for comfortable circulation, even when all the chairs are occupied.

Eating-rooms
8/9 Subdividing

The problem of separating the cooking from the eating is one that faces everyone starting to plan a house in detail. The simplest, cheapest solution is a door – there are several that can be made to fit an existing frame.

Swing door

Hinged to swing in both directions, it works well only if there is *plenty* of room on either side of it. Make sure that the return spring is gentle so that the door does not close with too much force. To allow the door to open easily, particularly if you have your hands full, a sturdy kick- or push-plate can be installed on the kitchen side. On the dining-room side, keep the original door handle. It is important that the floor joint between the kitchen and the dining area is trip-proof; a steel or aluminium floor-plate may be the answer.

Other door variations that can be fitted into an existing frame include the "stable" door – this is a door split across at waist level: it has the advantage of letting you see into the dining area while maintaining a certain amount of privacy in the kitchen.

Where there is little spare space, the door can be split down the middle. Narrow louvred doors work well, are strong and don't look too solid.

Hatches

The time-honoured hatch only really works if the meal is served by two people, one on each side. Often the standard hatch is too shallow. It should be deep enough to allow everything needed to be waiting in the wings, with enough clear space to take returning dirty dishes. In this way the complete meal can be served without traffic jams.

Large units, with upper and lower storage and generous working-tops, might have cupboards running through with doors on either side. The drawers can also do this, but will limit the depth of the unit; a drawer that is longer than 22 in./560 mm is rather more trouble than it is worth, because it is impossible to find the things at the back without rummaging.

1 A drop-down hatch-way opens to form the sort of table at which four people can eat in comfort on either side.

2/3 This circular table is designed for movable feasts; it slides through a slit underneath the hatch. It can accommodate snacks in the kitchen or meals in the next room, where upholstered seating arrangements complement its shape and create an eating alcove in a defined area.

1

2

3

4 Hatch opens like a sash window. The glass in the panel makes the effect of a stained-glass window.

5 Wall-to-wall louvred doors divide this Dutch dining-room from the kitchen.

6 A curtain is the most versatile and inexpensive of all partitions. When it is drawn open, there is no sensation of divided space; when it is closed, it promotes a feeling of cosiness, besides hiding possible untidiness in the kitchen and counteracting draughts.

7 Dresser-partition, designed by Paul William White. The door-opening between the dining-room and the kitchen goes straight up to the ceiling, emphasizing the continuity between the two areas.

8 If they are conveniently placed, kitchen and balcony can interrelate for summer meals.

9 Another example of the satisfactory effect of a floor-to-ceiling opening between kitchen and dining-room. Wide-slatted tongue-and-groove boarding is used above and below the hatch.

10 In photographer Roger Gain's kitchen, there is not so much a wall, but more a room-divider, with high level storage space and a working counter in the middle.

11 Kitchen and dining-room divided by a fold-down counter, to which stools may be drawn up for casual eating, and which acts as a side-table when meals are served in the dining-room.

12 The simplest partition of all – a run of standard, open-back cupboard units set at right angles to the wall, backed with chipboard or hardboard.

4

5

6

7

8

9

10

11

12

Eating-rooms
10/11 The living-room/the work area

The dining area must earn its keep by being put to other uses. If the walls of the dining area are covered with built-in storage units the table can become a working study, a sewing-room or area kept separate for study. It is important that clutter can be quickly put away when a meal is in the offing. And it is extremely important to plan for enough power points in appropriate places. The section might be turned into an area for watching TV or listening to music, so lighting must be suitable. If the table is to be used to most advantage, plan a ceiling light that can be lowered or raised, dimmed or brightened; for reading or study, an Anglepoise lamp can be plugged in for good, economical light.

Table surfaces

With this sort of all-purpose use, the table should be more durable than would be necessary in a conventional dining-room. Polished walnut or mahogany is asking for trouble. Laminated plastic is practical, if not aesthetically pleasing, but it can always be covered with a pretty cloth when a meal is on the way. At the opposite end of the scale, style-wise, is an old oak table so impervious to wear that only an extra polish is necessary to bring it up to entertaining standard.

Or a glass table can be covered with a cloth for activities between meals so that it is kept clean and unscratched. A melamine table is impervious to most marks, and can be quickly sponged.

Seating

The chairs, for this sort of table, should not look too "set" and arranged in the formal way. Chairs of bentwood, metal or wood and canvas that can be easily moved around are the best answer.

1/2 Slim table and chairs are sensible in a living-room : they look less conspicuous when not matched up "en suite".

3 If a room is to work as an all-purpose place, chairs with arms are essential.

4 Interlübke table folds up into the storage unit. Chairs fold and stack, too.

5 Flowered wallpaper, lacy tablecloth and cottagey things all contribute to the relaxed atmosphere of this friendly room.

6 Round tables, like Enzo Apicello's, don't look expressly designed for meals and, in a busy area, are less likely to bruise passers-by than tables with corners.

(Opposite) Overhead lighting makes this dining-table practical for typing or reading.

1

2

3

4

5

6

Eating-rooms
12/13 Other places/low-level dining

For a family whose space is really limited, there doesn't have to be one set place for eating at all. It helps if your family enjoys picnics! And it depends on the size and shape of your house or flat. In some older flats, for instance, the entrance hall may be big enough for eating in (with a table that can be moved to one side and with chairs that can be stacked). In houses where the staircase construction is suitable, there may be room on the landing for a small dining area. Draughts may be a problem, so the hanging of curtains or the placing of a screen might be necessary. Curtains should be on a ceiling track so that they pull into neat columns by day. In some cases it might be possible to arrange a "tent" for comfort, or to enclose an ugly or badly-proportioned room. But this would need specialist skill, and only the most dedicated DIY enthusiast would be able to make the arrangement elegant enough, with striped canvas and tented top, shaped on to a light wooden frame.

Almost anywhere, an instant dining-room can be made with a hinged table, preferably one to fold and fasten back into a storage unit or cupboard, and with light chairs brought from other rooms. Where the fireplace or kitchen range has been taken away, there is often a recess which could conveniently be used in this way with the chairs dispersed between meal times. In these circumstances, smaller children can sit on stools to bring them up to a comfortable level, and these, too, can be taken away when the meal is over.

Low-level eating

Older and larger people may not like it but the fact has to be faced that, where space is restricted, there is a lot to be said for low tables and even lower seats or chairs. This applies particularly to bed-sits, studios and other rooms which are all-purpose to say the least, and to situations where people like to watch TV during meals.

Low-level eating, however, does present some problems when it comes to serving the food. Carving meat or serving food from bowls is out. This must be done near the stove and food is best carried on trays to the tables. And separate courses which need constant bobbing up and down on the part of the food-provider are relaxing to no one. So it is better to have starter or soup/main course and pudding on the same tray. Or a compromise may be made by having a separate low table laid with the bread/butter/drinks/fruit, etc., to which people can help themselves. For four people you need a low table about 36 in./915 mm square. This works better than a long, narrow table as there is room in the middle for a low bowl of flowers, the bottle of wine, the ash trays and the salt and pepper mills.

Ideally, this sort of low table should not be as low as all that. The average coffee table is about 15 in./380 mm, but for eating, the table should be at least 22 in./560 mm, which means that guests can be quite comfortable sitting on the sofa or in a low armchair. If your table is lower than this, it may be better to provide thick comfortable cushions on the floor. If these floor cushions or bolsters can be put against a wall so much the better, as guests can then make themselves really comfortable with extra cushions for their backs. This type of floor cushion is most comfortable and practical if it is made of foam rubber with covers that can be unzipped for easy cleaning or washing. The leaning cushions, however, can be softer and filled with crumble-foam or feathers.

Where the living-room for a large family is the biggest in the house, there is much to be said for *small*, low tables, one for each person. If food is put on a side-table or buffet, or on a trolley wheeled in from the kitchen, each viewer or listener or reader can eat at his own pace, getting up to serve himself – and possibly clearing away afterwards. Incidentally, the old "hostess" trolley that went out of fashion some time back is reappearing, and extremely useful it is.

1

1 *Low table in the family room doubles for casual meals or Scrabble: floor cushions here are pads covered with grass mats from the Far East.*

2 *Variation on the low table theme, with monster bolsters to lean against and comfortable, draught-free carpet.*

3 *Coffee table laid for buffet supper in the living-room. If you can't find a big enough table, cut down the legs of a non-valuable old side-table.*

4 *Avoid claustrophobia in a passage-way dining area: use floor-to-ceiling mirror to create an illusion of space. Painters' trestles make useful narrow tables, which can be stored flat, taking up the least possible space.*

5 *Dining-table conveniently masked from the main study area by a bookcase unit set at right angles to the wall.*

(Opposite) Hall leading to the garden door has just enough room for a table which can be pushed against the wall between meals to make passageway.

2

3

4

5

Eating-rooms
14/15 The formal dining-room

A single-purpose dining-room serves a very distinct function in the house; it is the room used for entertaining; the room which is "shown off" on special occasions.

Consequently the decoration should be a little special too, and the scheme can afford to be more emphatic. Traditional colour schemes for dining-rooms tended to be dark. Today the most favoured dark colour seems to be chocolate brown. One of the obvious reasons why dark walls are often chosen as a background to formal meals is simply that they look their best by artificial light, throwing the glitter of glass and silver into sharp contrast, and isolating the diners in a pool of light.

It is the dramatic isolation of the dining table, focusing the function of the room, that makes for the most coherent decoration.

The one place where the strong centre-light really works is over the dining table, but the height at which it is hung is crucial and the shape of the shade is important too. The deeper bowl will always work better than a shallow one. If the shade is made of some translucent material, coloured plastic or stained glass, which needs a strong light to show off its colour, fit it with a bulb that has its lower half silvered. This shows off the shade to the full without blasting too much light down.

Other lights in the dining-room should be positioned carefully to throw light only where it's needed – on the serving table, for instance – and not detract from the main lighting over the table.

The other furniture

It's best to keep the other furniture in the dining-room down to a functional minimum. The traditional Georgian sideboard was ideal in a big room as it combined storage with a serving table, deep drawers for bottles, shallow ones for linen and cutlery. The modern equivalent is often too large for a small dining-room and protrudes too far from the wall. (A serving shelf need not be deeper than 15 in./380 mm, but the wall behind it should be well protected by a sheet of glass from splashes.) In a larger dining-room, where space permits, such additions as a small refrigerator built into a storage unit is by no means such a fancy luxury at it sounds.

1 *Ceiling-recessed pin spotlights shine down and the wall sculpture by D'Arc Angelo is dramatically lit.*

2 *Formal dining in the cosy Victorian manner. Dark walls and a low-slung pendant lamp combine to create a glowing pool of light.*

1

2

An uncluttered, functional dining-room shows off the classic lines of Aalto laminated plywood chairs and the oval table. The patterned rug focuses attention on the dining area.

A thoroughly grown-up formal dining-room has pale leather Bauhaus chairs and a round marble-topped table standing ankle deep in soft, pale carpet. A circular mirror repeats the rounded motifs.

In a comfortable Swedish farmhouse a large tile-topped table is surrounded by comfortable cane armchairs. (Extra leg-room is needed if chairs are lower than usual dining height.)

A large, farmhouse-style dining-room has red floor tiles, wheelback chairs and a big wooden table. Willow-pattern plates and dishes are displayed in a well-proportioned, tall wooden dresser, which complements the proportions of the room.

Natural colours and textures of rush seats, tiles, patterned plaster walls and beamed ceiling for a dining-room that is both rural and sophisticated. The splendid rocking-horse makes an unusual focal point at one end of this long room.

A cosy and welcoming garden-room houses an interesting assortment of collectors' pieces. The old apothecary's chest makes a splendid sideboard as well as providing useful drawer-space for small items such as cutlery, napkins, table-mats and so on.

Eating-rooms
16 Details

On the table, it's again the details that count – not just the plates and glasses and knives and forks, but the accessories, some that you mightn't have thought of, like, perhaps, a centre-piece made of fruit and vegetables.

Choose the kind of china that suits the kind of food you enjoy. Simple food tastes best off simple country pottery plates, and the simpler the design of the dishes the more versatile they will be. Obviously it is best to start by buying china that will be easy to replace and match, but you can easily ring the changes by serving the pudding course on a totally different style of dish. And some of the nicest looking meals are served on china lovingly collected from various sources.

Soup bowls are more useful than soup plates, they keep the soup warmer and can double up as small serving dishes. Keep the size of the dishes generous and this applies to glasses as well (tiny wine glasses, whatever their quality, look really stingy). The standard round-bowled French Burgundy glass is probably the best glass ever designed; use the size larger than the standard pub wine glass (12 oz) and you can drink anything from coke to cognac from it. Beer, however, does need a half-pint tumbler.

The decoration of the table is a matter of inspiration. Sheets, bedcovers, or lengths of any material for that matter, will enlarge your repertoire of table cloths. Remember that a table setting should be a bit dramatic.

Flowers, used skilfully, add enormously to a dining table. Remember not to leave them too tall – it's difficult to talk through a bush. A lot of the same flowers in a small bowl look better than the same number of flowers thinned out in a larger vase. For a simple table arrangement either keep the same flowers in a bunch, or mix flowers in one colour. The effect can be stunning.

1 *White china makes any food look delicious.*

2 *Breakfast – French coffee is reinforced with a Provencal print.*

3 *Lunch – things needn't match to look good, and can be picked up at odd sales and auctions.*

4 *Tea-time – an opportunity for nostalgic delights served on fine bone china.*

5 *Lacy cloth, china and polished fruit for a festive dinner setting.*

Kitchens/1

The easiest way to plan a new kitchen is to treat it like cooking a good meal. You have to make many of the same decisions: whom is it for? how many? what are the ingredients? how should they go together? and what should it cost?

To start with, make a list of the equipment you would like. Kitchen design has changed a great deal since the introduction of many reliable and well-designed mechanical items which take the slavery out of cooking. For instance, a large refrigerator/freezer not only keeps a variety of foods at different temperatures but is a long-term store so that you don't constantly need to go marketing.

Mixers and blenders, provided they are ready to hand, make food preparation much quicker; gas and electric hobs give you a combination to beat power-cuts, and a double-oven will allow you to cook two quite separate dishes at the same time. A waste-disposer will consume all the revolting smelly kitchen waste.

Some dishwashers now not only deal with saucepans and baked-on food, but wash much better than most people can by hand. Extractor fans keep the kitchen clean and clear of fumes and humidity.

If you cannot afford all the equipment you want at once, try to allow space for future installation. Too many kitchens have been planned so that it cannot be added without expensive redesign.

Having decided on what you need, check that the kitchen space is large enough to accommodate it all. In many houses, especially new ones, kitchens are too small, but with a builder's help could be extended by taking down a wall or walls, which may in the end save money.

Here are some questions you should ask before you plan your kitchen.

- [ ] Where should your kitchen be in relation to the eating area?
- [ ] Do you want a kitchen for cooking only or a family room where the children play?
- [ ] What sort of cook are you – bachelor, family, convenience, continental?
- [ ] How many do you usually cook for?
- [ ] How often do you shop? Therefore, how much storage space do you need?
- [ ] Are the existing supplies of water, gas and electricity adequate?
- [ ] Is the ventilation adequate?
- [ ] Do you live in clean air so that you can have open shelves; or dirty air where you should have cupboards?

1 *Warm and welcoming: here, natural materials, wood, copper and brass, create an atmosphere of workman-like comfort.*

2 *Stark and clean: stainless steel and plastic laminates are used for a kitchen which is simple, striking, efficient.*

Since the kitchen is the hub of the home it is essential that it should be positioned conveniently. In old houses planned for servants, the kitchen is often quite wrongly located – as for example the front basement kitchen. Here the floor is often rotten and the walls damp, so you have a good excuse while renovating to do a major conversion: knocking the front and rear basement into one to make a long living/dining-kitchen with a view into the garden at the back.

Better use of spaces

Between-the-wars houses often have inadequate kitchens, planned before dishwashers and split-level cookers. But they sometimes have unused coal cellars, an outside wc, an over-large larder or a small breakfast-room or scullery. You could knock all these areas into one, or make a kitchen/dining area by taking down the dividing wall to the dining-room.

In the larger detached houses of the 1870s, where the best rooms looked out on to the road, the bathroom, outhouses and kitchen were at the back with no access to the garden except by a side entrance. By rearranging the kitchen inside it is possible to provide doors opening on to the garden and perhaps a terrace for summer eating. The small artisan-type terrace house usually has the kitchen in a rear extension with a large chimney breast which housed the old range. This is best removed to make room for a dining area.

Country cottages and farmhouses present no problems of space as they usually have fairly large kitchen/eating areas and sometimes an old buttery which can be incorporated into your plan.

Forget the dream world of the advertisements and think the kitchen out as a natural extension of the design and feeling of your house or flat. It is more economical to plan a convenient kitchen using standard units within an irregularly shaped room than to use tailor-made units to follow all the curious shapes of the wall. New walls can be simply formed with timber stud partitioning faced with plywood, which adds little load to the floor. Often the spaces behind can be used for hot-water cylinders, pipework or cupboards – there can never be too much storage space in the kitchen.

Existing kitchens

Close problem gaps between a freestanding stove and adjacent unit with a heatproof top or widen the gap to about 6 in./152 mm to provide a space for oven cloths, paper towels or implements which you need at hand while cooking.

The best overall answer to units of differing heights, and window sills below work-top height, is to remove the highest work-tops and then put in one new top to fit both units and window opening. Or build up the lower work-tops with marble pastry or sycamore chopping areas. There are often gaps at the back of units, especially where the wall is uneven, and these can be covered with an angled fillet scribed to the wall.

Safety

The kitchen kills as many people as our roads, so safety should be a prime consideration. The hob is one of the most dangerous things in the kitchen. Ideally, the gas burners should be in a row at the back of the work-top so that it is difficult for children to pull a saucepan down, and it is a good idea to have the controls out of reach, too.

Pipes

In older houses pipes are often left exposed and may have rusted or corroded. Check which pipes are no longer necessary, and have them removed. Sometimes it is possible when putting in new plumbing to re-run the water pipes – either along the wall at the back of the units, or in the ceiling. For pipes in corners, an angle casing straight across is better than boxing them in.

Finishes

Kitchens get a great deal of hard use. Choose materials, both for work-tops and floors, which will mellow well or be impregnable. There should be at least one surface for cutting (apart from loose chopping boards and bowls), so that you are not tempted to use the laminated top and leave permanent marks which spoil the surface.

Rented accommodation

A short-term kitchen system for a rented flat is an adjustable shelving system which will take 2 ft/610 mm brackets. But make sure the fixings are strong enough. The main work-top shelf can have cut-outs for a sink and hob with a shelf above to accommodate a rôtisserie, or a small oven below the work-top. Small whitewood chests of drawers or mobile office equipment can be fixed below the top for further enclosed storage. If and when you move, you can not only take these pieces with you, but also redesignate them for other uses.

Tidying-up the looks

The most typical problem of all is lack of money. Even so, most existing kitchens can be made more attractive with only a small amount of expenditure. A great improvement can be made straightaway to a hodge-podge of units and equipment by painting everything, including refrigerator and cooker, with one colourful heatproof paint. Replace non-matching handles with simple white china or brass ones. Even exposed pipes will look more cheerful when they are painted in bright colours, which will make them into a deliberate, decorative, feature.

Before painting, remove all unnecessary wires, old pipes or bell indicators, and replace all the badly designed implements, old clocks, battered calendars, ugly dish-cloths, with new and better-designed ones that fit your new colour scheme. Add flowers, plants, a bird cage or goldfish bowl; a sofa or china cabinet; cheap wine racks or saucepan stands painted white.

Fix a small shelf for spice and herb bottles by the cooker with a rail below for hanging cooking implements, and cut a slot in the work-top where you chop to keep knives safely.

1 *Simple layout for a small square kitchen in a Nash terrace house in London. All work-top, storage and equipment are built in along the two side walls with the table doubling as eating and extra work space. Work-tops are lit by concealed lights under the high-level storage cupboards. The kitchen is entered from the rear end of a dining-room and the tall window lights both rooms.*

2 *An old dresser and cooker have been painted red to match the walls, which adds gaiety as well as unifying odd pieces of furniture and irregularities of the room. The dark colour also shows up the dresser clock and a lively collection of china.*

3 *Exposed pipes lose some of their ugliness when painted in strong colours; the paint must be waterproof, emulsion will not do.*

4 *A large kitchen/dining-room in a late-Georgian house has a central work unit, incorporating the hob, which divides the dining area from the kitchen. Equipment in constant use is stored on shelves below.*

5 *The glazed door – in the same kitchen – leads into a conservatory where potted plants and climbing greenery make an all-the-year-round garden.*

6 *The dining end has a carpeted floor. The large windows, with the original glazing bars preserved, throw plenty of light on the work-tops. At night the room is lit by recessed downlighters.*

7 *At the kitchen end, louvred doors ventilate a storage cupboard. The painted match-boarding is useful for hiding pipework as well as giving enclosed cupboard space.*

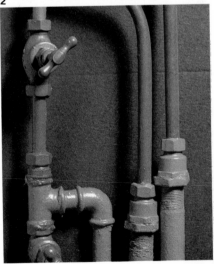

4

5

6

7

Kitchens
4/5 Plans for layouts

The layout of the kitchen depends upon the size and shape of the room. In conversions where a certain amount of compromise is always necessary, it may be cheaper to alter a window or door position to achieve a good, simple layout than to go to great lengths to fit a kitchen into an awkward space.

Working out a layout is like playing a game of chess, with almost as many permutations. These are the basic rules:

(a) You need the food storage area near the door with space to put the shopping down.

(b) This must be near the preparation space, which should not be less than 3 ft/ 914 mm long and adjacent to both oven and hob. It is not necessary to have the hob and oven close together.

(c) The hob must be near the sink so that pans can be filled for vegetables and afterwards drained.

(d) The hob should be near the hatch, if there is one, or serving area.

(e) If there is a dishwasher, this should be fitted into or next to the china and cutlery store and be near the sink and waste disposal so that dishes can be quickly cleaned before loading the machine.

The "passage" space between units should not be less than 4 ft/1.25 m if two people are working in the kitchen, although in small "single" kitchens it can be cut down to about 2 ft 6 in./760 mm. The round walking distance between the main cooking areas should not be more than 20 ft/6.10 m. If possible, the kitchen should not be a main traffic route. If there is room, a lobby with two doors between the kitchen and the garage or back door will provide a useful airlock against cold entering the house and can also be used for deliveries, tricycles or boots.

Types of plan

Simple layouts are the cheapest and usually work best. Keep the tall cupboards, built-in refrigerator, dishwasher and oven in one group if possible so that the rest of the space can be uninterrupted. Kitchen planning books usually show three typical kitchens: the U-shape, L-shape and galley plan. These can sometimes be difficult to adopt in existing kitchens because of the layout of doors, windows and plumbing, and there is no reason why you should not have any plan you like provided that it works, and suits your own requirements.

There are a number of mobile kitchens which can be pushed from room to room and plugged in where necessary. Another idea, the module kitchen, consists of a number of fully equipped units each designed around one particular process. For instance a mix-area for pastry making, with built-in electric mixer,

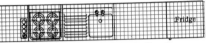
Single line : often the only solution for a narrow kitchen or bachelor flat.

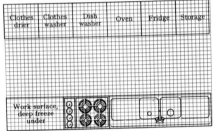
Parallel or Galley : here everything is within easy reach.

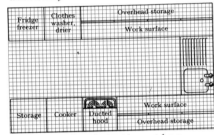
U-shaped : often the best layout for a medium, regular shaped room.

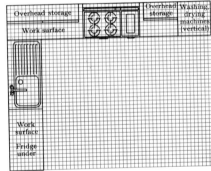
L-shaped : this leaves rest of the room traffic free.

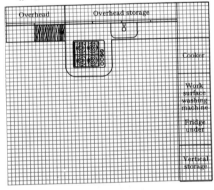
F-shape : really a combination of U and L.

marble slab, storage for mixing bowls, casseroles, baking sheets, rolling pins, etc. Careful, integrated design of this kind can lead to great economies in space, and make kitchen chores more enjoyable.

The vertical layout of the kitchen is just as important as the horizontal. It is difficult to achieve the ideal width standard units but the following dimensions can be taken as a guide. All units with work-tops should have a toe recess at floor level at least 3 in./76 mm and 6 in./ 152 mm if the flooring turns up. For most women a convenient work-top height is 2 ft 8 in./810 mm (depth of 2 ft/610 mm, to include working space plus an area where things can be pushed back). There should be a small upstand at the back to prevent spillages into the storage below. The most comfortable storage space is above the work-top, where it is useful to have adjustable shelves 4 in. or 5 in./102 mm or 127 mm deep.

Wall cupboard units can start about 1 ft 4 in./410 mm above the work-top and should not project to more than 1 ft/ 305 mm from the front edge of the work-surface. The highest shelf in wall units should not be more than 5 ft 6 in./1.7 m for comfort and the cupboard tops about 6 ft 4 in./1.93 m. Fill in the space between the shallow cupboard tops and the ceiling with a vertical panel to align with the front edge of the work-top. This eliminates the dust trap on top, and makes a useful space for running ventilating ducts and service pipes, and is a good place for lights so that you will never stand in your own shadow.

Refrigerator and cooker doors

All too often the swing of the refrigerator door (which must clearly open towards the preparation area and a convenient place for setting down) dictates the whole plan of the kitchen. Most refrigerators are hinged on their right-hand sides, but some manufacturers do provide optional door swings.

Of course, when cookers have let-down doors the problem does not arise, and most built-in ovens can be bought with optional door swings. In small kitchens the drop-down door may take up too much room, as you have to stand well away from it and stretch into the oven.

Cabinet doors

The layout of the kitchen may also dictate the type of cabinet door you choose. In narrow kitchens it is better to have sliding doors (if possible use projecting handles which catch, so that you can slide two doors at once), or very narrow, hinged doors, ideally on a linked rod so that two can be opened together for easier access.

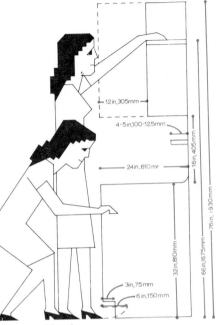
Diagram showing average comfort heights and widths of units and high-level storage.

1

2

3

4

1 The layout of the work area in this kitchen ensures that, although the room is large, moving about is kept to a minimum during the preparation and cooking of food and well away from the eating end.

2 A neat U-shaped/galley plan which makes full use of all available wall space. Where storage cupboards are ceiling height, least-used items should be stored at the top and these can be reached via a stepladder or sturdy chair.

3 A pair of butcher's chopping blocks have been made into a central island work-top in this Cambridge, Massachusetts, house. The hob and oven are built into a brick dividing unit between kitchen and dining areas with light and extractor outlet above. The floor is also brick.

4 Small compact kitchen with cooker, sink and storage, all fitted into one recess, is an ideal arrangement for a bedsitter. The pinoleum blind pulls down to hide the units when they are not in use.

Kitchens
6/7 Making a meal of it

It is often best to have the eating area in the kitchen, but if there is also a separate dining room, the layout should also relate to it. There must be a convenient door, wide enough for a trolley, and no awkward jutting-out corners from units or shelves to get in the way. A hatch can be useful, particularly if it's combined with two-way storage.

Allow for a safe area where your pets can eat their food without being tripped over or having their bowls trodden on.

1 *Dining and kitchen areas are divided by a work-top doubling as a sideboard.*

2 *French doors are better than a window if the kitchen is at garden level, or if a terrace can be built up to it.*

3 *A simple breakfast bar is useful for snack meals.*

4 *Horizontal hatchway with tiled work-top on kitchen side deep enough to take a plate-warmer, and lower sideboard shelf on the dining-room side.*

5/6 *The area below the hatch has become a wine rack. When open, the wooden portion of the hatch cover disappears into the ceiling, the stained glass remains.*

7 *The sink under the window enables you to keep an eye on children in the garden while washing up.*

8/9 *Bachelor kitchen: an efficient solution for a bed-sitter or small flat is to confine equipment to one wall, hidden behind a Venetian blind.*

10 *Kitchen in a cupboard: another means of shutting off a kitchen area.*

1

2

3

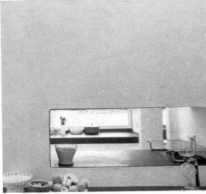

4

5

6

7

8

9

10

Elegant upholstered dining chairs and highly polished mahogany tables are out of place in a working kitchen. Scrubbed pine, bentwood and laminates are better choices. If space is limited, have seating that can be pushed right under the table out of the way.

You must make sure that there is enough room to move around comfortably between worktops and dining areas when the family or guests are seated.

Check that the ventilation is first-rate, and the lighting adjustable for the different uses.

1 *The dining table in this all-pine kitchen designed by Peter Bell is fixed to a batten on the back of a central island work-top unit. The raised back and sides of the unit shield the work-top from the diners.*

2 *Scrubbed kitchen table and wooden trestle benches add to the old-fashioned farmhouse look of this kitchen.*

3 *Natural wood and white predominate in a simple uncluttered room with pine table and bentwood dining chairs. All vertical surfaces are white; the work-top is of wood, the floor cork tiles.*

Kitchens
8/9 Storage

One advantage of planning a kitchen round standard units is that you get a good idea of what it will look like by studying the catalogues. Some manufacturers also have a free planning service. However, if you know exactly what you want or are employing an architect/designer and have an odd-shaped kitchen, you might find it better, and not necessarily more expensive, to have custom-built units which will fit into all the difficult corners.

A good compromise is to choose standard units you like in a neutral finish such as white, and have the work-top made up with special non-standard design points – solid marble for pastry making, sycamore chopping blocks, stainless steel hob and sink unit in one piece. Remember that special fittings like bucket holders and wire racks can be bought separately.

Standard kitchen unit sizes are related more closely to equipment than to practical dimensions for storage. Most food-stuffs can be stored on 5 in./127 mm shelving and things like spice jars on 2 in./51 mm shelving. The advantage is that everything is on view, and as there is no reaching over to the back, shelves can be closer together. This way you often get as much effective storage space as you would with bigger, deeper cupboards. Walls which cannot be used for conventional storage cupboards, because they are too close to other equipment, can be used in this way. Except for large items like jam pans, practically everything in a kitchen will fit on a 12 in./305 mm deep shelf quite comfortably.

Where you have a deep cupboard, use a hinged door with racks on the inner face which project into the cupboard, so restricting the shelf depth inside to a convenient size. Horizontal sliding doors, useful in confined spaces, should have projecting handles so that one catches on the other and they are pushed along together. The ideal doors for wall cabinets above work-tops slide upwards on a sash mechanism. They give full access to the contents, unlike horizontal sliding doors, and do not project into one's face like a hinged door.

In a clean-air area, open shelves are practical and can visually link the kitchen to the room. This is particularly important where the kitchen is not being entirely altered but simply having a little spent on it to bring it up to date. If you are really saving money, it is often possible to buy old kitchen units from a builder who is putting in a new super-kitchen for someone else. Check the fittings, and possibly renew the handles and catches. On strong walls, industrial-quality wall-mounted suspension systems can be used with open shelves.

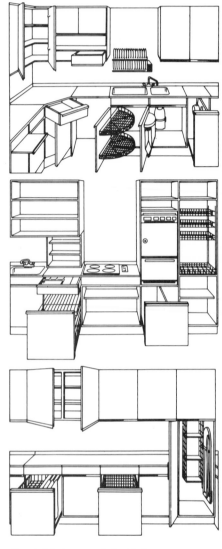

Special fittings made by kitchen manufacturers to make life easier for the housewife – condensed into three drawings.
Top, *from left : corner cupboard wall unit ; plate rack over sink; pull-out shelf ; corner drawer and cupboard unit ; door with swivel wire storage trays ; door-hung holder and lid for plastic or paper refuse bags (note electric waste disposal unit) ; narrow pull-out drawer for hanging saucepans.*
Centre, *from left : Shelves of different sizes and widths ; cutlery drawer ; drawer with vegetable racks ; wide pull-out drawer with centre partition for saucepans and lids ; wire pull-out storage trays.*
Bottom, *from left : High-level storage cupboards ; pull-out drawer with towel rails ; pull-out drawer with wire basket for laundry, etc. ; cleaning cupboard incorporating ironing board.*

1

1 (*Opposite*) *Open shelving is storage at its simplest and most convenient – if you live in a clean-air zone – and if the shelves are spaced to take items of differing heights there is no wasted wall area.*

2 *Well-designed, carefully-planned units in an Italian range provide ample storage space for everything from china and pots and pans to tinned and fresh foods and cleaning items. Cupboards above the work-top, with sink and hob set in to allow headroom, vary in width to store bottles and herb or spice jars. There is also a very wide cupboard incorporating a plate drainer rack. Note the pull-out unit on castors.*

3 *Built-in cupboards may be preferable if you like everything out of sight. China stays cleaner, and can be stacked more economically. Here a ventilation hood has been incorporated above the hob.*

4 *Pine units in this Habitat range have a country look and make efficient storage easy.*

5 *Differing heights of units look more interesting than standard ones. This custom-built kitchen is by Max Clendinning. A pull-down table top conceals a toaster and other breakfast essentials. The shiny red ceiling adds warmth to efficiency.*

Kitchens
10/11 Storage details

Gadgets can complicate life unless conveniently to hand – it can take longer to lift, use, wash and put them away than to do everything by hand. One answer is a cupboard with adjustable shelves and pegboard back, so that each appliance has its own allotted space.

Open shelving can be rationalized too, with items roughly graded by height and width.

Manufacturers of kitchen fittings have some clever space-saving ideas – well worth looking into.

1 *Small items lined up on a narrow shelf above the work-top with larger pots, casseroles and trays stacked underneath.*

2 *Staggered shelving eliminates wasted shelf space. Cups and saucers can be stored at the top, heavy casseroles and meat dishes on the wide bottom shelves.*

3 *Saucepans and lids neatly stored in roomy drawers below a work-top.*

4 *The plastic-coated wire trays in this corner cupboard swing out on their hinges when the door is opened.*

5 *Another hinged wire basket, attached to the inside of a cupboard door.*

6 *Shelves above a tiled work-top take bottles, tins and jars.*

7 *A wire basket bottle-holder fits neatly into a cupboard below the work-surface.*

8 *Electric mixer fixed to a pull-out shelf with all removable extras below. When not in use the mixer shelf swings down into the cupboard.*

9 *Another standard unit extra – a plastic drawer for keeping bread.*

1

2

3

4

5

6

7

8

9

238

1

4

7

2

5

8

3

6

9

Utensils, gadgets, tins, boxes and bottles come in so many different shapes and sizes that it needs some ingenuity to fit them all in comfortably. Odd corners can be put to good use, and the undersides of shelves can have cup hooks fitted under them or runners for drawers.

1 *The end of a partition wall turned into a tall, narrow drinks cupboard.*

2 *The end support of a table/work-top divider with shelves for cookery books, herbs, sauce bottles. Shelving is carried on over the doorway.*

3 *Custom-built white tiled work-top with handled pots and pans within reach on hanging rail above, mixing bowls and casseroles below.*

4 *Stacked white bricks support slate shelves.*

5 *A slot at the back of the chopping board keeps sharp knives safe but handy. Ladles, graters and other items hang on a stainless steel rail above.*

6 *Old kitchen range transformed into a useful storage area. Larger pans, colanders and garlic hang on hooks above.*

7 *Pegboard mounted on a kitchen wall can be used to hang up a collection of copper pans.*

8 *Dresser cupboard unit built under a curved ceiling combine open shelves with cupboards and drawers. Upper shelves lit by a recessed light accommodate cups on hooks, china, etc. Larger items, including bottles and nylon-coated vegetable trays, are below.*

9 *Dark dresser and wallpaper complement the neatly arranged white china. Note the wine rack at the top.*

Kitchens
12/13 Refrigerators/cookers

Even the smallest refrigerator is quite a bulky object and the best idea is to build them at a convenient height, leaving adequate ventilation to the top, bottom and rear. The larger ones can go on a plinth to line with the rest of the units and make the floor easier to clean.

Small refrigerators are generally put under the counter. This means that you have to stoop, and it is difficult to see right to the back. Instead you could have a wall-hung model, or build one into a cupboard. One advantage of small refrigerators supplied with doors opening either way is that they can be bought in pairs and placed side-by-side, handles to the centre. They can be run at different temperatures, and are useful in the case of a growing family since you can start with one and add another if and when it becomes necessary.

Large refrigerators often have a variety of extras apart from a deep freeze unit. There are places to keep butter from getting too hard, automatic ice makers which produce a continuous supply of ice cubes (given a water supply), and the better models are frost free.

Vertical deep freezers are more practical, though more expensive, than the chest type as everything can be seen at a glance; chest freezers are apt to be less convenient and therefore less fully used.

Refrigerator/freezers can have the freezer either in a separate top unit or at the side, which reduces the width of the door; useful in a small kitchen.

The door swing can very often affect the whole planning of the kitchen, since it is essential that there should be a good setting-down space on the opening side. Most refrigerators are still cold white statues to hygiene and not friendly places to go for a coke or the eggs for breakfast. Some makers now use colours in a limited way and, better still, some use a thin metal trim, so that a sheet of copper, stainless steel or a plastic can be used to cover the front to match the rest of the kitchen. Large transfers or stencils are another way of adding variety.

Larders

Refrigerators and freezers are not always the best place for perishable foods and any serious cook should also consider some kind of ventilated larder storage; and certainly think twice before pulling down an old one. The simplest is just a wall cupboard with a vent top and bottom to circulate the air. If on an inside wall, the air can be brought in through tubes in the floor and ceiling. The air must come from the cool side of the house, and vents be fly-proofed with gauze. One shelf should be cold: marble or slate is the ideal material.

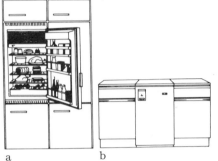

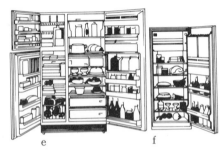
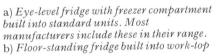

a) *Eye-level fridge with freezer compartment built into standard units. Most manufacturers include these in their range.*
b) *Floor-standing fridge built into work-top units.*
c) *Chest-type freezer with top opening lid. Usually holds more, but is wasteful of surrounding space.*
d) *Fridge/freezer with separate doors.*
e) *Three-door double-width frost-free freezer and fridge for large families.*
f) *56 inch-high floor-standing fridge with 2-star frozen food compartment.*

1 *Small refrigerator and freezer are built into unit next to eye-level oven and grill.*

2 *Refrigerator built into a dividing wall.*

3 *Full-height freezer/refrigerators next to twin ovens take up the whole end wall of a large, well-equipped kitchen.*

4 *Both refrigerator and oven are placed under the work-top in this small kitchen where work surfaces are at a premium.*

Cookers

Long ago the gas cooker reigned supreme. But today there is little to choose be-between electricity and gas. They both take about the same time to heat up a kettle, though an electric kettle is quicker than either. Cheap electric ovens, how-ever, usually take longer to heat up than do cheap gas ovens.

Gas is more flexible for cooking a deli-cate sauce. Electricity keeps its tempera-ture more accurately for long-term cook-ing. The newer electric induction hobs, astronomically expensive at present, remain cool while cooking and react instantaneously to changes in control, since there is no residual heat. So far there is no gas alternative. The most sensible thing is to back both fuels with electric ovens for cleanliness, even temperature and their extra gadgets, and a gas/electric hob for flexibility.

Conventional cookers have several disadvantages, though they are easier and cheaper to install. They usually have a gap at the side which is difficult to clean and they do not fit the wall behind. One answer is to use a split-level hob set into the work-top with a bulit-in oven below. You can even have two ovens built into one unit. If there is room this pro-vides an ideal arrangement. The oven and its controls are out of the way of children: it can be opened, loaded and unloaded in perfect safety, and the contents watched without stooping. There must always be a convenient heatproof setting-down space beside the oven. Similarly the hob should have a convenient setting-down space on either side or – as the safest arrangement is to have the burners or rings in a row at the back of the counter – in front.

Ovens

Built-in ovens usually come fitted with a grill, following continental and Ameri-can practice. This has the disadvantage of occupying the oven at a time when you may well want to use it for something else. A cheaper alternative to two ovens is to have a wall grill, which can be either gas or electric. Wherever it is, the grill must always have very good ventilation. If you really want to be traditional, you can dispense with the grill altogether and use an iron salamander heated up on the hob, for all browning purposes. Some small ovens are designed so that they can be built-in or hung on the wall, which saves buying a cupboard housing.

Microwave ovens are quickest of all, making many delicious traditional dishes, once slow to cook, as fast to prepare as convenience foods. They are particularly useful in conjunction with a deep-freeze as they eliminate the chore of defrosting food beforehand.

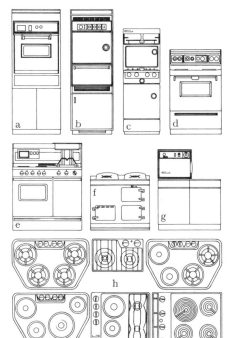

a) *Built-in electric oven/grill unit.*
b) *Built-in oven with separate grill unit.*
c) *Gas cooker with eye-level grill.*
d) *Roomy electric cooker with self-cleaning oven, automatic timer.*
e) *Double oven gas cooker with four burners plus grill/rotisserie.*
f) *Gas, oil or solid fuel cooker/boiler with fast and slow oven, two hobs.*
g) *Table-top microwave oven.*
h) *Some hob combinations and shapes.*

---

1 *Cantilevered kitchen unit with wall-mounted oven.*

---

2 *No need for too much bending with double oven and grill unit. Glass doors mean you can watch the soufflé rise.*

---

3 *Hob below full-length window allows plenty of space and light, and hot pans can be put down on the tiled surface.*

---

4 *A charcoal grill is worth the extra space for delicious steaks and kebabs.*

---

5 *Cooker cum boiler with two hotplates and ovens is fired by oil, gas or solid fuel. Larger models heat radiators as well as water.*

---

6 *Even things like ice-cream stay cool on an electric induction hob.*

---

7 *Easy-clean electric hotplate has its own tiny sink.*

---

8 *Cooker in tiled fireplace opening makes use of the old flue for ventilation.*

A stainless steel sink unit is resilient and should be satin finished and 18/8 grade not to show marks easily. Ceramic and enamelled cast iron sinks are colder to touch but possibly more sympathetic in an old kitchen. If the work-top is a laminate the neatest way of fixing the sink is to glue and screw it up from below.

Since the sink should be near the hob, a stainless steel drainer can double as a useful place for putting hot pans. The flat, ungrooved, recessed continental type of drainer is better than the conventional grooved, sloping British type, since there is not so much danger of anything slipping into the sink. Teak drainers, on the other hand, should be slightly sloped and can be used in conjunction with stainless steel bowls fixed from underneath.

If you do not have a dishwasher, a double sink is essential for quick washing up. Ideally a waste disposer needs its own small sink so that rubbish accumulated does not interfere with the main sink.

Although a sink below the window is pleasant, it is not necessarily the ideal place (unless you have small children to watch in the garden), because the best place for a plate rack is over the sink. Then china can be washed, rinsed and stacked in one operation, and if the rack is in a cupboard unit you don't have the bother of carrying china away.

The sink should be as close as possible to the hot water supply. If it is not possible to have it within 20 ft (6.10 m), consider using a separate electric storage cylinder. About 15 gallons (68 litres) capacity should be enough.

The best mixer taps are wall-mounted, since they make cleaning much easier. If you have to use a mixer on the sink, choose a single-stem type – much neater than the two-pipe variety. There should be a store for detergents and other cleaning equipment by the sink, a soap dish, and a place for towels.

Waste disposal

Food waste is best put straight down a waste disposer or through a chute in the wall or counter top leading to a sealed bin outside. Cans and bottles can be thrown into plastic or paper containers fitted on the inner doors of the units or fed from a hopper to the outside.

Paper and cartons are bulky and difficult to fit through domestic waste hatches. Have a large plastic container attached to a cupboard door, which opens as the door opens, or use a gas or electric incinerator which will burn everything to a fine ash, or have one of the central heating boilers which also burns waste. (This, however, does little towards the recycling process; if you are waste-conscious, use separate bins.)

Single and double inset bowl units.

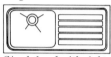
Single bowl with right-hand drainer.

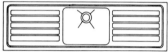
Single bowl/double drainer unit.

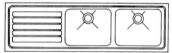
Double bowl and left-hand drainer.

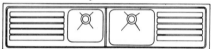
Double bowl/double drainer unit.

Single unit plus oval waste bowl.

Double unit with central waste bowl.

Flat unit with corner waste bowl.

Taps: two mixer, two single and one lever.

1 *Stainless steel sink, shallower than usual, means that users do not crick their backs.*

2 *Waste disposer in a small central sink unit is ideal where there are three sinks.*

3 *Stainless steel sink set into teak work-top has a two-ring electric hob next to it.*

4 *Waste disposal unit with its own separate sink in a corner of a work-top aids tidiness.*

5 *Enamelled steel sink can add colour to all-white kitchen units.*

6 *Plate rack above the sink both drains and stores crockery.*

1

2

3

4

5

6

1

3

5

2

4

6

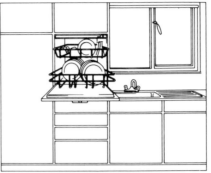

Dishwasher built into units at eye level.

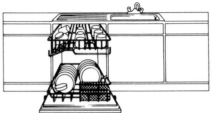

Floor-standing model at work-top height.

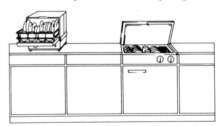

Small free-standing model and top-loader.

7

1 *Low dishwasher built into a storage wall below the china cupboard.*

2 *Dishwasher housed below work surface next to built-in refrigerator.*

3 *At work-top height a dishwasher is easier to load. Here crockery is stored in the cupboard beside it.*

4 *Corner arrangement of hob, sink, refrigerator and washing machine.*

5 *The electric hob in this island work-top unit has its own small sink. The washing machine is built in below, while the main sink, oven, dishwasher and refrigerator have been sited along the outside walls.*

6 *Separate oven and gas hob are adjacent and their control panels line up. The drainer is made of a solid wood block with circular holes for the steel sinks.*

7 *Top-loading washing machine rolls out from below the work-top between the sink and the oven.*

Dishwashers

A dishwasher is like an extra helper in the kitchen who is always there to take care of the worst chore of all. Early dishwashers were bought more for prestige than anything else. They took longer to load and unload than it took to do the job by hand and in any case washed only the easiest things well. This has given the dishwasher a bad name and provided an excuse for all the men who say they already have a dishwasher at home – and it's called a wife.

Good dishwashers may seem expensive, but they will quickly justify themselves in time saved. It is a mistake to buy too cheaply because this is one piece of equipment which can be genuinely useful two or three times a day. If it is not large enough, or is noisy, or breaks down constantly, it will prove a false friend.

Siting

The very best place for a dishwasher is to have it built in to a china and cutlery store preferably at waist height so that it is easy to load. The service man will often need access to the back of the machine and, unless the dishwasher is fitted in a cupboard partition with a door in the back, it will be necessary to have a simple wooden framework made, so that the dishwasher can be pulled forward on-to it. When not in use the framework can be unscrewed and stored away.

In any hard water area it is essential to have a water softener, and many machines now have them built in as standard. Even the best machines have been known to flood, and no matter whether the ceiling in the room below is yours or belongs to a neighbour's flat, you should have some kind of small floor drain. This will also be useful for washing down the floor. (It is frowned upon by some local authorities and insisted upon by others, so check with yours before taking any expensive steps in that particular direction.)

Siting other equipment

If you have several different large pieces of labour-saving equipment you will have to do some careful layout planning to make sure they really are saving labour (which is not always the case).

Washing machines and tumble dryers are often most useful when fitted in under work-tops or built in to kitchen units. You have to consider not only the plumbing limitations but also whether the laundry will get in the way of the cooking on wash days. If the laundry units are likely to crowd you in a small kitchen, perhaps you should find a home for them elsewhere in the house, perhaps tucked into a passage, close to the bathroom, or in the bathroom itself.

Kitchens
16/17 Surfaces/floors, walls, ceilings, work–tops

The ideal work-top surface takes the hottest pan, is pleasant and resilient to work on, is cool enough for pastry making, soft enough to chop on without blunting knives, mellows beautifully – and does not exist! The only answer is to use a number of different materials.

Stainless steel will take any degree of heat, and since the hob is best near the sink it is sensible to combine sink and hob unit in one.

A satin or imprinted pattern finish 18/8 stainless steel wears well and cleans easily, but a less good stainless steel *can* stain and scratch. It is noisy unless insulated below with some materials such as asbestos fibre.

Although the best chopping boards are portable, so that you can shake the bits into the sink, it is sensible to have a large area, at least 2 ft/610 mm square, for occasional chopping. Use end grain sycamore or maple. Feed it with olive oil to keep its appearance. For pastry making, the best is Sicilian marble. Slate is a good alternative.

Walls

Where a wall surface has to take extreme heat over a hob, or is subject to splashing, ceramic or stainless steel tiles are best. The junction of wall and work-top should be curved for easy cleaning.

In areas where there is not much heat, cork, vinyl or timber can be used. Timber boarding fixed on battens can hide electric wiring, and with suitable water-proofing and rot-proofed battens can also be used to cover a damp wall.

If you paint the wall, use a high-quality paint recommended for kitchen use. Semi-gloss is better than gloss paint as it does not show condensation runnels and is easy to clean. Insulating cork is a good wall covering above a desk area for pinning up notes and reminders.

---

1 *The food preparation surface is made of three quite different slabs – marble, laminated and wood.*

---

2 *White-jointed tiles filled with white Parian cement are set into a work-top surrounding a sink.*

---

3 *Wooden work-top next to cooker has pans hung from rack above.*

---

4 *Wood – for cutting bread and vegetables – and marble – for pastry-making – have rolled flanges and coved edges.*

---

5 *Marble is best for pastry making because it stays cool and very smooth.*

---

6 *Small charcoal fire set into the back of a work-top in Oliver Gregory's London house.*

1

2

3

4

5

6

Floors

Unless you are struggling with an old-fashioned range and dropping hot ashes all over the floor, sealed or vinyl cork is a good choice. For colour or pattern, vinyl, battleship-quality linoleum or ceramic tiles could be your choice. Ridged ceramic tiles are slightly warmer than flat tiles.

Think twice before taking out a wonderful old brick or stone kitchen floor. It will never be possible to recreate its qualities in modern materials, but today it can be easily sealed with the appropriate plastic (matt finish) coating. This will make it look splendidly mellow, and it will be easy to keep clean.

Ceilings

To counteract the hum, rattle and roar of waste disposers, washers, mixers and refrigerator compressors, you could put up a ceiling of acoustic tiles, but you must have a very efficient extraction system or the ceiling will be permeated with grease and the kitchen full of unpleasant smells. Tongued and grooved boarding cuts down noise and is not subject to condensation.

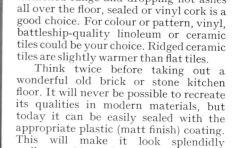

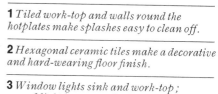

1 *Tiled work-top and walls round the hotplates make splashes easy to clean off.*

2 *Hexagonal ceramic tiles make a decorative and hard-wearing floor finish.*

3 *Window lights sink and work-top; a roof-light increases daylight. Ceiling-mounted diffusers give general illumination and a pendant lights the table.*

4 *Spotlights on a matchboarded ceiling adjust to light work-tops or cupboards.*

5 *Tiled floor with a geometric pattern in a kitchen/dining room.*

6 *Sill-height shelf makes kitchen counter; the effect of cold air is counteracted by the hot-air grill in the floor.*

7 *Stainless steel tiles on kitchen walls look opulent but are easy to maintain.*

8 *Stripped board floors wear well if thoroughly sealed and maintained.*

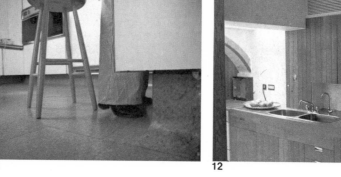

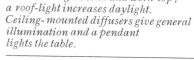
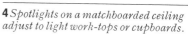

9 *Tubular neon curlecue exudes from a 3-D aeroplane on a blue wall.*

10 *Painted murals liven up built-in storage. Note wall-mounted liquidizer.*

11 *Coved edges to cupboard bases and round the walls make cleaning easier, and prevent water from getting underneath.*

12 *Wood-panelled walls match unit fronts.*

The kitchen and the bathroom are the only rooms in the house which create their own heat. Refrigerators and freezers produce a gentle, continuous form of heat and the larger they are the more heat they produce. Ovens, hobs, washers and the sink all produce quite large amounts of heat at times when it may not be wanted. Extract/intake fans, on the other hand, can produce quite dramatic drops in temperature by drawing in cold air from outside doors, windows and other parts of the house. Conventional forms of heating such as radiators are therefore quite inappropriate in the kitchen, unless it is part of a large living space where local changes of temperature in the kitchen area can be readily absorbed.

Forms of heating

The ideal form of heating should be thermostatically controlled to react immediately to any changes in temperature. Fan heaters meet this requirement and can be time-set to switch on early in the morning to warm the kitchen up for breakfast. In summer they can be used without their heating elements to provide a cool breeze, since any air movement feels cooler than still air. Another advantage is that they are small and can be easily fitted into plinths of units or over wall cupboard units and do not ever get in the way.

Small portable electric fan heaters can be hung on the wall, but with a piped central heating system it is better to use a fan unit designed to blow air across a finned pipe inserted into the central system. Most of these units also have electric elements so that they can be used for heating on cold summer days when the central system is switched off. They should also have a filter bag to take the troublesome dirt out of the air.

Radiators do have one advantage in the kitchen: they provide a good place to dry the dishcloths, but it is much better to use a proper heated towel rail for this purpose.

Where fluctuations in temperature are not important, consider putting in a floor heating system, either electric, or water borne. In an old farmhouse this would allow you to keep the romantic old stone floor which otherwise would be too cold unless you habitually wear carpet slippers; it would warm a floor in quarry or ceramic tiles.

Ventilation

A badly ventilated kitchen will suffer from condensation and the smells of your last meal, which will probably find their way into the rest of the house. The hob, particularly gas hobs which create a lot of water vapour in burning, is the most important area to ventilate efficiently.

An overhead hood is the most acceptable method, and if vented directly to the outside air it does not really need a fan at all, though it is much better if there is one. The problem with a conventional hood over a four-square hob is that if it were low enough to do its job really efficiently you would not be able to see to cook. If possible, the cooking rings should be placed in a line at the back of the work-top, which is also much safer with children, so that the hood can be brought down to a convenient height above the saucepans; that is, about 1 ft 4 in./407 mm. If possible the hood should contain a grease filter, which will save the fan being covered with fat, which greatly impairs its efficiency. The filter should be easily removable for washing – you'll be amazed at the dirt it picks up.

With an island unit, a circular or square hood can be brought down from the ceiling. The extract pipe can be inserted between the ceiling joists and taken to the outside air. Some fumes are bound to escape from under the edge of the hood, and being warm will rise to the ceiling, where there should be a secondary extract, off the same fan, at high level.

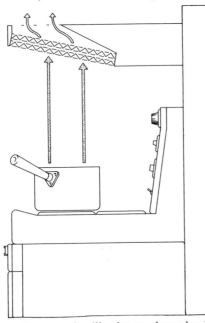

Ovens and grills also produce clouds of cooking smells, but they are often forgotten. Built-in ovens should have small extract hoods above them perhaps connected to the same system as that of the hood. Separate wall grills should have the same extract as the hob unit. There are a number of hoods which clean the air by passing it through filters but they have a limited capacity. Their advantage is that they do not create the same degree of heat loss caused by fans sucking the warm air out of the kitchen and into the garden.

Where a hood is impractical, or too expensive, a ventilating fan should be placed as near the offending apparatus as possible and as high as it will go. Wall-mounted fans are more expensive to install but less unsightly than window-mounted fans. If you have a large chimney, consider siting the oven in the embrasure and fitting the fan into the chimney. In older houses, a simple solution to a rotting, ugly window is to replace it with a single, fixed pane of glass uncluttered by dirt-catching window bars, double-glazed against condensation if you can afford it, with a wall-mounted fan for ventilation.

Some appliances now contain their own ventilating system. There are ovens with built-in extract fans, hobs and counter-top grills which extract air downwards using very strong fans, with a duct at low level to the outer wall.

Lighting

Although the kitchen is primarily a work space it is also in many ways a living area, and the lighting, whether natural or artificial, should be efficient and stimulating. This means that although the work areas must be well lit, so that you are not standing in your own light, there should still be some variety in light intensity.

For efficient work-top lighting fit tungsten tubes behind a pelmet below the front edge of the wall cupboard units. If there are no wall cupboards, then put the tubes behind a pelmet fixed horizontally about 4 in./102 mm from the wall, so that the light can shine down on the work-top. It can also be allowed to shine up the wall for a decorative effect, but you may prefer to fill in the top of the pelmet with a shelf.

Further work-top lighting, and lighting for inside wall cupboards, can be achieved by a line of small, adjustable spotlights recessed into the ceiling. Larder cupboards can be lit with a simple recessed light holder at the top connected to a door switch. Adjustable spotlights at ceiling level will light the room generally and can be trained on to eating areas. With care, it is usually possible to find sufficient space between the ceiling joists for recessed spotlight fittings, which give a much cleaner appearance to the kitchen than surface fittings. Otherwise use the smallest surface-mounted spotlight fitting you can find.

If you have a dining area, you can fix an adjustable pendant light over the table and by turning all the working lights off when entertaining enclose the diners in a cosy circle of light.

Fluorescent lighting is not suitable for kitchens unless it is part of a closely integrated system in the rest of the house. Stepping from a carefully thought out and sensitively lit room into a dazzling bright shadow-free kitchen can be like stepping out of a Rembrandt into a supermarket. Some fluorescent lighting also tends so to distort the colour of food as to make even the best cut of meat look thoroughly unappetizing.

Windows

Work-tops can be lit by placing them below a window, but although the light and possibly the view is then satisfactory, one cannot use the wall for essential storage. In this case, one can have wall cupboard units with strip windows below them about 1 ft 6 in./457 mm high and put another window over the eating area, perhaps facing the view, where storage is not critical.

If the kitchen is below a flat roof, roof-lights will provide very efficient lighting. They must be double-glazed against condensation, but you can use a much smaller area of glass for the same amount of light as a window in the wall, since the roof-light gets light from all directions from which the room naturally benefits.

Doors can also be used as windows. An old back door enlarged and converted into a floor-to-ceiling sliding window will turn a dingy kitchen into an attractive living area. Ideally, one window should face east so that you are welcomed by the morning sun while cooking the breakfast. If you have a good view to the south and are worried about heat in the kitchen, plant a fig tree outside which will provide marvellous dappled shade in the summer and allow plenty of light in winter when the leaves have dropped off.

Louvred windows are particularly useful in the kitchen as they can control ventilation without causing a draught problem.

Blinds are more efficient than curtains in the kitchen and also collect less dirt; if you must have curtains make sure they are fireproof or can never blow over the hob when the window is open. For super cleanliness you could fit the blind between double glazing.

Day and electric light combine to make this windowless kitchen a pleasant place to be in. The daylight comes from the double-height ceiling above the breakfast bar/work-top and at night this is lit by two wall-mounted downlighters. A recessed ceiling spot lights the cooker and hob, which has an extractor hood and ventilation grill above it.

Kitchens
20/21 Heat, light, ventilation/other details

1 *A narrow shelf parallel to the horizontal glazing-bar continues round above the sink. Plants stand on the lowered window sill behind the hob.*

2 *A glazed door panel can add daylight. At night the white enamel sink and work-top are lit by pendants.*

3 *Strip lights above and below high-level cupboards ensure good working light without glare.*

4 *Louvred windows let out steam and smells efficiently and can be left open even in very bad weather.*

5 *An extractor fan fitted to an outside wall above a gas hob unit is an efficient way to control ventilation.*

6 *Strip lighting and a down-lighter recessed in the ceiling combine to give good light where needed.*

7 *An extraction slot straight into the chimney above double grill units in the Conrans' kitchen.*

8 *Coloured hood over electric hob matches things on the shelf.*

9 *Extractor hood over a built-in double oven unit.*

10 *Small deep drawers with recessed handles under a stainless steel work-top hold flour, oats or breadcrumbs.*

11 *Paper towel holder – a minor but useful detail.*

12 *Plug outlets for electrical gadgets have been neatly placed between two heights of tiled work-top.*

13 *A small chopping-block table with hinged flaps can become extra work-space.*

14 *White-painted dresser with china display above, scales and birdcage below.*

Lighting and extractor hood are combined in one neat unit above a central work island in this French kitchen/dining-room which is as beautiful as it is efficient. The island unit incorporates a double sink in stainless steel, the hob and an adequate, easy to clean work area.

Kitchens
22/23 Batterie de cuisine

By far the best part of furnishing a house is the setting up of a kitchen; after mulling over such things as paint and door knobs, kitchen pots seem very cosy and rewarding. It can be done in one exciting swoop, but since saucepans and knives will be used daily as the implements of your trade as cook, it is probably worth buying these essentials first and spending as much as you can afford on them. The salad shakers and serving dishes can be bought later in the local junk shop or antique market and will be all the nicer for it.

Saucepans

When you are buying saucepans keep your cooker in mind – any pans can be used on gas cookers but electric stoves and solid-topped stoves need solid ground bases, or you will waste fuel. If you can't stock up with really good pans buy them cheaply and gradually replace those that give you positive displeasure. A thin enamel pan will have to be replaced pretty quickly – everything sticks and burns and they chip badly; in fact thin pans in general are scarcely worth the space they take up. Probably the best buys are heavy-gauge steel for omelette pans, heavy enamelled-iron for frying pans and thick aluminium or heavy well-tinned copper for saucepans. But don't buy copper pans old or new unless you know of somewhere that re-tins them when the inside tinning wears out – copper taints food. (Restaurants may advise on where to go.)

One cheap, frequently replaced non-stick milk pan is invaluable for scrambled eggs, milk and porridge; it saves hours of scrubbing and irritation. As far as buying giant pans goes, leave it until you actually need one for jam-making or a huge party as it will take up a colossal amount of space and can anyway often be borrowed for the few times it is needed.

Oven dishes

Casseroles for stews and pot roasts are best in enamelled cast iron – choose them with white linings to lid and pots, to avoid any risk of toxicity. It is useful to have a large deep earthenware pot or two for dishes such as Boston baked beans, cassoulet or chili con carne – it seems to make them mellower. An oval casserole holds a chicken or duck better than a round one.

Gratin dishes – flat oval earthenware dishes without lids – are needed for pies, lasagne, apple crumble and any dish that needs a nice brown top; they are the right shape to go into the oven and under the grill, and food always looks good in them.

You may find it nice to buy an oblong enamelled iron or earthenware terrine for pâté, although this can always be made in a straight-sided round or oval casserole or even in a simple pie-dish. But a terrine for pâté making can also be used for fish mousses, galantines and brawns.

Knives

Good French cook's knives and a solid chopping board are just as important as good pots and pans. If you think of the different kinds of cutting you do in the course of making a simple meal you will see how many different knives are needed; you will use a heavy, sharp but not too large knife for cutting up meat; a small, very sharp knife for preparing vegetables and pulverizing garlic; a serrated knife for cutting bread – many knives are serrated and call themselves tomato knives or even carving knives, but these are the worst knives you can buy, only useful to people with no skill who don't mind hacking things into pieces. A well-sharpened French cook's knife with a 5- or 6-in. blade is far more useful and enjoyable to use. For carving you will use a 7- or 8-in. bladed knife, the former for straightforward joints, the latter for jointing a chicken or duck.

The ham knife hardly ever gets any use, but a good-quality magnetic steel and a carving fork are essential. The art of sharpening knives is gradually learned but eventually it takes no effort at all. Wheel knife sharpeners are inclined to eat up the knife too quickly and leave a sharp but thin wobbly edge. If your knives live in a drawer, keep them well oiled and wrapped in a soft cloth.

The stainless-versus-carbon-steel argument has been waging for too long to go into again, but stainless knives are definitely harder to keep sharp. Carbon-steel knives stain but are quickly cleaned with Scotch-brite or other plasticized scrubbing pads, or in an emergency with scouring powder and a cork, but don't do this too often as it makes the surface even more vulnerable to the acid in fruit or vegetables.

Other essentials

Apart from the pots and pans and knives there are numbers of invaluable things for the kitchen drawer – although a better plan is to have a large jug or pot beside the cooker where wooden spoons, tin openers, potato peelers, ladles, strainers and the inevitable fish slice can be ready to hand. Another deep pot next to it containing loose salt is a good friend to the cook. To keep knives sharp and in good shape the ideal solution is a magnetic knife rack.

The list opposite does not put implements in order of importance, but things used often will be found at the top.

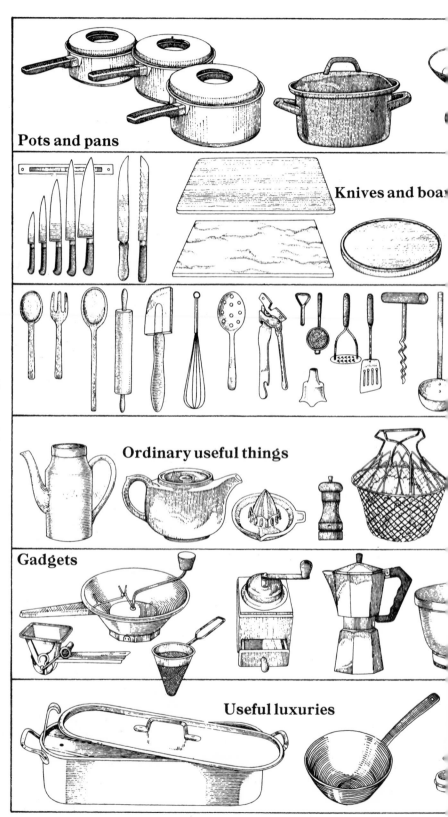

Pots and pans

Knives and boa

Ordinary useful things

Gadgets

Useful luxuries

Baking tins

Bowls

Kitchen drawer

BREAD

*Here are all the utensils
you'll be needing*

Pots and pans

3 saucepans
(*in different sizes,
with lids at least*)
2 iron casseroles
(*with lids*)
1 omelette pan
2 frying pans
1 colander
2 pie dishes
1 soufflé dish
2 gratin dishes
8 cocottes
1 roasting tin
(*usually arrives
with the cooker
for some reason*)
1 small, thick pan
(*for making sauce*)
1 non-stick milk pan
possibly 2 sauté pans
1 deep frying pan
(*with a basket*)
1 oblong
or oval terrine
1 double boiler

Knives, boards

2 cook's knives
(8-9 *&* 6-7 *in. blades
for carving*)
2 or 3 cook's knives
(5 *in. bladed
for vegetables, etc.,
so helpers can help*)
1 sturdy meat knife
1 bread knife
1 magnetic steel
chopping board
marble slab (*pastry*)
small bread board
demi-lune chopper

Baking tins

1 cake tin, 8 in.
2 loose-bottom
sponge tins, 8 in.
1 loose-bottom
flan tin, 10 in.
2 loaf tins
2 baking sheets
2 jam-tart tins
2 tin pie plates
set of biscuit cutters

Bowls

2 large bowls
2 pudding basins
(*at least*)
salad bowl
3-4 small bowls
(*for keeping dripping,
salad dressing
and the like*)

Kitchen drawer

3 wooden spoons
1 wooden fork
rolling pin, spatula
fish-slice, egg whisk
large metal spoon
tin opener, corkscrew
bottle opener
strainer, soup ladle
steak basher
pastry brush
grater, masher
perforated spoon
scissors, skewers
salad servers
scraper, strainer

Gadgets

mandoline, mincer
moulin-légumes
coffee-grinder
coffee-maker, timer
juice-presser
mixer, liquidizer
poultry shears
mouli-parsmint
wire grill
(*for open fire cookery*)

Useful things

kettle
piping bag, nozzles
nutcrackers
coffeepot, teapot
glass lemon squeezer
salad shaker
funnel, pie-funnel
measuring jug
pestle and mortar
jelly mould
salt box, peppermill
toast rack
strainer, scales
oven gloves
bread bin, cake tins
glass storage jars
(*large and small for
beans and herbs*)
hair sieve tamis
(*pointed metal strainer*)
dustpan and brush

Useful luxuries

preserving pan
fish kettle, steamer
asparagus kettle
pressure cooker
round-bottom pan
(*for hollandaise, etc.*)
sugar thermometer
meat thermometer
ice-cream maker
oyster opener
rubber ice-cube tray

251

Kitchens
24 Batterie de cuisine

Enthusiastic and versatile cooks simply can't help accumulating enormous numbers of implements in all shapes and sizes. In this Californian kitchen, an island site contains everything that the most dedicated chef might need. Pots and pans are suspended from a steel frame high above the wooden chopping board; smaller tools hang from hooks fixed to the vertical supporting posts. Staple foods are stored under the working surface in canisters decorated with Toulouse Lautrec posters; the knives are lined up on a magnetic band, out of harm's way.

Built-in knife rack helps to make the cook's life easier and to keep blades butcher-sharp. The tiled area beside the cooker can accommodate whatever you are likely to need close at hand when preparing a meal. The wooden spoons, the tin-opener, the garlic press and other gadgets live in good-looking white earthenware jars, and herbs and spices are within reach on a narrow shelf.

Work areas/1

There are plenty of routine jobs that need to be done in the home, like writing letters, laundering, ironing, or a bit of carpentry. And many more that you may undertake for pleasure or profit.

Any such task becomes less arduous if you are doing it in pleasant surroundings: the duller the job, the more stimulating the workplace should be.

It is often impossible to give over a whole room to a hobby or specialized activity. But however small the space allocated, and particularly if it has to serve a dual purpose (like a dining-and-sewing-room or a study cum everything), you must think the arrangements through in every detail.

There are two rules that apply to all workrooms – always allow for more storage space than you think you will need or things will pile up, and always have glare-free lighting.

Most work-rooms should be kept warm and well ventilated, so that things don't rust or get spoilt. If there is no central heating, a blow-heater will warm the place up and disperse condensation quickly.

The most common kind of work area is the study. Then there are sewing and utility rooms, which need plenty of storage space and a sizeable work-top. There are workshops proper, which may be rigged out with benches, vices and power-tools; equipped for pottery and all the mess this entails; or for model-making with its thousands of bits and pieces, glues, paints and lengths of string.

Last of all there are those areas which get used spasmodically, like boot rooms, flower rooms and store rooms. These need not be the neglected, untidy spaces they so often become. With a little planning, even the smallest space can be made useful and efficient.

If you're starting from scratch make a check-list before you start laying plans. Look ahead – you don't just want to cater for your immediate needs, but for future eventualities:

☐ Privacy – will you need absolute quiet and isolation?
☐ The comfort of others – will there be noise, vibrations from machinery, smell from varnish or glue, dirt that might invade the rest of the rooms?
☐ Services – will water, gas or electricity be needed?
☐ Safety – yours, and others'.

Best of all possible worlds – designer Alan Fletcher's gallery drawing office. It's not too far away from the life of the house, but far enough to allow concentration. Shelving and bookshelves give ample storage space. The filing system sits snugly under the work surface – an idea that's easily adaptable in less lavish surroundings.

Work areas

Even if you don't do much more than write the occasional letter, it is useful to have everything to hand, without having to clear a space and assemble from various parts of the house everything that you are going to need.

When houses were built with plenty of rooms, studies were the rule rather than the exception. Nowadays, space is at a premium, so office furniture is being made as compact as possible. This makes it ideal for the home, particularly where you want to get better use out of a tiny nonentity of a room.

Thus in a small third bedroom, with a window on the wall facing the door, you would put the desk under the window; your filing trolleys on castors would go underneath, out of the way.

Ideally you should not have to get up to answer the telephone, nor to stretch across the work in hand for it.

Have the typewriter on a separate table, placed so that you can swivel round to it. The ideal height for this table is 2 ft 4½ in./725 mm – not higher.

To muffle sound, line the walls with felt or hessian. Softboard panels, fitted to the walls and similarly covered, can turn them into huge pinboards.

Although some office equipment is very good value, it can still cost a lot. If you have to furnish your office on the cheap, consider using a trestle table as a desk, and get hold of a third-hand filing cabinet; it may look heavy but you can paint it with enamel or polyurethane paint to lighten its bulk.

Wherever possible, hang all shelving on the wall. If you can't afford to buy matching DIY fittings, set up rough-and-ready shelving with planks supported by bricks. White bricks look good, or you can paint everything in a bright colour. For a really tough finish, such a job should be done with a spray gun – try your garage or motor repair shop, they'll probably oblige.

For a less business-like room, any small table will serve as a desk. A chair, a shelf for directories and dictionaries, some objects on the walls, and you have an inviting retreat.

If the only corner available is in a room used by the whole family, and if you're particularly bashful – or untidy – you'll be glad to hear that screens are enjoying a revival.

1 *Maximum working surface for spreading out the work is achieved by wall-to-wall desk top. Any old chest of drawers, imaginatively painted, can become a filing cabinet.*

2 *Writing-room in Sissinghurst Castle, inspiring with its mixture of old furniture, modern shelving and Elizabethan brick.*

1 *It is possible to devise a small study area almost anywhere in the house. In the kitchen, most house-wives will appreciate the bonus of having a small work desk, with a pinboard for notes and recipes, somewhere to keep the bills, and a telephone.*

2 *In the bedroom (there's a lot to be said for having a quiet study area). This desk can double as a dressing table.*

3 *In a living room, a small study area, with bright, attractive equipment, can become a decorative asset.*

4 *In a narrow passageway or hall, desk area can be increased by making it triangular. This is how it works :*

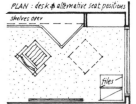

5 *On the landing, an unused patch of space can be adapted into a study as long as you can keep out of draughts, and don't need absolute privacy.*

6 *In an open-plan living/dining-room, a study area can become an attractive and useful room divider.*

1

2

3

4

5

6

Work areas
4/5 The workshop

A home workshop can be anything from a small work-top in a corner to a fully fledged purpose-built outhouse. If you just need a place for odd jobs, a recess in the hall, or the end of a corridor, may be suitable; or your garage, if it is big enough and has good light, would do. For more ambitious work, involving heavy machinery and a lot of mess, the workshop should have its own access, well away from the living areas.

The basics

For many jobs you will require supplies of water and power, so unless you get these facilities installed separately, the workshop must be attached to the house.

Good artificial light is vital, so placed that you never stand in your own shadow. Fluorescent tubes above eye-level are best and also glare-free. A spotlight is useful for close work.

Floors must be tough, easy to clean and easy on the feet. All heavy machinery should stand on a solid floor rather than joists, because of the vibration.

Safety

Workrooms are full of booby traps. Keep tools and switches activating machinery out of children's reach. Have a first-aid box and a fire extinguisher handy in case of emergencies.

Noise

Airborne noise can be deadened by insulated walls and shutters; a trickier problem is caused by noise carrying through a building's fabric, so keep machinery well away from structural walls. See that electrical equipment is fitted with suppressors. This is in fact required by many local authorities.

Storage

Use brackets for lengths of wood and piping; racks for sheets of wood or plastic. Screw-top glass jars fixed to the undersides of shelves are ideal for nails.

1 *Tools on pegboard; a painted outline will help you spot what's missing at once.*

2 *Transparent plastic or glass containers make contents easily identifiable.*

3 *A do-it-yourself storage system enables you to plan the shelving to fit your needs.*

4 *Brightly coloured boxes hooked on pressed metal sheeting store odds and ends.*

5 *Track with movable power points and spotlights eliminates tangles of flex.*

6 *Carpenter's workshop kitted out with adjustable metal shelving.*

1 *Specialist workrooms have different needs, but, equipment apart, they can be simple and inexpensive. This weaving room, with good light, has a natural background of wood and rush – the hanks of wool and yarn provide all the colour one could wish for.*

2 *Architects and designers usually manage to have offices as nice as their living quarters. Note the shelving unit and the shallow, swivelling containers of the storage unit – infinitely useful for things other than pencils or paints.*

3 *A carpentry workshop with thoughtfully fitted equipment in a basement passage. Storage facilities under work-top are augmented by ingenious slide-doored cupboard, built on the slope to allow maximum headroom.*

4 *Artists need space and tranquillity in their studios. Good light is essential ; the daylight source, whether skylight or high-up window, usually admits a cool, even work light. Here, the white brick wall reflects both the light and the warmth from the old-fashioned stove.*

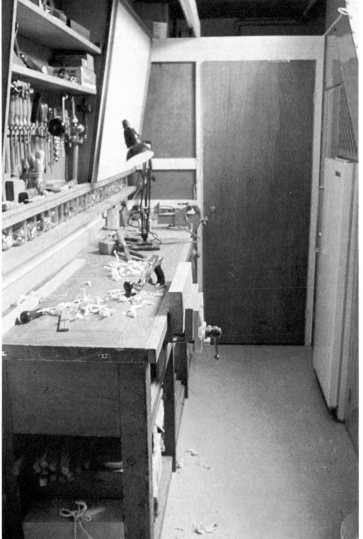

257

Work areas
6/7 Laundries and sewing rooms

Laundry units usually go in the kitchen, not because this is the best place, but just because there often seems nowhere else for them to go. But think very hard before establishing a laundry in a small kitchen, with all the disadvantages of three-course meals and dirty washing getting tangled up with each other, and the lack of space for sorting and ironing. When deciding on a location for your laundry, bear in mind the plumbing and drying facilities you're going to need, and do not forget that laundering machines do make some very irritating noises so the further out of earshot they are, the better it is.

Laundry equipment

You will certainly require a sink for soaking bulky things, some sort of counter for sorting clothes as they come out of the machine, and a wall cupboard (with a lock if there are children) for all the detergents, bleaches, bowls and plastic buckets that are part of washday.

Washing machines

The washing machine itself, twin tub or automatic, will need a cold water supply and a waste outlet. Most machines now pump the waste water away, so it is not essential to have them near a drain. But a hot air dryer, integral or separate, will have to be vented, which means positioning the machine close to an outside wall.

In selecting the right kind of machinery for the amount of laundering you have to do, there is no need to install expensive equipment you may never need. There are devices similar to waste disposal units which will convert your sink into a washtub of sorts, and this, with a small spin dryer or a strong clothes line may be all you need.

Drying

If there is enough space, have a tall cupboard for a fold-out ironing board and do your ironing there too. If you don't have a tumble dryer, any large, well-ventilated cupboard can become a drying place once you have put in a low-kilowatt heater. Have movable slatted shelves, so that you can make hanging space for drip-dry shirts and dresses, and socks, if you should need it.

Floors and walls

Remember that even the best machines flood sometimes, so be prepared with a flooring and skirting that can stand up to possible soaking.

There's no reason why you shouldn't lash out with bright colour on the walls. Water-tolerant paint or wallpaper is available, easy to apply and will help to make your laundry sessions less dull.

1

2

3

4

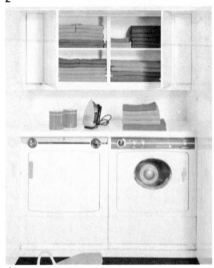

5

6

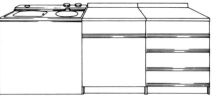

Top-loading washing machine and dryer unit go side by side. A similar layout is efficient for a twin-tub washing machine.

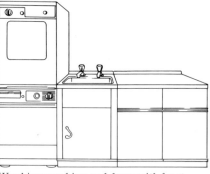

Washing machine and dryer with front loading and controls stack up and need a minimum of floor space.

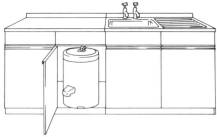

Small spin dryers can disappear out of sight when they are not in use.

1 *A sealed-off passageway behind the kitchen – perhaps an old scullery – provides a practical and self-contained laundry.*

2 *In-built equipment ranges neatly along the wall. There's no reason why laundry machinery should not be next door to the oven, as in this multi-purpose kitchen.*

3 *Stacked washer and dryer beside storage cupboard and drawers take up the least possible kitchen space.*

4 *Laundry-in-a-cupboard has plumbed-in washer and dryer and storage shelves.*

5 *Now you see it, now you don't. Purpose-built laundry and ironing unit on which you can close the doors.*

6 *Corridor-laundry at the top of a house, close to bedrooms and bathrooms, which saves much carrying of bed-linen.*

Sewing room

Rooms for more genteel activities, like sewing, are a different matter. They will almost certainly be in the main part of the house and can have pretty, soft furnishings; except that a smooth floor surface is more easily swept and kept clean than carpeting – vinyl or plastic-coated cork tiles would be suitable.

Avoid polished boards; however well they're sanded there are likely to be splinters to snag delicate fabrics, and pins will disappear between the cracks.

A large trestle table, covered with dressmaker's dump or PVC, makes a good cutting place. Have a separate, lower table for machining. There should be one chair for machining, and another, less upright, for hand-sewing.

This sort of room probably needs more storage-space than any other. There should be deep cupboards with fairly widely spaced shelves for folded lengths of cloth; deep, narrow drawers for patterns; shallow, wide drawers for trays of pins, scissors, silks, chalks, tapes and similar items. Also there might be a shallow cupboard with an ironing board fixed to the wall inside, to be let down when needed.

In the best of all possible worlds, there will be a small sink for hand-washing, damp pressing and spongeing. A full-length mirror, however, is essential for fitting.

If shortage of space makes an arrangement of this nature impossible, or if the type of sewing you do is more in the mending than the dressmaking line, you can make do with a small sewing trolley. The solid top can be used as a work-surface for modest tasks, or the carrier for the machine, and the whole thing can be trundled from room to room with ease. Lighting is important. There should be a background of good general daylight, either natural or simulated. If your machine does not have its own light, an adjustable lamp is advisable. For hand-sewing, you should have something like an Anglepoise anyway, because it's portable and can be adjusted to cast light directly on to the fabric, not into the eyes.

1 Sewing room with everything to hand, with storage space provided by desk drawers, little box shelves, filing drawers and larger shelves for fabric.

2 Vinyl-tiled sewing area with large cutting out table and desk for machining.

3 This sewing room has a pinboard and a wall-tidy for odds and ends. Roller blinds can be drawn to hide the contents of the storage-cupboards.

Work areas
8/9 Using odd corners

It is not easy to be too specific about these, since only you can really know where they are located in the house. The intention should be the same whatever shape or size they are: to create order without spending too much money. Often this can be done with quite a small outlay, perhaps some simple shelving, seating if there's room, a little paint and the necessary lighting.

There is no need to build complicated structures for storage. Shelves provide a home for all sorts of things: suitcases, picnic baskets, shopping baskets, tennis rackets, fishing rods and what have you.

Some of these oddments can have clips fitted on the wall especially for them, and the more shelves, clips and racks you provide, the more you can store tidily, so that there is no need to rummage around when things are wanted.

Psychology plays a part here too. If these nooks are brightly lit, there is far less excuse for anyone to leave junk heaped up in the corners. If you add brilliant glossy paints or hang breezy wallpapers, it will encourage everyone in the house not to sort through the contents in a frenzy, hurling them here and there with abandon, but neatness will be preserved for longer stretches at a time, far fewer things will get lost, and tempers will get less frayed.

Toy cupboards

Your under-the-stairs, or any reasonable large cupboard, providing the access is safe and near enough to the children's main play areas, can become something of a miniature Father Christmas land.

Walls can be lined with pinboard, or cork, where the kids can stick up their pictures and posters. Quite large toys can make their home here. Be certain that the place is well ventilated throughout, and that children cannot lock themselves in or be incarcerated by their playmates.

Food and drink

A niche not usually on public view could well take a deep freeze and all the accessories like plastic boxes and labelling equipment. Or it could become a drinks cupboard – with racks for wine, shelves for other bottles, olive jars, cocktail onions, tins of peanuts. And on a nursery floor, it might be a practical place to have an extra station for heating the baby's bottle or even for preparing children's meals.

Where floorboards are uneven and will not take much weight, but there are strong beams above (such as in an old cottage), hang storage from the ceiling by using a rough fabric like hessian, with a wooden batten inside to hold it steady.

1/2 *Pull-out storage fitments make under-the-stairs a neat place to keep bulk-purchased dry goods, wines, cleaning materials, or any other equipment for which there's no room elsewhere. The sections operate on castors and runners, and there is no need to rummage for what you need, for everything is tidily organized. When the pull-out storage fitments are removed, they reveal other good ideas, such as the shelves fitted under each riser, and the baskets, used for dusters and brushes, on the inside of the cupboard door. A pull-out box for household tools is under the bottom tread of the staircase.*

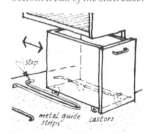

3 *A storage unit on castors folds out to provide a desk, dressing table or storage in one half and clothes hanging space in the other half. When closed, the unit can be pushed into a small alcove against the wall.*

4 *Quite another way to make the most of under-the-stairs is to use it for storing drinks and hi-fi equipment.*

1

2

3

4

Work areas
10 Cleaning cupboards

In a cloakroom, extra storage space is provided by boxing in the w.c. and fitting shelves across the other half of the alcove. Both halves are covered by louvred doors.

Broom cupboards in kitchens can be kept tidy by hanging up as many items as possible. If you run out of room on the base, fix shelves or wire baskets to the sides.

Storage for soaps, detergents and other cleaning materials is provided in an otherwise dead space above a door in a hall. (Note the washing machine under the stairs.)

Polishes don't need shelves wider than they are. All brooms and broom-shaped objects are suspended, and the cupboard is easily kept looking tidy.

The cupboard

The first thing to decide is what you want to keep in your cleaning cupboard.

Install some shelves at eye-level to hold your basket of dusters and tins of polish, or hang a wall pocket on the back of the door. This should be canvas, or plasticized fabric, so that it can be washed from time to time. Hang all the light, awkwardly shaped things, like mops and brooms, on clips and hooks and they will then have a better chance of airing or drying and therefore will last longer. By staggering the hooks on the wall you can fit in more broom-like objects than if you hang them in a row. For plastic buckets, screw a hook into the ceiling half-way down the slope.

Fix as much as you possibly can to the wall, and try to keep things off the floor, though upright vacuum cleaners and heavy galvanized buckets will have to live there.

Floors

Try to run the hall flooring right into the cupboard, because if your flooring material is continuous it will be easier to manoeuvre heavy objects in and out. (However, nobody in their right mind would lay carpet in a cleaning cupboard!)

Bear in mind that the floor will come in for some fairly rough treatment, and that there'll be damp mops and dripping cloths.

Lighting and ventilation

Organize your lighting in this cave so that you can see everything without shadows and without getting yourself between the light and the object you are searching for. Fluorescent strip lighting gives general light and is cool enough not to overheat in a confined space.

Ventilation is most important, not only to make life sweeter for you, but for the good of the things stored in your cupboard. A few holes in the door may be adequate, or fit a louvred door in place of the original.

Meters and fuse boxes

If these unlovely things are lurking in your cupboard, do remember that they must not be covered up. It is a good idea to have a torch clipped to the inside of the door, and fuse wire within easy reach, for emergencies.

Upstairs

You may find that you use some of your larger pieces of cleaning equipment almost exclusively upstairs. You may prefer to keep your shoe-cleaning gear near your bedroom and your shoes. Maybe the windows and mirrors upstairs need frequent attention with polish and rags. So provide somewhere up there to take these items – there may be room at one end of the landing to put in a cupboard with louvred doors.

Bathroom-cleaning equipment normally amounts to little more than a couple of cloths and some tins of powder. For these, you could build a little cubby hole or shelving into the panelling surrounding the bath.

Elsewhere

If you live in a flat, your broom cupboard will probably be in the kitchen. Several manufacturers make specially designed cupboards to hold cleaning equipment, but try not to put one too near the food preparation area.

Alternatively, you could screen off one corner of the kitchen to hide large objects, and hang brooms and mops from hooks on the inside of the screen. The outside might then serve as a pin-board for memos, shopping lists and recipes.

Lastly, if you have small children, and you keep metal polish, bleach or any other toxic or dangerous substances in your cupboard, do think seriously about locking the whole cupboard when it is not in use.

Bedrooms/1

All of us in our mind's eye have some idea of the kind of bedroom we would ideally like to inhabit – and no other room in the house is more personal, even if it is shared. The trouble is that by the time you have spent most of your cash and ingenuity on the rest of the house, too often there is nothing left for that precious room of your own. So faced with an empty room and an already depleted bank balance, your mind will probably register a disconcerting, hopeless blank.

This will probably take your mind straight back to the prosaic master bedroom at a point when you really ought to be ditching conventions to look at the problem with a fresh eye. When you consider that space in most households nowadays is like gold, a whole 14 hours a day of room going empty, however small, seems an unthinkable waste. It is clearly absurd to attempt to cram all the family's activities – television, homework, dressmaking, listening to records, children playing – quite apart from entertaining friends – into the confines of the living – room space, while the bedroom half of the house is under-used, under-exploited and under-enjoyed. Central heating has made the proposition of the round-the-clock bedroom increasingly viable, and incidentally a far more interesting, less stereotyped room to plan. However, before planning a more ambitious multi-purpose scheme, you must first consider the basic bedroom – taking into account not only essential ingredients like the bed, storage and general furniture groupings, but also other things like the plumbing and whether it is feasible to install a basin or link the bedroom to a bathroom.

In any case, not everyone has the good fortune to be able to start completely from scratch. So you may also find yourself having to decide what to do with Gran's useful but ugly cast-off cupboard, or even how to play down the heavy feminine overtones of an existing pink carpet in a room exclusively masculine. As you plan each bedroom, ask yourself:

- [ ] Is the room for one or more persons?
- [ ] Have they been consulted?
- [ ] How near is it to the bathroom/lavatory, and would installing a basin be worth while?
- [ ] Do the windows fit or will they need draught stripping, double glazing?
- [ ] Could the room usefully serve a second purpose – is there room for a desk or table?
- [ ] How much storage space do you need?
- [ ] Does the room get the sun in the morning, evening, no sun at all?
- [ ] How much room is left for circulation after you have positioned the bed?
- [ ] Is there somewhere to put up visitors, children's friends?
- [ ] What kind of wear will the floor get and will noise penetrate and disturb people in the room below?
- [ ] Is there a socket outlet near the bed, a switch by the door?

(Above) Farmhouse bedrooms are conducive to sound sleep: all is simple and restful, and this airy look is achievable by town-dwellers.

Bedrooms
2/3 Basic styles

Decoratively speaking, bedrooms should be restful, welcoming and uninhibitedly personal. If you see yourself surrounded in flowers and frills, then stick out for it bravely. The atmosphere of the room is more likely to come off for being authentic than it would be were you to curb your inner longings and end up with a half-baked compromise – or a style that's plainly not you.

Finding your style

If you're not sure what kind of style to aim for, you can do a fair amount of effortless spade work by leafing through magazines (and of course the illustrations in this book). Stop and chew over the photograph which catches your eye, and analyse its ingredients. Quite often it's one carefully worked-out detail which provides the key – like a crisply tailored bedspread in a particularly subdued, ordered atmosphere you happen to like. Other times it's the paradoxical absence of certain things. A rural bedroom, for instance, with white-painted floorboards, gingham bed drapes and white-painted wooden shutters at the window, owes its simple freshness to the deliberate absence of curtains and rugs on the floor. This sort of thing works equally well in urban surroundings, just as a streamlined sophisticated set-up would work beautifully in a country house – particularly because of the pleasant surprise element that it provides in each case.

The same goes for rooms owing a debt to exotic influences – where else would the stuff that dreams are made of be as suitably housed as in a bedroom?

1 *High under the ridge-pole, the roof provides a pyramid-shaped recess for the bed. Fur covers make a luxurious contrast with the stark geometric lines of the ceiling.*

2 *Here the paraphernalia of dressing has been banished to the adjacent bathroom, and calm and peacefulness are the order of the day. The tweed-upholstered bed has tailored cushions and bedcover to match.*

3 *Dreams of an eastern bazaar have inspired this bedroom arrangement. The exotic look is achieved by using colour, pattern and pictures on every available surface, the more you can collect together, the more authentic will be the result.*

(Opposite) Warm and seductive, this free-standing bed is surrounded by a cushioned lip, with hi-fi equipment at the head. Only the blind and cushions provide contrast and pattern. Lights, set in a platform, illuminate the ceiling, and extra storage-space is provided by a drawer underneath.

1

2

3

Bedrooms
4/5 Finding the right style

The most successful decorative schemes are, almost without exception, the most consistent. If for example you happen to love dark brown, but have reservations about painting the entire room in that colour, don't adopt the usual half-hearted compromise of painting one wall brown and the rest another colour. Instead, you could paint the walls white and pick out the window frames, doors and even ceiling mouldings in dark brown, or paint a band of dark brown – 4ft/1.2m – around the lower half of the room. The result will be more coherent, restful and harmonious.

Colour and pattern

As a general principle, the monochromatic schemes are inherently easier to live with in a bedroom than are different colours on walls, ceilings and floor. Keep the basic shell of your room as simple as possible. Later, you can always add small dollops of colour – in a bedspread or brightly lacquered piece of furniture.

All-white bedrooms with a touch of sunflower yellow somewhere look crisp and bright even on a fogbound winter's day. Yellows and golds, or a combination of sandstone beige and off white, look marvellous in the morning sun. Pastel shades, provided they are not too sickly, are flattering to the skin. Dark muted colours, and even terracotta in a room that's naturally rather dark anyway, have a soft, gentle sophistication about them. Remember that whatever you choose will be what you wake up to; strong blues and bilious greens could be ghastly on the morning after the night before. You may tire very quickly of jazzy patterns in strident colours; and large pronounced florals, with large areas of plain between the motifs, tend to dominate to distraction.

Walls

Generally speaking, bedrooms as compared to living-rooms have to stand up to considerably less wear and tear, so you can afford to be relatively less practical with your choice of wallcovering. Paper-backed felt is available in a range of lovely colours; plain velvet paper looks appropriately sensuous; cork walls are warm and quiet.

Handwoven or handprinted Indian bedspreads are cheap and make serenely beautiful hangings. They're washable, don't crush easily and you can of course use them to make matching curtains or blinds, bedspreads, and to cover cushions. Car carpet (strictly not recommended for floors outside the car) is relatively inexpensive and easy to stick to the walls. (Particularly good as a cover-up for bumpy walls and provides absolutely splendid insulation.)

Floors

The bedroom is, in many people's opinion, the one room in the house which should be close carpeted, if funds permit. You can get away with using an inexpensive quality carpet, even exhibition felt, provided you invest in a hessian-backed foam underlay. A good underlay is in any case important in the bedroom. In an old house a fitted carpet extended to cover the skirting board cuts down draughts and sound, and makes the edges of the room easier to clean (below).

If you can't afford to carpet the entire floor area, raise the bed on a carpeted dais – 7 ft 6 in. × 9 ft/2.2 m × 3 m for a standard size double bed – and cover the rest of the room with a hardboard sub-floor and vinyl tiles or sealed plywood squares. Alternatively, if the floorboards are relatively even, sand and seal them, or you could paint them.

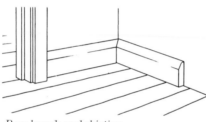

Bare boards and skirting

Extend carpet up over skirting-board

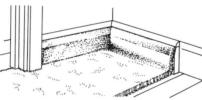

Extra carpet strip, wooden quadrant beading to hide carpet tacks

Ceilings

Considering the amount of time one spends lying in bed thinking – staring up at the ceiling (particularly during an ill spell in bed) – bedroom ceilings deserve far more attention than they get.

Here are some ideas:
Choose the most dominant colour in your scheme (or one to contrast with it), and paint a band of that colour around the edge of the ceiling – or pick out the ceiling cornice, if there is one. Finish the inner edge (the most conspicuous) with a narrow band of mirrored or coloured sticky tape to blend.

A stylish *trompe l'oeil* bed canopy, painted on to the ceiling and continued down the wall behind the bed, can look very effective and unusual. Or simpler – a random collection of non-directional white billowy clouds painted on to a sky blue ceiling; or a spattering of large self-adhesive paper stick-on stars dispersed over a dark blue night-coloured ceiling. If in doubt; experiment first with test shapes, cut out of brown paper.

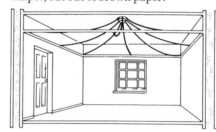

How a "tent" ceiling works

Any stark little bedroom can be made infinitely more intimate if it is given a lining in the form of a bell tent (above). What you will require is a really strong centre light fitting (the type designed to support old-fashioned chandeliers) which must be properly secured to a central ceiling joist. Attach eight (or more) lengths of curtain wire to it, stretched and fixed to the wall at various points around the room, equidistant from the floor (6 ft 3 in./1.9 m, ideally, to clear the top of the door frame). Next run a length of wire horizontally around the room. Finally drape your lengths of fabric – gathered at the top end to cover the frame. You'll need yards and yards of cloth, so choose something cheap, crush-resistant and washable, like Indian cotton, or sheeting. You could of course use the same idea, on a smaller scale to encircle the bed (below).

"Tent" canopy

Windows

Even if you can afford to double glaze only one set of windows in the house, consider the bedroom windows first, not so much for the extra warmth as the extra peace and quiet which double glazing provides. Unless you're lucky enough to live in the wilds of the country, the problem peculiar to most bedroom windows is how to provide adequate privacy during the day, without unnecessarily blocking out natural light. Net curtains are relatively easy to wash, but tend to look grubby in no time at all and do little to mitigate the dreariness of a typical back street view. Sheer fabrics such as a pretty patterned terylene, or a heavy lace cotton, are good alternatives. So is a muslin blind, ready printed, or tie-dyed at home, which, if you shine a spotlight on it at night, will prevent people outside from seeing in. Or even an Indian sari, or printed chiffon scarves sewn together.

Tinted glass, opaque Perspex, or mirrored paper (Melanex, which lets through daylight) also make excellent daylight filters cum view obscurers, but they are all relatively expensive to buy and fit properly. A less expensive alternative – stained glass windows – can be made easily and very effectively with tissue paper. Paste the inside of the glass with ordinary wallpaper paste and build up a pattern, overlapping and re-pasting as necessary. It does fade after a few months in the sun, but it's easy to scrape off and start a new design.

1 *The stained glass around the door and the floor and wall tiles lend coolness to this bedroom in Marrakesh, which is dominated by the parasol-shaped canopy.*

2 *Twin beds are partitioned off from the rest of the room. The thin fabric wall can be lowered at night.*

3 *Chrome yellow is a good colour for a permanently sunlit look.*

4 *Uncluttered modern; one wall is given over to cupboards, and there is a painted tester which incorporates overhead lighting.*

5 *Carpeted platform, matching the rest of the floor, provides bedroom seating. This is particularly nice in high rooms.*

6 *Horizontal wall treatment: strong colour contrast makes this high room feel low and cosy. Note the way colour outlines the door.*

7 *Sumptuousness, created with Oriental embroidery. Indian cotton prints could have a similar effect, provided there is enough variety in pattern and colour.*

1

2

3

4

5

6

7

We spend over a third of our lives in bed. Considering how often bed manufacturers remind us of this fact, it's surprising how many people there are who will spend hours fussing about which car to buy, its performance, potential and looks, while a bed, in which they are destined to spend infinitely more time over the years, they fondly reckon to select in one ten-minute shopping spree in their lunch hour.

Enough to say that beds must be chosen with care, and it's pointless going out to buy a new one without having done some elementary homework.

The first job of a good bed is to support the body's natural posture during sleep, taking over as muscles relax. If your body isn't properly supported, muscles get no rest, you may wake up snappish, and you may have built up aches and strains during the night. Too soft a bed does nothing to support you. Too hard a bed will leave your body unsupported in the hollows of hips, hips and knees, knees and ankles, straining your back, thighs and calves.

Points to watch

The very worst bed is an old sagging hammock-shaped mattress mounted on a soft divan base, which bends you in the middle and restricts blood circulation and body movement, ultimately damaging to the spine. Manufacturers' sales talk is inevitably misleading on this score. Beset with the tricky problem of selling comfort, they find that depth sells best. But although a deep bed may look more comfortable, the fact is that what matters most is your own personal preference in softness or hardness.

Generally speaking a hard bed provides far better postural support than a soft one (which is why people with back troubles are often advised to have a harder bed).

Ideally most beds are mounted on smooth-running castors, but if you don't have enough space or energy to want to move them about to clean below, choose a bed on a drawer base that's completely boxed in under the mattress.

Choosing a bed to buy

An adult should have a new bed at least every ten years, and if a bed in daily use is to last a decade, you should be prepared to spend every penny you can afford.

Cheap beds are suitable only for *small* children or occasional guests. As with most other furniture, there are few bargains to be had. Beware of false discounts: beds are sometimes displayed in shops or discount warehouses at an artificially high price for a short period. Later they are discounted to the normal retail price. A gullible shopper could be misled into thinking he was getting a bargain when often this is untrue.

Types and sizes

The main difficulty in choosing a new bed is that you cannot see what is inside it, so you need a competent retailer to guide you. It helps to know about springs and how the bed is made as you will command more respect from an expert if he feels that you know what you are talking about.

A bed should be at least 6 in.–8 in./ 150–200 mm longer than the sleeper, so if you are over 6 ft/1.8 m tall, you should order an extra-long bed. Allow at least six weeks for the order to reach you. Make sure the bed is wide enough. Stretch out full length on the mattress, link your hands behind your head and let your elbows relax on to the bed. If your elbows protrude over the edge, the bed is too narrow. You will find that a tall person needs not only a longer bed but also a wider bed.

Married couples should test a double bed together. If there is a big difference in their weight, the lighter of the two risks sleeping on a slope and rolling on to the other person during the night. A firm mattress should be able to compensate for this, but in case of difficulty or different taste in the firmness of mattress required, order matching twin beds with different mattresses zipped and linked to form a double bed.

Mattresses

There are three basic types: foam, old-fashioned stuffed and interior sprung. Foam are made from rubber or plastics in a honeycomb-type structure with thousands of air bubbles. They are lighter and easier to handle than most other kinds, they distribute weight evenly, and they don't develop lumps or lose their shape. A good one should be at least 4½ in./114 mm thick, but thickness is again a matter of personal preference.

Stuffed mattresses are cheaper than other types and rely for their support on the quality and resilience of their filling and on a proper sprung base designed for the mattress. There are two basic types of sprung mattresses (both consisting of coiled springs sandwiched between insulating upholstery): those with pocketed springs, and those with open springs. Pocketed springs (above) are contained under pressure in individual calico pockets, unaffected by the compression of neighbouring springs and so particularly good for double beds.

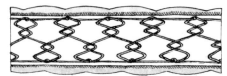

Open spring mattresses (above) on the other hand are made up of coils or a network of linked hour-glass-shaped springs. The denser the springs in either type of mattress the better. The British Standards Institution recommend a minimum of 288 springs in a 4 ft 6 in. × 6ft/ 1.4 × 1.8 m bed, but the average is 500, with up to 1,000 in the very best beds.

Bed bases

The bases of most of the divan beds sold in England are usually one of two kinds: *Sprung Edge* (below): The springs are continued to the very edge of the bed and stand up out of the wooden base frame. Sprung edge divans are more expensive but help prolong the life of the mattress. They have the added advantage that the bed remains equally soft right to the edge.

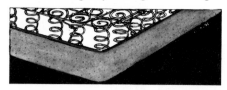

Firm Edge (below): The springs are contained within an outer frame. Firm edge divans are less expensive and usually stand higher off the floor – an advantage for anyone who likes to be able to clean under the bed without shifting it.

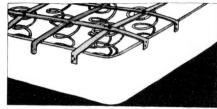

Sleeping on the floor

A note to all exponents of the now fashionable Eastern cult of sleeping on the floor: some sort of base under your bed is vital. Moisture condenses in mattresses at an astonishing rate (during one night the body releases up to half a pint of liquid in vapour form); besides which, lifting the mattress just a short distance off the floor keeps the sheets clean longer and prevents mildew. It's pointless to buy a new mattress to put on an old sprung base (or vice versa), since each deteriorates at an equal rate. One way to economize, however, would be to buy a good mattress and make up a simple bed base by resting a flat door – or two for a double bed – on two pieces of 3 in. × 4 in./76 mm × 102 mm timber at head and foot. You must drill plenty of holes all over the doors, though, for ventilation.

Basic mattress upholstery

This is basically a buffer – designed to prevent the sleeper from feeling the springs. It is made from coir (coconut) fibre, or curled black hair, needled to hessian; rubberized curled hair; wire cord insulator; or all cotton. On top of this is the surface upholstery, which provides softness made from woollen mix with felt, cotton felt, curled hair, white wool or polyether foam or man-made fibres.

New developments/special beds

Water beds and hanging beds have tended to steal the limelight over the last few years, but the list of available beds is long:

Adjustable (below): Beds with an electric mechanism for lifting the head and foot are the ultimate luxury for anyone who likes to spend a lot of time in bed and a boon to anyone who is bedridden. These beds are expensive, but one manufacturer will convert existing beds or allow you to hire a bed for a few months.

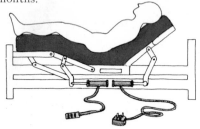

Folding: Beds designed to fold up and store during the day, leaving the floor space entirely free for other activities, have until recently been rather expensive or more of the camp-bed style. You can now get quite reasonably-priced ones that fold away into a cupboard, sometimes incorporated into a whole storage system. Avoid a folding bed which creases the mattress as it folds away.

Fourposters: From a practical point of view, many fourposters – particularly those with hard wooden top canopies – do collect dust. You might consider enclosing this space flush to the ceiling, as extra storage space, particularly suited to stowing away bulky items like suitcases – or extra blankets – or babies' paraphernalia – whatever is not in constant use.

Hanging beds: Most people are understandably very dubious about the idea of sleeping in a hanging bed, for fear of feeling sea sick. In practice, once you're in bed it's very little different from sleeping in an ordinary bed. They are specially easy to clean under and don't leave pressure dents in the carpet as do four-legged beds. The beds are fixed to the ceiling with coach screws and hung on tough nylon chains; the manufacturers strongly advise that they should be fitted by a builder.

Moulded plastic shapes: Increasing in popularity, they not only look extremely stylish but the best incorporate an ergonomically shaped back rest, foam upholstered with a washable stretch cover. They are easily kept clean with a vacuum cleaner.

Orthopaedic: Many doctors recommend that we all sleep on harder beds and in recent years the sale of firm and extra-firm mattresses has increased.

Several manufacturers now make what they call orthopaedic beds. In many cases these are extra-firm mattresses, sometimes on a bedboard rather than a sprung base. However, some orthopaedic beds are different in construction and are intended for people who are subject to backache.

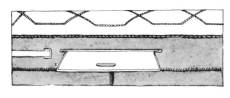

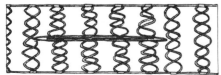

Mattress consists of a sandwich of spring units, with a removable hard centre panel. One side of the mattress is softer than the other but for an extra-firm sleeping surface, the centre panel can be slotted in between.

Retractable: The idea of a bed which disappears into the ceiling by a sophisticated pulley rope system is quite feasible, and one double bed size model is now available. The system is counterweighted, so there's no danger of the bed suddenly descending on you because you haven't fixed the pulley rope properly. Theoretically it can be installed in an average 8 ft 6 in./2.6 m high room, but psychologically it feels and looks less conspicuous in a high-ceilinged room where it's least likely to cut out the natural light.

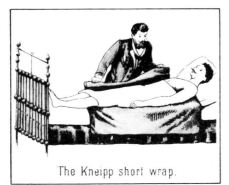

The Kneipp short wrap.

Water beds: Water beds aren't a new invention. The London *Times* carried an ad. in 1854 proclaiming the comforts of Kneipp's waterbeds for those suffering from fractures, paralysis, etc. Apparently the reason people toss and turn in their sleep is because the small blood vessels become constricted, causing minor discomforts. Enthusiasts claim that this doesn't occur to nearly the same extent on a water bed, which supports the body more uniformly and sympathetically than a conventional mattress. But they make sploshy noises unless great care is taken to smooth out the air bubbles after filling. They aren't cheap, but don't be tempted by cut-price offers: go for the established firms who can offer a guarantee of at least five years. They will also tell you all you need to know about setting up and filling a waterbed and many will set up their beds on delivery, although they may make a small charge. Basically a water bed is made up of an ultrasonically welded vinyl bag, which contains around 150 gallons of water weighing about half a ton when full. If you've got squeaky floorboards or you're worried about whether your floor will withstand the weight, check first with your surveyor or architect.

---

1 *Bedcover and valance are redundant in this simple modern bed. Its base is encased, and its top tightly covered with a blanket.*

---

2 *Victorian brass and enamel bedsteads, large and decorative, are becoming collectors' pieces but can still be found.*

---

3 *Romantic fourposter of cane looks light and delicate. Colour and pattern in the rest of the room have been kept to a minimum to let it come into its own.*

---

4 *Beds which can be concealed during the day behind wall units can provide accommodation for visitors. They're a special boon in small apartments.*

---

5 *Bedhead upholstery in fabric matching the counterpane gives a nice tailored quality.*

Bedrooms
8/9 The software

Not since fitted sheets first came on to the British market has anything promised to alleviate the wearisome chore of bed-making to the extent that the continental duvet does. Duvets are not only light and cuddly but equal in warmth to three good blankets and an eiderdown, which together cost more. Experts recommend you buy them a foot (305 mm) wider than your mattress for one person and 18 in./460 mm wider for two people.

Duvets

Another labour-saving virtue of a duvet is that, unlike blankets, it drops no fluff, so that you find yourself vacuum cleaning the floor less often. This may sound unimportant, but if you have three or four bedrooms in constant use, it can make a big difference to the housework.

Choose the filling of your duvet with care. Down, the most expensive, is also the lightest and the best insulant in relation to its weight. Next in order of price comes down and feather, and then feather and down. (Where the filling is a mixture, the constituent which predominates is listed first.) The more feathers the quilt contains the heavier it tends to be. The quality of a polyester filling also varies, so it's best to stick to one of the branded varieties, as the fibre manufacturers only permit manufacturers of good-quality products to use their label. The advantage of polyester is that it is washable and non-allergenic.

If you like the feel of blankets but would prefer the convenience of a duvet, buy a wool-filled quilt – it is warm and drapes well but looks flatter than its feather or polyester counterpart. If you take care of your duvet it should last you for many years. You should always keep a duvet in a cover, even when it is not in use, to protect it from dust and dirt. If you have a garden with a clothes line, hang a feather or down duvet out to air from time to time to prolong the life of the filling. Feather duvets should not be washed or sent to the dry cleaners but polyester-filled duvets can and should be washed. (Never dry clean a quilt as fumes from the cleaning fluid trapped in the fibres can be dangerous so close to the face all night.)

Duvet covers

Duvet covers are like giant-size pillowcases. Made from matt cotton, cotton seersucker or polyester/cotton, they don't slip off the bed as easily as a shiny eiderdown does and they can be bought with matching sheets and pillowcases in some lovely colours, either plain or patterned. You could make these yourself perhaps using some of the top sheets made obsolete by your new duvet.

Pillows

Pillows will vary enormously according to the filling. Think what you need. The most expensive (pure down) is not necessarily the best for you. The function of a good pillow is to support your head so that your neck and back remain in alignment. This explains why in certain parts of the world the natives sleep soundly with their heads supported on blocks of wood. The softness of a pillow is a matter of taste and habit rather than essential comfort. So choose a pillow that will give you good support. Pure down pillows are soft but not resilient, and unless they are used with a feather or foam under-pillow they do not give adequate support. A good compromise is a feather and down mixture filling. Choose goose- or duck-feather filling, as these have a natural curl and remain resilient much longer than chicken feathers, which are put through a curling machine.

Recently two pillows have appeared in British shops aimed specifically at providing surface softness with inner resilience. The first is made under licence from its German inventor. Seemingly a normal pillow, it contains an inner feather-proof tick filled with resilient feathers; this in turn is surrounded by down and the normal outer tick. The second pillow, rather less expensive, has a firm foam core wrapped in polyester.

When pillows are filled with polyester they usually carry the manufacturer's brand name on the label.

Polyether foam is produced from chemicals and can be controlled to be more or less dense and therefore firmer or softer. Like latex foam, which is made from rubber, it is non-allergenic and can be washed. Always store foam pillows in a pillow case as sunlight can damage them. If, like most people, you cannot remember when you last had a new pillow, carry out an inspection. Fluff up the pillow and put your hand under the centre of it to hold it in mid-air. If it sags down sadly on both sides of your arm it is time you threw it away and bought a new one.

Blankets

Always allow at least 10 in./254 mm for the tuck in. There are four main varieties of blanket on the market – traditional woven, cellular, knitted and needle punched. Traditional woven are hard-wearing and warm. Cellular blankets are more recently invented and based on the same principle as a string vest. Many hospitals use pure cotton cellular blankets and not many of the patients complain of the cold – their main advantage is that they are light and easy to wash and dry at home. Knitted blankets

are usually less expensive and are made mostly from synthetic fibres. They are soft and warm with a pretty lacey appearance. Needle punching is also fairly new in blanket manufacture.

Electric blankets

Avoid buying one without a thermostat and make sure it is of a sort officially approved. The others may be cheaper, but could be dangerous, or at least uncomfortable. On a bed that's not used consistently, in a weekend cottage, say, electric blankets are a particularly worthwhile investment as they dry out any dampness quickly.

Sheets and pillowcases

Before setting out to equip your linen cupboard, know the exact measurements of your bed. Ideally, a bottom sheet should cover the top and all-round depth of the mattress, leaving a 12 in./305 mm edge to spare for tucking in on all four sides. The edge also allows for shrinkage. This rule also applies to top sheets. Pillowcases should be 2 in. – 3 in./51 mm – 76 mm longer and wider than the pillow. For extra-bulky, restless or unruly sleepers the top sheet could do with being at least 12 in./305 mm wider and longer than the bottom sheet.

Rather than experience the bother of having to store and retrieve different sized top and bottom sheets, stick to one sort only (unless you go in for fitted sheets). Beware of sales and bargain stores, where one can easily be misled into buying skimpy sizes and poor quality. Sheets vaguely described as "large" or "double" too often turn out to be just large singles.

Linen sheets are extremely hardwearing, wash well and don't show dirt quickly, but they also cost the most. Cotton sheets vary from a top grade fine Egyptian percale to a loosely woven, relatively coarse yarn. Nylon and polyester sheets are strong, easy to wash and dry in a day, but because they are less absorbent, they need changing more often. For this reason polyester cotton sheets are more practical, particularly during the summer or for someone ill in bed. Cotton flannelette sheets feel warm.

There are excellent ranges of plain strong-coloured sheets, and a wide choice of patterned sheets in pretty geometric or floral designs. Some have matching wallpapers, fabrics and bedspreads.

Many sheets are quite pretty enough to leave uncovered – particularly dark plain and dark boldly patterned ones. Whether an uncovered bed is practical depends on the dirt and dustiness in the air outside, and on whether you lie on your bed during the day.

Duvets or continental quilts make bedmaking easy and eliminate blanket dust. Covered in nice strong designs, they act as bedcovers, too.

Double bed with matching sheets and blankets for the traditional look. Patchwork quilt and wall-hanging add colour.

(Opposite) Fourposter, with sheets, covers and curtains in matching gingham. This arrangement practically makes a room within a room, which has deliberately been kept sparse and plain.

Bedrooms
10/11 Storage

While a whole wall of cupboards built flush to ceiling may sound like a good continuous space-saving idea in principle, it must be handled carefully to be really successful. This kind of storage needs to be thought of as an architectural element and not stuck on as an ill-considered after-thought. And remember it is often the more distinguished, well-proportioned rooms which take least kindly to any kind of superimposed building work. On the other hand you can enhance or even improve the existing shape and character of a less inspiring room.

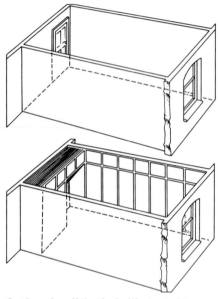

Cupboard-wall that looks like part of the room's structure.

For instance, the 7 ft × 11 ft/2.1 m × 3.3 m bedroom shown above was turned into a cosy little square simply by building a wall of cupboards across one end of the room, leaving a gap for the door. The walls of the room were covered in a module of hessian panels to match the cupboard doors, and because the cupboard unit stretches across the top of the door, you are deceived into thinking that the cupboards are just a marvellously thick old wall – part of the existing structure – until the doors are opened by concealed touch-push latches.

The second example (above right): an engulfing rambling country bedroom 22 ft × 14 ft/6.7 m × 3.2 m, was turned into a more interesting L-shaped bedroom – enabling the occupants to use the fireplace end as a private sitting area during the day, and for quiet TV evenings. The new dressing room built into the lower right hand corner provides more storage space than the old tallboy, wardrobe and kidney-shaped dressing table

put together, and in a far more compact, logically laid out way.

A separate dressing room presupposes a fair amount of space, but you might be able to adapt this idea in a smaller house by knocking a hole through the bedroom wall, dividing off a small area of an adjacent corridor, landing, bathroom or spare room to use as a closet.

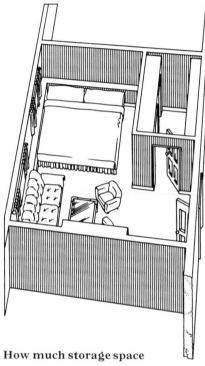

How much storage space

It's patently wiser to overestimate the amount of storage space you need, than to find yourself having to rip out inadequately small, jam-packed cupboards at a later date.

You could, if your present budget is tight, invest in a storage system designed to be added to, or at least allot extra space now in your plan (perhaps putting up open shelves which can have cupboard doors added later). A lot of space is often wasted at the bottom of hanging cupboards, so divide a section of the cupboard either into a two-tier rail system or with shelf space at the bottom.

Shoes are always a problem to store, particularly tall boots. Be careful to see that they don't obstruct hanging clothes. They also distribute a fair amount of dust and dirt, so you could install a wire basket rack below a bottom shelf at the foot of the cupboard, lined with silver foil or wax paper to keep it clean, and away from the clothes. A tiered shoe rack is useful if you have a reasonable amount of vertical but very little horizontal space.

Blankets, extra pillows, sheets, heavy pullovers, suitcases, hats and anything else not used every day, can be stored at a higher level, but make provision for anyone shorter than yourself by keeping a wooden chair or stool near at hand. To get to any shelf that's plainly out of reach, you might be able to build a narrow flight of steps into the cupboard base.

Drawer space

Folded clothes can of course be stored in a chest of drawers, but rather than waste valuable floor space, you can buy wall-hung sliding trays to attach to the wall inside a built-in fitment, or there are several interior drawer fittings designed to sit inside hanging cupboards. If you've inherited an old chest of drawers, which you don't particularly like the look of, it's possible to make your cupboards deep enough to accommodate it. The space above is useful for hanging "short" clothes like skirts or shirts. (Shirts, by the way, are not often hung up in Britain, although it saves time in folding and they look better when you put them on.)

On the whole it's easier to take out clothes from shallow drawers, but if you prefer deeper ones, see-through Perspex or wire trays allow you to see below top level and save you from rummaging for elusive-seeming items.

Cupboards

Doors for custom-made, built-in units can cost a relative fortune, depending on the materials and finishes used. Whether you make the cupboard frames yourself or get a carpenter to do them for you, here are some ideas to keep the cost down.

Solid-backed or open slatted louvred doors, and space-saving "bi-fold" doors can be bought ready-made to your size requirements from door specialists who often also supply frames in kit form. Unfinished panel doors can be bought in the same way to be covered with your own choice of fabric or wallpaper. Alternatively, fabric-covered doors battened to a simple wood frame (with a diagonal cross member support) can look marvellously dramatic, particularly with a large bold print, or a tiny patterned paisley print with matching wallpaper will effectively tie together a small room with lots of nooks and crannies.

Alternatives to built-in cupboards

Considerable space is often wasted under, around and above the bed which can be used for storage. Here are some of the most workable ideas:

Under the bed: Several firms make drawers on castors or with wheeled bases to put under the beds. Recessed handles

are of course vital for under-the-bed drawers, as protruding ones could be decidedly dangerous. Avoid massive-sized drawers. They are difficult to manoeuvre, and tend to get crammed full of heavy books and blankets. By raising the bed base 3 ft 6 in. – 4 ft 6 in./1 m – 1.4 m off the ground, the area below the bed is lofty enough to be used as a hanging cupboard.

Around the bed: Storage units at the head and foot of the bed don't get in the way of bedmaking quite to the extent that units at one side of the bed do. You can also use them to lean up against when you're in bed, they cut down draughts and the topmost units can be two-way – accessible from the bed on one side and used to house drawers or proper hanging cupboards on the other. However, it is more practical to have units in an L-shape along one side and at the foot.

1 *Open shelves under the window provide space for bedside storage.*

2 *Bedbase composed of Palaset storage units – the interchangeable drawers come in bright colours and can be worked into any decorative scheme.*

3 *Cavity beneath high-level bed becomes hanging space for clothes. This unit was specially designed by Peter Murray for its owner, writer Molly Parkin. It's made up of a simple wood frame, clad with chipboard.*

4 *The wall at the end of a series of staggered floor-to-ceiling cupboards is faced with open shelves and a neat control panel of switches.*

5 *Wall-to-wall-to-ceiling-to-floor fitted cupboards in the Conrans' bedroom become an architectural feature with no furniture connotations. Needing no tops, sides or backs, these cupboards are not all that expensive to install.*

6 *Since fitted cupboards are usually a long-term investment, it's best to keep them plain. The linking shelf between the cupboards forms a desk which could double as a dressing table.*

7 *A bank of low-level storage units at the foot of the bed provides useful and attractive storage facilities, and the top comes in useful for anyone wishing to watch television in bed.*

8 *Bed set in an island of low storage units, the tops of which provide a continuous surface, broken only by the entrance-gap.*

9 *Bedhead shelving with lamp contains a small library and makes for comfortable bedtime reading sessions.*

1

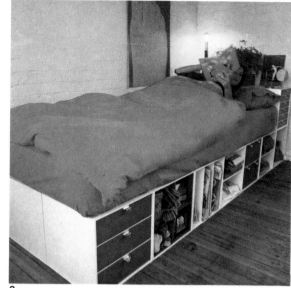

2

3

4

5

6

7

8

9

Bedrooms
12/13 Other furniture

It's too easy to forget just how much junk tends to accumulate beside the bed, and that while some things – telephone, lamp, torch, radio, books, magazines, watch, water jug, glass and ashtray – look decorative enough to expose on a shelf, other things like pills, teeth, electric razor, piles of unread newspapers, knitting, mending gear, paper hankies and cigarettes are clearly better tucked out of sight in a drawer or cupboard. It all depends on what you keep beside the bed, but most people need more than one little shelf.

Free-standing units

These usually hold more, but require floor space. Low table-cum-cupboard units are an obvious choice if you like to be able to change the position of the bed from time to time (which will incidentally help to prolong the life of the carpet). Some units are designed to be placed at the back of the bed and these are useful in a small room where there is no space for conventional bedside tables. Any storage chest behind the bed should incorporate at least two lift-up tops, so that you don't have to clear the entire table top to get at what's stored below.

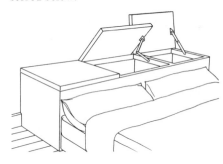

Some units are basically headboards with storage at either end. Some also have pull-out table extensions. Some incorporate swivel mirrors and lights, so that the bedside tables can act as dressing tables.

Wall-hung units

These get less in the way of bedmaking and floor cleaning, but if possible you should provide some shelf and cupboard space below the level of the bed – shelves above the bed are impossible to reach from a lying-down position. A neat solution to this is a shelf with a drop-front cupboard door to form a table top *below* the level of the mattress. If you haven't got enough room at the side of your bed leave a gap behind the bed for a low shelf. If you have shelves directly above the bed, be careful to leave at least 36 in./914 mm between pillow level and the shelf above, or you'll be knocking your head every time you sit up in bed. Also, for safety's sake nail an edging to shelves

above the bed. (Imagine your collection of books descending upon you, dislodged while you thrash around – a nightmare.) But there's no reason why they shouldn't be attached to furniture flanking the bed,

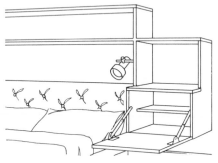

where you can see where things are, without having to sit up and pivot backwards.

Headboards

The first question to ask yourself is do you need a headboard at all, and, if so, why? A divan-type bed in a frame which holds the mattress and base in alignment and fixed to the wall clearly doesn't require one, except as a decorative addition.

If you are worried about greasy headmarks on the wall, avoid slatted or open lattice headboards, however pretty. Headboards should preferably be soft and warm to lean against and washable as well as pretty. Many headboards which look terrific are hopelessly impractical, don't protect the wall, are difficult to clean and uncomfortable to rest against. Even the most expensive padded and buttoned fabric-covered headboards can be spoiled by a brass surround. (Try leaning against cold metal first thing in the morning.) Some of the best headboards are homemade. Drapes with some padding behind them, hung just below the ceiling (velvet, thick cloth, candlewick, flannelette or just plain cotton feel, as well as look,

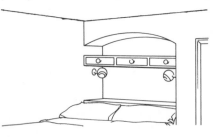

sumptuous). Or you could create the illusion of a grand headboard by placing the bed inside a recess (above).

The bedroom is not necessarily the best place for a dressing table. If there's room, consider the possibility of a Vanitory unit in the bathroom to safeguard the bedroom carpet against possible spillages.

Dressing tables

Make-up isn't easy to store. Jars, pots, flagons, bottles and lipsticks come in such an odd assortment of sizes. Plastic cutlery drawers are a good, cheap stopgap. And a wide shelf spanning two inexpensive whitewood chest makes a single effective dressing table/work-top.

However, an ideal dressing table – see below – might combine a shallow unit for small items like lipsticks, with a flap-up mirror top and built-in tungsten strip light (on an automatic switch); a lockable jewellery drawer; a deep drawer for larger bottles, shampoo, hairspray; a built-in waste bin and a stool (possibly cum laundry basket), mounted on castors and sized to slide into the unit, flush, to look like a huge drawer.

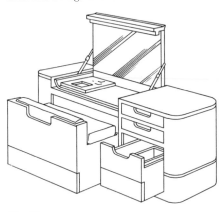

Trolleys

A trolley (see below) – not usually thought of as essential equipment – can be invaluable as a bed-table during sickness. The main disadvantage is that it does tend to clog up circulation space when it is not in use.

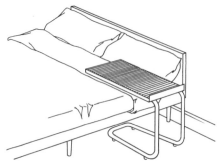

Chairs

Most men prefer a chair to the edge of the bed for putting on socks. And although most clothes keep better shape in a cupboard than dumped on a chair, there is no use pretending that most of us don't leave at least some items lying about

overnight. If you have room for only one chair in the bedroom, it may have to double as a dressing table stool. You may be able to squeeze in a low stool at the foot of the bed. Topped with a block of foam, covered in the same fabric as the bedcover, it won't harm your shins as you stumble hurriedly into bed on late nights.

Lighting

Electric lighting in the bedroom should be soft, warm, flattering and variable. Avoid a central overall light which tends to flatten and deaden a room. Concentrate on separate light sources, which in a bedroom will have to illuminate some, if not all, of the following activities: reading in bed, seeing to dress and undress, doing hair, making-up or shaving, as well as sewing and writing.

Mirrors should be placed near a window, but not where they block out daylight. Dressing-table lights should be in front of your face and not behind it. Bedside lights in a double room should if possible be capable of being angled, or dimmed (or both) so as not to disturb a sleeping partner. If you remove a central light, make sure that at least one light can be switched on from the door, and that all lights in the bedroom can be operated from the bed.

Good concealed lighting inside the wardrobe can illuminate hanging rails as well as full-length mirrors backed on to the cupboard doors. The next best thing is a ceiling-hung lamp between you and your reflection. Extra table lamps, or uplighters which spotlight the ceiling or alcoves with concealed lighting, add interest and warmth.

1 *Cantilevered Vanitory unit and tulip chair with fold-away mirror looks unboudoir-like and works well in a bedroom with a tailored look.*

2 *Built-in dressing table that vanishes out of sight – when the lid shuts, the bedside table unit's surface is continuous.*

3 *Glass is still the most practical dressing-table surface. Except possibly for the laminates, it is the only material resistant to spilling of nail polish and remover. Used here as a neat tray, it is a far cry from the old bit of kidney-shaped glass-over-fabric affair.*

4 *The dressing table that isn't – all make-up clobber has been swept to the bathroom.*

5 *Set of Victorian bedroom furniture includes this neat, alcove-fitting, dressing table on wheels. The mirror matches it, but odd ones can still sometimes be picked up in junk shops.*

1

2

3

4

5

Bedrooms
14/15 Planning a basic bedroom

Once you have established each bedroom's location in relation to the rest of the rooms in the house, you should now take calm, considered stock of the empty room – its shape, character, size, and the position of any special structural features such as windows, doors, fireplace alcoves or any existing built-in fittings. Note the position of power points, gas supply (if any) and the overall plumbing plan for the house. (It may not concern your plans for the moment, but should you be planning to install at a later stage a washbasin or showers, make provision for them, so that the present work is not wasted.) Bear in mind any minor alterations which may seem worth while. Quite often simply rehanging the bedroom door will enable you to make fuller use of the floor space available. Alternatively a sliding door would take up no floor space at all.

Fireplaces

There is often a strong case for removing any bedroom fireplace not in use. Whether it's boarded up or left in its original state, it nearly always looks somehow unloved and uncared for, wastes the valuable floor space in front of it and more often than not occupies the strategic position overlooking the rest of the room. Victorian gentlemen customarily stood with their backs to the fire, as much to enjoy a position of psychological command as to warm their behinds. To have a fireplace taken out, then bricked up, ventilated and plastered will cost you money and may seem a lot for disposing of a mere redundancy, but the sizeable piece of flat wall you acquire as a result will increase the room's potential in terms of layout and flexibility. Depending on the width of the chimney breast, it could accommodate a single or double headboard with flanking bedside tables and alcoves or alternatively a dressing table shelf as wide as the chimney breast, with hanging space on either side.

Layout

To get down to the nitty gritty of drawing out a detailed layout, map out a scale plan of your room and jot down a list of your requirements in terms of activities, necessary furniture and space allotment. Work out the best possible positions of the furniture and workability of the space. If, for instance, the 1 ft 10 in./560 mm recommended minimum circulation space around the foot of the bed is overlapped by the 2 ft /610 mm of standing space in front of the washbasin, don't expect to be able to walk past the washbasin when it's in use. Accuracy is all-important. A small bedroom which can look quite spacious in plan is bound to become a muddle if the bed can't be made

properly or open doors and drawers clash. Alternatively, a plan which looks a little congested on paper, can turn out to be quite satisfactory in real life if the furniture is limited in height. Ankles need less space than shoulders.

Top priority position should be given to the bed. To avoid draughts, the bedhead shouldn't go under the window (unless the latter is professionally double glazed), nor should it go in a direct line between the window and the door. Directly facing the only window in the room can be trying; sleeping with one's back to the door can be disturbing.

Having found the best position for your bed, or beds, think in terms of logical furniture grouping specifically related to

your own particular daily round of activities: i.e. washbasin, dressing table, wardrobe equals getting up in the morning; washbasin, chair, light-switch relates to going to bed at night; bedmaking, linen store, dirty-clothes basket relates to changing sheets on laundry day. As a general rule try to avoid an equal distribution of clutter around the room. Separate dressing table backing in to the bay window (blocking out light and view), tallboy and wardrobe set diagonally across different corners of the room, chest of drawers in the middle of one wall, separate bedhead and bedside tables, bookshelf chairs, stools and a small table or two, strewn higgledy-piggledy around the room, are guaranteed to make even

the largest bedroom seem crammed.

The eye registers unbroken areas of floor and wall, and the same area broken up will look half its size. For this reason furniture with light legs or bases, or wall mounted, will make a room feel far larger than the same pieces solid to the floor.

Aim to leave at least one wall completely free of furniture and plump for one distinctive type of furniture grouping aimed to unify the space. Consider the following alternative plans for an average box-like modern bedroom – 11 ft × 12 ft × 8 ft 6 in./3.3 m × 3.6 m × 2.5 m high: Everything amassed on to one wall – bed head included. Same treatment, except that the bed is treated as a separate entity, occupying a space apart.

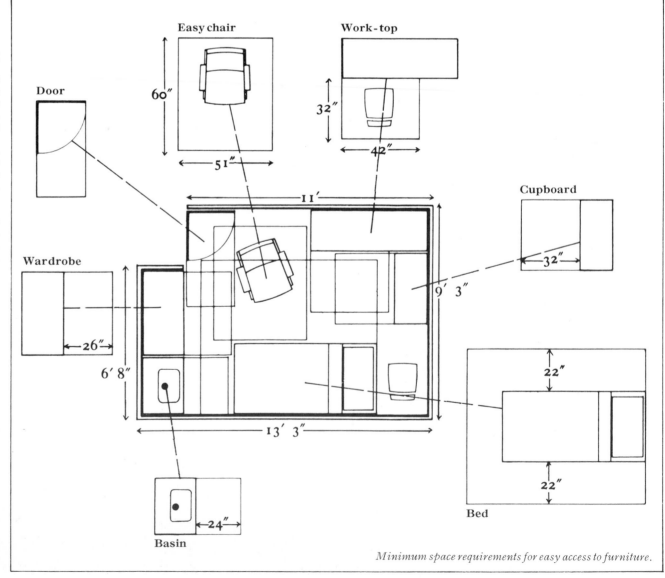

Minimum space requirements for easy access to furniture.

1 *Fireplace wall with blocked-up chimney breast accommodating headboard and double bed. All bedside things, including telephone, books, hi-fi speakers and lamp, are arranged on shelves with storage units in the alcoves. Clothes are kept in built-in cupboards on the opposite wall. The purple velvet chaise-longue is both decorative and a temptation to retreat from the hustle and bustle of family life for a quiet read or daytime snooze.*

2 *Low-level storage link-up. A wide shelf carried round the edge of the room, about 1 ft/305 mm off the floor, integrates bed, bedside table, seats and chest of drawers. So as not to detract from the floor area, it is cantilevered off a narrow plinth, painted in an anonymous cream colour in contrast to the bright yellow shelf edge. The dressing mirror module is the same as the chest: and cushion seats as the bedside table top. In a larger room, the plinth could be designed in sections to accommodate storage, with flap-up lids. The plinth idea is particularly useful as a means of boxing in unsightly pipes.*

3 *Floor-to-ceiling storage built in along one wall of a room with the bed treated as a separate entity, backed against the window wall. The cupboards have louvred doors, the open shelves incorporate books, TV and general display. Note the white sheer roller blind emphasizing the monochromatic colour scheme.*

4 *Central bed with storage at head and feet. A wide brown band over walls, ceiling and floor plus brown bedcover and cushions makes the sleeping area into the focal point of the room.*

Bedrooms

From a purely decorative point of view, the decision to use your bedroom for other uses besides just sleeping, changing, and storing clothes, doesn't automatically commit you to adopt the usual bedsit policy of disguising the bed as a divan during the day. On the contrary, why, at the risk of ending up with a blank depersonalized hotel-room atmosphere, go to the trouble of playing down the bedroomy aspects of the room at all?

What about the bed itself?

The bed, being such a conspicuous and cumbersome object by nature, is far easier to emphasize than conceal. Make a bold feature of an old-fashioned four-poster, team it with a clean-lined modern sofa and perhaps a Davy Jones-type coffee table cum linen chest and the chances are the room will achieve far too distinct a pedigree to come into the bedsitter class.

Bedroom cum private sitting room

In theory everyone would like one, and yet few attempt it. Compared to designing a study bedroom or a seamstress's bedroom, it's by far and away the hardest of dual-purpose bedroom formats to bring off successfully, simply because comfortable seating requires so much extra room, as well as money.

One armchair, or even a sofa, isn't on its own enough to induce one out of the albeit noisy family living room into the bedroom for a quiet evening's read on one's own. A solitary armchair looks sadly lonesome (too reminiscent of old people's homes, perhaps?), and a sofa without a coffee table, or some kind of equivalent dumping ground for books and magazines, tends to get dreadfully littered up so that there is soon hardly any room to sit down.

Ideally one should aim to create a separate seating area within the bedroom, complete with low tables and lamps. But without the space and funds to install a complete second living-room suite – sofa, two armchairs and coffee table – what are the alternatives?

Floor cushions arranged around a group of small low tables, pushed together is one of the least expensive solutions. Both cushions and tables can be neatly stacked out of the way when not required, and bookshelves or a corner bookcase could be tucked into the seating end of the room – to keep current reading material permanently off the floor.

Another seating idea, which requires less space, is to raise the bed on a platform and build seating in step formation around two, if not three, sides. Carpeted to match the floor it forms a stylish sculptured extension of the bed.

Carpeted platform around bed forms seating.

Bedside tables could be added – made out of simple hollowed-out box shapes and carpeted as part and parcel of the same unit. Glass table-tops are a practical extra, but should be inset to prevent them from sliding off the carpet. Seat cushions should fit into a module – or at least match the width of the seating surround so that you can pile them out of the way at night (top right). In a tall, narrow room, you might be able to put the bed out of the way on a platform and use the space below, à la Pullman sleeping car, for a comfortable sofa. The upright supports to the platform incorporate a ladder at one end, and shelves for books at the other. Behind the sofa is an extra shelf (below).

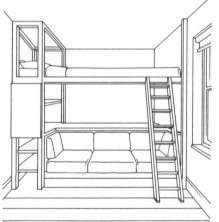

Platform bed with seating alcove.

The safest way to build this kind of structure is by nailing vertical supporting struts to the wall on either side, fixing horizontal 3 in. × 2 in./76 mm × 51 mm timbers along the full length of the bed. A blockboard sleeping floor would take less time to erect than ordinary planks, but would need plenty of ventilation holes drilled into it. Ventilation holes aren't necessary with planks – but these take more effort and skill to lay.

Platform bed leaves room free for other uses, and itself becomes a high-level sitting area.

Another way of achieving this effect is to buy bunk beds, to sleep on the top bed and to add masses of extra cushions to the bottom mattress, so turning it into a sofa. You may have difficulty in finding British made bunks with sufficient space between the two beds for an adult to be able to sit up straight, but Scandinavian bunks, which are built for adults as well as children, are more spacious.

Sewing

Quite apart from the fact that bedrooms are ready rigged up to use as fitting rooms with a full-length mirror and hanging space, the advantages of being able to dressmake in one's own room as opposed to the kitchen, dining- or living-room, are obvious. When visitors drop in unexpectedly, you don't have to hastily tidy away a half completed cutting out job. While men may marvel at the budget-saving art of home dressmaking, not one of them enjoys having to pick his way through a sea of material, paper patterns and pins strewn across the living room floor. A sewing trolley, designed to slide in and out of a wall of built-in bedroom cupboards, is a good idea. It makes it quick and easy to tidy sewing away and you can lock the machine out of reach of small children.

Alternatively you can buy, or have specially made, a cupboard unit with a flap-down door cum table top resting on folding legs, designed to flap up out of the way and store flat just like a wallpaper table, or the classic British bridge table.

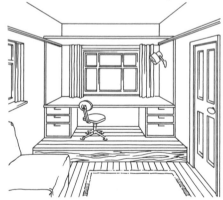

Above-window storage for fabrics.

The area under the bed could be used as a fabric store: or you could run a wide shelf above the sewing area at picture-rail height. Everyone drops pins, so invest in one of those extra large magnets which you can run over the table and floor when you have finished work.

Ironing

Having found a place for a machine, it's rather a tall order to expect to fit an ironing board into the bedroom as well: but it may be possible to install an ironing

Bedroom dressmaking is convenient when all the gear can be neatly stored.

Bedroom doubles as sitting room; the upholstery matches the tight bedcovers.

board top which swivels out from under a sewing work-top, rather like a blade on a penknife.

Alternatively, you could hang an ironing board on the back of a cupboard door, or fix an ironing board top to it, designed to flap down on to a cantilevered support, like those folding tables in train carriages. Don't forget to work out a place for the electric socket, and a safe asbestos-lined locker in which to store the iron. Provide yourself with a hook or rail beside the ironing board where you can hang up freshly ironed clothes on a coat hanger. Everything creases less if it is folded when it is cold and dry, so it is worth hanging up shirts and blouses even for half an hour. One of the best hooks for this purpose is a copy of a brass Victorian cloakroom fitting with 6 or 8 little hooks along an extended arm. You can find this at most architectural hardware shops.

Study/bedroom

Any bedroom which is also intended to double up as a study will benefit if all the paraphernalia of clothes and dressing can be confined to one area. The less vivid images and visual clutter assail the eye, the easier it is to concentrate. For the best light, the desk should be set at right angles to the window – right-handed people should sit with the window on their left. If there is only one window in the room, avoid facing the desk directly on to the window. It causes eye-strain. For people who only study at night, the question may not arise, but if you have to choose between placing the bed or desk to face the window, far better to give the desk preferential treatment. Sometimes, if the window wall is long enough, it is possible to squeeze in a desk and bed at right angles to the window. The back of the desk is padded to double up as a head rest for the bed, and the desk light can also be used from the bed.

Sitting bent over a desk all day (people cramming for exams are the worst offenders) isn't ideal. It is possible to provide a well-lit armchair as an alternative reading position. A narrow wooden board, sized to span the arms of the chair (to which the student could attach a pencil

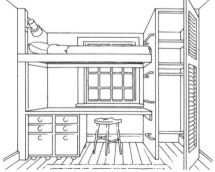

Sleeping facilities on top of the job.

and notepad), is an incredibly simple but worthwhile extra.

You can even buy a desk with a bed above, on a 5 ft/1.5 m high platform. The bed and platform come in kit form (see drawing), with optional extras to slot into the space below.

Work storage

If your work involves lots of papers and much reference material it is well worth investing in a filing system. You may be able to manage with pocket files stored in the existing drawers, but otherwise buy yourself two table-height filing cabinets and have a work-top cut to go over them, making a knee-hole desk. You can get filing cabinets in white or bright primary colours, so this need not wreck the look of your bedroom. You could have the work-top faced with laminate in a contrasting colour, or to match.

Televiewing

Watching TV in bed doesn't necessarily mean you have to be a two-telly family, but it helps if you have a set that's portable and can plug headphones or individual ear plugs into the set, so that one partner can go to sleep, if the other one wants to view on late into the night.

The most strategic position for the set is on a shelf (built into the foot rest) at the end of the bed, between a foot to three feet above the level of your pillows. This is better than directly on a line with the pillows, which forces you to crane your neck into an uncomfortable position, pushing your chin into your chest.

Two ways to ensure the set won't fall forwards on to the bed when your husband cheers on his favourite football team – either fix the television set to a wall bracket secured to tall foot posts (e.g. as on the fourposter, see drawing) or set it on a trolley, designed to slide over the foot of the bed.

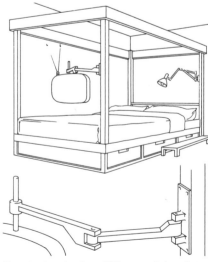

Fourposter viewing: TV on angle bracket.

Bedrooms
18/19 Linked to the bathroom

Along with central heating and a good fitted kitchen, there is nothing like a bedroom/bathroom suite to bump up the value of your property.

Basins

Installing a basin to each bedroom in the house is a good first step – especially if the one and only bathroom in the house clearly isn't coping with the early morning rush. Start with the master bedroom or the bedroom farthest away from the bathroom. In theory, installing a basin is a relatively simple and inexpensive operation. Since bedrooms are nearly always at the top of the house nearest the water tank, your bill for copper piping should be minimal, but this depends on how you heat your water (you could if necessary install a small instant water heater). If possible place the basin (and this also applies to shower or bath) against or as near as possible to the outside wall. It makes for a shorter run of unsightly waste piping.

If the outside wall happens to contain your one and only span of fitted cupboards, it's quite feasible to fit a basin or shower cubicle into one section – preferably a corner. For a basin, you might simply board up the side next to the cupboard with a timber frame, plyboard facing and tiles.

A small Vanitory basin fitted off centre in a laminate surface can become part of a built-in dressing table. After all, most women use some water for their make-up even if it is only to wash out a brush. For a room used by a man, fit a razor plug. If the mirror runs the length of the laminate surface, the plug is best fitted away from the basin. For a narrow mirror, you can buy a strip light with a built-in razor plug. A woman who uses heated rollers needs a 5 amp socket near her dressing table.

Provide a rail or ring for towels. You can fix this to the wall or, if you have a deep facing panel along the front of the basin, fix a towel ring to it.

Possible snags with installing bedroom plumbing, which may only become apparent after the event are nocturnal gurglings and knocking pipes. These can be avoided by a competent plumber, but make sure he knows you *mind* about this – *before* he quotes for the job. Silencing pipes once they have been connected can be prohibitively expensive.

Another common problem is how to protect the area around the basin or shower. Rubber mats are hopeless (the water eventually drains off into the carpet). Thick twist pile cotton rugs mop up splashings, but need frequent drying out and washing. Rot-proof carpets, made from synthetic fibres, are

a sensible choice, like extremely tough, hard twist, non-crush 80/20 Acrylic/nylon carpet tiles – laid loose which looks like fitted carpet.

Tiles have non-fray edges, which means you can easily replace individual ones when you've spilt innumerable amounts of toothpaste, powder, nail varnish or deodorant without having to invest in a whole new carpet to re-cover the entire bedroom (but remember to buy spares to start with).

Showers

If you are short of space, fit a fold-away shower which can be bought ready made, and which when closed up looks like a shallow cupboard measuring 7 ft 1 in. × 3 ft × 9 in./2 m × 1 m × 228 mm, finished in white melamine. To use it, you merely open the cupboard doors, fold down the base section and turn on the taps.

Top floor or attic bedroom showers are often impossible to install for lack of the necessary clearance between shower head and water storage tank to provide adequate pressure. There is a small instantaneous water heater with an integral shower head which can be plumbed direct to the cold water mains and overcomes this tiresome problem.

Planning a bed/bathroom link

A large L-shaped bedroom lends itself perfectly to an open plan bed with bath. The long arm of the L can make an adequate size bedroom to walk into, with a wall of built-in cupboards on one side of the door and a double bed backing on to open shelves on the other. The bathroom need have no door, perhaps just a change in level, loosely divided from the bedroom area by a mirror. The basin and bath can be built into one continuous unit. If you want to install a w.c. you must check the local bye-laws.

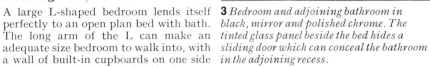

A wall of built-in floor-to-ceiling cupboards can make a natural screen between bed and bath; a high headboard divider is another alternative (see below).

If you are worried about the possible claustrophobic effects of dividing one large room into two, there is no reason why you shouldn't decide on a completely open plan bathroom/bedroom – providing the room is well heated.

1/2 Two views of a bathroom linked to the adjoining bedroom by an intermediary dressing room, lined along one wall with mirror fronted wardrobes. A feeling of unity is given by the polished wood floor used throughout and the striped cotton runner linking the bed to the bath. White is used throughout on the walls and woodwork and continued on the bedspread. The bath is centrally placed between two louvre-fronted cupboards and set in a surround of travertine effect tiles, which also form a splashback for the overhead shower.

3 Bedroom and adjoining bathroom in black, mirror and polished chrome. The tinted glass panel beside the bed hides a sliding door which can conceal the bathroom in the adjoining recess.

4 Bath and bedroom all in one in a pine-clad attic room. The bath placed across the narrow end of the room is panelled in pine and top lit by a skylight. The bed in the main part of the room has a white bedspread.

5/6/7 Large, open-plan bedroom and bathroom takes up a whole floor of the house, and so has light coming from windows on all four sides. In the bedroom area the stripped and polished floorboards, antique furniture and shiny brass bedsteads filled in with panels of fabric, give a cosy feeling to the sleeping and sitting areas. The bathroom is defined by a change of flooring and screened off by the glass showcase on a base which is flush with the bath and houses the heater.

6 The dressing table, laminate topped for practicality and mounted on brass brackets to match the pedestal of the harp stool.

7 The bathroom seen through the glass case, showing the high-level storage unit above the dressing table. The underside of the unit conceals a strip-light.

1

2

3

4

5

6

7

Bedrooms
20 Spare room corners/sofa convertibles

Few people now can manage to set aside a complete room specifically for guests. Dank, musty, immaculately empty rooms, only broken into when visitors were imminent, are (happily in many ways) a thing of the distant past.

Bearing in mind all the ghastly lessons to be learned from bad nights spent in other people's houses – sagging beds, lumpy pillows, not enough air, no bulb in the bedside light and fumbling frantically along pitch black corridors to find the bathroom – here are some solutions.

A guest room cum hobby room

This isn't as far-fetched as it may sound, provided junk and hobbies can at a moment's notice be packed out of sight, It is, after all, the small thoughtful details – a bowl of flowers, ashtrays, lighter, boxes of tissues, writing paper, large fluffy towels, the latest issue of some glossy magazine – which make guests feel well cared for, far more so than grandly spacious amenities.

Any bedroom systematically emptied of all trace of previous human existence is likely to give a chilly, if not positively eerie, impression, rather like a hospital or international hotel room.

The most effective way to divide junk and hobbies from the spare bed area of the room is to utilize space below or above the bed to best advantage.

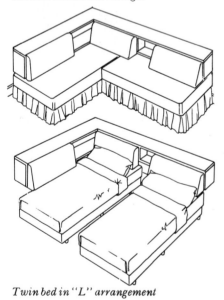

Twin bed in "L" arrangement

If you own a spare room that's large enough for two twin beds, as opposed to one large double, are always more useful in the long run, particularly when elderly relatives come to stay. They can be pushed out of the way, leaving the floor clear for children to use as an extra play room. Or, pushed against adjoining walls to form a corner settee (see above).

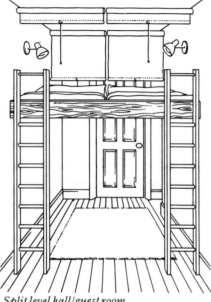

Split level hall/guest room

A bed niche spare bed corner

For a night or two away from home, most people are prepared to be a good deal more adventurous in their sleeping habits.

In a large Victorian house with high half landings, or even in the hall, you can make use of any spare areas, providing the house is well heated. (No guest will thank you for a cold night spent in a draughty hall, however romantic the setting.) The owners of one house built a platform just above the tops of the doors opening into a long, narrow hall. The platform, which spans the width of the hall, is just wide and deep enough to accommodate two twin foam mattresses (above). Duvets do away with conventional bed-clothes and bedmaking, which would in this case present major problems. Two sets of roller blinds were set into the ceiling at either end of the beds. Each bed has a wall-fixed light and its own securely fixed vertical ladder.

The same platform sleeping idea can be adapted to fit into a half landing at the top of the house. Cantilevered over the stairwell, it could have an L-shaped writing desk cum dressing table below,

linked to the sleeping area above by an old Victorian spiral staircase (e.g. an exterior fire-escape). The sleeping area can be divided from the stairwell by roller blinds recessed into the ceiling. Guests could hang their clothes on a Victorian hat stand

A bed in someone else's room

An ideal solution for children's friends staying overnight – a pair of nesting beds for the space of one. The lower bed slides out on castors and can be stowed away ready made up. Also made are triple nesting beds which work on the same principle.

As an extra spare bed in the living room, a truly elegant sofa which converts quickly into a reasonably comfortable bed for an occasional guest is not always easy to find. Many which could be described as comfortable beds are too deep in the seat to sit on comfortably during the day. Others are visually marred by untidy upholstery ridges and furrows, or are far too complicated to convert.

The great merit of a camp bed, not to be scoffed at as a last-resort emergency spare bed, is that it folds up right out of the way into a neat, light, tight bundle. An optional extra would be a thin polyether foam mattress, which can also be stowed in a roll.

1

2

1 Unless you have a lot of overnight guests, a spare room can end up by being rarely used. One way of overcoming this problem is to butt two beds up together into a corner, tight cover the mattress and store all bedding out of sight in the drawers in the base. With banks of cushions forming a backrest, the room becomes an extra sitting room.

2/3 Foam-filled sofa/convertible covered in natural canvas is a satisfactory way to put up guests overnight in the sitting room. The arms and backrest are held in place by Velcro, and when they are removed, the seat opens out to form a comfortable double bed.

3

One-room living/1

One-room living isn't necessarily confined to any one particular age group, income bracket or type of person. A comfortable and practical bedsitter can solve a living-in granny's or grandpa's predicament as well as the problems raised by an independent teenager clamouring for a room of his or her own.

Of course there are hundreds and hundreds of students who need the isolation of living alone to concentrate on studies, and can't afford much more than a bedsit anyway. But living in one room need not be looked on as a wholly bad option.

Many enthusiastic exponents of this life style are people who have become very weary of negotiating passages and opening and shutting doors in a rabbit warren of tiny rooms. When the internal partitions are down, the whole area can be turned into one stimulating and surprisingly flexible room in which multitudes of different activities can peacefully co-exist.

However, living in one and the same room, day-in, day-out, can become tedious and claustrophobic. It's therefore important for a bedsitter to have some of the qualities of a chameleon. It must be easy – very easy – to change about to suit the activities of the moment. Dual-purpose adaptability is an attractive concept, which may make for interesting picture material in home magazines. But in practice it can be very difficult and awkward. Anything more ambitious than fold-away beds, stacking chairs, sliding doors, folding screens or mobile furniture mounted on large, safe castors should be regarded with suspicion. And any so-called flexible furniture ideas which really mean involving yourself in constant switching around – like using the bath as a base for the kitchen table – should be avoided. Whether you are thinking of turning a bedroom in your home into a bedsit or revamping a dreary one on a shoestring; or just enjoying open-plan living, you should check the following points.

☐ Do you want to sleep in your living room or live in your bedroom?
☐ Do you need to cater for washing and cooking?
☐ Do you want to eat/study/work/entertain?
☐ Can all your possessions be contained in one storage system?

How one virtually penniless pair set up home starting with nothing more than a mattress and an old chest of drawers. They made shelves out of painted bricks and wooden planks (which don't have to be wall fixed in a rented place), and invested in large floor cushions and stacking tables, which will be useful in any future home.

One-room living
2/3 The practicalities

Irrespective of your budget or the style of one-room flat you have in mind, the overriding problem which invariably tends to beset each and every one-room occupant is one of space.

It would be well-nigh impossible to begin making provision for eating, sleeping, cooking sitting, working, washing and ironing without some idea of how much space to allow for each activity. You may never cook another meal if every time you want to open the oven door you find yourself having to rearrange the tables and chairs and push the bed against the wall.

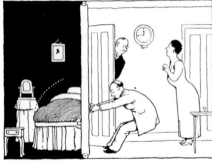

Space-problems solved by Heath Robinson.

Apart from needing upright chairs for eating and working, you'll also want a comfortable sofa. You will probably be tempted to combine sleeping and sitting arrangements: there are ways to do this.

Even in a very small room, it's usually quite possible to place your bed on a low seating platform – using the mattress as a prop for your back, not as a seat (below).

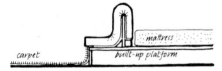

Low seating formed by taking 2 in. (50 mm) foam rubber over vertical board.

Alternatively, you could raise the bed on a high platform and use the area underneath for a seating arrangement.

If you are very hard pressed for space and you have to use a conventional sprung divan to double as a sofa, better turn the mattress in all directions fairly often so that you and your friends are not always sitting on the same edge. The only mattress that can withstand constant pressure round the edges has to be made of foam rubber.

A convertible sofa-bed could solve your space problem, but beware of one that is neither a comfortable bed nor an adequate sofa. There are Italian convertible sofas that cope beautifully with sitting, lounging and lying down, on the principle of a mattress that simply folds over (see below).

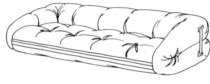
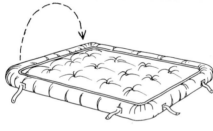

Fold-away furniture always seems the obvious answer for bedsitters, but the perpetual bother of opening and shutting complicated pieces of furniture often becomes a tedious chore. If you still feel it's the only answer, consider buying the very, very best designed versions you can afford, otherwise they tend to look gimcrack and not work at all well.

Several firms do now produce a good bed-in-a-cupboard, which means that the bed disappears behind the wall storage units during the day. If none of these camouflage arrangements will work in your room, don't forget to avoid all the obvious reminders of bedsit life. Flounced floral bedspreads and dressing tables belong strictly to one-purpose bedrooms.

1/2 *Revolving shelving and fold-away bed unit, incorporates a drop-down table big enough for four people.*

3 *Panels either mask the bed or the kitchen/wash slot. Sliding gear for the panels is concealed in a beam running across the room. A wardrobe storage unit solidly divides the areas.*

1

2

3

4 *For the agile – a sleep shelf from wall to wall in a room only six feet wide. Add a comfortable mattress, a clip-on light, and install wall bars; these work as a ladder to the bed, and a challenge for owners in need of a work-out! Warning: this kind of shelf needs to be very securely fixed – either with battens at each end plugged firmly into the wall or supported by a beam slung across and run into the wall: a job only for a competent DIY man or builder. If you tend to thrash around in your sleep, do have a guard rail.*

5 *Attics tend to be full of water tanks and nicked out corners to give head room below. One way to rise above such problems if your bedsitter is under the roof, is to build a big platform right across the offending bumps. Here almost half the attic is jacked up to make an area big enough for sitting comfortably or for putting up overnight visitors. Hinged lift-up flaps in the floor of the platform to give access to water tanks, and storage tucks all the way along the front end.*

6 *In a high-ceilinged room, stove enamelled piping or glossy scaffolding, a well-constructed deck and a comfy mattress can all add up to make a two-level room. In most parts of the country, you're supposed to have planning permission for this sort of internal mezzanine – not because the local authorities are nosy, but for your own protection. It's very important to know whether the floor can take the load of the scaffolding and whether the steps are safe enough to scuttle down in the middle of the night. It's a job for an architect, not a DIY idea.*

7 *One-room living needs adaptability – yours, the layout's and the furniture's. Any module system can be used in an almost endless variety of combinations – the trick is to choose unbedroomy colours and to keep all the dressing and sleeping paraphernalia out of sight during the day. Here, the dressing table is at the back of the storage unit – where the clip-on Guzzini lamp can direct its beam when needed. For reading in bed, there are twin lamps under the shelves by the bedhead.*

4

5

6

7

One-room living
4/5 Basic considerations

As long as your table is well supplied with adjoining storage space for books, crockery, cutlery, glasses, sewing machine, typewriter, there is no reason why one large table shouldn't double up as an eating-cum-other activities surface. Nine times out of ten, a fixed table with storage space above and below is less trouble than tables which are designed to fold out from the wall, or trestle tables designed to stack away – both of which are likely to involve you in endless back-breaking possession-shifting manoeuvres. Table-height mobile storage units with flap-up extensions are a good compromise.

Heath Robinson's space-saving ideas.

If you are going to use your all-purpose table for preparing food as well as eating it, make sure that it has a wipable surface; and if you are using a laminated plastic, have a chopping board handy, else the table will soon be ruined.

Cooking

If at all possible, set aside a separate area for cooking with washable surfaces and floor, and allow yourself the option

to screen it off – perhaps behind roller blinds or sliding doors. Good ventilation, preferably an electric extractor, is vital, otherwise the whole room will get overheated and full of cooking smells.

You should allow a minimum of 7 square ft (0.65 square m) of shelf space for dry foods and equipment, including crockery and cutlery, but take heart, people living in caravans often manage with a good deal less.

There are several good-looking and efficient off-the-peg mini-kitchens on the market. One of the best incorporates sink, fridge and two electric cooking rings, as well as an instant water heater. If space is your problem again, a small sink/drainer/work-top and three cooking rings unit is made for caravans – obtainable through caravan dealers.

Washing

Unless you have the necessary plumbing for a separate basin and sink, the sink will most probably have to double up as a washbasin. Either stock up with two plastic bowls – one for washing dishes and one for washing you, stored as near as possible to the sink, or if you have enough room you could be very Victorian and invest in an old-fashioned washstand.

If you are planning your washing facilities from scratch, but again you have provision for only one source of plumbing, a deep ceramic washbasin set into a laminated work-top, which would double as a sink, rather than vice versa, would be far pleasanter to wash yourself in and would be quite adequate for doing the dishes. Ideally, of course, a separate washbasin should be built into the dressing area of your room.

1 *You can fit a workable kitchen area into the smallest nook or cranny – here a compact sink/hob/fridge combination slots into a cupboard. The whole lot is shut off from the main room with a pair of concertina folding doors, a good idea for any one-room flat as they take up virtually no space once they are open and folded against the wall.*

2 *Bachelor's breakfast cum washing cupboard – with mini-water heater, plug-in toaster and electric kettle and a generous-sized ceramic basin.*

3 *Here today, gone tomorrow. Moonlight flit solution for a washing-up corner in a large, virtually unconverted Paris warehouse. Cupboards, sink and cooking units are all supported on scaffolding, lit up with the kind of rubber insulated wire-shielded lights used by mechanics to peer under cars. The whole thing takes apart in half an hour, with the help of a plumber.*

1

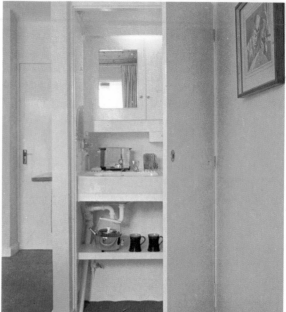

2

3

Even if the bedsit you are planning is a room in your home for an au pair or an elderly relative, it's a good idea to install some simple washing and cooking facilities, even if they are not going to be used every day. It gives them a feeling of independence and you peace and quiet in your own domain. If you are furnishing a room for granny, take care with the seating. Don't be misled by comfortable-looking overstuffed armchairs – tiny frail grannies won't be supported properly by them and large grannies will have difficulty getting out. Older people are generally much happier with an upright, upholstered chair with arms.

4/5/6 *Here's the kind of pretty, elegant, self-contained room that could have a lot of appeal for grannies. The gentle, all-over pattern on the wallpaper and fabric helps to bind the various elements together and makes the bed less prominent. Round tables are good in smallish rooms, as there are no corners to bruise oneself on. They also look less functionally like a dining table. Upright chairs are light enough for someone elderly to move about easily. By the way, if the person is fairly frail, they will probably find bedmaking simpler if the bed projects out into the room, rather than being pushed against the wall.*

4

5

6

One-room living
6/7 Visual variety

To build visual variety and interest into your bedsit, try incorporating a change in floor levels, and avoid an unbroken expanse of wall-to-wall cupboard units. Punctuate built-in units with an open alcove here and there to create a feeling of space continuing beyond and behind the unit, and to make the space seem larger.

To divide one area of activity from another, quite ordinary free-standing folding screens are hard to beat. More sophisticated screening can be mounted on runners or set into the ceiling to operate as you would a roller blind. A translucent effect, like that of pinoleum blinds, has the advantage of letting through daylight, but at night one side of the room can be hidden from sight simply by switching off its lights. It is very appealing to be able to half-glimpse through from one area to the next, but dull to be able to take in the entire room at a single glance.

1–6 This apartment, on the top floor of a small warehouse, includes a main living area with a corner neatly snipped off to accommodate the kitchen and bathroom.

To create a sense of spaciousness the architects designed curved corners for partitions and stairwell since they are visually less obtrusive than a series of right angles.

When the bed unit is folded up, its underside becomes the focal point of the whole space, with chromed metal strips set into the black painted timber base. Six heavy-duty springs attached behind the headboard take most of the weight when the bed is being raised or lowered.

Shelving runs along the wall and returns to form the stair treads to the roof garden above, while the lower tread is widened to form, with the addition of cushions, a low-level seating unit. Another visual space maker is the carpet carried up the 6 in./150 mm- plinth which runs under the seating and storage units. Electrical outlets are also sited in this plinth.

The dining table/work-surface folds out from a cupboard unit. All doors have touch latches so there are no handles to catch people in this relatively small area.

Colours are kept to an absolute minimum throughout. Natural hessian, small areas of sepia hessian, matt black timber with chrome hand rails and motif on the underside of bed, beigey carpet – virtually everything else is white including the bathroom and kitchen floors.

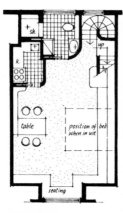

1

2

3

4

5

6

7 /8 /9 Room designed for spry girl who climbs up a ladder to get into bed on the top of her gallery. Underneath, believe it or not, there's a bath, a washbasin and a mini-kitchen. Demolition sites provided most of the materials – the decorative rail along the edge of the gallery is a communion rail from a church, complete with fold-back section, and the doors below were all rescued from a builder's bonfire.

10–12 Designer Linda Brill uses great big floor cushions and a screen to make her bright, fresh apartment work. The wicker screen hides her bed, but if there is a party on, it can be folded back to make more floor and sitting space. Floor cushions give a sense of freedom and informality since they can be moved around, rearranged more easily than conventional chairs.

13 Linda Brill likes to keep lots of cut-outs, design ideas, and snippets around her, but she makes sure they're confined to two definite places so that the room never gets out of hand. The detail of her studio corner shows how an Anglepoise lamp leaves the decks clear for designing, and how useful all the softboard panelling is for pinning up bits and pieces.

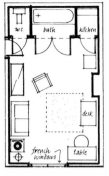

7

10

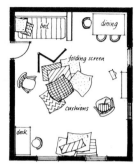

8

11

9

12

13

One-room living
8 Vistas

One of the problems of one-room living is that you're looking at the same four walls day-in, day-out. A screen means a variety of views and gives different areas a feeling of their own. If the screen is curved it will break up the squareness of the room.

This room is all lit up so you can see everything at once, but normally the lights are used to "shut off" various parts, and to define different areas by creating warm pools of light.

This deceptively simple layout is in fact extremely sophisticated. One continuous curving white band links all the various elements and the wall around the sunken bed.

Privacy is no problem in this Californian home. As the nearest house is half a mile away, there is no need for curtains or blinds. This room includes a studio bay, an area for eating, and a large iron bed which also serves as a sofa.

Children's rooms/1

Having children means that your home is no longer yours alone. It's theirs too. If they can't do a lot of what they like in it without a background of constant nagging, who can blame them if they leave it at the earliest opportunity.

Some young children speedily learn that other people's property must be respected, and precisely those who are rigidly relegated to their own rooms at home often become fiends of destruction when visiting other people. But most parents feel it desirable – in the interest of sanity all round – to have a certain amount of segregation. Perhaps specified places – maybe a study, maybe a living room – could be for adults only, admitting accompanied children (like cinemas showing A films) on special occasions.

Children have a pronounced sense of fair play and will, in time, expect a certain privacy in their own quarters too, and a great say in the decoration.

Whether or not you're going to see eye to eye with them, some basic considerations will apply: children's rooms have to adapt to different needs in a relatively short time – even a "baby" room meant for a number of infants in turn. Furniture should, if possible, be more or less in scale with the child. Storage needs to alter as toys give way to records, and tiny garments in drawers to full-size things on hangers.

So where do you begin? First, make a mental checklist of all your ideas, on the size and upbringing of your future – or existing – family. It doesn't matter that you may drastically revise these as time goes on – it's a starting point for some of the questions that you will ask yourself.

☐ Once your offspring are no longer tiny and asleep for most of the day, will their room be mainly a bedroom, or their playroom too?

☐ Given the available space, have you weighed up the advantages of positioning their room (a) near your own bedroom (b) close to the family's living quarters?

☐ If you are doing up not only a nursery but the house, are you child-orientated when considering stairs (safety), walls (washability), storage-facilities (child-height), garden layout (somewhere to play), hall (muddy feet)?

☐ Children up to the age of four will want to be where you are. Have you thought of arranging a play-space where they can be under your eye without being under your feet?

Consider the practicalities from the start but pull out the stops when it comes to decorating the nursery. Don't feel wedded to pink and blue, but make the baby's room the wittiest, prettiest place in the house.

Children's rooms
2/3 Newborn babies

Many loving parents keep their newborn bundles close to their quarters at night, either in their own or in an adjoining room with the door left open. Tiny babies do not yet need, or want, large cots, but will be happiest in fairly enclosed spaces, whether it's a drawer lined with foam or the whole flounced bassinet bit. There's a huge range of cribs on the market – from clear Perspex ones to traditional wicker-baskets. Or use one of those baskets that has handles like a shopping basket, or the carry cot from a transporter.

In any case the baby will be out of this basket in about three or at the latest six months, and many people consider the expenditure on quickly outgrown things unnecessary. But if you can afford them, they are very nice indeed; since having a baby does not automatically bring out the maternal instinct, make the business of baby-care as pleasant as possible – the best crib in town or really lovely baby clothes definitely help.

A room of their own

By the time that babies really take notice and can stand and crawl, it is time to arrange for a separate room. Babies often wake in the night long past the age of needing food, but will soon go to sleep again if there's no one there with whom they can socialize.

Intercom

An intercom relaying any cries or demands will come in useful. It will alert you when you really need to pay attention, and save you much rushing upstairs and downstairs to see that all is well – particularly if your house is of the tall terrace variety. At night, as the separate-room routine is being put into practice, it will help to reassure you by transmitting the baby's regular breathing (or snoring, if the volume is turned high). It will not be an extravagance, as it will come in useful later as a link between other parts of the house, for instance between the kitchen and the workroom.

Cots

When the time comes for swapping the crib for a cot, investigate types that convert into beds at a later stage. If you settle for a non-convertible cot, a fairly traditional, high-sided one, plain or painted – you can get them without transfers these days – might be best, as many of the glamorous, shallower cots aren't much good for athletic babies.

Furniture

Baby bouncers, walkers, playpens and high chairs should be sturdy. Feeding chairs that hook over dining room chairs are a good idea, but won't work on curved back chairs, so check yours. If you don't want to buy a "nursing chair", a low one, perhaps with its legs bobbed, in which your elbows are unimpeded will probably do.

Day-time baby-care

However nice the nursery, it's no good expecting young children to spend much time in it on their own. They'll want to be where they can keep tabs on you. However, a sizeable chunk of your time is bound to be spent in directly ministering to the child, and the nursery could well be the place where you do all the wiping, wrapping and unwrapping that will punctuate your day. Keep all the baby's toilet things together on a tray in easy reach of the work-top, and avoid having to turn your back on the child as you fish for safety pins, as babies can be very slippery and roll about a lot.

Bathtime

Baby baths, once awkward things to store, are now up to all sorts of useful vanishing tricks, like those that double as a nappy-changing table. But little baths, like cribs, won't be in use for long; the baby will be happier in one where he can splash and kick very soon.

Floors

The surface should be smooth and washable – babies dribble and spit food around, and carpet is difficult to clean. The floor also needs to be smooth for the day when the child crawls, and there should be nothing to trip you up when you carry the baby about.

Lighting

It should be bright so that you can see what you're doing, and there should be a soft light for nightfeeds: bright lights tend irrevocably to wake up all concerned. A dimmer switch can be very useful here.

Heating

Especially for a tiny baby, the temperature must be kept even – 18°–21° Centigrade (65°–70° Fahrenheit) is about the mark. If there's no central heating, an oil-filled radiator with thermostatic control will maintain a comfortable temperature without getting too hot in itself. It's too heavy to be knocked over by the tiny baby, but not safe for bigger children, so other arrangements will have to be made as time goes on.

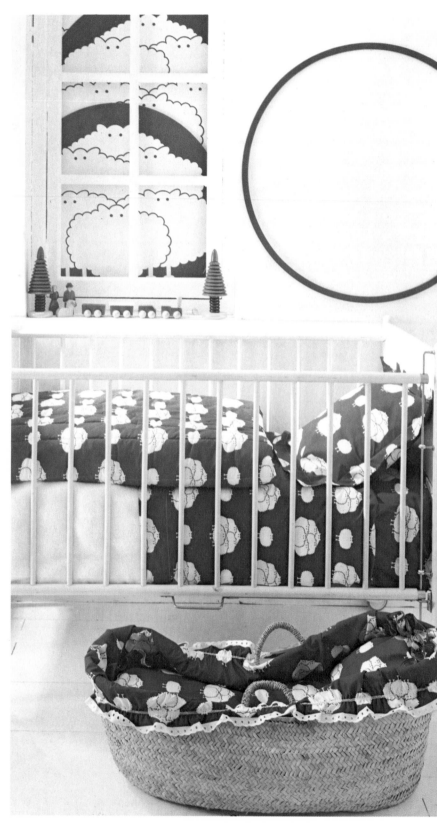

The strong colour and bold design of this Scandinavian print make a convincing case against the usual run of pretty-pretty nursery fabrics. Parents of insomniac babies please note the soporific potential of the sheep.

1

2

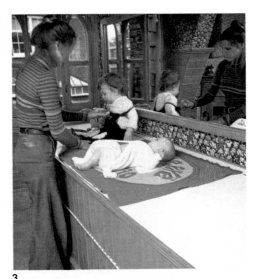

3

1 *A bright and practical nursery that will adapt to a child's needs as it grows older. There is a useful changing table at waist height which projects from the storage unit.*

2/3 *Work-top here goes over the bath at working rather than bathing level. The melamine-laminated blockboard top panel is hinged above splashback.*

4 *Bold decorations make this little attic room a cheerful nursery. The bright yellow ceiling gives a sunny glow to the whole room.*

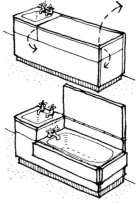

5 *There is an enormous range of cribs, ranging from traditional wicker ones to this bright, modern plastic buttercup, which can be used in later years as a decorative storage unit for toys.*

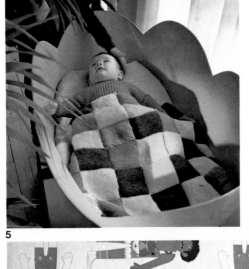

4

5

6 *A storage pillar, which opens to reveal hanging space and shelves to hold clutter and clothes.*

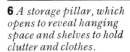

7 *A baby's-eye-view of a portable changing table cum bath, a washbasin and nappy bin, which makes this a completely self-contained nursery.*

6

7

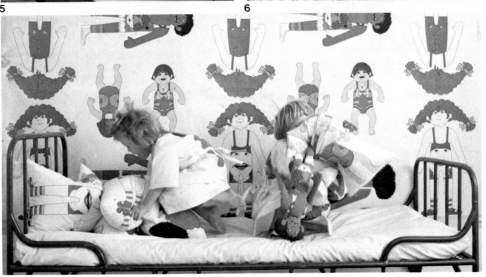

8

8 *Don't throw out an old iron bedstead, which for the price of a few coats of paint and a new mattress can look very pretty and will withstand a great deal of punishment.*

Children's rooms
4/5 Three to ten years

It's to everyone's advantage if children find their room sufficiently attractive to spend quite a lot of time there. Its position in the house may affect this, although that, of course, is usually dictated by available space. If there's a choice, remember that while closeness to the parental bedroom makes for feelings of security at night, being packed off to bed to an otherwise deserted floor of the house can create an acute sense of isolation. It may be preferable to bed young children down at the living room level – the hum of adult conversation will reassure them rather than keep them awake. Banishments like "go to your room and stay there" tend to backfire, and it is useful to get rid of the idea that healthful sleep can be obtained only in near Siberian temperatures.

Heating

Even if there's central heating, it's a good idea to have some extra form of heating in the children's room: they may need warmth when the heating for the rest of the house is turned off. A convalescent child, for instance, may need to be kept warm at a constant temperature, and not be prepared to stay under the covers.

Safety is, of course, vital. Never make do with anything portable in the heating line, anything with loose connections, frayed flexes or exposed elements, even if these are protected by a wire grid. Electric fires should be fixed high up, out of reach. Get all power points positioned out of the reach of toddlers' fingers and/or fit the type of point that needs a plug pushed in to open up the power outlet. Never allow radiators to get too hot; a burn or a nasty sore place is a horrible way of learning by experience.

A flat radiator has been boxed in with hardboard, which in turn has been painted with blackboard paint. Vents have been left to allow the heat to rise, but the structure never becomes too hot for comfort.

It's pointless spending a lot of money on decorations for young children. They won't appreciate the financial sacrifice and will feel highly indignant when you nag about scribbles and dirty marks. Cheap and cheerful wall coverings are the answer for the messy age. Modern emulsions have a plastic content which makes them durable and washable; strong, bright colours are easy to get, and they're cheap and easy to apply even over old wallpaper.

Pin-up boards

A small area covered in blackboard paint (from builders' merchants) theoretically helps to cut down scrawlings on the wall (an idea to be regarded with cynicism), but an area on which children can pin up drawings or cut-out pictures is helpful.

Wall coverings

These should be applied with dedicated paper pickers in mind: stick down all edges and joins really firmly, so that nothing can be pulled off in great nasty strips. Make a periodic check for areas that may be working off the wall.

More expensive than papers, but a good investment, are vinyl coverings. They are washable, virtually indestructible and resistant to scuffs. But buy an extra roll (this also goes for paper) for possible repairs – designs get discontinued with maddening rapidity.

A grown-up who can make a cut-out animal for the children to paint themselves would be popular. Free standing, this could be moved around like a screen to hide clutter.

Encourage the pictures but save the walls. If there's no pinboard, give them paper-hangers' paste which can be sponged off.

Furniture and accessories

Children need horizontal surfaces for drawing, painting and homework. You could make this adjustable by fixing a broad shelf on to brackets fixed into slotted metal uprights. This way, you could gradually move the whole thing higher, and a typist's adjustable chair could be lowered as the child grows up.

Scaled-down furniture makes more sense if it can be handed down from child to child – pleasant though it is, it's rather a luxury. However, low children's tables can make quite useful bedside tables for later on.

Tidiness need not mean grumbling if putting clothes away is fun: goose-pegboard, made by one imaginative handyman father tired of wading through casually discarded clothes, worked wonders; and the idea could easily be adapted to many other nursery characters.

Most toys are eventually replaced, but old favourites need not be abandoned if they are settled comfortably in baskets, tuckboxes or wall-hung storage-pockets.

Lighting

When you first plan the nursery, the chances are that you design the lighting scheme from your own rather than the children's point of view, but it is they who will ultimately benefit, or otherwise.

Lighting is too often a neglected aspect of children's rooms. Children need good light in the right places, or they're going to strain their eyes and store up lots of trouble for themselves. Obviously, you need something that turns on at the door, but it does not need to be a central fitting. It could be a wall light that also supplies a good light for reading in bed.

The switch by the door should be low enough for children to reach, so that they can pop into their room at any time. A dimmer switch is worth considering, particularly if your child likes a light to be left on at night. Older children need a good light on the surfaces they're using for hobbies and homework; wall-mounted spotlights would be fine. And those in bottom bunks tend to get the black hole of Calcutta feeling if nobody thinks about their gloomy position. Again, you could have a little clip-on spot, or a wall light, so that they can read independently of the top occupants' activities.

Clip-on lamps boost the light in this room-within-a-room, and help the users of the table top to concentrate on what they are doing.

Pendant lamp illuminates the room-dividing play and toy-storage unit.

Floors

Floors in children's rooms get filthy. Face up to that fact from the start and you are half-way to making a good choice. It's no good (and not fair) to expect that you can ever make children be careful with furnishings in their own room. So choose something that won't look sordid when messy. Smooth floor coverings such as linoleum and foam-backed vinyls are especially easy to clean thoroughly.

But children spend an awful lot of time on the floor, and might want something with a bit of softness and warmth, but still smooth so that toy cars can run easily. Some forms of cord carpeting are ideal. They are cheap, come in good colours, and you'll approach them with the assumption that you'll get rid of them when the peak years of dirty activities are over.

Sisal is more durable but hard on knees, and stains are hard to get out. The new cords made from polypropylene are a good idea: the colours are bright and spills can be mopped up easily. Cork is excellent for children's rooms, provided it is correctly sealed right from the start, before it has had any rough treatment.

Carpets are impractical, but rugs, especially cotton ones that can be washed in the machine, look and feel nice on smooth floors.

Practical flooring in children's rooms is essential. A tiled pattern lino – or vinyl in tiles – helps with the invention of games.

Hardboard, tacked down on a wooden floor, can be stained or painted to please the child. Some might like paths for cars; train enthusiasts a simulated railway track.

Beds

Good firm beds are essential to support young spines. Small-size children's beds are rather a waste of money because they are soon outgrown. However, there are several that extend and grow along with the child.

Bunk beds are a good idea if you are short of space. No child under four or five should sleep at the top; the accident statistics are frightening. Check that the ladders have smooth slats, and can be firmly fixed, preferably permanently.

All top bunks should have full-length safety rails, double ones if possible. Most bunks split into two single beds. It is a bit of an operation to stick them on top of each other during the day and separate them at night, but it is useful when the children get older and, perhaps, move into separate rooms. An alternative to bunks are beds that slide one underneath the other – a great space-saver.

Practical fathers could make a climbing frame to incorporate a platform.
Strictly for older children: the frame must be sturdy and fixed both to wall and floor.

Bunk beds are comfortable and space-saving. Many are now made so that they can be transformed into separate beds if the children move into separate rooms. Box-storage underneath can be a useful bonus.

Storage

Children are hoarders, and since you are expected to respect their possessions although not to the point of drowning in a sea of them, the best thing to do is to provide the children with sufficient storage-space to put them in.

Most bunks have storage drawers as an optional extra; very useful for blankets, toys or linen in what would otherwise just be wasted space.

Schoolchildren view with scorn bunnies decorating those small-size storage units designed especially with children in mind, and mini-cupboards and drawers are useless for coping with clothing that gets larger and bulkier every year. Anyway, a lot of things you need to store for babies are large and bulky to start with.

You'll need a certain amount of small-size storage for babies' clothes but you can provide for this with small trays and boxes. Try to make as much of your storage as possible accessible to the child; avoid handles that are out of reach, and doors and drawers that are difficult to manoeuvre. In this way you can encourage children to put away their own things. You can try, anyway. Labels for what goes where might help. You could use symbols for younger children and non-English speaking help. A good idea for storing socks, vests, jumpers and other small items is to buy coated wire trays from a stationer (the sort used for filing) and to use them on shelves, with or without a door (a roller blind could be used as a cover-up). For toys, look for big plastic boxes that stack up, or you might use huge plastic waste bins or laundry baskets into which the children themselves can "post" their belongings, making tidying up a game and not a chore.

Tidiness in children is usually only feasible if storage is easy. Plastic bins or baskets hold a lot of clutter and are quicker to use than drawers and cupboards.

Safety

Most accidents take place in the home, so it is up to parents to remove all hazards.

Open fires must have a childproof fireguard – ugly but vital, and required by law. Windows are a danger point, and a child should never be left alone in a room with an open window of the type he could climb on or fall out of. The old sash-type windows are safer than many modern ones as you can simply never open the bottom half. Children do lean against shut windows and although bars may be unsightly, an hour or two of do-it-yourself carpentry putting them up is worth it. Make sure the bars are vertical – horizontal ones merely provide footholds. Good lighting, especially on stairs, is essential, and nursery gates across the stairs are a must for children who are still unsteady on their feet. Bolts on the insides of doors, such as bathrooms are best removed – small children are adept at locking themselves in and panic when they can't undo the bolts. Free standing cupboards are another hazard – they can be toppled over by junior Tarzans.

These are a few of the many points to remember. There can be no definitive roll-call of potential accident areas because every house is different, with its own black spots that need watching. To list every eventuality is futile, particularly since safety, when all is said, is largely a matter of common sense.

In a house with stairs, a safety gate is essential once a child can crawl. Difficult to buy to the exact size, a home-made gate with narrow vertical spaces, painted to match the stairs is the answer. An old set of bannisters will serve admirably. When the gate is not in use, bolt it flush against the wall, making sure the bolts are sturdy.

Children's rooms
6/7 Furniture

1 *Scandinavian shelf and work-top unit that grows with the child by means of stacked raisers; it graduates from nappy-changing surface via nursery table to desk.*

2 *Maximum floor area, that comes up smiling no matter what, is achieved by ranging all the furniture along the walls.*

3 *Ceiling-suspended table and off-the-floor beds for multi-level nursery life.*

4 *End-to-end beds with flaps make long play-surfaces comfortable.*

5 *Double unit creates two useful hideouts from one awkward room. Central partition and ladder are bolted to ceiling and floor. Bunks are supported from ceiling, shelves by cupboard tops (below). Work-tops are cantilevered.*

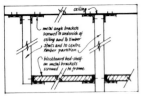

6 *Duplex apartment with platforms everywhere makes maximum use of available space – for older children only.*

7 *Shallow-shelved table support and wall tidies.*

8 *"Environmental" toys need not cost the earth. This one is not only cheap and collapsible, but stimulating to the child's imagination.*

9 *Sitting and study area – adapted dresser makes storage-seating unit (built around meshed radiator for cosiness).*

(Opposite) Play-floor (as shown earlier) obviates the need for space-consuming tables altogether.

Children's rooms
8/9 Playing and sleeping

There comes a time when it becomes clear that children, who have comfortably shared all available accommodation for years, would be happier in separate rooms. Even children of the same sex may differ enough in personality, interests and habits to become very tired of sharing.

So at this stage, provide them with bed-sitters, so that they can do their own thing in the privacy of their own room.

The best way to prevent yourself from constant worry as to the whereabouts of your older children is to make it easy for them to bring their friends home. This means arranging for conditions in which they don't have to make conversation with you all the time, so a room that isn't just a bedroom is all-desirable.

The bed will have to serve as the sofa/lounging area for entertainment purposes, and the bedcovers or counterpanes will come in for some hard wear. A spare bed – perhaps a stacking one – is a good idea to put up friends from far afield; it is one of the delights of bigger girls to have someone to stay and to giggle with.

Bedroom-type storage should, if possible, be unobtrusive, although a lot of hanging space is usually needed. Storage for smaller things could be kept low and include a surface for doing homework. Perhaps you could run a counter-height surface all along the wall and provide simple storage facilities underneath, such as a low chest of drawers, and something like a simple office filing cabinet for hobbies that need space, like stamp collecting or dressmaking.

By the time that children have reached the bed-sitter stage, they will have a taste of their own. It may be frightful, but it must be considered; to ban everything that you don't consider impeccable does not guarantee that they'll grow up with faultless tastes of their own; they're that much more likely to rebel against yours as soon as they have the opportunity.

It is also useless to expect your children to have the same feelings about neatness as you have. So don't blanch at displays of whatever they collect – just keep the door shut and realize that a tidy room is far more unnatural to most young people than an untidy one. Messiness, in any case, is a passing phase, and provided that there is enough storage space, strewn floors and heaped chairs will miraculously clear – in time. All you need is patience and understanding.

Duplex arrangement for an independent teen-ager: there is an extra bed for an overnight guest (or for an extra surface) and plenty of well-organized storage. Records and player have their own slots, and the "cave" under the top-structure is lined with shelves.

1 *Conversation well is easily arranged and adjusted according to the size of the party if soft furnishings are really soft and easily movable.*

2 *A room in which boys can be boys. Rope ladder must be very firmly fixed, to take both inhabitant's and his visitor's weight.*

3 *Storage pillar divides sleeping area from working area.*

4 *Ideal conditions for earnest concentration on games. Wall-fixed bolster stays put, unlike cushions, when room becomes bedroom.*

1

2

3

4

Children's rooms
10 Teen-age pads

Teen-agers will have very definite ideas on the kind of room they will want to call their own. Let them have a room that suits their personality and caters for their hobbies; after all, you won't be living in it and they will.

1 A pop fan lives here, and posters of her current idol adorn every inch of available wall space. The record player and guitar take pride of place and the spare upper bunk can be used either as a huge storage tray for records and mementos or to put up a friend overnight – hopefully one with similar tastes in pop stars.

2 A simple and practical desk for a teen-age room. The track-mounted light is always just where it's needed; there is a pinboard for photographs and messages, and the desk-top is wide enough and sturdy enough for a record player.

3 A peaceful haven for two quiet, studious teen-agers, with plenty of well-lit desk and table space for getting down to some serious homework.

1

2

3

Bathrooms/1

Attitudes to bathrooms have been changing. These rooms are no longer limited by Puritan traditions according to which you used them only for ablutions, if not cold baths, or groped your way through clouds of rolling steam and yards of pipes. Standards and expectations of comfort have risen dramatically. New materials like Perspex, plastics, polyurethane seals and nylon have opened up new possibilities. More important is the feeling that a bathroom should be a pleasant place where you can relax and pamper yourself.

We illustrate bathrooms large and small; some expensive and some really quite cheap; some designed with children in mind, some for bachelors. Each has its own personality which results from the owner's tastes, needs, space and funds. All show that there is more to planning a nice bathroom than arranging a bath, basin and WC neatly round a small room.

In this chapter we discuss how you might set about creating this new sort of bathroom, whether your resources stretch to planning a new one from scratch or making radical improvements to an existing one; or whether you mean to transform what is there with some deft decoration and new detailing without spending too much.

However, if you own your house, don't dismiss the idea of making improvements on the grounds of cost alone: they will materially add to the value of your property – and that includes not only bathrooms, but downstairs WC cloakrooms, basins in bedrooms, and showers.

Before you look at your bathroom in a new light, or decide to embark on making yourself a present of a new one, ask yourself the following questions:

- ☐ How many bathrooms, showers, WCs does your house need ideally?
- ☐ Will you have to make provision for old people or small children?
- ☐ Exactly what fittings and what kind of plumbing are you going to need?
- ☐ Are you planning the bathroom for other uses?
- ☐ Will you install a washing machine, work-top and extra storage?
- ☐ What sort of atmosphere do you want in your bathroom – practical, luxurious, private or social?

Warm to look at, warm to the touch, this bathroom, designed by Juliet and Peter Glynn Smith, has polyurethane-sealed cork tiles on the walls – darker to dado height, then a row of tiles, then paler cork above, topped off with a row of chequer-board. Cork tiles cover the plumbing and the basin surround. Everything is beautifully streamlined – a bidet is masked from view on the right.

Bathrooms
2/3 Basic ingredients/the fittings

Consider the fittings (bath, basin, WC, etc.) from two points of view: their actual size, shape, the space needed round them, and whether they work in practical terms for you. Then you have to think of the design and colour of the fittings. Shapes are now simpler, more streamlined and sculptural, and colours are more interesting.

The bath

British Standard sizes are basically 5 ft 6 in./1.7 m long, 2 ft 4 in./711 mm wide and between 20 in./508 mm – 24 in./610 mm high. Variations go up and down in 4 in./102 mm steps for length and width, 2 in./51 mm for height. 6 ft/1.8 m means that unless you are exceptionally tall and long-legged you can't reach the end with your feet if you want to lie back and read. The shorter lengths are useful for small spaces. Some hip baths (where you sit on one level and have your feet lower down) are only 3 ft/914 mm long. It is also possible to get baths that fit into a corner (see diagram A).

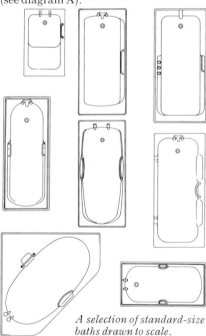

A selection of standard-size baths drawn to scale.

If your bath doubles as a shower, choose a flat-bottomed one as wide as possible – at least 26 in./660 mm wide.

Low sides look more in scale with low-ceilinged rooms. 16 in./406 mm is ideal for small bathrooms and small children. Older people find higher baths easier to get in and out of.

There are many subtle shape variations within the standard dimensions. To see if they suit you, try them – bath at friends' houses, or climb in shoeless in the showrooms!

Cast-iron and steel

Beautiful Victorian baths and, until recently, the best new baths, were made of porcelain-enamelled cast-iron. They are the most hard-wearing and good-looking of all baths. Unfortunately, these are hard to come by, as very few are made today. Vitreous enamelled steel is normally used instead.

Acrylic

Baths are moulded either out of thick acrylic sheet or synthetic resins, reinforced with glass fibre. Both kinds need a firm steel frame supplied by their makers to hold them rigid. Their light weight makes handling and transport easier and cheaper. Acrylic baths can be moulded into more varied shapes and are made in richer colours than traditional baths, often with a slip-resistant finish. They are also warm to the touch.

Minor snags: they're not so rigid even with the best of frames; although they won't chip, they do get scratched (use only liquid detergent for cleaning): they melt if a cigarette burns on them, so don't smoke in the bath!

Panels

Baths today are made to be built in. Some have panels as part of their integral design. Builders' merchants supply standard hardboard panels with chrome corners. Or you can have your own made and covered with what you want. Most panels go down to the floor, but where the bath is raised, a large drawer can fit underneath.

Tap positions

You should specify where you want your taps. Most baths have taps at the plug end, but this need not always be so (see diagram B). You save a few millimetres by putting them on the side or across the corner. Or they can sprout from the wall at the side or end – but allow for concealing the plumbing behind a false wall or having the pipes chased into the plaster.

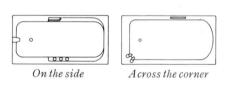

On the side   *Across the corner*

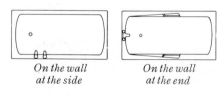

On the wall at the side   *On the wall at the end*

Handles and hand grips

These are worthwhile extras, standard on some baths, optional on others. Or attach grips to a strong wall just above the bath.

A custom-built bath

If you want a really exotic bath, you can have one tailor-made in glass-fibre or designed and built in rather like a miniature swimming pool.

Showers

There are various ways to provide a shower: (a) with the bath, (b) install a separate shower cubicle, (c) arrange for the bathroom to have a shower corner, (d) buy a ready-made unit. The crucial dimensions are the amount of room you need under the shower, and the amount you need outside to dry and dress. Shower areas vary, the most usual being 32 in./813 mm or 36 in./914 mm square. The drying/dressing area needs to be 28 in./711 mm × 36 in./914 mm if the shower is enclosed – less if it's not (see diagram C).

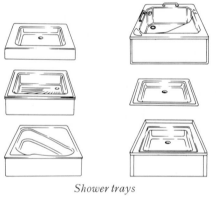

Shower trays

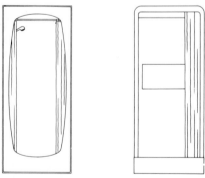

Shower cubicles

Waterproofing

The walls and floor of the shower area must be properly waterproofed. Ideally, the ceiling, too, because there is so much steam and condensation when you take a shower.

Shower controls

Take care to choose the correct shower fittings. The head, where the water comes out, should be movable. It can be fixed to the wall, or it can come on a flexible lead with two or three fixing points. Or you can simply hold it. Water temperature is controlled by a mixer valve which you set. Because a change in water pressure changes the balance of hot/cold in the shower, and as there is only a small difference between being comfortable or scalded, it's worth fitting an expensive thermostatically controlled mixer valve. Then the temperature remains constant. That's important if children use the shower. If the shower unit is part of the bath taps, look for one which automatically turns itself back to "bath" after "shower". You can then avoid those unwanted showers as you turn on the bath.

Finally, you must have enough pressure or head of water. The head of the shower has to be at least 3 ft/914 mm below the bottom of the cold water tank. If this isn't possible you'll need an electric pump attached to the shower to boost the water pressure (see diagram D).

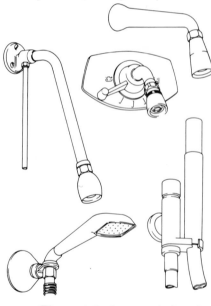

Thermostatic shower controls and shower heads.

Plugs, overflows, etc.

There is a certain amount of choice here. Many built-in showers and shower trays just have a drain. If you want to use the shower tray to double as a bath for small children, you can specify a plug, in which case it is wise to specify an overflow. The drain/plug positions vary, too, so match up to your waste with the minimum of extra pipework.

*A beautiful exercise in streamlining – one continuous surface takes a drop-in basin,
an access flap to the lavatory cistern, then turns into a shelf above the boxed-in
plumbing. Access to stopcocks and cisterns is behind the mosaic panel beside the bidet.*

Bathrooms
4/5 Basic ingredients/the fittings

So many different basins are made now that almost any space can be provided with a basin to fit. Think in terms of the space you have and what you want the basin for. 24 in./610 mm × 16 in./406 mm is adequate for hair washing. A tiny basin projecting only 6 in./152 mm is just big enough for hand washing. For laundry work, get the largest basin possible; even a sink in the bathroom can be practical.

Basins are made in various materials: fireclay, vitreous china, vitreous enamelled steel, acrylic, even marble. Some of the new rounded shapes are very elegant, but the neatest thing in basic design is the Vanitory unit, where the basin is set in a work-top with shelves, cupboards or drawers underneath. Pipes are concealed, and the top, in any reasonably waterproof finish, terrazzo, tiles, Formica, hardwood, lino, vinyl, is invaluable for make-up/shaving gear, or for changing the baby.

Basins

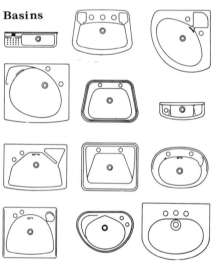

Siting the basin

32 in./813 mm is a good compromise between the best height for washing hands and washing hair or face. Allow space in front of the basin. You need around 28 in./700 mm for hair washing.

With poor walls it is safer to choose a pedestal basin.

Wastes

Basins come with pop-up or cheaper plug-and-chain wastes. A chrome trap, unless concealed, looks smarter than a plastic one.

Taps

Some firms who make sanitary ware also make taps, but there are also specialist tap-makers. If you choose your taps separately they seem to cost a disproportionate amount.

Choice is between shapes (whether you like them, whether they are comfortable to use) and quality (some are more carefully finished than others). Most are chrome-finished on a brass base, some are gold-plated! There have been efforts to produce good plastic taps or at least plastic tops, some of which have not lasted so well in use as the traditional chrome ones.

Mixer taps are often used in baths and basins. They are particularly useful when you just want to wash your hands under running water, or, of course, for hair washing. There is even a thermostatically controlled tap which maintains the water at a pre-determined temperature. It's good with children.

Taps

A,B,C Showertaps with thermostatic controls.

D Mixer taps for bath with shower attachment.

F Nozzle on/off tap for hand washing.

E Concealed bath mixer taps with pop-up waste.

G,H,I Alternative shapes for bath or basin taps.

If you never want to change washers, choose taps with ceramic cartridges which don't have washers. A special check valve at least means you don't have to shut off the water at the mains. You can get the same result by having a stopcock fitted to the supply pipes to each tap. Even if you only do this to the hot taps, it saves having to drain the hot water system before replacing a worn washer.

Anti-splash rim

If your family is messy, there are basins with a lip along the inside which prevents the water from slopping.

WCs

Although a WC with cistern is seldom more than 28 in./711 mm from front to back and 16 in./406 mm across, you have to allow at least 4 ft 8 in./1.4 m × 28in./711 mm floor area if you are not going to feel cramped using it. But the cistern

and the pan can be tucked under a sloping ceiling, for instance, with full ceiling height in front only. This way WCs can be fitted into small spaces under stairs. The height of the pan itself is usually 16 in./406 mm, which is a compromise between the ideal heights for sitting users and standing ones. But many manufacturers make pans 12 in./305 mm, 14 in./356 mm and 15 in./381 mm high.

Types of WC

If you choose your pan and cistern as one unit you can have them close-coupled or with the cistern a little higher on the wall. If you choose them separately, you can have the cistern either high or low.

WCs

A Conventional WC suite.

B Close coupled WC suite.

C Slim-line cistern.

D High-level cistern.

E WC with concealed cistern.

F,G Cantilevered WCs with concealed cisterns.

Most WCs can turn to right or left or go straight back into their waste and soil pipe: you can specify which when you order. Some flush by depending on the flush of water to wash waste away, while others have a siphonic action in the pan itself. The cantilevered WC is fixed to the wall and rests on invisible brackets which go under the floor finish. A compromise is a WC which has a minimal part of it resting on the floor – this just has wall fixings rather than brackets. Both have to have their cisterns concealed behind strong false walls, and you have to provide access to them.

Cisterns

Another recent design improvement is the slim, plastic cistern: the slimmest projects only 4½ in./114 mm from front to back, and can be used to replace an old high-level cistern without moving the whole pan and plumbing forward. They can be ordered with special top-fixed handles so that they can be boxed in.

Seats

Some manufacturers provide seats specifically designed to fit their pans, but often you have to buy the seat separately. They are mostly made of plastic nowadays. If you envisage using the WC as a seat (while bathing children for example) or for standing on to reach light fittings, choose the most expensive rigid plastic you can find. For good quality fittings choose nylon ones. Cheaper plastics are liable to snap, and brass ones to corrode.

Bidets

These take up the same floor area as the WC: 28 in./711 mm from the front of the bidet to the wall; but in practice you need a further 24 in./610 mm in front, and an overall width of at least 28 in./711 mm. The height is also usually the same as the WC – 16 in./406 mm. If you have both, they look better if they match in style and dimensions. The cheapest and simplest just have taps, over-flow and a plug waste. Expense mounts as a flushing rim, pop-up waste and spray mechanism are added. Although the dimensions don't vary much, it is worth getting the largest possible bidet.

Bidets

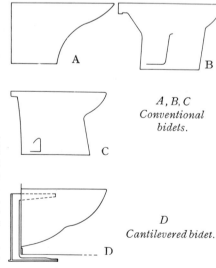

A, B, C Conventional bidets.

D Cantilevered bidet.

Alternative styles and shapes of bidets.

1 *Before you decide to rip out old fittings and modernize, consider whether all you really need to make bathtime a pleasure would be good modern heating. Here, a few coats of crisp white paint have given a new lease of life to a pretty, old-fashioned bath-tub.*

2 *In this Californian bathroom with an uninterrupted view of hills and woodland, wide oak planking is used for the walls, ceiling and huge bath, which has been given a coating of epoxy resin.*

3 *Built-in soap dishes keep soap dry and leave the sides of the bath free of clutter.*

4 *A collection of stream-lined, matching ware making the best use of a small bathroom.*

5 *Luxurious circular bath in actor Christopher Plummer's bedroom has a wide marble surround and theatrical lighting effects from the circular diffused ceiling light. The lavatory is encased in a steel tube to the left of the picture.*

6 *A Vanitory unit with a circular basin has been slotted into a recess in this tiled bathroom. A thermostatically controlled mixer tap is set into the back panel which conceals all the plumbing.*

7 *Shower cabinets are one way to squeeze an extra wash-place into a crowded home, as they can slot on to landings or into a corner of a bedroom – like this one – where it takes up less space than a wardrobe.*

8 *Not a bathroom, but a room with a bath, which projects into the centre of the room, and is inset into a tiled island – somewhere to park soap, towels, sponges, loofahs and everything associated with bathtime.*

1

2

3

4

5

6

7

8

Bathrooms
6/7 The plumbing basics/the space basics

Two things will regulate the plumbing. One is the Building Regulations which have been evolved to ensure plumbing of an acceptable standard of quality and hygiene; the other is the cost of the work.

In England in recent years the Building Regulations have changed to make the installation of bathrooms easier. Internal bathrooms and WCs with no outside window are now permitted, provided there is the approved amount of mechanical ventilation to the outside. Drains and pipes can run inside instead of outside the house. Walls between bathrooms or WCs and bedrooms or living-rooms can be light partition walls instead of solid ones, which makes it cheaper to steal space from a room to make a bathroom.

Rules about ventilated lobbies have also been eased. At one time no WC was allowed to open off a habitable room or kitchen without a ventilated lobby in between; that is, a small space with either an opening of its own to the outside, or a duct to the outside. This rule is usually relaxed for open-plan living quarters, where definitions of rooms don't apply.

It is permitted to have a WC opening directly off a bedroom. provided there is either another WC in the home or another entrance to it not through the bedroom. All blueprints must, of course, be checked by the Public Health authorities when you make your planning application.

Other regulations refer to the quality of the fittings, which the manufacturers should take care of. Also the qualities and dimensions of drains, soil pipes, stacks, septic tanks, cesspits and even earth closets, a good builder will clear these details with the authorities. You need worry only if you are employing direct labour. But do bear these regulations in mind when planning any new bathroom or renovation, and don't forget to include drains and cesspits in your budget.

The high costs of plumbing make it worthwhile getting a really streamlined solution for bathrooms. This can make the difference between a job you can afford and one you can't.

The service core

The architect's concept of a "service core" or "plumbing wall" is one to aim for. And the cheapest – because with a service core you have all your services (like drains, hot and cold water, electricity) in one duct. Pipe runs are short. Everything is accessible. It can work in new houses and also in old terrace houses: there you can use one of the recesses of the chimney breasts to carry all services up to the house and steal space from the

middle of the floor to sneak in an internal bathroom or WC at whatever levels you want them.

With a plumbing wall you back all the rooms needing water supplies and drains up against each other (usually kitchen on one side and a bathroom or two on the other) and run all the pipes and drains within that wall. This is very often how blocks of flats are planned, and is a good principle to bear in mind if you are converting a house into flats.

Keeping down the costs

Plumbing costs are high because a plumber's time and his materials are expensive. Plastics have revolutionized things like drains and external gutters, but it still has disadvantages when used for supply pipes.

You can cut down plumbing costs in various ways by careful planning. Here are a few ideas:

Bringing water to the bathrooms and cloakrooms. The nearer these rooms are to the source of supply, the better. Cold water has to come down the house from the tank, but hot water comes from the cylinder, and bathrooms and cylinders should ideally be placed in close relation to themselves with not too long a pipe run to the boiler or other source of hot water.

Taking away waste. Most houses have their waste run into one main drain or a drain leading to a septic tank or cesspit. The wastes from the WC, basins, baths and kitchen sinks all eventually go into this drain, so obviously it is cheaper to site kitchen and bathrooms on the same side of the house.

WCs also need a soil stack to disperse fumes and smells. Two or more WCs can share the same stack if they are sited correctly in the house.

Pipes in the bathrooms. The modern technology is to box in and conceal pipes. This in itself is not cheap. If you plan the individual bathrooms with the minimum of pipe runs possible, you can make savings here.

Wastes in the bathroom. These have to *slope gently* down until they get to the main downpipe. They can't cross a floor horizontally and you should bear this in mind when siting an internal bathroom disgorging into an external waste. Baths also need a trap under the plug hole (like sinks and basins) and this means there has to be an extra 4 in./102 mm below the bath. This is usually easily fitted in between the floor of the bathroom and the ceiling of the room below, but not, for instance, if the ceiling below has exposed beams, or is very shallow. The bath then has to be raised.

Heads of water. The cold water

tank must be above all installations. For showers and bidets, its base must be 3 ft/914 mm above the shower head or taps respectively. You save on piping and plumbing if the cold tank is immediately above the bathrooms/WCs.

Overflows. These used to stick out of the wall at random: landladies could always hear when tenants had too full a bath. You are now allowed to plumb overflows from baths and cisterns back into their own wastes. This is sensible and avoids soaking the brickwork of the walls, which is often the beginning of dry rot.

Access. This should be provided to tanks, pipes and stopcocks.

Space basics

When you have decided what fittings you want in a bathroom/cloakroom, and considered the plumbing in the house, the question of space arises. At this stage, the easiest way to solve problems is to make a scale plan with doors and windows indicated, cut out scale diagrams of the fittings, and do a jigsaw (see Co-ordination). There are a number of ways of arranging two or three applian-

Bathroom layouts

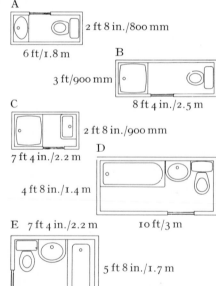

A

2 ft 8 in./800 mm

6 ft/1.8 m

B

3 ft/900 mm

8 ft 4 in./2.5 m

C

2 ft 8 in./900 mm

7 ft 4 in./2.2 m

D

4 ft 8 in./1.4 m

E   7 ft 4 in./2.2 m   10 ft/3 m

5 ft 8 in./1.7 m

Plans A, B and C have been chosen to show how two appliances can be fitted into the smallest possible area. Doors should preferably be sliding or outward opening.

Plans D ana E show two bathrooms with the conventional appliances (bath, basin and WC) fitted into a compact arrangement, with economic pipe runs, and good wall-space for towel rails, etc.

ces with allowance for the minimum space you will need between the fittings to use them comfortably.

To provide one child with shower and basin the minimum size of 3 ft/914 mm × 5 ft 4 in./1.6 m could do. A downstairs WC with a small basin, opening off a place to hang coats, can be 2 ft 8 in./813 mm × 5 ft 4 in./1.6 m, or even 4 ft 4 in./1.3 m. But the moment more than one person is to use the room at one time, or small children have to be supervised, you need to allow extra space.

One useful space-saver is to change the door from opening inwards to opening outwards, or even to a sliding door. Or hang two half-width doors (Mississippi steam-boat style).

What is striking when you make scale plans is how often it is possible to steal sufficient space off a bedroom to make a second bathroom. Or to find a corner for the very useful downstairs WC in halls and lobbies.

Building on

If you can't fit in your bathrooms, you sometimes have no choice but to add on. This will involve you in the extra expense of new foundations, walls and roof, and you will have to go through the rigmarole of getting Planning Permission. Prefabricated units (pod bathrooms) are usually more suited to multiple projects such as hotels or large-scale housing schemes. But there are new developments in this field which are simpler to install. At the moment it may be cheaper to get your own built.

---

1 *A small bathroom symmetrically planned for maximum use. The stainless steel bath matches the wash-basins which are, in fact, small kitchen sinks.*

---

2 *The luxury of a sunken bath – the floor has been raised to the level of the top of the bath, and covered in studded rubber. The hot-water system and the plumbing are under the platform, with a warm air heater. Grilles are set into the risers of the steps.*

---

3 *A central bath makes a room look less like a bathroom. This one has been boxed in with white tiles to hide all the plumbing for the waste and the taps.*

---

4 *Easy-to-copy idea for a bathroom that is going to be used by growing children. The adjustable board is held in place by battens firmly fixed to the wall and slotted into the bath surround.*

---

5 *Tiny space under the stairs has been fitted out with a basin, mirror and good lighting to provide guests with a place to wash and brush up.*

1

2

3

4

5

Bathrooms
8/9 Floor/walls

It is just as important to budget for finishes as for the plumbing and fittings. You will need to allow nearly as much again for this work.

Floor finishes

The floor should be as waterproof as possible. A damp-proof concrete floor presents no problems, but make sure that the builder uses the right adhesive for the floor-covering you have chosen. A wooden floor needs additional preparation. An expensive solution is to lay a concrete sub-floor on a damp-proof membrane in place of the original floor. It is usually enough to put down a sub-floor on top of the original floor (and a damp-proof membrane) and lay the new floor on that. The best sub-floor is marine ply, but you can use hardboard.

The joins between floor and walls or floor and fittings must be made as waterproof as possible. This is always a problem, as the various surfaces and materials move and expand or shrink at different rates. Coving, where the floor runs up the wall a little way, is the best solution between floor and walls or bath panels, storage units, or boxed-in pipes. Between fittings themselves and walls or tiles, there seems to be no perfect solution except to use one of the proprietary compounds for the purpose, and renew it as it cracks or shrinks.

Cheaper finishes include vinyl, in sheet or tiles, either plain or with special foam backings. Also lino in sheet or tiles, but it shouldn't be polished because this makes it slippery.

Inexpensive fitted carpet ought to be in a non-rot synthetic fibre with its own foam or rubber backing, but *not* jute. Otherwise you must check frequently that the jute backing is not rotting, and replace when necessary. Rush matting makes a cheap temporary finish for a damp concrete floor.

Medium price finishes include cork or the more expensive vinyl-topped cork (see Floors), also non-slip rubber tiles, and Flotex, an all-nylon plush pile invention (available only through a floor contractor).

Expensive finishes include tiles, terrazzo and expensive deep-pile nylon carpet. These materials themselves are costly and need professional laying, which can cost as much again. Once again, carpet must have a rubber backing, otherwise it will rot. Tiles must be laid on a properly prepared floor. Terrazzo is made and polished on the spot and can be laid only on a concrete sub-floor This is expensive but it does make the most beautiful hose-down floor, ideal for family bathrooms, and can be under-floor heated.

Wall finishes

You give yourself a greater choice if you differentiate between the walls that are going to get splashed a lot and those that 'aren't. Splashed walls are those surrounding shower cubicles about 8 in./205 mm above the bath – or shower height if it is to double as a shower – and behind the basin

Cheap waterproof walls: For small areas, white tiles. Clear Perspex sheet over wallpaper or paint.

Medium price waterproof walls: Plastic laminate, but it is hard to waterproof joints. Flotex, Cork.

Expensive waterproof walls: Tiles, which don't have to be as thick as floor tiles – $\frac{1}{8}$ in./3 mm rather than $\frac{1}{4}$ in./6 mm – or mosaics. Glass or mirror, but, like Formica, the joints are hard to waterproof. Other walls not directly in the splashing area can be treated normally.

Cheap ordinary finishes: Plastic emulsion paints are easy to put on, cheap to touch up and come in lots of colours. Tougher but still with a matt finish are the new silk vinyl paints. If you have a condensation problem, gloss paints will aggravate it, so keep gloss for woodwork. Cheap wallpapers can be protected if necessary with Perspex or a coat of sealer or varnish.

Medium to expensive wall finishes: Vinyl wallpapers or more expensive waterproof wallpapers. Panelling is a good solution for bad walls provided there are enough firm places to fix the battens on which to mount it. Tongue-and-groove pine or panelling survives well in bathrooms, sealed, stained or painted gloss white. Softwood is inclined to "move", but cedar panelling is more stable than most – and more expensive.

Woodwork is traditionally finished in gloss paint; it could also be sealed or stained. Work-tops, for Vanitory units, can be finished in plastic, laminate, hardwood, tiles, or marble.

---

1 *All-in-one bathroom on different levels has a basic wooden framework. The bath and basin unit are covered in flat sheets of sponge rubber.*
Inside-out foam rubber gives the bath surround and floor a knobbly texture. Rubber used in this way should have a high plastic content and a waterproof coating, otherwise it will rot.

2 *Tongue-and-groove timber panelling is an attractive way of covering up shabby walls and festoons of pipes. After filling the joints with waterproofing this timber has been treated with a white stain to take out the bright yellow look and then coated with waterproof polyurethane.*

1

2

1 *Don't rush to plaster stone walls. They look splendidly primitive in hot climates, Elsewhere you need to be sure the central heating is effective.*

2 *Suitably watery pop art by Mediocre Murals covers the whole of the far end of this bathroom. The wall fixed light becomes a centre point.*

3 *A small slot of a bathroom, made rich and glowing with dark cork tiles on all the walls. Note how the mirror fits exactly into the recess so that the reflection of the wall continues unbroken.*

4 *A very tailored use of pine panelling. The narrow strip of floor-to-ceiling mirror carries the ceiling and floor line right through.*

5 *An attic conversion. The terra-cotta tiles are lozenge-shaped and the detailing of the step round the bath runs on to make a window-sill.*

6 *Marbled wallpaper costs less than marbled plastic laminates, and looks more exciting. If not ready-coated, spray on a layer of sealer against steam and scuffs.*

7 *More wood. Rugged pitch pine boards on the walls, and a stainless steel basin dropped into a sealed cedar slab.*

8 *This bathroom floor slopes gently towards the central drain, doubling as a shower tray. Coving prevents water from getting into the cracks.*

9 *Caramel tiles and crochet-pattern carpet tie together the various elements in this neat attic conversion.*

Bathrooms
10/11 Open storage and concealment

One of the advantages of a good plumbing system is that the pipe runs which show are minimal. The aim of modern bathroom design is to have no pipes showing at all, so many fittings are designed for concealed plumbing.

1 *Walls faced with riven slate make a marvellous foil for the brilliant colours of modern bathroom ware. The twin basins are sunk into a unit which conceals the plumbing and provides a sunken area for plants.*

2 *Boxed-in bath makes the best use of a small awkwardly shaped bathroom unified by an all-over covering of cork bought by the yard.*

3 *There is more to building in a bath than a hardboard panel along the side. Baths without tap fittings have all the plumbing built into the wall.*

4 *Tiny bathroom covered in tiles. The plumbing is hidden behind a false wall built out to form a reveal for the window.*

5 *White tiles form a simple, continuous shape that hides all the pipes no one wants to see, and displays to good advantage a collection of plants.*

6 *Horizontal tongue-and-groove boarding, painted a glossy white, boxes in the bath and makes a false wall behind the basin to hide the pipes.*

7 *A fireplace has been blocked in and the plumbing and recesses streamlined behind hardboard panelling faced with dark cork tiles.*

8 *A patchwork of old tiles collected from demolition sites and junk shops by designer Jan Pienkowski. The basin has been plumbed into a marble-topped washstand.*

1

2

3

4

5

6

7

8

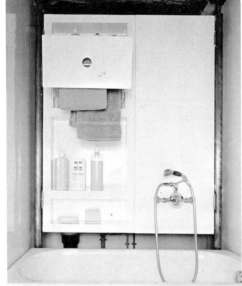

1-2

3-4

5-6

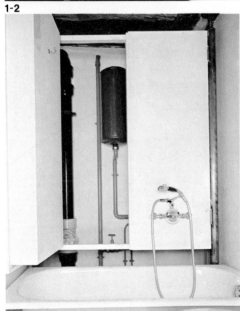

1-2 *A portable, compact bathroom, which could be installed in a building that can't be touched structurally. The same system works too for anyone proposing to rig up a temporary bathroom in a warehouse or barn. Wall panels and bath are supported by scaffolding with adjustable floor and ceiling clamps. The plumbing is hidden in the storage unit.*

3-4 *A trap door above the bath opens up to reveal a washing line which can be hauled up into the attic space above by a rope and pulley system. An ingenious idea for anyone living on a top-floor with nowhere for an outside line.*

5-6 *A wall of neat cupboards. The louvred doors allow air to reach the gas water heater and heat from the radiator to get out into the room. Solid doors prevent dust getting into the airing cupboard, which is warmed by the radiator below. Flush ring pulls are sensible in constricted areas like bathrooms, as they don't stick out and bruise people.*

Bathrooms
12/13 Lighting/ventilation

The thing people complain of most about internal bathrooms is that they are gloomy places. Nine times out of ten this is the fault of poor lighting. It also shows that you should regard windows, as a valuable asset, rather than obliterating all trace of them with severely frosted glass and layer upon layer of net curtaining.

Lighting

All bathroom lighting, but especially lighting in internal bathrooms, has to be well thought out. You need a general light, plus very good light for shaving and make-up if you do that in the bathroom. And don't forget light to read by if you like to read in the bath.

Some of the most successful lighting for bathrooms is created by indirect rather than direct light sources: bounce light off a white ceiling, conceal strip lights behind battens, use mirrors to reflect light. Where ceilings are low, choose flush recess fittings so that you don't hit them while drying.

Lighting can also create focal points, which is particularly important in an internal bathroom to make up for the lack of windows; it can even be used to create a fake window effect.

Safety

Safety for all electrical fittings in a bathroom is something you must not ignore. There are a number of regulations about the use of electricity here: shaver sockets have to be low powered fittings: lampholders for lights have to have an extended cover to prevent direct contact with the live part: lights have to have pull switches: heavy machinery (immersion heaters and washing machines) has to be fixed permanently into a socket with warning lights: infra-red fires have to be out of reach of a person standing in the bath. This is because a wet, naked person is far more vulnerable to a fatal electric shock than a dry, fully-clothed one. So all wiring should be done by a good electrician, and not on the cheap. Catalogues usually indicate which fittings are suitable for bathrooms: if in doubt check with the manufacturer. Everything must be properly earthed. When siting electrical fittings, avoid placing them near areas which are likely to suffer from condensation or damp.

Windows

Windows add another dimension to a room, as well as providing ventilation. Unless there is a real lack of privacy try to make the most of them. Early-morning sun streaming in to a light, airy bathroom is one of the greatest pleasures in life.

Ventilation

If you have an internal bathroom, Building Regulations dictate the size of fan and duct to the outside. It is worth finding ways to cut down noise and vibration.

Extractor fans

Even if you have a bathroom with a window, sometimes some extra ventilation is needed, especially if there is a shower. An extractor fan often helps: firms who make them will advise on size, and it always pays to choose the largest they suggest.

A refinement which is particularly welcome where the only WC is in the family bathroom is a mechanical ventilation unit wired into the light-switch. It turns on automatically when you put on the light and mechanically wafts away smells. This is much more efficient than scented sprays and deodorizing.

Heating

Good heating, like ventilation, cuts down condensation as well as making the bathroom a nicer place. A bathroom temperature of 72°F–75°F is pleasingly un-Puritan.

One way of achieving this is for the bathroom to be on the same central heating system as the rest of the house. This is fine in winter but in summer it leaves you short on ways of drying towels.

Alternatively you can have a radiator which works off the hot water system in the bathroom, but the bathroom needs to be close to the hot water cylinder for this to work. Or an electrically-heated towel rail, which will heat a small bathroom but not a large one. Possibly the best solution is an electrically-heated towel rail as well as central heating.

Infra-red heaters need to be turned on at least half an hour before you go into the bathroom and can only be expected to heat up small rooms.

Finally, under-floor heating is exceedingly pleasant – especially if you are in the habit of doing your exercises in the bathroom.

---

1 *Porthole shutter, mirrored on both sides, reflects the daylight when open, and works as a mirror open or closed. Lights are four downlighters fixed to the wall at right angles.*

---

2 *A mirror under a roof light immediately adds to the brightness. Note the high spout on the basin, which is perfect for hair-washing.*

---

3 *A battery of 40 watt round bulbs looks doubly effective when the light is reflected by rich, glossy paint.*

Everything adds up to make this streamlined bathroom look restful and spacious – bath and shower compartments are the same height ; one warm tone has been used for the tiles over all the walls, rather than little bits of contrast here and there. Vertical louvre blinds provide a softer, warmer light than venetian blinds, and even better privacy, because they filter light through the slats themselves. The spillring downlighter in the ceiling throws down a beam of light, but the bulb itself remains virtually invisible.

Bathrooms
14/15 Adding personality

Think of what makes you relax physically and feel at ease; after all, the bathroom is where you take care of yourself physically. To look and feel your best afterwards, your bathroom should be a sympathetic place.

If you find harsh, garish colours oppressive, avoid them. If plain white does nothing for you, don't have it. Choose colours you and your family will feel comfortable with.

How do you respond to scents? All the unguents, bath salts, and soaps, that usually live in bathrooms, can help you feel at ease.

What about your reactions to sound? Eliminate all functional sounds like dripping taps, knocking pipes, or gurgling cisterns. They are all curable. Add your own as you like: but if you want to listen to the radio or cassettes in the bath, plan a safe, dry place for them.

Pleasant accessories

Although the atmosphere of your bathroom will be helped tremendously by good heating and intelligent lighting, floor finishes and wall finishes play their part. They will to some extent dictate the colour scheme.

Careful accessorizing rather than a quick trip to the nearest ironmonger can contribute a lot to the final effect. Things to consider are:

Mirrors. Essential for shaving and making-up, bathroom mirrors are very decorative. As a wall covering they are expensive but do more than anything to lighten and brighten an internal bathroom or enlarge a small one.

For steamy bathrooms, there are plastic mirrors, vacuum-coated with aluminium to minimize misting up; and silver coated acrylic ones which can be cut by sawing, and come in a wide range of sizes and colours. They are much cheaper but not as good as glass.

Matching sets of towels and flannels in good strong colours revive a dreary bathroom. If you do your washing at home or at a launderette, you need to allow only one bath towel per person and a few extra for guests.

Small fittings. Soap dishes, racks, toothbrush holders and all the other little things that clutter bathrooms are now being designed in sets. Good storage means that most of them are no longer necessary. Soap dishes are best built-in: most tile manufacturers make them on the same module as their tiles. If these small fittings all have the same style, they help a bathroom scheme; if they don't they can simply give an impression of clutter and mess.

Plants. Some potted plants positively thrive in the slightly steamy atmosphere of a bathroom providing they have enough light. Philodendrons, ficus elastica (rubber plant), Tradescantia and Begonia Rex are all good choices, provided the room is not overheated.

Doors, furniture, handles, etc. These should also be of the same style. You may think it worth while to sacrifice Victorian locks and bolts for one of the small neat vacant/engaged fittings which can be opened from the outside in case of an emergency.

Shower curtains. There is no need to accept as final the choice offered by the local department store. You may be lucky if you want a standard length 6 ft/ 1.8 m and the standard widths for baths or showers. But there are many alternatives such as PVC coated fabric from furnishing or dress fabric departments, plain cheap plastic lining for the inside, and on the outside, virtually any material – perhaps to match curtains or wallpaper. Even a printed sheet might do. Plain unbleached cotton makes an excellent shower curtain. You can hang shower curtains from curtain rails (two rails if you want a double thickness) or from chrome bars across the top of the shower cubicle: either way, there are various methods of hooking the plastic to the rings or runners without tearing it: for example, use a belt hole punch for the curtain, with hooks; or plastic hooks and hoods designed to hold fabric which need no heading tapes at all.

1 *Collages, press cuttings and political posters make this bathroom into an interesting art gallery. Brightly coloured towels that complement the colour scheme can also be an attractive wall decoration.*

2 *If the room is virtually no bigger than a corridor, mirror will multiply the size by as many times as there are walls covered with it. The steam-loving plant is a large and shiny-leaved philodendron.*

3 *One way to give a tall, narrow bathroom a dazzling new look – fill in the area between tiles and ceiling with one-inch-square mirror tiles. The owner of this bathroom has gone even further with a silvery array of mirrors, mirrored vases and boxes which tie the whole scheme together.*

4 *One way to make sure there's plenty of room for drying all the towels in the house is to get a metal-worker to make you a long serpentine tube: with some ingenuity, a plumber could even incorporate it into the central heating system, making it into a heated towel rail.*

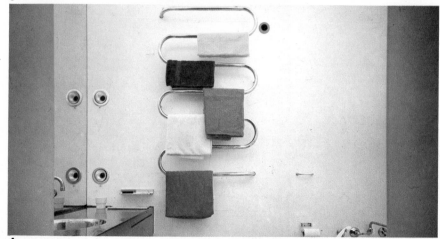

1

2

3

4

1 *Focal point here is made up from panels of tinted acrylic mirror glass mounted over the bath which won't mist up when the atmosphere gets steamy.*

2 *Panels of engraved sand-blasted pub glass, lacy curtains and a deep-pile red carpet makes bathtime an Edwardian luxury.*

3 *Streamlined and smooth with rounded corners, the shower alcove is built on to the end of the bath. Two fluorescent tubes are concealed behind an acrylic diffuser panel set above the bath and basin unit.*

4 *Tiny bathroom designed by Conran Associates that has everything – bath, shower, basin, WC and bidet. The fittings are of solid mahogany treated with bar-top lacquer to prevent the wood warping or splitting. Mirrored walls on three sides make the room look larger and reflect the patterned wallpaper on the end wall.*

Bathrooms
16 Improvements

Dark, poky internal bathrooms: These usually need a re-think of their lighting. Try mirror surfaces for reflection, and perhaps a few plants to give an airy, outdoor impression.

Builder's pastel suite and matching tiles: Replace tiles with others at key points (round bath, basin and shower). Use bright paints or wallpaper. Choose towels and bathmats in dark, rich variations of the suite colour – navy or purple with pastel blue; brown or deep gold with primrose yellow.

Walls in bad condition: If it's just old plaster, face it with tongue-and-groove pine panelling. If the walls are damp, it's cheapest in the long run to cure the damp and then start afresh.

Large cold bathroom: Put in heating, or double up what is already there. Take up some of the draughty space with useful cupboards.

1 *An ordinary white bath cheered up with new tiles and surrounded by the display of a plate collection.*

2 *A coat of bright paint covers the wall and the tangle of pipes. A lack of storage space is solved by fixing shelves across the window.*

3 *Dramatic floor-length curtain for a utilitarian, white-tiled bathroom.*

4 *A splash of colour is the easiest way to brighten things up.*

5 *A collage of pictures cut from magazines is a simple and effective way to brighten any wall.*

6 *Another collage: maps of far away places to induce bathtime daydreams.*

7 *A check pattern of vinyl tiles on the floor and round the bath is balanced by a frieze of ceramic tiles around the walls The recessed end of the bath makes a shaver cabinet.*

8 *The top of a boxed-in lavatory cistern is turned into a bookshelf for browsers.*

9 *Simple shelf units display a collection of pretty bathroom paraphernalia.*

10 *An oddly shaped bathroom becomes a flexible visual experience. Row upon row of hooks hung at random with anything that takes the owner's fancy.*

11 *Glossy brown paint from floor to ceiling is accented with yellow.*

12 *Un-bathroomy wallpaper, shelving unit and light fitting make for an elegant, restful atmosphere.*

Details that count/1

When Arne Jacobsen built St Catherine's College at Oxford, he not only designed the building and landscaped the grounds, but he also designed the furniture and fittings, right down to the knives and forks and salt cellars. When you visit the college, whatever your reaction to the building itself, it strikes you as all of a piece: everything contributes to the architect's idea.

In the same way all the components contribute to the style of your house. But while you may be confident about colour schemes, soft furnishings and furniture, and while you probably know just where to go to buy the china, kitchen things, bath towels and lampshades, and while you might possibly be able to select good antiques, interesting bric-a-brac and paintings in a salesroom, you are a rare person if you can pick your way through the so far uncharted chaos of ironmongery and come up with a well-balanced selection of door knobs, locks, bolts, window fittings, hooks, cupboard fixtures, hinges, light switches, latches and shelf brackets.

Yet these are details which do count, not just in what they contribute to the style and feeling of the whole house, or any intrinsic value they might have, but also in convenience, ease of use, smooth working over the years with the minimum repair and maintenance.

This is why it is worth considering carefully what you would like and working out conscientiously how to get it. Otherwise you know the scene: just as you are dashing out, the builder comes up to you with a catch in his hand. "This do for the bedroom cupboards?" he asks cheerfully. You have no time except to agree. Or, the electrician comes with his own supply of switches and sockets, and unless you have already ordered or got the ones you like, you use his or the job is held up.

The ironmongery business is still organized on Victorian lines, though unfortunately many of the products have lost their Victorian charm. Even if the manufacturing firms are large (but most aren't) the suppliers are usually small concerns, many of the goods unbranded and the distribution erratic. There are some majestic specialist shops left, whose goods are more often than not in boxes, and out of sight: you have to know what you want to benefit from their stock.

So you don't have an architect to advise you (let alone design for you), how can you start?

New way with door furniture – clean new designs are now being produced in nylon-plastic in bright and beautiful colours, simple and sophisticated shapes.

Details that count
2/3 Choosing ironmongery

For ironmongery which shows, your first step is to decide which "family" or style suits your house. We show the main ones here. Family members include door and drawer knobs, doorstops, latches, door-knockers, locks, hinges, letterboxes, door-plates, handles, brackets and hooks.

Contemporary

If your house or conversion is modern in fact or feeling, the Modric range is an instant solution. Is it surprising to discover that one of its designers, Knud Holscher, was site architect at St Catherine's? The hidden achievement of this range is not only the large number of items in it, not that they fit together in style and size, but that their finish (matt anodized aluminium) exactly matches throughout the range. Ironmongery is made by various processes (some items are cast, some extruded, some wrought, some made from sheet) and it is very hard technically to get these to match. When you choose from a number of unintegrated manufacturers' ranges, you will find it hard to find knobs to match bolts to match hinges to match locks.

No other range is so complete. Most modern ironmongery has an aluminium/silver finish of some sort, although some firms are experimenting with other looks. By and large, the more you pay, the better the quality.

Traditional urban

Many older houses need more traditional ironmongery. Some sources for this are antique shops, junk stalls or demolition sites. Sometimes it works out less expensive, sometimes more, to buy things this way. Otherwise the traditional patterns are still made, and you can match up practically any size or pattern of knob, knocker or door plate, not to mention drawer handles, fire guards, hinges, in the traditional patterns and materials.

Traditional rural

Sometimes, in the country, there is a local tradition for door closures and window fittings which spring from local materials and style of building. Some old houses in Sussex have thick wood latches which you pull open with a strip of leather. There are many local variations of this sort. If your house has some of these genuine fittings, keep them and add more of them throughout the house – they add enormously to the intrinsic country feeling. Don't despise the ubiquitous country style curly iron door and window fittings. These also reinforce the country atmosphere in a country house – although they won't ever turn a suburban villa into a cottage.

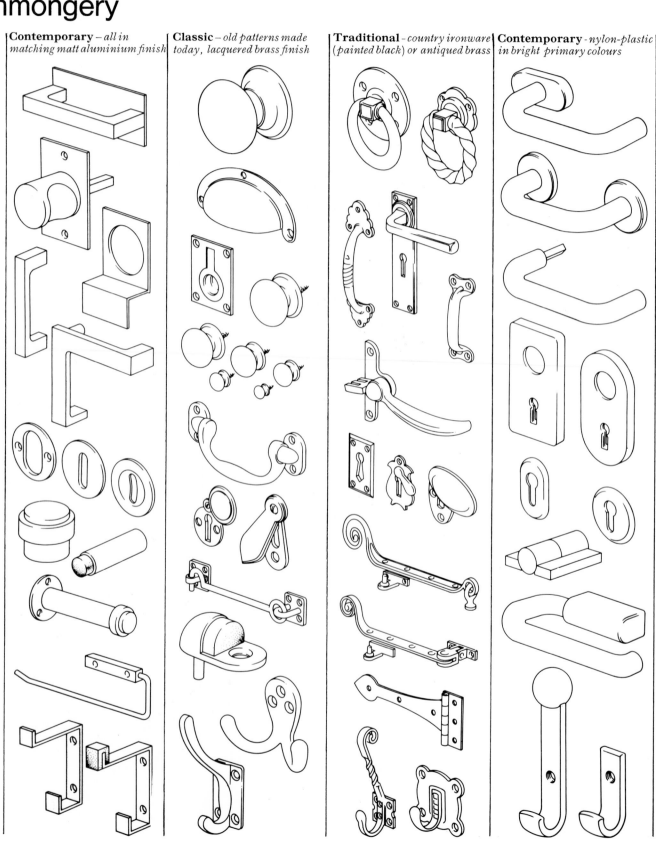

Contemporary – *all in matching matt aluminium finish*

Classic – *old patterns made today, lacquered brass finish*

Traditional – *country ironware (painted black) or antiqued brass*

Contemporary – *nylon-plastic in bright primary colours*

The look-no-handle solution

This can work quite well on doors and cupboards inside the house: the drawer, for instance, you open by a bottom lip or finger hold (A); the sliding door that has a wood edging instead of a handle; the cupboard door with a touch latch; the thick timber door with a hand-hole hollowed out of the wood itself (B).

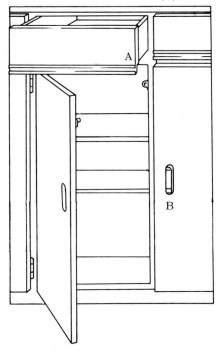

Which materials to choose

The style dictates the material the fittings are made in. If you choose brass, be prepared to look after it lovingly: even if lacquered, the lacquer deteriorates and has to be renewed from time to time. In fact all handles of whatever metal need care because the acids from the human skin cause them to dull.

Most contemporary fittings are made from either plated metals or anodized aluminium. Plating is a chemical process, and its quality can vary depending on its thickness: the final price is in direct relation to the quality of the plating. Anodizing means processing so that all the molecules are in a regular order which gives the surface a better finish. As anodizing shows up any surface imperfections, anodized fittings are, by definition, of good quality. The problem with iron is that it has to be kept rust-free. The really easy materials, like glass and china, are suitable only for knobs and handles and finger plates. Plastics are definitely overtaking the cheap end of the market, but only a few ranges are really well-designed.

Detail on detail – the door here and its architrave have been covered in soft warm felt, which is reflected in the neat knob, not in brass but matt anodized aluminium.

The solid brass doorknob which feels good when you use its classic shape. Make sure the brass is lacquered or you will have to keep it polished unendingly.

A doorstop, like this one with thick rubber, can cut down the noise that children make banging and slamming the door. It also protects the wall/furniture from scuffs and knocks.

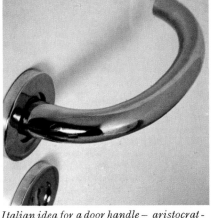

Italian idea for a door handle – aristocratically curved in shining chrome with matching plate. (Usually you specify what locking mechanism you want behind the plate.)

Another classic, in plain white china which is better for not being painted or embellished with bands or floral designs. Eminently practical, as it just has to be wiped clean.

Old military chests have inspired this handle. It fits flush into its recessed plate and swings out for turning – an essential detail when officers' possessions went into the field, and came in for rough handling.

Invisible ironmongery

There is a great deal of ironmongery which you don't see, but which makes its presence known by the way it functions – or doesn't. Door-hinges are an example. A hinge can lift an opening door over a thick carpet or uneven floor; this is known as a rising butt hinge. There are lift-off hinges, which enable you to lift a door off easily. Some hinges stop a door opening too wide, others make it fold back on itself, and butler's doors have hinges so that they can open both ways.

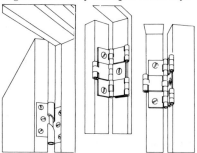

Rising butt   Fold both ways

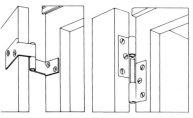

Fold back   Lift off

Door fastenings

Doors can be shut in several different ways. The traditional latches, catches and turning knobs can sometimes be replaced by ball catches, push-button catches, touch latches. An interesting development is in magnetic catches and seals.

Magnets

There are two parts to a magnetic catch: the magnetic part and its pole pieces go on one side, the counterplate on the other. The catch won't be efficient unless you get one of sufficient power for the weight of the door, but the fact that they are chosen for use on yachts and liners (the QE2 for instance) where the tossing of the ship puts a greater strain on catches, shows how superior they can be to normal mechanical catches. Good quality is important here, too: the match between the magnet and its counterplate must be accurate. The finish has to be accurate too, so there is no air. And in order to compensate for warping and movement, good magnetic catches are made with one half flexibly mounted so that they are self-aligning.

Details that count
4/5 Electrical fittings/alarm systems/budgeting

The self-closing mechanisms for doors are now designed so that they can be fixed into the door: instead of seeing a big round pressure unit squatting above the door, you simply see the arm. (See A.)

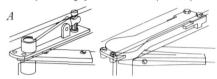

A

Opening and shutting windows

The way windows open is also important to get right, not just for opening but also for cleaning. Side opening windows can double out so that you can get your arm round to clean the outside. Top hung windows can pivot over for the same reason. Friction stays can eliminate casement stays, and this neatens up a window sill. Sash windows can be fitted with a spring mechanism instead of weights and cords. They can be closed by any number of fittings varying between the fitch, the claw, the lever or the quadrant, not to mention the locking devices. (See B.)

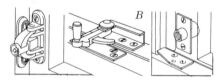

B

Sliding gear

There is some extremely sophisticated ball-bearing gear capable of making heavy doors – garage doors for instance – slide smoothly; while the drawers of kitchen cabinets run on simple filing-cabinet runners. Sliding gear is extremely versatile: the only proviso is that you get the right gear for the weight of the doors.

Quality

Much of this ironmongery is covered by the British Standard for Builders' Hardware (BS 1331). This governs the quality of the material used in manufacture and the fixings supplied (where applicable). Most of the materials used are still metal: surprisingly little ironmongery is simulated in plastic, though no doubt it will be. The newest, toughest plastics which might be suitable are still in specialist use. It is obviously more sensible to choose hardware which conforms or is superior to BS 1331 than stuff which doesn't.

Locking up

A very important section of ironmongery is locks and bolts, which all add up to "security". Here there is more to consider than the visual impact or your preference for a pretty brass-finished key. First you have to analyse what sort of security you need. Helpful for this is the new police policy to have Security Officers attached to local stations who will come round and advise you: it is really the next best thing to having a master burglar case the joint out loud for you. Contact your local station. Also, the major firms have representatives whose job it is to come round to advise you, plan a secure system and submit an estimate of what it will cost – all free of obligation. Of course your problem is harder if you have notable valuables which burglars might plan to steal, in which case you need a sophisticated alarm system. But the majority of burglaries are "petty", unconsidered and not carefully planned: they are committed by people on the look-out for opportunity and who aim not at valuables but the easily-disposed-of loot: transistor radios, colour TVs, silver, money, drink, etc. To deter this sort of burglar, you need proper locks on all doors and ground floor and basement windows, plus anywhere someone might climb in easily and unseen.

The proper front door lock is a mortice dead lock. The British Standard for Thief-Proof Locks for Hinged Doors (BS 3621) specifies that this lock should have at least 1,000 differs (i.e., that its mechanism has to be capable of 1,000 variations to be opened by 1,000 different keys, before any repeats can be made). The lock has to have a minimum of five levers inside plus a resistance plate inside (i.e. a shield which comes down as the first lever is turned so that you cannot turn other levers without the proper key). It has to have a bolt to specified strength and throw. Mortice dead locks have to be fitted into the door and their plates into the frame. You have to lock and unlock them when you go in and out.

The more common rim latch does not deter professional burglars. This is because the latch itself is easy to pick and easy to force, particularly when it is screwed on to the inside of the door rather than set into it. In this case there are only the screws holding the lock against the determined strength of a man.

The sight of a good mortice keyhole is often enough of a deterrent to the casual burglar. (It means, if it is locked, that time has to be spent sawing through the bolt.) You can further strengthen the door by having locking mortice bolts at the top and bottom (two more bolts for the burglar to saw through) and hinge bolts on the hinges. Other safeguards on the inside, like chain bolts and peepholes, are helpful in that you can see for whom you are opening the door before you do, or you can open the door just enough to take in a parcel or speak to someone on the doorstep.

A mortice dead lock is advisable on all outside doors or doors giving access to the house. You don't need keys for each one: manufacturers supply sets of matching locks.

Doors such as up-and-over garage doors, or sliding door units which have keys like mass-produced car keys are not really very safe: experts can quite easily pick these locks. Door units can usually have an additional mortice fitted. Garage doors sometimes have nothing strong enough to fit a mortice on to: so even if the lock held, the door would not. This is why doors from garages into houses should be just as secure as an outside door.

Glass doors are a weak spot, especially where neighbours couldn't hear or notice the smash or breaking glass. French windows with small panes can be treated like front doors and given a mortice dead lock and locking bolts. Large areas of glass can only be protected by a burglar alarm; or you could fit wired glass or a jeweller's grille which would have to be fitted with a secure lock.

Should internal doors have locks? These are probably more for the benefit of the owner of the house than a deterrent to a burglar. If a burglar has got in unnoticed, once alone inside he can take his time and make quite a bit of noise breaking down internal doors, which in any case are not usually as solid as front doors. But at night, when you are in bed, it could alert you and provide you with the few minutes necessary to raise the alarm.

Windows do need locking, certainly ground floor windows and basement ones. These lockup devices are certainly worth getting, especially if you live in a frequently burgled neighbourhood.

When you move into a house, it is advisable to get the locks checked – and it is very important to check up on the previous distribution of all the duplicate keys.

Only you can judge how vulnerable you are to being burgled. A residential district where the neighbours are neighbourly often protects itself. Where there are no neighbours to watch out for you, or where the neighbourhood is so busy that strange comings and goings do not attract attention, you should consider installing an alarm system.

Alarm systems

There are many alarm systems on the market. Most of the big lockmakers make alarm systems, and so do many other "security" firms.

Doors, windows, floors can all be sensitized and connected to the central alarm. More elaborate are the devices which work like radar, picking up infra-red energy from intruders. The central control box has to be switched on and off each time you leave the house empty and return. The most useful, probably, are connected to a telephone which automatically dials 999 when activated and relays a recorded announcement via the operator to the local police. The telephone line is a second line, outgoing only, ex-directory and, to avoid it being cut, should be concealed as it leaves the house. The boxes on the fronts of houses contain the alarm bell to alert neighbours, if any, and are considered to be psychological deterrents to casual burglars as well as advertisements for the security firm.

Choosing electrical fittings

Another range of details that count are electrical fittings. These have their British Standards (BS 3676 for switches, BS 1363 for plugs and sockets), and because the standards require a minimum quality for the materials used as well as minimum requirements for performance and insulation, it is worth making sure all your switches and sockets at least con-

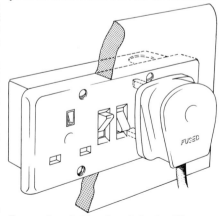

Recessed socket is almost flush with the skirting board.

Four switches on one switch-plate in an elegant matt anodized aluminium finish on a wall of natural hessian.

Electric switches look much better grouped together on one plate. These rocker switches are in white plastic.

Air-conditioning controls and two dimmer switches are lined up together and share the same finish.

A double dimmer switch – two dimmers on one plate. This switch has a press on/off control.

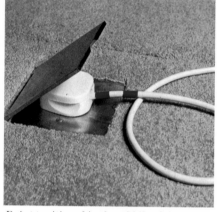

Point positioned in the middle of the room is covered by a flap which snaps shut when not in use.

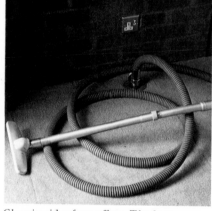

Cleaning idea from offices. The dust collector is built into the walls. Just plug in the pipe to an outlet in each room.

Bold anodized aluminium grille is set low in the unplastered wall, echoing its sharp lines. The grille is in proportion to the module of the bricks.

Radiator grilles come in all shapes, sizes, and thicknesses, so choosing a grille to blend in discreetly with your room will not be difficult.

A radiator grille facing upwards under a window to counteract down draughts. It is set into a shelf unit made of unusual narrow tiles.

form to these standards. There is some choice in the style of switches and sockets: in recent years they have improved in design. The finish can vary. Mainly it is white plastic, but switch-plates can be made with aluminium, copper and brass finishes.

Sockets

It is well worth considering the distinct advantages of getting sockets which are inset flush into the wall or skirting: they look neater, are not so vulnerable to knocks and don't collect dust. It is always worth having double (two-gang) sockets put in rather than single ones. It costs very little more and is much safer than adaptors branching out. Switches that say "on" are good reminders that the appliance is live.

Budgeting for ironmongery

Most people are surprised by a simple rule of thumb which puts the cost of ironmongery (including the conspicuous bits like the knocker on the front door) at $1\frac{1}{2}\%$ of total building costs on a new house. Although no one item (except perhaps a sophisticated burglar alarm system) is all that expensive, together they mount up.

The money will be well spent. It is very important to get ironmongery that works well: stuff that breaks, sticks or gets loose is unbelievably irritating. However, one can be economical by choosing the simple way of, for instance, hinging cupboard doors instead of going for electrically-operated sliding doors. But it is never worth letting the builder or supplier fob you off with a cut-price import saying, "Well, there's no difference really, is there?" There usually is. The minimum standard to insist on is the British Standard where it exists.

If you take the $1\frac{1}{2}\%$ standard and apply it roughly, you get a cost in proportion to the quality of the rest of the house. Where you can cut down is in choosing the simpler, more available alternative: the Habitat ironmongery department, for example, has a good selection of things for an unpretentious inexpensive conversion. It is folly, for instance, to buy anything way above the ambitions of the house. The mortice dead lock and bolts only make sense in a solid front door, because there is not much point in the lock holding if the door itself is easily broken by an expert shove of the shoulders. If you want to save money on your actual front door you might as well forget about security and just have an ordinary latch. You could say a house is as good as its details, but there is no point in expecting rich details to cover up larger economies.

Details that count
6 Double take

The doorknob is real, as is the painted knocker; but the rest, including even the wood grain, is an amazing example of trompe-l'oeil, by an artist with an eagle eye for detail.

Things/1

Within most of us there's a collector trying to get out; but although everyone may be a magpie at heart, not everyone is blessed with an unerring instinct for placing things, beautifully, in relation to others.

Agreeable arrangements don't necessarily come up if you let the accumulation of objects take its natural course. Unlike lovely drifts of spring flowers that materialize when, instead of poking in the bulbs one by one, you close your eyes and scatter them anyhow before planting, things have a nasty habit of conglomerating in an untidy mess. Conversely, too rigid a discipline might land you with the equivalent of a regiment of municipal tulips standing to attention.

The process of arranging what are essentially still lifes on walls, shelves, and table-tops has much in common with flower arranging: colour, shape, texture and proportion all contribute to the result. There are fewer guidelines, however, for while a lily is a lily is a lily, flowering at the same time as late roses and the early chrysanths, objects and pictures come in all shapes and sizes and may crop up at any time.

Generally speaking, things on display look happier and will make more of a point if they're grouped rather than dotted about. Less, in this instance, is not more (it seldom is), though a single fine piece, dramatically lit, can make a splendid effect – on the principle of a single hothouse bloom in a special vase.

There can be no cast-iron rules. What looks right to one pair of eyes may look wrong to another. There's the case of the former director of one of our great museums who stayed with an equally renowned art-expert; every afternoon he would surreptitiously move a little Renaissance *maquette* a fraction to the right in accordance with his own sense of spacing, only to find it in its original position by the time dinner was served.

What applies to museum-pieces also applies to less exalted objects – pictures, toys ancient and modern, left-overs from the Industrial Revolution, china, enamel signs and birdcages. All of these, nicely displayed, will moreover belie their humble origins and look like works of art. Unlike flower arrangements, they won't ask for your attention by drooping or wilting – but watch out – familiarity breeds not so much contempt as blind spots. When you no longer feel some positive pleasure while looking at your things, it's time to rearrange them.

The collection of bottles, on a glass shelf by the window. Glass gains immeasurably from the play of light – and the lamp that provides it by night is itself decorative.

Things
2/3 Things on shelves

Books are well known to furnish a room, but bookshelves are too useful for display purposes to be given over to the library alone. Tomes get interspersed with objects; this looks nice, although the removal of even one slim volume will cause the rest to tilt, shifting decorative arrangements and flattening fragile ones. Vertical dividers prevent this from happening, as will segregation by shelves, but if you're after a more spontaneous effect, make sure that you set up your decorative groups near to the books that don't get read much.

Shelves come in so many shapes and sizes, and are so versatile that it should be possible to create suitable spaces for whatever you wish to display. Since books are getting huger all the time, and having them forever lying about on coffee tables isn't everybody's *cappucino*, you'll most likely space out one lot of shelves to take the giants. (If your collection doesn't quite fill a whole shelf, you might place the occasional volume not "spine-to-camera" in the usual way, but cover-to-front so that especially nice covers become decorative items.

The only snag about shelves not crammed, library fashion, with barely a finger's space between the top of the books and the shelf above, comes with dusting. Bits and pieces are hell to cope with, there's no getting away from it, but at least make life easier for yourself by seeing that your shelves are smooth, whether hermetically sealed and polished, or painted in a high gloss.

Alternatively, you could always put your objects behind glass, either sliding panels or hinged doors; and don't forget, when you divide your shelves into display areas you can treat them like so many different stage-sets and give them backgrounds of different colours.

1 *Show-case treatment for this handsome collection is achieved by the simplest means: white-painted boarding forms the background to these open shelves, and the arrangement is strictly linear.*

2 *The wall beneath the bookshelves has itself become part of the display, pictures are evenly spaced underneath the bottom shelf.*

3 *Each set of items in this vertically divided shelving unit sits in a space in sympathy with its dimensions, so that each partition becomes a small showcase.*

4 *This wall of shelving is made up of different materials. Glass shelves support the objects, white-painted wooden shelves encase the books, and the sloping shelf for magazines becomes part of the unit.*

1

2

3

4

1 *This cool shelf arrangement of china is extended to the shelf above the fireplace: shelved alcoves do not need to be self-contained compartments.*

2 *If light shelves are set against a dark background and dramatically lit, everthing happening on them is invested with special drama.*

3 *Alcoves in Georgian rooms make tall and slender "display columns" – even if the shelves do not go right down to floor level. Any piece of furniture drawn into the area immediately becomes a display piece.*

4 *Light-box arrangement above and below paired bookshelves gives the display areas, and the objects in them, an extra dimension.*

5 *Lit-up display cases visually break up any wall to which they are fixed, and the objects they hold are seen as though on a stage.*

Things

Don't hang your pictures too high. Don't space them out too far. Don't hang them so low above sofas, or on walls that are part of the sitting area, that the heads of sitters knock against them. Don't hang them arbitrarily, but don't, on the other hand, treat them merely as decorative objects; and resist matching them to the general colour scheme. Warnings abound, but positive advice is hard to come by since pictures vary as much as walls in size, and as far as colour, tone and content go, the permutations are endless.

Here's a rough guide to picture hanging:
vertical arrangements will make the room look taller, horizontal ones, wider (see Walls).

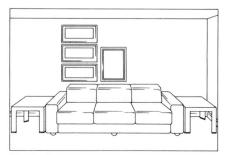

Vertical group accentuates the room height.

A plain background suits most pictures best so if you are faced with a strongly patterned wallpaper, use large mounts to create islands of calm around the pictures, or frame them so that they don't, metaphorically, spill over. Contrary to common belief, it is not white but very dark, almost black walls, that make pictures sing out most. Since pictures are there to be looked at, take the eye level of standing or sitting viewers into account when you hang them. If you plan to make a large dynamic arrangement of a lot of pictures, some large, some small, some middling, still bear this eye level in mind.

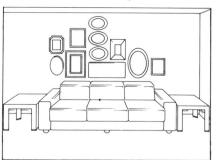

Assorted sizes and shapes grouped together.

Reckon that the viewer's gaze will come to rest somewhere in the centre of the group, unless you deliberately lead it on from this focal point by other judiciously placed items.

Whether you aim for a symmetrical or asymmetrical arrangement, keep a bit of tension going between the pictures you're grouping together. That means the spaces between them should not exceed half the width of the smallest item you're hanging. And do range them somewhere, top, bottom or side, and the more of them there are, the more important it becomes to make them look organized, enabling each picture to come into its own.

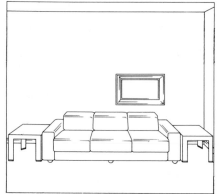

Single picture lined on one side.

Pictures of varying size ranged above head height.

Symmetrical position echoes furniture arrangement.

1 *Symmetrical arrangement of an uneven number of pictures. Note the space between them in relation to their width.*

2 *Fireplace group, dominated by a large painting. The smaller pictures on the over-mantel, as well as the objects, become part of the same group.*

3 *Huge blow-ups side by side become one immense photo-mural.*

4 *This picture-covered wall has been successfully organized by an amalgamation of distinctly separate groups.*

5 *This arrangement of diverse shapes gains by the structural elements of the fireplace and the large "L" (for its owner, Louisa).*

6 *The eye sees this interesting picture arrangement as square, and supplies the outline as though there were no gaps.*

7 *Pictures, ranged to form a straight line at the bottom, are hung above the sofa (high enough for reclining heads not to displace the arrangement).*

8 *Pictures do not necessarily have to hang on the wall – leaning side by side against the wall they produce, in this case, the effect of a collector's "cabinet".*

9 *Time-honoured "up-the-stairs" arrangement – with this difference, that they crowd their way upstairs instead of tiptoeing one by one.*

10 *Strict organization, pictures ranging both horizontally and vertically.*

4

5

6

7

8

9

10

Things

The rule is to consider the object in relation to the piece of furniture on which it is to sit and the arrangement, as a whole, in relation to its background and the space surrounding it. Great big things teetering on little tables destroy the proportions of both, and tiny bits and pieces on a large surface tend to become entirely invisible. After all, sculptures have their plinths made to complement them, and making 3-D still lifes is a form of sculpting, albeit with ready-made components.

Keep it low

Tabletop arrangements which are to be seen from above become, by that token, a form of bas-relief – kept low enough for people to see each other as they talk across them. Having to crane one's neck when having a conversation is as irritating at the coffee-table as it is in the dining-room.

What makes an arrangement

The most disparate and surprising objects can be happily brought together. They may be related in shape, in genus, in colour or not connected in any way – there for the simple reason that their owner likes the look of them. Junk and non-junk mix quite happily, and so do things of quite different periods; they are all grist to our decorative mills.

The idea is to have fun, to give one's inventiveness a free rein, and to resist the temptation to think of any arrangement as final. Reshuffling pays off in the satisfaction of feeling mildly creative, which is as well, as table-top still lifes tend to become disarranged more quickly than any other form. One shove, and the balance has gone.

Positioning

A thing to remember is that in the case of a low table by the sitting area, space must be allowed for setting down the odd cup and saucer, or a book or a magazine. These spaces left vacant should in themselves contribute to the design.

A frail arrangement can't be expected to last for five minutes even on the fringes of the circulation area, let alone in the middle of it – its back to the wall should be your rule. For easier dusting – of the table-top, not the arrangement – it's not a bad idea to contain it on a tray.

A polka-dot arrangement of massed spices in oriental bowls for a subtle, enticing colour scheme that could not readily be matched by any other known material. Not suitable for a household with small children who would get a horrible shock when licking fingers that had been poked into curry, ginger or ground cinnamon.

1 *Simple flower in simple glazed stone bottle – things don't have to be complicated to look effective.*

2 *A city made up of boxes, lollipops, Perspex cubes, jars filled with assortments of nuts, all sitting on an island which is a tray, its skyline against the painted wall.*

3 *Tiles don't need to be confined to going under dishes too hot for the table, but can sit effectively on narrow ledges.*

4 *Purist ensemble, white against beige, with a touch of greeny yellow and chrome, and looking as though suspended in mid-air.*

5 *Massed circles, ellipses, and cloverleaf shapes. The surfaces are at different levels; the flowers, particularly the long-haired chrysanthemum, add further variety.*

6 *Merely by putting objects into the radius of light from an opaquely shaded lamp you can "frame" the display area as well as highlight it.*

1

2

3

4

5

6

Although most plants are gregarious and seem to get on well together, indoor plants come from a wide variety of habitats and climates and you can't expect a desert plant like a cactus or a succulent, used to cold nights and dry hot days, to flourish happily next to a

Saintpaulias are happy in normal room conditions if sunk in a peaty box and kept damp

damp-loving denizen of the steamy green Amazonian rain forests.

As our houses get hotter and hotter every year with central heating, we have to decide which we are going to pamper most, ourselves or our plants. The reason why those wonderful arrangements of geraniums, bromeliads, cyclamen, begonias and echeverias flourish so beautifully on cottage parlour window sills is mainly because they are cool and *undisturbed*. It is not so much the overheating but the lack of humidity that some plants cannot survive. Some plants like more heat and some less; some like lots of light, some do not. Generally it is better to group your pots in a metal or plastic trough or tray with a layer of pebbles or gravel on the bottom, and peat or sand round and between the pots, and peat or moss on the top. This will keep the plants from losing moisture through the earthenware pots; they will stay damper and need watering less often. Few plants like standing in a pool of water so it is better to put a little gravel in individual plant pot saucers too. Knock the side of the pot; if it sounds hollow the soil is probably too dry; if this is the case, immerse the pot in a bucket of water until the bubbles stop rising. This will thoroughly soak it. Most plants should grow well in a south or southwest facing window, except those naturally found in a shady jungle. These prefer to be away from the sun in an undisturbed corner. Some, like *Aralia*, *Cissus*, *Saintpaulia* and even cyclamen

would be happy in a north facing window.

More pot plants die from drowning by being over-watered than from any other cause, so if in doubt give less (yellow and falling leaves are not necessarily a sign of drought, they can also, more often than not, mean over-watering). In the dormant season of winter they need very little water, but in summer, while new growth is being made, they are very thirsty. Ideally, use rain water, which is lime free; but if this is not available boiled tap water will do. All water should stand for an hour or so at room temperature before being fed to plants – icy rain water or water straight from the tap is too much of a shock. Most plants respond well to some time spent out of doors during the summer. They also benefit from an occasional shower bath of rain. Large leaves (not the furry or hairy ones) should be gently sponged to rid them of dust; cacti and succulents should be dipped in tepid water.

The aspidistra was called the cast iron plant as it flourished in Victorian interiors lit by town gas, which is poisonous to most plants. There are a number of tough and adaptable plants easily available which show the same willingness to live with us. Group them to contrast feathery fronds with glossy, leathery leaves, stiff sculptural spikes with trailing tendrils; if one plant begins to look sickly separate it (a few days in a steamy bathroom does wonders, especially for begonias) and try to find a place where it can thrive more readily. If you are successful with one variety make a group of them (one avocado looks dull, four make a little grove – much more interesting). If one gets huge and dwarfs

Sparmania africana is a very easy-going indoor tree with large soft green leaves.

its neighbours in the trough (as a *Ficus* or a *Sparmannia* might) grow it alone in solitary splendour.

Monstera deliciosa is a climbing member of the arum family from the Mexican jungle.

Of the large Arum family, the Dumb Cane (*Dieffenbachia*) has many varieties. They like to be comfortably warm and not too dry.

Hurricane Plant (*Monstera deliciosa*) is a large tree climber from the Mexican jungles and has aerial roots and shiny leaves which look as if someone has done some decorative cutwork. It is very tough and amenable and likes some time in the garden in the summer. Philodendrons (*Philodendron* sp.) are all tree climbers from Colombia, climbing high from a box or trough or trailing down a wall. They like water but dislike being waterlogged and should be regularly sprayed.

The Rex Begonias (*Begonia rex*) from the Himalayas come in every imaginable leaf colour, from velvet red to silver. They grow well in cool, shady places and do not like full sun.

Bromeliads are, perhaps, the perfect house plants, being happy in sun or shade and capable of standing neglected for weeks on end. They come from Central America and are called "Air Pines" as many are epiphytes and live on trees and roofs. The Pineapple (*Ananas comosus*) is an example of a terrestrial species. They have stiff, curving blades of leaves in a rosette or crown with a hollow centre, and many flowers. *Aechmea fasciata* has greyish curving leaves of great sculptural beauty and an amazing pink flower which blooms for months. Like all its family it likes water in the central vase formed by the leaves. Rain water is best, or boiled water cooled to room temperature. *Neoregelia carolinae tricolor* can grow to two feet across with long, narrow leaves striped with green, pale pink and cream, and before it flowers, will produce shorter crimson leaves. It likes semi-shade and, like most bromeliads, is lovely in a low position so that its rosette can be seen in plan.

Cryptanthus are like flat little tabby starfish, some with stripes of silver and purple, some silver with deckle edges; they are tolerant and easy going. *Billbergia nutans* has narrow, spiny, dark green leaves and fantastic drooping flowers of green and blue with red bracts; it will tolerate a cool position.

There are several good members of the Fig family. The Rubber Plant (*Ficus elastica*) is too well known to need description; it is happy in reasonable conditions, even suffering cool corners. Moreton Bay Fig (*Ficus benjamina*) is a delicate tree with pale bark and short, broad leaves.

Some other tolerant and undemanding good plants are the Kangaroo Vine (*Cissus antarctica*) which has rather large, dark green leaves and which, being a climbing plant, needs support. The Spider Plant (*Chlorophytum comosum variegatum*) is like a fountain, with striped green and white leaves and stems ending in small plantlets which will root round the parent or in other pots. The ivies (*Hedera* sp.) are easily grown, thriving in cool rooms; they climb or trail. The Wax Flower (*Hoya carnosa*), with its pink, sweet-smelling flowers, is a climber, liking rich soil and shade.

Gardenias are delicate creatures and really need a glasshouse environment so enjoy them while they last – even the greenest fingers can't keep them alive for long in a warm, dry room.

Peppers (*Peperomia* sp.) are small with decorative leaves and like moist shade. Mother-in-Law's Tongue (*Sansevieria trifasciata laurentii*) is a tall erect plant with sword-like leaves striped grey-green and yellow, liking light but tolerating most situations as long as it is not over-watered. Finally, the Tradescantias and Zebrinas are the easiest of all to look after; the leaves of this family of plants are striped green and white, some silver and pink, of trailing growth, and easy to propagate from cuttings.

A Busy Lizzie will thrive on a window sill. It loves the light and will grow into a gigantic bush from which it is easy to propagate more and more plants.

Things
10/11 Indoor plants

1 *Almost the nicest thing about growing avocados from stones is the waiting for them to split and sprout, which they happily do, either in water or soil, becoming large-scale glossy-leaved plants.*

2 *The unique decorative effect of graceful palm leaves was first appreciated in the Victorian drawing room and conservatory, and is seen to the full in a pale modern interior. The small neighbour is a pretty Ficus Benjamina.*

3 *Plants do not have to be large scale and dramatic, even the smallest have presence and are effective.*

4 *Chlorophytums, or spider plants, striped green and yellow, love light, and as they fall in cascades of firework-like stars, are particularly good high up, as here in a passage.*

5 *Nephrolepis and trailing ivy are among the most accommodating of plants, particularly in hanging baskets. Here, under a skylight, the leaves will show silvery pink.*

6 *If you really want, not just a plant, but a tree in the room then the lovely Sparmannia or zimmerlinden (Chamber Lime) is for you. It has pale green, furry leaves, spectacular flowers in spring, is very good natured and easy to keep happy.*

7 *Glass shelves across a window make the happiest environment for a gaggle of plants, here echevarias and other succulents.*

(Opposite) All the arums have great sculptural quality; here a Dieffenbachia is seen at its best as a centrepiece on a low table.

1

2

3

4

5

6

7

1/2 *Bottles, filled or empty, look best when light can shine through them.*

3/4/5 *Toast-racks, the white china sort, keys from long-forgotten doors, wood blocks that were used in Edwardian printing works, all good on their own, but infinitely better in an organized mass.*

6 *Open-shelved room-divider is used as a pottery and china cabinet. Each jug, pot and jar sits cheek by jowl with its neighbour, and the result is a rich decorative panel.*

7 *Collections of botanical specimens, in assorted frames, make an intricate, delicate filigree design when they are hung close together.*

Serious collectors of all the things that customarily get hoarded are not usually in any doubt as to how to deal with their butterflies/stamps/minerals/coins and so on, but tentative collectors are not always in this happy position. In fact, a great many things get accumulated simply because one liked them at the time and can't quite bring oneself to throw them out. Pebbles and shells from holiday beaches come into this category, and once they've come home, they lie about in the backs of drawers, yet, they could be stored in goblets or glass jars.

As for the endless bits of Victoriana/Edwardiana or any other -iana that people tend to acquire without much purpose, they can be seen to be collections (with a capital C) as soon as they are given a bit of space of their own. Even if you don't want to go as far as lit-up glass-fronted cabinets, a shelf or tabletop covered with some generically connected items can look great. Or have a simple pinboard for two-and three-dimensional objects with a common theme; it will make a collection screen on the principle of those varnished Victorian screens.

Quite modest, pleasant things can look disproportionately stunning when they're seen in the mass, so it's well worth keeping one's eyes open for possible bargains in whatever line you've chosen, or have made a start on without realizing it. And then, of course, there's always the pleasant thought that a junk-shop bargain today may be tomorrow's highly priced antique, or at least a cherished heirloom.

8 *Max Clendinning lined a large recessed area of this room with glass shelves, indirectly lit, so that the objects and their shadows seem to pattern the wall.*

9 *(Above right) Kites, in their extraordinary oriental colours, make an interesting 3-D mural.*

10 *John Stefanides' baskets, all in different shapes, sizes and colours, suggest that it is Christmas every day of the year*

11 *A collection of native combs takes the place of pictures on this wall.*

Things
14/15 Kitchen things

It is almost impossible to go wrong with the arrangement of kitchen things. Their very shapes have something so satisfying about them that it seems a shame to hide anything at all away.

1 *Dressers are "naturals" for displays of china, interspersed or not with other things. The Conrans' shelves hold soup tureens, platters, scales and their weights, vegetables in a basket, a posy or two and an intergrated telephone, wall-hung, with a mug for pencils nearby.*

2 *The more stainless the steel, the more welcome the food still-lifes and greenery in pots.*

3 *Copper always makes a brave show. Long-term polish takes the fag out of caring for it, but don't forget about re-tinning.*

4 *Massed pewter, or any silvery metal, looks particularly spectacular against a very dark background.*

1

2

3

4

5 *It always seems a shame to see the utilitarian objects of yesterday incarcerated in museum-like isolation. They were made to be used – certainly one needs to be extra careful in handling them, but why not?*

6 *John Stefanides' plate-rack dressed with local pottery has the decorative quality of a folk painting.*

7 *Paint the wall behind a set of shelves in a colour to flatter your things on display: a pale sharp pink marvellously complements white china.*

8 *Pudding and cake moulds on individual nails make nice decorations for the kitchen wall.*

Things
16 Visual puns

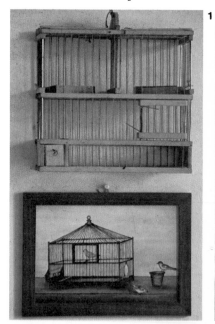

Every arranger of things is allowed a number of jokes: wit pays off in this as in all other fields. Whether you pair objects that relate by association, or by genus, witty juxtapositions tend to give more point to all of them. Too many visual puns would be tiresomely side-splitting, but a few, even if they are quite subtle, can be a treat.

1 *A real birdcage closely associated with a picture of another makes a telling unit on the wall.*

2 *Exotic-looking wood-pigeon – really a child's paper-lantern, part of a whole menagerie stocked by stationers – is at home here in a jungle of house-plants rampaging up a window.*

3 *Real palm leaves echo the frond in the picture in front of which the plant is placed.*

4 *A decoy duck carries a small mechanical duck on its back, while Mexican pottery animals sit solemnly on small marble blocks in the shelf above, pretending to be serious sculptures on plinths.*

5 *London bus by André Francois, Mexican mule (less fuel, more speed?) and Coronation coach all tell a transport story. Note: goblets make marvellous "display-cases" for all manner of small things – from seaside pebbles to dice.*

Attics/1

If the roof on your house is pitched you have an attic or loft. If you are not already making full use of it you should certainly consider how best to exploit this valuable space.

External appearance

The top floor of a building is highly visible, so extra care must be taken to ensure that your attic conversion is not unsightly; this is particularly important if you live in a building of architectural or historical merit. In this case you may be required to get special permission from the ancient monuments division of the local town planning department for your alterations.

Professional advice

Attic conversions are extremely complicated and particularly vulnerable to the practical constraints of every authority imaginable, including your neighbour. So if you plan to make any structural alterations to attic or roof you will certainly have to consult an architect.

Points to consider

☐ Will adequate use of this space mean a great deal of structural work and alteration of the roof line?

☐ Are you prepared to employ an architect and go through the formalities of obtaining planning and bylaw approval, dealing with the health inspector and fire authorities and probably agreeing party-wall awards with your neighbour?

1 *Adjoining attic conversions to three terraced houses in Hampstead. The first and second roofs have been completely rebuilt. The first house has a dormer across the whole width of the house, forming a tall room with french windows on to a balcony. The second has a narrower dormer of the same type.*

2 *By converting a former attic, two extra storeys have been built on to this tiny terraced house facing the Thames. The main area is a double-height living-room with big studio dormer window.*

3 *A new floor built in a London house. The roof over the staircase has been built higher so clerestory windows can be formed to light the stairwell.*

4 *A window has been built across the width of the house, forming an attic room the same size as the rooms below.*

5 *Another example of an attic extension over the whole building, with side party-walls built up to the heights required by the authorities.*

Attics
2/3 Exploring structural possibilities and plans

Even the most experienced architect will blanch slightly when you describe the attic conversions you have planned. Apart from the many approvals he will have to obtain there are various unforeseen troubles that can arise from altering any part of the roof. For instance, it may be discovered that the whole building needs underpinning to carry the extra weight, and it is not unheard of that a whole wall – several storeys high – may have to be rebuilt when, at a late stage, the builders discover that the roof of your charming period house has for many years been supported by a couple of bricked-up windows or a timber lintel, riddled with dry rot.

Whenever a roof is opened up, sooner or later your upper floors will be partially open to the elements, and however good your builder, and however much he insists that he will provide adequate protection, considerable mental anguish is likely to be caused to the owner.

Advantages

In spite of all this, the advantages of obtaining a larger house without moving from your home may be so great that you may decide to proceed. As long as you are prepared for a great deal more expense and temporary worry than you originally expected, you will be delighted with the result when it is finally achieved.

Access – stairs

If your new rooms are so-called "habitable" – i.e. living-rooms or bedrooms – they will require, in some parts of the country, a permanent access stair, 3 ft/ 1 m wide and rising at an angle of no more than 42°. The Greater London Council is more lenient about this provided that it is a private stair used only by the family.

An open circular stair (as shown in diagram A) looks attractive and doesn't appear to take up so much room.

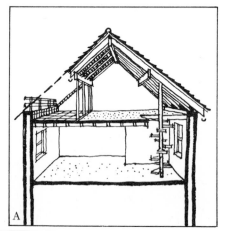

A step-ladder, or extendable loft-ladder, which can be pulled up so as not to obstruct the floor below, would be adequate for lofts used only for storage. Wherever you are, you will have to ensure that the entrance into the converted space provides headroom of at least 6 ft 6 in./2 m, or head injuries will result (see diagram B). Stairs can be juggled and the direction changed in mid-flight by means of half-landings, which will give the necessary headroom.

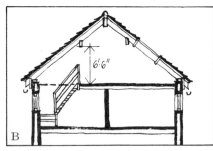

Heights in habitable rooms

The height required in this type of room is a minimum of 7 ft 6 in./2.25 m over at least half the existing "unobstructed" floor area. If the space does not meet this requirement there are various solutions. One is to cut down on the floor area by building cupboards and other fitments and even "non-habitable" rooms (i.e. bathrooms, store rooms) in the more awkward spaces.

If an existing chimney is not being used, and is not necessary for stabilizing the structure, you might be able to add some full-height floor space by removing the chimneybreast in the attic. Special permission will be needed for this.

It is sometimes possible to borrow headroom from the floor below. In this conversion (see diagram C), part of the attic floor was lowered 2 ft 6 in./762 mm in step formation into the bedroom below, increasing headroom below the roof purlin and providing standing room in the new dormer window. The raised part of the room could form a base for a platform bed. The new lowered ceiling is incorporated in strategically placed built-in cupboards in the bedroom below.

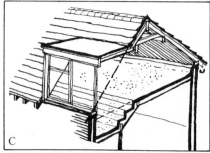

Needless to say, extra square footage of flat ceiling provided by a dormer window often helps to give the requisite height (see diagram D). Extra headroom can also be provided by other methods, such as raising the purlins to a higher level, removing old ceilings and exposing collars or trusses or making slight alterations to the roof structure – without altering the roof.

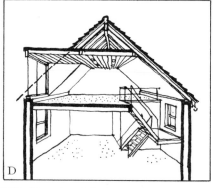

Windows/roof-lights

The least complicated windows to install are roof-lights set within the thickness of the roof. Unfortunately, the ventilation bylaws, which apply in attics as everywhere else, do not allow for incorporating opening lights in sloping windows in the required ventilation area calculation for a habitable room.

Roof-light blinds

Considerable thought should be given to providing protection from solar heat-gain in an attic space with roof-lights. Remember when you order blinds to fit sloping windows to give the suppliers all the details of the slope of the window as well as the size, so that the necessary supporting wires are included. Roller blinds of cedar slats connected by copper links, or weather-proofed green pinoleum as supplied to commercial greenhouses, fixed externally and operated from within, might well be considered.

For safety a very large roof-light should be of wired glass.

Dormer windows

There are several forms of dormer window. The conventional projecting dormers can have a glazed roof and cheeks, which will give sideways views never seen before. The inverted dormer window is set back in to the roof to form a balcony (see diagram E). The advantage of inverted dormers is that they open up the roof space to views and sun and provide the chance to plant a small roof garden or build a barbecue. They also enable you to fit full-length windows on

to a small balcony – not frightening as it is set into the roof. The disadvantage of the inverted dormer is the difficulty of waterproofing and strengthening the balcony floor – formerly only an attic floor. Unless very well built, this could cause troublesome leakages.

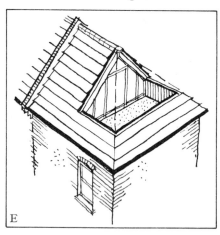

Maintenance of windows

Repainting and general maintenance of windows in these high and inaccessible positions might be difficult. Glass-fibre windows, double or single-glazed, or aluminium windows with permanent acrylic finish – neither of which requires repainting – might be the answer.

1 *The Velux-type window is one of the most practical. It comes with its own waterproof flashing, it is double glazed, and you can buy it with a pleated paper blind between the sheets of glass.*

2 *In a house with gable end-walls that can be opened up without much trouble, the problem of providing light and air to attic spaces is much reduced. Big windows can be fitted into most of the A-shape of the end-wall, as the main roof structure is supported by the purlins and the side walls. It is safer to separate a big window in this position into small panes.*

3 *An intricately woven hammock has been slung from two of the white-painted exposed timber trusses and across the window.*

4 *A new sleeping platform in an old house. The new bed is at sill level and the room has standing room only in the centre.*

5 *An attic bedroom over the whole top floor of this house with two dormer windows built in below the purlins. The ceiling has been boarded up to the peak of the roof to make the most of the space. Extra windows have been built into both gable walls.*

1

2

3

4

5

Attics
4/5 Knocking top floor and attic into one

Attic rooms have a special character of their own and are capable, after conversion, of becoming the most pleasant in the house. Some modern houses, such as the A-frame structure, have been designed as a whole house within a giant loft. But if your loft space is meagre and there is no way of building extra windows or obtaining the necessary floor-heights, or if you do not want to alter the roof, the attic will not be wasted if you open it to the floor below, and line the underside of the rafters to form a new high ceiling (see diagram below). Your top floor will become much more spacious and impressive. Some of the adjoining attic can be made into a sleeping or study gallery – with headroom as low or as high as you choose – overlooking the double-height area. Any young adults in the family will, if allowed, at once lay claim to your refurbished attic. They will not be worried by the climb and will be charmed by the wider outlooks and views, and the informal atmosphere created by the irregular shapes of walls and ceilings.

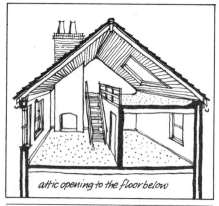

attic opening to the floor below

1 *The attic has been opened to the room below, which has gained impressively in height. The exposed roof timbers, painted black, contrast with the white walls.*

2 *A new flat on a top floor has gained a double-height dining-room by exposing the attic. An adjacent attic bedroom overlooks this space through a grille.*

3 *The attic has been opened, a roof-light built in, and a low-level sleeping gallery has been formed behind one of the roof trusses.*

4 *Another example of a gallery room built into an opened-up attic.*

(Opposite) In its original form this attic would have been almost useless, but opened up to the floor below, leaving the old timber tie beams, the combined area has been given a new dimension as a living-room for the family.

1

2

3

4

Attics

Heat rises, so once you have opened up the attic to the rest of the house, it should not be difficult to keep it warm, provided that the roof itself is thoroughly insulated. The attic roofs – directly exposed to the weather and of comparatively light construction – will require a great deal more insulation than any other part of the house. Formerly, they may well have formed the only insulating barrier between the upper rooms and the roof.

Probably the easiest way of insulating an existing roof is to nail insulating board, of which there are many different kinds, to the underside of the rafters, leaving the collars and purlins exposed. Make sure your local building inspector approves the type of insulation you have chosen. If the cold-water storage tank is above the roof, it will require lagging and boxing-in separately – more so, as a well-insulated roof will let no heat through to prevent the water from freezing.

Weatherproofing underside

If your slate or tile roof is leaky, there is a new sealer available which, sprayed on the underside of the roof, will weatherproof it completely. It forms a thick layer, bonded firmly to the roof structure, is fire-proof and eliminates condensation. It is guaranteed to remain effective for 25 years by the specialist firm that applies it for you.

Walls and ceilings

Attic walls and ceiling may be one and the same surface. Timber boarding or panelling, set between the joists or nailed over them, looks pleasing and natural, but will require insulation such as glass-fibre quilting. If you want a smooth finish or a plain surface to contrast with exposed purlins and trusses, a laminated plasterboard has internal lining, insulation and vapour barrier in one component. Any sheet material can be used, providing it is painted with a fire-retardant finish.

Floors

An attic floor is usually of timber-joist construction. Originally, it was probably considered only as a ceiling, so make sure it is strong enough to form a floor. A plywood or blockboard surface over the joists will be required for any floor finish other than boarding. Close carpeting is perhaps the most pleasant covering as it helps form a sound-insulation barrier to the floor below. About 40 per cent of attic space is inaccessible, but do not box it in. Continue your floor covering to its utmost limits for a greater illusion of space. If you need the space round the edge for pipes and electric wiring, enclose the awkward angle of floor and roof, hiding unsightly tangle.

1

2

3

4

1 *A raised platform has been formed by boxing in the lower member of the roof truss. The natural coloured carpet covering the main floor has been carried up over this and forms a shelf and bed-back. Even the timber purlins have been constructed so as to double as bookshelves.*

2 *A domed and boarded false ceiling in this attic bedroom gives an attractive shape to the roof and covers insulation pipes, built-in tanks and a multitude of sins.*

3 *The unusually shaped roof trusses in this Italian attic have been emphasized by leaving them their natural dark colour; the walls and ceilings, covered with insulating board, are painted white; the living-room furniture is arranged in geometric patterns around the floor. The white and wood-brown colours have been carried through the general scheme.*

4 *An obvious way of using the low-ceilinged part of the roof is to build a bed into it. Here an extra-large bed has a shelf around and a drawer under to store bedding.*

5 *In this flat the roof has been built so that the owner has been able to suspend an insulating (both sound and heat) board over the roof trusses before replacing the rafters and roof covering. The rather fearsome trusses have been left fairly rough and painted white to contrast with the very smooth finishes elsewhere in the room. They also form partitions between the different rooms. The daylight comes from roof-lights.*

5

Attics
8 Kitting it out

1 *The boarded ceiling follows the roof line up to the highest collar. Part of the lower side of the room has been cut off to form a roof-garden terrace accessible by glass doors.*

2 *Children's room in attic: a large area of loft with low head-room can form an excellent play-area for children. Adults – whose progress through the room would have to be on hands and knees – will not be able to insist that train layouts and dolls are put away every evening. You may well find that this becomes, unofficially, the favourite recreation space for the whole household.*

3 *Another example of using a Velux window and placing a table and shelves in a low-ceilinged corner.*

4 *Attics are usually nice and warm, and good places for drying and ironing clothes.*

1

3

2

4

Basements/cellars/1

For some years houses built in this country have not included cellars and basements, but in many old buildings there is a great deal of waste space in the areas below ground level. These basements are often dark and damp, and there is a tendency to think of them as useful only for storage – particularly of food or wine – because of the all-year-round equable temperature.

A basement is also the obvious place for anything large and heavy, such as machinery, because the strengthening of supporting walls and floors that would be required anywhere else will not be necessary here. It is a good place for heavy oil-storage tanks for central heating, especially where the local authority insists on a catchment pit – that's an extra impervious surround to the tank in case of leakage. In some buildings, where a pump is needed for distributing water, the tanks may well be stored in the basement; but except for these and similar examples, better use for this valuable space should be considered.

Town planning/bylaws

When deciding whether to give planning permission for new houses or changed usage in existing houses, the authorities consider rooms as "habitable" (bedrooms and living-rooms) or "non-habitable" (bathrooms, storage, garages, workshops, etc.), and all building land is zoned to dictate the number of people permitted to live in any given area, taking only habitable rooms into account.

Complications will of course arise when changing the use of space from non-habitable to habitable. You will have to take questions of access, drainage facilities, security against unwarranted entry, means of escape in case of fire, and many others, into consideration, but first the new room will have to conform to local regulations concerning provision of adequate daylight, ventilation and minimum heights of rooms.

If you own a house with a basement here are some points to consider:

- ☐ Are you making the best use of it?
- ☐ What would the planning and bylaw authorities let you do with the underused space?
- ☐ Could the room usefully serve a second purpose?
- ☐ Is it free from moisture?
- ☐ If damp, what type of damp-proofing would be most suitable.

A large basement store has been turned into the perfect living-room. The ceiling has been covered with acoustic board. The existing Rolled Steel Joists (RSJs) have been painted with red-lead oxide paint – decorative as well as rust-proof.

Basements/cellars
2/3 Habitable rooms

Building laws require that habitable rooms – bedrooms, living-rooms, dining-rooms or kitchens – shall have window area equal to at least 1/10th of the floor area, and that half of this window area must be able to admit fresh air. If this is not possible, approval can usually be obtained for the use of mechanical ventilation connected with a duct to an outside wall (for 22 cubic metres of air per hour per occupant, or 5 cubic metres of air per square metre of floor space: whichever provides the greater ventilation). The building bylaws also require a minimum height of 7 ft 6 in./2.3 m for any habitable room.

Self-contained flat

The most economical use of a basement might be to turn it into a self-contained flat. Various problems will arise when you consider this.

Rates: If you propose to let the new flat you will probably have to have it rated separately from the rest of the house. This may result in an increase of rates for the whole building.

Separate entrance: It is advisable to give your new flat its own entrance, otherwise you may have difficulties with the local fire authority regarding the rest of the house. A floor with some fire-resistant qualities will be required between basement and ground floor.

Basements in town houses generally possess areas with their own entrances. This type of basement often includes potentially useful coal-cellars beneath the road.

General planning

To allow maximum ventilation and light into your habitable rooms, it will be advisable to keep the plan of your basement flat as open as possible, though bathrooms and storage could be tucked away in dark corners. Room heights might be a problem. Lowering the floor – which would mean disturbing foundations and certainly upsetting any existing damp-proofing – would probably be impossible, although this course of action is sometimes feasible providing that you keep well away from the structural walls. A better idea would be to consider opening part of the basement to the first floor, which can give interesting vertical and horizontal space relationships.

The coal-cellar under a typical 19th century terrace house has been used to increase the area outside this basement conversion. The brickwork has been treated with a waterproof plaster, and painted white. A floor of marble chippings and plenty of green plants have transformed this cellar into a pleasant garden room.

1

2

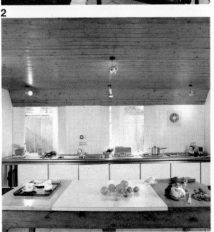

3

4

5

Living-room or bedsitter

An extra living-room or separate bed-sitting-room can be a great source of pleasure. The sound-insulation of the heavier walls and floors makes it the ideal place for young people to play music and entertain friends.

Kitchens

A kitchen may be considered a habitable room in some parts of the country, so check with the local authority. For many reasons – easy access to plumbing and services, easy delivery of goods, but perhaps mostly for traditional reasons – it seems natural for the kitchen to be in the basement.

Border-line habitable rooms

The bylaws that apply when you wish to build a recreation room in the cellar will depend on the local building inspector, or the district surveyor in London. If the problems of creating habitable rooms in your basement appear insurmountable there are plenty of alternatives.

1 A view through the window of the conversion shown opposite. The arched cellar which has been incorporated into the spacious basement flat has been opened out. An extra cavity wall lined with a damp-proof membrane has been built inside the main arch.

2 The interior of the self-contained flat shown opposite and in (1). Furnishings have been kept simple, and in neutral colours to make the most of the relationship between indoors and out.

3 The architect has designed a two-storey flat by opening part of the basement to the first floor. The main living-room and bedrooms are at basement level. Main entrance is at ground-floor level.

4 The greatest advantage has been taken of all available daylight in this basement kitchen, where a plain stainless-steel working-surface incorporating sink and all cooking appliances has been carried across the whole window wall. Light is reflected into the room from this and the shiny, white-tiled walls. More light is reflected back from the white area-walls outside.

5 Long narrow dining table facing french doors opening on to basement area. The area wall has been stepped back into the garden. Although this enlarged area may take up a lot of space in a tiny town garden, it makes the basement much lighter and more useful, and you can bring greenery and colour into the area with flower pots and shrubs. It can also act as an extension to the dining-room for summer parties.

Here's a conversion in the basement of a large terraced house in London. Long, thin and gloomy it had to be turned inwards upon itself. The main problems were the lack of daylight and view to the outside. The front half is covered by the house that rises four floors above. Over the back part daylight comes from a series of roof-lights. Two schemes were proposed, both providing two bedrooms.

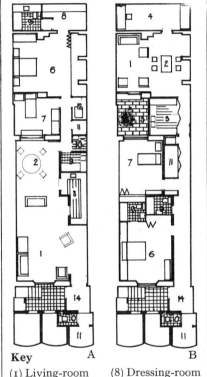

A **B**

Key

(1) Living-room
(2) Dining-room
(3) Kitchen
(4) Study
(5) Storage
(6) Main bedroom
(7) Second bedroom
(8) Dressing-room
(9) Bathroom
(10) WC
(11) Cupboard
(12) Boiler
(13) Courtyard
(14) Lobby

Plan A shows the large living-room looking on to the front area. The internal dining-room and kitchen are lit at high level. The bedrooms and bathrooms are also lit from above. Access to the private areas is through the living- and dining-rooms. Plan B is the scheme selected. Focused on an internal courtyard, the living-room, kitchen and one bedroom are grouped around it. The main bedroom looks on to the front area. This is planted and painted brightly. Artificial light, colour and textures add interest inside the apartment.

Basements/cellars
4/5 Non-habitable rooms

Storage

You can turn the whole basement into a really well-considered storeroom. The best place for storing wine is in the basement because temperatures vary very little all the year round. Ideally wine should be stored on its side, tilted slightly downwards, so that the cork is kept permanently damp.

"Dutch" cellar

When designing a new house with no basement, if storage is likely to be a problem, a "Dutch" cellar could be formed. This is a half-depth cellar, accessible by a trapdoor, usually situated in the hallway so that the entrance will not be obstructed. It is used by the Dutch for storing wine, preserves, etc., which require a constantly low temperature. The bottles and jars are stored around the edges of what may be an area of only 4 ft × 6½ ft/1.2 m × 2 m and about 3 ft/1 m deep. It could also be constructed in an old house, especially where there is a hung timber floor.

---

1 *There is no oppressive feeling in this basement bathroom. Full advantage has been taken of the arched ceiling, and an illuminated panel in the end wall gives the impression of leading outdoors.*

---

2 *Instead of building your bath into the floor, you can build up the floor and sink in the bath. The strength of floor required to carry the weight of this enormous purpose-built bath would make the basement the only possible place for it. The waterproofed walls and tiled surround are impervious to splashing and soaking.*

---

3 *Walls and ceilings have been boarded in with pine planking, following the somewhat untidy structural shapes to give the necessary feeling of unity. The floor has a thick pile rug, and the general effect is plushy.*

1

2

3

Workshop

No family could be happy without some sort of workshop. Ideally this should be planned to fit the various activities of each member of the family, and ideally it should have separate access from outside. The basement is the best place for storing the heavy machinery you might require, and from there the noise of an electric drill will not be too disturbing to the rest of the household. Gadgets that make a continuous noise, such as a stone-polishing machine, can be hidden away in dank and distant corners.

Photographic darkroom

Your windowless space would be suitable for a photographic darkroom, but mechanical ventilation would certainly be necessary. The higher the ceiling the better, if you want to make big enlargements. A sink will be needed for washing finished prints.

Laundry-room

This would need some special ventilation and some form of steam extraction. You must check that any drained appliance is well above the level of the drainage system, or a pumped system will be required.

Garages

If you have the space and headroom to build an outside ramp, or can afford a lift, you can make a garage, but remember that fire regulations require that the walls and ceilings between a garage and the house shall be fire-resistant; any door should be self-closing and fire-resistant. A step or raised threshold may be required to prevent any inflammable liquids cascading into the house.

1 *Front gardens such as these are almost invariably waste space, used only by local cats and dogs. Much better to have an attractive garage workshop.*

2 *Basements are usually cool, which makes them excellent places for larders. If the larder door opens into the kitchen, it pays to make it look as friendly and warm to look at as possible – like this arched door in natural waxed pine.*

3 *If you use machines such as welding apparatus in a basement, you must take special precautions against fire, such as lining the ceiling and walls with asbestos.*

4 *Perhaps the most satisfactory way of using the cellar – certainly the best place for storing wine. Rare flagstone floors such as this should never be tampered with. You can seal them with a heavy polyurethane seal to make them easier to maintain.*

Basements/cellars

New buildings have a damp-proof membrane built into the ground floor and through the outside wall, and they usually have cavity-walls contruction – two skins of $4\frac{1}{2}$ in./114 mm brick or block with a 2 in./51 mm cavity between. This should give sufficient protection above ground level, but if your wall extends lower, a problem of drainage arises. The usual practice is to incorporate a vertical damp-proof membrane – usually asphalt – or to build a solid wall, from ground level down, of concrete with a waterproof additive. A further waterproof rendering on the inner surface of the wall should keep your basement doubly dry.

Old buildings: Most cases of damp trouble come under three headings: (1) rising damp; (2) penetration owing to building faults or deterioration; (3) condensation.

Expert advice may well be necessary, as damp-proofing is hardly a do-it-yourself job.

Horizontal damp-proofing

A damp timber floor which is basically well built and in good condition may be cured if you clear away all the earth and rubbish which has blocked up the air-bricks in the outside walls, but you may have to install new air-bricks to ventilate the underfloor area. A wooden floor in bad condition will have to be replaced with a solid concrete slab incorporating a damp-proof membrane. The DPM should be taken at least 11 in./279 mm up the walls and linked to any vertical damp-proofing. Asphalt, as a floor finish combined with DPM, is a possible solution. Asphalt now comes in colours other than black.

Vertical damp-proofing

Infusion or transfusion: A solid wall can be dried out by infusing a chemical, generally a latex siliconate, through small holes distributed throughout the structure. This chemical can be introduced by pump pressure, or it can be transfused by gravity from containers or "pots" placed round the walls. The manufacturers claim that it takes no more than three days to damp-proof an average three-bedroom house, and the process is guaranteed for twenty years.

The electro-osmotic system: This method makes use of a small electric charge, always present and linked with the rise of water through bricks and stone. The specialist firm concerned maintains that when the charge is removed the rising damp will be controlled. Copper strips are inserted into holes and chases in the brickwork, connected to a small brass junction-box linked to a copper rod driven

into the earth for a depth of between 12 and 20 ft/3.7–6 metres. This system works like a lightning conductor. The copper strip and rod safely conduct the electrical wall charge deep into the earth. This system (also guaranteed for twenty years) is suitable for a basement with earth behind, as a vertical grid of copper strips can be built against the wall, preventing penetration at all levels.

Impervious rendering: Several firms provide a chemical which can be mixed with plaster to form a waterproof rendering for walls and ceilings. If, however, the wall behind the rendering is subject to water under pressure, this may curl off or crack.

Newtonite lath: This is a form of bituminous dove-tailed lathing which, when fixed to the wall with rust-proof nails, forms a cavity isolating the damp and forming a key for plaster.

It is possible to get a government grant for these kinds of improvements, but you must check with your local authority first.

Condensation

Internal vapour condensing on cold outside walls or windows can be cured by balancing the relative temperatures of the air in the room and the inside face of the outside wall, perhaps with additional insulation in the walls and windows. It is unlikely to occur except in a new house, where the drying out of concrete, plaster and paint produce abnormal conditions requiring special treatment.

Tanking

Tanking may be necessary where a building is subject to water under pressure. In this case, nothing less will keep the damp out. It is an expensive process, requiring that a skin of damp-proofing material be laid over the floor and walls, up to the necessary height; this layer has to be protected by a further skin of brick or concrete to keep the impervious layer from being forced in by water pressure.

In cases where tanking is necessary it may be wise to use the basement for basic storage only, perhaps with some sort of a raft to keep possessions off the ground and away from the walls.

Decorations and finishes: walls

Unless you are absolutely certain of your damp-proofing it is wiser not to paper or paint the walls with anything that creates an impervious film, as it is more than likely to peel off. An unpainted fair-faced brick finish requires no maintenance and hides many faults, such as quite heavy condensation. Panelling or boarding makes a pleasant wall-covering

but should be nailed on battens that have been treated with creosote or a similar material. For extra protection, impervious building paper or PVC sheet can be inserted behind the boards.

If you are hanging pictures or other ornaments on walls that might be damp, it is a good idea to glue slices of old bottle corks to the back of the ornaments, creating a barrier which will help protect them from mildew.

Ceilings

The same rules as for walls generally apply. An arched or vaulted ceiling helps to prevent a closed-in feeling. An illusion of a vault can be created with a false ceiling, behind which can be concealed lights, pipes, insulation or undersides of old floors.

Acoustics

The thick walls, lower ceilings, solid floors and small windows of basement rooms give satisfactory sound insulation from the rest of the house, but produce increased resonance within the area. The obvious answer to is have as many sound-absorbent finishes on ceilings and walls as possible.

Floors

The existing floor will almost certainly be of solid construction. A timber floor below ground level would be too difficult to ventilate. Where there is a damp-proof membrane in the floor any finish can be used.

An asphalt layer over the floor provides a combined DPM and rough floor finish. It is not very attractive in appearance, but if covered with carpet or matting it would also give extra sound absorption.

A quarry-tiled floor is perhaps the most suitable and offers some resistance to damp in its own right. It is easy to maintain and clean and probably the most suitable finish, if you decide to install under floor heating.

Windows

You will want to make the most of these, so enlarge them wherever possible. There are other ways of admitting extra light. A ventilation or lighting shaft, lit from above, can be built into the walls. Glass bricks or pavement lights can be built into the structure – for instance, into the risers of front-entrance steps. A type of prismatic glass which deflects the angle of light might be a help. If the ceiling is close to ground level, it might be possible to dig an area or drained trench outside, so that you can fit in some high ground-level windows looking into it. There may be legal objections to

this: in some areas certain unobstructed light angles are required.

Artificial lighting

This is likely to be used continuously and is therefore very important. It might be a good idea, for psychological reasons, to design your lighting to give an illusion of daylight. You could conceal it subtly round windows or false windows – perhaps with stained glass, or shining indirectly from behind curtains. Walls and ceilings are better lit round the edges, if you want to make the room appear less oppressive. It is better not to be able to see your source of light, except where a special lighting effect is required. A mirrored panel gives a feeling of space.

Heating

A good dry basement is in theory so equable in temperature that you should not have to provide a great deal of extra heating. It can be incorporated in your general heating system, but radiators and pipes should not be below the level of the boilers for safe drainage.

If you install independent heating, electrical storage-heaters or underfloor heating worked off cheap night rates would be very suitable. Floor heating coils should be laid on an insulating layer over the damp-proof course to ensure no loss of heat through the floor.

If you have installed mechanical ventilation in your basement, why not build a heater into the duct which will heat the air as it enters the room?

1 *The work-top in this basement room is level with the window sill. There is a positive pleasure in looking out at eye-level on to the paved area and the garden beyond.*

2 *Duplex basement/first-floor room has a huge picture window, which has sliding panels in its lower part.*

3 *If you do not like steps and stairs to your basement, you could build a ramp.*

4 *In a house that's light and airy (note the through-view from front to back), the basement window should not be forgotten. In this conversion, by Heber-Percy Parker Perry, a strong exterior spotlight boosts the natural light.*

5 *If you can get light down to floor level it helps enormously. In this kitchen, the solid door has been replaced with a glazed "stable" door.*

6 *Cellar transformed into music room. A false vaulted ceiling has been constructed of plywood and painted with metallic paint.*

1

2

3

4

5

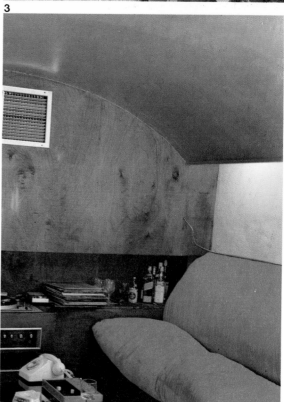

6

Basements/cellars
8 Something different

Picture windows in the basement presuppose a pleasant outlook. There is a great deal that can be done even to the most uncompromising area or wall.

1 *The area wall is clad in mirror-panels, making the transition from indoors to outdoors invisible. The illusion is reinforced by white paintwork outside and in, and by the white panels which are taken up to the top level of the railings.*

2 *Bright yellow paint on the facing wall makes for a sunny outlook. The radiator below the window brings the colour scheme indoors.*

3 *Mosaic paving, extended to the stairs and the wall facing the basement window, makes this area a civilized place where trailing and climbing plants thrive in their mosaic-covered troughs.*

4 *A strict arrangement of tiled seating that continues the design of the floor is accentuated by formal bay trees in their tubs. The centre-piece, a giant Busy Lizzie, is dramatically spotlit at night.*

Adding an extra room/1

An extension room may be the best or only way to achieve the extra space you need – a third bedroom, a study, a dining area, or a playroom. It could be designed as a conservatory, so that you can look the whole year long at leaves and flowers and enjoy their scents; it would also give garden enthusiasts a place for potting up plants, propagating and so on. If the windows are double glazed, it can serve as a dining-room all year provided some topping-up heat is available.

A room that catches the sun adds considerable vitality and pleasure to the character of any house. It becomes somewhere to take sewing, coffee, drinks, and vegetables to prepare, or a place for a toddler's playpen, and is of value in a household where there is an elderly parent or invalid who can't get out.

Consider very carefully what the space is for, then you can decide where to build on and what sort of construction to use. Another room at ground floor level may improve access to the house, as well as to electricity and water supplies. Or perhaps there is a flat-roofed garage over which to build an extra bedroom. However, if you just want a large room for older children's play, a sunny garden room, a simple workshop/hobby-room or a really generous store, it could be far less expensive and less disruptive to erect a prefabricated cedar shed or summerhouse in the garden – trellis and pergola framing covered with quick-growing climbing plants will soon soften its boxy form and link it into the garden scheme.

Here are some questions you should ask when adding on an extra room:

- [ ] What is the extra room for?
- [ ] Does it need to be self-contained?
- [ ] To which room should it be adjacent?
- [ ] Could it be used for several purposes?
- [ ] About how much space is required?
- [ ] Is it mainly for summer, or for use all the year round use?
- [ ] Would it get plenty of sun, yet not cut off light from other parts of the house or from your neighbour?
- [ ] Would it have easy access to drainage, mains, etc. where needed?
- [ ] Would a prefabricated timber structure be visually compatible with the existing house?
- [ ] Or would a solid-wall structure be more appropriate?

One reason why the Victorian or Edwardian conservatory is still so successful lies in the fact that the proportions of windows and glazing bars usually follow the style of those in the principal structure, while the lightness of walls and domes is in marked contrast with the heavy, often ponderous masonry.

Adding an extra room
2/3 What kind of extension?

You have to decide how you are going to construct your extension: whether you will buy a package kit, go to a specialist firm, get a builder to make it up from standard parts or have it specially designed.

Most kits as they stand will not provide a room that can be used the whole year round, but by lining walls and floors and ceilings you can improve their insulation sufficiently to use the room in this way. It would be unfair to say that they are flimsy, but they are not very sturdy structures and need regular maintenance if they are to have a long life.

Although they offer various permutations of elevations – combinations of window and door panels – there are few that offer really good panel proportions. Some manufacturers provide drawings and specifications for the local authority when you apply for permission to build. Some provide an assembly service; with others you will have to call in a builder.

You can go to a package deal firm and have the whole problem taken care of. The service can include taking measurements, preparing designs, making applications to local authorities, arranging finance, carrying out the work and in some cases giving a written guarantee at the end of the job. The advantage is that you have only one firm to deal with. It is in their interest to get the job done as quickly as possible. The one great disadvantage is that their design skills may be limited.

If you are not sure of what you want, you would be better advised to get in a local architect who specializes in conversions and extensions. You could use him to carry the job right through, getting quotations from builders, supervising and checking final accounts, or look after these stages yourself.

Adding a storey

Of course, there may already be a structure which you can build on top of your existing garage, for instance. If it is structurally linked to the side of the house and built of the same material, its foundations should be substantial enough to carry an additional floor. Well designed, an extension of this kind can often add considerably to the appearance and value of the house, making it look wider and more substantial.

However, to achieve this effect it is essential to carry the existing roof across so that the finished job looks as though the house had been built in this way from the beginning. Don't try to save money by having a flat roof over the new room where the existing roof is pitched. A gable-ended roof is easy to extend – you just carry the roof structure through.

(A) *A timber-framed extension is related to the house by a section of matching brickwork.*

(B) *A brick extension can easily be painted to blend into the walls of the house. The woodwork should be painted to match the existing window frames*

(C) *An extension which runs the entire length of the house means that drainpipes have to be re-routed.*

(D) *A timber-framed porch extension matched to the fascia of the house.*

A hipped roof is rather more difficult, as you need to dismantle the existing hip and remake it at the end of the new extension. Try, too, to match the existing bricks or wall finish. Where this is not possible, you could build up the outer walls with timber framing or insulating building blocks. Clad this in weatherboarding, tile or slate hanging – whatever is the local idiom or would best suit the house.

If you have red tiles on your roof, you should match them in any tile hanging you may decide to have on the walls. If you have a slate roof, then use a matching slate. Windows, too, should match in type and scale those in the rest of the house.

Some townhouse gardens are overshadowed for most of the day, making an additional room at ground level less of an amenity. However, the sun may penetrate at a higher level and as this type of house frequently has an existing single or double storey extension, it might well be developed to provide the sort of additional conservatory/sun room suggested earlier at an upper level. Usually the sill of the window on the half landing can be dropped to provide access to it through a glazed door. Extensions may have flat or pitched roofs. The flat-roofed ones are usually covered with felt or asphalt which can easily be peeled off, and the joists below can usually be strengthened and stiffened to enable them to carry a floor load.

Preliminary checks

Before you go ahead with any alterations and additions, you should check the following points. You must find out from your solicitor whether there are any covenants in the title deeds of the house which might restrict what you can build. If you are hoping to extend your mortgage to cover the work – and this is a very good idea – the scheme will require your building society's approval. You will need to check with your local authority whether the proposed structure will comply with Building Regulations.

Planning permission

The addition which you're proposing may be of a kind to require planning permission as well, and should you be lucky enough to own a listed house, then there will be fairly stringent limits on what you can and cannot do.

Before they will grant you permission to go ahead, the local authorities will want you to fill in forms describing the purpose and structure of the new work and provide drawings to illustrate it. If you are using an architect or a package deal firm, they will look after this part of the operation for you.

(E) *An extension built on piers incorporates space beneath for storage or garages.*

(F) *The horizontal accent of this extension is accentuated by the strong lines of the handrail on the balcony.*

(G) *Prefabricated timber-framed extensions are easily and quickly erected.*

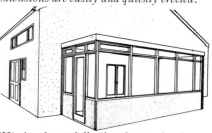
(H) *An almost fully glazed extension is integrated with the house by a matching base.*

However, should you feel you can go it alone with a builder, or even try building it yourself, the responsibility for providing this information will be yours, and you should consult the local District Surveyor or Building Inspector, who will give you a list of all the approvals you require and names and addresses of the appropriate authorities.

Match or contrast

In relating the extension to the house, form, material, colour and the character of windows and doors can all play a considerable part. Obviously if you plan to build a brick extension you should try to match the brick with that of the house. But, if you can't find the right one, it would be better to go for a contrasting treatment using colour wash, weatherboarding, or tile or slate hanging.

Where you have a red brick house with white paintwork and propose to add an extension kit type room, it would be better to choose one with a white finish, or paint it white yourself, than one in treated cedar which could look unsympathetic against the red bricks.

Cedar, unlike most other woods, is proof against rot and decay but unfortunately often comes treated with a preservative to retain its ginger colour. Left untreated, it weathers to a soft silvery grey which blends attractively with stone and grey brickwork. If you're stuck with "ginger"-treated cedar you could always darken it with a dark brown or black water-repellent wood preservative.

Climbing plants help to soften the differences between old and new structures, but avoid ivy, which can damage both timber and brick. Quick growers include honey-suckle, Virginia creeper, Russian vine or clematis. Evergreens do a cover-up job all year round, but need to be lifted so that walls can be re-created or painted during the winter – wood preservative, incidentally, needs renewing less often than paint.

Where the walls are going to be largely glazed in a panel construction, the most attractive proportions are those which have the sort of vertical accent one finds in old greenhouses. Most of the big joinery firms make floor-to-ceiling framed units which can be fully or partially glazed or totally panelled. The proportions of these tend to be simpler and more satisfactory than kits, and the timber sections more substantial. The frames are designed to sizes which will take standard double-glazing panels, and using such framed units with their related doors is a simple way of designing an extension yourself which your builder could construct.

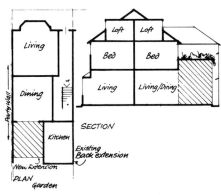

TYPICAL TERRACED HOUSE

An extension with a greater height than existing ground floor rooms can create a light and spacious feeling. A balcony or flower bed can be made on the extension roof.

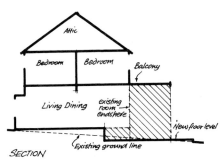

HOUSE ON SLOPE

A virtue has been made of the sloping site, and the new floor level of the extension is carried back into the existing room to create a split level effect. The balcony/flower bed treatment of the new flat roof is an added possibility.

1 *A glass-roofed verandah in a London house has a flourishing vine growing over the dining table. The yellow kitchen units and shelves add cheerful warmth on sunless days.*

2 *The kitchen extension is built as a projecting bay on the first floor of a small house. The sloping roof-light admits daylight while preserving privacy. Work surfaces are of teak and the walls are clad with Canadian Douglas Fir.*

3 *The living-room in this conversion by Aram has been extended into the garden – the new end wall has become a large sliding window and the sloping roof has been glazed. Wooden-slatted venetian blinds have been stained dark brown to match the leather furniture.*

Adding an extra room
4/5 Siting/structural materials

Where there is a great difference between the interior and the outside levels, it is simpler to lay floorboards on rot-proofed floor joists set on or over the slab rather than to build up the concrete to a sufficient thickness. Suspended floors take most floor finishes except heavier ones like quarry and ceramic tiles, stone slabs etc.

Heating

As mentioned earlier, underfloor heating could be installed when laying a new floor slab: where there is a suspended floor, night storage radiators give reliable background warmth and if you have one of the new kind, a booster can be turned on when you need to use the room. If the rest of your house is centrally heated, the boiler may be able to cope with an additional radiator. A good type would be a fan-assisted one which leaks enough heat to keep the chill off and can be turned up when the room is in use. Electric ceiling heating is another possibility, or, if the structure is really well insulated, oil-filled or convector electric heaters controlled by thermostats, which cost very little to install.

Walls and windows

Structures using mainly glass can be a problem. It is no good insulating the solid wall-sections unless you double-glaze the windows too. Choose a make of window frame which can take standard double-glazing units glazed in directly like a single sheet of glass. Otherwise the glass will stream with condensation and the heat loss will be considerable. This isn't just a question of heat-waste; the place will be too uncomfortable to use.

Where solid walls are to be timber framed, pack between the framing with fibre glass, and panel them on the inside with insulation panelling of some kind – ply, chipboard, flaxboard or tongued and grooved boarding. Where the walls are to be of cavity brickwork, infill the cavity with insulation material and use insulating blocks for the inner skin. This can look very good left unplastered and simply painted.

Roofs

Decide whether you want the roof to be solid or to let in light. Most building kits offer both kinds. There is a rule about this that you should observe. A solid-roofed conservatory or verandah may be added in front of an existing window even if the window is the only one in the room, so long as it does not project more than 5 ft/1.5 m. If the addition is to project more or unless the room has a second window, the wall between the room and the verandah must be removed or totally glazed. French doors alone are not considered to provide adequate ventilation – some additional means must be provided.

A solid roof clearly provides the best insulation, and if additional light is wanted a flat roof could be given a domed skylight immediately in front of and over the window or windows of the neighbouring rooms. Where the roof of the extension is to be sloping, then a flat double-glazed form would do a similar job.

Choose a roof form that will marry in with the house. It may be possible to run an existing sloping roof down over the new roof extension. This would make it appear as an integral part of the building with the bonus of a high sloping ceiling inside to give the new room greater contrast and interest. Avoid, where you can, sloping roofs that are not at the same pitch and covered with the same materials as those of the house.

The only shallow-pitched types that really look well are the ones covered with zinc or lead, as the Regency and Victorian ones were; these are not cheap materials, but properly laid have a far longer life than bitumenized felt. Where you want a transparent roof, the corrugated plastic kind is the cheapest, and very light to support. But for a more permanent structure, plain or wired glass, carried by timber sections or the sort of aluminium framing used in larger conservatories is more appropriate.

How to handle a flat roof

There are several good ways of linking a flat roof with the main structure. It could double as a balcony to the rooms opening onto it. Trimmed with an open balustrade, the otherwise thin line of the roof will develop a more substantial character. Or you can achieve this effect by giving it a wide fascia board extended into the garden, with sturdy posts at intervals – a pergola treatment that could be used to define a paved sitting area. Infilled with trellis perhaps, covered with climbing and trailing plants, this could add enormously to the attractiveness of both house and garden.

When working out the best site for an extension, check where your drains are. Try to avoid manholes; although if you badly want the room in a certain position it should be possible to adapt the drains in some way to suit your scheme. You may need power as well as lighting points. Perhaps you want a sink, in which case you will need a water supply and access to a galley or manhole. You will also need to think about heating.

Any room extension will benefit from the heat loss of the room or rooms opening into it. The way you heat the house and how you plan to use the room will determine what sort of heating and insulation you should have.

What kind of floor?

If you simply want a sunny sheltered place where you can sit for half the year, bring in tender plants for the winter or let the children play on rainy days, then a simple paved floor matching and running into the paving of your terrace would be sufficient. But if you want a room that is comfortable to use all the year round, then you should insulate the floor. This doesn't mean that you can't have quarry or ceramic tiles, or even the same paving as outside, but it does mean that you should lay them on a good concrete foundation with a proper damp-proof course and a layer of polystyrene foam or glass quilt before the screed carrying the tiles or slabs is laid. Where a White Meter for night storage, space or water heating is already installed, you might consider laying cables for underfloor heating. It will give a pleasant background heat up to about 60°–65°F/16°–18°C, easily topped up when the room is to be used, but warm enough for children's play and plants. Because it provides a large area of low temperature heat, floor heating doesn't dry the air in the way that a small source of high temperature heat does.

Floor coverings

Sealed or clear vinyl-topped cork tiles make a sturdy warm floor for a year-round playroom and will continue to look well even when the room changes its purpose in later years. Insulation backed lino or vinyl sheeting are both good alternatives.

Carpet can be laid directly onto a dry concrete floor slab, but you should either choose one which incorporates a heavy foam backing or lay a thick foam underlay first. Such underlays can give good insulation, but only lay them where there is some kind of damp-proof course. Rubber or plastic foam provides insulation but isn't proof against rising damp.

Floor levels

It is generally safer to keep an extension room at the same level as the rooms from which it opens out. This is particularly the case with kitchen/playroom link-ups. Where there is a more definite change of mood, say from a sitting-room into a dining-room/conservatory, then a change of level is more acceptable, but the steps should be clearly visible. Different coloured flooring in the two rooms helps – or if you want to keep them the same, a constrasting nosing for the step.

Another point to watch is which way the doors swing. It is dangerous to open a door outwards and step down at the same time, but with a door that opens inwards you have time to become aware of the step. The same thing applies to sliding doors.

If you plan to step down to somewhere near outside paving level or just 6 in./152 mm above it, the simplest way to construct the floor is to lay a concrete floor slab, put in a damp-proof course topped with screed, and use this as a base for your floor finish. Bear in mind that a new solid floor level alongside an existing suspended timber floor must not inhibit the free flow of air which is essential if dry rot is to be avoided.

1 This large extension, which could overwhelm the original house by its bulk if it were less well designed, blends in perfectly: its stark modernity does not clash with the classical proportions of the house but complements them to produce a genuine extension rather than an awkward addition.

2 A pergola can act as an extension to the living-room, defining the area in front of it and making the room itself look larger.

3 A glazed extension, continuing into a balcony verandah, which leads into the garden is upheld by a framework of classical simplicity.

4 Buildings placed over open spaces can have a look of instability. This problem is overcome here by keeping the construction looking light – as with this painted weatherboarding.

5 The formal arrangement of stripes in the paving is continued in the symmetrical windows, and the slab making the balcony.

6 Sunshine on the balcony can mean shadow beneath, but here the use of industrial mesh provides support while allowing light to penetrate below.

7 The framework of this modern conservatory is set out with classical discipline.

8 A basement kitchen has been created out of the space beneath the stairs, which has been extended into the well.

9 Glazed conservatories are traditional in Victorian houses. This modern equivalent sits snugly against the house.

10 Small additions at the back of large houses can be diminished by the sheer size of the surrounding buildings. A blend of simple massing with delicate glazing has given this extension an individual validity.

1

2

3

4

5

6

7

8

9

10

Adding an extra room
6/7 Furnishing/uses

A ground floor conservatory can provide a valuable store for garden furniture during the winter months. Used in this way, it argues for buying the sort of cane, rattan and bentwood furniture that can be easily moved in and out, depending on the weather. This type of furniture is always worth considering in such rooms where most of the walls are glazed, as it responds more sympathetically to the slender lines of stems and branches, trellis and pergolas than the bulky sort.

One of the pleasures of rooms of this kind are the long horizontal vistas they can create Looking through a room extension into the garden beyond will give a far greater sense of space than looking from the same room directly into the garden. You become aware of the middle distance.

Choosing a style

If you have added on a solid-walled room with ordinary sized windows, there's no problem. But if it is an off-the-peg, sub-greenhouse kind of structure, heavy curtains, wall-to-wall carpeting and substantial furniture look thoroughly out of place.

The answer is to sympathize with the basic greenhouse character, perhaps mentally ennobling it with the title of "conservatory", and then think of the most attractive way of interpreting your needs for a playroom, dining-room, sewing-room, or extra sitting-room on these terms: metal, bamboo, cane and bentwood furniture as well as country beech and pine furniture will all look right. Colours should be muted neutrals. Use blinds instead of acres of (expensive) curtains. Pinoleum blinds are useful for screening out strong sunlight – a cheaper alternative to venetian blinds.

Rather than fitted carpet, consider quarry tiles, rush matting or sisal. And of course some mature plants.

Another look in sympathy with the glass and wood construction is boat style: solid built-in wall-to-wall locker seats with piped linen covers; sealed wooden floors with woven cotton rugs; plain canvas awnings, half-louvred Mississippi steamboat shutters and doors, slatted teak tables and chairs or canvas director chairs, or steamer reclining chairs with footstools and armrests for drinks. (Locker seats are in any case a useful form of storage in a room with more window than wall space.)

In the same way, colourful, shiny plastic furniture will look well with boldly patterned roller blinds, as long as everything is kept streamlined as much as possible. Or, if you want to create a more exotic atmosphere in your garden room, you may find inspiration in looking through photographs or paintings of Far Eastern pagodas.

Flexible uses

An extension room can be a means of providing the children with a playroom, so that the living-room can be kept comparatively toy-free. It can help considerably if the room is planned so that it is immediately accessible from the kitchen and children are reassuringly within sight and sound.

There is no reason why children should not have as many meals as possible there; it can make for a far more relaxed atmosphere when other children come to tea. When you are planning a room of this sort, it is obviously worth looking ahead to the time when the children are older and will be happier to go off to their own rooms to work and play. It might then become a dining-room/conservatory

Where you have a garage adjacent to the house with some space behind it next to the kitchen, such an area could be usefully developed to provide a utility room/workshop: a place to keep the washing machine and deep freezer, dry the clothes on rainy days, do the ironing, with room for a work bench and all those half-used tins of paint; a place to have a housekeeping desk and keep your cookery books, where sewing can be left overnight instead of being gathered up off the dining-room table when it is time to lay the supper.

A detached or semi-detached house could have a glazed verandah running across the entire width and doubling as a greenhouse/sitting area.

Sometimes, of course, it won't be another room that you need but an existing one made larger. If the ground plan of your house is L-shaped, for instance, infilling the internal angle will not only give you the amenity of extra room but improve the circulation and seem to double the size of the ground floor area. Or an extension might project from the house to break up the garden into more conveniently usable areas, dividing the service area with its dustbins and washing line from the terrace where you loll in the sun.

Extension rooms can provide useful shelter against prevailing winds and can be a valuable means of linking up the back of the house with the odd mixture of outbuildings one frequently finds too useful to pull down.

1 *An open verandah in California is an extension of the garden into the home.*

2 *A first floor extension is a dining/kitchen area entered from the living-room.*

1 *Oliver Gregory has replaced the window in his kitchen with a white painted timber-frame glazed extension which stands out as a balcony over the basement area. Indoor plants and wicker chair make this kitchen a pleasant place to work and sit.*

2 *View from outside showing fast-growing Russian vine. This kind of extension can be adapted to open up a dark passageway at garden level, creating space and light for wintering geraniums, raising seedlings and general potting up.*

Adding an extra room
8 Case history

1 *This house had previously been converted into two flats. The bottom flat had a very inconvenient layout, and architect Adrian Gale was given the problem of creating a kitchen and eating area. This extension has been built on to what was previously a vestibule leading on to the courtyard. The roof has been tiled to match the existing roof as closely as possible and the brickwork chosen to match the quoins of the original building.*

2 *Plate glass sliding doors are double glazed, and the rectangular quarry tiles are continued out into the courtyard.*

3/4 *General lighting comes from downlighters, working light from tungsten strips under the high-level storage units. Curtains can be pulled right across to shut out the outside world on wet and windy nights, and thanks to underfloor heating and an extra radiator this room is as warm and welcoming in winter as in summer.*

1

2

3

4

Outdoors/1

When you buy a house, it's rather like dropping a stone into a pond. The building itself is obviously going to be the centre of your interest. But then comes the garden, the street, the neighbourhood, the whole area.

We are now concerned with the first ring around your home, the garden. It contributes to the impression everyone will have of the place in which you live.

Getting it together

From inside your home, your own view of the world outside is coloured by your garden too. It can be nothing more than an expensive picture to look at, or an extension of your way of life, furnished as carefully as any room.

The relationship between inside and out can be developed in even the smallest way: between window and planting-box or balcony in a flat; between penthouse and roof garden; town house and yard; terrace house and modest garden; and so on up the scale.

Just as you put together the interior of your house, deciding why a table should stand here or a sink go there, so you should consider the things that go to make up the garden.

The elements that will make a useful gardening plan depend on what you expect from it.

For instance, you'll need shelter from draughts (in town) and from winds (in the country). And since the most useful part of a garden is often the terrace (and this applies particularly to small town gardens) it is often better to spend more on paving and sheltering the terrace, leaving a minimum for the remainder.

If your plan has no logic to it, and you have not dealt with, say, the odd step or retaining wall, the chances are that the result will have no logic either. And although much of the bones of your plan might ultimately be covered by planting, one can nevertheless immediately sense whether a scheme has been properly resolved.

What is a garden for?

If it is for looks alone (and very few are, when you come to think of it) your plan will largely depend on what you plant to provide an interesting all-year-round setting for the house.

But what if you have a chilly garden facing north? What will you do about walls or fencing, the drive-way – if you have one – a car wash, outside tap, lighting, drainage and dust-bins?

Every kind of garden benefits from having the correct boundaries, the right pavings, seating, statuary, pots and light fittings, to hold it together, and link it with the inside of the home.

When considering the boundary to a garden, one tends to think of marking the limits with the material of one's choice. But to be properly functional your garden may need privacy from the neighbours on either side, and in certain situations from above, too.

All these things must be considered from the beginning as part of the basic plan, before you can start getting down to the horticultural side.

If the front garden is public, the back is a more private area and should be designed for the personalities of the family. Children will not become tidy the moment they step out-of-doors; expect a conglomeration of their toys; and take this into consideration.

In fact, consider all the roles a garden might play during a lifetime.

Its changing role

Newlyweds may have little money to spare for gardening on the grand scale, but can plan the area so that it develops with their family and their resources. They might settle for a terrace at the beginning, and a hard-surfaced area connecting the kitchen with such services as the dust-bins or garage.

As the family grows, the hard-surface region may have to expand to take a sandpit, or a circular path for the children to pedal their tricycles.

At this stage, a small vegetable patch might be planted, with a plot of herbs, and a bed to provide flowers for the house.

As the children become older, there might be a barbecue, to cater for fry-ups during the holidays or at weekends, and perhaps an area for ball games.

Other things permitting, a swimming pool may appear, with its attendant gear; or a sauna. At the same time, the flower-beds will need territorial expansion, and a frame or small greenhouse may have to be fitted in. Parents by now are probably deciding that they enjoy gardening, and the garden has come a long way.

Sooner or later the young will leave home, and the garden will seem empty. The parents may want more horticulture; the greenhouse may get larger; a conservatory might be built. This is the stage at which the older gardener must take stock. An area that is easy to weed or mow at 40 or 50 becomes more of a burden as time goes by. Then the garden must be made easier to care for.

Your garden plan, then, should be adaptable, able to expand and contract, as different demands are made on it.

Cool, crisp white paving contrasts with old, weathered stone and the warm earth and grass of the great outdoors.

Outdoors
2/3 View from the inside out

Whatever you plan for your garden, it will be more than worthwhile to try to link the inside of your house with the space outside it.

The more glass you have in your house, the easier it will be to create this feeling of an inflow of space from outside. The effect of bringing the outdoors inside can be even further enhanced by having an abundance of plants in the house; or you can use flooring or walling materials that are continued from the inside to outside, or see if you can co-ordinate your interior colour scheme so that it relates to the flowers or foliage outside.

Terraces

The terrace, if you have one, will be the transitional area between house and garden, and is the one place outside that is likely to get the greatest amount of usage. You might create the feeling of a green room by having some sort of overhead structure supported by the run of wall which often separates properties. Or you might achieve this indoors/outdoors feeling by sinking an area of the terrace.

If you can afford to instal heating on the terrace, it will make it possible for you to use the terrace or patio more, so that it virtually becomes a room.

It is all too easy when trying to create a terrace-room to build an arid platform which simulates the balustraded and urned terraces of grander houses. This terrace solution was often more to enhance the house and impress visitors than for family enjoyment.

Having decided what you want the terrace to do, decide on your flooring material. This might pick up the structural character of the house and its style (old stock brick walls, used York stone paving, for instance).

Work to the module scale of your flooring material and pattern, fitting in the elements you want – built-in seating, perhaps, a sandpit, a pool or areas of planting, so that the plan relates logically to the house, the walls, and even the overall garden pattern.

Styling the garden

You must establish in your own mind the style of your house and interior, and aim for a co-ordination of their style with the furnishing and planting of your garden.

To some extent, this will determine the pattern of your garden. There are situations where a clash in style will work visually, but it's generally safer to stick to one system.

For instance, the formal Queen Anne type of house with an equal number of windows on either side, and a splendid front door, will probably need an equally formal symmetrical layout.

A modern building may demand equal formality, but, in view of modern trends an asymmetric layout might be best. Such a layout is well suited to many of the modern patio or courtyard-type houses.

When a more flowing design is called for, perhaps to link the garden with a wooded area beyond, use bold curves to make up the plan. This is not to say you cast all discipline to the winds; try to keep the shapes interlocking, related to one another (use a pair of compasses on the plan to keep the curves simple) and you will find they will fit the site better.

Few free-shaped gardens work well visually when their curves are just pointless wiggles. In nature, a curve is usually smooth and generous because of the force that creates it. Think of how water flows in looping meanders or of the gentle-curved path that cows wear across a hilly pasture.

If, subsequently, the outlines you create for your garden become fringed with plants, and they flop over the edge of a clear area the plan you conceived should still be discernible through all the greenery.

Rambling on

The apparently rambling informality of a cottage garden is one of the most difficult to create particularly since, if some underlying discipline is not imposed, it all too easily becomes a mess, smothering your plan.

In nature, the strength of a wild-growing group is often derived from one kind of plant forming 85% of the picture, with other things interspersed. This way, all the elements hold together.

A cottage garden often relies on its path, box hedging, a piece of topiary or a well-formed shrub to provide the necessary quiet discipline to the whole.

Do not skimp on planting in an informal garden, even though bold planting arrangements may be expensive. As your garden matures the time needed to maintain it is reduced. Much, though, will depend on your outlook, and whether you are a stickler for tidiness. A more relaxed approach makes life a lot easier.

Start thinking now about the house, since it is the background mass to your garden. The right shaped tree, a horizontal pergola, the line of a fountain jet, become important elements in the final composition. All these features should, of course, be in the style of the house. The aim is to make your house sit in its site, not on it, and use all these elements to bind house and garden together.

A successful plan should not only be in a style referring back to the house, but provide an extension of your internal family life – but outside.

1

2

1 *In this view of a town garden the eye is led out by the leaves of a climbing vitis to a neat path and lawn where buddleia, fig and other leafy plants flourish.*

2 *A lovely, inside-outside desk view on to a London street through a curtain of climbing beans grown in tubs. Inside a fibrous begonia, outside a tall pink hollyhock.*

(Opposite) The room becomes part of the garden and the garden part of the room with this wall of glass to a patio garden, neat and architectural, burgeoning with leaves and a tree in perfect scale. The floor texture changes from shaggy rug to cool tiles to white paving; house plants stand inside and the creepers on the garden wall become part of the decoration of the room.

Outdoors
4/5 Planning

It is essential to get your thoughts on paper, no matter how simply you do it, as it is only on a plan that you can see the relationship between house and garden. This way, too, you overcome the impulse to take the easy way out and plan with plants only.

With luck, you might well get a plan of your site, either old or new, with the deeds of the house or in the estate agent's brochure.

If you find you have to draw a plan of your garden to work on, do the drawing on graph-paper.

Offset

An offset is a measurement taken at an angle of 90° from a fixed line whose position is established to an object, line or boundary whose position is not known, in order to locate it. The fixed line is normally a physical line, such as a wall or fence, but it can also be a datum line established in order to take offsets from it. Normally a series of offsets is taken from the fixed line in order to establish the profile and position of the unknown object or boundary (see below).

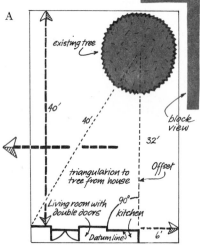

Plot the house, after taking measurements round it, marking windows and doors to scale or, if you already have a house plan, trace its outline on to a larger sheet. Working to the same scale, take offsets at 90° to the house to boundary points and establish the perimeter of the site. Then take offsets from your house again, or the boundary, and fix the position of any key features within the site; a large tree, for instance. To really fix the position of something which will line up with anything else, take two offsets from the object back to fixed positions, so forming a triangle, and here is the process, in its simplest form, of triangulation. You are now beginning to have a site plan.

Now note banks or hummocks on your drawing, and indicate with an arrow any particular view you think worth preserving, or blot out any area to be hidden, like a nearby power station.

Put the points of the compass on your drawing so that you can see where the sunny or sheltered spots of your garden will be.

You now have in front of you a plan of your site (see drawing A). If you have not already done so, write down what you want by way of features in your site. Now you will be able to position what you introduce into the area to its best advantage. Now block in:

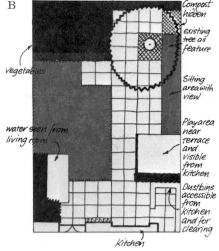

(a) The terrace area, taking into account the sun and the view. Make sure it's big enough.
(b) The dust-bins – near the kitchen but easily accessible for bin collection.
(c) A drying line – not too far away, perhaps masked by judicious planting.
(d) The route to the garage on wet mornings. If it is across the garden, no tripping about on stepping stones.
(e) The compost heap – out of sight and smell range.
(f) A greenhouse or garden shed.
(g) A small vegetable plot or flower-bed.

With luck some sort of pattern might now be emerging. Think first in terms of blocks linking your areas together, or try making bold sweeps with circles (see B).

Having formed some sort of a pattern, try infilling; a block of planting here, paving there and so on (see C). If you have an uneven site, mark in retaining walls and/or steps.

Now look at your plan and try to visualize it from ground level. Laid flat, lines running from the house will visually increase the length of the site, while lines running across the site will give it

breadth. Lines running towards a feature will emphasize it, and curves will be laid flat and foreshortened.

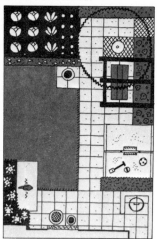

Just as the flat lines in the garden are important, so too are the vertical ones. The difference between the line of a strongly horizontal tree, like a Cedar of Lebanon and the strongly vertical line of a Lombardy Poplar, must be obvious. These shapes, even on the smallest scale can be made to contribute to the third dimension of your garden.

You might well think here about stage design. "Wings" at either side of the stage give the whole setting depth.

You use your "wings" of plants to direct the view, hide eyesores, and generally give the garden some element of mystery, so that when you look at it from indoors not everything is visible all at once.

Instant gardens and no-care gardens

Both are a myth. It *is* possible to build a garden quickly, as long as you are willing to pay for fairly large plants; but the area will still look raw and new. In this case,

plants have to be put in with all the space they need for their subsequent growth.

The demand for an instant garden presupposes that a garden remains static. It does not. It is a pleasure at all stages. It is possible to buy semi-mature trees (see PLANTING). There are shrubs like buddleias, brooms, and lupin trees which grow quickly and which can be interplanted amongst slow-growing specimens, to be removed in 5–7 years' time. Annuals, too, can add bulk. Sunflowers grow to 10 ft/3 m or more; verbascums and hollyhocks (perennials) up to 5 ft/1.5 m or 6 ft/2 m at least. Then there are very quick climbers: the Russian vine, honeysuckles, clematis montana, for instance.

For quick effect, and to cover bare earth, scatter packets of nasturtiums, marigolds or California poppies, though you might live to regret it since they go on seeding themselves. Also, use annuals generously in tubs and pots.

The other myth is the no-care garden. There is no such thing. A labour-saving garden is a possibility, but there is always some work to be done.

If your pavings have been well constructed, and don't grow weeds; if you don't have a rockery; if you don't have rubble walls; if you don't have a pool; and if you don't have grass, you will cut down on labour. But then you won't have much of a garden either.

One way to save labour is by your planting. Plant broad simple masses, preferably of evergreen material; there is a vast range. Keep your annual colour restricted to a few pots on the terrace. Roses, of course, will be out, since even the floribunda needs spraying for black spot and mildew, and they all need ground treatment in winter. Choose shrubs that sweep to the fround, blanketing weed.

If any kind of planting out seems too much like hard work, you could pave the area totally and rely on shrubs and/or potted plants for colour. Care will be reduced to the minimum.

---

1 *An interesting juxtaposition of camomile lawn and zigzag paving.*

---

2 *This traditional garden plot has a lawn of curves and straight lines with a formal stone edging.*

---

3 *Shrubs and foliage plants like hostas show up well against stone paths.*

---

4 *An ideal proportion of stone to greenery. Lavender, bay, broom, grasses, laurel and pelargoniums soften a concrete path.*

---

5 *A brilliant yellow-green acacia frames and shades a square of paving with a gravel area for pots of bright pink pelargoniums.*

Outdoors
6/7 Levels

A garden plan is often complicated by the fact that the garden is not flat, and changes of level have to be incorporated.

Broadly, though, initial thinking remains the same. The retaining wall, bank or steps necessary for the level change must fit into the same basic pattern. If you have planned a crisp town layout, with wall surrounds, then your retaining walls will be in the same material, or in concrete block.

A larger lawned area might call for ramped banking when levels change–making an ideal place for bulbs – or the bank can be planted solid with a ground cover, which is easier to look after.

The country garden might need a more random approach. Old railway sleepers could look attractive, with ferns and mosses creeping through them.

Beware, however, of the rockery. A stock solution that is invariably inadequate, difficult to maintain, and after spring flowering looks a mess. It should appear as a natural outcrop, not a heap of earth with stones stuck in it.

Whatever you choose, consider drainage as water will inevitably flow from top to bottom. When it can get away, or be caught by a drain, all is well. But if water is trapped behind your structure the whole is eventually weakened.

In a solid wall include weep holes every 6 ft/2 m in the horizontal run, but above the bottom level, so that water building up behind the wall can escape.

You will lengthen the life of a solid retaining wall by including some form of damp-proofing up the back, by painting it with a Bitumastic finish, or running a plastic sheet up it, and incorporating a damp-course in the structure to avoid damp rising within the wall.

The steps linking two levels should be in the idiom of your layout; crisp in some places, relaxed and gentle in others. Try to get away from flights of steps and instead create an interesting series of levels. This will add much interest to the site. Turn your steps, curving them or staggering them so that you progress across the level change rather than straight up it. Steps can make occasional seats when near a terrace; but when there are children with cycles, or elderly people who find steps difficult, consider a ramp.

Steps should not be too steep; the tread should be wide, 18 in./457 mm is ideal, and a 6 in./152 mm riser is adequate. They should be sound and dry throughout the year, or they become a hazard. This is particularly important when the first access to the house is up or down steps.

Steps can be built in most of the materials considered for outside use. The larger the element they are made with, the safer they will be.

When traversing a bank, one often finds that the small area on either side of the steps presents difficulties if the steps are not bordered by retaining walls. Good evergreen ground cover like juniper or hypericum plants make an ideal muffle to these tricky changes of level.

Points to remember

(a) Unless you particularly want a very crisp feel to steps, always allow between 1 in/25 mm and 2 in./51 mm overlap of the tread (the bit you walk on) over the riser.
(b) Keep your steps as shallow and wide as possible. The garden is not a place in which to move about quickly, and the width and height of your steps controls the pace at which you use them.
(c) Make allowance for water to drain off steps quickly so it can't freeze on them, particularly when they are a main access.
(d) The detail on either side of steps is tricky, resolve it before starting off.

---

1 *On a wooden wall, triangles of timber make massive steps giving dramatic shadows.*

2 *Bare stone steps have white alyssum nestling in the corners.*

3 *Huge slabs of stone make a romantic flight of steps in a steep woodland garden.*

4 *Brickwork edges a flight of grass steps.*

5 *A wide flight of stone steps lead to a wooden seat framed in climbing roses. Poppies and purple clary grow by the steps.*

6 *Terraced steps planted with rosemary, thrift, galeobdolon and silver centaurea.*

7 *A sunken eating area with an elm table and benches. The paving stones are planted with fig, ornamental nettle and euphorbia, and set about with pots of geraniums.*

8 *A sculptural and prehistoric-like edging is a palisade of stout posts of varying heights.*

9 *Here retaining walls for terracing are made of solid horizontal timbers.*

10 *Large saracen stones mark a corner in a garden where steps meet a cement path.*

11 *One change of level edged with stone slabs and cobbles divides up a carpet-like lawn. Red and white floribunda roses are effective in this simple garden.*

12 *Raised steps or boxes with plants on different levels can be interesting.*

13 *Stone paving leads to shallow stone steps to lawn, then to another plane of lawn, framed in stone, to end in a mass of roses.*

1

2

3

4

5

6

7

8

9

10

11

12

13

Outdoors
8/9 Enclosures

Since the possibilities for planting, boundaries, and general pattern are endless, a garden can be an expression of your own personality.

Not everyone needs, or wants, their garden enclosed. They may have a fine view, no neighbours, or just like watching the world go by. But some form of screening will probably be necessary to block out draughts and wind.

A *brick wall* makes an excellent permanent enclosure. If built of the same material as your house, an arm of it is straightaway established outside. If a wall is 9 in./229 mm thick, it will need a coping of stone, paving slab or slate. A 4½ in./114 mm wall can usually only take a coping of half a brick.

A far cheaper solution to walling is *concrete block*. Different types, sizes, and colours are usually available locally, or the names of local distributors can be obtained from the Cement and Concrete Association.

Less satisfactory against sound, and with a shorter life, are *timber panels* which come in many patterns and heights, but should be used with care. Too much timber fencing surrounds you with a dark strip, and the creosote or preservative on new panels scorches plants growing against it, which makes immediate softening difficult. A timber capping to the panels, and a gravel board along the bottom to stop it rotting, will increase its life span considerably.

Hurdles can be used as a short-term measure (three to five years) to enclose a site while planting grows up. Made of wattle, osier or reed, their character is distinctly rural.

Made of softwood rails fixed on alternate sides of a timber vertical, *ranch-type fencing* does not give complete privacy, but offers a solidity lacking in wooden panels. Allow plants to grow through any gaps, softening the effect.

External strip lighting or planting boxes can be worked into the wall to provide a very pretty terrace screen. This works well on roof gardens.

Palisade fencing gives little enclosure, although high panels, mixed with plants, can be effective. Normally 3 ft/1 m–4 ft/1.22 m high, painted white, it gives a front garden a cottage effect. The tops of the verticals, set about 2½ in./63 mm apart, are pointed or rounded.

Chestnut pale fencing should be supported either by galvanized wire fixed and strained between timber verticals, or, more expensive, by a timber horizontal rail. It is bought in rolls of up to 50 ft/15 m lengths, and should always be erected with the pales strung a few inches above the ground to prevent them from rotting.

Patterned blocks available for pierced screen walls.

Post and rail fencing is attractive for its comparative cheapness. It comes sawn, either in oak, when no treatment is necessary, or softwood (which needs a preservative), or, more rustic, in cleft chestnut or cleft oak.

Single-bar fencing has a crispness about it suitable for defining a front garden. It often surrounds village greens.

Timber and wire fencing, cheap and cheerful, defines a site when the view is to be preserved. Galvanized wire is strained between sawn larch or cleft oak posts. Concrete posts can be used, but they seem out of place on the domestic scene. Chain link or plastic mesh might be used between timber verticals, but look unsightly left unadorned.

Metal fencing: vertical-bar railings could not be more urban for front gardens. Their counterpart, with horizontal rails, is essentially rural.

Gates

A gate takes very heavy wear, so keep its design strong and simple, and above all else, in style with fence and house.

Walls

1. It is obviously cheaper to build a 4½ in./114 mm wall than a 9 in./229 mm one, whether in brick or concrete block. Both need piers or buttresses for support. Consider building the thinner wall in staggered bays to provide 9 in./229 mm piers at 6 ft/2 m – 8 ft/2.4 m intervals.
2. If your wall is in a different material from a hard surface nearby, consider capping or coping the wall with the paving material to get a tie-up. Use brick, slate, tile, or concrete paving slab.
3. Consider a damp-proof course. When building retaining walls, consider water building up behind them, and allow for weep holes every so often, so that water can escape. Consider waterproofing the rear of a retaining wall.

---

1 *A vertical slatted fence gives you both privacy and a through view.*

---

2 *Rough softwood poles with small transverse dividers make a lovely palisade.*

---

3 *A wall of rough stones and old bricks makes a perfect background for roses.*

---

4 *A solid wall, pierced with a "window" can be dramatic and evocative.*

---

5 *A bright mural of comic-book characters livens up a children's play area.*

(Opposite) Grey stone walls make a perfect enclosure for plants. Here the paths are kept neat and clean, but Welsh poppies seed themselves in every crevice.

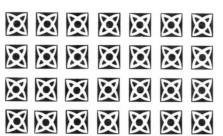

Various sheds are combined under one roof. Timber contrasts with gravel and stone.

Harsh car-port wall angles camouflaged by jasmine and clematis montana.

A sand-pit for tots penned in with a seat-height brick wall.

A compost heap, walled with brick and separated from the garden by a high beam.

Few house designers consider outside storage space, and the little Noddy structures they often produce are difficult to hide, as the scale is all too often wrong. Most outside structures are too high for their ground size, and tend to be blemishes. For the same reason, the siting of a bought structure is usually difficult too. For convenience it should be near the house, but for a good visual effect should be hidden; whether it's a shed, a fuel store or the oil storage tank.

Early on in planning a garden group the essentials together. Consider extending a roof, or just a fascia line, to become a pergola. Anything, in fact, to make a mass so that the garden does not look cluttered. The back of one structure can be the prime wall of a lean-to, and an odd angle become a dustbin enclosure.

Or, with simple timber screening, block out eyesores and distract the eye.

It seems a pity that no manufacturer copes with garden structures in this light. In our age of prefabrication, one ought to be able to add to structures as one builds up a garden over the years, so that different elements are all held together.

Such an all-embracing scheme like this might well be too big for many a garden, but there are many occasions when the do-it-yourself handyman can put up a pergola beam over his terrace, or link his shed to his kitchen extension, to good effect. The resulting covered area, helped with a vine or clematis grown through it, provides a perfect place for eating out, and also becomes a green transition from house to garden.

It is the style of pergola which matters. If the lines of your house are clean and simple, keep your structure that way too. In an older garden, avoid the rustic pole or brick piers with sagging ropes between.

The space saved in a small garden, by clever grouping and building-in, is enormous. Consider seating in this light too. If you are going to use your terrace for the occasional cup of tea or evening drink, you won't want to drag out chairs from the back of the garage. (By then the sun will have gone in.) So give retaining walls a good wide top on which you can perch; or for half the width of the odd terrace step, miss a riser so that you get some double height steps, each making a seat. Build in a whole bench in brick or timber, with a lift-up lid, in which you can store toys or gardening boots. Build in a table, which is there all the year round. You will find that this type of all purpose furniture gives you immeasurably more service than an iron pub table or hard metal chair. It will look more welcoming to.

Consider your children's play equipment in the same way. Most metal structures are garish when new, sordid when not. A swing can hang from a reinforced pergola beam and be unhooked.

Build in a sand pit along with the terrace. Make it large enough to get into, with a shelf inside for sand pies.

With three brick or concrete-block walls supporting an old bootscraper, you have a suitable barbecue on which to cook. Remove the scraper, use it as the fourth wall, and you have an incinerator.

Fitting in garden structures

The siting of any building in the garden is crucial. If the service units can be screened, or added to existing structures, so much the better; but the feature buildings need more careful handling, since they will probably be standing on their own.

The secret seems to be to site any feature structure so that it appears to sit *in* the garden, couched in greenery, and with a green backdrop, rather than *on* the garden in splendid isolation. The detailing of the surround to the building is important, because it can make a 'tidy join between the vertical and horizontal planes. Lastly, the materials used in the structure should be in sympathy with the whole.

(Opposite) Pergolas must be strong enough for robust nature to climb and entangle. Here large beams jut out from a wall giving stripes of shade on to a sitting area. Underneath is a planting of cottage pinks, roses and cardoon thistles.

The ultimate in formal outdoor entertaining a well-designed barbecue fireplace.

Pierced openings in solid walls on to a view – the cottage window secret.

The shallow stone steps of this low eating area double as seats with squab cushions.

A stone pit to play in, surrounded by a romantic and secret garden.

Outdoors
12/13 Surfaces

Once you have sited the major functional areas of your garden, you will need some sort of surface to get to them.

Decide how much hard surfacing, like paving, you want; how much soft surfacing like lawn; whether you want any gravel.

The type of surfacing you choose will depend on the function, character, and size of the area.

For a domestic setting, a smaller element, like brick, or granite sett, looks more sympathetic.

Smoother surfaces in larger elements, like concrete slab, brushed *in situ* concrete, call for more attention if they are not to look arid. Pots should be stood about, and the furniture of a family garden. In a more traditional setting the compromise is a surfacing of old squared York stone.

The drive-in, taking the heaviest wear, might be in tarmacadam or asphalt, in varying colours according to the chippings rolled in; or in brushed concrete; or, newly on the market, a heavy-duty interlocking concrete block.

To break up what can easily become a desolate area, mix the materials. Try to include one which was used in the structure of your house or boundary walls.

You might try a squared pattern of brick, granite sett or paving slab, with an infill of tarmac or brushed concrete. Brushed concrete has the gravel aggregate showing, giving the surface a pleasant texture.

Whatever pattern or shape you conceive for your paved area, it should obviously relate to the remainder of the garden plan.

When evolving a scheme, be generous in your areas of paving. A terrace for sitting, eating, or sunbathing should be at least 6 ft/2 m wide. Consider the run back for table tennis, and the space necessary for changing a cycle tyre.

It is a good idea, when initially conceiving your garden plan, to think in multiple dimensions of the paving you have chosen – provided it is a regular one. This way you save on cutting, and don't end up with all sorts of odd shapes and corners.

In a small town garden decide if a lawn is practical. It is often considered both cheap and easy, but if the grass is to be of a good standard, and free of weeds, it will need fairly frequent attention.

Pets tend to foul up a lawn, and an area of *gravel* might be a good compromise. It is comparatively weed-free if properly laid, and looks pleasant enough with occasional plants growing in it.

Washed pea gravel ranges from gold to brown and comes in varying gauges from gravel pits and river beds.

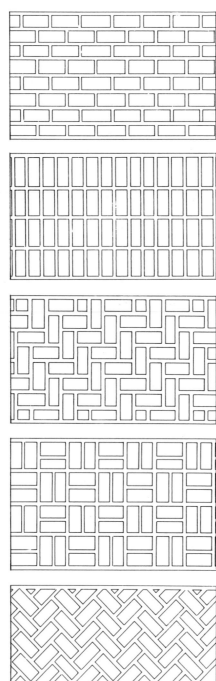

Patterns for laying bricks.

White gravel chipping is good in a dark area. It is readily available.

Hoggin – a mixture of brick dust and clay – used with, or instead of, gravel.

A few materials lend themselves to use both inside and out: for places like a small garden area, terrace, or roof garden, which have to relate to a room adjoining them, such as a conservatory or playroom.

In a sheltered area where they are not likely to get exposed to severe frost, *quarry tiles* are admirable for use inside and out. First quality tiles are of a standard colour. Enquire about seconds, which often have variations in them. They therefore don't look as flat, and are a little cheaper.

Engineering (hard) brick can be used both inside and outside. It is only 2 in./51 mm thick and easy to lay. A good range of colour is available.

Slate looks superb inside or out but it is expensive and becoming difficult to get.

Granite has a similar feel, but needs polishing for inside use.

York stone or pre-cast concrete slabs can be sealed for use indoors, and outside look good over a large area.

On roof gardens, where weight is a problem, consider cobbles, asbestos, or composition blocks.

Pavings

1 Always lay surfacing with falls away from the house into the garden. A cross-fall of roughly 1 in./25 mm in 6 ft/2 m is adequate. The garden will soak up surplus water unless the area is too vast. You might consider a drain across the edge of the main flow, or an open gully, leading to a soakaway pit. This is a sunken area about 3 ft × 3 ft × 3 ft/1 m × 1 m × 1 m at the very least, filled with brick rubble, which soaks up the drain run.

2 Paving with the joints pointed can either be laid flush or rubbed back ⅛ in./3 mm or so. This looks better. Paving laid without jointing, or "butted up", will drain quicker, but tends to grow weeds.

3 It is not necessary to put in a curb at the edge of paving to retain earth; the paving will do that itself, unless the surrounding ground is much higher.

4 If you are putting steps in a paved area, stick to the same materials for their construction. A change will only break the flow of the pattern.

5 Lay paving ½ in./12 mm below that of abutting grassed areas, so that the mower goes over the edge of the paving without any damage to the blades.

6 Always ensure that hard surfaces and earth levels are at least 6 in./152 mm below the damp-proof course to your house, and do not cover over air bricks,

Going Metric

Much of the building industry has already gone metric. Bricks, concrete blocks, and paving are available in new sizes.

New paving sizes are:
450 mm (18 in. approx) × 600 mm (24 in. approx)
600 mm (24 in. approx) × 600 mm (24 in. approx)
600 mm (24 in. approx) × 750 mm (30 in. approx)
600 mm (24 in. approx) × 900 mm (36 in. approx)
Brick sizes vary, but an average one is 300 mm (12 in. approx) × 100 mm (4 in. approx) × 100 mm (4 in. approx). Concrete block sizes vary, but the following might be typical sizes, with varying combinations:
400 mm (16 in. approx) × 200 mm (8 in. approx) × 150 mm (6 in. approx).
450 mm (18 in. approx) × 225 mm (9 in. approx) × 200 mm (8 in. approx).

1 *A large area of outside floor made subtly interesting with square granite setts, like giant mosaic – meeting and curving.*

2 *A good contrast of two materials – white cobble steps with patterned brick.*

3 *Vaguely medieval and lovely to walk on, a contrast of mown turf and level stone paving inset in the sward. You can have your velvet turf continuous with no fear of wearing it bald by walking on it.*

4 *Tiles, bricks and paving stones have a special charm when unevenly laid. Here the floor is made of old tarred wood blocks which used to form city roads. Ferns in the wall make feathery shadows.*

5 *The epitome of a formal garden walk: pleached limes, neatly clipped, line a stone-flagged path which has granite setts on either side with small plants growing. The perfect surroundings of velvet lawns with old-fashioned roses.*

6 *Beautiful to walk on, if hard to find: slices of conifer trunks, laid in sandy gravel, give an orderly fish-scale effect with subtle differences of size and shape.*

7 *A courtyard floor worthy of Peter de Hooch: yellow and grey bricks in subtle geometric patterns.*

8 *Patterned brick remains one of the most successful garden floors. Here it is laid in simple alternate horizontal and vertical squares round an old apple tree, with a riot of grape hyacinths and forget-me-nots neatly enclosed.*

9 *Nature just being kept in check. York stone paving in a beautiful country courtyard, with camomile, poppies, scarlet pimpernel and grasses rioting out of every crevice.*

1

2

3

4

5

6

7

8

9

375

Outdoors
14/15 Planting out

We have considered the advisability of small lawns, and there are cases for a piece of grass even in the smallest plot: to sit the baby on, or to pen a pet rabbit, for instance. Where grass is wanted on this scale, it is worth thinking of it as a bed which might otherwise have contained geraniums, built into the terrace. The grass should be ½ in./12 mm above the surrounding surface for easy mowing. This is also a cheap way of enlarging a terrace, but the grass must be in the area of surrounding paving, not next to it. Otherwise it becomes a separate feature.

What shape of lawn?

Undoubtedly the chief glory of the English garden is its fine sward of grass, usually attained at great cost in time and money. There are, however, different standards of grass suitable for different needs. The weediest lawns can often take quite the hardest wear.

When evolving your lawn shape, keep it as simple as possible, avoiding tight little corners which you will have trouble negotiating with a mower. Consider how you will mow the area, and make the runs up and down as simple as possible for yourself. If your mower is electric, make sure that a tree will not foul the flex on each turn.

It goes without saying that a lawn surface should be as level as possible, but grass banks can add interest, be enjoyed by children, and be left as rougher grass in which you grow spring and autumn bulbs. Failing this, group your bulbs so that the shape of the long grass in which they grow appears as part of your overall plan, even though you may mow it all down in June.

Lastly, avoid creating island beds or planting specimen shrubs all over your lawn. The effect becomes spotty and unrestful, and the lawn becomes most difficult to look after!

Seeding v. turfing

The pros and cons of seeding your lawn as opposed to turfing one are worth considering at the outset.

The surface for turf needs less preparation than for a seed bed, and if well laid and watered, the turfed result is very quick indeed. Ensure that a good fine grass meadow turf is laid, and that it is comparatively free of weed, though any weeds remaining can be later eradicated. It is seldom worth even considering sea washed turf for a domestic situation.

A seeded lawn will probably take a whole season to establish itself properly; this can be a problem when young children are bursting to use it. Provided a good seed has been used and the area has been maintained through that first season, the result will be better than a turfed lawn. In terms of money the seeded lawn is cheaper, but more demanding in labour and time.

Planted areas

Before you begin filling in the garden with flowers, select the trees and shrubs which will form the background to your plan, choosing those which will reach the height you want. Many should be evergreen, if the area is not to be a lattice of twigs in winter. Some can be decorative, others sculptural in quality.

Trees

Start with the trees. Will your space allow for the development of a forest tree, or only small flowering ones? Remember that a tree grows outwards as well as up.

It is possible to buy large trees, in a good range of varieties, but –
(a) They must have been properly and professionally prepared;
(b) They must be expertly moved and planted by the correct mechanism;
(c) They must be properly guyed for up to three years;
(d) They must be watered and maintained constantly for at least the first year in their new position.

In most domestic situations, it's far better to buy large nursery stock trees.

One outsize tree in a small town garden can be magnificent, and the shade it casts will determine the planting under it.

Shrubs

The types of shrubs which are good all-rounders for backyard infill are really very limited for general use.

They might include some of these:
Berberis
Buddleia (the butterfly bush)
Cotoneaster
Cytisus
Fatsia
Hibiscus
Ilex
Prunus
Ligustrum
Mahonia
Veronica (Hebe)
Viburnum

Select and plant your specimens in groups or drifts. Have two or three to a group in a small garden, a group of seven to ten in a larger area.

Climbers

Climbers are often high on the priority list of plantings, to soften hard new walls and muffle fencing. Wires or timber horizontals running along the line of your brickwork provide the simplest and least conspicuous support. See that they are firmly anchored.

Here is a list of what to plant where.

For sunny positions:
Berberis
Buddleia
Caryopteris
Ceratostigma
Choisya
Clerondendron
Convolvulus
Crataegus prunifolia
Cytisus scoparius
Fuchsia (hardy)
Genista
Hibiscus
Lavandula
Olearia
Perovskia
Potentilla
Prunus (some)
Rhus cotinus
Rose (various)
Rosmarinus
Senecio
Spartium
Tamarix
Ulex
Veronica
Vinca

Shrubs for shade:
Arundinaria
Aucuba
Camellia
Chaenomeles
Cornus alba Elegantissima
Cotoneaster
Daphne
Euonymus
Fatsia
Fuchsia
Gaultheria
Hydrangea
Hypericum
Mahonia
Pieris
Pyracantha
Rubus flagelliflorus
Rubus tricolor
Skimmia

Rampant:
Convallaria majalis
(Lily of the valley)
Cornus canadensis
Gunnera manicata
Hedera helix Hibernica
(Ivy)
Hypericum calycinum
(St John's wort)
Luzula maxima
(grasslike)
Lysichitom (Arum-like)
Trachystemon
Verbena corymbosa
Vinca major
(Periwinkle)

Plants for shady walls:
Camellia
Chaenomeles
Clematis montana
Cotoneaster horizontalis
Enonymus radicans
Hydrangea petiolaris
(climbing hydrangea)
Jasminum nudiflorum
(winter jasmine)
Pyracantha
Roses (some)

For town gardens:
Acer platanoides
(Norway maple)
Ailanthus altissima
(tree of heaven)
Arbutus unedo
(strawberry tree)
Aucuba japonica
Berberis (deciduous)
Betula (Birch)
Buddleia davidii
Catalpa (Indian bean tree)
Chaenomeles japonica
Cornus
Cotoneaster
Crataegus (thorn)
Cytisus scoparius (broom)
Daphne mezereum
Deutzia
Euonymus europaens
(spindle berry)
Fatsia
(false castor-oil plant)
Ferns
Forsythia
Hedera
Hibiscus
Ilex (holly)
Jasminum
Laburnum
Ligustrum (privet)
Mahonia
Malus (crab apple)
Pernettya
Philadelphus
Prunus
(flowering cherry varieties)
Prunus laurocerasus
(common laurel)
Pyracantha (firethorn)
Ribes sanguineum
(flowering currant)
Senecio
Sorbus aucuparia
(mountain ash)
Spiraea
Symphoricarpos albus
(snowberry)
Syringa (lilac)
Veronica
Viburnum
Vinca (periwinkle)

More sober:
Alchemilla mollis
(Lady's mantle)
Anaphalis triplinervis
(grey leaves)
Anemone hupehensis
Artemisia abrotanum
(Southernwood)
Artemisia canescens
(grey)
Artemisia pontica
(grey)
Aruncus silvester
(Spiraea-like)
Asperula odorata
(Woodruff)
Astilbe
Bergenia
(Elephant's ear)
Brunnera macrophylla
(Anchusa)
Calluna
(Bell heather)
Campanula latiloba
Centaurea dealbata
Cyclamen neapolitanum
Daboecia
(Tree heather)
Dianthus Highland Hybrids
Dicentra formosa
Epimedium
Erica
(Heather)
Eryngium bromelifolium
(Thistle family)
Euphorbia robbiae
(green flowers)
Ferns
Geranium
(herbaceous)
Helleborus
(Christmas rose)
Hemerocallis
(Day lily)
Hosta
(Funkia)
Iris (several)
Lamium maculatum
variegatum
(Variegated dead nettle)
Monarda
(Bergamot)
Nepeta mussinii
(Catmint)
Origanum
(Marjoram)
Pachysandra terminalis
Paeonia
Polygonatum
(Solomon's seal)
Polygonum
Pulmonaria
Rodgersia
Ruta graveolens
(Rue)

The traditional velvety English lawn with a riotous and burgeoning herbaceous border divided by a geometrically paved stone path. From crevices in the path grow clumps of alchemilla mollis, *in orderly disorder.*

Topiary – even on a smaller scale – needs constant attention.

Formal planting of "island units" in lawn beds ; standard floribunda roses with small clumps of lavender, and sage.

A mixed mass of vegetation makes a very effective feature exploding out of a well-kept lawn. Here the plants are globe artichokes of silvery grey-green, the misty mass of crambe latifolia. *Especially effective because of lack of obvious colour, this is a good example of a massing of different plants.*

White-painted walls, wood (as here), brick or stone are a good background for climbing plants : here the rose "Zepharine Drouin", and the fronds of berberis.

Vertical features are important ; here a clematis montana *will soon cover a wall. The combination of dark painted building and plain white picket fence is perfect.*

377

Water livens up a terrace area considerably but before introducing it, decide how you want to use it.

Fountains

The submersible pump has made fountains a very easy proposition. The pump sits in the bottom of the pool, with a lead back to the mains electricity. This should be adequately concealed and covered, preferably by a pipe to stop perforation by a spade or toy.

Before deciding to have one, though, listen at your local garden centre to the different noises the fountains make, and be sure that you will be able to stand it.

Some firms have a scheme whereby you can borrow a series of fountain jet fittings and can choose the type of spray you like *in situ*.

Ponds/pools

A well-balanced pond will keep itself fairly clear, but there is a certain amount of maintenance to be done throughout the year. Too many small areas of water have no real character.

A raised pool is attractive to sit around, but where a pool is below ground level and surrounded by paving, the water level should be just under the paving.

Some of the pre-formed plastic pools, when of a geometric shape, can be successfully worked into your plan.

A plastic sheet cannot be recommended for domestic use as a pool liner, since the folds are always visible, and the edges of the sheet present problems.

Complicated water supplies and outlets are not needed for small pools as you seldom need to change the water.

Submersible plants

Submerged oxygenating plants, along with fish and snails, will establish balance in your pool. Allow about 12 plants for each 24 sq ft/2.2 sq m of surface water area. Here is a list:
Callitriche verna – starwort
Ceratophyllum demersum – hornwort
Eleocharis acicularis – hair grass
Elodea canadensis crispa
Fontinalis antipyretica – willow moss
Myriophyllum verticillatum – milfoil
Potamogeton crispus – curled pondweed
Ranunculus aquatilis – water crowfoot

Among these you can of course plant water lilies too, but get the right lily for your depth of water. Lilies do not like moving or running water.

The best snails for your pond are black ramshorn snails; one dozen should be introduced for each 24 sq ft/2.2 sq m of water surface area.

Water, an important space-giving and magical element in a garden.

1 *Dripping water and senecio and flag iris.*

2 *The splashing of water into a cistern – an ancient and magical sound.*

3 *Sculpture made of water: three constantly changing fountains growing from a square of pebbles. An exciting mixture of sight and sound.*

4 *Beautifully severe red brick cisterns containing water have an ancient simplicity; here water reflects sky and vine above a shady patio.*

5 *Small feet on cool, wet stone. A submersible pump can make the supply seem endless.*

6 *A beautiful arrangement of levels and rectangles, some stone, some water, with iris growing and a Chinese vine above.*

7 *Paving, gravel and rectangular pool with yellow roses and silver senecio greyi.*

8 *Stepping stones cross the water, joining two paved areas.*

9 *A stone-framed pool in white gravel with a mass of reeds and grasses.*

Outdoors
18/19 Living outside

We have considered building timber, brick or concrete seating, and, near the kitchen door or window, this makes sense for children's play, shoe cleaning, a quick cup of coffee, or shelling peas in the sun. With little adaptation, and a long lead, the ironing can be done outside too.

Hong Kong basketware, for more elegant seating, looks decorative, but stands little more than one summer outside. Morning dew rots furniture just as much as rain.

Since, ideally, it remains outside throughout the summer, a seating group should look sculptural, and as with all else, be in sympathy with the style of the house and garden.

Wooden furniture, stained or painted, does withstand the English weather and, being more massive, looks good outside. Much of the best comes from Europe.

Metal furniture is even tougher, but then you have to be too, since it can be extremely uncomfortable. A lot of it is rather fey in design.

From the Continent comes some very fine "plastics" furniture. Although expensive, it is completely weather resistant but not very sympathetic to the garden. Metal and canvas furniture from Scandinavia is tough and good looking.

Bamboo, rush, and basket furniture is comfortable to sit in, but as it does rot, it is more suitable for the sun-room or conservatory.

Good value, light, and easy to store, aluminium chairs and loungers are universally available.

Cooking

Our requirements for eating outside are quite humble: we are still a nation of soggy-sandwich eaters in the main.

Various types of barbecue are available. The cheaper Japanese grill barbecues are ideal small fitments, and not unattractive in themselves. You can even take them in the car boot for picnics.

Design for a barbecue

The whole mechanism of the barbecue need be very simple: a grill for the meat, and a tray for the charcoal underneath. What most barbecues do not provide is working space. An adjacent flat top is essential, with perhaps a light and a place for storing charcoal.

By building one's own cooker corner, Mum can cope at very short notice with outdoor meals.

Movable furniture in a garden should never obtrude; old-fashioned white-painted cast-iron and marble always were and still are about perfect. Shade is important for eating and nothing beats a leafy bower for lunch on a hot day.

1 *For a formal meal white-painted chairs and an elegant old wooden table are here moved outside. A level floor, here brick, is essential to avoid wobbling.*

2 *Creaking comfort is part of the pleasure of sitting outside. Woven slat, basket and wicker, being natural materials, are always right out of doors. Chairs should be comfortable and light to move about. These, under the catalpa tree, are from the Perigord district of France.*

3 *Given a pair of half-way suitable trees, just about the nicest piece of portable garden furniture is a hammock.*

4 *Cooking outside is an enormous pleasure made even better if you have the right equipment – a simple block - built barbecue is always the nicest answer.*

5 *Shade is often essential for eating out. Failing a pergola or handy tree, light, movable cotton screens can be slid easily into the right place, also giving privacy and keeping off a cool prevailing wind.*

6 *Colours used in painted furniture and fabrics such as tablecloths must always harmonize in an outdoor setting.*

1

2

3

4

5

6

Outdoors
20/21 Lighting outside

When you have spent time and money on building your garden, and are justifiably proud of the result, use it at night as well – visually, at least. Floodlighting can be magical. You can get results by the correct placing or even a single light source. The good points are emphasized and no one will see the terrible mess round the corner. You can draw people outside with lighting on a warm evening, in a sheltered garden, to enjoy the evocative scents of nicotiana, night-scented stock, and lilies.

Floodlighting on any large scale is probably an expert's job. Adequate insulation and earthing of all fitments is vital. However, for the small point of interest, inexpensive floodlights are available which can either be stuck in the ground on a spike, and moved from one spot to another throughout the season, or set on a bracket for rigid fixing.

Generally, the floodlight source should be low, shining up into the flowers or tree branches. It is fun experimenting with different effects. One of the most beautiful vistas is of a garden floodlit in snow, or with a heavy frost on the ground. Use candles in barbecue lanterns, or old-fashioned, twinkly, rough-pressed glass candle-holders, or oil lamps in a sheltered corner. Oil lamps are splendid for outside use, but have to be sited on a firm base.

Flares in holders or traditional flares on a stick give a festive feel on a mid-summer evening. But be careful in your selection as some of the coarser ones give off a black smoke.

If children are around, the naked flame should be well out of their reach.

One of the drawbacks to small-scale night lighting, especially if you live in the country, is that the light attracts insects and moths. But against that, it can also work as a burglar deterrent.

Lighting on a more utilitarian scale should not be forgotten, for instance the lights that guide you from the garage to the front door, up the steps in winter, and provide a glowing welcome for the visitor.

The positioning of a light source is important. Don't think that if you position the light high up, one will do. Apart from casting a ghostly light, the unwary are still likely to trip over low objects which remain in darkness. Two lights at a lower level are far better, or even one low spot on steps. Do avoid lamp posts: they are not suitable for gardens.

Lighting sources for decorations should, when visible, again be low; on average, about eye level. Manufacturers are at last producing a wide range of outside light fittings, modern as well as traditional, suitable for all styles of garden.

1 *Wall lights should not be dazzling but, like this one, give just enough slightly mysterious light.*

2 *A spotlight on a house number or name is useful and decorative.*

3 *A light for a path or courtyard is essential; it can be a decorative feature, as here, a globe on an Edwardian curly iron bracket.*

4 *One of the most effective and magical forms of lighting in a garden is the floodlighting of trees at night.*

(Opposite) Still probably one of the best forms of outdoor lighting, here helped by lights from the house – candles in lanterns hanging from trees.

Outdoors
22/23 Play

A normal family garden is an extension of the children's playroom. And as children grow and as their interests widen, it will have to be changed and adapted.

From the youngest upwards, children will need/appreciate:

(a) Space for a pram to stand.

(b) A small grass piece to sit the baby, or a place for its pen.

(c) A small sand pit, even if only a large tyre with sharp sand in it, which in winter is cleared away.

Builders' sand is soft and when damp becomes soggy and takes ages to dry out. Sharp sand is made up of minute particles which dry out far quicker.

(d) Youngsters up to six or so prefer a sand pit they can climb into, for making their own small messy world. The container then becomes a house, a ship, or a desert isle. This element of fantasy is an essential part of growing up and other parts of the garden can encourage it, with small winding paths and places for little dens. Flowers fascinate many small children, so encourage them to grow their own packets of seeds. Do not expect this to be a decorative element of the garden, though. Water is appreciated, although its hazards are obvious.

(e) A hard circular route for cycling or tricycling, without steps of course.

(b) As children become more robust, something to climb. For example, a climbing frame cum swing can be made with larch poles. The swing need have only one rope and a big knot in the end, or a timber disc to sit on.

(g) Inevitably somewhere is wanted for cricket or football. The garden has to be designed to this end, or a complete veto rigidly applied, since horticulture and small boys' footballs do not go hand in hand.

(h) A corner for pets is often necessary, screened probably, but near the house.

(i) A place for table tennis, such as under the carport, is a good idea. This can double as a place for mending a cycle tyre, or building a boat.

(j) If you want a swimming pool, provide an adequate, dry, non-slip surround; and changing space if possible. Eliminate passage through the house, since you won't have only your own children splashing in and out but all for miles around.

If thought of in time, many of these elements can be incorporated in the initial garden layout, and can be adapted to something else when their usefulness is outgrown. The sandpit can become a pool, the climbing frame a pergola or trellis.

Ideally playhouses should merge, and be part of the garden, like this treehouse, constructed of indigenous wood.

1

2

3

4

5

The idea of a place-of-their-own is very appealing to children, and left to their own devices the dens, or treehouses, they build for themselves, are much more ingenious than the dull, scaled-down garden sheds sold as children's houses. Four walls are not enough, the structure should have some element of ingenuity about it, like an entrance that's too low for adults to crawl through, or an approach up a precarious rope ladder. The structure will probably be an eyesore in the garden, as children are not concerned with adult aesthetics. So the siting is important.

1 *Like a blown-up doll's house, a real proper little "house" with a proper door you can shut, traditional and unobtrusive.*

2 *A traditional climbing frame, at its best when occupied, needs a firm base.*

3 *A really dramatic touch with gigantic chessmen moving on the black and white tiles of a paved garden.*

4 *This simple wooden structure is house, castle, tower — and very good to look at when uninhabited.*

5 *A leafy play pit with solid log walls for young troglodytes.*

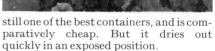

1 *An alabaster head set against a brick wall.*

2 *White dovecots with black roofs are beautiful, especially when inhabited.*

3 *A sculptural, globe shaped container, lovely against a large acanthus.*

4 *Earthenware pots, some empty, some full, make a sculpture in themselves.*

5 *A central group – a statue among rambling roses.*

6 *White-painted stand raises up plants level.*

Things in a garden stamp it with the character you want to give it; but objects are not enough, the basic proportions and layout have to be right.

Pots

There is a large range of available containers for plants, but one still has to look around for something very special.

Glass fibre, moulded vinyl, or asbestos composition containers are light and come in a range of colours. White, honey and chocolate show plants off best. They are also ideal for a roof or terrace. The latest have a saucer device built into the base, providing an automatic suction watering system.

Concrete pots, though heavy, are safer on a terrace where children might play.

Red terracotta pots, either plain or decorated, mellow with age. The large old 12 in. or 14 in. terracotta plant pot is still one of the best containers, and is comparatively cheap. But it dries out quickly in an exposed position.

Stone composition pots, tubs and troughs look well in the country, though somewhat brash when new. "Mossy age" can be encouraged by painting on a watery solution of cow dung.

Cast-iron urns look superb in old gardens. There is a Victorian pattern and an 18th century one · get the right one for your house.

Timber containers, either in hardwood,

often teak or iroko, or softwood, painted. For the country garden feel, with white timber furniture, the painted half-barrel, white with black bands, looks best. If possible, paint inside too; this will lengthen the life span considerably. Do not use a preservative and then plant straight into it, the toxicity is too strong for plants. Square Versailles tubs, available either in fibreglass or timber, should be planted up permanently with some form of shrub and not used for annuals.

Make sure that the plant you use in your pot is in scale with it both in height and breadth.

Sculpture/statuary

The range of pieces the average person can afford is slowly growing. For all too long, all that was available was the coy nymph or the ugly little "mannequin pisse" but it is now possible to obtain, at reasonable prices, small copies of classical pieces in reconstituted stone.

Small modern pieces are more difficult to obtain, other than through the sculptors themselves, but then the prices are likely to be high. So try a local art school, or sculpt your own. Since most statuary/sculpture works well in association with fairly strong, architecturally-shaped plants, home-made defects can be fairly easily screened.

1 *A large curving shell gives magic to a wild corner among ferns and greenery.*

2 *A wood and metal container for sedums and grasses.*

3 *They were right for Versailles and are still right for your orange trees – Louis XIV white-painted square wooden tubs.*

4 *Japanese-inspired Easter flag by Peter and Alison Smithson.*

5 *In front of french windows geraniums hang on white-painted railings.*

6 *A tall stump in grass has sculptured stone birds pecking on and around it.*

The smallest garden of all, after pot plants, is the window-box. Not only does this give pleasure to passers-by and to you, but your outlook on the world improves as you gaze at it over and through its contents.

Any box or container must have drainage holes, covered with crocks and a layer of gravel. In window-box and pot gardening it is essential to have good soil. Plants can go directly into boxes or stand in their pots with soil or peat round them, which makes changing easier.

There is a large selection of tubs and boxes nowadays; some have castors which make it easy to wheel them into a protected position at the onset of winter.

Plant small trees and shrubs in containers in winter and spring; put alpines in sinks or troughs in April, and sow hardy annuals in April/May; plant bulbs in September. Hanging baskets are planted in May and like all box and pot gardens need a lot of watering. Use damp peat for top dressing in the hot summer days, and water daily. For hanging baskets, use plants which trail or dangle naturally like lobelia, pendant begonias, nasturtiums, fuchsias, petunias, ivy-leaved geraniums and zebrinas.

In winter, boxes and pots can be filled with everygreens like small junipers, cypresses, winter-flowering heaths and ivies. A charming miniature garden, extremely easy to grow, is a collection of houseleeks (sempervivum) in a sink or trough, perhaps mixed with miniature alpines.

The old-fashioned stand-bys of petunias, lobelia, begonia semperflorens, fuchsia, heliotrope, pelargoniums of all sorts, and verbena, are tough and immensely rewarding as riots of colour in window-boxes and tubs. Take off dead flowers constantly and they will go on and on. Rosemary and lavender are fragrant box plants, and look particularly lovely with marguerites (chrysanthemum frutescens).

Have a box on the window-sill or roof for your herbs. Given enough water, thyme, marjoram, chives, rosemary, savory, chervil and parsley should thrive. They are highly decorative and fragrant, as well as essential to good food, whether cooked or eaten raw.

1 *Blazing annuals, aloes and ferns make a splash in pots and boxes.*

2 *Old chimney-pots are full of personality and in a courtyard or on a roof double as sculpture and flower-pot holders.*

3 *Favourite pebble gleanings from holiday beaches look lovely among pots on a roof or in a yard.*

A bay tree is another good pot subject, clipped formally or allowed to flourish in its natural way. While we are on herbs, put mint and tarragon in separate boxes from other herbs and from each other. Their roots run everywhere and are best kept in solitary confinement.

Although you can mix colours successfully in a small space, it is equally effective to have a mass of one colour in a large pot or box, like calendula for a crock of gold; Tom Thumb nasturtiums for orange-vermilion with bluey leaves in late summer; ruby velvet wallflowers in May.

If space is short and the position sheltered, there are a number of annual climbers that are happy in pots. They will cover your walls by climbing up trellis, bamboo canes, string or plastic mesh. *Cobaea scandens*, the cup-and-saucer plant, has greenish white/blue flowers and can cover a wall in a season. It can be grown from seed under glass in April/May. *Thunbergia alata* (Black-eyed Susan) has yellow flowers from June till autumn and does best in semi-shade. Perhaps the most beautiful of all is *Ipomoea rubrocaerulea* (Heavenly Blue), which needs a lot of sun and a sheltered place and produces vivid blue trumpets which last for a day, climbing up canes or strings in an unbelievable blue curtain.

Even on a small balcony or roof it is worth putting some climbing French or runner beans in a large pot and letting them curl up sticks or canes in a decorative obelisk. They'll look lovely, smell superb, and taste delicious.

A few pots of tomatoes in a warm sheltered place will give you pounds and pounds, picked warm from the sun. There are some pretty miniature tomatoes called Tiny Tim, which are brilliant scarlet, taste delicious and are the size of marbles. Courgettes, too, will grow in a large pot with good rich soil.

If you have a dark little yard, pave it and surround it with ferns, hellebores, Solomon's seal and lilies of the valley. If you have a hot little roof, fill it with dazzling vermilion and white geraniums and scent the whole area with fragrant tobacco (Nicotiana) and stock.

1 *A balcony is a hanging garden, plants everywhere making a blaze of colour.*

2 *Even the narrowest area can make a happy home for a packed mass of plants, both decorative and useful (as herbs).*

3 *About the smallest plant-growing area you can use is round a window and round its sill. Most herbs thrive like this.*

4 *A traditional conservatory is for plants and people: a light, warm extra room.*

1

2

3

4

Finishes/1

It is not always easy to know what to do and what not to do to furniture, upholstery and work surfaces to keep them looking good.

There's been a "plastics revolution". Plastics have triggered off some of the most exciting developments in furniture and finishes in the past 20 years. Because plastics have different structures from traditional materials, they can be used in quite different ways. For furniture, this has given designers a great new freedom to experiment with shapes. For surfaces, a plastic finish can give the user more variety, greater toughness, easier maintenance than with traditional ones. All over the house we benefit from the helpful qualities of the various plastics: in paints that are easier to apply and keep bright; in floors that just need wiping over (instead of scrubbing/polishing); in wall coverings which are washable; in wipe-down kitchen and bedroom units; in light acrylic baths, bright cheap kitchen things, and so on.

Already there are many different plastics and since polymer technology is a growth industry, there are likely to be many more.

Some worth remembering are: polypropylene and ABS (Acrylonitrile-butadiene-styrene) for furniture, polyester and acrylic for fibres, PVC (polyvinyl chloride) for sheet plastic, polyurethane and melamine (pre-catalysed and acid-catalyst) for seals and surfaces; polystyrene for rigid foam and polyester for squishy foam and fillings. In the chart at the end of this section there is a summary which includes uses, advantages and maintenance hints for all these plastics. Here are some of the ways plastics are being used.

Furniture constructed in plastics

This is usually moulded. Sometimes it is solid: as for example Jo Columbo's Kartell chairs or Magistretti coffee tables. The finish can come in a wide range of colours and often (though not necessarily) that pleasing mirror-like flat surface. Sometimes, plastics are used in a rigid expanded foam moulded to a shape: for example many "shell" type chairs and sofas have this basic foam construction around which their upholstery is applied. Other moulded things, like drawers, record-player cases or TV cabinets are also made of expanded rigid foam, not solid plastics.

Prices: The original mould is very expensive, but mass-production (if it is achieved) lowers unit prices.

(Opposite) Glass, not the easiest surface to maintain in pristine condition, repays care by looking marvellous.

Decorative panels

Moulded plastic can also be used to make an outer skin to furniture or fittings: for example, some louvre doors consist of a chipboard core with a plastic front.

Plastics laminates

Laminated plastics (for example Formica or Warerite) are now widely used for work-surfaces in kitchens, offices, bathrooms. These are made from layers of Kraft paper impregnated with phenolic resin bonded together at very high temperatures. As the top layer of paper can be printed any colour or pattern, this kind of plastic laminate can simulate any texture or material (see the section on Wood finishes overleaf). Melamine is a harder, clearer resin used to coat the surface of the bonded material. The thicker the Melamine layer, the higher will be the quality.

Plastics films/seals

A clear plastic film or seal is often used to protect a surface: for example, pine tables nowadays are sealed like this, so the wood is visible, but the surface is practical for everyday family meals. It can be wiped clean rather than scrubbed or polished. The same treatment is applied to flooring: for example, vinyl-topped cork tiles. The plastic film is very tough, but can be scratched and burnt, and, if it is, is marked permanently.

General care: Although plastic is tough and practical it needs some care if it is to keep looking good for any length of time. On the whole, the finishes are tougher than solid plastics, because a different type of plastics resin is used in these circumstances.

1. Regular cleaning is important. Use a cloth dampened in mild detergent solution. This will help control the static electricity which plastics produce and which in its turn tends to attract dust and grime.

2. Very few plastics withstand scratching. If used to cut on (e.g. kitchen work-tops) they mark. For this reason, avoid scouring powders or wire wool.

3. Most plastics cannot withstand extreme heat: each different plastic has its own burn point. Cigarettes left burning on any plastic surface (except for melamine) always leave a permanent mark. It is unwise to put very hot dishes (straight from the oven) down on an unprotected plastic surface.

4. Most plastic furniture is not very easy to set fire to, but if it does burn it produces a dense, choking smoke which can be lethal.

5. Plastic surfaces tend to stain unless spills of such things as tea, coffee, Ribena, paint, ink, whisky, red wine, etc. are mopped up quickly. But if cleaned with mild cleaning paste or detergent, the stain is seldom permanent.

Most of the metals fashionable now and widely used in the home are in the mechanics/structure, the plumbing, the central heating, possibly the window frames, sometimes the beams and joists. But some are suitable for furniture, fittings and surfaces. Here are some you are likely to have in your home.

Stainless steel

This is a remarkable alloy of steel; a small proportion of chromium (and sometimes nickel also) is added to give it its heat-resistant non-corrosive quality. Just how practical, hygienic and hard-wearing this surface is can be judged by the way stainless steel is used for work-surfaces in hospitals and professional kitchens. But it is expensive, so its use in the home is usually limited to kitchen sinks and drainers, trims, handles and cutlery. It is used rather less frequently for cooker hobs and work-surfaces *per se*, or tiles. Big expanses of this material are too costly for most people even to think about.

Care: Stainless steel stands up to a great deal of wear and tear, but is not entirely scratch-resistant. Clean with a mild detergent. To polish up, use a mild (non-abrasive) cleaning paste, or a special stainless steel polish.

Steel

Most radiators are made from steel, which rusts without proper protection. Radiators nowadays usually arrive with their protective primer and undercoats on – ready for the final decoration. If they get scratched it is important to rub down around the scratch, apply a rust inhibitor, then a primer, then undercoat(s) before redecorating.

Care: Depends on final finish. If gloss or emulsion paint (always oil-based), wash down to keep clean.

Cast iron

Hospital-type radiators, decorative railings, outdoor furniture, Victorian spiral staircases, are usually made from cast iron. Like steel, cast iron rusts if not protected. As for steel, make sure it is properly primed and painted. Deal with any chips or scratches straight away.

Care: If finished with paint, wash down from time to time.

Chromium-plated steel tube

This is a finish that is fashionable for furniture at the moment. Chairs have chromium-plated legs and arms, glass-topped tables have chromium-plated legs and supports. Chromium-plating is a method of electro-plating steel tube – first with nickel, then chrome, to give it protection and a shiny finish. The best chromium-plating has a slightly watery effect – like old-fashioned car bumpers. The quality depends largely on the care with which the steel tube has been prepared in the first instance. No amount of plating will compensate for a bad base, whereas a good one might only have a very thin application of plating. Cost, unfortunately, is no reliable guide to its quality.

Points to check for are: a uniform surface and unflaking joins and welds.

Care: Keep clean by washing with warm soapy water, and dry carefully afterwards. Avoid abrasives, and use cleaners sparingly. Should your chrome peel or crack, the only known remedy is to have it first stripped and then replated.

Epoxy resin or stove enamel finishes

Steel can also be protected by either of these methods, and, in fact, any piece of furniture which is obviously metal but has a coloured surface has usually had one or other of these finishes.

Epoxy resin is a plastic finish sprayed on to the metal and fixed at a high temperature. Stove enamelling means the metal is sprayed with special paint before being baked at a high temperature. Both give hard and long-lasting surfaces.

Care: Clean with warm soapy water and dry thoroughly. Abrasives damage the surface and create little dirt-traps, so it is important to avoid.

Plastic-coated metals

Steel mesh is sometimes given a coating of plastic, usually nylon, to create a very tough finish indeed: some Bertoia chairs, and many less distinguished chair legs are treated like this.

Care: Wipe over with damp cloth. Although tough, if the coating does get chipped, it is impossible to repair.

Anodized aluminium

Aluminium creates its own protective layer of aluminium oxide against corrosion. This is why aluminium window frames don't need painting. But where it is handled a lot, as in door furniture, the extra protection anodizing gives is desirable. Anodizing is a chemical process like electroplating which re-arranges the molecules so that the metal has an improved resistance to corrosion and staining. In this process, the metal can be satin finished or dyed another colour.

Care: Clean with a damp cloth quite frequently in the case of door-furniture, to keep the acids from the human skin at bay.

Finishes
2/3 Wood, surfaces and how to treat them

Timber is classified as hardwood and softwood. Softwood, from conifers which grow fast, is comparatively cheap. It is used for constructing buildings and cladding. Formerly it was used only for cheap (nursery and kitchen) furniture, but now "pine" is fashionable and not so cheap. Hardwood has denser grain, matures more slowly and is therefore always more expensive. It is used for fine furniture and sometimes for parts of a building that show – the doors, the window frames and occasionally also the wall cladding.

Because both mass production methods and the prevalence of central heating call for a dimensionally stable material which solid timber is not, it is being replaced by veneers on cheaper wood products such as chipboard, ply or blockboard. Another reason is that there is a demand for uniformity, e.g. matching wardrobe and drawer fronts, which can only be achieved with veneer, although it is often more expensive to make, certainly in the case of softwood and even the cheaper hardwoods.

This section aims to help you identify the various woods in your home and care for them correctly.

Pine

Most softwoods are called "pine". In fact there are differences between softwoods from different species and different countries.

Douglas fir – also known as Columbian or Oregon pine – comes from North America and is usually referred to as Knotty pine. It has a straight grain, pretty markings and is reddish gold in colour. Much used for "pine" furniture and tongued-and-grooved pine boards.

Parana pine from South America has a more interesting grain and comes in wider boards but it is temperamental as it dries, and so is less widely used.

Red Baltic pine – or Scots pine – comes from northern Europe and is best known as "red deal". This is what is mainly used in house construction and what you get from a woodyard unless you specify something else.

Norway spruce – from northern Europe and North America – is known as "whitewood" or "white deal". As it "works" well and – as its name implies – keeps its pale colour, it is used widely for cheap whitewood furniture and units which are to be painted.

Cedar – from western North America – is different from other softwoods, having natural oils which protect it from attack by insects and make it very durable. The timber is mainly used for outside cladding for houses, tiles, sheds, greenhouses, etc., but could be useful for cladding bathrooms since it is not affected by damp.

Yew – from Europe – is the only hard softwood. Very rarely used now except for small turned woodware.

Beech

This is a European hardwood. It is a straight-grained, light-coloured and very strong timber which machines to a high-grade finish and polishes up well. Although it is not suitable for outdoor conditions, solid beech is typically used for chairs and upholstered chair frames, tables, tools , etc.

Teak

Teak is an Eastern hardwood from India and Burma. It has a long, even grain, is mid-brown in colour and contains a very high proportion of natural oils which make it resistant to rot and decay. It is extensively used wherever an attractive and water-resistant wood is needed – i.e. for decking, outdoor furniture, draining-boards, etc. Much top-quality Scandinavian furniture is made from teak or uses teak veneers.

Two timbers closely resembling teak and often used as substitutes are Afrormosia and Iroko. Iroko is slightly coarser and oilier than Afrormosia. Both these woods are considerably cheaper than teak.

Oak

Hardwood, the best of which comes from Britain. Now rare and expensive. Grain depends on the way the timber is cut. Oak starts light and darkens with age and polish. Can be used outdoors or inside. Much early English furniture – refectory tables, coffers, Jacobean chairs, etc. – was made from solid oak and since oak is virtually indestructible, a lot of it still survives, having mellowed with age. Veneers are also used today.

Mahogany

Hardwood from Honduras and West Africa. Many varieties: Gaboon, Sapele and Utile are types of mahogany. It is beautifully grained, deep rich red and easily worked. Typical use: a favourite for large formal Victorian pieces such as side-boards and tables for dining-rooms, and wardrobes and imposing bedheads for bedrooms. Veneers used today.

Rosewood

Hardwood from Brazil, Honduras, East Indies. Beautiful and expensive timber. Dark chocolate or purple with irregular very dark striped graining. Typical use: pretty antique inlaid furniture. Today as a veneered finish for dining tables, coffee tables etc.

Walnut

Hardwood which varies according to country of origin. Curly black veining is typical of English walnut, now almost unobtainable. Top-quality furniture wood. Typically found in antique pieces like Queen Anne chairs or bureaux.

Traditional veneering

Veneering is an age-old craft, practised by some of the most famous furniture makers in their day. It means overlaying one wood with a very thin layer of another timber, for a decorative finish. Expensive and beautiful hardwoods such as rosewood and English walnut have seldom been used except as veneers.

Allied to veneering is inlaying. Here the top veneers are of contrasting woods designed to fit together in a pattern.

Care: Veneers are finished as solid wood – either french polished, wax polished or oiled.

Modern veneers

The same methods are still widely used today both for reproduction and good quality modern furniture but there is usually a coat of synthetic lacquer.

Care: As described for french polish, wax polish or oiling as applicable.

Laminated veneers

A recent development is that instead of a craftsman making a piece of furniture and carefully laying on his veneers, the veneer is laminated at a factory on to one of the constructional boards – either chipboard, plywood or blockboard. The pieces for the furniture are cut directly from the veneered board.

Care: These veneers are likely to be finished with a cellulose or polyurethane seal. They just need wiping clean and occasionally brightening up with furniture cream or spray.

New developments

Wood surfaces are now being laminated with clear plastic melamine as well as veneers, to give a tougher wipe-clean finish. Technological advances have also made it possible to lay a coloured/patterned plastic directly on to board. This can give an impression of a wood veneer under melamine.

Another new process is the use of "fine line" veneers. These use the cheapest wood veneers possible; their effect comes from stacking and sticking layers of veneers together and slicing them down vertically.

The third method is a very ingenious technique in which cheap veneers are over-printed with expensive teak or rosewood patterns (from photographs) then sealed with clear seal. Most people find it hard to tell these apart from the real thing.

PVC foil

PVC foil is the most widely used finish for cheap furniture. It can be in plain colours or be printed to look like teak or other wood. Much softer than melamine, it scratches easily and is unrepairable.

Care: As all these have clear plastic top surfaces, they can be wiped clean and just occasionally polished.

Plywood

Made from veneers and can be between $\frac{1}{8}$ in./0.8 mm and 1 in./25 mm thick. Odd numbers are bonded together with the grain running in opposite directions: this equalizes the tensions and tendency of the wood to warp. So you can get 3, 5, 7, 9 or 11 ply. It is made from various timbers – Douglas fir, Parana pine, beech, birch and West African hardwoods. It can be laminated with melamine or treated for outdoor use.

Finishes: Clear cellulose or polyurethane seal, coloured stain, paint.

Uses: Furniture, cladding, flooring.

Blockboard

This is made from vertical strips of softwood bonded together at high pressure sandwiched between two layers of thick veneer, usually birch.

Finishes: On both sides or the balance is destroyed. Clear cellulose or polyurethane seal, coloured stain, paint.

Uses: Built-in furniture, doors, etc.

Chipboard

This is made from softwood chippings bonded together under high pressure. It is 50–60% cheaper than blockboard. Can be used with no facings, if good quality, but is very often the core on to which veneer facings are laminated. Must not be allowed to get damp.

Finishes: Clear polyurethane seal, coloured stain, paint.

Uses: Floors, furniture.

Flaxboard

This is like chipboard but made from flax straw bonded under high pressure. Usually the core to laminated veneered boards, but on its own looks better.

Finishes: Polyurethane seal, paint.

Uses: Furniture, building, interior wall cladding.

Doing your own finishing

Some furniture made from chipboard and a lot made from whitewood is sold for you to finish:

1. Clear polyurethane seal or lacquer. Paint on as directed. Usually three coats.

Sand before each.

2. Coloured stain – in shades of brown or a range of bright colours. Paint on, three coats, sand before each.

3. Paint. Use emulsion paint as a primer and first coat on both chipboard and whitewood. To get a gloss finish, use gloss paint or a clear polyurethane seal.

Wax polish

The glowing patina of antique chairs and tables is not only the result of ageing but also of years of burnishing with beeswax. This is the oldest finish for wood. There are still some special wax polishes produced for antiques which are very satisfying to use. However, for the purists who wish to use genuine beeswax, this is how you make it:

1. Buy beeswax in either block or flake form. If in a block, the first step is to grate it into flakes.

2. Put the flaked wax into a container such as an old mixing bowl or clean paint can, and cover it with white spirit.

3. Place this container in an outer vessel such as a saucepan, and pour boiling water into the outer vessel. This is to melt the wax. You have to keep renewing the boiling water in the outer vessel until all the wax flakes have melted.

N.B. Do not whatever you do put the saucepan and inner container over a gas jet or electric ring. White spirit is very inflammable and can explode or catch fire very easily, if it gets too hot.

To apply: All wax polishes should be spread very sparingly on to a clean dry surface, left a few minutes to dry and then buffed off. A shoe brush is said to be very good for this. Some people prefer using old pyjamas or tea-towels. On flat surfaces (tables) the polishing brushes and lambswool pads on a shampoo polisher give fine quick results.

Care: No one can pretend that a wax polish on furniture gives a trouble-free surface. Wood treated with wax is affected by heat – especially damp heat. It stains with alcohol, soft drinks, tea, coffee – even water. (Wiping over the surface with a cloth that is too wet can discolour the wax polish!) Minor stains can be removed simply by polishing with good quality furniture polish. Difficult stains need rubbing off with fine sandpaper, followed by repolishing. So, while wax polish will make furniture look very handsome, it is hard work keeping a wax polish immaculate on, say, a dining-room table used every day.

Sometimes furniture with wax polish which hasn't been polished regularly, needs redoing. In this case, clean off all old polish with a cloth (unfluffy) moistened in turpentine. Rub off all traces of turps with a clean cotton cloth. Put on a new, thin layer of polish and polish off as above. Another way to remove old polish is with a solution of vinegar and warm water: one tablespoon of vinegar to one pint of water. Dry thoroughly and repolish as above.

French polish

Think of a highly polished Victorian dining table or grand piano, and you have an idea of what french polishing achieves. It was the glossiest highly-finished surface for wood. French polishing was a skilled craft practised by thousands. Now used mostly for high-class reproduction work and restoration purposes.

French polish has a base of shellac dissolved in methylated spirits. The colour varies from dark french polish through garnet, button and white to transparent. New proprietary brands make french polishing easier.

First the surface has to be well sanded and filled. A rubber (a pad of cotton wool inside a soft cloth) is the only tool. The cotton wool holds the polish which is poured on to it in just the right amount. The polisher then works the pad over the surface in a slow figure of eight, so the wood gets a series of thin even coats. When a deep even polish is achieved, it is left to dry for eight hours, after which the second stage of "spiriting off" can begin. The rubber now has a double thickness of cotton outside, and the cotton wool inside is dampened with methylated spirits. The wood is rubbed as before to remove all marks from the surface, but carefully or the polish would be taken off too. The last polish is with the grain of the wood. Then the piece is left to dry for several days.

Care: At the end of all this, the piece of furniture is beautifully finished, but needs regular attention. If it is a chair, bureau or grand piano this means dusting daily and polishing (thin wax) regularly. But if it is a table or surface in daily use, more care is necessary. French polish does not stand up to prolonged contact with heat, water or any other liquid. It is easily scratched. Heat-proof mats have to be used and it needs to be cleaned after each meal with a damp cloth, then dried. Polish (thin wax) once a week. Bad heat marks and white rings can be "spirited off", using meths in an improvised rubber, very cautiously.

Removal of extensive marking or restoration needs a professional. If the piece is not valuable, there are proprietary polish revivers on the market.

Oiled furniture

Teak and its substitutes, Afrormosia and Iroko, are most often oiled. Rosewood, mahogany and oak can be oiled, but not ash or sycamore except where air and surroundings are ultra-clean.

Teak oil: Is the up-to-date version with additives to speed drying and resist marking, but you can use a mixture of 25% linseed oil and 75% turpentine, which is cheaper though slightly harder to apply. Use on indoor or outdoor woodwork.

To apply, use a fluff-free oil-impregnated cloth and rub very sparingly well into the wood. Remove excess oil by buffing up with a second fluff-free cloth. Repeat the whole process even more sparingly next day. This treatment can be repeated when the wood begins to look dull. Do not over-oil or a sticky deposit will form (i.e., not more than twice a year). Oil can be cleaned off by rubbing the surface with fine wire wool dipped in a little white spirit. When dry, oil again sparingly.

Care: Just wipe down when necessary with a damp cloth – or dust. Never polish. Marks or rings can usually be removed by sanding lightly and re-oiling the area very carefully. Let dry, then rub as hard as you can.

CAUTION: Oil-soaked rags are highly inflammable – and have been known to ignite spontaneously. After use, put in a can (or something fire resistant) and place in dustbin. They can be burnt in a garden incinerator, but great care should be taken during this operation.

Care of modern furniture

Modern furniture is considerably easier than antique furniture to look after. Modern glues are stronger. Modern polyurethane (even cellulose) seals are tougher. In addition, plastic seals and bonded wood chips do not encourage furniture beetles or woodworm.

Most pre-war modern furniture was finished with clear cellulose finish.

Care: Wipe down, polish with furniture cream or spray. (Just as these are wrong for furniture used to wax polish, so wax polish is wasted here.)

Post-war furniture increasingly has clear plastic melamine or polyurethane finish, both of which are tougher than cellulose.

Care: Wipe down.

Occasional care: Brighten up with any furniture cream or spray.

If the wood has a matt finish or a semi-matt one, don't polish it at all or it will turn into a glossy one. Just wipe with a damp cloth occasionally.

Care of old and antique furniture

Old furniture is vulnerable to certain conditions occurring in the home, such as excessive heat, or very strong sunlight. Polishes (french, wax, oil) do not protect wood as well as do some of the plastic finishes. To keep wood in good condition you have to make some effort to maintain the right atmosphere.

1. Keep the temperature more or less constant and temperate. Wood warps and veneers crack if furniture is placed right in front of a direct source of heat.

2. Protect furniture from strong sunlight which bleaches out the colour. Venetian blinds or sheer curtains filter the effects of sunlight quite effectively.

3. Keep humidity at a comfortable level. A very dry atmosphere is as bad for furniture as a very hot one, particularly for antiques which have spent a century or two in homes which were not well heated and tended to be a little damp. Wood takes up and loses moisture, swelling and shrinking as the relative humidity changes in the atmosphere.

When central heating is installed, the atmosphere becomes drier and wood shrinks more than it swells in ordinary unheated conditions. Eventually it may develop cracks and the veneer may begin to lift. Some timbers move more than others – beech, birch, oak and pine move more than teak, Afrormosia and rosewood.

To put back some of the moisture an electric humidifier can be switched on for a few hours each day. Water troughs can be fitted over the radiators, and indoor plants, lots of them and well watered, put back some of the moisture into the atmosphere.

Furniture pests

Woodworm is the most usual furniture pest; it attacks softwood, and prefers unpolished surfaces. The insides of drawers, the back of a cupboard and the base of a chest of drawers are likely hiding places. The first signs of the pest are little piles of sawdust, followed shortly by their egress holes. Isolate the piece of furniture, because the adult beetle will fly about and spread the trouble. Brush or spray the whole of the affected piece with a woodworm destroyer, and inject the fluid into the worm-holes (important, as grubs may not be reached by a surface treatment). There are special nozzle-kits available which allow you to get the liquid deep into the wood.

A second application may be needed the following spring, as further eggs may hatch. (A bad infestation needs professional treatment.)

Furniture polish containing insecticide may help, and so may occasional waxing of unpolished areas, or treating these with a wood preservative which is designed to keep this pest at bay.

Finishes
4/5 Upholstery materials

The best way to keep upholstered furniture looking good is to ask yourself the right questions before you buy anything. Silk upholstered chairs or pale suède sagbags have a role they can play for years in some homes, but not in those where they will come in contact with children, pets, mud, food, drink, grease or ball-point pens. The amount of wear you expect to inflict should be an indication of how tough and practical your furniture need be. This can vary not just from home to home, but room to room. A pretty Victorian chair could survive intact for years in the bedroom of a house where the daily onslaught in the living-room would destroy it in a matter of months. Meal-times are much more relaxed if you are not on edge in case something gets spilt: dining chairs need to be easier to keep clean than those in a study. Outdoor furniture should be able to survive outdoors without having to be brought in to shelter every time it rains. Obvious things when you think about them, but often forgotten at the moment of purchase.

General maintenance

Regular care is the most important rule. What is quite a quick and simple matter to remove each week becomes difficult, often impossible, if left to accumulate over months.

Every week: The whole piece should be vacuumed thoroughly, using the appropriate attachments. Dusting or brushing down is not so satisfactory.

Turn the cushions if possible: some which are shaped have to stay in the same position. Spot check for any stains and clean them. (N.B. It is much better to deal with these as they occur, before they have time to sink in.) How to get rid of them depends on the fabric of the covering.

If covered with PVC or polyurethane hide, wash with warm soapy water, dry and buff up.

Spring-cleaning: This should only amount to washing or dry-cleaning removable covers – whichever is appropriate for the fabric. Feed leather.

Accidents: Deal with these straight away as they occur – stains get progressively harder to remove as time goes on.

Manufacturers' instructions: The complexity of blends and synthetics and cleaners makes it very important to get these with the furniture. Keep them safely, and follow them.

Checking the structure

When the structure is hidden under layers of soft foam and/or cushions, it is important to demand information from the shop/person you are buying from. The frame (its design, suitability for use, etc.) is the responsibility of the manufacturer.

Today, completely upholstered furniture usually has either a wood frame or an expanded plastic shell. In traditional upholstery the wood frame supported the springs, which were held in place and padded out for comfort with horsehair and wadding of various kinds. Nowadays plastic foam is used for padding. Foam can be sprayed on to the wooden frame as well. In the same way, foam provides the cushioning round a plastic shell.

Problems arise more often with antiques than with new furniture. Here no one is liable and much can have gone wrong with the frame unnoticed.

When the structure is visible, check its qualities for yourself – although its suitability is still the manufacturer's responsibility. These pieces usually have their arms, legs and sometimes backs and bases made from wood or metal.

Care: As advised on instructions or sections here on wood and metal.

Basket chairs: With these, structure and shape is the same. Cane, white willow and rattan are the most usual materials. Although these chairs, sofas and stools give a summertime alfresco atmosphere, they should not be left outdoors, let alone kept outside. When choosing, try to pick those which feel solid and have no loose bindings to come undone. Price tends to be related to design rather than expected life.

Care: Wash with a mild detergent.

The upholstery and cushions: Plastic foam of various kinds has revolutionized upholstery. The most expensive chairs and sofas still have down top cushions – there is nothing quite so soft and resilient – but foam is better than inferior feathers.

Solid foam (usually polyether) is used for the bases of chairs and sofas and unit seating. It is so strong and adaptable that it is successfully used on its own for chairs.

Squishier cushions are usually made from shredded foam or crumbs. Sagbags which mould themselves to your shape are filled with polystyrene granules.

Provided the right grade of plastic is used for the purpose, this upholstery will last for years with minimum care (i.e. none at all).

Foam is not fireproof. As with most plastics, foams do not catch fire easily, but if they do, they burn with a particularly noxious smoke. A sensible precaution is to have covers in wool or flame-retardant (if not flame-resistant) fabric, and to keep well away from intense heat, e.g. electric fires.

The life of a piece of furniture is more often determined by the life of the covers than that of the frame. When choosing upholstery, fixed covers, difficult and expensive to replace, should be in the toughest possible material, whereas loose covers need only be washable (or dry-cleanable) and reasonably hard-wearing. Price is a guide, but not an infallible one, to quality. This depends on what the fabric is made of, how it is woven and finished. In the survey that follows we begin with the natural fibres.

Wool fibre

Wool is an ideal upholstery fibre – soft and comfortable. It takes dyes well, and normally does not fade noticeably. It is flameproof. The International Wool Mark is a guarantee of high quality, and the fabrics which carry it are reliable.

Because of the great variety of yarns wool can be woven into many different fabrics. Tweedy fabrics, for instance, get their interesting textures through the yarns: knops (knots), bouclés (or loops), slubs (irregular thick and thin yarn).

Weaves

Wool can be "flat-woven" so that it makes a close-textured, very strong repp (a practically indestructible corded cloth with the rib running across the width), or tweeds. Wool jacquard upholstery fabrics are also "flat" and usually smooth in texture. The designs can be large or small.

Wool can also be woven into "pile" fabrics. Uncut moquette was the great Victorian invention for upholstery, so hard-wearing it was once in every front parlour, but now more often used for contract or public-transport seating. Moquette is patterned; plain wool pile is known as plush.

There are some very attractive loosely-woven, shaggy wool fabrics with tremendous character. While suitable for upholstery, these fabrics don't wear as well as the close-woven ones as they tend to catch and are harder to keep clean. A good rule of thumb is: the closer the weave the harder the wear.

Care: Wool upholstery covers are best dry-cleaned. Spots and stains can be removed with a dry-cleaner or tepid soapy water or a special shampoo: but test in an unobtrusive place first. Care instructions are usually supplied; if not, ask for them, and make sure that you get them even if the shop has to get on to the manufacturer for them.

Silk

Silk is a luxury fabric for upholstery and very impractical. Some antique chairs and chaise longues traditionally demand silk upholstery (but it is never satisfactory for normal use and seems to lead to such horrors as protective polythene covers). Silk is usually closely woven, but traditionally was also used for the richest velvets and brocades. It is, and has been from time immemorial very expensive indeed.

Care: Dry-clean. Possibly some stains could be removed with tepid soapy water, but test first, again in an unobtrusive place, and watch carefully whether the surface of the fabric remains unchanged after being damp.

Cotton

Cotton is used a great deal for upholstery, particularly for loose covers. But it is important to choose solid, good-quality cotton fabrics. Canvas and denim are tough and hard-wearing, strong enough to be used even on sling chairs, and so are cotton repps and twills of the right weight. Cotton takes dyes and prints well, is easy to wash, and has been comparatively cheap until recently; prices are now on the increase.

When choosing cotton (and linen too) avoid fabrics that have been heavily "dressed" to give an impression of better quality. The test is to rub the material between your thumb and forefinger. If white powder appears, there is excessive dressing.

Cotton is also made into "pile" fabrics: needlecord, corduroy and velveteen. These all have a pleasant, natural, unpretentious look, but for upholstery it is important to get the right quality. (For instance, if you are buying by the yard, do not be tempted to economize by selecting a curtain-quality fabric to cover a button-back chair.) Because there is very little "stretch" or give in these fabrics, "cord" upholstery tends to lose its crisp new look quite quickly, but having acquired its "lived-in" look, it stays that way without deteriorating further for quite a long time.

Care: The beauty of most cotton is that it can be either washed or dry-cleaned. The velvets, etc., are more safely dry-cleaned.

Linen

Linen fibres are much firmer and more lustrous and stronger than cotton ones, but they also tend to crease more easily. Linen can be woven in the same ways as cotton and is very often found mixed with it – Linen Union is the traditional blend for loose covers and is still being printed with some of the best fabric designs there are.

Care: Washable or dry-cleanable. Keep and follow any instructions.

Rayon

Synthetic fibres, with their own qualities and properties, are often used in conjunction with natural fibres.

Rayon was the first synthetic fibre and is still probably the most widely used. One of its great advantages is its cheapness, compared with the ever-rising prices of natural fibres. It is about half the cost of other synthetics. Within the last ten years rayon has been greatly improved and Evlan now has more "body" and better abrasion-resistance than its predecessors. Rayon is used by itself, but probably more often in blends with wool, cotton and other synthetics. It can be treated in all ways: flat-woven to resemble close repps, tweeds, or brocades, or used for pile fabrics – rayon-velvets and figured rayon-brocades – giving you rather grand effects in a reasonable price range. In fact, this is the way to think of rayon: its use in (or in addition to) a fabric makes the price come down as well as the wear. This is often acceptable when you want a cheaper or shorter-lived piece of upholstery rather than one to last your lifetime.

Care: Rayon is not always washable. Unless so described, it is better to dry-clean it and use dry-cleaning preparations to get out stains, spills, etc. Test first. Keep and follow instructions given by manufacturer.

Nylon

A percentage of nylon is generally used to give additional toughness and abrasion-resistance to other fibres, wool especially.

The most important other use for nylon in upholstery is for stretch covers. These were invented for nylon, because it has a high degree of elasticity and is given a two-way stretch when knitted. It can be so knitted into plain or textured fabrics in one or more colours. It is eminently washable. The one snag is finding the ready-made cover to fit your chair in the colour/pattern you like. And there are problems in making up stretch fabrics at home.

Care: On its own, nylon can be washed. In a blend, follow instructions.

Acrylics

The Acrylic family of fibres has not been used for woven fabrics. Knitted fabrics may become more common as the rising prices of other fibres make acrylics comparatively cheaper. But one acrylic, Dralon, has entirely transformed, and now dominates, "pile" fabrics, particularly velvet. Dralon is tough, washable, almost dog-and-cat-and-child-proof. Dralon is widely used as an upholstery fabric on sofas and chairs, and

is also available by the yard.

Care: Remove stains and keep clean by scrubbing with mild detergent or upholstery shampoo.

Melded fabrics

These are synthetics but instead of being made into fibres and woven, the fabric is produced as a continuous sheet. One such nylon, Cambrelle, is already used for loose covers.

Blended fabrics

It is possible to combine the qualities of natural fibres and synthetics at an acceptable price by blending them.

Wool blends: When wool is combined with synthetics, such as nylon or acrylics, it often becomes less expensive, while gaining qualities of durability and increased resilience. The International Woolblendmark on a fabric is a guarantee of a high-quality blend, containing a minimum of 70% wool. Blends of wool and rayon bring the price down considerably.

Cotton and linen blends: There is no guide like the Woolblendmark for these blends. Linen Union was one of the first upholstery blends and still exists. It is a mixture of cotton and linen, ideal for loose covers.

Other blends: Synthetics (particularly rayon and to some extent nylon and acrylics) are put into blends with wool or cotton to give the fabric easier cleaning qualities, bring down the price and/or give better abrasion-resistance. These blends vary widely. The manufacturer or retailer should provide full details of the blend and how to care for it.

Natural hides

All hide is first treated in some way to make it usable. Most of it has the surface treated to improve or change the colour, to give it extra softness and resistance to staining. This gives the leather a slight shine. Some leather furniture uses "natural" leather which has not had the protective surface treatment. This is a lovely pinky creamy colour with a matt surface, but it stains all too easily. It is simply no use trying to keep it "looking new", it won't, but it can age – stains and all – quite handsomely.

Care: Natural leather – Wipe over with a clean, dry, soft cloth. If something more is necessary, rub very carefully with a clean cloth well wrung out in cold water. Never use a detergent or soap on this leather. Obviously, with no surface protection, it stains irremediably very easily.

Treated leather – Clean with a soft cloth wrung out in cold or lukewarm water. Stubborn marks can be rubbed

lightly using lukewarm soapy water. Avoid detergents. Spirits, tea, coffee, all stain leather, showing up as a light patch. Grease also stains it, showing up as a dark patch. Clean any spills immediately to prevent staining. Get a professional cleaner for really bad accidents.

Leather needs feeding so it should be treated regularly with a proprietary brand of hide food, applied with a slightly damp cloth. This cleans the leather, helps keep it supple and conceals scratch marks which are difficult to avoid.

Leather is almost unbeatable for upholstery. It is tough, wears well, looks good whether it is new or shabby, is comfortable summer or winter, has that beautiful leather smell. Its only disadvantage is its price, which is high.

What to beware of

Pets: In a short time dogs and cats can do more damage to a chair, sofa or cushion than human beings do in a lifetime. It isn't just those cats who sharpen their claws. It is the grease and dirt of their coats, not to mention the shed hairs and their all-pervading scent, which seems to cling forever.

People who perch: However politely they are perching, they are also causing interior damage to the arms and the base of your chair or sofa.

Cigarettes: Air the room thoroughly after it has been subjected to smoke.

Sun: Bright sunlight can fade fabrics, causing especially the blues to discolour, so draw blinds or curtains whenever this is possible.

Heat: Direct heat from radiators, for instance, can cause wooden frames to warp over a period of time. Do not allow your furniture to stand too close to the heating source.

Condensation: Upholstery placed under windows can be stained by condensation running down the window-pane and on to the fabrics.

Suede

Suède is more expensive than plain leather, needing even greater care if it is to stay looking good. (The way suède coats and shoes wear out gives one an idea of what to expect from suède upholstery.) There are now ways of treating the surface of suède to protect it from water and grease marks: you should make sure any suède furniture you buy has this kind of protection if you want it to last.

Care: Most manufacturers recommend a solvent cleaner for maintenance purposes and some provide their own. There are also proprietary brands available. When you buy, you should insist on getting the manufacturer's maintenance instructions and also his

recommendations for professional cleaners in your area – all suède things need one at some point.

A great deal of "leather" upholstery on sale today is synthetic. Since the days long ago when "leathercloth" (a cotton fabric coated with nitro-cellulose which looked and smelt horrible, went hard, cracked and peeled and generally misbehaved itself) put people off imitation leather, the scene has completely changed; the best of the products now offered look and wear well.

Synthetic leathers

PVC *fabrics:* Until four or five years ago, most synthetic leather for upholstery (car seats especially) was made from PVC (polyvinyl chloride). PVC is a plastic fabric squeezed out in a solid sheet. Grain, pattern and colour are embossed and printed on to the top surface. Sometimes PVC is used on its own, more often now a thinner layer is bonded on to a knitted fabric. PVC is extremely tough and hard-wearing.

An improved, but slightly less tough, fabric is Expanded Vinyl or PVC. This is the same old PVC but in the form of a foam with a thin top skin, usually supported by a knitted cloth. It feels softer, and it can be grained, dyed, textured, patterned. It simulates leather quite convincingly, except that it hasn't the same porosity, which is why it is sticky and rather uncomfortable to sit on in hot weather which is rather a drawback.

Polyurethane fabrics: The latest simulated leathers are made from sheets of polyurethane bonded on to fabric backings. These have a feel and appearance which is very close to leather, plus some porosity. They feel cool in summer and warm in winter, and are very soft and fine. They allow designers great freedom in styling, although the life-span of the earliest types that were used was short, particularly when they were to cover button-back furniture.

It is difficult to tell PVC and polyurethane leathers apart. In fact, to bring down the price of furniture, manufacturers sometimes use the more expensive polyurethane leather on the parts of the chair/sofa you see and feel most and PVC elsewhere.

Care: Both fabrics need to be wiped clean weekly with a cloth just dampened in mildly soapy water, dried carefully and buffed up.

Stains can be absorbed by PVC, so it is important to deal with them as they occur, especially ball-point ink. Use a proprietary ball-point ink remover. Make sure you get cleaning and care instructions from the manufacturer and follow them carefully.

Finishes
6/7 Surfaces chart

Surface	Uses	Performance	Snags	Stain removal
Float or plate glass.	Table tops. Shelves. Over wood on serving tables and dressing tables to protect surface.	Is impervious and unaffected by most household chemicals. Don't put very hot dishes directly on to glass – it may crack. Ditto very cold things. Sharp-edged items can scratch glass.	Avoid using for heavy-duty shelving. Even plate glass can shatter, so don't use glass tables where children play. Although resistant to acetone, wipe up mild acid stains quickly. Avoid strong acid solutions which may cut into the glass.	Rub with methylated spirit on a cloth, or use a proprietary cleaner.
Toughened glass.	As above. Also door panels, oven doors, etc. Heavy-duty shelves.	Able to resist extremes of temperature. If it does break it disintegrates into fragments instead of shattering.	Avoid strong acids.	As above.
Marble.	Table tops. Pastry-board let into working surface. Fireplace surrounds.	Although polished, marble is slightly porous, and stains quite easily. Marks should be rinsed off immediately.	Wine and coffee stains not quickly removed mark marble. Cigarette burns and spirits penetrate surface and professional repolishing is needed to remove these stains.	Make solution 2 teaspoons borax to $\frac{1}{2}$ pint water. Rub over surface. Rinse well and polish with dry cloth. Dabbing with vinegar removes stubborn stains, but don't leave on the surface for more than 2 minutes. Rinse thoroughly.
Wood (wax polished).	Furniture and panelling.	Wax polished furniture that has developed a patina over years of polishing will withstand some spills provided they are wiped up quickly, but it is not a practical surface if sticky children abound.	Not resistant to spilt liquids. Acids will mark, and so will ink. Water leaves rings, so beware damp vase bases and glasses. Not heat-resistant.	Rub surface with fine grade steel wool lubricated with white spirit. Rub with clean cloth and re-apply wax. Antiques need professional attention.
Wood (french polished).	Furniture (mainly antique).	French polish gives a high gloss finish, and is found on antiques more than modern furniture. If damaged, it can be stripped off and re-applied by a professional polisher. Minor repairs can be done by an amateur.	Does not resist heat or mild acids or alcohol. Will scratch if misused. Water leaves white marks.	1 Heat or water marks can be rubbed with cloth dipped in a solution of $\frac{1}{4}$ pint of turps and 1 pint of linseed oil. Leave overnight on surface. Remove and polish. 2 Dissolving the polish a little may also help. Use a thick cotton pad and moisten with two drops meths (no more). Cover with thin lint-free cotton and rub lightly on and round the stain. Leave to dry and repolish.
Wood (clear cellulose finish).	Reproduction antiques and some modern furniture with high gloss finish, although some matt cellulose finishes available. Used mainly on less expensive furniture.	Cellulose is a thin lacquer finish which comes in many qualities, but is easily damaged. Needs regular polishing (except matt finish) to avoid marking.	Poor resistance to marking by various liquids and to heat. Easily scratched.	As method 1 for french polish. Surface can be repaired with proprietary pastes.
Pre-catalyzed melamine.	Dining and bedroom furniture.	Thin one-pack lacquer which is easy to repair when needed. Will withstand water, moderate heat (up to 100°C) and some liquids, but wipe up spills as soon as possible.	Household acids and alkali solutions can impair surface. Low resistance to scratching. Ammonia can attack surface. Don't clean with silicone polish. May chip if mishandled.	Rub with paste cleaner on dampened soft cloth. Do not use scouring powder.

Surface	Uses	Performance	Snags	Stain removal
Acid-catalyst melamine.	Medium-priced bedroom, dining-room and occasional furniture.	More durable finish than the one-pack melamine above, it provides better resistance to wet and dry heat, liquids and dilute household acids and alkalis.	Better scratch resistance than above, but don't use as chopping surface. Ammonia can attack surface. Do not clean with silicone polish.	As for pre-catalyzed melamine.
Polyurethane.	Good-quality furniture finish. Garden furniture. Kitchen and bedroom units, etc. Also used for boats.	Very good wet and dry heat resistance. You can pour boiling water on it without harm. Resists staining by most household liquids including nail varnish remover and does not mark easily. Can provide high gloss or matt finish, and is difficult to repair.	Although resistant to scratching, it can be scored with a sharp instrument, e.g. a pocket knife. Avoid prolonged contact with petroleum, undiluted disinfectant and dry-cleaning solvents. Avoid scouring powders.	Use liquid detergent to remove sticky deposits. A cleaner/polisher can also be used.
Polyester.	Good-quality bedroom, kitchen and dining-room furniture.	Excellent resistance to wet heat. Fair resistance to dry heat (100°C). Very good mark and liquid resistance. Also very good for scratch resistance.	Affected by petroleum. Difficult to repair if it becomes chipped or dented. Avoid abrasives.	As for polyurethane.
Polypropylene.	Chairs and occasional pieces, e.g. linen hampers, bathroom stools, coffee tables, storage boxes, etc.	Fair resistance to heat up to 100°C. Good resistance to liquid spills and most marks. Retains its high gloss in wear.	Avoid cigarette burns, abrasives, nail varnish and remover, chlorine bleach, petrol and cleaning solvents. Liable to scratch unless treated with reasonable care.	As for polyurethane.
Laminated plastics.	Table tops, work tops, dressing-table tops, shelf surfaces, splash backs, bath surrounds, etc.	Laminates are heat-resistant up to 120°C/150°C, according to make, and unharmed by boiling water and hot fat. Casseroles or pans direct from stove top or oven may damage surface. Don't use as chopping board as the surface will scratch.	Cochineal, concentrated fruit juices, hydrogen peroxide, hair-colourants, iodine and nail-varnish remover. Coffee, tea and red wine will stain if left on surface. Mop up quickly.	Rub stains with a paste or liquid cleaner and rinse. Never use scouring powders – they scratch the surface.
A.B.S. (acrylonitrile butadiene styrene co-polymer).	Occasional furniture, and domestic appliance housing. Lavatory seats, telephones, and television and radio cabinets.	Resistant to 80°C heat, and has impact strength. Resistant to dilute acids, most alkalis, oils and dry-cleaning fluids.	Undiluted bleach, benzine and petroleum based products attack the surface. Avoid prolonged exposure to sunlight.	Polish out scratches with metal polish. Use liquid detergent or paste cleaner (not abrasives) to remove stains.
Acrylics.	Sinks, baths, shower cabinets, occasional tables, trays, door furniture, etc. Trade names: Perspex, Plexiglas.	Good resistance to sunlight, dilute acids and alkalis, oils, fats and petroleum. Keeps its surface finish well in wear and is easy to clean. Warm to the touch, too.	Do not use abrasive cleaners. Avoid nail varnish and remover, dry-cleaning fluids, paint strippers and undiluted bleach. Do not use heavily alkaline bath salts. Will not withstand hot dishes or pans direct from stove or oven. Cigarettes burn the surface.	Remove small scratches with metal polish. Clean with liquid detergent or cleaner/polishes.

No matter how cleverly everything is planned to be labour-saving, there are still a lot of day-to-day maintenance jobs to keep machines running smoothly, carpets stain-free, linen well aired and cutlery well polished. In the past a trusty housekeeper knew all these secrets. Now it is up to you.

The cleaning cupboard

Now contains more than the odd broom, ragged mop and yellow duster, though you still need these as well, but your armoury is extended; these are the weapons you will need:

Vacuum cleaner: Upright or cylinder? Uprights have been demonstrated to be more efficient at picking up dog hairs from carpets. Cylinders are more convenient for hard floors because of their attachments. There is an attachment for more powerful cylinders that does do carpets well and, equally, uprights can come with as varied a range of bits. What is important is to get the most powerful suction possible.

Dustette: Small hand-held vacuum cleaner. Good for quick clean-ups and stairs. Favoured by those who don't like/can't lug the real thing about.

Shampoo/polisher: A good investment if you do shampoo carpets and polish floors or tables.

Brooms and brushes: Soft head for sweeping up in the house. Harder for outdoors. Choose nylon and keep clean by dunking in mild detergent solution. Dustpan and soft brush for dust and hard brush for getting up mud/dirt from carpets. Choose nylon/plastic; keep clean as above.

Squeegee mop: Essential for cleaning hard floors.

Polish-impregnated mops: Good for going over regularly-polished floors.

Cellulose sponges, cloths, dusters, etc.

Bucket.

Cleaners: Detergent, paste cleaner (non-abrasive), paste stain remover, liquid metal polish, silver polish, oven cleaner, stainless steel polish, antistatic polish, bleach, disinfectant, lavatory cleanser, window wiper.

For stain-removal: Dry-cleaning solvent, alcohol, methylated spirit, surgical spirit, bicarbonate of soda, salts of lemon, hydrochloric acid, india-rubber.

Emergency electrical box: Fuses, spare plugs; an electrician's screwdriver; a pair of pliers; Stanley knife; a torch and fuse wire in various ratings.

How to care for rugs

Dhurries: Indian cotton dhurries should be dry-cleaned. When dealing with stains and spills, first remove the dhurry from any soft floor covering underneath, so there is no transference of dye.

Flokati: These rugs can be handwashed in cold water using a mild detergent suitable for woollens. Rinse thoroughly. Dry naturally. Comb and brush pile.

Skin rugs: If you can clean off a stain without wetting the skin, it is safer. The skin of a goatskin rug, for example, may harden if it gets wet and for this reason professional cleaning is recommended.

How to care for carpets

When carpets are new they should be treated gently for the first month. Handbrush in the direction of the pile, daily if necessary. When the carpet has settled, vacuum about once or twice a week. Don't shampoo early in the life of a carpet. If single tufts in a pile carpet stand proud, don't pull them out. Cut them level with scissors. Crepe sole shoes, metal tips and high heels, all accelerate carpet wear.

Occasional care: Carpet squares should be turned about twice a year to equalize wear. If the carpet is fitted, rearranging furniture would change the direction of heavy traffic. If furniture has crushed the carpet pile, hold a hot iron just clear of a damp cloth laid on the flattened area, steam, then brush up pile.

Stair carpet should be about 18 in./ 457 mm longer than necessary so that it can be slightly moved to spread wear, say twice a year. Never turn the carpet round completely: pile should run from top to bottom. If it doesn't, carpet will wear out very quickly.

Cleaning: Carpets can be cleaned professionally at home or in the factory. Most can also be shampooed at home.

If you shampoo a carpet yourself, vacuum it thoroughly first. Be sure to use a proper carpet shampoo, and carefully follow the instructions.

Shampoo is easier to apply with a carpet shampooer (you can often hire them very cheaply from local ironmongers). You will get far more foam, and avoid getting the carpet too wet.

If it is the first time a carpet has been shampooed, do a trial patch somewhere it won't show. (Occasionally colours – the reds especially – bleed.) When you know that it is safe to proceed, start at the wall farthest from the door; never put furniture back before the carpet is thoroughly dry.

Long pile carpets may need two shampoos for a thorough job.

Emergency carpet treatment: If a carpet is badly stained or damaged, or very valuable, it is better to call on professional advice, but the following will help you to deal correctly with minor accidents.

It is always safer to test first on a corner. Use as little cleaner as possible, avoid soaking the carpet and do not rub too hard.

Speed is important. Cope with the carpet – then with the culprit. Sponge or wipe gently as much of liquid spills as you can. Use a knife or spoon to remove grease or solids.

There are then two methods, depending on the stain, but in each case, wherever possible, lift the carpet off the floor so that air can get to its back.

Method 1: Use dry-cleaning solvent. Apply to absorbent cloth – not directly on to carpet – start at outer edge of stain, work towards centre. Work with window open. Take care if carpet is rubber-backed; solvent may damage it.

Method 2: Add one teaspoon of white vinegar to a pint of correctly diluted carpet shampoo. Apply lather with sponge or absorbent cloth. Rub gently. Repeat until stain is gone. Rub gently with clear water. Leave pile sloping in correct direction.

Alcohol: Method 2, then surgical spirit if necessary.

Beverages: Coffee, tea, milk – Method 2 followed by Method 1.

Burns: Extensive burns need expert attention. Blackened fibres can be removed with scissors, then Method 2.

Fruit stains: Method 2. Then if some colour remains, methylated spirits or surgical spirit.

Grass stains: Mop with methylated or surgical spirits as for fruit stains. Then Method 2.

Ink: Method 2 will cope with freshly spilt writing ink. Ball-point pen needs methylated spirits, as above, with a little white vinegar added. Apply with absorbent cloth to prevent spreading. Finally Method 2.

Oil and grease: When excess has

been blotted or scraped off, use Method 1, then Method 2. Grease may reappear later and need a second treatment.

Paint: As for oil and grease.

Salt: This affects carpet colour and attracts moisture; remove thoroughly.

Shoe polish: Scrape off excess; Method 1, then Method 2.

Soot: Vacuum lightly, holding machine just clear of carpet so as not to rub soot into pile. Method 2 followed by Method 1 if necessary.

Starchy foods: Scrape, Method 2.

Tar: As for oil and grease above.

Urine: Mop or blot. Method 2.

Water: If wetting is widespread but the water is reasonably clean, mop and dry as quickly as possible. Raise wet carpet from floor to allow air to circulate. For flooding, burst pipes, etc., call in professionals.

Wax: Scrape off as much wax as possible with a table knife. Cover stain with tissue or blotting paper and hold hot iron just clear of paper but near enough to soften residue of wax. Blot off, constantly moving to a clean patch of paper. For fabric which can be ironed, sandwich stain between two pieces of blotting paper and iron, again moving paper so that there is always a fresh patch of paper next to the stain.

Then clean with a spot remover, carefully following instructions. Use a clean absorbent cloth, put solvent on cleaning pad and gently smooth stain, working from edge to middle so that you don't spread the stain even further. If the wax was coloured, you may need to finish off by sponging with a little methylated, or surgical, spirits, and if so, you finally sponge with water.

Care of sisal

A stain resistant finish provides a good barrier to liquid stains such as spilt coffee or Indian ink and prevents major accidents from causing permanent staining provided, of course, that spillage is mopped up as quickly as possible.

Regular care: If the carpet is reversible, reverse from time to time because the colours on the underside are always fresher. Hard, dry brushing will not harm the carpet but too much water will, and could cause shrinkage.

Shampoo: Use a solution of soap liquid with about one teaspoon of vinegar per pint. Apply evenly and gently in small overlapping areas. Finally, sponge with clean, cold water. Don't use synthetic detergents, ammonia, washing soda or strong alkalis, all of which may affect dyes. Don't use household soap because it leaves a film which attracts more dirt.

Emergency treatment: First aid for

stains on sisal carpets is similar to that given in the section on *Carpets* but these are the manufacturers' recommendations: Act quickly. Remove loose dirt with knife or brush. Blot up as much liquid as possible without spreading stain.

Blood, milk, grease, gravy, oil, paint with oil base, paraffin, petrol, polish, tar, wax: Remove stains with carbon tetrachloride or branded dry-cleaner. Then make a solution of carpet shampoo adding one teaspoon of vinegar per pint. Apply gently with sponge. Do not overwet the carpet. Rinse with clean cloth and cold water.

Beer, chocolate, coffee, fruit, ink, jam, water-based paint, tea, wine: Gently sponge with carpet shampoo added per pint. If any stain remains, try dry-cleaner or 1 part Milton to 2 parts water. Remember, Milton is a bleaching agent. So rinse away after using.

Soot, urine, animal dirt: Remove excess with a stiff brush if dry, or blot up if wet. Gently sponge with carpet shampoo adding one teaspoon of vinegar per pint of solution.

Rush mats

Rush and sisal should be looked after in the same general way.

It is important when buying rush matting to find out the type and the correct care. For some rush mats watering is recommended; for others it is disastrous and makes the rush rot. When cleaning is necessary, the mat should be thoroughly dried, as quickly as possible, before putting back.

Windows

Dust or wipe the frame first. Don't clean in frosty weather when the glass is brittle and liable to break, or when a hot sun is shining on the windows. You can use virtually anything for cleaning windows from cool tea to crumpled newspapers. Faith and elbow grease can make them all work. Once you get the hang of them, those rubber-bladed wipers which professionals use are very quick.

Curtains

Curtains should be hung as far as possible from the glass because condensation will shorten the life of a fabric.

Lined, interlined and large curtains are best dry-cleaned. For curtains suitable for washing, here are some general reminders. Remove hooks. Release simple gathers. Soak for ten minutes in cold water and a little liquid detergent. Rinse, remove as much water as possible, then launder in the correct way for that fabric. It is always better to wash separately. Don't wring or wash too energetically – daily exposure to sun and elements may have weakened fabric.

Acrylics should be washed according to HLCC (Home Laundering Consultative Council) wash code No. 6. Nets, particularly in towns, should be washed very frequently. Glass fibre curtains should be washed gently by hand, never wrung, rubbed or put in a spin dryer. See HLCC wash code No. 8. Put a not-too-heavy rod through the hem of net and lace curtains when you hang them up to dry. It will ensure that the hems hang evenly and they will need very little ironing.

Blinds

Venetian: Keep dust-free. When they need washing, try wearing a pair of old fabric gloves, dip your fingers in warm, not too soapy water (lather is difficult to get rid of) and run your fingers along the slats. Or you can unhook the blind and wash it in the bath.

If venetian blinds are hung in a kitchen, clean frequently before there is any build-up of grime.

Pleatex: Pleatex blinds are made from strong Kraft paper and need a minimum of maintenance. Dust with vacuum cleaner attachment.

Roller: To clean blinds made from cotton impregnated with polyvinyl acetate, and wipe with sponge wrung out in clean lukewarm water. Don't immerse in water, scrub, or hang in humid atmosphere. Holland blinds need dusting only. Some with a special finish can be wiped with detergent and water.

Baths, basins, bidets

Ideally these should be cleaned immediately after use before soap and grime have a chance to harden. If you do it then, no special cleaners other than hot soapy water are needed.

Prevent lime forming round waste hole, by making sure taps don't drip.

Change the washer in time. To clean cast-iron or vitreous enamel or porcelain appliances, use mild abrasive paste, rinse off and dry. For difficult stains, rub with a little vinegar—but rinse away thoroughly as quickly as possible. Avoid abrasive remedies which may also remove enamel. A paste or jelly stain remover is easy to use and will remove stains with minimum damage to surfaces.

To clean acrylic (Perspex) baths, use mild detergent. Warm soapy water and soda only if it has got greasy. Liquid metal polish only if the surface has got scratched.

Showers

China tray should be cleaned like a vitreous enamelled bath; acrylic trays like acrylic baths.

In hard-water areas, the tile surround needs wiping down to keep off the white lime deposits. The rose, if it gets blocked, can be pricked clear with a pin.

Lavatory pans

Keep clean with daily shake of lavatory cleaner or bleach, but do not mix the two as they can combine to form a poisonous gas.

Alternatively, let one of those foaming, cleaning colouring blocks that hangs in the cistern do the job for you.

For bad lime and other stains, treat with spirits of salts (hydrochloric acid). Use carefully as these are poisonous and corrosive. Mix in glass or china container, pouring one measure of acid into two of clean, cold water. Use rubber gloves and apply with a brush on a handle (old lavatory or washing-up brush). If the stain is below water-level pour in acid mixture, leave a few moments and scrub off with brush. If above water-level, apply with brush, doing a section at a time.

This treatment can be used for sinks and baths, but the acid must not touch metal (smear a protective layer of Vaseline over waste hole and taps if necessary) and it must not remain in contact with enamel for too long.

How to care for wallpaper

Use bread, squeezed into large pellets, or a clean india-rubber to remove dirty marks. Rub gently. Dab greasy marks with a pad slightly moistened with carbon tetrachloride or any proprietary brand of dry-cleaner. Wise to test first in a corner. Don't rub or the pattern may come off. You can replace badly-damaged patterned paper by tearing an irregular patch (hold the paper pattern-side down) from a left-over piece. Paste over damaged area, carefully matching pattern. If paper is plain you will have to replace at least a complete length.

Muraweave: Muraweave, grass paper, bamboo wall coverings, etc., should be dusted with a vacuum cleaner attachment. For stains, use a good upholstery fabric dry-cleaner. Test first.

Washable: Washable doesn't actually imply sluicing down or scrubbing. Wipe them with a damp sponge; don't wet them more than necessary. Work up and down to avoid lifting at seams.

How to care for paintwork

Always rinse off all detergents and cleaners after use. Read instructions. Don't use too strong a concentration of any cleaner, otherwise you will remove gloss, and paintwork will get dirtier more quickly in future. A little furniture polish helps protect window sills and areas that get heavy wear.

To wash walls, start at the highest possible point – but don't embark on the job unless you are prepared to do at least all of one wall.

To remove stains, try a mild paste cleaner, then polish.

Wall tiles

Normally wall tiles just need wiping with a damp cloth then lightly buffing. They will need an occasional spring clean to remove dirt and grease, particularly in bathrooms and kitchens. Use a mild paste cleaner – anything harsh may scratch the glaze.

Wood

If sealed, wood darkens on exposure to light. Wood behind pictures remains lighter unless the pictures are moved every few months. To get wood light again, it has to be sanded and re-sealed.

If the wood has been stained, the darkening process is hardly noticeable, so it just needs to be kept clean with regular dusting, wiping down. If painted, it needs washing down at regular intervals. A solution of ammonia and water gives good results.

Mirrors

Clean as windows; take care not to let water seep between glass and backing. There are preparations which you apply at intervals which stop the mirror from steaming up. To remove hair lacquer, use surgical spirits.

Much of the sheer labour of housework can be taken over by machinery, but the machinery needs to be taken care of.

Keep instruction books: Don't read them once and throw them away. Re-read them from time to time. You may find you are not using the machine quite correctly or not exploiting it to the full.

Organize servicing: It is better to buy a more expensive machine which can be serviced easily, locally and at short notice than a bargain which no local retailer would touch. This is something to settle before you buy.

Servicing comes in various ways:
(i) The manufacturer runs his own servicing. This can be an advantage, but not if the firm is employing too few engineers and supplying a limited range of spares, and letting no one else service his machines.
(ii) The retailer arranges servicing (this usually applies for the period of the guarantee). Good if they have their own engineers, not so good if they contract servicing out.
(iii) The manufacturer appoints an agent. This depends on the quality of the local men; also how they are spread about the country.
(iv) You go to an independent engineer. However obliging and clever, these men always have terrible trouble getting the manufacturers to give them the necessary spares.

Usually you ring up when things go wrong, but some appliances can be put on to a regular service contract. It is a good idea to take advantage of such schemes.

The cheaper the appliance the harder servicing becomes, as the cost of a replacement and labour may well exceed the cost of a new appliance. Friends and national press comment can keep you up to date on which retailers/manufacturers have good reputations for servicing.

Fuses are graded into 2 amp, 3 amp, 5 amp, 10 amp and 13 amp capacities. The more power an appliance uses, the stronger the fuse required. A bedside lamp should have a 2 amp fuse, a washing machine a 13 amp one.

Wire up correctly with the right fuse: Modern ring main plugs have three pins and a replaceable fuse. The diagram shows how to wire up.

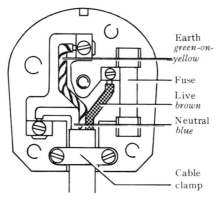

Earth *green-on-yellow*
Fuse
Live *brown*
Neutral *blue*
Cable clamp

Guarantees: Keep these with your instructions. In law, your contract is with the retailer who sold you the goods: it is his job to put the faults right.

Dishwasher

This is one of the most complicated pieces of machinery in the house. Regular servicing and maintenance are advisable. Most manufacturers recommend the detergent and softener. Daily maintenance is confined to keeping filters clean.

You put silver, cutlery with wood, bone, horn or some plastic handles, fine antique or cut lead crystal glasses, and gold painted crockery in at your own risk: dishwasher detergents and temperatures are adjusted for ordinary things.

Cooker

A daily clean with mild abrasive paste, and, if necessary, wire wool, combined with a periodic onslaught with a strong caustic cleanser, is all most gas and electric cookers need.

A gas, self-cleaning oven, and stainless steel hobs have their own instructions. Otherwise cookers go on cooking.

Refrigerator

Seldom goes wrong, but you should know who would repair it. Keep the firm's telephone number handy.

Most, except fridges with automatic defrosting, need emptying, defrosting and wiping clean (use a mild bleach solution to disinfect) occasionally.

Deep freezer

Seldom goes wrong either, but as the value of the food is often so high, get the telephone number of an engineer who would come to see to it. Some big companies organize maintenance contracts and insurance schemes.

Deep freezers need clearing out about twice a year, if only to scoop up the unidentifiable little packets that have dropped to the bottom. Use warm water

and a plastic scraper to hasten the defrosting. Wipe down with weak bleach solution and dry thoroughly. Meanwhile keep food wrapped in blankets or eiderdowns or even newspaper. Do not put back until the freezer has reached the correct temperature again.

Electric kettles

Elements can be replaced if they go wrong. Kettles often suffer from flex damage, which is easily put right.

Mixers, blenders, beaters

Make sure there is a retailer manufacturer to honour obligations under the guarantee. Keep these machines clean, but don't put plastic parts in very hot water. Be careful not to use them so hard that they burn out.

Vacuum cleaners

Empty out the bag frequently. Do not ask it to do too much. Tugging can break cables in the flex. In time the motor loses some power: often it can be replaced.

Washing machine

A really labour-saving machine, especially if it is fully automatic. To get the best from it, follow the programmes for different fabrics carefully. If something is very dirty give it a separate pre-wash; rub collars and cuffs of shirts with detergent before machining.

In 1966 the Home Laundering Consultative Council (HLCC) published a care labelling scheme so that what you see on clothes coincides with instructions on your washing machine.

Since one comes to rely on one's washing machine, it is well worthwhile having a regular maintenance contract with the manufacturer or retailer. It seems expensive to begin with, but is worth it in the long run.

Tumble dryer

Immensely useful, especially if there is not much space to hang out washing to

dry. Used skilfully it saves a lot of ironing. Practically trouble-free – but check service arrangements just in case. Remove the fluff from the filter.

Irons

Most likely accidents are the flex burning through, or damage through dropping, but hardly anyone will mend an iron. Steam irons last longer if you use only distilled water, and carefully empty them out after use.

Lighting

Clean appliances regularly – not only shades but bulbs too, otherwise half the light you are paying for will be obscured. Fluorescent tubes in kitchens get particularly dirty – if you take them down they can be safely immersed in warm soapy water for washing. Dry them thoroughly before you put them back and switch them on.

Lampshades

Lampshades attract dust, because of the heat of the light, and need regular cleaning if they are not to cut down on the amount of light.

Japanese paper lanterns should be lightly dusted with a vacuum cleaner attachment or feather duster.

Cotton shades should never be gripped by the side, only by the wire fitting. If the shade should get dented, hold the dent against a gentle source of heat for a few minutes while pressing it out from the inside. Remove from source of heat but maintain pressure until the lampshade has cooled. Dirty marks can often be removed with an eraser or bread. If this does not work, try a barely damp cloth.

Fabric-bound shades are not washable and should the frame get wet by accident, dry as quickly as possible—with a fan heater or hair dryer if you have one. Brush the shade lightly to remove dust.

Acrylic shades can be washed in warm soapy water. When rubbed dry, they tend to get dusty relatively quickly. You can cut down on static either by finally wiping with a cloth damped in detergent and water or by using a special anti-static Perspex polish. The polish should be used very sparingly and thinned with water if necessary. Finally buff until shiny.

General: Always switch the light off before cleaning the shade. Don't let the shade get too dirty or you will find it difficult to apply sufficient elbow grease *in situ.* Choose the right shade: a washable one for the kitchen; keep fabric eons for living rooms and bedrooms.

Mattresses

All polythene wrappings must be removed before using a divan or mattress; otherwise condensation, followed by mildew, will occur.

If you have a bad back and want to put a stiffening board between mattress and base, the board must have holes to allow ventilation.

Foam mattresses do not need turning but others should be turned once a week for the first few months so that fillings can settle evenly. After that, then turn alternatively from top to bottom, and over completely, once a month.

If you sit on the bed – bedsitters please note – sit well back to avoid distorting the border springs.

It is worth putting a special fitted cover on a new mattress. Try cleaning marks from the ticking with dry-cleaning fluid, but do not wash. Brush to remove dust. Vacuum cleaning can disturb the upholstery.

Occasionally shake and air out of doors. To store, make sure blanket is clean and well aired. Protect from dust with a polythene bag.

Blankets are made in a wide range of materials, and the method of washing and cleaning depends on the kind you buy. For all wool blankets, dry-cleaning is recommended. After cleaning, iron satin binding with a cool iron.

Sheets

Deep-dyed cotton sheets should be washed separately for the first three times. Any colour that comes out of the sheets during these initial launderings is surplus and does not mean that the sheet is getting paler each time it is washed. Follow HLCC washing code No. 2. Iron while damp or with a steam iron. Cotton fabrics should not be left rolled up damp for any length of time. Do not use bleach on coloured sheets.

Follow washing instructions for permanent press and easy care sheets.

Quilts, duvets

Duvets take the place of top sheets, blankets and eiderdowns. They can be filled with pure down, a mixture of feather and down or a synthetic fibre. The quilt should always be used in a washable cover.

Quilts should be plumped up each day and occasionally given a shaking on a fine day out of doors. They should not be vacuumed or beaten.

Quilts with synthetic fillings can be dry-cleaned, hand or machine washed. If they are dry-cleaned, they should be aired for 48 hours to get rid of cleaning vapours. Clean fluid must be used, otherwise the quilt acts as a filter and strains off the dirt. Although they can be hand washed, tumble drying is essential to fluff them back into shape.

Down, and feather and down quilts should be dry-cleaned. Wrong cleaning can spoil the cover, resilience of the filling and the insulation properties.

Emergencies: In the case of accidents, act quickly. Remove cover at once. If stain has seeped through, smooth filling away and treat gently; do not allow the quilt to get really wet.

Pillows

Fillings for pillows include down, various qualities of feathers, latex foam, plastic foam and synthetic fibres.

Down and feather pillows: A down pillow will last about ten years; feathers, depending on quality, rather less. Down is soft and light; feathers are heavier and firmer. Shake daily. Air occasionally in the sunlight. Keep clean by using a pillow slip under the pillowcase. They can be professionally dry-cleaned (the easiest) or they can be washed at home, although they tend to lose some of their bounce; the ticking, too, may become less featherproof.

A washing machine and a tumble dryer will, of course, make washing a pillow easier. If you have to dry a pillow on a clothes line it may take several days. Shake it frequently while drying.

Foam pillows: A foam pillow should last for five to seven years. If the cover of a foam pillow needs washing, handle the foam interior with care so that it does not tear, and keep it in a pillowslip because exposure to light can damage it. Do not use the foam until it has been stitched back into its cover.

If the foam gets soiled, try gently sponging with suds, wetting as little as possible. Sponge suds away with clear water, mop with a towel. Then stitch back into cover, and dry in airing cupboard or near fan heater, but not near source of direct heat. If the foam needs washing completely, leave in its

own cover; gently squeeze in warm suds, then rinse until water is clear. Don't twist or wring. Wrap in towel and press out as much water as possible; dry in a warm place. This may take some time.

Terylene pillows: In the past Terylene pillows tended to go lumpy when washed, but the filling now used is said to make laundering easier. Use HLCC code 6. Tumble dry if possible or fluff up well. Do not dry-clean.

Household linens

Household linens mean everything from sheets to tea towels, and not all are made of linen, of course.

If you send linens to the laundry they should be marked with your name. Keep a list of items inside the door of the linen cupboard, writing down the date of purchase, description, label and price paid. If you do lose a sheet at the laundry, it's not much help describing it as a "double white one". Linens should not be stored for any length of time in a heated cupboard. If they discolour, wash and bleach in the sun.

Towels

Terry towels should be washed before using for the first time to tighten the basic fabric and prevent loops being pulled out. If deep-dyed, wash separately for the first three launderings, as we advised for deep-dyed sheets.

Laundering

Always check instructions carefully. The properties of special finishes may be spoilt by washing at too high a temperature or by wringing instead of allowing to drip dry. Some detergents and biological washing powders may change the colour of fabrics if incorrectly used. Follow instructions on packet carefully and don't soak above 30°C.

Circular table-cloths should be ironed from the centre to keep their shape.

Stain removal

To list possible stains for all the different fabrics is impossible. This brief list contains remedies for accidents most likely to happen to table linens. Very extensive, very stubborn stains, or very delicate fabrics, are best sent to a good laundry with details of stain.

Grease, oil, gravy, butter: Use warm

thick suds on stains, rub between hands. Wash and rinse.

Tea and coffee: Remove stain at once. Stretch linen taunt over a bowl, pour boiling water on stain from a height.

Egg: Soak in cold water. Wash, rinse.

Cream and milk: Wash immediately in cold water. Wash and rinse.

Tomato juice and ketchup: Sponge with cold water. Wash in hot suds.

Ink and rust: On white linen, remove with salts of lemon. (Salts of lemon are poisonous. Handle carefully.)

Fruit and wine: Cover stain at once with salt. As soon as possible stretch linen taunt over a bowl and pour on boiling water. If unsuccessful, rub stain with lemon juice and salt and pour on boiling water.

Indelible lipstick: Rub lard into stain. Sponge with dry-cleaning fluid. Wash in warm suds and rinse. Always try to remove stains before laundering.

Cutlery

All cutlery should be washed as soon as possible in warm soapy water. Salt, vinegar, lemon juice and egg can pit and blacken cutlery. Water will mark it too, although only temporarily. If you want it to look good, it should be dried and lightly buffed by hand – even if it is machine washed.

Stainless steel

Don't use a silver dip on stainless steel, it will turn it dull grey. There are special stainless steel polishes.

Silver and silver plate

Sterling silver and plate should be kept in a baize-lined box or drawer so that the pieces do not get scratched or rubbed. Storage for silver not in use should be airtight. Remove egg tarnish from silver spoons with table salt.

Handles

Cutlery with handles in natural materials such as wood, horn, mother of pearl, ivory, and some plastics cannot be put in the dishwasher and should not be soaked in water. Immersion in hot or even cool water may not only spoil the look of the handle but soften the adhesive fixing it on. Wash such knives by holding the handle and drying immediately, or place them in a heavy, stable jar, handles uppermost and above the waterline until you are ready to wash or dry them.

Kitchen knives

If you buy professional cooks' knives – and it is worth it – you need to lavish a bit of professional care on them.

Carbon steel knives should be dried or wiped clean immediately after use. Lightly grease with edible oil before putting away unless they are in constant use. Vinegar, fruit, onions, even raw potato will stain carbon steel if knives are not wiped immediately. If stains do occur, remove them with an abrasive pad, wet-and-dry emery paper or something similar.

Stainless steel blades can also be marked by salt, lemon juice, etc., so wash and dry quickly after use.

Do not immerse knives – especially wooden-handled ones – in water and do not put in the dishwasher. Apart from spoiling the handles, it is not safe to wash very sharp blades other than by holding them by the handle.

Storing

Properly planned storage saves time, temper, labour and breakages. Keep pieces in constant use readily accessible.

Use plate racks inside cupboards if you can. If not, stack plates of the same size only, so that you never have to take a plate from the bottom of a pile. If plates are richly decorated, put tissues or pieces of kitchen paper between plates. If you don't, you will scratch them.

Don't store pottery at too high or too low a level. Things that are difficult to get at are more likely to get broken.

Breakages

Eating off cracked tableware isn't very hygenic. It doesn't look very good either. Obviously it is better to replace broken pieces, but if you can't, some breakages can be successfully mended with an epoxy resin. Handles are a cinch to stick back; multiple fractures require time, patience and skill.

Washing up

If dishes are left to soak, leave in clear water. Use hand-hot liquid detergent suds for washing. Don't use soap powder or boiling water. In time the pattern will

be ruined. Spring-clean china regularly. Use a soft nail brush or washing-up brush to clean round handles, etc. Remove tannin stains with a damp cloth dipped in bicarbonate of soda or borax. Vinegar and water followed by brisk rubbing will remove hard water scum.

Tin trays

Tin trays are made from tinplate, litho printed. Each colour is separately stoved and the tray is finally given a protective coat of transparent varnish.

Trays should be wiped with a damp cloth and dried before putting away. Dunking them in hot washing up water will soften the protective varnish and the decoration will then get worn very quickly. Don't use anything abrasive and avoid scratching with knives, etc.

Glass

Table glass is tough provided you follow a few simple rules:

Don't subject to sudden temperature changes. If you want a hot drink in a glass, put a spoon in first, pour the hot drink in slowly. If you wash a glass under the hot tap (not really a good idea), at least heat the outside first to allow expansion and prevent cracking.

Don't store glasses upside down, the rim is invariably the weakest part. When you do turn glasses upside down to drain, do it carefully.

Don't force your hand inside the bowl of a glass. Wash with a soft bristle brush, dry with a rolled up ball of drying up cloth (non-fluffy).

If stacking tumblers stick, stand the bottom glass in hot water and fill the top one with cold. Not ice cold and boiling though, or you will have a different problem.

To clean stained decanters and carafes, try swilling round with vinegar and sand, or vinegar and cooking salt. If you have any, lead shot and hot water works the same way. You may need to repeat several times. Vinegar removes marks caused by hard water.

Washing up

Glasses used for milk should be rinsed first in cold water. Wash glass in warm water and detergent, rinse in clear warm water, drain and dry with a non-fluffy cloth. Use a soft bristle brush for

inside vases and decanters. A soft nail brush is useful for cut glass. Glass seems to sparkle more if rinsed in slightly soapy water and polished immediately, though it probably shouldn't be recommended for drinking glasses.

Woodware (illustrated heading)

Wooden equipment is best kept on open shelves so that it keeps fresh and dry. Don't leave it soaking in water and don't put it in the dishwasher. Always wipe dry after washing and leave to air and dry completely before putting away.

It is usually sufficient to wipe salad bowls with kitchen paper after use but you need to wash them in clear warm water after a potent fish salad for example.

Lemon juice will whiten bread boards and chopping boards. Keep a special board for chopping and cutting raw meat: it will need more vigorous cleaning. Scrub with cleaning powder or sluice down with a solution of household bleach. Rinse thoroughly in cold water.

Never dry any woodware near direct heat. When wood is cracked it will, like pottery, harbour dirt and germs.

Pottery

This section deals with cooking ware.

Check when you buy earthenware that it is ovenproof. Occasionally you will find pieces that have the robust look of cooking pots but are in fact only serving dishes. Earthenware should be heated gently, never put in the oven unless. it contains liquid, fat or food. It will crack if you subject it to drastic changes of temperature. Always allow to heat and cool slowly. Wash and dry carefully before putting away. Earthenware is porous under the glaze and if chipped or cracked will pick up stains.

Fireproof earthenware

Elizabeth David gives the following advice for French fireproof earthenware

designed for use over direct heat, such as *pot-au-feu*, *marmites* and *poelons*. It is advice worth following for all ceramic cooking pots if they are designed to be used on the stove. Always heat slowly. Keep heat very low and steady throughout cooking. Earthenware retains heat well so even if initial cooking is over direct heat, a mat should be used to check and reduce heat once simmering point has been reached. Don't add cold liquid to a casserole containing hot fat or food. Hot casseroles should be left to cool before they are washed.

For safety, the cooking ring should not be smaller than the base of the pot. Oval baking dishes, for example, are safe under the grill and in the oven, but smaller sizes only should be used on top of the stove. Large oval earthenware terrines or casseroles should be used only in the oven. For safety and to reduce and regulate heat, casseroles should be used with a heat diffuser mat.

Sometimes the glaze inside earthenware cooking pots looks crazed as soon as liquid is poured in. This does not mean the glaze is faulty.

Stoneware

Stoneware is a hard tough vitreous body which is ovenproof and occasionally flameproof. It is non-porous and will not stain if you chip the glaze. It can be used for storage containers. If manufacturers say a stoneware cooking pot can be used on top of the stove, it is wise to follow the advice laid down for French fireproof earthenware.

Patent ceramics

These are comparatively new, usually marketed under brand names—"Pyrosil" is well known in this country. They are ovenproof, flameproof and will withstand extremes of temperature far better than other ceramic pots, but even here it is safer to underestimate their strength.

Aluminium

Aluminium pans are light, easy to clean, don't tarnish and don't rust. Just remember three things. (1) Don't use washing soda for cleaning. It has a harmful chemical action on aluminium. (2) Don't store liquids and food in aluminium pans. Water, as well as some foods, can cause pitting. It doesn't affect the efficiency of the pan, only its looks. (3) Don't use metal spoons and sharp implements for stirring. They will scratch and cause pitting.

Cleaning: Wash in hot soapy water, rinse and dry before using for the first time. After that, wash in liquid detergent, using a saucepan brush, nylon scourer or fine steel wool but not copper scouring pads or harsh scouring powder. Rinse thoroughly and dry. If the inside discolours, don't worry; it won't affect food or flavour. You can remove the discoloration by boiling up some water with apple peeling or a lemon when you've used the juice.

Frying pans: Should be heated gently with plenty of fat. Never plunge a frying-pan into washing-up bowl after use; it will buckle. Allow to cool first.

New aluminium kettles: Make curiously coloured tea. If you bring the kettle to the boil repeatedly, emptying and using fresh tap water each time, it will rapidly form a protective coating on the inside and the tea will improve.

Stainless steel

As stainless steel is a poor conductor of heat, stainless steel pans have to have an applied, or sandwich, base of copper or aluminium before they can be used on top of the stove.

Although stainless steel has a tendency to develop blue heat marks, the material retains its good appearance easily with a minimum of labour. Simply wash in hot soapy water and dry to avoid water marks.

There are special polishes for stainless steel: don't use silver dips.

Scratching shows less on satin finishes than mirror finishes.

Copperware

Copper preserving pans and bowls for beating eggs are unlined. All other copper pans for cooking are usually lined with tin, nickel or silver, and should be relined when necessary.

Use wood or plastic for stirring in lined copper pans.

Tarnished copper can be cleaned with half a lemon dipped into a tablespoon of salt and vinegar. Rub hard. Then wash in hot soapy water and dry thoroughly.

Non-stick

Non-stick coatings vary in quality and the way they are applied. It is important therefore to follow the manufacturer's own care instructions.

The following notes on the care of Tefal, where the metal is etched before the non-stick polytetrafluorethylene

(PTFE) is poured on to the surface, are good guide lines for all non-stick pans:

1. Before using for the first time, wash in soapy water using a sponge or cloth. It is suggested that the cooking surface of frying-pans, etc., are oiled by wiping with kitchen paper soaked in salad or cooking oil.

2. Best results are obtained at medium settings.

3. Empty pans should not be left on hot burners or in heated ovens.

4. At temperatures above 450°F, the cooking surface may discolour. This does not affect the efficiency, but discoloration can be removed, in the case of Tefal pans, by mixing two tablespoons of baking soda and half a cup of liquid household bleach with one cup of water. Boil this solution for five to ten minutes in the stained pan. Wash thoroughly, rinse and dry. Then wipe with oil again before using. Repeat if necessary.

5. Although metal utensils can be used with Tefal pans, they should be used gently. Sharp implements should not be used. Wooden spoons and nylon spatulas are best for using with all non-stick pans.

6. If you use a non-stick pan correctly, washing in hot soapy water is sufficient. Do not use abrasives or scourers. Provided handles are dishwasher proof, non-stick pans can be put in the dishwasher.

7. Protect non-stick lined pans by not storing other pans inside them.

Enamel

There are two kinds of enamel used for household products. They are quite different and need different care.

Vitreous enamel: Vitreous and porcelain enamel are two names for the same finish: glass fired onto metal. Vitreous enamel is used for baths, cookers, cooking pots, sinks, etc. It is tough, scratch-resistant finish but abrasive cleaners are not recommended.

To get rid of food burnt onto enamelled cooking pots, soak in detergent and water until food is easily removed. If the inside of the pan gets discoloured, fill it with the correct solution of household bleach and leave it to stand. Wash thoroughly before use. Cast iron should always be heated gently; sticking is usually caused by too much heat.

Avoid hard knocks which may cause vitreous enamel to chip. Avoid sudden changes of temperature and do not heat when empty or the enamel may spit off.

Stoved enamel: Stoved enamel is paint baked on at a low temperature. Tougher than ordinary paint, it can nevertheless easily be scratched.

Frying-pans

A frying-pan is probably used more than any other cooking pot so it is worth having several, and cherishing them.

For greatest efficiency, a frying-pan should relate as nearly as possible to the size of the cooking ring. Make sure the pan is suitable for the fuel with which you cook.

Generally speaking don't use more heat than you need, and wipe or rinse in clear water after use rather than wash so that a natural non-stick patina builds up. To a great extent, however, care will depend on the material from which a frying-pan is made.

Steel frying-pans and omelette pans

These are lightly greased before they leave the factory to prevent rust. Before being used, they have to be cleaned. Put a good measure of oil into the pan, heat it well and then leave it to cool. Pour off the oil and wipe with kitchen paper. Wash well with liquid detergent, scour with a soft nylon pad if necessary. Dry pan very thoroughly – in a still warm oven is fine – and coat thinly with more oil before storing.

A steel pan should not need washing after use – usually a rub with kitchen paper is sufficient; it acquires its own patina and surface protection, which should not be disturbed unless a piece of food sticks. If this happens, clean the pan like any other but without soaking and not with a coarse cleaner. Dry thoroughly and re-oil. Don't put steel pans on the stove without some fat or oil in the pan. Don't put a hot pan direct from the stove into the washing-up water. Leave it to cool, pour off the cooking fat, clean it, wipe it dry, oil before putting it away.

Tinned ware

Tinned ware is mild steel coated with tin, and is used for cake tins, ring moulds, baking tins, wire whisks, etc. The tin is silvery when new but darkens with use. Don't use abrasive cleaners which will scratch the tin coating. Soak off burned-on food. If pieces get really dirty, soak in weak solution of bicarbonate of soda or boil up in a solution of washing soda. Rinse. Always dry very thoroughly so there is no chance of the base metal rusting.

Flameproof

If a cooking pot is flameproof it can be used on top of the stove. The commonest are cast iron, enamelled steel and enamelled cast iron, glass ceramics, porcelain, stainless steel with an applied base. Sometimes ovenproof glass, earthenware and stoneware can be used on

top of the stove but it is very likely that a heat diffusing mat should be used, and extra care taken.

Read manufacturers' instructions carefully. Always heat gently, avoiding extremes of temperature.

Casseroles

Casseroles can be made of many materials: cast iron, glass, earthenware, stoneware, porcelain, patent ceramic, etc. The important difference is whether they can only be used in the oven or whether they can also be put, for the initial browning, on top of the stove.

Fireproof or ovenproof

Ovenproof dishes can be used in the oven but unless they are also flameproof, they cannot be used on top of the stove – see *Pottery*.

Ovenware dishes should not be subjected to high temperatures unless they contain fat, food or liquid.

Don't take dishes straight from the oven and put them onto a cold working surface or plunge into the sink for washing. They won't stand up to sudden changes of temperature. Allow to heat and cool gradually.

A dish cannot be put in the oven if the handles are plastic or any other material that won't stand up to the heat. This is most likely to apply to stainless steel pans.

Cast iron

Cast iron conducts heat evenly and can be used on the stove, with gentle heat, or in the oven. It is a tough, durable material if treated with reasonable care, but may fracture if dropped on a hard surface. Because cast-iron pots are heavy, they should not be chosen by people who have real difficulty in lifting heavy weights.

Most cast iron is vitreous enamelled (see *Enamel*) or has a ground coating of enamel, usually black or grey, which gives it protection against rust and, if applied inside the pot, gives an almost non-stick finish.

If cast iron is untreated – rare these days – it should be seasoned before use as follows: pour a good measure of olive oil into the pan. Heat it well and then leave to cool. Pour off the oil and wipe with kitchen paper. Wash well with liquid detergent, scour with a soft nylon pad if necessary. Dry thoroughly and coat thinly with olive oil before putting away.

After use, wash in hot soapy water, scrub with a stiff saucepan brush. Always dry thoroughly (in a still warm oven is fine), then lightly oil against rust before tidying away.

Most people who have ever employed a builder will confirm that the relationship starts with great enthusiasm and confidence on both sides and usually ends with one or both parties hating the very sight of each other.

It is not inevitably the case, of course, but it is frequent enough to justify the generalization. Normally the blame can be apportioned retrospectively in equal parts to just about everyone involved; consequently everyone feels wronged, but none more so than the client – you.

After all, it is *you* who has had to fork out all the money, it is *your* home that has been bashed about and trampled underfoot for weeks and *you* are going to have to live with the result.

Appropriately enough, whether or not you suffer escalating acrimony and aggravation throughout the project is also largely up to you. For the foresight and attitude of the client is the make-or-break factor in any situation which involves employing other people to improve your home. You *can* end up all friends together, regardless of whether you are simply knocking two rooms into one or tackling a major conversion. It depends, to a large extent, on how you plan to go about it.

First you need to know what you want to do, and second you need to be able to communicate your plans to whoever is going to execute them. Simple enough? No, not really.

Knowing what you want

Mistakes at this stage are no joke except when they happen to other people. It may be a bit of a laugh to see the builders arriving next door to put back the wall they have just taken away or take away the window they have just put in, but it is difficult to see the funny side if it is happening to you.

The real problem, to paraphrase the Victorians, is not so much knowing what you want as knowing what will be best for you. If, for example, you decide you want a spiral staircase in the hall, it may look just as you imagined it in your dreams. But when you discover that it is impossible to carry anything up it . . .

Fortunately, there is no shortage of advice available to prevent such disappointments. Much of it is free: from trade advisory bureaux, local consumer groups, department stores, manufacturers, local authorities, and all those with a vested interest in persuading you to use certain of their products.

Probably the only advice worth paying for at this stage is that of an architect, designer or surveyor, particularly if you want a major alteration or improvement. A surveyor's report on an old house in

The relationship between you and your builder can easily deteriorate.

need of conversion is an invaluable document because it will tell you what work must be carried out to put the house in a sound state of repair.

An architect worth his salt should be able to reveal the full potential of a house by suggesting the best ways it can be made to work for you and your family. A consultation fee paid for an architect's advice before you formulate final plans could, in the long run, *save* a great deal of money, either by avoiding disastrous mistakes or simply by finding cheaper and more efficient solutions to your particular problems.

Getting the work done

First, catch your builder, handyman, plumber, electrician, etc. Second, tell him what you want him to do, being aware that nowhere is the communications gap greater than between client and builder, handyman, plumber, *et al*.

Easy (and expensive) way out of the problem is to retain an architect to supervise the whole job. Difficult (but possibly cheap) solution is to act as your own main contractor and employ the various trades needed to complete the work. A reasonable compromise can be arrived at by using an architect's or surveyor's advice in the preparation of a specification, then asking three or four local builders to quote a price for the job.

Whichever method you adopt, the specification is the most vital document. It should list, in great detail, all the work to be carried out in such a way that there can be no misunderstanding.

Provided that the specification is clear, if the builder or any of his merry men does something wrong you can make them put it right at no cost to yourself. If it is not absolutely crystal clear then you and your builder are well on the way to loathing each other.

Like many other things, money is the real key to the ease or otherwise with which you can improve your home. If you can afford full architectural services, just sit back and let it happen. The tighter the budget, the more effort and irritation you may have to suffer. If you decide to act as your own main contractor your problems will be multiplied by the number of trades you employ.

Advice and where to find it

If there is a drawback to the advice generally available on improving houses, it is less its quantity than its quality.

There is certainly plenty of it. Do-it-yourself enthusiasts are always ready with tips; manufacturers of building and decorating materials churn out "advice" by the ton, dozens of magazines are devoted to telling us to do it this way or that way, and a large chunk of the advertising

industry peddles home improvement "advice" through the media.

Much of it is useful if the interests of the "advisors" are borne in mind. In addition to all the commercially-motivated counselling, there is unbiased (and therefore possibly more helpful) advice available from all kinds of sources to those prepared to seek it out.

On structural alterations or additions: First source to tap is the borough surveyor's department of your local authority. Find a good man and get him on your side, and he will guide you by the hand through the amazing complexities of planning permissions and building regulations in addition to telling you what you can and can't do. The public health and planning departments may also be helpful. Architects and surveyors will cost you money (see *Buying a House*) but charges need not be exorbitant if you are seeking only straightforward advice on the feasibility of your plans. If you are thinking of making an extension, there are plenty of ready-made units or factory-built components on the market. Most of the manufacturers offer a planning or design service, although it's likely to be pretty uninspired. But it's free, so probably worth the effort on the off-chance that they might just come up with something that suits. Advice from the Building Centre in London is free. Normally if they can't answer your questions they can put you in touch with whoever can.

On heating: Best sources of free information are the four main sources of fuel – the local electricity board, gas company, coal board and oil distributors. All of them are liable to tell you their system is best and most suitable for what you have in mind, whatever that is.

Impartial advice about central heating is available from The National Heating Centre but you have to pay for it: fees are charged both for interviews and for postal enquiries.

On electricity: Make your local electricity board work for you. Representatives of the board should be able to advise you on all matters concerning electrical appliances, wiring and re-wiring, as well as recommending reputable electricians to carry out their work. If you can't get much sense or action out of your local office, write to the Marketing Department of the Electricity Council.

On plumbing and drainage: Your local authority will tell you all you need to know about drainage – usual contact is the public health inspector's office. For plumbing problems, general advice is readily available from the National Federation of Plumbers and Domestic Heating Engineers.

On general household problems: The Consumers Association or the Design Council will be able to answer your questions or point you in the right direction to find an answer.

Countdown what happens then

If you are employing an architect to supervise the whole job:

Discuss with him what your requirements are going to be.

Tell him what you like and don't like.

Tell him how much you can afford to spend.

Make sure you know what his fees and expenses will be.

When he comes up with his suggestions, don't approve them unless you are sure that they are what you want – his job is to give you just that, not satisfy his own ego.

Having agreed a plan, sit back and let it happen; don't interfere.

If you are employing an architect for advice and drawing up of plans:

Find out how much he will charge and what you can expect him to supply for your money.

Discuss with him your requirements.

Make sure he knows what you like and don't like.

Tell him how much you can afford to spend.

When he comes up with his suggestions, don't approve them unless you are sure they are what you want.

If you are employing an architect for initial advice only:

Find out how much he will charge.

Tell him what you want to do and what you want to end up with.

Make careful note of his suggestions.

If you are going it alone, before you do anything yourself, make sure you have the best possible plan.

TEST: Will it work for the whole family? Have you considered all the alternatives? Will it add to the value of your home?

More questions to ask – and where to find the answers:

Is it structurally possible?

(Local authority/architect.)

Do you need planning permission?

(Local authority.)

Can you get a grant?

(Local authority.)

Can you afford it?

(Ask a couple of local builders for a rough estimate without obligation on either side.)

When you are satisfied (and remember mistakes are much more expensive later on), first task is to write the specification in the order in which the work is to be carried out, and get drawings prepared if necessary.

Then follow this timetable:

(a) Apply for local authority approval (if necessary).

(b) Apply for an improvement grant (if applicable). Remember: no work can start before the grant has been approved.

(c) Draw up a list of four or five recommended builders and ask them to quote for the job on the basis of the specification and drawings.

(d) Choose your builder on the basis of his price, reputation and estimated time for completing the job.

(e) Pare his estimate down to your pocket, agree to the final price and the dates he will start and finish work.

(f) Supervise the work: check every day that it is proceeding exactly according to the specification.

(g) If extras crop up during the course of the work, make sure that you get the cost confirmed in writing.

(h) After completion of the job, retain a small percentage of the final account for six months to cover the cost of faults which appear after the builders have left. (This has to be agreed at the time he gives you his estimate.)

Who needs an architect?

"The architect's function is to translate the client's needs into a building that will serve his purpose in every way and represent good value for money, within agreed limits of time and cost." Excerpt taken from a RIBA brochure.

An architect is trained to recognize the full potential of a house for the people who are going to live there. He should be fully up to date with the latest building techniques and materials, the restrictions likely to be placed by local authorities and the approximate cost of any improvements, alterations or additions you may have in mind.

It is not his job to take over your home and turn it into an architectural design exercise which forces you to change your life style or taste. His job is to accept and analyse your way of life, your needs and your tastes – *then* use his skills to provide the best possible living arrangement within the confines and limitations of your own home.

By virtue of his training and experience, he may be able to suggest solutions that may never occur to you – like making maximum use of all the available space or a small change in room layout that alters your entire vision of your home. Naturally, you have to pay for the services of an architect, but it need not be a lot of money and it could save you making expensive mistakes or living in an arrangement of your own making that patently doesn't work.

Ultimately only you can decide whether an architect's fees are worthwhile. Plenty of people consider them to be an expensive and unnecessary luxury; others think of them as indispensable to any house-improvement project.

Either way, whether you employ an architect for half an hour's advice or for building your dream home, the important thing to remember is that the only one he is working for is *you*.

How to find an architect

Architects are not allowed to advertise or solicit for work in any way, but the Clients' Advisory Service of the Royal Institute of British Architects keeps a register of practising architects covering the entire country.

The register includes details of their completed work as well as the kind of jobs they are prepared to tackle – you won't therefore find yourself with an architect who normally builds tower blocks of flats if you only want to add a single storey extension out at the back.

Members of the public are welcome to call at the RIBA headquarters in London to look through photographs of work by different architects.

Alternatively, you can write to the RIBA and ask them to send you the names and addresses of suitable architects near your home.

Approaching an architect with details of your project does not commit you in any way. You are free to see as many architects as you wish and to discuss your scheme with all of them before making up your mind which of them you want.

How much an architect costs

Most architects are happy to give you a "partial service" – that is preliminary advice at the planning stage or a recommendation on the best way to achieve your object. A standard fee per hour is payable for employing an architect for advice; for lesser fry, a small hourly fee is agreed on the basis of his gross salary. This complicated latter arrangement has an advantage – you can employ a principal for expert advice, but one of his minions (at a cheaper rate) to handle the routine work like the preparation of the drawings you will need.

The hourly rate is normally used as the basis for calculating a fee for the first two stages of an architect's work – inception and feasibility. The fee for full architectural service on an existing building is based on a percentage of the cost of the total job.

Between the hourly rate and the full fee, there is yet another scale of charges dependent upon just how much work you want your architect to do, and how much you will want to do yourself.

If you want him to put forward outline proposals of what you should do, he can charge 15% of what would have been his full fee. For a "scheme design", that is drawings showing room placing and spatial arrangements, an outline specification and estimated cost, he can charge 35% of the full fee.

For all architectural work up to the point of putting the job out to tender, the charge is 75% of the full fee.

What you can get for your money

The more complex the improvements you are planning to make, the more help you are liable to need from an architect. For simple alterations or improvements, buying an hour of an architect's time could be the best investment you could make. It could open up totally new possibilities or suggest simpler and therefore cheaper methods of achieving the same end – saving you the architect's fee many times over. Asking an architect to

You and your architect: Are you on the same wave-length?

put forward outline proposals will cost you around 2% of what you intend to spend on your house.

For this fee you can expect him to analyse your requirements and suggest the best solution within the limitations of your budget and your home.

For a scheme design you pay a larger fee and you will get enough information to obtain any necessary planning permission and to approach a builder for a quotation. What you won't get are detailed drawings and a detailed specification.

Complete architectural work up to putting the job out to tender would cost about 10% of what you intend to spend on the job. For this you will get a complete set of working drawings, detailed specification, planning permission and everything that a builder will need to complete the job. All that is left to you is to find the builder and supervise the work. Full architectural service will cost about 13% of the total price of the job, but relieves you of all the responsibility after you have agreed with your architect the optimum course of action and the price.

You and the surveyor

It is always advisable to deal only with properly qualified chartered surveyors, who are members of the Royal Institution of Chartered Surveyors.

As far as private individuals are concerned, surveyors have two useful functions – first, they are trained to value property, taking into account both the state of the market and the condition of the house, and second, they report on its structural condition and the estimated cost of necessary repairs.

You have to pay for this survey, but until recently you were never allowed to see it or know its contents. And if you wanted to have your own private survey, you normally had to add the full cost on top of the fee demanded by the building society – which meant that you were obliged to pay for a surveyor to visit the house *twice*.

However, the increasing power of the consumer over the last few years has induced some building societies to provide a valuation and structural survey for one fee, and to let you see it.

If you are buying a reasonably new house or flat there is very little point in paying extra for a structural surveyor, but the older the property the more useful it can be. A survey listing the vital repairs necessary and their estimated cost can be a useful lever in screwing down the selling price of a house and in addition is a good starting point in the preparation of a specification for a builder.

Negotiate a reasonable price.

There is no standard scale of charges for a structural survey, so it is worth shopping around among the professionally qualified surveyors to find the cheapest you can.

In theory, if your surveyor makes a terrible boob and omits to tell you that the roof is about to fall in or some such, you should be able to sue him. In practice, it's virtually impossible, because no surveyor will commit himself to passing as sound any parts of the property which are unexposed or inaccessible.

The surveyor's report will generally include details which may appear patently obvious – so if you don't want to pay someone to tell you that the paint is chipped along the skirting or that the bathroom mirror is cracked, you should make this clear.

To sum up:
(a) Never employ a surveyor who is not professionally qualified.
(b) Use your building society surveyor if possible.
(c) Negotiate a reasonable fee by telling him what you want to know, or, more important, what you don't want to know.

You and the Town Hall

Are the men in grey suits at your local Town Hall interfering busybodies or helpful advisors? Well, it rather depends on which way you look at it.

Certainly local authority regulations can impose very real restrictions on your freedom to make your home as you want it and they can also force you to carry out work which you might consider to be both unnecessary and undesirable.

On the other hand, the Building Regulations (the national book of rules which lays down what you can and can't do) were not written just to make your life difficult. They set desirable standards of light and ventilation and space and so on – standards designed to make your home a reasonable place to live in. Whatever alterations or improvements you are intending to make, you can be pretty sure there will be someone at your Town Hall who would like to know about it. Because of the complexity of the Building Regulations and the existence of bylaws which vary from place to place, the Department of the Environment advises everyone who is planning to improve their home to contact the local authroity for help and advice.

That's all very well, except that "help and advice" can mean that you will be told that you can't do this unless you do that and so on. All aimed, of course, at saving you from yourself.

Some unscrupulous people have been known to disregard the Town Hall's "help and advice" and just get on with whatever it was they wanted to do on the assumption that what the Town Hall doesn't see the Town Hall doesn't know or care about. Such a course of action could not be by any means recommended, even though it might save a lot of time, trouble and expense.

Planning permission is a rather different kettle of fish. If you add a couple of rooms to the back of your house without getting the necessary permission, the council could, if they felt really nasty, send someone along to knock down the results of all your time and money.

To avoid this unpleasantness, not to mention pointless expense, no one should start building anything, anywhere (not even a garage) without first ascertaining whether or not planning permission is needed and, if it is, getting it.

Improvement grants

If you are intending to apply for an improvement grant then you have got to put up with the Town Hall having a say in your plans. And what is more, they won't give you the money until the work is completed to their satisfaction.

Criticism of the whole grant procedure

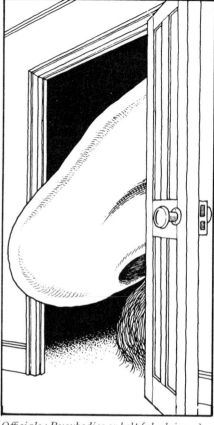

Officials : Busybodies or helpful advisers?

was that the extra work on your house demanded by the council cost more than the money they were dishing out and therefore the whole deal became rather pointless.

This situation has been improved a great deal as the Government, at both local and national level, has gradually woken up to the importance of preserving the nation's stock of old houses.

There are two kinds of grants: the standard grant for putting in "standard amenities" is yours as a right provided that you fulfill a few simple conditions; the discretionary grant is for a thorough modernization job but is available only at the local authority's discretion.

Normally you can be pretty sure that if your house has no proper lavatory or drainage or bathroom or kitchen you are a good candidate for some kind of improvement grant. The council will only ever agree to pay for half the cost of improvements, so expect to match this half.

Local authorities really enthusiastic about house improvements programmes often agree to lend rate-payers their half of the grant. Full details of grants and your council's attitude to them are available at their offices.

You and your builder

Finding a good builder is not easy because any get-rich-quick bodger can set himself up as a builder and plenty do.

Safest way, of course, is by recommendation. If a builder has done a really good job for someone you know, the chances are that he will do the same for you. In the country, licensees of pubs, who listen to most of the local gossip, very often know who are the best local builders.

If you can make friends with the local borough surveyor or one of his staff you may be able to persuade them – unofficially – to tip you off about the reputations of builders. They obviously know who is good and who is terrible, but because of their positions they can't officially give you a recommendation without laying themselves wide open to accusations of favouritism.

Failing satisfactory recommendations, the National Federation of Building Trades Employees are always prepared to put you in touch with reputable firms in your locality.

One of the aims of the NFBTE is to combat all forms of sub-standard building and poor workmanship and encourage its member firms to provide an efficient service to their clients.

Specification

To safeguard all parties, no builder should be asked to give an estimate for a job without being shown a written specification of the work involved.

The moment you give any builder leeway to choose a size or height or detail is the moment trouble starts. His choice may well not be yours – and if you haven't covered yourself in the specification, then you are stuck with it.

If, for example, you wanted to knock two rooms into one, your specification might read something like this:

Specification for proposed work at 77 Acacia Drive, Sometown

[1] Remove partition wall between front and rear rooms on the ground floor.
[2] Make good any damaged plaster in the ceiling and plaster across the gap where the wall has been removed so the ceiling is flush from front to rear.
[3] Ditto for walls on each side.
[4] Replace floorboards, if necessary, to fill gap where the wall has been removed, so that the floor runs through flat from front to rear.
[5] Use skirting from removed wall to make good gaps in the skirting between front and rear rooms.
[6] Remove door and door frame complete from front room.
[7] Block the gap and plaster over on both sides.
[8] Use skirting from removed wall to fill the gap in the skirting on both sides of the wall.
[9] Make good decorations on entrance hall side of blocked door.
[10] Re-decorate the new large room formed from front and rear rooms – two coats of emulsion on the ceiling, wallpaper all walls.
[11] Ensure all work complies with local authority requirements.

For bigger and more complicated projects he may also need drawings. If you are employing an architect, obviously he will supply these. If not, you should be able to find a local draughtsman or architectural student who will be able to prepare the necessary drawings for a small fee. (This is much cheaper than an architect's fee.)

Builders are often able to put clients in contact with technically-qualified individuals who earn extra money in their spare time by writing complete specifications and preparing drawings. You should not, however, rely on such people for design advice.

Bigger firms may even have their own drawing office and take on the whole job in a similar way to an architect – but you will obviously be expected to pay for this additional service.

If you are planning to write your own specification, the main thing to remember is to leave absolutely nothing to the builder's discretion. You need to write down every step of the job you want done from start to finish.

It does not have to be in technical jargon; but it does have to be sewn up so tight that if the job does not turn out as you envisaged you can wave your specification in your builder's face and make him put it right at his own expense.

Writing a specification can be a slow and laborious business, but it is time well spent. You do not need to spell out *how* the job is to be done – that's the builder's problem. What you *do* need to spell out, in great detail, is what you want to end up with when he's through.

Without a specification, had you simply asked a builder to remove the partition wall, you could easily find that the extensive making good required was not included in his price, or that he had not allowed for finishing the floor between the two rooms. With a detailed specification you are safe.

Estimates

Always try to obtain estimates from at least three separate builders. As well as the total cost of the job, you should also establish the exact date on which they can start work and how long they anticipate the job will take.

Because of the nature of their work, most builders will start a job with great enthusiasm, putting in as many men as possible to get the work under way. But as the job approaches completion busy builders are already negotiating their next contract and their initial enthusiasm may well dwindle.

For this reason it is important not to allow progress on your job to get slower and slower as the builder needs more of his men to make a start on his next contracted job.

Variations

If you need to change your mind after your builder has started work, nine times out of ten it is an indication that insufficient forethought has gone into the project. It is a mistake that you may have to pay dearly for.

When a builder has to start undoing what he has already done, it is a tiresome and expensive business for him just as much as you. It means he will be longer on the job than he anticipated, and therefore his subsequent contracts are placed in jeopardy. So you can expect to pay through the nose for changing your mind halfway through.

There is also a great temptation, once the builder has started work, to get extra jobs undertaken "while he is there".

He may, or may not, welcome additional work to that originally agreed. Whatever his attitude, it is important to remember that instructions for extra work should be given only to the builder – and not to his workmen; a price should be agreed with the builder at the time and the agreement should be confirmed by both of you in writing.

It is also worth a husband and a wife agreeing beforehand who is responsible for making decisions on any minor problems that crop up during the work. The situation of a wife telling a builder one thing and the husband contradicting it a few minutes later, or vice versa, has provided the stuff of many a slapstick film.

Supervision

Your builder won't appreciate your looking over his shoulder every minute of the day – neither will you appreciate it if you leave him to it and then find he has made a muck of it.

The possibly obvious compromise is to have a good look round at the end of the day, after the builder and his men have packed up.

It helps a lot to dish out appreciation as the work progresses: inevitably, any workman is going to care more if he thinks you are interested and care about what he is doing.

It also helps if you raise problems as soon as they occur. Your builder won't thank you for swallowing complaints and only raising them when the remedy is far more complex than it would have been had you spoken up at once.

Payment

On small contracts, lasting less than four or five weeks, most builders will not expect payment until after completion of the work.

On bigger jobs, he is likely to ask for interim payments as the work progresses. It is a fair enough arrangement: small building firms cannot be expected to finance the cost of materials and wages over a long period.

If you have an architect supervising the job, he will discuss with the builder the value of the work completed and agree an interim payment. If you are on your own, you will have to use your own judgement about this.

It would be reasonable to be suspicious of a builder who wanted a large sum in advance of starting work. The building trade is notorious for the number of bankruptcies it suffers every year and any builder without sufficient funds to start a job is a potential candidate. Even though

Do you and your builder speak the same language or is it double-dutch to you?

Employing others
5/6 Going it alone/woodworm and other pests

you will already have got an estimate before your builder started work, it is essential to keep tight control of the purse strings, particularly if you are getting involved with "extras".

Some estimates will include "provisional sums". These are normally used for work which the builder has to sub-contract and for which he has been unable to obtain a firm estimate.

He may, for example, charge a "provisional sum" for re-wiring, having based this figure on his experience rather than a quotation from an electrician. Normally you can expect "provisional sums" to be reasonable guesses at the real cost of the item – if it is wildly out, then something is wrong.

Always ensure that you are consulted before a "provisional sum" is converted into a firm price, otherwise you may find your original estimate has escalated.

Finally, you are entitled to retain between 5% and 10% of the total cost of the job for a period of between three and six months after work has been completed, provided the builder is told that you intend to do this at the time he makes his estimate. This retention is to cover the cost of any defects that may arise due to faulty workmanship or materials.

It is your builder's responsibility to make good defects which are his fault. And it is a powerful incentive to get him to fulfil that responsibility if you still owe him money.

Make/stay friends with your builder

Before the work even starts, completely clear the rooms likely to be affected. This helps the builder enormously to get on with the job.

Agree with him a convenient place where ladders, scaffold boards and other equipment and materials can be stored during progress of the work.

Set aside reasonable accommodation for the men to have a mid-day meal or to shelter if the weather is bad and they are working outside.

Make sure they have access to whatever services they need – water, electricity or the lavatory!

If you can't make them a morning and afternoon cup of tea, at least make sure they have facilities to brew their own.

Going it alone

Everyone will advise you not to do it, particularly those people with a vested interest like builders and architects. Plenty of people, however, do get through the difficulties and traumas – and they normally save a great deal of money, even if afterwards they claim it has taken years off their lives.

Acting as your own main contractor simply means that you employ – direct – the different trades required to carry out whatever work is required. In effect you are replacing the builder, although not the skilled trades that work for him.

Clearly it is fraught with problems for the inexperienced, but all can be overcome by applying foresight and common sense. You will have to be prepared, however, to devote a considerable amount of your time to the project – far, far more than you would if you were employing an architect to see the whole thing through.

First step is to go through the process a designer or architect would go through when deciding what needs to be done. You should face up to drawing a reasonably accurate plan of the house in order to analyse its layout. You should discard the existing concept and consider carefully what is required to meet your particular needs.

Insurance

Most bona fide building firms are covered by employers' and public liability insurance in respect of accidents at work, whether to persons or property.

If your builder is something of a

LATER THAT YEAR...

Do not allow things to slow up.

one-man band, make sure of your insurance cover before he starts work, otherwise you run the risk of heavy financial liabilities if he has an accident.

Don't be hamstrung in your thinking by how the house has formerly been used – consider it simply as a shell within which you are going to create the optimum comfort and convenience for yourselves.

It might be a help to actually write down how you like to eat and play, what activities will be going on in the house, which rooms should be closest to which. If you are committed to keeping your current furniture, measure it up and cut out scale outlines to arrange on your plan.

Assume – initially at least – that any of the interior walls can be removed if necessary or new ones put up, that doors can be blocked in and new openings made elsewhere, that windows can be enlarged, moved or removed. Simply lowering a window sill, for example, can make an enormous difference to a room. It is that kind of detail which you should consider.

Can you do it?

Having worked out in detail exactly what you want to do, the next stage is to find if you will be allowed to do it. The Town Hall should be able to help you here, if you give them a rough idea of your plans.

If you need to get planning permission, get the local bureaucrats to help you with it. It's not unknown for them to actually fill in the forms for you, but if they won't go that far they will certainly tell you what to put down in answer to any questions that mystify you.

Once you've got over any objections from the local authority, you need to know if you can afford the work. If you were employing a builder, his estimate would tell you soon enough. But as your own main contractor you need to get separate estimates from all the trades involved – carpenters, plumbers, electricians, plasterers, etc.

Each trade will have to be supplied with a separate, detailed specification of the work proposed. As usual, it is best to get at least two or three separate estimates from firms or individuals.

Finding your tradesmen

Sometimes it is not very easy to get a firm recommendation from someone whose opinion is worth respecting. And very often the chap whose work is of a very high standard as well as being reasonably priced will be too busy to take on any other jobs for six months or more. (Before you ask any firm for an estimate, it is always worth checking in the first instance to see if they are able to take on the work within a reasonable period, otherwise everyone's time is wasted.)

If you can't get a recommendation and are finally obliged to pick out trades from the Yellow Pages or the local Chamber of Commerce directory, a simple safeguard is to ask for the names and addresses of recent clients and to check with them, making sure that the work done was satisfactory.

To pare the total cost of the work down to the size of your pocket, you'll need estimates with every item separately priced. (Some firms often complain about doing this on the grounds of all the work involved – what they are really objecting to is that an itemized and separately priced specification gives them no leeway to bump on a little extra profit for luck.)

With all the estimates in, you should then decide which work is essential, which is highly desirable, which is desirable and which is unimportant. Hack away at the bottom of the list until the total price matches what you can afford.

Co-ordinating the work

Having lined up all your tradesmen and agreed to their estimates, now comes the tricky bit: organizing a sequence of work so that they are not constantly being held up by each other. (For more detailed information, checklists and work-flow charts, see *Co-ordination*.)

It helps, first, if all the trades are aware of each other's existence so that in an emergency, if you can't be contacted to sort out the problem, the plumber or whoever can contact the chap who is causing him difficulty direct.

If you are lucky, all the blokes will work it out between them as to who does what and when and the job will proceed to its conclusion without any real strife. But if that happens you *will* be lucky.

To sort out a working schedule for everyone's benefit, you should know the sequence in which trades normally work. It is as follows:

Any demolition or shoring.
Earthwork – digging out foundations, etc.
Concrete work – laying foundations.
Brickwork and partitions.
Fixing drainage and sewage connections.
Laying solid floors of concrete or asphalt, etc.
Masonry work.
Roofing or tiling.
Timber and hardware fittings.
Plastering.
Fixing rainwater gutters and downpipes, etc.
Plumbing.
Heating.
Electrical.
Glazing.
Painting and decorating.

That is the sequence for new building, but it is substantially the same for conversion work unless woodworm or dry rot has to be dealt with.

The easiest way to work out a reasonable dovetailing of the work is to analyse the jobs that have to be done and then list them in order so that no one job is holding up another and nothing has to be undone in order to allow progress to continue.

The situation to avoid is each trade pressing on regardless of the others. If the electrician has to hack away new plaster to get his cables through or if the plumber has to take up floorboards that the electrician has just nailed down, everyone starts getting a bit cross.

As a guideline, on a reasonably simple conversion job, the sequence of work could run something like this:

Demolition and stripping out. Taking out walls that are to be removed, removing unwanted plumbing, etc.

Woodworm or dry rot treatment, if required.

Damp-proof treatment, if necessary.

Replacing or repairing brickwork where necessary, building new partitions where required.

All exterior drainage and sewage work plus connections to the house.

Structural repairs and roof repairs.

Laying solid floors, if required.

Carpentry – wooden floors, doors and frames, windows, etc.

Plastering.

Plumbing and central heating.

Electrical, re-wiring, etc. (including installation of telephone).

Painting and decoration.

No list of this kind can ever be rigid because of the variety of work that can be involved and the different conditions met in individual houses. It may be that for what you are planning to do it would be preferable for the plasterer to come in after the plumber, or the electrician before the plasterer, etc. The way to sort it out is to get together with the different trades before work starts and mutually agree a workable sequence, then to keep in close touch with the work.

Payments

As your own main contractor, you might find several of your sub-contractors will need interim payments to help meet the cost of the materials they need. This is more likely if they are self-employed tradesmen working as individuals.

It is fair enough to start making interim payments after work has started. But never agree to pay an initial amount before the tradesman has done anything (you may find he will never turn up) and never pay the full amount until the work has been completed to your satisfaction.

...one may wonder how houses stand up.

You and your woodworm

Surveys and estimates for dealing with woodworm and dry or wet rot are always free. They are usually extremely thorough, very detailed and often they are absolutely terrifying.

A comprehensive woodworm and rot survey report, particularly on an old house, can often leave the owner wondering how on earth the house can still possibly be standing.

That is not to say that the companies operating in this field set out intentionally to cause alarm – they are, however, in the selling business and therefore nothing even remotely deserving of treatment goes unremarked. In addition, most of the reputable operators offer a 20-year guarantee that their treatment will work and so they play absolutely safe.

Shop around

As the surveys are free, it is well worth getting as many as you can – the different results and estimates should also make interesting reading. As an experiment, *The House Book* had a large house in Suffolk surveyed by six different companies. While all of them agreed on the

extent and siting of the main damage caused by wood-boring insects, each of them discovered totally different, allegedly serious, attacks in different parts of the house. Not one report seemed to cover everything and the estimates for treatment varied greatly.

It is not worth bothering with any companies that do not offer a guarantee, but most do and their terms are usually similar. Some unscrupulous people, having got together all the surveys to determine the extent of the problem, simply buy a couple of gallons of proprietary wood preservative and do the job themselves. This is not always a very wise thing to do.

Their estimates tend to be disproportionately expensive to the amount of work involved and the skills required because someone has got to pay for all those costly surveys never taken up by the clients.

Most of the timber preservation companies now also undertake damp-proofing work, using a number of different techniques. If you have a damp problem it would be worth asking for an estimate for remedying the difficulty at the same time as they turn up to look for woodworm.

You can get a grant for installing a damp-proofing course (up to half the total cost), but not normally for dealing with woodworm or rot.

Identifying the problem

Only an expert can identify the precise species of insect attacking timber and establish whether or not the attack is still active. But if you find a series of little round holes in any woodwork you can be fairly sure that you probably have (or had) woodworm.

More than three-quarters of all woodworm damage in Britain is caused by the common furniture beetle. The females lay their eggs in cracks or crevices in unpolished woodwork and the small grubs that hatch from the eggs bore into the wood for two years or more before they finally bite their way out and fly away. The holes that you can see are where they have left, not where they have entered. The powder post beetle and the death watch beetle are less common in ordinary houses, but they can cause more damage. The powder post beetle feeds on the sap of hardwoods (often hardwood strip or block floors) and eats happily away until there is sometimes only a thin crust of sound timber left on the surface between you and the floor below.

Death watch beetles usually go for structural timbers of old houses, particularly oak beams, which are either damp or affected by fungal decay. A quite

DEATH-WATCH BEETLE

COMMON FURNITURE BEETLE

POWDER-POST BEETLE

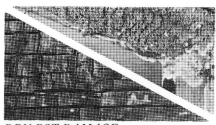

DRY ROT DAMAGE

WET ROT DAMAGE

HOUSE LONGHORN BEETLE

Employing others

simple test to indicate whether or not a woodworm attack is still active is to rap the timber hard with a hammer or mallet. If fine white powder or dust jumps out of the holes, the little devils are probably in there eating away. But even if this doesn't happen, you should not assume that they have gone away.

Woodworm can be eradicated by coating the affected timber with an insecticidal fluid that penetrates the wood and destroys the larvae and renders it immune from further attack for a long period. Wood that has been severely damaged has to be replaced.

Dry and wet rot
Of the two, dry rot is the more dangerous form of timber decay because it is usually not discovered until it is well advanced and it can spread very rapidly. It is a fungus that is attracted to timber that is slightly damp or is poorly ventilated – it therefore normally starts in cellars or underneath ground floor timbers.

Once established, the spores of dry rot fungus spread rapidly in all directions, even through brickwork or masonry. It sucks the nourishment from the timber, quickly making it brittle and finally causing it to crumble away.

First visible sign of an attack is a fine white growth, like cotton wool, on the wood, but because it usually starts underneath floors it can be very wide-spread before it is discovered.

To eradicate dry rot, the cause of the original dampness or lack of ventilation has to be remedied, otherwise it can easily start up again. Then the badly affected timber has to be cut away and replaced and the remainder treated with a fungicidal fluid.

Wet rot: This sounds alarming but in fact it is far less dangerous than dry rot. Wet rot starts, logically enough, when timber is allowed to become saturated with water over long periods. However, the fungus does not spread far from the damp area and therefore the damage is usually far less widespread.

Treatment is obvious – remove the source of damp. When this is done the wet-rot fungus will die. But the timber should still be treated with a fungicidal fluid just in case the dreaded dry rot spores leap in and get a hold as the wood is drying out.

You and your electrician
Local electricity boards are always prepared to take on any domestic electrical work, from fitting an additional socket outlet to a complete re-wiring job. For reasons best known to themselves, their prices normally tend to be between 5% and 10% more expensive than those of private electrical contractors.

The advantage of getting the board to do the work is that they can't moan about it afterwards, but this problem can usually be overcome by making it the responsibility of the independent contractor to ensure that all the work complies in every respect with the requirements of the relevant electricity board.

To safeguard yourself, get this agreement in writing and ask for it to be included on the estimate.

In fact, no qualified electrician should ever undertake a job that he knows would not be approved by the electricity board, but often the rules and regulations are ignored, particularly on a small job that is unlikely to be inspected by board representatives.

When a complete re-wiring is involved, the electricity board have you over a barrel because they won't connect up the supply until the installation meets their requirements in every respect. It is for this reason that you must ensure the onus of responsibility is on the contractor – otherwise you might be asked to lay out more money to pay for additional work insisted on by the electricity board.

As always, make sure you know exactly what you are getting for your money before you agree the price. What

Get some light thrown on the cost.

kind of fittings are to be used? Are all the cables to be concealed? Is all the plasterwork and decoration to be made good?

It is natural for any tradesman to choose the quickest and cheapest way of tackling a job. For an electrician working on a re-wiring installation, that means fixing the cables along skirting boards and up architraves – and a network of exposed grey cable in and out of every room may not have been what was in your mind when you started out. That is why it is so important to get the details tied up at the beginning.

Planning new electrical installations
All new wiring in Britain today is installed on the "ring main" principle, which means there is a loop of cable running round the house linking all the switches and sockets. It starts and finishes at the fusebox.

The advantage of the ring main system is that it allows extra sockets to be installed cheaply and easily and every appliance has a fuse in its plug so that if something goes wrong it blows its own little fuse – not the whole circuit.

Then what do you want the switch to control? Ceiling points? Or wall lights? Or low-level lighting plugged into sockets near the skirting? If you decide on ceiling points, do you need more than one and which pieces of furniture will they hang over? For wall lights, which walls and what height? For low-level lighting, which pieces of furniture will the lamps be stood on and where will they be positioned? If you want a lamp on a low table in the middle of the room, will a socket in the floor, perhaps, be the most sensible solution for you?

Next thing to think about is which electrical appliances will be used in the room. Where is the television going to go, or the hi-fi, or the radio? Are there enough sockets for everything?

In halls and landings it is important to work out the sequence of circulation – can you turn off the light downstairs from upstairs and vice-versa?

In the bathroom you must have a pull cord switch, by law, to avoid any danger of shocks from touching an electrical fitting with wet hands. And you won't be allowed to install any socket outlets at all in your bathroom.

It is false economy at this stage to cut down on the number of switches and socket outlets if you are eventually going to need more. During re-wiring, the approximate cost of each additional point works out at only a few pounds. Calling in an electrician later to fix more points is liable to cost two or three times as much because of the extensive cutting away and making good required.

In order to avoid misunderstandings, electricians being asked to estimate for re-wiring a house should be supplied with rough plans as well as a specification. The plans do not need to be professionally drawn up – provided they are clear and roughly to scale they will be sufficient.

The symbols used to indicate the size and type of outlets and which switches control what, are shown below. The drawing is a sample of how architects indicate type and placement of outlets, switches, cables, etc.

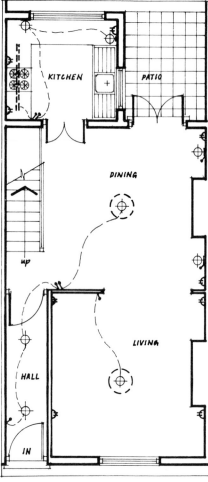

Planning the re-wiring of a house is very difficult because it means you have to decide virtually how each room is to be furnished before you know where the points and plugs should go.

It is almost inevitable that when the builders and electricians and plumbers and decorators have all finally packed up and gone home, you will find some sockets just where you didn't want them and none where you did and making any changes at this point is always an expensive and time-consuming proposition.

To reduce the chance of this frustration, each room should be considered separately and in detail when you are thinking where the electrics should go. You should consider first what activities are liable to take place there, what the natural lighting offers, which electrical appliances will be needed there, where the furniture is likely to go and what atmosphere you want to create.

Start with the wall switch. It normally goes just inside the wall on the opening side of the door – but does it really need to be at the traditional height, just too high for small children? Would it be better, for example, at waist height? Why not?

As an added precaution, before the electrician starts work, go round the house marking the positions of everything on the walls and ceilings with a piece of chalk or a thick crayon. Then there is no excuse for his making a mistake and, if he does, he will have to put it right at his expense.

Re-wiring an old property normally qualifies for an improvement grant.

You and your plumber

It is illegal to make any alterations or additions to the plumbing or drainage of a house without reference to the Public Health Department at your Town Hall.

So before you even think about getting estimates from plumbers for what you want to do, go down and make friends with the Public Health men at the Town Hall and get their approval first.

If you are installing a bathroom or inside lavatory for the first time, then the cost should qualify for a grant.

Bureaucratic interest in your plumbing arrangements is mainly confined to traps and vents and falls and their main purpose is to prevent you and your neighbours dropping like flies from some dreadful medieval ailment because the drains aren't working properly.

If you are lucky you will be able to get all the information you need at the Town Hall to write a specification for the work.

Regulations and requirements vary from one local authority to another, so it is not possible to lay down a precise guideline to follow when you are making plans for the positioning and layout of bathroom and lavatory, etc.; however, there are a few points worth bearing in mind. Both the bathroom and the lavatory must have adequate ventilation, preferably via a window. Forced ventilation by an automatic fan operated by the light switch is sometimes acceptable, but it is usually more difficult to get through the council.

If you care about the exterior appearance of your house, plan for most of the plumbing (particularly the soil stack, the thick pipe which carries the waste from the lavatory) to be fitted internally. They can normally be boxed in fairly unobtrusively.

In order to estimate for a plumbing installation, plumbers need to be supplied with a detailed specification indicating which fittings are to go where. A drawing is a help, but it is not essential. The specification should make it clear that it is the plumber's responsibility to ensure that all work complies with local authority requirements.

If you have not decided which make of fittings you want, ask the plumber to allow a "p.c. sum", but let him know as soon as you have decided, to avoid possible hold-ups because of delivery delays.

As always, get at least two or three estimates and try to use firms which have been recommended. If you have difficulty finding suitable firms, contact the National Federation of Plumbers and Domestic Heating Engineers, who will be able to help.

Because of the possible danger to public health from faulty drains or plumbing systems, the council will always take on – promptly – the job of clearing blocked drains or sewage pipes. That doesn't mean to say that they'll come and unblock the kitchen sink, because they

An urgent call to your plumber . . .

won't. But if you've got a terrible smell in the back garden and a strange seepage coming from under a manhole, they'll be round like a shot.

Security

Free professional advice is available to every householder about how to keep burglars away. Ask for the crime prevention officer at your local police station. His job is to recommend the best locks to use for doors and windows, the best place to keep the family jewels and the various precautions you can take to discourage unwelcome visits by a thief.

Good door and window locks only buy the house owner time, because in the end they can all be opened by a really determined burglar. But the theory is that the more difficult it is for him to get in the less likely he is to bother.

Cheap "warded locks" (the ones that have old-fashioned keys) hardly offer any protection today against a burglar worth his salt. Any model of this type of lock can be opened in seconds with a single skeleton key.

The conventional cylinder rim latch is not much better – a strip of celluloid will ease back the latch bolt.

All exterior doors should be fitted with locks that will at least provide a bit of a challenge to a thief – and windows, particularly on the ground floor, should also be fitted with key-operated locks. The police crime-prevention officer will tell you the best ones to use for your particular needs. His advice is free.

Decorators/designers/landscapers

Not many professionals in the field of interior and landscape design are controlled by a professional body; you are therefore not protected in any way from unprofessional practice. Similarly, there is no set scale of fees.

Most of the top interior designers calculate their fees as a percentage of the total cost of the job on a sliding scale basis – a smaller percentage the larger the cost – although some of them charge their clients no fee at all and earn their money by buying all the materials required at trade price and charging the client full retail price.

Despite claims from some of them, they are not really interested in helping Mrs Bloggs decide between the blue or the pink for her new bedroom suite. They are normally commissioned to complete the interior design to the last detail – and the cost, consequently, of such a project is normally beyond the reach of the majority of people.

Top decorators are internationally recognized and incredibly talented, but underneath them there is the entire

Not every designer belongs on a pedestal.

spectrum of people who claim to be designers or decorators, sometimes with absolutely no talent, ability, or training to back it up with.

If you are going to pay for advice from a decorator, or indeed pay him to see the job through, you should satisfy yourself first of all that he has got (a) talent and (b) ability. If he has neither, you'll be much better off alone. Insist on seeing what work he has already completed and talk to some of his former clients, if possible. Agree before he starts *exactly* how much the bill is going to be, find out on what basis he calculates his fees, and what you are getting for your money. Be sure to get any verbal agreements finalized on paper.

Largely the same advice applies to using a landscape designer to transform your garden into a joy for ever.

A number of shops and nurseries offer their customers a design service to help them with design problems. If the service is free, there's no harm in using it, although you can hardly expect the advice to be unbiased. If there is a fee involved, be chary; find out if previous clients have been satisfied with the service rendered.

Glossary 1/2

Acid: Opposite to alkali. Substances which neutralize and are neutralized by alkalis. Examples of household acids are vinegar and lemon juice.

Aggregate: The major component of plaster, concrete, asphalt or tarmac-adam. It is usually broken stones, slag gravel, or sand. Fine aggregate passes through a screen of $\frac{3}{16}$ in./5 mm holes, coarse aggregate doesn't.

Airbrick: Perforated block built into walls to ventilate a room or the underside of a wooden floor.

Alkali: Opposite to acid. Includes soda, potash, ammonia, etc. Produces caustic or corrosive solutions which neutralize acids.

Alkali resistant: Paint used on new plaster which is durable in contact with lime.

Apron: Horizontal panel or board underneath a window and projecting slightly into the room.

Architrave: Wooden trimming round door and window frames to cover the joint between the frame and the wall.

Backfilling: Hard rubble, earth or stones used to fill excavations after the foundations have been laid.

Backing coat: The first coat of plaster on walls.

Backing up: Using cheaper bricks behind the facing bricks of a wall.

Balanced flue: System which enables a gas-fired boiler to be installed in a room or cupboard with ventilation through an air brick.

Balustrade: A coping or handrail with its supporting balusters or banisters.

Banisters: Posts in the balustrade between the handrail and the stairs.

Ballast: Unscreened gravel comprising sand, grit and stones.

Barge board: Sloping board fixed along the gable, covering the end rafters.

Bat: A half or portion of a brick.

Batten: Timber strip for fixing slates or tiles.

Beading: Semi-circular moulding used to cover a joint.

Bearing plate: Plate in a wall which supports a beam and spreads its load.

Bevel: The slope formed when surfaces meet not at a right angle.

Bitumastic: Proprietary trade name for a spirit paint made from refined coal-tar pitch, etc.

Bled timber: Inferior wood from trees which have been tapped for resin.

Bond: The systematic overlapping of bricks in a wall for structural strength.

Breast: Projection into a room containing the flue and hearth of a fireplace.

Building blocks: Hollow or solid blocks of clay, gypsum or concrete, cheaper and quicker to lay than bricks.

Building paper: Fibre reinforced bitumen between layers of paper, used as sheathing for walls and roofs.

Butt-joint: Two edges which meet but do not overlap.

Calcareous sandstone: A kind of building stone, most of which comes from the North Riding of Yorkshire.

Carcase: The main loadbearing part of the house, without floors, windows, doors, plaster or finishes.

Casement: A window hinged to open about one of its vertical edges. (The hinged part of a window.)

Cavity blocks: Pre-cast concrete blocks shaped to form a cavity wall.

Cavity flashing: The damp course which crosses the gap in a cavity wall.

Cavity wall: A wall consisting of two layers with a 2 in./51 mm gap between.

Chair rail: Old-fashioned wooden moulding fixed to a wall at dado height.

Chamfer: A bevel or slope made by paring off the edge of anything originally right-angled.

Chase: Groove cut into wall or floor to take pipes or cables.

Chipboard: Reconstructed wood compressed from waste wood and resin.

Cladding: Any material fixed as "clothing" to walls and roofs.

Clapboard: Weatherboarding, thicker at one edge than the other, fixed with thick edge overlapping thin one.

Conduit: Metal or plastic tube for casing cables.

Coping: Brick, stone or concrete protection at the top of a wall.

Course: Horizontal layer of bricks or slates throughout a wall.

Coving: Curving cover for a junction between two surfaces, e.g. floor and wall or wall and ceiling.

Crazing: Hairline cracks on the surface of concrete or cement rendering or paintwork.

Crocodiling: Bad crazing on paintwork.

Cutout: Fuse, or any other circuit-breaking device.

Cutting in: Painting a clean edge, usually a straight line, at the edge of a painted area.

Cylinder lock: Latch operated by a small key from the outside, and by a knob from the inside.

Dado: Beading or panelling fixed on the lower half of wall above the skirting.

Damp-proof course or dpc: A layer of asphalt, lead, slates, zinc, plastic, polythene, copper or any impervious material laid in a wall (usually about 6 in./152 mm above the ground) to prevent rising damp. In basements the dpc has to be fixed vertically behind the plaster.

Deal: A softwood board of a standard size. Red deal is Scotch pine, white deal Norway spruce.

Devilling: Scratching plaster to prepare the surface for the next coat.

Distribution box: Small metal box joined to conduit and giving access to the cable for the connection of branch circuits.

Doors–ledged: Vertically boarded door with three horizontal battens.

Doors – braced: Ledged and vertically boarded door with horizontal and diagonal supports.

Doors – framed: Wooden door with strong outer frame.

Dormer: Vertical window protruding through sloping roof.

Downpipe: Pipe which carries rainwater to the ground from the roof gutters.

DPM: Damp-proof membrane. Large area of damp-proof course (q.v.) laid, for instance, under a basement floor.

Drain cock: Tap fixed at lowest point of a water system through which the system can be drained.

Dralon: Acrylic fibre used mainly for furnishing fabric.

Dressing: Masonry or moulding round openings or at the corners of a building of better quality than the rest of the walls.

Dry rot: Timber decay due to attack by certain fungi.

Eaves: Lowest overhanging edge of a sloping roof.

Efflorescence: White crystalline deposit left on brickwork as it dries out.

Elbow: Any sharp corner in a pipe.

Embossed: With a pattern standing out in relief.

Emulsion: A liquid mixture containing globules of fat, resin, etc.

Engineering bricks: Very strong bricks sometimes used for damp-proof courses.

Escutcheon: Metal plate round keyhole.

Expansion pipe: Pipe leading from hot water tank to point over cold water cistern (supplied from the mains) so that, if water boils, water or steam can be discharged.

Facing bricks: Bricks of a decent colour and texture used for the visible parts of any wall.

Fair-faced brickwork: A neat and smooth, unpainted brick surface.

False ceiling: Ceiling built with a gap between it and the floor above to provide space for cables and pipes or to lower height of room.

Fascia board: Wide board which carries the gutter round the eaves.

Fibre board: Stiff boards of compressed vegetable fibre used as insulating material.

Fireback: Wall behind fire.

Flange: Projecting flat rim or collar.

Flashing: Flexible metal seal laid round junction between two surfaces, e.g. where roof meets chimney, to make it watertight.

Floor loading: The weight that the structure of a floor is capable of supporting.

Flush door: Door faced in hardboard or plywood.

Footing: Wall foundations.

Formaldehyde resin: A plastics resin.

Friable mortar: Crumbly mortar.

Frieze rail: The rail next to the top rail in a six-panelled door.

Gable: Triangular area of the end wall of a house with a sloping roof.

Gasket: Hemp fibre wound round joints on water pipes; it expands when wet to make watertight joint.

Georgian glass: Thick glass with square mesh steel wire embedded in it.

Glazing: Term used for fitting glass into window frames.

Glazing bar: Wood or metal bar holding the panes of glass in a window.

Glazing bead: Small hard strip used to fix glass instead of putty.

Gravity system: Hot water system which works without a pump, by virtue of the different densities of hot and cold water.

Grinning through: Undercoat of paint showing through the topcoat.

Grouting: Filling up or finishing with thin mortar.

Header: A brick which is laid across a wall as part of the bonding pattern.

Hipped roof: Roof which has a slope at each end as well as the two of a conventional gabled roof.

Handed: Describes building parts which match each other as if mirrored.

Handrail: A rail to hold on to, as on stairs.

Holland: Tough linen fabric used for roller blinds, etc.

Hollow core door: Flush door with hardboard or plywood faces glued to skeleton framework.

Hungry: Describes surface which is too absorbent for the amount of paint.

Jamb: Vertical face inside window or door frames.

Jamb lining: Timber facing over the jamb.

Jerry builder: What you don't need – someone whose work is as shoddy as his materials.

Jib door: Door fitted flush with wall and disguised by the decorations.

Joists: Wood, concrete or steel beams supporting the floor and/or ceiling. Steel joists are normally called RSJs.

Joist hanger: A steel plate or shoe to carry the end of a wooden joist.

Key: Preparation, e.g. roughening of a surface which enables plaster or mortar to grip it.

Kick plate: Metal plate fixed to bottom of door as protection.

Lagging: A non-conducting covering round pipes, etc. for insulation.

Laminate: To make by putting thin layers together, as in laminated plastic, where sheets of cotton, paper, etc. are impregnated with a resin, dried and pressed together.

Latex adhesive: Substance containing rubber, often synthetic.

Laths: Rough strips of wood used as a base for plaster in older houses.

Leaf: One solid half of a cavity wall; one part of a pair of doors or windows; one of the movable parts of a table top.

Light: A glazed or unglazed opening admitting light to a building; a single division of a window.

Lining paper: Plain paper pasted on to plaster as base for wallpaper or paint.

Lintel: Beam over a door or window carrying the load of the wall above.

Loadbearing wall: Part of the structure of the house – it can't be removed without being replaced by a joist.

Make good: To repair as new.

Mastic: A bituminous or oily cement.

Matchboarding: Boards laid side by side so that the tongues and grooves on opposite sides can fit together.

Melamine: An organic substance used to make, for example, break-resistant plastics suitable for tableware.

Melinex/Mirrorlite: Trade names for flexible mirror available in rolls.

Microwave oven: One that cooks food in a few minutes even if straight from a freezer, breaking down the food particles by radiation.

Mitre: Joint cut so that the straight line of the joint bisects the angle.

Module: A self-contained unit or a dimension for regulating proportions of other parts.

Mortar: Mixture of cement, sand and water for laying bricks, etc.

Multigroove: Fitting for spot- or floodlight which concentrates beam of light and conceals its source.

Muntin: The vertical framing piece between door panels.

Newel: Corner or end post supporting a handrail.

Newel cap: Ornamental top of the newel post.

Nogging-pieces: Short horizontal timbers which stiffen the studs of a partition frame.

Non-bearing wall: Wall which carries only its own weight.

Nosing: The projecting rounded edge of a step or moulding; strip of covering material for this edge.

Oleo-resinous: Made of a solution of a resin in an oil.

One-pipe system: Heating circuit in which all connections to radiators come from the same pipe.

Oriel window: Type of bay window supported on brackets or corbels.

Panelaire: Trade name for decorative perforated hardboard panels.

Parabolic reflector/strip: Light fitting which looks dark from most angles.

Party wall: Wall separating two properties or houses.

Pebbledash: External plaster surfaced with small stones.

Pediment: A triangular, rounded, or otherwise shaped structure over a portico, door, window or niche.

Pier: Loadbearing brickwork between doors or windows; a short buttress bonded to a wall.

Pinoleum: Very thin wooden reeds used for blinds.

Pointing: Raking out the old mortar from joints of brickwork and re-filling them with new, normally cement, mortar.

Polyether: A kind of plastic, used instead of rubber for foam fillings.

Polypropylene: A tough plastic used for furniture frames, etc.

Polystyrene: A plastics compound used for tableware and in an expanded form for insulation.

Polyurethane: A plastics resin used for foam cushioning, etc.

Primer: First coat of paint on a bare surface such as new wood or plaster, applied to seal pores of material before painting.

Purlin: Horizontal member laid across the principal rafters and supporting the subsidiary rafters.

PVC: Polyvinyl chloride – kind of plastic in sheet or tile form.

Quoin: Outside angle of house.

Rafters: Sloping timbers which support the roof.

Rendering: Coarse material applied to a wall to cover the brick or stonework.

Return: A change in direction of a wall, usually at a right angle.

Reveal: Outer part of the jamb visible in door or window openings and not covered by the frame.

Ridge tiles: Special tiles to cover the ridge of a roof.

Ring main: Standard method for wiring 13 amp power circuits.

Riser: The vertical piece connecting two treads of a stair.

Rising butts: Hinges which lift the door as it opens so that it clears the carpet.

Rising main: Mains electricity, gas or water supply pipes passing up through a building.

RSJ: Reinforced steel joist.

Riven: Split.

Screed: Plaster, concrete or mortar finishing layer of floor surface.

Screeded concrete: Concrete with smooth top layer.

Seal: A preparation used to coat a surface and protect it from soiling and wear; water contained in a trap in a drain pipe, which prevents foul air escaping out of the drain.

Seconds: Used bricks – very often more attractive than new ones.

Secret nailing: Nails driven at an angle through tongue of one board and covered by the groove of the next.

Septic tank: Independent drainage system used when main drainage is unavailable. Sewage is purified by bacterial action.

Services: Supply and distribution pipes for water, gas, electricity, drainage.

Sisal: Fibre used for ropes, mats, floor covering, etc.

Skirting board: Wooden board set on edge round the foot of a wall to protect the wall from kicks and scuffs.

Shiplap boarding: Weatherboarding, but of rectangular cross-section, with a rebate cut along each edge.

Silica coated: Describes a kind of light bulb which has uniform brightness.

Size: Liquid sealer applied before paint on wood to prevent too much paint being absorbed; also applied to plaster walls before papering to ease hanging.

Slatted: Made of thin/narrow strips of wood.

Sleeper wall: Brick wall under the ground floor supporting the floor joists when there is no basement.

Small bore system: Central heating with small diameter pipes through which water is driven by a pump.

Soffit: Any under surface except a ceiling, e.g. the underneath of a cornice, stair or beam.

Soil pipe: Vertical pipe, ventilated at the top, which carries sewage into the soil drain and then to the sewer.

Spill ring: Ceiling light fitting which gives concentrated downward beam. The light source itself is invisible.

Spirit-based: Descriptive of wax, pigment, shellac, etc. dissolved in a volatile solvent.

Stile: An upright member in framing or panelling.

Stop cock: Control tap by which gas or water supply can be shut off.

Stretcher: Brick laid parallel to length of wall.

Stringer: Sloping board on each side of stairs carrying treads and risers.

Strobe lights: Stroboscopic flashing lamps, electronically synchronized.

Struck joints: Mortar joint in brickwork, raked back at an angle.

Structural: Said of all parts of a building which carry load in addition to their own weight.

Stucco: Smooth plaster on exterior wall.

Stud: Vertical timbers of partition framework.

Sub-floor: Concrete base, or boarding laid over joists on top of which the flooring is laid.

Tester: Canopy over a bed.

Tick/Ticking: Special kind of closely woven fabric for covering mattresses or pillows.

Tongue and groove: Joint made by a tongue on one edge of a board fitting into a corresponding groove on the edge of an adjoining board.

Transporter beam: Loadbearing beam.

Trap: U-shaped bend in pipe so arranged that it always contains sufficient water to seal the air.

Travertine: Calcareous stone, usually light cream in colour, used for floors and work surfaces.

Tread: Top surface of a step, i.e. the flat portion on which the foot is placed.

Trimming: Frame round any opening in floors, roofs, ceilings or walls.

Truss: Framed structure for supporting a weight, such as a roof.

Tungsten bulb: "Ordinary" light bulb, i.e., not fluorescent.

Two-pipe system: Heating circuit with flow and return pipes to each radiator.

Urea resin: A light plastics resin.

Valance: Short curtain, often gathered, hung round base of bed.

Vanitory: Unit combining hand basin and dressing table. (Trade mark.)

Variation order: Written authority to a builder to carry out extra work to that agreed in the contract.

Varnish: A resinous solution applied to wood, metal, etc. to give a glossy surface.

Velcro: Special patented tape used for fastening.

Vermiculite: A mineral substance which is very water absorbent and very light – used for insulation.

Vinyl: See PVC, polyvinyl chloride.

Wainscoting: Wood panelling up to dado height.

Wallboard: Panels used for surfacing rather than insulating walls and ceilings.

Wall plate: Horizontal timber along the top of the walls at eaves level to which rafters and ceiling are fixed.

Waste pipe: Pipe carrying water from basin, bath, or sink.

Water-based: Descriptive of wax, pigment, resin, etc. dissolved in water.

Winder: Triangular or wedge-shaped tread changing direction of stairs.

Window board: Horizontal board fixed like a shelf at sill level inside a window.

Just as every child under seven can paint delightful pictures, so every reasonably intelligent adult can tackle many jobs about the house. Everything is going for the do-it-yourselfer: new developments in paints, papers, glues, seals, power tools, sewing machines, etc., put much once left to a craftsman within your reach. In fact it can be argued that to persuade someone else (builder, plumber or little woman round the corner) to do things for you is harder, messier, takes far longer and costs much more than doing it yourself. Don't think of do-it-yourself in terms of Knit-your-own-Royal Family: it is as accessible to you as cooking or driving a car.

To start you off, here are some detailed but simple step-by-step directions for decorating, laying floors, tiling walls and ceilings, fixing hooks, shelves and tongued-and-grooved panelling, making curtains, blinds and soft furnishings. As the secret of success at first is not to aim too high, these directions give you the straight-forward way of doing a few obvious things.

Start Decorating

This section includes painting, papering and tiling walls and ceilings: read it in conjunction with the section on *Walls*. The first part is about the one thing common to all decorating – preparation. Don't skip preparation even if it seems tedious.

No paint, paper or tiles can adhere properly to a surface with dirt, grease or tiny fingermarks on it; nor to crumbling plaster, flaking paint or powdering distemper; nor to bulging, peeling or mildewing paper. If you allow at least as much time for preparation as for decorating, you'll find that not only will the painting, papering or tiling be easier to do, but it will look and last much, much better.

Preparation that pays off

Woodwork :
(i) Good condition. Sand lightly with fine sandpaper. This gives a "key" for the new paint. Wash.
(ii) Poor condition. Sand more thoroughly to smooth down bumps, flaking patches, etc., using first a medium sandpaper,

then a fine one. Fill in noticeable holes with Polyfilla. Wash down.
(iii) Discoloured pine panelling. Sand off top layer of wood. The quickest way is with a sander on a power tool, but it can also be done by hand.
(iv) Stripping. Only necessary before repainting if too many old layers have obscured the moulding profiles. Otherwise the more layers of paint the better the wood is protected. But all badly-flaking or blistering paint should be removed with a knife or sandpaper before repainting.
(v) New wood. If not already sanded and primed, sand down. Seal knots with shellac to prevent resin oozing. If already primed, clean; sand if necessary.
Metal :
(i) Good condition – e.g. previously painted, or new radiators ready primed. Remove any grease with turps substitute. If necessary to give a "key", rub down the surface lightly with fine sandpaper. Clean off any other dirt that still remains.
(ii) Where rusty – remove all traces of rust with wire brush or wire wool. Paint these areas with rust-inhibiting primer.
Plaster walls and ceilings :
(i) New plaster. Prime with thinned emulsion paint or alkali-resistant primer. If you don't want to wait through the "drying out" period before decorating, be prepared for a crumbly, mouldering efflorescence to appear from time to time. Rub this off with a dry cloth. It is unwise to use gloss paint on new plaster within a year because it prevents the "drying out": emulsion paint allows the plaster to breathe.
(ii) Emulsion paint in good condition. Wash down with detergent. Fill in holes with Polyfilla.
(iii) Emulsion paint in poor condition. As above, but remove all flaking, loose paint with a stripping knife. Fill holes with Polyfilla. If surface is very bad, line with paper before painting, or conceal behind tongue-and-grooved panelling.
(iv) Distemper. Non-washable distemper should be washed off completely as nothing will hold over it – distemper being merely a mixture of paste and whitener. It is wise to take off washable distemper because almost in-

variably it has been sloshed over old ordinary distemper. Wash a second time to remove all remaining traces of glue.
(v) Gloss paint in good or bad condition. Sand down thoroughly to give a good "key". Fill holes with Polyfilla. Wash.
(vi) Wallpaper in good condition. If you want to paint over it, check that the colours won't bleed through the paint. If they don't, clean with brush or vacuum cleaner and only wash off any grease marks. If colours do bleed, seal with primer.
(vii) Wallpaper in bad condition. Strip it off. Soak with water alone or a preparation like Polypeel. Give water/Polypeel time to dissolve paste, so that most of the paper comes off in long strips. Use a stripping knife for hard bits. (Washable papers need scoring so that the water can penetrate washable coating to paste underneath. Exceptions: those with a plastic coating which is meant to peel off leaving the paper as a lining for next one.) Wash wall clean. Fill holes with Polyfilla. If you plan to paper again, size the plaster with a weak solution of wallpaper paste (like Polycell) first.
(viii) Building boards – plasterboard, chipboard, hardboard, insulation boards, etc. If previously painted, wash down and paint as you like. If new, use a primer which can be used on any surface, including metal.

Brickwork indoors :
(i) Good condition. Clean – your aim being to remove any bits of mortar and flaking brick. You can then either leave it, seal with clear seal or paint it with gloss or emulsion. If painting, the first coat should be either an alkali-resistant primer or thinned-down emulsion paint.
(ii) Poor condition. As above. It probably needs repointing with mortar, but you can usually manage by filling the worst gaps with Polyfilla and painting thickly.

Tools for preparation

Washing down : Big sponges. Rubber gloves. Strong detergent – Flash is good because, if you change the water often enough, it doesn't need rinsing.
Sanding : Coarse sandpaper (for gloss paint on walls and poor woodwork). Fine sandpaper (to give "key"). Block (to wrap sandpaper round when sanding large flat areas). Power tool with orbital sander (for large flat areas), disc sander (for coarser work), drum sander (for finishing), wire brush (for metal).
Filling : Filling knife. Polyfilla – buy it as a powder and mix it up yourself or, more expensive, buy it ready-mixed. Step 1. Clean and wet hole or crack. Step 2. Get blob of Polyfilla on knife. Step 3. Force into hole or crack. Step 4. Smooth over, with knife or damp cloth. If hole is

large, fill in two or three goes, leaving it to dry in between.
Stripping : Using paint stripper, as instructions, which you paint on and scrape off with either a stripping knife or shave hook – whichever is appropriate. Start at bottom. Cover floor. Be careful to wear rubber gloves as paint strippers are caustic and burn the skin.

Using a blow lamp. Play flame up and down a small area until the paint begins to blister, then immediately scrape off with stripping knife or shave hook. Take care not to burn the wood, but if you do, sand off blackened areas afterwards. Keep flame away from glass, asbestos and plaster.

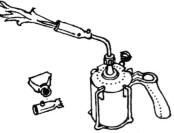

Using a sander on a power tool. This is good for large flat surfaces. No good for architraves or Victorian woodwork.

Using a Scarsten stripper knife. Score with one blade, scrape with flat blade. Sharpen blade on oilstone as you work. Good for small areas only. You need practice to get the angle of the tools correct.

Ladders: You need one ladder which enables you to reach your highest ceiling and/or top of the stairwell. Professionals often use two ladders with a scaffolding board in between to reach high ceilings and walls. There is movable scaffolding, but this is worth getting only if it enables you to do all your outdoor decorating, or if your rooms are vast enough to contain it.

Painting tools

Brushes: 5 in./127 mm or 6 in./152 mm brushes for large flat surfaces with emulsion paint. 4 in./102 mm brush better for large areas of gloss. 2 in./51 mm, 1½ in./38 mm and 1 in./25 mm brushes – choose the best for your problems and the one you find easiest. Sash brushes, crevice brushes. Get these only if you have to paint sash windows or behind awkward pipes or radiators. N.B. Some people keep brushes used for gloss and emulsion separate from each other. Others keep one set for white paint and one for colours. But now that so many paints can be cleaned so easily in water this isn't so important as having enough brushes so everyone who wants to help paint, can!

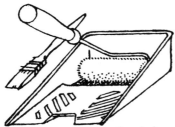

Roller and tray: Good for applying emulsion paint to large flat areas. (You still need brushes for joins and corners). All rollers leave a more textured surface than brushes.

Spray: Spray guns are very hard to handle. The paint has to be thinned to exactly the right consistency, and even then is very difficult to apply without blobs and runs. Small aerosol packs are useful (though expensive), particularly for chairs.

Which paint?

For the different paints professional decorators use, see *Walls*. But if you have not had a lot of experience, there is no doubt that the best thing for you to do is as much as possible with good quality emulsion paint. Stick to good quality because, as emulsion is water soluble, it is all too simple to cut the price dramatically by stepping up the water content. Result: thin paint, low opacity, more work involved in putting on extra coats.

Emulsion paint will go on anything, even act as its own undercoat (just thin with water: directions are on the tins). If you want a matt finish, you can use emulsion paint on wood. It comes in any colour. If the shade cards in the shop don't thrill you, the range of British Standard colours is made by all leading manufacturers and can be quickly ordered. Colorizer ranges and Mixmaster machines in shops can produce a wide range of pale to medium colours. Finally, most good paint shops can put you in touch with a manufacturer who will match a paint to your sample.

Ordinary emulsion paint has a matt finish of course. But if you want an effect such as the old eggshell lustre finish, try the newer silk finishes.

There is no mystery about using emulsion paint. Just use a brush load and spread it medium-thick as far as it will go! Cleaning up (and mopping spills) is done with water while the paint is still wet.

For woodwork, if you want a gloss finish, there are two alternatives: use a water-based undercoat, putting on one, two or three coats as necessary, with a thin final coat of an oil-based gloss with polyurethane. (This will have to be cleaned up with turps substitute.) Or there are water-based acrylic gloss paints, but, as yet, these are not quite as tough as the oil-based ones, though they can be cleaned up, like emulsion, with water.

Occasionally, if you are painting woodwork which has been stained or treated (like old ceiling beams), you need to apply first an undercoat of aluminium primer, otherwise the stain will "bleed" through.

If the wood has not been painted before or you have just stripped it, there are alternatives to painting: you can seal it with a clear polyurethane seal – which may need several coats and light sanding between each; or you can stain it with a coloured wood stain; or, if it isn't going to get hard wear or dirty, you can polish it with beeswax or a wax-based polish.

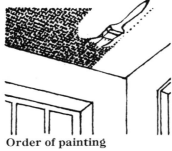

Order of painting

Ceilings: Start at the window end and work along towards the opposite wall in strips.

Walls: Start at the top and work in bands downwards, aiming to join up new paint before the previous band has dried.

Windows: Sash – work from the outside in.
Casement – do the window before the frame.

Doors: If panelled do the panels before the main door; the door itself before you begin on the architrave.

Hanging wallpaper/tools

Decorating table – the light folding table sold by decorating shops is worth investing in if you plan to do your own papering. It is a convenient size, light to move about, firm, folds flat for storage and isn't expensive.
Painting brush – for applying wallpaper paste.
Hanging or smoothing brush – for smoothing paper on wall.
Roller (sponge or boxwood) – for pressing down edges.
Bucket – to mix paste in.
Plumb line – to mark vertical against which to hang paper.
Wallpaper scissors – long, with blunt ends.
Stanley knife – for trimming.
Long steel rule and folding rule (metric).
Soft black pencil.
Sponge and rags – to mop up.
Adhesive – different papers need different pastes, so buy whichever the supplier advises for the wallpaper you choose. The advantage of using something like Polycell is that if it gets on to the front of the paper it can be wiped off without leaving a mark.

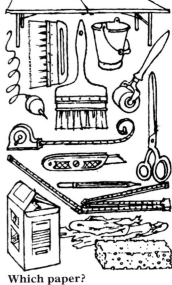

Which paper?

Some papers are very much easier than others to hang. Some rooms are easier to paper. So, make your first attempt on a room with flat wall surfaces and the minimum number of obstacles (pipes, shelves, radiators, light switches, doors, windows, etc.). Choose a firm, good-quality paper remembering that it is obviously easier not to have to match a pattern the first time.

Beware of papers which have to have the paste soaking on them for a period: they almost always stretch alarmingly. Very thin papers tend to tear easily and the paste can stain them: this of course doesn't matter with lining paper. Heavy coverings – like paper-backed hessian, vinyl, Anaglypta, Lincrusta Walton – are harder to handle than ordinary papers and sometimes the wall needs special preparation. Ceilings are hardest of all to paper, whatever you choose, because the lengths of paper are so long and gravity is working against you.

Where walls are uneven, the final effect is much improved if they are first lined with lining paper. Some people say all walls should be lined first. Lining paper comes in several grades, so choose something not too flimsy to learn on – certainly a heavy quality if it has to cover up defects on the wall.

Most papers are sold ready-trimmed, and you can just butt-join the edges. If the paper you want isn't trimmed, get the dealer to do it for you. It is not advisable for the beginner to trim his own paper or attempt to follow counsels of perfection and join a hand-blocked paper with a mitred overlap!

How much paper?

See the chapter on *Walls*.

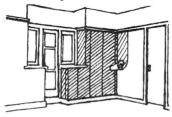

Step-by-step paperhanging

Where you start: In theory this is where the eye first goes when you enter the room. Usually this means starting at a corner near the main window and working round both ways to the door. If, however, there is a chimney breast and recesses, and you have a large patterned paper, it looks better to centre the pattern on these features, doing non-matching joins on the corners where they won't be noticed. (Ceilings are usually started across the window end of a room.)

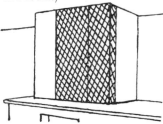

Mark up your starting place: Starting from a corner, mark the wall so that the paper will turn the corner by just 2 in./51 mm. (You always turn corners by a small amount, partly because corners are seldom completely vertical and partly because a large overlap is difficult to manage.) With the plumb line mark a vertical line on the wall: this is your guiding line for your first length of paper. If the corner is vertical your second piece will butt the first; if not, overlap the second length so that it is hanging true.

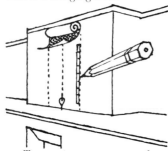

To centre paper, mark a straight line down the centre of the chimney breast or recess, then mark a parallel line to the right, half the width of the paper away. Line the first length of paper against this second line.

Cut lengths of paper: When the paper has no pattern or random repeats, cut the first length, allowing 4 in./102 mm each end for trimming.

Where the paper has a definite pattern to match, find the dominant motif, assume that will be the top of the wall and cut 4 in./102 mm above to allow for trimming. Measure to bottom and allow another 4 in./102 mm. For the next length, check whether starting any other roll would be more economical than matching up from the first one. You always waste paper matching up patterns, but the whole point of the pattern is lost if you don't match it properly. Match end piece with the one it is butting up to.

Pasting: Put the paper face down on the table with the top edge on your right, the bottom overlapping if necessary, and the far edge just overlapping. Paste down the middle. Spread the paste out over the far edge. Arrange paper so the near edge just overlaps the table.

Make the first fold by taking up the two top corners and folding the paper on itself.

Pull this fold so it overlaps the top end of the table, and paste the rest of the paper in the same way. Some people pick the paper up like this with one corner in each hand and "offer" it to the wall. Others make a second fold and carry the paper over their arm, then unfold this and place the paper on the wall.

Hanging the paper: Taking the two top corners, place or "offer" the paper to the wall, so the side matches the mark from the plumb line and the top overlaps about 4 in./102 mm.

Stick the paper by brushing with the hanging brush from the middle outwards (to get out all the air pockets).

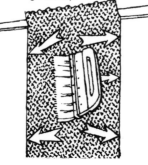

To trim, run the blunt end of the scissors along the join at the ceiling, pull the paper off the wall gently and cut along the mark of the scissors. Brush again to stick. Trim bottom of paper in the same way.

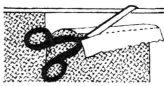

Use the roller to stick the edges really firmly down. When joining two pieces make a butt join. Don't overlap.

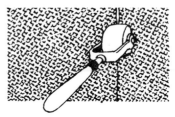

Inside corners. Cut the paper beforehand, so that only about 2 in./51 mm overlaps. If corner is not true, either overlap the next length, or cut with your Stanley knife) so that the untrue edge is made vertical.

External corners. Treat in the same way. Not more than 2 in./51 mm wraparound.

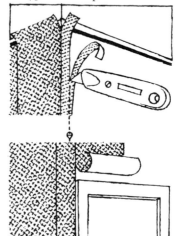

Doors and cupboards. Cut a narrow length to bring you to the edge of the architrave. Cut a short length to go above.

Or, if a wide width is needed before reaching the door, stick paper up to architrave, cut so that you can stick the top bit.

Then trim paper down the architrave by marking with the blunt end of the scissors as for top and bottom trimming.

For round or square light switches, cut star from centre of switch, mark round edge of switch, trim and stick down.

Ceramic tiles

If you have a firm, flat wall, choose thin modern tiles which have their own built-in spacer lugs, and get the correct adhesive – you will not find wall tiling very difficult.

Estimating the number of tiles: Tiles are being made either 6 in. × 6 in. × $\frac{1}{2}$ in./152 × 152 × 13 mm or $4\frac{1}{4}$ in. × $4\frac{1}{4}$ in. × $\frac{5}{32}$ in./106 × 106 × 4 mm. Tiles to join up on all edges are REX tiles, and are used on edges to prevent chipping. Plan to cut tiles to fit in at the ends of walls, the base of the area, at the least noticeable points. For baths there is ceramic coving for the gap between bath and tiles.

The tools you will be needing: Filling knife. Knotched spreader (often comes with adhesive). Tile cutter. Sponge for grouting (often supplied with grout). Adhesive – as advised by tile supplier. For bathrooms, get a waterproof adhesive. Where temperatures are likely to get high (behind cookers, fireplaces), do get a heat-resistant adhesive.

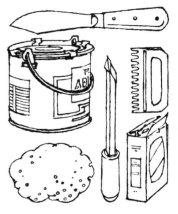

Grout – this seals the gaps between the tiles after you have laid them. Get waterproof grout for bathrooms and behind kitchen sinks.

Aim to get a very firm, flat wall. Paint in good conditions on plasterboard, plywood, hardboard, chipboard, etc., just clean. Plaster, if new, should be left for at least a month to dry out. Old, not very solid plaster should be evened up with Polyfilla and primed (thinned-down emulsion paint) so that it doesn't absorb the water in the glue too much. Old ceramic tiles, if firmly stuck to the wall, can simply be cleaned, levelled and scored (to give "key"). If the wall is very uneven line with Marine ply on battens before tiling.

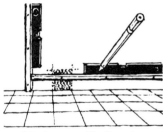

Mark yourself a base to work from : This can be done with a pencil line, but if the adhesive is going to be spread over the wall, it is worth the trouble of fixing one batten to make the horizontal guide line, another to make the vertical one.

If you are doing the whole wall, the batten or mark should not be more than one tile width from the floor or skirting.

If you are tiling round a bath, above a basin or along a sink, put your batten or mark so there is never more than one tile width between the bath, etc., and the batten.

Using a tile, mark off tile positions on your horizontal. At the end of the last complete tile on the left, make your vertical guide, checking with spirit level or plumb line that it is level.

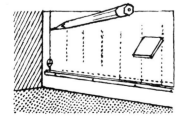

Adhesive is best spread on the wall – thickly covering about a square yard/square metre at a time, then even it out with the knotched spreader. Squidge the first tile into place so it is firmly embedded in the adhesive. Work in horizontal rows. You can butter the back of the tile with adhesive, but you have to be careful to make sure every bit of the tile is covered so there are no air pockets behind. Air pockets allow the tile to crack more easily if it gets knocked. When the whole area has been done remove the battens and put up the last rows, cutting if necessary.

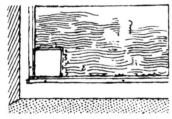

Cutting : Mark as for floor tiles. To cut thin, modern tiles, just score with tile cutter and gently break across score.

Accessories : Various soap dishes, lavatory paper holders, toothbrush holders, etc., made to the same module as the tiles. These can be stuck to the wall in place of one or two tiles. While adhesive is setting, hold them in place with tape.

Bath coving : Comes in packs with rubber-based adhesive. Stick it on after the tile adhesive has dried. Grout with the other tiles when its adhesive has set.

Grouting : Mix as directed; apply with sponge all over the tiles so that every gap is filled. When dry, wipe it off the tiles. Perfectionists smooth the grout between tiles with a rounded stick.

Mosaic wall tiles

You can get mosaic tiles in self-adhesive sheets. They are fixed to a net backing which is protected by a paper backing which you peel off. Techniques of applying these are similar to putting up single ceramic tiles.

Estimate the number of sheets you need – checking size of sheets available first. There is no difference between inside and outside tiles (no RE or REX to think of).

Prepare the wall so that it is clean, dry and firm, as above.

Mark the horizontal base line to start on, and the vertical one, as for ceramic tiles.

Stick by peeling off the backing paper and sliding the sheet of tiles into place. But if this is to be waterproof, check that the self-adhesive back is in fact waterproof. If not, use another waterproof adhesive, spread as above, and stick down sheet.

Apply grout as directed.

Cutting can be done with scissors between the little tiles. Cutting the tiles themselves is fiddly but can be done with the tile cutter.

Cork wall tiles

You can use either floor tiles for walls or cork panels. Tiles are easier to put up than ceramic tiles as you are dealing with a material that is very easy to cut and not brittle.

Estimating : Standard size is 12 sq. in./305 mm², and you can use the thinnest for walls. Other sizes are available too. No difference between inside and outside tiles. Coving is available.

Preparation : A smooth, clean, firm surface to stick the cork to is important.

Mark the horizontal base line with batten or pencil.

Sticking : Use the recommended adhesive as directed –

preferably one like Thixofix, which gives you a little time to manoeuvre the tiles into position before it begins to grip.

Cutting : Simple with a steel rule and Stanley knife.

Finishing : No grouting. Either seal as for floors, wax polish or leave natural.

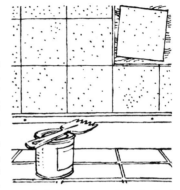

Panels are made of dark grainy cork and come in panels three times the size of the floor tiles. Estimate accordingly. Preparation of wall and marking the horizontal line is as above.

Stick : With recommended adhesive, but cut with Stanley knife and rule; as material is very brittle, the knife should be very sharp. No sealing or polishing necessary.

Ceiling tiles

It is very tempting to cover up a defective ceiling with cheap expanded polystyrene tiles. But resist this solution in rooms where people are to sleep. Polystyrene tiles are a serious fire risk because, even if they are flameproof, they give off asphyxiating black smoke. They also melt when hot and drop in hot gobs, setting fire to floor and furniture underneath. Pay more for ceiling tiles made from mineral fibres which you can track down through builders' merchants. Most of those designed for offices and factories to be fixed on to grids can equally well

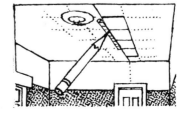

be stuck on to your ceiling.

Estimating numbers : Most mineral tiles come in the 12 in./ 305 mm size as well as other square and rectangular sizes.

Preparation : A smooth, clean ceiling is necessary, but the tiles will cover up cracks and stains.

Establish your starting line : draw a straight line either:
(i) across the centre of the ceiling (if there are no light fittings to accommodate).
(ii) along a line looking from the centre of the doorway (again if there are no light fittings).
(iii) through the centre of a ceiling rose.
(iv) along a fluorescent fitting.

Stick : Using recommended adhesive for tile and surface. Use a large, flat, clean wooden pad to hold tile to surface while it sticks firmly.

Finishing : No finish necessary, but most can be painted.

Floors

Many floors are better left to the specialist, but there are a few on which you can save a lot of money by doing yourself. As with decorating, success starts with proper preparation: getting the sub-floor right. Also you give yourself a better chance of doing a good job if you stick to materials which are easy to handle – vinyl rather than ceramic tiles, sanding rather than wall-to-wall carpeting. Read the section on *Floors* for basic information.

Preparation for all floors

All flooring must be laid on a firm, flat foundation. First, because any unevenness shows; second, because it is very much harder to lay a floor on an uneven sub-floor; third, because an uneven floor wears unevenly and therefore has to be replaced much sooner. Make sure any electrical work or pipework has been completed.

(i) Concrete floors
If these are level and damp-proof with a good cement screed on top, all you need do is to clean off the surface dirt.

If the concrete is old, have it relaid or prepared with a cement screed professionally before laying anything new on top.

(ii) Wood floors
Go over each floorboard and make sure it is firm. If not, nail about ⅛ in./3 mm from the edge of the board along the line of the joists with floor or oval nails.

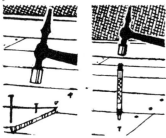

If the boards are old or uneven, you can lay a hardboard sub-floor (over latex screed). Buy in sheets appropriate to size of room: i.e. use standard sheets for large areas, but get suppliers to divide into halves or quarters for small fiddly places. Lay rough side up, using sheets as big as possible.

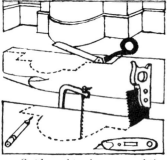

Cut board to shape round the edges by making templates from brown paper. Use a panel saw to cut straight edges, a coping saw for round ones, or a very sharp Stanley knife.

Nail down with ¾ in./20 mm panel pins very firmly – i.e. one pin about every 6 in./152 mm round the edges and across the centres of large panels.

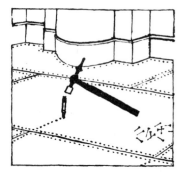

Lino or vinyl tiles
(i) Choose ordinary vinyl or lino tiles. (Not vinyl asbestos tiles which need warming before you can cut them. Nor vinyl-topped cork, which is stuck with an impact adhesive. Nor extremely hard inlaid vinyl tiles, which are as hard to cut as ceramic tiles.)
(ii) Estimate tiles needed by drawing a plan of the room on graph paper and decide on the scale so that a square or squares can represent the size of the tile you plan to use.

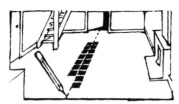

(iii) Mark the guide lines for laying tiles on the floor. You should start in the middle and work towards the edges of a floor because (a) floors are seldom truly square and (b) even if they are they are never an overall measurement so the tiles fit exactly. The simplest method is to start from the doorway. Mark the centre and mark a line direct to the opposite wall. Lay the first two rows of tiles back to back along this line.
(iv) From the central tiles along this line mark another guide line at right-angles across the room. Lay tiles up and across the room until you are so near the edge that a complete tile won't fit.

(v) To measure tiles to fit, lay the tile you are to use on top of the one already laid. Take a second tile and use it to mark off distance from wall. Cut first one accordingly.

To fit a tile round a corner, do the same thing from each side.

To fit a complicated pattern, use the second tile to mark off a number of measurements and connect and cut accordingly.

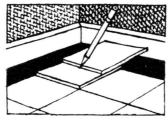

Sheet vinyl or lino
(i) Choose any sheet lino or vinyl which is easy to cut and stick – you can have jute, foam or composition back.
(ii) If there is a choice of widths, choose the one which means the least number of seams.
(iii) Cut into rough lengths which are too long and overlap 2 in.–4 in./51–102 mm. Put these on the floor in position, don't stick but leave them like that for a week or so to settle and stretch.
(iv) To fit seams: place a long, straight rule or piece of wood down the centre of the overlap and cut through both thicknesses with a sharp Stanley knife. This will give a perfect butt join, when you take away the surplus from each side.

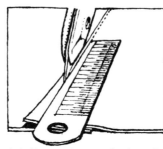

(v) To mark round obstacles, make a template from brown paper. To mark the edges very accurately first make a "scribe" by getting a smooth piece of wood about 18 in./757 mm long sticks out about 1¼ in./32 mm, about 6 in./152 mm from one end. Mark the vinyl or lino 8 in./

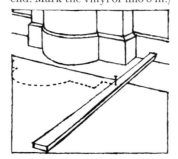

203 mm in from the wall or skirting. Pull the sheet away from the wall and make a second mark 8 in./203 mm out from the first one. Using the scribe, put the nail on the second mark and the short end of the wood against the wall (adjust the sheet), slide the whole scribe along to make an accurate cutting mark.
(vi) Stick by using double-sided tape at seams and edges. Stick the floor first, then place the sheet on it. Adhesive is more difficult, because getting the whole sheet into position without its sticking in the wrong place is tricky.

Sanding/sealing/staining
(i) In addition to nailing down the floorboards it is essential to punch down *all* the nails in the boards at least ⅕ in./5 mm into the wood. Use a punch and hammer so the sander can strip off the top ⅛ in./3 mm of wood without being damaged.

(ii) Hire a big sander. Follow all instructions. Always sand with the grain of the wood: old floorboards for this reason are easy to do, parquet and woodblocks are best left to professionals. Clear room completely as the mess and dust is dreadful.
(iii) Sand edges with a hand machine: orbital sander or discs on a power drill.
(iv) Dust exceptionally well.
(v) Paint on clear polyurethane seal, white shellac, or coloured stain. Plan for three coats, sanding by hand in between for a long-lasting tough finish.
(vi) If painting, do undercoats and gloss in normal way. Choose a really tough gloss for top coat.

General carpentry
However humble your aims, it is important to have a place for a firm, solid workbench (it can be an old table, but it must be solid)

where you don't have to clear up all the time and where you can store all your tools together.

On the workbench you need: A vice and a benchhook.

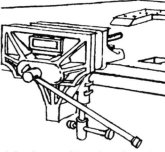

A basic set of hand tools – claw hammer, ratchet screwdriver, bradawl, hand drill, countersink bit, Surform plane, plane, panel saw, tenon saw, coping saw, spirit level, try square, long rule, folding rule, pencils. Rawlplugs, nails, screws and collars, masonry fixing pins.
Power drill – choose a two-speed one at least. One speed is for drilling wood, the other for drilling solid walls.

An extension flex and plug is useful. Choose attachments that help you do the jobs you most need help with. Sanding attachments are particularly useful: discs (for rough sanding), drum (for sanding with the grain), orbital sander (oscillates and gives a good finish). Sawing attachments are less useful as most yards cut to size.

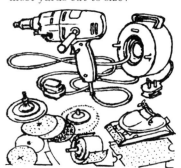

Ordering wood
Metrication has altered the way you order wood. You order lengths of wood by the wood unit. This is equivalent to 11 13/16 in./300 mm. Of course, while staff at woodyards remember the old feet and inches, they will convert for you, but you have to buy to the nearest wood unit.

Some widths have altered too, but this only affects you if you are trying to match up old widths. Floorboards are very difficult, for instance. But it makes no difference if you are starting from scratch.

Fixing to walls

There are two different ways of fixing to walls: one is direct on to the wall, the other is to fix a batten (wood) to the wall, and then fix what you want to that. In each case, the first thing to find out is what sort of wall you are fixing to.

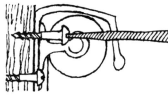

(*i*) *Solid walls:* Made of brick, stone, breeze blocks or plastered brick. Usually these will be outside, or load-bearing walls inside. To nail: use a long enough masonry fixing pin to penetrate the brick, about 6 in.–8 in./152–203 mm.

To screw: make a small hole to house the screw, fill the hole with a fibre plug and drive the screw into that. (To make the hole, you can use a hand boring tool and hammer, but a power drill with a masonry twist bit is much better.)

To screw into concrete (some modern houses have concrete lintels above the windows), use a power drill on a slow speed with a durium-tipped bit.

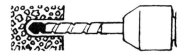

(*ii*) *Stud walls:* Made from plasterboard fixed at intervals to upright wood beams. In old houses these walls are often lath and plaster fixed to beams. Safest (and only solution for lath and plaster) is to locate the upright beams and use nails or screws.

To locate beams: bang the wall with your fist – the plasterboard or lath and plaster will sound hollow – where the beam is will sound solid; then prod with a bradawl.

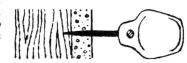

If the wall is plasterboard only, there are special toggle anchors which you hammer or screw through the board and which unfold the other side to provide a better grip.

Wood which is simply cladding (like tongued-and-grooved) won't take anything heavy. Fix either to battens supporting tongue-and-groove or locate studs in the wall behind.

Fixing direct to the wall

(*i*) *Curtain rails:* Fix to the window frame itself or use Rawlplugs with screws through wall. The number of fixings depends on the final weight of the curtains: the heavier the curtains, the more fixings.

(*ii*) *Roller blinds:* These usually come with small screws suitable to go into the wood of the window frame.

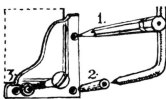

(*iii*) *Heavy mirrors, pictures:* These frames usually come with key plates. Mark position of plates on wall then put in Rawlplugs, and screw through eyes into Rawlplugs. On stud walls the eyes, if possible, should be fixed to beams – or at least the top central one should.

(*iv*) *Shelving systems:* On solid walls use Rawlplugs and screws to fix the vertical supports. On stud walls use the upright beams.

Fixing to battens

The advantage of battens is that you can fix the batten solidly to the beams and this gives you more freedom to fix other things anywhere you like along its length: you are not stuck with fixing them to a solid part of the wall. Battens can also support furniture or shelves on the wall.

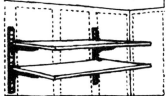

(*i*) *How to make the batten:* Unless you want the battens to match other hardwood in the room, they are usually made from softwood, 1 in./25 mm thick and as wide as looks good. Plane or sand (with Surform) the sharp edges in front and at the ends. Sand the front. Seal or paint. Measure carefully so that the holes you make for the screws coincide with the position of beams in the wall if you are fixing to a stud wall.

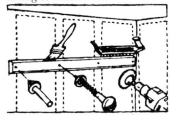

(*ii*) *Hooks on battens:* As coat hooks frequently get overloaded and winter coats are pretty heavy, it is better to mount them in a row on a strong batten than singly. Use a 1 in. × 3–4 in./25 mm × 76–102 mm batten as long as you want. Fix it to the wall with intermediate screws every 8 in.–12 in./203–305 mm.

(*iii*) *Shelves on battens:* A very simple way to make shelves for recesses is to fix 1 in. × 2 in./25 × 51 mm battens, a little shorter than the depth you want the shelves to be, into the recesses.

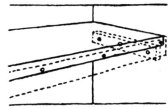

Make the shelves from 1 in./25 mm planks cut to size and planed, sanded and sealed. They can just rest on the battens.

To conceal battens, put a lip along the front edge, glued, nailed, or screwed on with a brass screw and collar.

Putting up t & g

Tongued-and-grooved and v-jointed softwood panelling, to give T.G.V. its full name, is often a good solution for walls which are in poor condition. If you can do it yourself it is a lot cheaper than getting a professional to replaster. Although it seems a big thing to tackle, handling the boards is much easier for the beginner than handling other panelling which comes in large sheets, so don't get carried away by t & g panels. They need much more battening and the joins between the panels are hard to get right.

T & g can run either vertically, horizontally or diagonally. Vertical is the best to start on. There are three main stages:

(*i*) *Putting up the battens:* T & g is held to the wall by a network of battens round the room, running the opposite way to the t & g itself. Use 1 in. × 2 in./25 mm × 51 mm battens, and if there is any chance of damp treat them with wood preservative before fixing them. As the battens are to hold the t & g firm, you need one at the top, one along the bottom and some in between

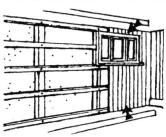

(the gap varies according to taste), between 20–40 in./508 mm/1 m. Around doors, windows, etc., either remove architraves, skirting, etc., put battens right up to doors, windows, etc., then t & g over and finally put back or renew the architraves, skirtings, etc. Or leave them in place and run battens round them. If wall is uneven pack out battens so that the face is even.

Fix battens firmly. If the wall is solid, nail them with masonry fixing pins. If stud, the battens should be fixed to the beams with nails or screws.

(*ii*) *Putting up the boards:* Boards come in different widths and thicknesses. When estimating how many you need remember the interlocking cuts about 2 in./51 mm off the width.

Cut the boards to length and sand each one. If you can't get boards long enough, either work out an interlocking pattern or decide to make random joins.

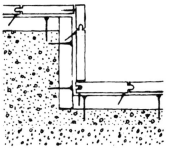

Fit the board into a corner so that its outside edge is truly vertical. Using panel pins, fix to batten in normal way, one edge inside the corner. On the outside edge, which should be tongued, secure diagonally across the tongue and shoulder so the next board will slot over and conceal the panel pin.

Internal corners: plane the slotted edge of the second board to fit flush with the first one and make sure it is vertical.

External corners: plane off the edge of the last board so that it is flush with the first one round the corner. Nail with a long nail into the next board.

(*iii*) *Finishing off:* Sand the boards before putting them up. Later, clean off any marks that have got on since.

Seal with a clear polyurethane seal, shellac or coloured stain. It needs three coats and sanding down in between each one.

If you are going to paint the boards, seal each knot with shellac first to prevent resin oozing.

After some years your t & g will have darkened, from the effect of light on the wood. To get it back to a paler colour, sand all over again; or paint it white.

DIY: Of course you can do it!
7/8 Soft furnishings: curtains and blinds

You can save a lot of money if you can tackle some of your soft furnishings yourself. There is a lot going for the home-soft furnisher. New sewing machines, new aids, all of which help you to achieve a professional finish with far less pain and anguish than ever before.

The secret of success for a beginner, we think, is to stick to simple straight-forward things, only branching into scalloped edges, decorator-style pelmets or button-back upholstery when you have confidence and experience. To get you going, we show you some very basic ways to tackle curtains and blinds, cushions and loose covers, bedcovers, duvet covers and valances. Once you have started this way, you will find that you can follow on, getting more ambitious as you become more experienced.

Getting the right tools

Tape measure: A flexible steel rule is more accurate for measuring up than an ordinary tape measure, and also easier to handle on long lengths like curtains. But you need a tape measure too. Both measures with metre, centimetre and millimetre markings as well as feet and inches.
Long cutting scissors, pinking shears and short snipping scissors.
Pins
Thread: Match to material. Use thick cheap soft cotton for tailor's tacks.
Straight edge: For marking long cutting lines if you can't follow the weave.

Curved needles: For fixing upholstery on the chair/sofa or mending carpet seams.

Sewing machine: Preferably – (i) electric (two hands are better than one at guiding material into long straight seams for curtains, etc.); (ii) easily adjustable stitch length and tension to sew heavy Dralon as well as thin sheers; (iii) various stitch options – zigzag is invaluable for seaming sheers and binding raw edges, especially blinds; (iv) choice of feet – e.g. zipper foot for piping; (v) choice of needles – to suit the thread chosen.
Upholstery tacks: For fixing material to wood frame.

Upholstery pins: For decorative finish on material tacked to wood. Choose in brass, chrome or antique bronze finish.
White string: i.e. piping cord, for piping.
Curtain headings and hooks: Choose the one to give appropriate height and pleating (see section on *Windows*).
Plastic weights: To make a curtain hem hang better.
Braids and trimmings: Choose them to match upholstery.
Velcro: Zips, press-studs tape for fastenings.
Polystyrene foam: For cushions.
Polystyrene beads: For filling cushions.
Terylene wadding: For padding out sagging upholstery.

Curtains

It is important to read our section on *Windows* before you try to decide on the sort of curtains you want and the kind of fabric and track to use. Think always in terms of ideas that are within your scope and materials which are readily available and easy to handle.
Measuring up and estimating material: There are three stages to this.
1 Decide on the width and length of the curtains. The key here is the width and position of the track. Is it to fit inside the window recess or outside it, and if outside, how much overlap on each side? Secondly, the length of the curtains has to be decided

on. Floor-length curtains should just clear the floor: if they reach down to the floor the hems get dirty unnecessarily. Sill-length curtains should just clear the sill for the same reason. Draw a scale picture of your window like the one here and fill in your measurements: A-B/C/D for track length, AX-/YZ for curtain length.

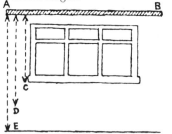

2 The amount of material needed will depend on the heading you have chosen as well as the width of material and length of curtains. Standard gathers, for instance, need material one and a half times as wide as the track. Pencil pleat heading needs material two and a quarter times the track width. Auto-pleat heading needs only twice the track width, while for pinch pleating, the amount of material needed depends on the number of pleats per pinch and the width of your fabric. Most fabrics for furnishing have been made 48 – 50 in./1.21 – 1.24 m wide: with metrication, the tendency is for fabrics to get wider.

If the material you choose is not wide enough for the curtain, you have to join widths or half widths. Allow 2 in./51 mm for each side seam. Allow 1 in./25 mm for each panel seam.

On the length, allow in addition: (i) turnover for the heading which will vary depending on the heading; (ii) turn-up for the hem, which is better if you are generous. A 6 in./152 mm hem is not too deep and some people also double the material over so there is more weight to make the curtains hang better; (iii) shrinkage. It is wise to allow 1 in./25 mm per yard/metre.

3 Finally, if you are using a patterned material, you have to allow for matching the pattern. You should add the amount of the pattern repeat on to every length of material you need. It is a matter of luck how much, or little, wastage this will cause.

Cutting out: It is much easier to cut out on a large table than on the floor. Your paper hanging table is better than nothing.

If the material is crumpled, iron it.

Mark the top line, using the weft – the line of the grain of the fabric. Pull a thread at right angles to the selvedge or tack along the grain of the fabric. If you follow the line of the design, and it isn't printed straight, curtains won't hang straight.

Choose part of the design that will look well at the top of the curtain, make allowance for the top hem and cut there. Measure the length required, and cut. Match the next length against the previous one so the pattern match is accurate.

Cut off all selvedges to prevent the seams and edges from puckering. Alternatively, clip selvedge at frequent intervals.

Cut the lining fabric shorter, by the height of the heading and its hem on the main curtain. Separate linings need not be quite so full as their curtains.

Making up: Join panels with ordinary seam and press flat. If you have to use half widths, join so that they hang on the outside edges of the window. For sheers try to choose in a width which needs no joins. If this is not possible make joins with a fell seam so that no raw edges show.

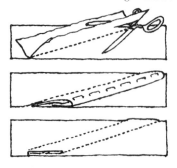

Tack down top edge to required depth for heading. Mitre corners and turn in each side hem, double width if you can spare the material. Machine

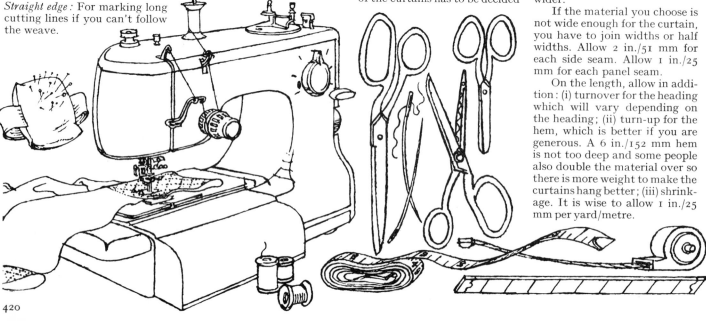

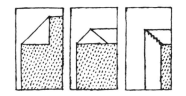

using a stitch which isn't too tight: real perfectionists do this by hand.

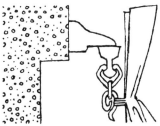

Put on heading as directions for tape. Make sure there is enough curtain above the heading to hide the track when the curtains are drawn, if you are having no pelmet. Tuck under ends of the heading tape, and knot the strings in one end. Tack and/or machine into place. Then pull strings to make pleats or gathers. Put in hooks and hang for at least 24 hours before hemming. You can hang lining at this stage – or later.

To hem: Pin while hanging. Take down and adjust line at the bottom. Press. Cut off any extra material remembering that the heavier the hem the better the curtains tend to hang. If you are going to weight the curtains, sew weights into position. You can now get weights threaded into a plastic tape. Hem, by hand or machine, having mitred the corners.

Lining: Sew as curtains. Make hem so lining is a little shorter than the curtains.

Roller blinds

The advantage of making your own roller blinds is that you are not confined to the manufacturer's choice of fabric. You can match up patterns and colours exactly. But, if you want either holland blinds or the fabric laminated so that it will always roll up as slickly as holland, you will have to get them made. Holland is virtually impossible to buy retail and lamination is only undertaken by firms when they make up the

blind as well. Roller blind kits, consisting of spring roller, base batten and necessary fixings, are quite widely distributed or available through the Habitat Mail Order Catalogue.

Measuring up: First decide where the blind is to hang – inside the window recess or outside it. Make a diagram similar to the one below for measuring up your windows. Blinds hung inside the recess look good, but it is crucial for there to be room for the material to cover the glazed area generously. Also there needs to be at least an extra 1 in./25 mm each end for "pin width", to take the brackets, pins and caps at each end. In the same way, blinds fixed outside the recess should overlap at least 2 in./51 mm each side to prevent their being sucked into the recess.

Measuring up

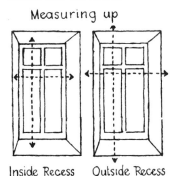

Inside Recess   Outside Recess

The brackets can be fixed to hold the blinds either from the ceiling or the top of the recess, or alternatively sideways from the window frame or the wall.

Which roller kit? Kits come in standard lengths. You cut the roller to fit your space exactly. Normally you get the kit which is just longer than you need. If your material is very thick or heavy or the drop is disproportionate to the width of the window, get the stoutest roller you can and cut it right down.

How much material? The width of the blind should ideally be less than the width of the material. Joins are possible but every extra thickness of cloth makes the rolling up less smooth. Seams and side seams for this reason should be as flat as possible: allow 1 in./25 mm each and no turn-in. The drop (length) needs an additional 12 in./305 mm per blind to allow for fixing

at the top and making a pocket for the batten at the bottom.

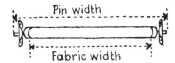

Pin width

Fabric width

Choosing the fabric: See section on *Windows* and above. Closely-woven fabrics roll up best and wear best. Those woven and printed truly square are easiest to make up. But if you want a particular decorative effect and don't mind the fact that your blinds won't roll up slickly at a touch, you can choose any fabric from figured velvet to cotton lace or semi-sheers.

Cutting-out: If the blind is to hang vertically, it is important to get the fabric cut square (this is why it helps if the material itself is true – not askew). Pull one of the weft threads and use this as a guide for the top. Cut as near a straight line from a right angle as you can. If the blind is wider than the material, join two widths. It looks better if you cut one width in half and join on each side symmetrically. Allow 2 in./51 mm each seam and side seam and 12 in./305 mm on the length.

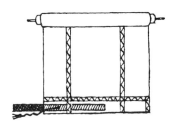

Making up: To minimize extra thicknesses, don't turn in side seams; either cut them with pinking shears or oversew them (zigzag stitch). Press all seams as flat as possible. For the batten pocket on the bottom: tack and press a strip 2 in./51 mm or the minimum large enough to hold the batten. Stitch close to the edge and down one end. Cut the batten so it is 2 in./51 mm shorter than the width of the fabric. Insert into pocket and stitch down the remaining end.

To fix the pull: Follow instructions if a pull holder is supplied. If not use a length of

blind cord and nail to centre of batten before putting into pocket. Cut a small hole in centre of material at pocket base and pull cord through.

To prepare roller: Cut roller to correct size, allowing for pin width. Fix metal cap on to the end of the roller, sanding if necessary where you have cut it. Drive in metal pin firmly.

To fix material to the roller: Lay the made-up fabric out flat, right side up. Lay the roller across the top with the spring mechanism (the end you didn't cut) on your left. Glue (some kits provide this, some don't, but it's a good idea) the material to the blind so it is quite square and true. Then tack (tacks are provided) the material on to the roller at 2 in./51 mm intervals starting at the centre and working towards the ends. Roll up the material on to the roller, with the right side of the material on the inside.

Attaching fabric to roller

Spring Pin

Putting up the blind: Mark bracket positions on wall. Start with right-hand bracket and fix (with screws to wood or use a Rawlplug if the surface is plaster). Use blind to check position is horizontal. Screw home left-hand bracket. Fit rolled up blind on its brackets. Pull down blind and adjust length of cord. Fit acorn.

To tension the spring: Take the blind off its brackets unrolled and roll up again by hand. Replace and pull down. It should now lock in the down position when required. If not, repeat. Be careful not to overload the spring by doing this too often either at this stage or later when, for some reason, you have to take the blind down.

Roman blinds

As Roman blinds are pulled up by strings (see section on *Windows*) instead of rolling up on a roller, they have some advantages over roller blinds if you decide to make them. Literally

any material which is not too thick to pull up and pleat prettily can be used. It is usual to line these blinds; you can use the same fabric so they look interesting on the outside as well as inside, or ordinary lining material. You must be able to sew long straight seams.

Measuring up: In principle as for roller blinds, except that as romans are mounted on a wooden batten fixed inside or outside the window recess, you do not have to allow any "pin width". Sometimes, if outside the recess, roman blinds are mounted on a decorative pole.

How much material? Each roman blind needs material the width of the blind plus 2 in./51 mm for each side seam, plus the length of the blind (or drop) plus an allowance 10 in./254 mm for top and bottom turnings. If you are lining your blind, you need the same amount of fabric for the lining.

Other haberdashery, etc.: Half-inch tape – enough complete lengths to do each side plus two in the middle or more if necessary. The tapes are usually spaced between 8–12 in./203–305 mm apart.
One-inch tape – to finish top of blind. Vine eyes – one for each vertical tape. Half-inch brass rings – to go every 8–12 in./203–305 mm along tapes.
Thin nylon cord – to go up each tape, across the top and down to fixing cleat. Wooden batten 2 in. × 1 in./51 mm × 25 mm – to fix blind at top – or decorative pole and brackets.
Batten or dowelling – for base stiffening on blind.
Fixing cleats – to attach to window frame.

Cutting: Pull a weft thread to get a straight top cutting line. If material needs joining, plan seams along under the tapes. Cut lining as blind.

Making up:
(i) Sew lining to top fabric. Press down 1½ in./38 mm side seams on top fabric and 2 in./51 mm seams on lining. Put wrong sides together and tack.
(ii) Stitch on tapes. Machine the first two lengths of half-inch tape along the joins of fabric and lining. Then stitch on central tapes.
(iii) Make pocket for batten.

Check length and turn up enough material for batten to slot through. Turn over edge, press in position and machine along top edge. Slot in batten and stitch ends by hand.

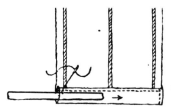

(iv) Fix top to batten. Finish raw top edge with one-inch tape. Fix to prepared batten along its top edge. If the batten is fixed to ceiling the material will be concealed between batten and ceiling. On wall-mounted blinds, tack material so that it is concealed between wall and batten.

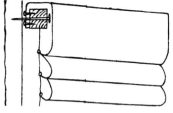

(v) If mounting on decorative pole, check length and turn over top to make a pocket big enough for the pole to slot through, as for bottom batten.

(vi) Sew rings on tapes. Space evenly 8–12 in./203–305 mm apart from top and bottom and each other. Sew on very firmly without going through front of fabric.

(vii) Fix cleats (to hold strings in place when blind is pulled up – or half up) on the most convenient side of the window, one low, one half-way up.

(viii) Screw vine eyes to batten to align with the top of each tape. Or back of the decorative pole.

(ix) Thread cord. Lay blind out flat. Start from bottom corner farthest from cleat (i.e. if cleats are on the right-hand side of the window, start threading from the ring in the bottom left-hand corner. Tie or sew cord firmly to first ring, then thread through other rings on the tape and all the vine eyes and leave enough thread for attaching it to the lowest fixing cleat. Thread other

tapes similarly. Tie all the cords together so that when you pull them the blind pleats up evenly.

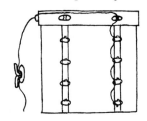

(x) Pleat up blind and leave for a day or two. This helps it hang well when in position.

To hang blind: Fix batten to wall / ceiling (see D I Y / carpentry). If possible conceal screws behind material, or fix from underside of batten. If using a decorative pole, fix the pole's brackets in correct position, check whether horizontal and set in blind.

Cushions

There are two things to consider when you are making cushions. First the cushion pad itself. This you can either make or buy. Then there is the cushion cover. This does not look good for long unless it can easily come off for washing or cleaning.

Making the cushion itself: A choice of fillings is available.
Foam – usually ready-cut into shapes of various sizes and thicknesses. You can cut it yourself; use a saw-edged knife (bread-knife) for thick foam, scissors for thin. Foam shapes still need an inner cover besides an outer one.
Kapok – traditional, but inclined to lump.
Polystyrene beads – often used for giant floor cushions. Does not lump like kapok. But it does compress after a while and may have to be topped up.
Terylene wadding – good because washable.
Feathers – lovely feel, but hard to handle. Close all doors and windows and handle in small fistfuls. Hard to buy but can be taken from elderly eiderdown and pillows.
Shredded foam – most used of all fillings now.
Cut foam – usually off-cuts. Makes springy cushions if carefully stuffed into a strong cover.
Odds and ends – nylon tights or other flimsy materials can be used shredded up very small.

Inner cover: Stout cheap material works well for the inner cover. But feathers need a feather-proof cambric.

The Shape: Virtually any shape or size of cushion can be made. The first step is to make a pattern in brown paper or newspaper so that when you come to make the actual cover, you can cut the material either to the same size (for foam cushions) or slightly smaller (for the rest).
(i) Square or rectangular cushions – just cut two sides the right size and join them. Corners are best rounded off, otherwise they stick up like floppy ears.
(ii) Round or odd-shaped cushions look better with a gusset around them. Boxed cushions and foam cushions need to be covered this way too. Cut the shape in the normal way, plus a straight piece long enough to go the whole way round.
(iii) Bolster cushions are made on the same principle except that the circular ends are small and the gusset is elongated to form the main part of the cushion.

Whatever shape you make you need to leave a piece of seam undone to take the filling. This should be just big enough for you to stuff in handfuls of filling. If you are covering a foam shape, it must allow the whole piece to get inside. Sew up by hand with strong thread and small stitches.

Making the top cover: If you have made your own cushion, use the same patterns for the cover. If you have bought cushions to cover, measure carefully and make the pattern slightly on the small side unless it is made of foam. Cut material carefully to make sure you are making the most of any pattern or border.

Fastenings: As all top covers should be removable, decide on the fastening and put in before sewing up the cover itself:
Zip – choose one a little shorter than the side of the cushion.
Press studs on tape – sew in so that tape and fastenings are inside the cover.

Velcro – a touch and close nylon burr fastening. Sew in as for press studs, tape, or in tiny dabs.

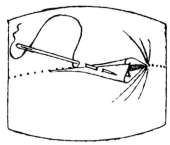

Slip-stitch – this is the cheapest solution. When cover is finished, put it on and slip-stitch into place. Slip needle in and out of alternate sides so opening is closed and invisible. Snag: you have to unpick it every time you remove cushion from cover.

Decorations: You can appliqué all sorts of decorations on to cushions – tapestry, ribbons, lace, braid, cutouts, etc. – or sew your own. These are best completed before you sew the pieces of cover together.

Piping: Optional. Sounds complicated, but isn't really. You need proper pre-shrunk piping cord. If you use ordinary string instead, shrink it by boiling it for five minutes. You also need long strips of bias-cut fabric 1½–2 in./38–51 mm wide. This is folded in half, the string/cord put in the fold and machined in, and finally the whole is fixed and seamed to the edge of the cushion or bedcover or whatever. To get long enough strips of fabric, you need to join them.

Piping

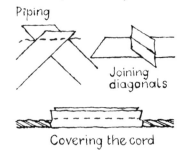

Joining diagonals

Covering the cord

To get really long strips, make a diagonal sleeve from which you can cut a continuous length of bias strip. Take a rectangular strip, say 9 in./228 mm wide, off 48 in./1.2 m fabric. Find diagonal by folding. Take chalk or crayon and mark parallel lines along fabric 1½–2 in./38–51 mm

apart. Join top and bottom together as shown here – right side in. Make sure corner E meets the top of line F. Press open seam. When you start cutting along the chalk line starting at F, you find you get a long bias strip, ready joined.

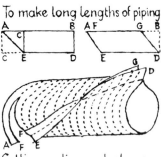

To make long lengths of piping

Cutting a diagonal sleeve

To join piping where two ends meet, cut with an overlap of 1 in./25 mm. Stitch the ends of the string inside the fabric firmly together. Smooth over one end of bias strip. Undo stitching on other strip, fit over, turn in raw edges and seam.

To join piping

Back stitch

Trim cord. Tuck one end of bias strip under the other. Back stitch ends.

Fold bias to cover ends of piping. Stitch down.

To fit piping, stitch along seam line on the right side of one side of the cover so that the seam will be as close in as possible to the string in the piping strip; this is when you need the zipper foot on the sewing machine. Clip edges at corners. Tack on second cover or gusset along same seam line. Machine (zipper foot again!) all thicknesses together. Turn inside out. N.B. – Try not to join the piping strip on a corner. It complicates things!

Cushion corners

Curved corners on square & jumbo cushions

Clip piping. Back stitch below clip.

Squab cushion with tie-ons: As for gusset cushions. Leave opening at back to be slip-stitched. To make the ties, cut two strips of fabric on straight of material about 16 in./406 mm long each. Fold in half lengthways and machine down length and each end. Fold again and pin on wrong side of base of cushion in appropriate place. Machine cover together. Turn right way out, press, insert cushion proper, slip-stitch the gap and tie to chair.

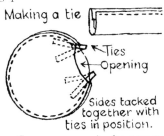

Making a tie

Ties
Opening

Sides tacked together with ties in position.

Square covers: As for square cushions whatever the size. Insert fastening into side seam.

Boxed cushion covers: As for gusset cushions also. If making a square cushion, cut the gusset and join at each corner and match the line of this seam with the corner of the material. Otherwise use a continuous strip. If the cushion has an underside, you can hide the opening by slitting the underneath panel and fitting the fastening in there.

Bolster cushion covers: As for bolster cushions. Fastening is fitted into back seam. Clip circle ends along edges of main fabric so it sits better.

Cushions on wood frame chairs and sofas: Use the same principles as for boxed cushion covers, adjusting the shapes.

Loose covers

Loose covers were traditionally made washable – that was the whole point of having loose covers. The best fabric is still tough hardwearing linen union, which is also probably the easiest to handle. Tweedy upholstery materials are difficult first go. Anything slightly flimsy is a waste of time and effort – it won't wear. If you have doubts about shrinkage, wash and iron before starting to make your covers.

Measuring up and making the pattern: It is always said that

if you measure the height of the back of the chair and multiply it by five, the answer is the number of yards/metres of 48 in./1.2 m material needed. You need to add an extra yard/metre of fabric if you want to be sure to match up and place a pattern correctly. To make a more accurate estimate add all these measurements together:
Back AB+2 in./51 mm seam allowance (sa).
Back-front AF+2 in./51 mm sa +6 in./152 mm tuck-in.
Seat FI+2 in./51 mm+6 in./152 mm tuck-in.
Arms LJ (twice)+2 in./51 mm sa+6 in./152 mm tuck-in.
Arms LM (twice)+2 in./51 mm sa.
Front IN.

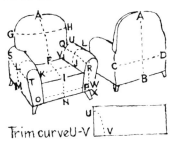

Trim curve U-V

For piping add on ½ yard/460 mm. For valance with box pleated corners add an extra ¾ yard/ 685 mm. For a drawstring, tie-under finish add 4 in./102 mm to the AB, LM and IN measurements making an extra ½ yard/460 mm of material altogether.

You can take detailed measurements and draw the pieces in chalk on the back of the material. However, the beginner is advised to make pattern pieces out of newspaper, carefully marked with the way the grain of the fabric should run. Seam allowance should be generous but consistent; we have allowed 2 in./51 mm per seam.
The following pieces are needed:
Back-panel: AB × CD (add 4 in./ 102 mm) to AB if tie-under required); one piece.
Back-front panel: AF × GH (add 6 in./152 mm to AF for tuck-in); one piece.
Seat panel: FI plus 6 in./152 mm tuck-in × JK plus 12 in./305 mm tuck-in; one piece.
Front panel: IN × OP (add 4 in./ 102 mm to IN if tie-under required); one piece.
Inside arm panel: LJ plus 6 in./

152 mm tuck-in × QR plus 3 in./ 76 mm tuck-in; two pieces.
Outside arm panel: LM × ST (add 4 in./100 mm to LM if tie-under required); two pieces.
Front arm panel: RW × PX (add 4 in./102 mm to RW if tie-under required); two pieces.

Cutting out: Place the patterns on the material, draw round them in chalk and cut the seam allowances. Then you have a chalk guiding line for stitching. Mark the centre of the grain on each piece with big tucking stitches.

Fitting: Mark the centre of the back of the chair also with pins or chalk. Place the back front panel AF/GH in position wrong side up, smooth it over the chair. Pin along the top to hold it while you push the fabric into the back and sides of the seat to work out what tuck-in allowance must be made. Trim off extra fabric to fit curve UV. Take off panel. Fold in half lengthwise and cut the other side to correspond. Do the same with seat panel FI/JK and the two inside arm panels LJ/QR, making sure to trim the panels so that when you join them, they give a smooth tuck in.

Arm & seat panels pinned to meet at V

Tuck in fabric and pin all the panels together.

Lay the back panel AF/GH back on to chair wrong side up again. Tuck it in at the base to hold it firm. Around the top, pin the outside back panel AB/CD into place. If necessary, make darts at the corners to fit. Pin around the sides to the arms. Put inside arm and seat panels into position. Pin all the seams together to meet at V, and tuck in on all sides so that the cover lies smooth and flat. Fit and pin all the rest of the panels together following the lines of the chair.

Piping: This is the time to put the piping in. Prepare lengths of piping as described

under *Cushions.* With the cover still on the chair and wrong side out, remove a few pins at a time and slip the piping in position between the seams. The corded edge will be against the right side of the material, the raw edges all next to each other outside. Pin close to the piped edge.

Remove the cover from the chair by opening the back seams as far as s (see diagram) leaving the piping pinned to the side panel. (This will be where you later put in a row of hooks and eyes or a zip for fastening.)

Stitching: First stitch any darts you had to make – around the top of the back panels, for instance. Then tack around all seams except the side back seam from s, using small firm stitches. Machine along tacking, using zipper/piping foot if you have put in piping.

Turn cover right side out and fit on to chair again. This is the time to adjust seams and make sure that the fit is satisfactory.

For the tie-under drawstring finish: Turn the cover inside out and stitch down the seams at each corner (except the one left open for the fastening) just ¼ in./ 6 mm beyond the bottom of the chair. Secure with strong backstitching. Turn the open edges of the 6 in./152 mm turn-under in at an angle to clear the castors or legs and stitch down. At the raw edge of each panel turn in a long narrow pocket 1 in./25 mm deep (for the tape) and machine, leaving ends open. Thread in tape, starting where the fastening will be.

Drawstring & valance finish

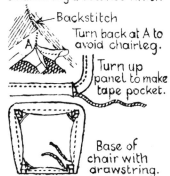

Backstitch
Turn back at A to avoid chairleg.

Turn up panel to make tape pocket.

Base of chair with drawstring.

For a valance with box-pleated corners: With the cover on the chair, mark along the bottom where you want the valance to hang from. If you

want to pipe along the seam, pin the piping on to the cover at this stage. Cut the valance out. You need four strips of material, one for each side of the chair. Add 12 in./305 mm to each length for the pleat. Add about 3 in./76 mm to the depth of each for a hem and top seam allowance. Stitch four lengths together but leave one end open for the fastening. Press seams.

Pin and stitch a 2 in./51 mm hem all round.

Make corner pleats as described for *Bedcovers.* Centre them on to the corner seams of the valance. Pin the valance along the pin or piping line on to the cover while it is still on the chair. Take the cover off the chair and tack and machine the valance into place, leaving the back corner open for the fastening. This will eventually be concealed by the pleat.

Section of valance with kick pleats

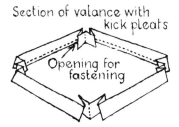

Opening for fastening

Putting in the fastening: Bind both sides of the opening of side back seam from s with a strip of material, sew hooks and eyes or zip or press studs tape.

Finishing off: Trim away excess fabric, clip the corners of the seams and oversew (by hand or machine, or simply trim with pinking scissors). Press thoroughly on wrong side, pressing carefully into every seam. Turn right way round, put on chair. Tuck in the seat and give the cover a final press on the chair. Use a damp cloth over the material. When you come to wash loose covers, it is often a good idea to replace them while still just damp and iron them back into shape on the chair.

Shaped foam chairs

You can buy these or other chairs cut out of foam quite cheaply. Sometimes they have covers, sometimes not, and even if they have you may prefer to use your own material.

Materials required: To cover

11/12 Chair and bed covers/valances

two chairs you will need 6 yds/ 5.5 m of material 48 in./1.2 m wide. It is best to choose a material with enough "give" to mould itself to the contours of the chair. If material is patterned you will need more if you want to match up the pattern carefully. You will also need 10 yds/9 m of 1 in./25 mm tape for tying on the covers.

To make pattern: Place foam chair sideways down on a sheet of thick paper at least 1 yard/1 metre wide. Trace around the outline adding 4 in./102 mm to the base. This piece will eventually fold under the chair to hold the cover in place. When you cut out the shapes, allow about 1 in./25 mm extra for seams.

Measure width AB, also the length CD. Add 8 in./203 mm to the measurement CD to fold under the chair and 1 in./25 mm all round for seams. If you are using printed fabric it is best to go to the bother of making a paper pattern of this rectangle to work out exactly where the print will fall. On a plain fabric you could cut it out without doing this, if you remember to cut along the grain so the cover lies smooth when it is finished.

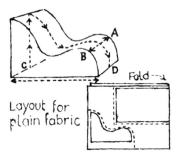

Layout for plain fabric

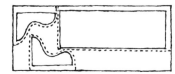

Layout for patterned fabric

Cutting plain fabric: Lay your fabric out double as shown and cut out the side sections. It is essential that the baseline lies as close to the selvedge as possible, otherwise you will not have enough material for the seat panel. Keep fabric folded double; cut seat section using the width AB and half length CD.

Cutting printed/patterned fabric: The material will have to be single thickness in order to get the design to match properly. The extra amount of material needed depends on the pattern repeat and also how fussy you are about matching the sides to the front panel.

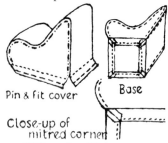

Pin & fit cover
Base
Close-up of mitred corner

Fitting: As with loose covers, you fit the cover on the chair. Place the centre panel of the fabric right side down on the chair, remembering to leave a 6 in./152 mm overlap at both ends. Pin on the side sections and fit round the curve of the chair. Ease out any wrinkles. When it fits perfectly, take it off the chair and tack together. Try it on the chair again, right way round, and adjust. Machine.

Put the cover back on the chair, inside out, to finish off the base. Pin a small double hem all round the raw edges. To mitre corners, at each corner take the extra fabric extending beyond the side seams and fold it back parallel to the lower edge of the chair. Mark along the fold line with pins, and allowing 1 in./25 mm for seam, cut off remainder of corner. Do this at all four corners. Take cover off chair, tack and stitch corners which should be beautifully mitred.

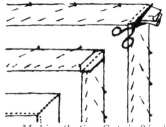

Making the ties: Cut six 8 in./ 203 mm strips and six 1 yard/ metre strips from the tape. Fold the 8 in./203 mm strips into loops and sew two to left-hand underside edge and one to centre edge. Sew the long strips to the corresponding sides, i.e. opposite

the loops. Slot the strips through the loops and tie.

To finish off: Clip the inside seams where the seat curves round the back and front so that the seams lie flat when you put the cover on. Turn corner right way round and press out the seams, using a damp cloth to get a really snug, smooth fit.

Re-upholstering seats

Assuming the seats themselves are in good condition it is very simple to re-cover them. This is true whether the seat is a lift-out panel or whether the cover is tacked directly on to the chair – as with some Victorian and Edwardian dining chairs.

Material: Always choose a firm material – preferably spongeable. It will be stretched and tacked down and therefore not easy to remove for cleaning or washing. As with loose covers, if you choose too flimsy a material which wears out quickly, you have to do the job of re-covering all over again.

Lift-out panel seats

Estimating material: Allow enough material to go round sides of seat panel and tuck under.

Preparation: Remove all extraneous nails and tacks. You can usually do this with pincers or the claw end of a claw hammer. Really awful ones have to be prised off with a hammer and screwdriver. If this removes the original cover, never mind. If the seat is sagging a little take the opportunity to pad it out. Either a thin foam pad cut to shape or some extra Terylene wadding usually does the trick.

Fitting cover: Place the chair seat downwards on the wrong side of the material, which you cut to roughly the right size. Pull the fabric over the back, and at the mid-point in the frame use a light upholstery tack to secure the material to the frame.

Take the material at the front of the seat and pull as hard as you can to fold it over. Tack to centre of front of frame.

Pulling and stretching and working from the centre outwards, tack down the material along the back and along the front of the seat.

Mitre the corners for a smooth fit and tack down sides.

Covering a fixed seat

Estimating material: The best way is to remove the original cover and use it as a measuring and pattern guide. If you have bought the chairs re-upholstered, but only temporarily covered, just allow a generous amount of material per seat. You will also need light upholstery tacks, some flat matching braid and possibly some brass-headed upholstery pins.

Preparation: Remove all old tacks and pins from the woodwork (see *Lift-out panel seats*). Sand down woodwork if necessary. If the seat has sagged a little, pad it out with thin foam cut to shape or with Terylene wadding.

Putting on cover: Start as with panel seats at the centre back. Put material over the chair so that the pattern, if any, falls in the right way, then, with the material slightly taut, hammer into the wood frame at the centre of the back. Put in one more tack each side.

Next tack the material to the front wood frame. In order to do this you must pull and stretch the material from back to front to get it as taut as possible before you hammer in the tacks. Where the chairs have shaped fronts, tack and stretch slowly bit by bit so that the shape of the seat is kept.

Tack down the rest of the back, front and sides and cut material to shape round the legs. Trim off material which hangs below the frame line.

Conceal rough edges and tack heads by putting braid around. First stick it down carefully and then, if you like, anchor it with decorative brass-headed upholstery pins, studded along the length of the braid at regular intervals.

Bedcovers

Some of the nicest bedcovers are the simplest to make. Just hem a piece of your favourite material large enough to cover the bed and throw it over.

But some bedrooms demand something a little more formal. Here is how to set about making a tailored divan cover, covers for single and double beds with bedheads, and covers and valances for beds with duvets.

Divan cover with piping

Measuring up: It is important to get a good fit over bedclothes. So measure over the bedclothes normally used on the bed. It usually looks neatest if the pillows are turned into cushions by day and kept in cushion covers. It is also very difficult to get a crisp tailored look over an eiderdown. The top panel needs to be the length of the bed by the width with a 1 in./25 mm seam allowance all round. For

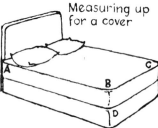

Measuring up for a cover

the neat straight-edged sides with corner kick-pleats, you need two side pieces measuring the length (AB) plus 12 in./305 mm for side seams and pleats, and the height of the bed off the floor plus 1 in./25 mm seam allowance top and bottom; plus two endpieces measuring the width of the bed (BC) plus 12 in./ 305 mm for side seams and pleats and the height of the bed off the floor plus 1 in./25 mm seam allowance top and bottom.

Materials: Uncrushable materials work best. Sides always tend to hang better if lined. Top is also best lined if the material is on the flimsy side.

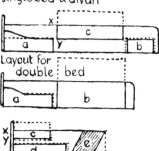

Pattern layout, 48" fabric
Layout for single bed & divan

Layout for double bed

Cutting out: See diagram. You should be able to get a single bed divan cover out of 5½ yds/ 5 m of 48 in./1.2 m material, but this does not allow for piping or matching up a pattern. See cutting plan and remember to get any pattern matching and/or the grain of the fabric going in the right direction. Cut lining similarly.

Join side to end panel

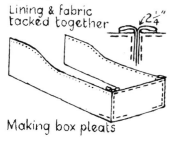

Right sides together, pin & baste fabric to lining

Making up: Join side panels with ½ in./12 mm seams. Join lining panels similarly. Press seams open. Right sides together, tack lining and cover 1 in./25 mm from lower edge. Machine. Turn right side out and press. (This is neater than a conventional hem, but you can hem if you prefer.) Tack top edges together.

Lining & fabric tacked together

Making box pleats

Making box pleats: With the right side of the material facing you, fold 2½ in./63 mm from side and end panels into each corner seam so the fold meets over the centre of the seam. Pin and tack pleats into position.

Piping: Make enough piping to go around the top – see how to make piping sleeve. With the right side of the material facing you, pin piping along the seam line with all the raw edges at the top. Machine piping as close to the cord as possible (use zipper foot).

Join top panel to side pieces: Put right sides together and tack side pieces along seam line. Machine along seam line close to piping (zipper foot again).

To line top panel: Turn in lining 2 in./51 mm all around and press. Lay on wrong side of cover, tack down at edges and then slip-stitch by hand to cover

all raw edges. Press thoroughly. Remove visible tacking.

Single bed with bedhead

This is very similar to the divan cover, except that as this sort of bed is not trying to disguise itself by day, all the bedclothes and pillows are left in place. So in calculating the shape, allowances have to be made for the pillows. As with divan covers, these fall better if lined.

Measuring up: The top panel is measured and cut in the same way as the top panel for a divan, but make sure the length is long enough to reach right over the pillows. The base panel is the same too, but you cut one instead of two.

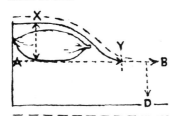

The allowance for the pillows is incorporated in the side panels. Measure AX and AY, as well as AB and BD. Make a paper pattern to exactly these measurements. Above AY incorporate enough fabric to make room for the pillow(s), and shape by eye. To the end of the panel at BD add on the 6 in./152 mm pleat and seam allowance. All round allow 1 in./25 mm for seam or hem turnings.

Cutting out: Follow the cutting pattern given earlier. Make the piping cover (if you are having piping) from spare pieces of material, or get another ¼ yd/ 228 mm to make a sleeve.

Making up: Join side panels with 1 in./25 mm seams. Join lining panels similarly. Press seams open. Right sides together, tack the three fabric and lining panels together 1 in./25 mm in from the lower edge. Machine. Turn right side out and press. (Neater than a hem.) Tack top edges together.

Make box pleats: As for divan cover, but you make only two, one for each of the corners at the bottom of the bed.

Piping: Make enough piping to go round three sides of the bed. Pin piping all along the top

of the side panels and bottom panel. Machine along seam line as close to cord as possible (zipper foot).

Join top panel to sides: Make a 1 in./25 mm double hem at the head end of the top panel by folding down 1 in./25 mm of fabric, pressing, then turning in another 1 in./25 mm and pressing again. Stitch by machine. Pin and tack the top and the side panels, right sides together 1 in./ 25 mm in from the edge. Begin along the end panel and do each side, working up towards the head. Machine stitch together, keeping stitching as close to piping as you can (zipper foot). Take out visible tacks, trim and over-stitch raw edges.

To line top panel: See divan cover lining.

To finish off: Before taking tacking out of corner pleats, steam press them into position. Steam press the rest of the cover on the wrong side, taking care to pull the piped edges taut so the seams all lie smooth and flat.

Double bed with headboard

This will differ from the cover for the single bed only in that you will need more material for the top panel. It is also unlikely that the top panel can come out a single piece of fabric. If you have to join two panels, it is much more professional to cut one in half lengthwise and have a wide centre panel flanked by two smaller side panels.

Cut out as shown. N.B. This guide does not allow for matching pattern.

Duvet covers

Duvets are possible to make up – you can get special kits. But even if you buy your duvet, you can save an appreciable amount of money making your own cover, as well as being able to match it up exactly to your colour scheme.

Material: Choose a light drip-dry material. Polyester/ cotton, Terylene, nylon or light-weight seersucker all work well. If you go for cotton sheeting or a heavier fabric, laundering the cover at home becomes a chore.

Measuring up: The size of the cover has to allow for the duvet settling itself around your body. It needs to be generous, on the

floppy side in fact. Go by bed size and allow 18 in./457 mm more than the bed's width (plus seam allowance) and 6 in./152 mm more than the bed's length plus another 12 in./305 mm if you want a tuck-in top like a pillow-case (the alternative is to make an opening in one side seam and do it up with ties at intervals).

Cutting and making: The problem is that unless you find 72 in./1.8 m material, it is not very easy to cut the cover economically – unless you use some of the narrow bits which will be left over for a valance. Here are some cutting guides for duvet covers with alternative openings.

To make tuck-in flap: Take flap piece and join it, right sides together, to one of the panels. Finish off other end of flap piece by machining down a small hem. Turn right way round and tack to sides of panel.

To join panels: Hem top edge of second panel. Right sides together, seam panels. Some people advise fell seams but pinking or binding with a zigzag stitch is usually quite adequate.

To make side opening: Decide where the opening shall be. Either hem, by machine, along each edge of the opening or press it open and finish with zigzag stitch. Cut tape or ribbon into four (or six) 8 in./203 mm lengths and machine on to sides of opening so that the ribbons face each other at regular intervals on the finished cover. Joining the panels is as above, except that you leave your opening open rather than the top seam.

Valances

These are a good solution when you have a pretty duvet cover which would be lost under a bed cover and which flops nicely over the mattress and sheet, but doesn't quite make it all the way to the floor.

The valance consists of a piece of material which goes under the mattress and on which you mount either a gathered frill which falls to the floor or some crisp box-pleated panels.

The material which goes under the mattress can be cheap sheeting – anything really, as it doesn't show – though if you plan to wash the valance, it is advisable to choose something

with a comparable washing performance to the material for the frill/pleats. You just cut it to the size of the mattress with a small seam allowance – 1 in./25 mm.

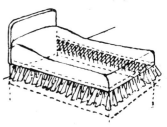

To make a frilled valance: You need to measure only three sides of the bed if the head is back to the wall. You need to make up a panel which is three times as long as this measurement. The depth has to be sufficient to cover the gap between mattress and floor plus a hem of say 2 in./51 mm and a top seam allowance of 1 in./25 mm.

Machine the hem all the way round the base of the frill. Gather along the top – two rows of stitching are better than one. Pull up the gathers so that the panel is the right length and, adjusting as you go, pin to the top panel. Tack and machine on to top. Press.

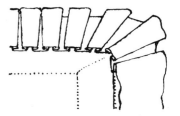

To make a box-pleated valance: You need the same top panel, and similarly a side panel in your nice material which is three times the length of the two sides and one end of the bed. Hem as above.

Either make a card marker or mark the top of the material directly with chalk every 4 in./ 102 mm. Pleat by folding the first and fourth marks behind the second and third and back again (see diagram). Tack each pleat in place. Press. Tack pleated panel on to top panel. Try to arrange: (a) that the pleats conceal seams, (b) that pleats fall centrally at the two corners. Machine on. Press again. Take out tacks.

Bonuses 1/2

Saunas are a recent innovation in Britain. Not until the mid-sixties did the idea start to catch on over here. The Finnish addiction stretches back over a thousand years.

There is now a growing choice of various imported saunas for the home: prefabricated, all sizes, for indoors or out, complete with stoves, stones and birch twigs, accessorized (if you want to go that far) with all sorts of extras like solariums and vibrating machines for setting up a regular home health farm.

How big a sauna and sauna area?

The three stages of a sauna can be described bluntly as: the Sweat, the Scrub and the Rest afterwards.

The Sweat takes place in the sauna itself, a log cabin in which the air is heated to temperatures between 80° and 120°C. This is the prefabricated package most firms are selling.

The size of the sauna you need depends on how many people you envisage using it at once. It is best to be able to lie

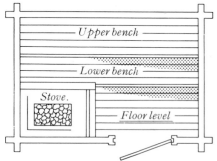

A floor plan of a sauna. The internal dimensions are 6 ft 1 in. × 4 ft 2 in./1.86 m × 1.73 m.

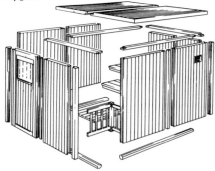

Cross section of a sauna with two benches. The higher you sit, the hotter you get.

down, so at least one bench should be bed length. You can also sit, but allow for calculations of capacity in the brochures packing people in like battery hens. A factor limiting size is that the larger the sauna the more expensive it is to heat.

For the Scrub (and cooling off) every sauna needs its complementary shower. Many people shower first to remove surface dirt. After a spell in the hot sauna, the idea is to wash, if not scrub, away the perspiration and hidden dirt, close the pores again and stimulate circulation. This is when Finns use birch twigs: when scrubbed on the skin they break and the smell they leave is very pleasant. While your body can take a cold shower after a sauna, it is obviously more sensible to have one with a hot supply too so that each person can regulate the temperature to his own taste. You alternate the hot and the cold, the sauna and the shower as often as you like. It is important to remember, before insisting on others sharing your sauna, that a sauna subjects your body to considerable physical stress, a stress which most people, even Finns, are not aware of. Anyone with a heart condition, diabetes, infection, or who has overeaten or has drunk too much, or who is simply doubtful, should check with his doctor before taking one.

The Rest you can take anywhere, but you should plan for somewhere nearby to change and dress and keep the towels. Some people like space to relax nearby as well; others like space for "health activities". After saunas, massage or electronic muscle exercisers have a really fantastic effect.

Solariums

A very pleasant thing to indulge in after a sauna is sun-ray treatment: for this you need a solarium, which is a glorified sun-ray lamp. A solarium suitable for home use usually has three or four lamps which give off both the ultra-violet and infra-red rays, with sophisticated controls, all set in one panel which is fixed to (or hangs from) the ceiling or wall. It needs nothing more elaborate electrically than a power point, and has a good "exposure field" (6 ft 6 in. × 5 ft/2 m × 1.5 m). But, of course, as with all sun-ray treatment, each individual has to time the exposure carefully.

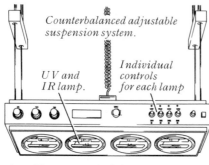

A ceiling-mounted Solarium with four individually switched lamps.

Indoors or outside?

Most prefabricated saunas are portable, easily erected cabins designed to be fitted inside a room, garage or outhouse.

A free-standing indoor sauna.

There are more elaborate saunas, more expensive, of course, designed as free-standing garden houses. If you have a swimming pool, and site your sauna beside it, you have the choice of taking a shower or plunging into the pool, in which case you can either buy the complete sauna/shower/changing house, or incorporate the sauna and shower into the existing changing/storage place.

Outdoor sauna with traditional roof.

Planning permission

If you are planning a new outside sauna, you need planning permission: the importers will supply plans for this. If the local Valuation Officer gets to know, which he does from the planning application, it is likely that the rateable value of your house will be put up. However, if you put a portable sauna indoors or inside an existing building, you don't need planning permission.

The structure

You can make your own sauna out of ordinary tongued-and-grooved pine boarding, but the Finnish logs are specially kiln-dried and treated so that the structure remains firm for years and the wood itself "breathes". This is important since the body stands the high temperature of a sauna only because the heat is dry not humid. Any humidity (caused by wet bodies or the "heat shock" from splashing water on the stove) is immediately absorbed.

The sauna's ceiling is similar to the walls, but insulated to keep the heat in. Indoor saunas tend to stand on existing floors with duckboards over walking areas. Outdoor saunas need a level concrete base.

The heat source

The air is heated by a small stove, of which there are several to choose from. Prices of saunas usually include and specify a stove. Most run on electricity but one runs on gas. Any stove using more than 3 kW needs its own circuit with its own fuse: most are between 5 and 10 kW. Because of the proximity of water to the sauna, it is very important to get the wiring done by a qualified electrician. He can also advise you if your household supply can take the extra load – it nearly always can. If the sauna is outdoors, it will need an underground 4 mm² mineral-insulated cable laid 18 in./457 mm underground and special earthing arrangements.

A thermostatically controlled sauna stove with periodotite stones.

In the sauna itself, the stove should certainly have a guard rail to prevent accidental touching.

On top of the stove lie the special peridotite stones. To get an extra "heat shock" a little water is ladled on to these from time to time – it hisses into steam at once which is absorbed by the dry wood walls. Although this lowers the actual temperature, you feel an extra wave of heat wash over you.

Extras

Thermostatic control of the heat is essential. You need to be able to see and set the temperature while in the sauna. A thermostat is usually part of the package. So are the wooden pail and ladle to hold the water for the "heat shock". They, like all accessories, have to be wood to withstand the extreme heat.

Water is usually classified into six groups: soft, moderately soft, slightly hard, moderately hard, hard and very hard. The degree of hardness depends on the amount of dissolved calcium and magnesium in the water. The more calcium and magnesium, the harder the water. Your Water Board will tell you how hard the water is in your area.

How does it affect you?

Very soft water, as occurs in parts of Central Scotland, makes marvellous lather for washing and laundry purposes, but you may find that rinsing takes a long time and a lot of water. The water doesn't taste particularly interesting either.

Hard water, on the other hand, can have quite a noticeable effect on washing, laundry, hair and skin. You will use more soap and detergent in a hard water area than you will in an area with softer water to obtain the same amount of lather. Hard water also produces scum – scum round baths and basins, and white deposits on anything washed in a dish-washer. Hard water is also responsible for scale in boilers, hot water pipes, washing machines, and, of course, kettles. Scale is caused by hard water being heated, which turns the bicarbonates in the water into chalk. As far as kettles are concerned, the effect is ugly but harmless and can be removed.

Don't worry that your central heating pipes will clog up; the same water goes round and round in the pipes and once the chalk has dropped, no more is formed.

Hot-water pipes supplying water to taps are a problem, as obviously the water flow is continually adding new deposits to the scale in the pipes. The build-up should not block the pipes completely, but it may narrow them and if it does, your fuel costs may rise. If your bills start rising inexplicably you will know there is something wrong, otherwise don't worry.

Old-fashioned boilers and washing machines can be descaled professionally; if you are considering changing to central heating and your boiler gets very scaled up, bear this in mind and think about mains water-softeners at the same time.

What can you do with hard water?

There are three main solutions to the problem: mains water-softening units, portable units, chemicals.

Mains water-softening units

All water-softening units, mains or portable, function on the same basis. That is, they immobilize the hard minerals by passing the water through a bed of resin. This contains sodium, which absorbs all the calcium and magnesium in the water until the sodium is saturated. The process is then regenerated by adding household salt to the unit which flushes out the deposits of calcium and magnesium. The sodium-impregnated resin is then ready for use again.

If you install a mains water-softener, it will be plumbed into your system and will then soften as much water as you want, automatically. The length of time before regeneration is necessary will depend on the hardness of your water, and the size of unit used. You should exclude your drinking water tap from the system as, apart from the fact that it is the minerals in water that give it its flavour, soft water tends to pick up metal from pipes – copper, iron, *lead* – more readily than hard water. If it is not possible to bypass the drinking water tap, do let the water run for a few minutes before drinking it.

The cost of mains units varies very considerably and the units themselves fall into three categories: manual, semi-automatic, fully automatic.

Manual: These units are not very popular as they have to be regenerated by hand each time the resin becomes saturated. The water supply to the softener has to be turned off, a measured amount of salt tipped in to clear the resin, then water run through to clear the salt. This process takes about one and a half hours – during which time the water will run hard – and requires almost constant attention, a lot of dial setting and fiddling about with controls. However, some manual units are less expensive than some semi-automatic ones. They have an average capacity of 1,500 gallons/6,820 litres before regeneration is necessary.

Semi-automatic: The only thing the user has to do is to initiate the regeneration process by setting a time-switch. This will operate the by-pass valves and controls automatically. The water during this time will, of course, run hard as the supply is bypassing the softener; but if you set the timer so that the whole process goes on at night, no one will be the wiser. Average capacity is under 1,000 gallons/4,546 litres.

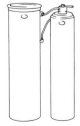

Semi-automatic unit with a brine tank which holds sufficient salt for 8 regenerations.

Both semi-automatic and fully-automatic units measure out the amount of salt they need – about 5–6 lb/2½ kg – from a salt storage tank which can hold anything from 50 to 200 lb/22 to 90 kg, and which would need topping up every few months. The salt, or brine, tank is often a separate unit connected to the resin tank by a short pipe. More compact models have a non-corroding salt reservoir built in.

Fully automatic: Once you have set the controls according to your requirements, it does the rest by itself. An automatic time-switch will initiate regeneration, usually in the early hours of the morning. All you have to do is top up the salt level from time to time. Average capacity – less than 1,000 gallons/4,546 litres.

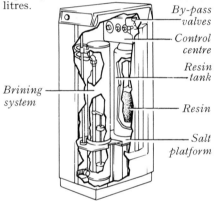

Automatic water softener with salt tank.

Your choice should be governed not only by cost but by the amount of water you intend to use per day, and the hardness of the water. These factors will determine the frequency with which your unit will need to be regenerated, which, because it can be a time-consuming and sometimes awkward business, is well worth considering. As a rough guide, 50 gallons per person per day is an average consumption. Work that out on a weekly basis and compare it with the capacity of each type of softener. The hardness of the water in your area will also influence your choice, because the harder the water, the smaller the capacity of the unit before regeneration is necessary.

Installation

In budgeting for a mains unit of any type, don't forget to include the charge for plumbing it into your water system. A good place to install a water softener is beside the tank, in the attic, but check with your local Water Board first to find out whether their regulations permit you to bypass the drinking water taps on this level or not. Some regulations insist that you should be able to drink from the cold

water taps upstairs as well as downstairs, and this may make a difference to where you install your unit.

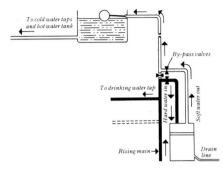

A typical installation showing by-pass system and drinking water outlet.

Portable units

The function of these units is identical to that of the mains installed units, but the portable unit is itself attached to the tap and softens the water as it flows out. If you are only really interested in soft water for, say, rinsing your hair, or doing the laundry once a week, then these units are quite adequate, but if you want all your water, or most of it, softened, a mains unit is better.

A portable water softener that fits any tap.

Chemicals

The third method of softening your water is to use additives to water you have already run, or are in the process of running – bath water, for example. The cheapest of these methods is washing soda, but it does make the water quite alkaline and may irritate your skin. There are other chemical softeners on the market which can be added to washing machines and dish-washing machines as well as bath water, and as long as you use these in the recommended quantities they will function adequately. (If you are using them for the first time to wash clothes, remember not to use as much soap powder as you normally do, or you will find it difficult to get the suds out.)

The drawbacks of this arrangement are obvious, but it is certainly fairly cheap in the short term, particularly if you only occasionally want soft water.

A house is bought more with the heart than with the bank balance. Agreed, that's true of so many things we buy. But most of these heart-stimulated purchases are small extravagances and not likely to break our banks or ruin our lives.

A house is the major investment in the lives of most people. A house is the one sure way open to most Britishers of turning their income into capital – of buying, out of their weekly earnings, an asset for the future, for their retirement,

Yet, nine times out of ten, people buy houses because they like the garden, the main bedroom or because there is a porch with roses round it, and lose sight of their proper priorities, like how many rooms they really need.

The size of your family will, of course, determine this, and the age of the children decides whether you want to live near a primary school, a secondary school, or any other kind of school. If they have to be chauffeured, long drives to and from school (remembering to multiply the mileage by four even if they stay for school lunch) are going to take a devil of a slice out of any housewife's day. And don't assume that the nearest place on the map is the quickest to get to. A fast 50-mile rail service may be better than a slow 25-mile one. But there are other, less obvious, points to check off. Think about your life style. So you loathe gardening? Then don't fall for a house if the garden can't be turned into a sweep-clean, paved patio or a near-meadow with some simply pruned shrubs. Watch it – gardens can be slavery unless they're your favourite hobby.

Nearly all home-hunting starts with the estate agent. First, use only those agents who have letters after their names. The letters mean that the agents belong to professional bodies that run schemes to protect initial, securing deposits paid by buyers – and we have all read those sad stories of trusting people who paid their deposits to some moonlighter.

So look for any of the following sets of letters. There are lots of associations, so here goes: MNAEA (Member of the National Association of Estate Agents); FRICS; ARICS; FIAS; AIAS; FSVA; ASVA; FRVA; ARVA; FFAS; AFAS; FFS; AFS; FNAEA; and ANAEA. If you find no letters after the estate agents' names, refuse to deal and don't pay any deposits.

They should send you lists of houses. But, since the palmy days when buyers queued up for property, a great many estate agents have become just plain lazy. So phone them every day to see if anything new has come onto their books. Buy local newspapers. Look up property advertisements in national and local papers (not forgetting that some vendors use the Personal columns instead). Just keep working at it and don't trust your agent to send you lists promptly.

If you see a house, or flat, and your spouse or whoever else might be involved in the purchase isn't there to corroborate, there's no harm in putting down a small deposit right away. Get a receipt for it if you pay cash and be sure one is sent on to you even if you pay by cheque. You can always change your mind on the following Saturday if those who are going to live with you hate the place. However, if you buy at auction – and more and more houses are bought in this way – you sign a binding contract on the spot.

There was a time when a buyer paid a deposit and automatically secured an option to purchase subject to contract. That meant that nobody else would get his house before contracts were exchanged, the acceptance of a price and a deposit being an implicit agreement to sell at that price. This no longer applies. Both buyers and sellers often change their minds before exchange of contracts. So we advise sellers to go on showing round prospective buyers and building up a waiting list while a house is under offer; just as we advise purchasers that they go on looking round for their second-best dream even after their offer for the dream home has actually been accepted.

Do have *another* cool, critical look at the house:

Is the place safe or are there danger traps for you, elderly relations or young children – tiny half landings, odd steps?

Can you get all your family together to eat? It sounds obvious but we have a friend whose only eating place is the kitchen and the family has to eat in relays.

Is the hot-water tank large enough for at least two baths running?

Is there somewhere to park the car? Or the pram? Or the bicycles, which never beautify the front hall?

Is there enough light in all the rooms, or can you enlarge the windows so that there is? Can they be easily cleaned?

Can you actually get furniture up those stairs or through an upstairs window without taking it all apart?

Do you own a lot of large furniture which will never fit into the small rooms of that newly-converted terrace house you like? And, if so, can you afford to get rid of the old stuff and start again? If you can, then for goodness' sake measure up the house you fall for very carefully, and before you start buying the new furniture.

Is the house sound? A surveyor will often tell you what is wrong with the place, but do specify that you want a thorough survey. If you are raising a mortgage, as most of us do, the mortgage company will insist on its own surveyor. You may be happy to accept his survey rather than pay for an extra one of your own. But remember that he is really studying the house to discover whether it is worth what you plan to borrow. His survey goes to the mortgage company and you will not see the details. The mortgage company will only tell you the salient points if they want things put right within a specified, limited period after lending you the money. Say, for instance, that a lovely old chimneybreast is damp. The mortgage company will want any vital restructuring to correct that. But you might then go back to the vendor and say "Hey, that chimney-breast needs work. What about cutting the price?" You would probably get a reduction to meet you halfway especially at times when houses are almost a glut on the market and vendors only too glad to conclude a deal. However, you'll be very unlikely to get any concessions when there is a seller's market: at times when people are up to the old gazumping tricks, arguing about a hundred or two to correct structural defects is going to lose you the house you covet.

If you are borrowing a high percentage of the purchase price, you might settle for the building society's survey report, since it will be careful to protect its own investment and is thereby more or less automatically protecting yours. If risking your own money to any great extent, get your own surveyor and make sure he is a member of either the Royal Institution of Chartered Surveyors or the Incorporated Society of Surveyors and Valuers (see *Useful Addresses*). Should the house be needing a lot of structural repair and alteration, you will need an architect and can probably dispense with your own surveyor, using the man or woman from the building society and your architect (unless the architect feels a survey is essential).

The surveyor might recommend other tests, like a drains test by a local builder. Get it done. Minor mistakes can prove expensive. Replacing a damaged air-brick can cost less than plastering it over or leaving it, which can lead to creeping damp that will ruin a whole chimney-breast or slab of wall. If you get a frightening survey report, showing that the cistern is askew and may topple; that damp is getting in through many cracks; that the damp course is defective; or that gutters need replacing and that gables need reinforcement or securer fixing, don't despair. Get a local builder to estimate for putting all these things right. He may charge for the estimate unless he is sure of getting the contract, but it may be worth it. If he finds that it is going to

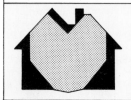 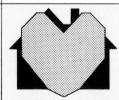 

cost a certain amount to put everything right, negotiate, even though the deposit is paid, for a reduction of that amount on the price of the house. You should get it, or nearly all of it. If you don't, give up and start house-hunting all over again – or sigh and pay up because you love and want the place whatever its condition.

Falling in love with the house and making the offer are only the beginning. After that, the real work starts and the paying begins. First, as soon as your offer is accepted by the seller, you pay the deposit. You should hand over 10 per cent of the full purchase price, but many estate agents, sellers and solicitors will accept a smaller deposit in earnest of intent to conclude the sale. Don't argue if you are asked for more, because you cannot win.

Even when the deposit is paid you are still not committed to the house. But do make absolutely sure that any papers you sign, or letters you write (or get written on your behalf) carry the phrase "subject to survey and contract". That is important even after a first survey. You may need another – it is not unheard of – if you plan to convert, modernize or something of that kind. The homework still has to be done – like finding out whether a motorway is scheduled to run through the dining room or a factory due to be built next door. Leave yourself an exit, just in case. Try, too, to get a written agreement from the vendor that the house is yours subject to contract, because he is no more bound to go ahead with the sale until after signed contracts are exchanged than you are. You may not succeed in getting a binding agreement to sell, but try.

If you are buying a freehold property, don't just assume that you will be free to do what you like there. Find out if there are any covenants attached to the land, the house, or sale of some of the land.

A leasehold property involves a contract between the leaseholder and the freeholder, the latter being the person or

company owning the land on which the house stands. Flats are almost always leasehold, and, by the way, we would not recommend buying a "freehold" flat. The laws are too complicated to make such a title as secure as it sounds, and you may be paying a bit of a premium for a freehold that isn't a perfect freehold. So go for a long lease.

Whether it's a house or a flat, ask to see the terms of the lease. You will find most of them pretty standard documents. You are not really likely to object to clauses forbidding you to run the place as a brothel. But you may jib at being forbidden to keep dogs, cats, any furred or feathered pets or even lodgers. You may want to hang out the washing in the garden and find that you're not allowed to do that. Quite a number of pretty ordinary pursuits may be banned.

If your coveted house is old, check on the local authority's attitude to grants for modernization and improvement. If the home is new, make sure it is registered with the National House-Builders' Registration Council. This does not guarantee you a perfect house. But it does entitle you to guaranteed minimum specifications; it protects your common law rights; and it gives you a ten-year guarantee that defects will be put right without eroding your bank balance. There are some other benefits, so this registration is worth having.

Now you should be starting on the legal work. You might do your own conveyancing. It is straightforward as long as your property is registered. But there's a wide gap between "straightforward" and "simple". Simple, it is not. It is decidedly complex, handling your own legal affairs. It is also hard work, involving carbon copies, files and many formidable forms. The money you save varies – solicitors no longer work on fixed charges geared to the value of the property. They charge according to the complications and time involved. Some expensive property can be conveyed

cheaply. Undertaking your own legal work may not save you very much money, and might land you in some expensive mistakes. If determined, get a book by the Consumers' Association called "The Legal Side of Buying a House". The figures will be out of date as money values and interest change, but the procedure guide is sound and clear.

Even when you hire a solicitor, keep your eyes on what he is doing and whether that lovely meadow next door is the projected site of an ugly housing or commercial development (there is a lot to be said for knowing the worst about your neighbouring buildings rather than moving to open spaces which may be turned into eye-sores).

Your solicitor can be checked up on. Make a visit to the local planning offices (usually at the Town Hall) and find out for yourself if anything is likely to happen near your future home.

Your solicitor will also work with the building society's solicitor. Now there are three ways of finding this building society. One is via the estate agent; another via the solicitor; and a third via a mortgage broker, who may be anyone from the estate agent to a bank to a specialist firm that advertises its services. Anyone can set up as a mortgage broker, so don't just sit down and study the yellow pages. Find a man with qualified rights to broke well, to both your advantages. He should belong to a reputable association (see our *Useful Addresses*).

If you are a first-time buyer, and have no knowledge of nor links with any building society or mortgage company, it is worth doing a little comparative shopping. Don't ask each of – say – three building societies for a survey and detailed offer. That's expensive. But get the terms from three or four societies or companies and weigh up the pros and cons. The finances will probably be much the same in each case. But the terms governing early repayment or death or some such eventuality may differ. A

broker will, or should, get the best deal for you. It will be tailored to your present income and to your prospects. The bigger companies, who advertise their mortgage broking services, usually have reputations to protect and are worth consulting. They charge no fees, getting their payment out of commission from insurance companies involved in mortgages. When employing individual mortgage brokers, be sure they belong to the Corporation of Mortgage and Finance Brokers; the Association of Insurance Brokers; or the Corporation of Insurance Brokers.

Before deciding just how much you need to borrow on a mortgage, work out exactly how much of your spare cash is going to be burned up by the mere mechanics of buying the house. The cost of it is one thing. The legal fees go on top of that; so does the stamp duty. You pay $\frac{1}{2}$ per cent of the total purchase price on houses costing between £11,000 and £15,000, and one per cent on houses of above £15,000. And do remember the duty is due on the entire purchase price, not just on the chunk that brings the house into the dutiable category.

You are also liable for the mortgage company's legal costs, although these are more often than not built into the loan and payable by instalments, as it were. Vendors pay the agents' commissions.

Having added up all that you pay for, throwing in the cost of new furniture, curtains, carpets and repairs, and the actual cost of moving, you will now have some idea of what you can afford as the actual deposit. Shave off 5 per cent for contingencies and try to borrow the rest.

What you can borrow depends on what you earn – or what you both earn if you are borrowing from one of those enlightened firms which take the earnings of husband and wife into account. Normally, you may borrow up to three times your annual salary. We must stress "normally", because since interest and mortgage rates started soaring, many lenders limit to twice or $2\frac{1}{2}$ times the

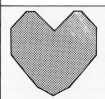 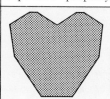 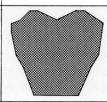 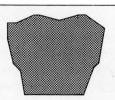

  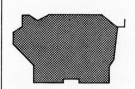 

salary of the applicant. The reason is simple. They are not as concerned with what you borrow as with your ability to pay it back. They may be more lenient if the wife is past child-bearing age and therefore likely to hold her job. They will still probably cut her income by a notional 30 per cent or so.

If you are buying a new house, one of many in a residential development by a building company, you may find pre-fabricated mortgages waiting for you and the whole thing becomes simple and relatively cheap. Their solicitors may act on your behalf, too, saving you quite a lot of trouble as well as a few pounds.

If you are buying an old house, or any property that is rather unusual, possibly even somewhat unsaleable, then you may be better off trying either local – often small – building societies with local knowledge, or the local council.

The council will often only lend if you can show that you've tried normal channels like building societies and insurance companies but failed to get a loan. If a council lends, it often takes a relaxed view of the whole project. Councils want their locales kept attractive and in good repair. They regard loans for house purchase as part of their rehousing plans. They tend to be rather more generous about valuing properties – building society surveyors are notoriously safe and even pessimistic.

A council will often lend 90 per cent or even more. It will often give priority to people with young children or to expectant parents. And it usually lends for long periods. While a building society will rarely lend for longer than 25 years – although 30 years is possible if you are young enough – a council will consider loans spread over 35 and 40 years. They want the loan insured, naturally. At one time, many council loans did tend to cost more than those of building societies but that is no longer true, and some are even cheaper now. Councils are not restrictive about earnings and often help

those with lower incomes, but their approval take longer. It's a good idea to apply to councils between January and March. They have to use up all their funds by March and they may find they have plenty of unexpected cash left.

And now to the building societies. They deal mainly in two basic categories of mortgage. There is the *standing mortgage*, whereby the sum owing is the same all through the repayment period. There is, in other words, no repayment of capital over the years, but only of interest on the loan. The loan is eventually paid off by an endowment policy (which also carries cover on the life of the mortgagee). Along with the interest repayment, there-fore, you are buying insurance and so paying out insurance premiums. The premiums and interest together will probably involve a rather higher monthly outlay. For example, a repaying mort-gage (described later) might cost you £90 a month gross. On the same size loan, you would be paying out about £104 a month gross for the standing mortgage covered by insurance. But you do get tax rebates on the insurance premiums, though to a lesser degree than on the interest.

Once you have got the net figures, after tax, you would find that the differ-ence lessens and the insured mortgage costs about £76.50 a month as against £74 with a repayment mortgage. The insur-ance scheme is, for most people, the wisest course: trouble-free, giving abso-lute security and building up some surrender value on the policy, which could be a great help in the event of en-forced, premature selling for some un-foreseen reason. If your income can run to buying a with-profits policy (which would add approximately £10 to £12 a month to your net payments), then you have a hedge against inflation and a lump sum share of the company's profits to come back into your pocket at the end of the mortgage-insurance term. Incident-ally, the examples given here have to be no more than approximate guides. The

age, state of health and prospects of the borrower or the insured can change them, as can the term of the loan. So the object is to give comparative examples of cost.

The *repayment mortgage* is the more normal type of mortgage. This is fixed up entirely through a building society and the loan is paid off, along with the interest, over the agreed term of 15, 20 or 25 years. At first the capital is being paid off only a little by little and most of the monthly payment is interest. Later, the capital begins to be reduced faster. Now there is a drawback to this kind of loan. The tax relief due on the interest is due *only* on the interest, without relation to outstanding capital. So, during the early years, there is a substantial element of tax relief, possibly when your income is too low for you to derive the fullest ad-vantage from such a benefit. As time goes by and the interest becomes smaller on the reducing capital, so does the tax relief. This is probably just the time that you could do with extra tax relief on your rising income. With the standing mort-gage, the interest and the tax relief are constant. This factor distorts a little the samples of figures given in the preceding paragraph and adds weight to the theory that a standing, insured mortgage may be the best for you.

You pay your mortgage interest gross; but you get a certificate for your accountant or tax inspector and you are then coded, or taxed if not on PAYE, to take account of the tax relief due to you. Your total interest is tax free. So, if you are paying tax at standard rate of 30 per cent, you are paying out only 67p for every £1 of mortgage interest you owe. If you are taxed at higher rates, your benefit is correspondingly greater.

Building societies are non-profit-making concerns. That doesn't mean that all their funds are available to lend, since they do pay their staffs and run a good many branch offices. But, after expenses, their funds are available for lending. They get the money from people

who put it on deposit with them, and deposits of this kind are likely to stay fairly low as long as there are so many rival schemes to tempt away savers.

If you happen to be paying less than the standard rate of tax, ask about an option mortgage. Under this scheme, you pay your interest net of tax, not gross. The result is that you are paying what a standard-rate taxpayer would pay on the same loan. Once the option mortgage has been in force for five years, the holder can change to an ordinary mortgage if his income has gone up. All mortgages, whether option or repayment, should be covered by some form of insurance so that heirs are not forced to sell the house to pay debts. The cheapest cover is whole-life, without an endowment. This pays out only in the event of death. Premiums add to the cost of the repay-ment mortgage as we have already shown it – by the cost of the premiums. Which brings us back to square one. Do consider a standing, insured mortgage scheme first and foremost.

If building societies and insurance companies fail, there is a very remote chance that your solicitor might know someone who will lend on a private mortgage contract. But, in these high-interest days, the chances are virtually nil and the cost will probably be high.

What you repay on what you borrow hardly bears thinking about. At 11½ per cent mortgage rates, you repay £25,900 gross over 20 years on a loan of £10,000. Net after standard-rate tax, that is £20,600. Appalling? Maybe. But, if you had the £10,000 cash you would expect to turn it into more than £20,600 over 20 years. A mortgage is still superb value, high interest notwithstanding. At 12 per cent for interest, the actual net interest rate to a borrower is only 8 per cent if he or she pays tax at standard 33 per cent. At higher tax rates, the interest becomes an actual 6 per cent or less. To someone in the top tax bracket, the interest is a net 25 per cent.

 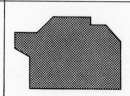  

   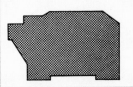

Not only is the interest low by comparison with industry which is now having to buy its loans at around 15 to 16 per cent, but you are buying a growing asset. House values may not continue to spiral as they have done in the past. But they are certainly likely to appreciate by more than 8.4 per cent a year. So, at low interest, you have a worthwhile, tax-free capital gain – provided it is your owner-occupied property. Second or third homes or letting property, as well as business property, are subject to capital gains tax. If a company could make its equity grow as house-owners can, they would think themselves lucky.

While on the subject of borrowing, don't think that building societies have noticeably relaxed their attitudes towards women. Some are inclined to think of women as continuing and reliable wage earners and to lend to women on their own. Most are still hesitant. Mortgage brokers may be of some help in pinpointing the few liberated societies.

There is a prevalent myth about how mortgages are heavily penalized for paying off their mortgages before the end of the agreed term. First, do think about paying off. If you are still earning and paying tax, it may pay you to use the money with which you would pay your mortgage debt for some other investment, and to continue with your mortgage payments. That is for you to work out. But never rush to repay.

Most agreements allow the mortgagee to pay all or part of the debt before time – which would be the case if the mortgagee wanted to sell and move to another house, for example. In such cases, the building society usually asks for three months' interest – that is the only penalty. It is not a harsh one. As soon as the contracts are exchanged, the seller can give notice to his building society. Completion of the sale will probably take a further six weeks. So, in the end, the penalty is reduced to a mere six weeks' interest. If the mortgage is a repayment

one, you could pay off as much as possible when you have the money and the wish to do so, but not quite all. Interest will be due only on the debt still outstanding after that part-repayment, and it will have been reduced to a small sum. So the three months' penalty will be negligible. Some societies block this loophole, reasonably enough. Some don't bother. The three months penalty clause can't be argued with since the original contract was to borrow for an agreed term. The society may not always enforce it, or may come to a compromise agreement. They are for the most part very humane bodies.

Under many mortgage agreements, you will be able to sub-let. But there are societies who ban it, so, again, look out for such a clause in the contract of offer from the building society. In fact, never sign anything without reading every word, even if it looks like a trustworthy, printed document that has obviously been signed by many others. The terms may not be bad (though they could be). But they may not suit you or your plans. Get your solicitor to explain anything that seems complex and don't be shy to ask him searching questions.

If you do let the house, it will become subject to capital gains tax when you sell. If you let part of it – say one room – you will be subject to capital gains tax on the proportionate sum represented by that room. You do not actually have to sell your existing home before buying another. There is some leeway for overlapping, but always establish your movements with the accountant or tax inspector as you make them. Or keep clear records.

The old business arises of who, in any kind of partnership, should own the house. If a wife is much younger or poorer than her husband, then it does make sense for the house to be in her name, even though he may be the mortgagee. That way, she pays no estate duty on it if he dies first. If both are much the same

age, then joint ownership is a good idea. Each person may leave his or her spouse £15,000 in property and £15,000 in cash or securities or other investments free of estate duty. But many houses are worth in excess of £50,000 these days, which might leave a surviving spouse lumbered with having to sell the home to meet duty (which is small in the lower financial ranges). You can't really legislate for who might get killed in air or car crashes, so the age rule is the sensible one. Solicitors ought to be consulted about estate duty problems. For example, you can leave the surviving spouse a life interest in the house, with the actual house to a son or daughter. That means she or he lives on rent free, and the offspring gets no benefit until the death of the surviving spouse. Then the offspring pays duty on the benefit of the house.

Briefly, we'd like to mention that elderly people can raise money on their homes which gives them an annuity to allow them to afford to stay on without having the upset of finding a new house. An insurance company will lend up to 80 per cent of the value of the house (assuming it to be fully paid for). The old man or the old lady pays interest on the mortgage, but gets a very beneficial annuity. (We do suggest a capital-protected annuity in case the older person is unlucky enough to die shortly afterwards.) Finally, the loan is deducted from the estate upon death. The insurance company doesn't just grab the house. It asks the heirs either for the money owing or asks them to sell the house to pay for it. There are many widows, and it could be true of widowers, who hate the idea of moving but cannot afford to live on in the old place, this is the scheme for them.

Housing groups are very much more prevalent than you might imagine. They start in all sorts of ways. Young, middle-aged or elderly people of like mind get together to build on a parcel of land, or to convert a London home or a country home into flats and/or maisonettes. The

end product for each member is cheaper than the cost of buying an ordinary house and it may soon be the only way for young people to acquire their first homes. You can obtain block mortgages, usually from your local council. You can get tax reliefs. You can have a say in the design, if you are literally in on the ground floor. But you never entirely own your own place and you do not get the whole profit on it when you sell because you are selling shares in a *project*.

You do, of course, get back your original deposit as well. There are pros – and many cons. But there are benefits for the broke or the lonely. We recommend careful reading of "Housing Associations", published by the Department of the Environment, Welsh Office (although it covers all of Great Britain). The book costs 80p from any of HM Stationery Offices, and some bookshops – but very few. Anyway, if you are thinking of a housing group, you first register with the Registrar of Friendly Societies. That affiliates to the National Federation of Housing Societies. And, if you still want to go ahead, you'll get all the help and advice you need from there, plus possible suggestions of where there might be building land, some associations now in train but with vacancies, etc.

There is one last thing. A number of people exist today who will offer to find properties for you at either a fixed fee or on a commission basis. In our experience, some of these people or agents are well worth commissioning but others produce contracts which give them some money for producing a few unsuitable places for you to see after which they disappear. Watch such arrangements. And, if you do hire an estate agent to hunt for a house for you, watch him too – not because he isn't honest, but because he may often be too busy to remember you unless you nag him.

And now, provided you think your bank balance can stand it, take your heart house-hunting.

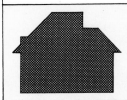   

Terence Conran, who has compiled this book, also runs the Habitat chain of stores in the United Kingdom and in France. Many of the things illustrated in these pages can be found in the stores, so we give you a list of their addresses:

Birmingham
41/43 New St Shopping Centre

Bolton
Ridgeway Gates, Knowsley St

Bournemouth
Parkway House, Avenue Rd

Brighton
11 Churchill Square
Western Road

Bristol (Clifton Heights)
Triangle West BS8 1ES

Bromley
12 Westmoreland Place
High Street

Cheltenham
108/110 The Promenade

Croydon
1111/1114 Whitgift Centre

Glasgow
140/160 Bothwell Road

Guildford
4/6 North Street

Kingston
14 Eden Walk

Leicester
13 Belgrave Gate

Liverpool
17/21 Dawson Way
St John's Centre

London
156 Tottenham Court Road
W1P 9LA
206/222 King's Road SW3 5XP

Manchester
14 John Dalton Street

Nottingham
144/147 Victoria Centre

Romford
The Market Place

Wallingford
Hithercroft Road

Watford
18 Queen's Road

York
26 High Ousegate

France
Tour Montparnasse
17 Rue de l'Arrivée Paris 75 015
La Maison Blanche RN13
Orgeval 18630
Centre Commercial Les Ulis 2
Burs-Orsay 91440

General

Advertising Standards Authority, 1 Bell Yard, London WC2 2JX, exist to endorse the code of practice of the advertising industry. Complaints should be made in writing, and should be accompanied by a copy of the advertisement, if possible.

Ancient Monuments Board for England, Sanctuary Buildings, Great Smith Street, London SW1, and the Ancient Monuments Society, 11 Alexander Street, London W2, are concerned with the preservation of ancient buildings.

Architectural Association, 34 Bedford Square, London WC1, will supply lists of its members willing to undertake domestic work.

Association of Flooring Contractors, 47 Great Russell Street, London WC1B 3PA, will recommend floor layers.

Association of Insurance Brokers, Craven House, Kingsway, London WC2 6PF, will put you in touch with insurance brokers in your district.

Beck & Pollitzer Ltd, Tower Bridge House, Tower Bridge, London SE1, specialize in overseas removals and packing.

British Ceramic Tile Council, Federation House, Stoke-on-Trent, will give addresses of recommended tilers.

British Colour Council, 21B Goodge Street, London W1P 2BN, advise on colours for paints, baths and a wide range of consumer goods.

British Woodwork Manufacturers' Association, Carrington House, 130 Regent Street, London W1, deal with finished woodwork.

British Waterworks Association, 104a Park Street, London W1, is the central body which can tell you all about local regulations governing water supply.

Building Centre, 26 Store Street, London WC1, have a permanent exhibition and information service on everything to do with building and building materials. There are also Building Centres at Colston Avenue, The Centre, Bristol BS1 4TW; 15 Trumpington Street, Cambridge CB2 1QD; 113 Portland Street, Manchester M1 6FB; 6 Newton Terrace, Glasgow G3 7PF and 18–20 Cumberland Place, Southampton SO1 2BD.

The Building Regulations 1972, obtainable from Her Majesty's Stationery Office, 49 High Holborn, London WC1, will guide you with regard to regulations which must be observed when building or converting. An architect or surveyor can also advise you about building regulations.

Building Societies Association, 14 Park Street, London W1, will help with queries concerning obtaining a mortgage. It also has a list of societies willing to lend money on older houses.

Chambers of Commerce exist in all local authorities. Most have offices in the Town Hall, where addresses of firms carrying out a wide variety of services can be obtained, e.g. glazier, sweep, carpenter, etc.

Chartered Auctioneers & Estate Agents' Institute, 29 Lincoln's Inn Fields, London WC2, will send a list of its members, who have to pass examinations and observe a code of professional conduct.

Consumers' Association, 14 Buckingham Street, London WC2, publish reports on a wide range of home equipment and furniture, and a monthly publication called *Which?* It also takes up complaints on behalf of its members.

Corporation of Mortgage and Finance Brokers, 6a The Forbury, Reading, Berks., advise on obtaining mortgages.

Cement and Concrete Association, 52 Grosvenor Gardens, London SW1, have invaluable pamphlets on particular aspects on the use of concrete.

Design Centre, 28 Haymarket, London W1, houses a permanent display of well-designed British products ranging from an egg spoon to industrial machinery. It also houses an index of modern consumer products.

Disabled Living Foundation, 346 Kensington High Street, London W14 8NS, have a postal information service advising people concerned with the disabled or elderly about aids available, ranging from a looped plug for easier connection to special equipment operated by the lightest touch. At the same address is an Aids Centre where equipment can be examined and handled, but visitors are asked to make an appointment so that they can be shown round by an occupational therapist.

The District Surveyor can be contacted through your local Town Hall.

Dyno-Rod Drain Cleaning Service, 107 Mortlake High Street, London SW14, will undertake drain clearance and unblocking for the householder. 24-hour service is available in most of the U.K. through local agents.

Electrical Contractors Association, 55 Catherine Place, London SW1, will supply lists of its members.

Federation of Master Builders, 33 John Street, London WC1, admits only experienced builders to membership and will supply lists of its members.

Fibre Building Board Development Organisation Ltd, Buckingham House, 6–7 Buckingham Street, London WC2, hold a reference library of over one thousand types and brands of fibre building board and displays of fixings and uses.

Incorporated Society of Valuers and Surveyors, 3 Cadogan Gate, London SW1, will put householders in touch with local surveyors.

Institute of Furniture Warehousing and Removing, 39 Victoria Street, London SW1, issues a useful booklet on moving house and will send the householder a list of its members.

Insulation Glazing Association, 6 Mount Row, London W1Y 6DY, have a list of members and will investigate complaints.

Insurance – before employing others make sure that your household insurance policy includes cover for anyone you employ in or around your home. A small additional premium may be needed in some cases.

Law Society, 29–37 Red Lion Street, London WC1, will supply booklets on legal advice. Your local Citizens Advice Bureau can put you in touch with solicitors working within the Legal Aid Scheme at much reduced fees.

National Federation of Building Trades Employers, 82 New Cavendish Street, London W1, will supply lists of its members in your area. The Federation accepts only experienced builders as members and will investigate complaints.

National Federation of Clay Industries, 30 Gordon Street, London WC1H 0AU, publishes the *Clay Tile Bulletin*, which gives details of its members.

National Federation of Housing Societies, 86 Strand, London WC2, advise on mortgages.

National Federation of Master Painters, 40 King Street, Manchester 3, will put householders in touch with its members. The Federation accepts only experienced painters as members and will also investigate complaints.

National Federation of Plumbers and Domestic Heating Engineers, 6 Gate Street, London WC2A 3HX, will supply lists of its members.

National Federation of Window Cleaners, 104 Hathersage Road, Chorlton-on-Medlock, Manchester 13, will supply lists of its members. If you live in Glasgow, Aberdeen or Huddersfield, where window cleaners have to be licensed, the City Hall will have their addresses.

National House-Builders Registration Council, 58 Portland Place, London W1, guarantee sound work in respect of new houses built by builders registered with it. Write for leaflet and names of builders in your area.

National Inspection Council for Electrical Installation Contracting, 1 Charing Cross, London SW1, will supply lists of qualified electricians.

Pescon, 645 Seven Sisters Road, London N15, eradicate home-based rodents and insects in the London area. This firm will also clean out empty houses before you move, including sterilizing drains and fumigating whole houses. This applies to the London area only.

Planning permission must be obtained for any alteration to your property, e.g. erecting a garage. Contact the Planning Department through your local Town Hall.

Post Office Users National Council, Waterloo Bridge House, Waterloo Road, London SE1, with offices in Belfast, Swansea and Glasgow, will help with difficulties and will deal with individual complaints against the Post Office.

Protim Services, Fieldhouse Lane, Marlow, Bucks., eradicate woodworm and dry rot and deal with damp proofing.

Public Health Officers (find the address through the Town Hall) will have to be consulted before any alteration to drainage takes place. Local Public Health Inspectors will also check cess pits and septic tanks and advise on their installation and use.

Registered Plumbers' Association, Scottish Mutual House, Hornchurch, Essex, will recommend names of its members. Members have to pass examinations to join the Association.

The Registrar of Friendly Societies, 17 Great Audley Street, London W1, is the person with whom to register a housing group.

Retail Trading Standards Testing House, 27 Bell Street, Henley-on-Thames, Oxfordshire, will carry out tests on merchandise such as carpets, clothes and bed linen for a fee, and issue a report.

Rentokil Laboratories, Felcourt, East Grinstead, Surrey, operate a guaranteed service for the eradication of dry rot and woodworm. Their Pest Control Division will also deal with pests.

Royal Institute of British Architects, 66 Portland Place, London W1, publish a useful book on employing an architect, and will send lists of names and addresses of architects on request. An idea of the type of work required, such as conversion (specialists), modern one-storey home, extension, etc. is helpful.

Royal Institute of Chartered Surveyors, 12 Great George Street, London SW1, will supply lists of its members, and will provide an expert to arbitrate between householder and builder. A fee is charged for this service.

Timber Research and Development Association at the Building Centre, 26 Store Street, London W1, has a display of timbers for walls and floors, and advice on decorative and constructional uses of woods.

Water Boards – local water boards should be informed about any alterations to plumbing (e.g. installing a new bathroom, putting in a shower, etc.). They will often re-washer taps for the householder free of charge, and will recommend qualified local plumbers in an emergency.

Weights and Measures inspectors can be contacted through your local Town Hall. Apart from complaints about short-weight, they can also help when equipment is taken away for repair and not returned, or where expensive equipment fails to perform adequately.

Specialists

Adding an extra room

Banbury Buildings, Banbury, Oxon., make sunrooms, play houses, extensions, etc. as well as garages.

T. Bath & Co. Ltd, 41 Norwood Road, London SE24, make extensions ranging from a porch to a medium-sized room.

Blacknell Buildings, Finehurst Avenue, Farnborough, Hants, also make several extensions and porches.

Boulton & Paul Group, 14 Stanhope Gate, London W1Y 5LB, make wooden porch frames, etc. in standard sizes.

Classic Buildings Ltd, 282 High Street, Rochester, Kent, make glass and aluminium extensions, with cedar bases which have built-in damp courses.

Compton Buildings Ltd, Fenny Compton, near Leamington Spa, War., make a range of extensions, porches and garages.

R. Hall & Co. (Kent) Ltd, Paddock Wood, Tonbridge, Kent, make a range of extensions, sheds and greenhouses in several designs.

Harry Hepditch, Martock, Somerset, makes several types of extensions.

K. Knight, 3 Reigate Heath, Reigate, Surrey, makes custom-built extensions.

Marley Buildings Ltd, Rees Marsh, Guildford, Surrey, make a range of porches and extensions, garages and sheds.

Westmere Ltd, Manor House, Church Street, Leatherhead, Surrey, make several extensions and porches.

Willan Buildings Ltd, 40 Strawberry Lane, Willenhall, Staffs., make porches and small extensions.

For architect-designed extensions, see "Architects" in General List.

Attics

Attic conversion specialists

Elite Loft Conversions Ltd, Holden House, Holden Road, Leigh, Lancs. Offices at: Newcastle-upon-Tyne, Harrogate, Birmingham, Bristol, Glasgow, Carlisle, Exeter and Nottingham.

Aluminium loft ladder with guide rail

Gravity Randall, Slinfold, Horsham, Sussex RH13 7RD.

Folding loft ladders

Ramsay Loft Ladders, Forfar, Angus, Scotland.

Basements

Air bricks and ventilation grilles

Automatic Pressings Ltd, Halesfield Industrial Estate, Telford, Shropshire.

J. D. Beardmore & Co. Ltd, 3–5 Percy Street, London W1P 0EJ, make brass and aluminium ventilation grilles.

Damp-proof floorings

Asphalt & Coated Macadam Association, 25 Lower Belgrave Street, London SW1W 0LS, will put you in touch with members in your area who would lay an asphalt sub-floor for you. Then you can lay any flooring you like over the damp-proofed floor.

Damp-proofing specialists

Peter Cox Ltd, 11 Wates Way, Mitcham, Surrey. Building restoration, water-proofing; woodworm and dry-rot specialists.

MDC Group Services, 77 Wyle Cop, Shrewsbury SY1 1UT, use the physical membrane system for damp-proofing. Nationwide service.

Phoenix Preservation Ltd, 62 Brookhill Road, New Barnet, Herts.

Preservation Developments (1972) Ltd, Victory House, 99–101 Regent Street, London W1R 8LJ, use the Vandex injection mortar system to deal with rising damp.

Rentokil Ltd, Felcourt, East Grinstead, Sussex, are damp-proofing specialists who will remove damp using the electro-osmotic method.

Bathrooms

Accessories

All Habitat shops.

Celmac Distributors Ltd, Hodford House, 17–27 High Street, Hounslow, Middx., French bathroom cabinets, lavatory seats.

Coverdale Marketing Co. Ltd, Bank Chambers, 6 Borough High Street, London SE1. Scandinavian and Italian bathroom cabinets and accessories.

Charles Hufton & Sons Ltd, Conybere Street Works, Birmingham B12 0YL. Good quality chrome and gold-plated bathroom fittings of simple and more ornate designs, as well as shower fittings.

Bathroom taps, shower fittings, etc.

Co-ordination of colour in the sanitary ware and ceramic tile industry is at last taking place. Ideal Standard Ltd, of Hull, are matching their colours to a range of tiles made by Pilkington & Carter, PO Box 4, Clifton Junction, Manchester M27 2LP.

Barking Brassware Ltd, Silver Road, Barking, Essex.

James Barwell Ltd, Great Hampton Street, Birmingham 18.

Belco Manufacturing Co. Ltd, Belco House, Park Royal Road, London NW10.

F. H. Bourner & Co. Ltd, Manor Royal, Crawley, Surrey. Spa and Supataps and shower fittings.

Finnish Valve Co. Ltd, Ascot Works, Kenley Road, London SW19.

Gainsborough Electrical Ltd, 105 Dollman Street, Birmingham B7 4RP, make shower mixers and shower heaters.

IMI Developments Ltd, Kynock Works, Witton, Birmingham 6, make plastic taps.

Meynell Valves Ltd, Shaw Road, Busbury, Wolverhampton, manufacture shower control valves.

Miraflo Ltd, Whadden Works, Cheltenham, Glos., make taps, shower fittings and controls.

Peglers Ltd, Belmont Works, Doncaster, manufacture a range of taps and shower fittings.

Walker Crossweller & Co. Ltd, Oriel Lodge, Oriel Road, Cheltenham GL50 1XN, make shower fitments and thermostatic controls.

Plastic mirrors that don't mist

AGP Plastic Ltd, 77 Cromwell Road, London SW7 5BN, market Plexiglass acrylic mirror.

Pearson Mirrorlite Ltd,
PO Box 48, North Point,
Meadowhall Road, Sheffield
S9 1SA, make Mirrorlite mirror
sheet.

Safety

Aygee Ltd, Century House,
Tanner Street, London SE1.
Safety rails.

Expandite Ltd, Western Road,
Bracknell, Berks., make safety
strips for baths called Safe
Trend. They do not harm the
bath surface and provide a grip
for the feet.

Charles Hufton & Sons Ltd,
Conybere Street Works,
Birmingham B12 0YL. Safety
rails.

Showers and cubicles

Dolphin Showers Ltd, Poplar
House, Poplar Road,
Birmingham 14.

Duraflex Ltd, Kingsditch Lane,
Cheltenham.

Gardex Ltd, Cromwell Road,
Bredbury, Stockport SK6 2RX,
make showers and shower
heaters.

Gardom & Lock Ltd, Alflow
Works, Pleasant Street, West
Bromwich, Staffs., make
shower units and heaters.

Alfred Goslett & Co. Ltd,
55 Great Marlborough Street,
London W1V 2NS, make
Swanlyne showers.

Heatrae Ltd, Norwich Airport,
Norwich NOR 29A, make
showers and heaters.

Johnson & Slater Ltd,
Westwood Works, P.O. Box 9,
Berry Hill, Stoke-on-Trent,
make shower trays.

P & R Electrical (London) Ltd,
Pearl House, 1 Berryman
Gardens, London W3, make
shower cubicles and electric
water heaters.

Osprey Industries Ltd, Elles
Road, Farnborough, Hants,
make shower cabinets.

Ventilators/extractor fans

Also see Kitchens.

Airflow Developments Ltd,
Lancaster Road, High
Wycombe, Bucks. Airflow
loovent toilet/bathroom
ventilation unit.

Morphy Richards
(Installations) Ltd, 50 Conduit
Street, London W1. Silavent
mechanical ventilation unit.

Stadium Ltd, Queensway,
Enfield, Middx., make a range
of plastic bathroom air vents.

Bedrooms

Beds and Bedding

All Habitat shops.

Airsprung Ltd, Ladydown
Industrial Estate, Trowbridge,
Wilts., make Ther-a-Pedic beds
for back care.

Dunlopillo Division of Dunlop
Pannal, Harrogate, Yorks.,
make foam mattresses and
foam pillows useful for people
who have allergies to wool,
horse-hair or feathers.

Hanging Bed Co. Ltd, 811
Fulham Road, London SW6,
make beds to hang from the
ceiling.

Heal & Sons Ltd, 196
Tottenham Court Road, London
W1, make beds and bedding to
order and will remake their old
beds. They also have a good
bed linen department.

London Bedding Centre, 267
Sloane Street, London SW1,
sell beds, including extra large
sizes, bedding and linen.
Countrywide delivery.
They have exclusive U.K.
rights to sell the French
"Treca" electrically-controlled
bed.

Price Bros & Co. Ltd,
Wellington, Somerset TA21
8NN, produce the Carlton
Relyon electrically-controlled
bed with adjustable head and
foot sections.

Tricar Holding Ltd,
17 Market Place,
Henley-on-Thames, Oxon.,
import the Tricamatic electric
push-button controlled bed
with adjustable head and foot
sections.

Bunk Beds

All Habitat shops.

Amba Furniture Ltd, Oxgate
Works, Oxgate Lane, London
NW2 7JN, make bunk beds
which convert to two single
beds when required.

Westnofa, 24 Rathbone Place,
London W1, import Ergolett
Norwegian bunk beds which
are large enough for teenagers
and smaller adults.

Two single beds which stack one over the other

All Habitat shops.

Hunkydory Designs Ltd,
10 Ansdell Street, London W8.

Pace Furniture Ltd,
Ravenscroft Road,
Henley-on-Thames, Oxon.

Bonuses

Saunas

Finland Saunas Ltd,
Ferringham Lane, Ferring,
Sussex.

Interscan Sauna Ltd, 61
Balmoral Road, Gillingham
ME7 4NT, Kent.

Nordic Sauna Ltd, Nordic
House, 31–33 Lesbourne Road,
Reigate, Surrey RH2 7JS.

Norpe Saunas of Finland (U.K.)
Ltd, Cleeve Prior, Evesham,
Worcs.

Water softeners

Cord Chemical Co. Ltd, Cord
House, Wirksworth,
Derbyshire DE4 4DS.

Permutit Ltd, Domestic Sales
Division, Permutit House,
632 London Road, Isleworth,
Middx.

Children's rooms

Nursery equipment

Mothercare shops in most
towns, or good mail order
catalogue from Mothercare
Ltd, Cherry Tree Road,
Watford, Herts.

Harrods, Knightsbridge,
London SW1, will hire out
cots, prams, pushchairs,
playpens, etc. through their
Catering Dept. Pram shops in
other cities may operate a
similar service.

Details that count

Alarm systems

Advanced Burglar Alarms
Ltd, 153 Fenchurch Street,
London EC3.

Associated Fire Alarms Ltd, 61
St Giles High Street, London
WC2.

Banham's Patent Locks Ltd,
233 Kensington High Street,
London W8. This firm also fits
locks, grilles, and other safety

devices for the householder.

Securicor Ltd, 17 Chelsea
Embankment, London SW3,
will keep a check on private
property while the owner is
away. They will also install
burglar alarms. This service is
nationwide.

The Security Officer at your
local police station will make an
appointment to call and advise
you on the best way of making
your home burglar-resistant.

Doors

Alcan Booth Industries,
Southam Road, Banbury,
Oxon., supply anodized
aluminium doors and threshold
units.

Door Store, 61 Judd Street,
London WC1, supply many
types and sizes of front doors,
and their next door neighbour,
Knobs and Knockers, the door
furniture to go with it.

The Lawrence Group,
Sawbridgeworth, Herts., make
solid wood, plywood-faced and
hardboard faced doors.

W.H.N. National Products
Ltd, 192 Ebury Street, London
SW1 8UP, supply
Georgian-style doors and
surrounds.

W. H. Newson & Sons Ltd, 61
Pimlico Road, London SW1,
make good range of solid wood
and faced doors.

Open Sesame Ltd, 1 The
Broadway, London SW13,
stock more than 70 designs of
modern and traditional doors
and supply good quality door
furniture to go with them.

Shapland & Petter Ltd,
Barnstaple, Devon., make wood
doors in wide range of designs.

Door furniture

All Habitat shops.

Albion Crystalcut Penthouse
solid acrylic striped and plain
door handles are available
through Albion Crystalcut Ltd,
Simon House, Middlefield
Industrial Estate, Sunderland
Road, Sandy, Beds.

G. & S. Allgood Ltd,
Carterville House, 297 Euston
Road, London NW1 3QA,
manufacture the Modric range
of fittings in black plastics and
satin chrome.

Comyn Ching, 59 Monmouth
Street, London WC2, is an

old-established ironmongers
where a wide selection of door
furniture may be found.

Eaton Corporation Ltd, Yale
Security Division, Wood Street,
Willenhall WV13 1LA, make a
wide range of door and window
fittings and locks, security
bolts, etc.

J. Legge & Co. Ltd, Willenhall,
Staffs., make reproduction brass
door fittings which retail at
reasonable prices.

Newman-Tonks Ltd, Star
Works, Moseley Street,
Birmingham 12, make brass
and satin chrome door and
window furniture and several
ranges of locks.

Door porter

Blick National Systems Ltd,
43 Causton Street, London
SW1, make the Ritto door
porter for do-it-yourself
installation.

Chubb & Sons Lock and Safe
Co. Ltd, also supply door
porters, but professional
fitting is recommended.

Electrical fittings

J. A. Crabtree Ltd, Lincoln
Works, Walsall, Staffs., also
make electric light and socket
fittings, dimmer switches, etc.

C. C. Friedland, Stockport,
Cheshire SK5 6BP, specialize in
all kinds of front door bells and
pushes.

MK Electric Ltd, Shrubbery
Road, Edmonton, London N9,
make dimmer switches, light
fittings, socket outlets, etc., and
will supply leaflets.

Locks

As well as those already
mentioned under door
furniture, lock makers include:–

Chubb & Sons Lock and Safe
Co. Ltd, Totfield House,
Tottenham Street, London W1.

Ingersoll Locks Ltd, Regent
House, 89 Kingsway, London
WC2.

Josiah Parkes & Sons Ltd, Bush
House, Aldwych, London WC2.

Floors

Carpets

All Habitat shops.

British Carpet Centre,
Dorland House, 14–16 Lower
Regent Street, London W1,

has a permanent exhibition of over 3,000 samples of British Wilton and Axminster carpets, and approximate prices.

Centro Carpets, 3–5 Swallow Place, London SW1, import durable cord carpets.

Copydex Ltd, 1 Torquay Street, Harrow Road, London W2, make Anticreep foam underlay to prevent rugs creeping.

Crossley Carpets Ltd, Dean Clough Mills, Halifax, Yorks., make Criterion Cord and a range of pile carpets suitable for stairs, etc.

Great Metropolitan Flooring Co. Ltd, 73 Kinnerton Street, London SW1X 8ED, will supply and lay all types of carpets and floorings throughout the U.K. They will also lay portable dance floors for weddings, etc.

Lancaster Carpets Ltd, Denton, Manchester M34 3SH, make carpets in tough synthetic fibres suitable for stairs, halls and landings.

Tintawn Ltd, Richfield Avenue, Reading, Berks., make sisal carpets in patterns and wide range of colours. Tough for halls and landings, but inclined to wear slippery on stairs.

Ceramic tiles

Candy & Co. Ltd, Heathfield, Newton Abbot, South Devon, import ceramic tiles and have a showroom at the above address and agents in most parts of the country including Manchester.

Domus Italian Tiles and Decor Centre, 260 Brompton Road, London SW3, import Italian floor and wall tiles.

Oporto Ceramics Ltd, Trendsetter House, Wortley Moor Road, Leeds LS12 AJA, import ceramic tiles and have a showroom with room settings of tiles. They will carry out installation work for the householder.

Reed Harris (London) Ltd, Riverside House, Carnwath Road, London SW6, import a wide range of Italian and Portuguese tiles. They have showrooms and orders can be placed through local builders.

Tanrae Tile Boutique, 857

Christchurch Road, Boscombe, Bournemouth.

Tile Mart, 151–3 Great Portland Street, London W1, import a wide range of tiles and also have shops within shops at Rackhams, Birmingham; Cavendish House, Cheltenham; Maple, Shepherd & Hedger, Southampton, and Robsons, Newcastle.

Tile Mart, 163 Borough High Street, London SE1 1HU, has a Tile Centre showroom.

Wall & Flooring Co. Ltd, 68 Liverpool Street, Salford 5.

Dennis M. Williams Ltd, 43 Thames Street, Kingston-on-Thames, Surrey.

Cork floors

All Habitat shops.

Wicanders (Great Britain) Ltd, Maxwell Way, Gatwick Road, Crawley, Surrey.

Cork flooring and stair-covering

Armstrong Cork Co. Ltd, Armstrong House, Chequers Square, Uxbridge, Middx. UB8 1NG. Specialist fitting needed.

Quarry tiles

Hereford Tiles Ltd, Whitestone, Hereford, supply quarries in several tones.

Daniel Platt & Sons Ltd, Brownhills Tileries, Tunstall, Stoke-on-Trent, Staffs., make Ferrolite tiles.

Wheatley & Co. Ltd, Springfield Tileries, Trent Vale, Stoke-on-Trent, supply Triton floor tiles.

Rugs and matting

All Habitat shops.

Afia Ltd, 81 & 85 Baker Street, London W1.

Benardout, 328 Kings Road, London SW3. Persian carpet specialists, who will also clean and repair them.

Carpetbaggers, 14 Kingswell, Heath Street, London NW3.

Eastern Carpets (Benlian) Ltd, 85 Clerkenwell Road, London EC1P 1BB.

Heal & Sons Ltd, 196 Tottenham Court Road, London W1.

La Cucaracha, 6 Halkin Arcade, West Halkin Street, London SW1.

Liberty & Co. Ltd, Regent Street, London W1.

Marshall & Snelgrove (Carpet Dept), Oxford Street, London W1.

Stock, 131 High Holborn, London WC1 and 236 Fulham Road, London SW10.

Studded synthetic rubber floorings

Dunlop Semtex Ltd, 24 Berners Street, London W1, import Pirelli studded and striped floorings.

C. Freudenberg, Lutterworth, Rugby, War.

Vinyl floors

Amtico Ltd, PO Box 42, Foleshill Road, Coventry and at 18 Hanover Square, London W1, make a wide range of vinyl floors.

Armstrong Cork Co. Ltd, Armstrong House, Chequers Square, Uxbridge, Middx., also make a wide range of vinyls.

Dunlop Semtex Ltd, 24 Berners Street, London W1, make a wide range of vinyls for amateur and domestic laying.

Gerland Ltd, 90 Crawford Street, London W1.

Marley Tiles Ltd, and Marley Retail Ltd, London Road, Riverhead, Sevenoaks, Kent.

Nairn Floors Information Bureau, 640 Fulham Road, London SW6, supply information on Nairn floors.

Wood composition flooring

Granwood (Wall & Floor) Ltd, Riddings, Derby DE5 4FT, make Granwood floorings and special cleaners for their floors.

Finishes and maintenance

Brooms, mops, carpet sweepers, etc.

Addis Ltd, Hertford, Herts.

Bissell Appliances Ltd, Highams Park, London E4 9HN, operate a hiring service for electric shampooers.

Briton Chadwick, Wymondham, Norfolk, make brushes of all types.

Kleeneeze Holdings Ltd, Home Care Service, Hamham, Bristol BS15 3DY, have agents who sell in most areas –

polishes, brushes and cleaning tools generally. They also do bulk packs of liquid detergent and washing up powder.

Plysu Housewares Ltd, Woburn Sands, Milton Keynes MK16 8SE, make good squeeze mops, including long-handled ones for washing windows.

Prestige Group Ltd, Prestige House, 14–18 Holborn, London EC1, make the Ewbank range of sweepers, mops and shampooers.

Sabco Housewares (U.K.) Ltd, 41 Hodford House, High Street, Hounslow, Middx.

Cleaning and polishing products

Amtico Floor Ltd, PO Box 42, 42 Foleshill Road, Coventry CV6 5AG, make Amtico Liquid Floor Cleaner for all vinyl floors which will remove build-up of polish.

Colthurst & Harding Ltd, Grosvenor Gardens House, London SW1, make Liquid Lino paint for painting over linoleum and other floor surfaces.

Coo-Var Ltd, Ellenshaw Works, Lockwood Street, Hull HU2 0HN, make Coo-Var Floor Formula polyurethane lacquer coat for floors which takes 48 hours to cure properly. It is not suitable for asphalt, thermoplastic or surface coated tiles.

J. Goddard & Sons Ltd, Nelson Street, Leicester, make a range of polishes for floors, furniture, metal, etc. and will send useful information on request.

Izal Ltd (Ronuk Division), Thorncliffe, Chapeltown, Sheffield, supply Colron wood dyes and Ronseal sealers for wooden floors.

Johnson Wax Co. Ltd, Frimley Green, Camberley, Surrey, make floor polishes, sealers and cleaners, and will advise on cleaning problems.

Marley Retail Ltd, Sevenoaks, Kent, make a range of cleaners and polishes for vinyl floors and will supply cleaning instructions and advice on request.

Reckitt & Colman, Dansom Lane, Hull HU8 7DS, make

Mansion polish for wood, floor, linoleum and furniture which needs wax; Seel self-shining wax for vinyls and lino.

A. Sanderson & Co. Ltd, Kingston Paint Works, Hull HU3 2BX, make Kingston Diamond Polyurethane Floor-Cote for use on most floors.

Watco (Sales) Ltd, 56 Buckingham Gate, London SW1, manufacture Watco cement paint in several colours.

Halls, stairs and landings

Stairs

Birmingham Guild of Architectural Metalworkers, Grosvenor Street West, Birmingham B16 8LH, make custom-made steel stairs and spiral staircases.

Crescent of Cambridge, New Street, Cambridge CB1 2RP, make spiral stairs to a modular construction.

Lewes Design Contracts Ltd, The Mill, Glynde, Lewes, Sussex, specialize in making spiral staircases.

Pedley Woodwork Ltd, Shirehill Works, Saffron Waldon, Essex, make a "do it yourself" stair unit.

Shirehall Works, Saffron Waldon, Essex, make wooden spiral stairways which are cheaper than custom-made steel ones.

Stairways Centre, Stairway Joinery Co. Ltd, 306 Upper Richmond Road West, Sheen, London SW14, specialize in open plan staircases.

Stair nosings

Gradus Ltd, Park Street, Macclesfield, Cheshire SK11 7NE.

James Halstead Ltd, Redcliffe New Road, Whitefield, Manchester M25 7NR.

Stair rails and balustrades

British Woodwork Manufacturers Association, 26 Store Street, London WC1E 7BT, will put you in touch with members supplying stair rails and balustrades in wood.

Ornamental Ironwork, 33 The Broadway, Thatcham, Berks.

Worshipful Company of Farriers, Moor House, London Wall, London EC2, will put you in touch with its members.

Heating

Cavity Foam Insulation Association, Audley House, 9 Margaret Street, London W1, will put the public in touch with its members and offer advice.

Electrical Floor Warming Association, 5 Roughlea Avenue, Culcheth, Warrington, Lancs., will advise about types of flooring suitable for use with this type of heating, and give names of qualified installers.

Electricity Boards all offer a free advisory service, and will send a specialist to advise on electric central heating and provide a detailed scheme and estimate.

Electrical Contractors' Association, 55 Catherine Place, London SW1, will provide a list of its registered members in your area and answer general enquiries. Don't use unregistered electricians for heating installations.

Electricity Council Marketing Dept, Trafalgar Building, 1 Charing Cross, London SW1, answer questions on electric space and water heating.

Esso Petroleum Co. Ltd, Victoria Street, London SW1, supply oil for oil-fired installations.

Gas Council, 59 Bryanston Street, London W1, supply a list of registered CORGI installers for gas heating. They also issue leaflets on their Guaranteed Warmth Scheme.

Heating and Ventilating Contractors Association, 172 Buckingham Palace Road, London SW1, supply advice on heating and ventilating and will put the householder in touch with members in his area.

Honeywell Ltd (Residential Division), Charles Square, Bracknell, Berks., make controls for every kind of central heating and air conditioning system and will send helpful pamphlets on the use of controls.

Humidifiers Advisory and Consultancy Service, 21 Napier Street, Bromley, Kent, advise on the use of humidifiers.

ICI Building Group, Rosanne House, Bridge Road, Welwyn Garden City, Herts., specialize in insulation.

Institute of Heating and Ventilating Engineers, 49 Cadogan Square, London SW1, is the professional body of qualified heating engineers whose members work as consultants for a fee.

Insulation Glazing Association, 6 Mount Row, London W1, will send detailed information and a list of its members who install double-glazing to the association's standard.

Megafoam Ltd, Morley Road, Tonbridge, Kent, specialize in wall cavity insulation.

National Federation of Builders and Plumbers Merchants, 52 High Holborn, London WC1, have over 300 Home Improvement Centres throughout the country where the public can get advice about heating. They will also send a list of builders' merchants who specialize in central heating equipment in your area.

National Heating Centre, 34 Mortimer Street, London W1, have a permanent exhibition and provide consultations on individual heating problems for a modest fee. Written enquiries are answered and heating systems designed. They also have a register of approved installers, backed by a two-year guarantee.

National Heating Consultancy, 188 Albany Street, London NW1, have members who are qualified consultant engineers who will, for a fee, visit a house and supply schemes or check a contractor's scheme. They will also act as arbitrators if legal action proves necessary.

National Fireplace Council, Churchill House, Regent Road, Stoke-on-Trent, publish a list of Approved Fireplace Centres and will send enquirers a booklet illustrating fireplace designs.

Ravensbourne Heating Ltd, 34 Cemetery Road, Lye, Worcs., supply do-it-yourself heating installations and advice.

Shell-Mex and BP Group, Domestic Heating Centre, 25 Bagleys Lane, London SW6, run a good delivery service and have a range of inexpensive heating systems with loans and guarantees.

Solid Fuel Advisory Service, National Coal Board, Hobart House, Grosvenor Place, London SW1, supply information on solid fuel heating, and a useful booklet, "Welcome Home", which details their loan schemes and lists registered contractors.

Kitchens

Batterie de cuisine

All Habitat shops.

Appliances

Philips Electrical Ltd, Century House, Shaftesbury Avenue, London WC2.

Rima Electric Ltd, 283 Ealing Road, Wembley, Middx. Also infra-red grills and blenders.

Servis Domestic Appliances Ltd, Hollies Drive, Wednesbury, Staffs.

Sinkamatic Domestic Appliances Ltd, 243 Finchley Road, London NW3, make a combined sink/washing machine unit.

Thermor, Madison House, Molesey Avenue, East Molesey, Surrey. Extractor/ canopy.

Vent-Axia Ltd, 232 Vauxhall Bridge Road, London SW1V 1AZ.

Xpelair, GEC-Xpelair Ltd, PO Box 220, Witton, Birmingham B6 7JH.

Showrooms

Humpherson & Co. Ltd, Beaufort Works, Holman Road, London SW11 3RL.

Kitchen Centre, 18 Berners Street, London W1. Scholtes and Westinghouse showroom.

Leisure Kitchens, 28 Brook Street, London W1Y 2DP.

Thorn Kitchen Advisory Centre, Thorn House, Upper St Martin's Lane, London WC2. Moffat cookers.

Wrighton Showroom, 3 Portman Square, London W1H 0JB.

Units

Beekay, 82 Cricklewood Lane, London NW2.

English Rose Ltd, Warwick.

GEC Anderson Ltd, 89 Herkomer Road, Bushey, Herts. WD2 3LS, make a stainless double sink with a separate slop sink.

Grovewood Products Ltd, Tipton, Staffs.

Leisure Kitchens, Nottingham Road, Chipping Norton, Oxon. Individual kitchens planned.

Multiflex Kitchens Ltd, Dafen, Llanelli, Carms.

W. H. Paul Ltd, Breaston, Derby DE7 3BQ.

Peerless Built-in Furniture Ltd, Western Avenue, Perivale, Greenford, Middx. Self assembly units.

Program Kandya, 2 Ridgemount Place, London WC1.

Qualcast Fleetway, Charlton Road, Edmonton WN9 8HR. Ready-form knock-down units.

SieMatic (U.K.) Ltd, 11–17 Fowler Road, Hainault Industrial Estate, Ilford, Essex.

Thames Eastham & Sons Ltd, Holmes Road, Blackpool FY5 2SQ.

Waste disposal units

Kenwood by Thorn Domestic Appliances Ltd, Kenwood Division, New Lane, Havant, Hants.

Colston by Colston Appliances Ltd, 30 Wellington Road, High Wycombe, Bucks.

Maxmatic by Bell Home Appliances, 240 Bath Road, Slough, Bucks.

Econa Parkamatic, made by Econa Parkamatic Ltd, Station Road, Coleshill, Birmingham 46.

Tweeny made by Haigh Engineering Co. Ltd, Ross-on-Wye, Hereford.

Pelican made by GEC-Xpelair Ltd, PO Box 220, Deykin Avenue, Witton, Birmingham.

Lighting

All Habitat shops.

C. M. Churchouse Ltd, 230 Tottenham Court Road, London W1, manufacture a range of simple modern lights, including exterior lights.

J. A. Crabtree Ltd, Lincoln Works, Walsall, Staffs., make light switches, socket outlets, etc. and issue helpful literature.

Concord Lighting International Ltd, 241 City Road, London EC1, manufacture a range of architectural light fittings and adjustable lighting tracks with spotlights.

Mrs M. E. Crick, 166 Kensington Church Street, London W8, specializes in chandeliers and will repair and replace missing parts.

Decorative Lighting Association, Llanerchymedd, Anglesey, North Wales, will supply information about its members and general advice on decorative lighting.

Edison Halo Ltd, 24 Avon Trading Estate, Avonmore Road, London W14, make light fittings.

Electricity Council, Marketing Dept, 1 Charing Cross, London SW1, provide advice on lighting.

Electricity Showrooms should also provide leaflets on the amount of lighting needed for a wide variety of activities in the home which will help when planning a lighting scheme.

Lighting Industry Federation, 25 Bedford Square, London WC1, will supply information on its members.

Lumitron Ltd, Chandos Road, Park Royal, London NW10, make wide ranges of lights and light tracks.

Nita Miller, 63a Grosvenor Street, London W1, cleans and re-covers fabric lampshades, and will make to order.

MK Electric Ltd, Shrubbery Road, Edmonton, London N9 0PB, make light switches, outlets, etc. and supply leaflets.

Osram (GEC) Ltd, PO Box 17, East Lane, Wembley HA9 7PG, Middx., make a wide range of bulbs and issue useful information about their use in the home.

Thorn Lighting Ltd, Thorn House, Upper St. Martin's Lane, London WC2, manufacture a wide range of light fittings and have a good showroom at the above address.

Christopher Wray's Lighting Emporium, 604 Kings Road, London SW6, specialize in Victorian oil lamps and will convert them for customers.

Living rooms

See under General, Walls, Lighting, Heating and Storage.

Fabrics and upholstery
All Habitat shops stock a range of materials including Marimekko fabrics from Finland.

Second-hand furniture
Austins, 11 Peckham Rye, London SE15.

Furniture Cave, 535 Kings Road, London SW10.

The Salvation Army, 124 Spa Road, London SE16, sell everything very cheap. Stock usually includes chairs, tables, carpets, good beds, kitchen furniture and cupboards. Saturday is the big day, and you need to arrive by 9.15 am. Doors open at 9.30 am and things disappear quickly. No cheques accepted, but they will deliver.

Second Hand and Junk City, 222 North End Road, London SW6.

Simmonds, 180 North Gower Street, London NW1.

One-room living

Folding beds
Heal & Sons Ltd, 196 Tottenham Court Road, London W1, make both single and double beds which fit into wall units.

Hille International Ltd, 132 St. Albans Road, Watford, Herts.

Slumberland Ltd, Redfern Road, Birmingham B11 2BN, make a single 2 ft 6 in./762 mm wide divan.

Staples & Co. Ltd, Staples Corner, North Circular Road, London NW2 6LS, make single and double beds which fold into the wall.

Wentelbeds, 15 Golden Square, London W1, supply single and double folding beds.

Furniture
Tetrad Room-Planning Service, Tetrad Association, Hartford Mill, Swan Street, Preston, Lancs., will design and supply furniture to fit particular needs. This service is expensive but should prove worthwhile for anyone who plans one-room living on a long-term basis.

Mini-kitchen
Beckermann Kitchens (England), 36 Sittingbourne Avenue, Enfield, Middx.

Blue Gate Products, Beautility Works, Kavanaghs Road, Brentwood, Essex, make the Cresta 500 range.

New Era Commercial Refrigeration Services Ltd, 82–106 Cricklewood Lane, London NW2, make the Beekay Banc.
See also under kitchens.

Wash-basin in a cupboard
J. T. Ellis & Co. Ltd, Crown Works, Wakefield Road, Huddersfield HD5 9BA, make small vanity units with cupboards underneath.

Shower unit in cupboard
Conseal Ltd, Bond Avenue, Bletchley, Bucks.

Outdoors

British Association of Landscape Industries, 44 Bedford Row, London WC1, have a list of approved landscape contractors.

Cement & Concrete Association, 52 Grosvenor Gardens, London SW1. Literature.

Country Gentleman's Association Ltd, 54 Regent Street, London W1. Invaluable catalogue to members on fencing, materials, gates, etc.

Institute of Landscape Architects, Nash House, 12 Carlton Terrace, London SW1.

International Garden Centres, Association, 44 Bedford Row,

London WC1, have a list of approved members.

Fencing and gates
Albion Box Co. Ltd, Dumballs Road, Cardiff, supply fencing by mail order.

Auriol (Guildford) Ltd, Trading Estate, Farnham, Surrey, supply chain link fencing, trellises, etc.

Banbury Buildings Holdings Ltd, Robins House, Royal Leamington Spa, War., supply Banbury concrete section wall, Coates fencing and Corbett Larch-Lap fencing through mail order.

British Gates & Timber Ltd, Biddenden, Ashford, Kent, make country and farm gates.

E. C. Cases Ltd, Taffs Wall, Cardiff, Glam., supply fences by mail order.

City Gate & Fencing Co. Ltd, 9 Sicilian Avenue, Southampton Row, London WC1, supply several types of fencing through mail order.

City Timber Co., Brasted, Westerham, Kent, supply fences by mail order up to 100 miles delivery.

W & D Cole Ltd, Ashford Road, Bethersden, Ashford, Kent, supply several types of fencing, and will fit for the householder.

Thomas R. Danby Ltd, 60 Basingbourne Road, Fleet, Hants, make electric gate operators which can be operated by remote control.

Devon Rustics Ltd, Moreton Fencing Works, Clovelly Road, Bideford, Devon., supply fences by mail order.

W. R. Farman, Cherry Tree Lane, North Walsham, Norfolk, supply fencing by mail order.

Groves Fencing Co. Ltd, Esher, Surrey, make and fit fencing over a wide area.

Kay Hopwood Ltd, Tuff Link House, Box 3, Ashton Road West, Failsworth, Manchester, make Tufflink and Trellex plastic link and mesh fencings and trellis.

Kencast Ltd, Chaddock Lane, Astley, Manchester M29 8HA, supply fencing by mail order.

Leander Products Ltd, 8a Horninglow Street, Burton-on-Trent, produce lap

fencing in several types and will supply by mail order in the Burton-on-Trent area.

Marley Buildings Ltd, Guildford, Surrey, manufacture concrete unit fencing which can be combined with timber panels, and timber fencing. All are supplied by mail order.

Nelton Sales Ltd, N.E. Wing, Bush House, Aldwych, London WC2, manufacture plastic mesh in several widths which is suitable for fencing. It is also suitable for trellis work and climbing plant support. Brochure and address of nearest stockist sent on request.

F. Selby Ltd, Leagrave Works, London E5, produce several types of wood fencing in kits for home assembly.

Wall blocks
Marley Building Ltd, Guildford, Surrey, with branches at Chorley, Lancs.; Cheltenham, Glos.; Poole, Dorset, and Carluke, Lanark, supply wall screening blocks.

Portland Block Co. Ltd, High Street, Swadlincote, near Burton-on-Trent. Portland screen walling blocks in several patterns. They deliver free within 100 miles.

Summer houses
Banbury Buildings Ltd, Ironstone Works, Banbury, Oxon., make summer houses.

L. Garvin & Co. Ltd, Glastonbury, Somerset, manufacture summer houses and children's play houses.

Robert H. Hall & Co. (Kent) Ltd, Paddock Wood, Tonbridge, Kent, make the Manhattan sunroom, and several other designs, as well as garden sheds and greenhouses.

Harry Hebditch Ltd, Martock, Somerset, make the Suntrent cedar summer house.

Holmes (Wragby) Ltd, Wragby, Lincoln, make a hexagonal summer house and several other designs.

F. Pratten & Co. Ltd, Norton Hill, Bath, Somerset, make several summer houses, including a revolving one called Solar which follows the sunlight or can be turned away from the wind.

Greenhouses and greenhouse heaters
Aladdin Industries Ltd, Aladdin Building, Greenford, Middx., make greenhouse heaters.

Edenlite Ltd, Oakdale Avenue, Northwood Hills, Middx., make a range of aluminium framed greenhouses.

Humex Ltd, 5 High Road, Byfleet, Weybridge, Surrey, make the Circulaire greenhouse.

Worth Buildings Ltd, Donnington, Wellington, Salop, make wooden greenhouses.

Tubs
Robert Barr, The Manor, East Haddon, Northampton, makes Haddonstone tubs, troughs, etc.

G. A. Harvey Group Services Ltd, Woolwich Road, London SE7, make tubs in Harcoster plastics. They also make water-butts in the same material.

Mitra (Plastics) Ltd, Arthur Street, Oswestry, Salop, make tubs and window boxes in glass-fibre.

Plastic Bunkers, 10a Freegrounds Road, Hedge End, Southampton, Hants, make polythene water-butts and plastic coal bunkers.

Paving
Marley Buildings Ltd, Guildford, Surrey.

Neolite Ltd, Borough Green, Kent.

Redland Tiles Ltd, Redland House, Castle Gate, Reigate, Surrey.

Used paving stones can often be obtained from the local council at reasonable cost. Make enquiries at the local Town Hall. You often have to arrange to collect the load from the council's depot.

Garden furniture
All Habitat shops.

Charlie Wearn, Wanders Ambo, nr. Newport, Essex, has an enormous stock of marble statues, pillars, etc. rescued from demolition sites.

Coates Ltd, 61 Fence Works, Bristol Road, Bridgwater, Somerset, make garden furniture kits in wood for home assembly.

Crowthers of Syon Park, Brentford, Middx., have a collection of antique sculpture suitable for gardens.

Easden Manufacturing Co. Ltd, Surbiton, Surrey, import swing hammocks from Scandinavia.

Geebro garden furniture made by Green Bros, Geebro Works, Hailsham, Sussex.

Lister & Co. Ltd, Dursley, Glos., make solid Burma teak garden seats, tables, etc.

Nor-Link Leisure Products, 24 Dudley Street, Grimsby, Lincs., supply cushioned loungers, etc.

Specialist nurseries

Hillier & Sons, Winchester, Hants.

Geo. Jackson & Son (Woking Nurseries) Ltd, Woking, Surrey.

Notcutts Nurseries Ltd, Woodbridge, Suffolk.

R. V. Roger Ltd, The Nurseries, Pickering, Yorks.

L. R. Russell Ltd, Windlesham, Surrey.

P. de Jager & Sons Ltd, Marden, Kent.

Highland Water Gardens, Rickmansworth, Herts.

Storage

All Habitat shops.

Doors to fit alcoves

Intermills International, RAC House, Lansdowne Road, Croydon CR9 2JD. Kayzed folding door system.

W. H. Newson & Sons Ltd, 61 Pimlico Road, London SW1.

Storemore Products (Door Drobe), 153 High Road, Luton, Beds.

Thames Plywood Mfg. Co. Ltd, Harts Lane, Barking, Essex. Slim-fold sliding doors.

Shelving systems

Design Shelves Ltd, 210 Monument Road, Edgbaston, Birmingham B16 8UU. Thor Module boxes and shelves from Denmark.

Nexus Manufacturing Ltd, 220 Queenstown Road, London SW8. Click shelving system.

Raaco Storage Systems (U.K.), Thames Industrial Estate, Field House Lane, Marlow, Bucks. Free-standing shelving system.

Shelvit, Belle Vue, Westgate, Burnley, Lancs. Steel shelving.

Things

Auctions

Look for auctions advertised in your local press. Old houses can often produce a wonderful collection of interesting pieces which can be obtained for reasonable prices.

Markets

Caledonian Market, Tower Bridge Road, Bermondsey, London SE1. Open air general market with a predominance of antiques. Open early morning to 4 pm, but go early.

Camden Passage Market, Islington, London N1. Antiques and objets d'art. Wednesdays and Saturdays, 9 am to 6 pm.

Chelsea Antique Market, 245A and 253 King's Road, Chelsea, London SW3. Antiques and bric-à-brac. Monday to Saturday, 10 am onwards.

Farringdon Road, Clerkenwell, London EC1. Second-hand books and old manuscripts. Monday to Saturday, 10 am onwards.

Leather Lane, Holborn, London EC1. Almost anything sold here, but it is good for cheap household goods. Monday to Friday from 9 am.

Portobello Road, Notting Hill, London W11, for antiques and bric-à-brac. Saturdays only, 9 am to 6 pm.

Prints and posters

Andrew Block, 20 Barter Street, London WC1, has a large collection of theatrical prints for sale at reasonable prices.

Francis Edwards, 83 Marylebone High Street, London W1, specializes in old maps.

London Transport Poster Shop, 280 Marylebone Road, London W1, sell London Transport posters.

Parker Gallery, 2 Albemarle Street, London W1, have an immense stock of old prints (and also sell old weapons).

Poster Shop Ltd, 43 Camden Passage, London N1, have a good stock of children's posters.

Radio Times Hulton Picture Library, 35 Marylebone High Street, London W1, have an immense collection of old prints for hire.

Victoriana

Bayly's Galleries, 8 Princes Arcade, Piccadilly, London SW1.

Victor Hall, 735 Fulham Road, London SW6.

Walls

Mirrors

APG Mirrors, 61 Connaught Street, London W2, produce plastic mirror tints.

Clark-Eaton Ltd, Southern Industrial Area, Bracknell, Berks.

Eden Mirrors Ltd, Eden Works, Charleswoods Place, East Grinstead, Surrey, market Verity mirrors.

Glass Advisory Council, 6 Mount Row, London W1, have a list of glass merchants throughout the U.K. who can supply and fix mirrors.

Hall & Keane Design Ltd, 93 Camberwell Grove, London SE5, will make screen-printed mirrors to order.

Pearson Mirrorlite Ltd, 15 Corporation Street, Sheffield, produce Mirrorlite.

Wall coverings

All Habitat shops.

Coloroll Ltd, 72 Tottenham Court Road, London W1, produce boldly patterned wallpapers and have a showroom.

The Felt & Hessian Shop, 34 Greville Street, London EC1, stock a very wide range of felts and hessians for walls, floors, cushions, etc. They also sell bags of oddments for collages, patchwork, etc.

H. & R. Johnston Ltd, PO Box 1, Tunstall, Stoke-on-Trent ST6 4JX, produce Ogee tiles from the Kasbah range, and many other ceramic tiles. See other ceramic tile suppliers under "Ceramic Tiles" in the Flooring section.

W. H. Newson & Sons Ltd, 61 Pimlico Road, London SW1, have a good selection of wood

panelling and plywood panelling available.

Osborne & Little, 262 Brompton Road, London SW3, specialize in hand-printed wallpapers, mainly from the United States.

A. Sanderson & Sons Ltd, 52 Berners Street, London W1, have showrooms where fabrics and patterns. can be selected and matched.

Tassor Decor International Ltd, Crossways, Silwood Road, Ascot, Berks., import glass fibre, hessian, linen and other wall-coverings. Write to them for local stockists.

Timber Research and Development Association, 26 Store Street, London WC1, have a permanent display of wood panellings and will offer advice.

Zealand Engineering, Ashford Road, Ashford Common, Ashford, Middx., produce stainless steel wall tiles in many patterns.

Wallpapers and fabrics are matched by ranges from Cole's of 15 Mortimer Street, London W1 and from Arthur Sanderson & Sons Ltd, 52 Berners Street, London W1.

Paints can be mixed to special colours to order from J. Tillyer & Co. Ltd, 1 Woodstock Street, London W1.

Windows

A. J. Jubb Ltd, 203 Arundel Street, Sheffield S1 1DH, make safety bars for windows.

Town & Country Aluminium Ltd, 103 New Road, London E1, replace old windows with modern ones, with or without double-glazing.

Velux Ltd, Gunnels Wood Road, Stevenage, Herts., make roof windows for sloping roofs.

Window Seal Storm Porches Ltd, 169 Cricklewood Broadway, London NW2, make storm doors to fit against existing doors and windows.

Frosted glass and patterned glass

Pilkington Bros Ltd, St. Helens, Lancs., will send you a leaflet and details of your local supplier.

Blind-making (own materials)

Dean's Blinds (Putney) Ltd, 478 Old Kent Road, London SE1, make all types of blinds and laminated ones. Will also supply fittings for making up at home.

Sandershade at Harrods, Harrods, Knightsbridge, London SW1, will laminate fabrics, including lace, and make up blinds.

Blinds—roller and venetian

All Habitat shops.

Curtain & Drapery Co. Ltd, 35 Upper Street, London N1.

Luxaflex Ltd, Wellington House, New Zealand Avenue, Walton-on-Thames, Surrey, make venetian blinds and roller blinds to measure.

Saltree Ltd, 152 High Street, Birmingham 17, manufacture vertical venetian blinds.

Sunvene Ltd, 5 Greenhays Lane, Manchester 15.

Tidmarsh & Sons, Transenna Works, Laycock Street, London N1, make slatted cedar venetian blinds.

Curtains

Sekers Fabrics Ltd, Whitehaven, Cumberland, operate a ready-made curtain service using Sekers fabrics.

Curtain tape, poles and tracks

Rufflette Ltd, 76 Laindon Road, Manchester M14 5BU, make Tervoil 60 tape.

Scandinavian Fittings Ltd, Canal Wharf, Langley, Slough, specialize in curtain poles for both modern and traditional styles of window dressing.

Silent Gliss Ltd, Starhare, Margate, Kent, make Silent Gliss track and fittings.

Swish Products Ltd, Tamworth, Staffs., make Swish Furniglyde and Slim-line tracks.

Shutters

C. F. Anderson & Son Ltd, Islington Green, London N1, supply Panelaire in a variety of patterns to make fretwork shutters.

R. Denny, 14 Neverwood Road, London W14, makes wooden slatted shuttering.

Charles P. Moody, Broadford

Mills, Shalford, Guildford, Surrey, makes window shutters.

Work areas

Workshop equipment

Black & Decker Ltd, Accessory Division, Cannon Lane, Maidenhead SL6 3PD. Workmate folding portable work bench.

Copydex Ltd, 1 Torquay Street, London W2, make tool-to-hand "basket".

Leisure Wood Products, High Road, Cowley Peachey, Uxbridge, Middx., import a Swedish work bench/storage unit.

Stanley-Bridges Ltd, Nelson Way, Cramlington, Northumberland, make several tool kits for the householder.

Services

Bath repairs

Newglaze epoxy bath coating kit is designed for do-it-yourself bath recoating. Obtainable from J. Hammersley, 22 Wolverton Road, Boscombe, Bournemouth, Hants.

Renubath Ltd, 596 Chiswick High Road, London W4, operate a service for recoating your old bath so that it looks like new. This firm provides a guaranteed service, and can also coat old tiles, etc.

To remove ingrained brown marks, try using Jenolite bath stain remover, obtainable from Allied Distributing Co. Ltd, Boundary House, Boston Road, London W7.

Bedding renovation

Mobile Mattress Re-maker, 2 Danemere Road, Lower Richmond Road, London SW15, will remake and re-cover any type of mattress, which they will collect. Also remake pillows. London area only.

Dolls and toys – repairs

Dolls Hospital, 16 Dawes Road, London SW6, will repair loved toys.

Carpet fitting, cleaning and repairing

Action Dry Cleaning Co., 88 Norroy Road, London SW15, clean carpets, upholstery, furniture, wall silks and tapestries.

Bissell Appliances Ltd, Highams Park, London E4 9HN, operate a hire service for an electric shampooer and shampoo through hardware shops in most large towns and cities.

Hardings of Kingston, Acre Road, Kingston-on-Thames, Surrey, will clean and dye carpets, including latex-backed ones, and furnishings. Free collection in Greater London

Kildew Ltd, Bolsover House, Clipstone Street, London W1, will repair, mothproof and clean any type of fur rug.

Patent Steam Carpet Cleaning Co. Ltd, 49–50 Eagle Wharf Road, London N1 7EW, clean carpets in their factory and in situ at home. They will also dye carpets.

Permaclean Ltd, 103 Brighton Road, Coulsdon, Surrey, will clean carpets and upholstery in situ, and deal with hard floors and walls, too. This firm also provides a 48-hour curtain cleaning service. Nationwide cleaning except for curtain cleaning.

Retufting service for cigarette burns on carpets, silicone treatment, general carpet repairs and refitting are all carried out by Carpet Care by Exclusive Interiors Ltd, Suite 3, Barry House, High Street, Potters Bar, Herts.

Stapco Ltd, Hove, Sussex, operate a silicone treatment for carpets.

Scott & Turner Co., St. Mark's Hill, Surbiton, Surrey, will hire out a Hoover carpet shampooer for use with their Shamporal shampoo through local hardware shops in most areas.

Clocks, musical instruments, objets d'art, paintings – repair and maintenance

Abbey Piano Factors, 53 Blenheim Terrace, St. John's Wood, London NW8, will provide day or evening service

for tuning pianos. They will also repolish the case and re-cover keys, restring, etc. Piano storage can be undertaken too.

Antiques Mechanical, 567 Old Kent Road, London SE1, carry out repairs to musical boxes and other mechanical instruments.

British Picture Restorers Association, 43 Albemarle Street, London W1, can supply a list of approved picture restorers.

Dunluce Galleries, 3 Beauchamp Place, London SW3, repair porcelain.

W. Holder & Sons, 60 Brook Street, London W1, repair, clean and restore paintings.

G. Garbe, 23 Charlotte Street, London W1, restores objets d'art, including antique clocks.

Equipment for hire

See also Floor-sanding

Hire Service Shops, 1 Essex Road, London W3 9JB, and branches in the home counties, hire out sanding machines, garden tools, decorating equipment, sewing machines, typewriters, camping equipment, wheel chairs and catering equipment. Catalogue is available.

Hire Technicians Group, 317–319 High Street, Watford, Herts., will hire electric tools and equipment, light ceiling props and saw benches to the householder. They operate a countrywide service and will send their catalogue on request.

Floor-sanding

See also Equipment for hire

Gt. Metropolitan Flooring Co. Ltd, 73 Kinnerton Street, London SW1X 8ED, will sand old wooden floors, seal and repolish. Nationwide service.

Nufloor Ltd, Rodney Road, Portsmouth, Hants, have a countrywide service for the hire of floor sanding machines. Write for full details and address of nearest stockist.

Furniture repairs, stripping, re-caning, etc.

Buttercups, 24 Church Street, London NW8, will strip old varnish off any furniture except mahogany. London area only.

Frederick Clarke (Furnishings) Ltd, 68 Pembroke Road, London W8 6NX, reglaze and mend chintz curtains and upholstery covers.

Macnabs, Inglesgreen Road, Slateford, Edinburgh, also reglaze chintz.

Maples Ltd, 247 Euston Road, London NW1, renovate antique and modern furniture and upholstery, clean upholstery, resilver mirrors and repolish furniture. They provide a countrywide service.

Town & Country Work Centre for the Disabled, Wychbars, Dedben Green, Saffron Walden, Essex, recanes chairs and re-rushes seats. Countrywide service, but limited collection and delivery service. Otherwise send via British Rail.

Leatherwork repairs and renovation

AXL Leathercraft Ltd, Coronation Works, Cobden Road, London E11, clean, renovate, retint and refinish leather goods, suède, sheepskin, etc. including garments.

Connolly Bros, Chalton Street, Euston Road, London NW1, repair leather upholstery and restore old, neglected leather. They also make an excellent hide food.

Silver and plateware polishing, repairs, etc.

Harris Plating Works Ltd, 18 New Wharf Road, London N1, will strip and repolish copper and brass. They will also replate silver, enamel, nickel, etc. and hold the Royal Warrant for this service.

W. E. Marshall, 62 Clerkenwell Road, London EC1, repairs silver.

Henry Savitt, 87 King's Road, London SW6, makes new glass liners for silver salt cellars.

Spring-cleaning

Servicemaster (Great Britain) Ltd, Little Square, Braintree, Essex, offer a countrywide cleaning service for carpets, walls, upholstery and will undertake whole house cleaning for the householder. Regular cleaning contracts can also be arranged. Smoke removal after a fire is another service.

Venetian blind cleaning

New Century Cleaning Co., 28 Eagle Street, London WC1, will clean and repair venetian blinds.

Walls, ceilings and roofs – repairs and maintenance

Action Dry Cleaning Co., 88 Norroy Road, London SW15, will clean wall silk and tapestries.

Majorcas, 38 Jerymn Street, London SW3, mend tapestries, antique wall hangings and textiles.

Marley Tile Co. Ltd, Sevenoaks, Kent, will carry out roofing repairs, stripping, retiling and re-guttering through their local branches and provide a countrywide service.

Servicemaster (Great Britain) Ltd, Little Square, Braintree, Essex, will clean fabric walls.

Walls & Surface, 19 Semley Road, London SW16, will clean walls and ceilings in a room without removing the carpet or furniture.

Getting rid of old furniture

The Salvation Army, 124 Spa Road, London SE16, will collect old furniture in good condition or take away the entire contents of a house which needs clearing.

Shelter Shop, 44 Queensway, London W2, will accept pieces in good condition which they sell to help homeless families.

Oxfam Shops in many towns are also grateful for gifts of small pieces of furniture, china, bric-à-brac, etc.

Some local RWVS units are able to put a householder in touch with a family in need of furniture. Also try local Welfare Departments (children's toys and books in good condition are most welcome), or Task Force, if a unit exists locally.

The House Book cannot claim personal knowledge of all the addresses given above. It is hoped that they will be useful. All information is correct at time of going to press, but owing to the vagaries of economic life, the editors cannot guarantee its continuing accuracy.

Going metric 1/2

First, a cautionary tale. A builder ordered boards in a size that would span the spaces between joists he was laying. When the boards arrived, they would not fit the space and work had to be delayed while the matter was put right. The reason? He had measured, and ordered, in inches; the boards are now sold in millimetres; and the nearest size was just not quite right. Similarly, to join new lengths of pipe (metric diameters) to old ones (imperial), a plumber may now need to turn up with a supply of special conversion joints to bridge the gaps between the two sizes.

Britain, the Commonwealth and the United States are all in various stages of going metric. Britain's changeover to metric measurements started a few years ago in the building trade, but is proceeding piecemeal, and some other industries have barely started. Not until 1975 (if then) will everything be sold in metric measurements or weights. Meanwhile some things will be marked in inches, some in centimetres and millimetres, and many in both.

The main difficulty will be knowing when the new metric measurements involve a simple ready reckoner conversion from the old, imperial measurement, and when they will constitute a rounding up or rounding down to a new set of metric sizes.

After metrication, a lot of products will in fact be exactly the same size as they were before – the 122 cm curtain fabric of the future is our familiar 48 in. width and there is no immediate plan to change it to 100 or 125 cm, say. But in other cases, like the boards and pipes mentioned above, the sizes are being altered slightly.

For example, single blankets which used often to be 90 in. long are being made 250 cm in length – which is about 9 inches longer. This is a more convenient figure to express than 228 cm, the exact equivalent of 90 in.; this is in fact an improvement in quality (for which we pay more, of course) as anyone who has suffered from chilled dawn shoulders will agree.

But other "rounding up" (or rounding down) to the nearest 10 cm, for instance, can cause problems, particularly if you are trying to fit an old product to a new one. Your present kitchen units, cooker, etc., may be 36 in. high. Metric ones are likely to be 90 cm, about half an inch lower, which could give a kitchen a higgledy-piggledy look if new units are added on to old ones. However, it is fortunately relatively easier to jack up new units on a half inch plinth than the other way about!

Apart from the top surface being lower, new metric kitchen units will of course have a lower under-work-top height, so you need to make sure that your old fridge or washing machine will slide under the new work-tops – though again, most kitchen machinery does have adjustable "feet" or plinths.

More difficult to overcome is the fact that the old units were often 21 in. from front to back, while the new recommended depth is 600 mm, i.e. about 23 in.

The same thing is also happening with some storage units, so if you already have some wardrobes or storage units, check the sizes against the new units in the current catalogues and make sure that, for example, new shelves will fit into old carcases. For a while we shall need to know the sizes of many items in both metric and imperial measures, and to keep a careful eye on how well old things and new marry up with one another.

Dual marking (of both imperial and metric sizes) will help. But as we've said, some firms when giving metric equivalents round off while others give more or less precise conversions. Look on three jars of jam, on which the manufacturers have printed the weight not only as "1 lb" but in grams too. You may well find one has put 450 g, one 453 g and one 454 g, but all will contain the same weight of jam. And it is likely to be with furnishing and decorating products too. Such small discrepancies may not often matter but can occasionally be crucial when trying to get a precise fit or to arrange things symmetrically.

There is, however, no means of knowing whether a floor tile described as 300 mm square really is now being made 300 mm square or is merely our old friend the 12 in. tile (which is in fact 305 mm big) on which the manufacturer has planted a new size description, neatly but inaccurately rounded down to 300 mm. So the first essential buy for any home-maker just now is a metal tape-measure with both centimetres and inches on it, with which to check everything!

Finally, there is the question of the use of millimetre (mm) versus centimetre (cm). The general public seems to find the concept of centimetres easier to visualise and it does mean that the numbers seem less astronomical when one is talking about room sizes, or lengths of curtain. However, the architectural and building trades have opted for millimetres in the main. If, like Italian lire, the figures seem incomprehensible, just put a mental point before the last figure and turn it into centimetres, or move the point up one more figure and turn it into metres – i.e. 789 mm is 78.9 cm, or 7.89 metres – which is certainly easier than turning yards into feet and feet into inches!

The following pages give some guidance on what sort of changes you may expect to encounter, where some of the most critical items around the house are concerned. The sizes quoted are ones likely to be found in the shops, now or in the future; but of course there are many other sizes which turn up, particularly in exclusive and hand-made designs.

Note where the sizes are ready reckoner equivalents, and where they have actually changed. You can use the right hand column to record any new sizes which have been agreed upon since going to press.

What metric measures mean

A metre is about $3\frac{1}{4}$ feet long, 10 centimetres are about 4 inches, a centimetre is about $\frac{2}{5}$ inch, a millimetre is about $\frac{1}{25}$ inch.

There are 10 millimetres in one centimetre; 100 centimetres in a metre.

The abbreviations for these are m, cm and mm.

To convert inches into centimetres, or vice versa, use the scale below.

(The conversions on the chart opposite are to the nearest mm or inch The conversions in the rest of the book are approximate.)

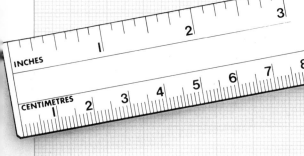

FURNISHINGS

Product	Some Common Sizes Now			Future Metric Sizes		
Carpets (Wilton etc.)	27 in. (686 mm) 36 in. (914 mm) 6 ft (1.83 m) 9 ft (2.74 m) 12 ft (3.66 m) 15 ft (4.57 m)			No plans for metrication		
Furnishing Fabrics	48 in. (1.22 m) 50 in. (1.27 m) 60 in. (1.52 m)			1.22 m 1.27 m 1.52 m		
Beds & Mattresses	Already metric – see opposite			0.9 × 1.9 m (3 ft × 6 ft 3 in.) 1.0 × 2.0 m (3 ft 3 in. × 6 ft 6 in.) 1.35 × 1.9 m (4 ft 5 in. × 6 ft 3 in.) 1.5 × 2.0 m (5 ft × 6 ft 6 in.)		
Sheets	(Still under discussion at time of going to press)					
Blankets	70 × 90 in. (1.78 × 2.29 m) 90 × 100 in. (2.29 × 2.54 m) 110 × 110 in. (2.54 × 2.79 m)			1.8 × 2.5 m (71 in. × 99 in.) 2.5 × 2.8 m (99 in. × 110 in.)		

Kitchen Units	Width	Height	Depth	Width	Height	Depth
Base Units	18, 24, 30, 36, 42, 54 in. (457, 610, 762, 914 mm, 1.07, 1.37 m)	36 in. (914 mm)	18, 21 in. (457, 533 mm)	400, 500, 600, 800, 1000 mm (16, 20, 23, 32, 40 in.)	900 mm (35 in.)	600 mm (23 in.)
Sink Units	36, 42, 54, 63 in. (914 mm, 1.07, 1.37, 1.60 m)	36 in. (914 mm)	18, 21 in. (457, 533 mm)	1.2, 1.5, 1.8 m (47, 59, 71 in.)	900 mm (35 in.)	600 mm (23 in.)
Wall Units	24, 30, 36, 42 in. (610, 762, 914 mm, 1.07 m)	20 in. (508 mm)	10, 12 in. (254, 305 mm)	400, 500, 600, 800, 1000 mm (16, 20, 23, 32, 40 in.)	450 mm (18 in.)	300 mm (12 in.)

BUILDING AND DECORATING MATERIALS

Product	Some Common Sizes Now	Future Metric Sizes
Wall Tiles	4¼ in., 6 in. (107, 152 mm)	100 mm (4 in.)
Floor Tiles	9 in., 12 in. (229, 305 mm)	300 mm (11¾ in.)
Sheet Floorings (Vinyl etc.)	6 ft (1.83 m)	2.0 m (6 ft 6¾ in.)
Paint	Already metric – see opposite	500 ml (½ litre) (about 1 pint) 1 l (about 2 pints) 2½ l (over 4 pints) 5 l (nearly 9 pints)
Wallpaper	21 in. × 11 yds (533 mm × 10 m)	533 mm × 10 m
Baths	67 in. × 27½ in. (or 31½ in.) × 19¾ in. 1702 × 691 (or 792) × 491 mm	1700 × 700 (or 800) × 500 mm
Washbasins	20 in. × 16 in. (508 × 406 mm) 22 in. × 16 in. (559 × 406 mm) 25 in. × 18 in. (635 × 457 mm)	510 × 400 mm 560 × 400 mm 630 × 460 mm

Index 1/2